Annotated Instructor's Edition

The Longwood Reader

Edward A. Dornan
Charles W. Dawe

Orange Coast Community College

Allyn and Bacon

Boston London Toronto Sydney Tokyo Singapore

Executive Editor: Joseph Opiela
Developmental Editor: Alicia Reilly
Series Editorial Assistant: Amy Capute
Production Administrator: Rowena Dores
Editorial-Production Service: Editorial Inc.
Text Designer: Pat Torelli
Cover Administrator: Linda Dickinson
Composition Buyer: Linda Cox
Manufacturing Buyer: Louise Richardson

Library of Congress Cataloging-in-Publication Data

The Longwood reader / [edited by] Edward A. Dornan, Charles Dawe.
    p.   cm.
    1. College readers. 2. English language—Rhetoric. I. Dornan,
Edward A. II. Dawe, Charles W.
PE 1417.L66 1991
808'.0427–dc20   90-19193
                                                                                  CIP

ISBN 0-205-12667-7

Acknowledgments

"Living Well Is the Best Revenge—Just Ask the Urban Coyote" reprinted by permission of the author, Michelle Huneven.

Acknowledgments continue on page 685, which constitutes an extension of the copyright page.

Printed in the United States of America

10 9 8 7 6 5 4 3 2 1   95 94 93 92 91 90

A Note about
the Instructor's Edition

We hope this special instructor's edition of THE LONG-WOOD READER pleases you. We have tried to make it as interesting as possible. As you thumb through it, you will quickly see that it is much different from the traditional "Instructor's Manual." Furthermore, its size is clearly larger than the student edition (which, by the way, you can order from Allyn and Bacon if you prefer it for classroom use).

The complete text of the student edition is printed in this outsized instructor's edition, but because of the additional space, we were able to pack the margins with commentary. This format has a clear advantage over a traditional instructor's manual: the commentary is where it should be—next to whatever it refers to instead of being tucked away at the end of the text or in a separate booklet.

The commentary is arranged under three headings: Teaching Suggestions, Marginal Notes, and Possible Answers. Our suggestions for teaching are just that—merely suggestions. You will find that they often give some background information to help set the stage for class discussion and then refer directly to the essay itself.

Marginal Notes are chock-full of observations on writing strategies, comments about allusions, information about references, and musings on culture. Sometimes the commentary may seem a bit esoteric. Would you know, for example, that the figure of speech Gretel Erlich uses in the opening of "About Men" is called *hysteron proteron*, a passage in which something that should logically come first comes last? Othertimes the commentary embodies what may be well known. You probably know, for example, that the Chisholm Trail, named after a American scout, Jesse Chisholm (1806–1868), led from San Antonio, Texas, to Abilene, Kansas, serving as a cattle trail for twenty years after the Civil

War. But do you know that Marlboro cigarette ads were once directed at women and that Marlboros once had red filter tips so lipstick traces would not show on them? Well, one of us didn't. In any case we hope the marginal notes, whether the information is esoteric or commonly known, interests you and enriches your experience with the essays and in the classroom.

Possible Answers offers answers to the questions that follow each essay.

E.A.D
C.W.D

Contents

> *"Negro girls in small Southern towns, whether poverty-stricken or just munching along on a few of life's necessities, were given as extensive and irrelevant preparation for adulthood as rich white girls shown in magazines. Admittedly the training was not the same."*

> *"The hangman climbed down and stood ready, holding the lever. Minutes seemed to pass. The steady, muffled crying from the prisoner went on and on, . . . never faltering for an instant."*

Thematic Table of Contents

Pairs of Essays

Although the selections in *The Longwood Reader* are arranged by rhetorical patterns, we have included a Thematic Table of Contents grouping the selections under seventeen subject areas.

In addition, we offer the following suggestions for those who wish to assign pairs of essays. Such pairing may be useful for discussion of contrary and/or complementary views of similar subjects or situations, choices of style and presentation strategies, as well as different ways of using a particular rhetorical strategy.

Individual teachers will, of course, discover additional pairings equally valid and informative.

Preface

Good reading influences good writing—this is an assumption embodied in *The Longwood Reader*. Are we referring to the techniques merchandised in speed reading courses that urge enrollees to scan a page merely for facts and information?

Absolutely not.

By "good reading" we mean the activity that engages a reader's imagination when he or she picks up a text. We mean the ability to question an author's ideas, to subject an author's argument to skeptical scrutiny, to use a pencil to note disagreements and counterpoints in a text's margins. By good reading we also mean the ability to read with a "critical eye," that is, to read with the ability to see an author's strategies: the way paragraphs are shaped, the way sentences create rhythm and impact, and the way images create feeling. Every writing course must then also be a course in reading with a second sight that sees beneath a text's skin to examine its bones and vital organs. Unfortunately, reading like a writer, reading with a critical eye, does not come naturally; students must acquire the ability.

How?

They must gather information about the writing craft, and they must study the craft at work. As we perceive the process, student writers must go into "training" much like student actors, dancers, musicians, or painters must train. A vital part of this training is studying the works of those who have mastered the art of writing, writers like Maya Angelou, E. B. White, Alice Walker, George Orwell, Maxine Hong Kingston, Gretel Ehrlich, and others represented in *The Longwood Reader*.

You will notice that the Introduction to *The Longwood Reader* prepares students to read with a critical eye. We explain the reader–writer contract: a reader must assume that a writer has created an understandable work; a writer must assume that a reader wants to understand the work. Together the reader and writer create meaning, relying on writing conventions to aid their effort. We explain the importance of reading to understand a writer's purpose, strategy, and style, a framework that establishes the pattern for the discussion questions that follow each essay. We also present five tips for the first reading of an essay. We then illustrate the practice of reading with a pencil in hand with Michelle Huneven's "Living Well Is the Best Revenge—Just Ask the Urban Coyote" accompanied by student notes. We close the Introduction with five tips for rereading an essay.

We arranged the nine chapters that follow the Introduction according to traditional writing methods, beginning with narration and ending with argumentation. We believe there is a slight risk in teaching rhetorical modes. When misunderstood, they may generate "cookie-cutter" prose, but we believe the benefit of mastering rhetorical modes outweighs the risk. When students understand these common development patterns, they can examine them at work in professional essays, thus sharpening their critical reading skills. By way of caution, however, throughout *The Longwood Reader* we discuss essays as having a dominant mode. We point out that during the composing process writers respond primarily to their material by selecting paragraph and essay patterns that best suit their subject and purpose instead of trying to fit their material into preselected patterns.

Each chapter begins with a detailed discussion that explains a writing method, offers strategies for using the method, and presents a sample of student work, several paragraphs in length, that illustrates the method at work in college writing. Here we wish to emphasize "detailed," for *The Longwood Reader* offers a thorough, though economical, discussion of each rhetorical mode and uses ample examples to illustrate major concepts. In the first chapter, Narration, for instance, you will find an explanation of narrative effect illustrated by a brief tale from Zen Buddhist lore. You will find advice on writing the opening, body, and climax of a narrative as well as a discussion of conflict, point of view, chronological and psychological time, and scene and summary. We use several examples to illustrate these concepts to help students understand them in the essays that comprise this chapter. In Chapter 3, Examples, you will find a detailed discussion of specific, typical, and hypothetical examples as well as the practice of mixing different types of examples in an essay. The discussion is amply illustrated by eight paragraph examples. We continue this practice throughout the text. Moreover, the student examples that conclude each chapter are fully annotated to reveal the writer's strategy.

Eight chapters have six essays each and the final chapter, Persuasion and Argument, has nine. Each essay is introduced with a brief biography of the author and brief comments to place the essay in context. Each essay is followed by questions grouped under the headings of Meaning and Purpose, Strategy, and Style. Two writing assignments follow the study questions, and each chapter closes with additional writing assignments designed to challenge students with a wide range of essay topics from which to choose.

The Longwood Reader offers several important reference features. The Glossary defines rhetorical terms that appear throughout the text. When a term first appears, it is highlighted in bold type to signal its appearance in the Glossary. *The Longwood Reader* also offers a thematic table of contents for readers who wish to read several essays on a common subject and a list of paired readings for those who wish to read for similarities or differences in perspective and style.

Of all the reference features, A Guide to Editing and Revising Sentences will have the most direct influence on a student's writing. The guide is arranged by rules: "Eliminate pretentious language," "Use technical language with care," "Consider the denotation and connotation of words," "Revise for proper coordination," "Place modifiers with care," "Provide variety in your sentences," and so on. Each of the rules is fully explained and illustrated, thus allowing students to use this appendix independently.

We thank those colleagues from colleges and universities around the country who offered indispensable advice while the manuscript for *The Longwood Reader* was being prepared:

Kathleen L. Bell, Old Dominion University; Michael Bobkoff, Westchester Community College; Judith M. Boschult, Phoenix College; Shirley Curtis, Polk Community College; Charles Dodson, University of North Carolina—Wilmington; Jane Dugan, Cleveland State University; Janet Eber, County College of Morris; Leslie Harris, Georgia State University; Elaine Sheridan Horne, Manchester Community College; Gloria Johnson, Broward Community College; Peggy Jolly, University of Alabama—Birmingham; Robert A. Kelly, Macon College; Joseph LaBriola, Sinclair Community College; Russell R. Larson, Eastern Michigan University; Barry Maid, University of Arkansas—Little Rock; Thomas E. Martinez, Villanova University; Jerry McElveen, Richland College; Gratia Murphy, Youngstown State University; Beth Richards, University of Nebraska; Connie Rothwell, University of North Carolina—Charlotte; Gerald Schiffhorst, University of Central Florida; David E. Schwalm, Arizona State University; Carole M. Sherman, College of DuPage; Laurence J. Starczyk, Kent State University; Jo Koster Tarvers, Rutgers University; Eugene Wright, University of North Texas.

We owe a special debt of gratitude to our sponsoring editor Joe Opiela for his trust, persistence, and wise counsel throughout a difficult process. We also wish to thank all the Allyn and Bacon professionals who worked on the text: Alicia Reilly, Amy Capute, and Rowena Dores. And we offer our appreciation to Kathy Daniel and David Lynch for masterfully overseeing the production of the final manuscript.

Finally, we wish to acknowledge an immense debt to our colleagues Don Pierstorff and Mike Finnegan for their extensive contributions to both the student and instructor editions of *The Longwood Reader*.

Introduction

    We heard a story recently about an event that occurred at a nearby campus. Campus officials, faculty members, and a contingent of dissatisfied students had been haggling over curriculum changes. Months of negotiation ended in deadlock. Frustrated, the students called a rally. A representative from administration began to speak, offering the "official" view. Suddenly, a student leader leaped to the platform and grabbed the microphone. Veins pulsed in his neck; his face turned crimson; his eyes spurted with anger. Everyone became excited, ready for a fiery attack on the administration and faculty, but instead he shouted, "Words, Words, Words! I'm sick of words!" He dug into a bag and began tossing lecture notes, essay shreds, and pages torn from textbooks

1

at the astonished crowd. "If words were feathers," he bellowed, "everyone on this campus would smother before anything changed." And then he stormed to the admissions office and promptly withdrew from his classes.

Or so the story goes.

A true story? Who knows for sure? It does, nevertheless, illustrate a common belief that words slow action. Indeed, taking direct action seems much easier than agonizing over a thoughtful, well-reasoned argument. But education relies primarily on words, written words—words *you* read and words *you* write. Reading and writing are sometimes slow, frustrating activities that at first glance may seem to oppose each other. On the contrary, though, reading and writing complement each other. The better reader you are, the better writer you can become.

Of course, you've been reading since grammar school. You probably spend some leisure time reading for pleasure, perhaps becoming engrossed in the psychological twists and turns of a popular thriller or enthralled by the intricate social weaving of a historical narrative. But you probably spend more time reading for information, gleaning facts from history, psychology, and science textbooks. While reading textbooks, you probably concentrate on a goal, which often has something to do with a midterm or final examination. In other words, you've learned efficient reading techniques. You've learned to approach a textbook as if it were a lake in which you troll for facts and theories instead of bass or trout.

Certainly, reading in this way helps you prepare for tests. It will also help after graduation when you face the heaps of memoranda, reports, and research every profession generates. It won't, however, help you become a better writer. For your writing to improve, you must learn to read like a writer. You can begin by learning to read with a "critical eye." The critical eye reveals a writer's purpose and strategies. It scrutinizes the way in which words work in sentences. The critical eye pierces a work's surface and reveals its bones and heart.

We offer the essays in this anthology as a means to help you develop a critical eye. The essay is often described as a well-organized nonfiction composition in which the author concentrates on a single aspect of a subject. Usually this kind of essay is written in formal English and designed to convey information. But essays as a group cover a much broader territory. Many are impressionistic or exploratory. Often they express personal feelings or attitudes based on the writer's experience.

Because essays are so varied, these selections represent a great range, all the better, we believe, to help you sharpen your critical eye. They include works by such well-known essayists as George Orwell, Joan Didion, and E. B. White, as well as works by lesser-known, rising essayists, such as Gretel Ehrlich, Phyllis Rose, and Elizabeth M. Whelan. The essays are from varied sources: newspapers, magazines, academic and scientific journals, and nonfiction books. They cover many subjects: crime and violence, men and women, work and play, country and city life, even culture and customs. The collection embodies several styles, ranging from the newswriter's objective report to the poet's subjective expression. Some are serious. Some are playful. All are worth your attention. As you study them, hold one idea in mind: you are reading like a writer; that is, reading to develop your writing skill—reading with a critical eye.

The Writer–Reader Contract

Pause for a moment. Imagine an essayist pushing back from a typewriter desk. The writer stretches and yawns before slipping a final manuscript into an envelope and sending it off for publication. You might think this is the critical moment—when the essay is completed and in the mail to the publisher.

But it isn't.

The critical moment comes when the work falls into a reader's hands—your hands. To begin reading an essay is the first act in a dynamic interaction—not between you and the writer, as you might guess—but between you and the essay itself.

This is not to deny that a relationship connects you and the writer. In fact, readers and writers are joined by an implicit agreement, a "contract" between writer and reader. A reader must assume that a writer has created an understandable work; a writer must assume that a reader wants to understand the work.

Unfortunately, communicating in written language is often difficult. A writer cannot gaze over your shoulder and whisper into your ear to make understanding an essay any easier. Only the essay speaks to you. To fulfill the writer–reader contract, a writer employs principles known as "conventions" to help you understand the essay. Even if the essay is difficult, you must trust that the writer has kept the reader in mind during the writing. You must trust that the writer has seen the essay through *your* eyes. In other words, you must trust that the writer has used the conventions of essay writing to help you understand the work.

Generally, these conventions dictate that essays have a purpose, use clear strategies to achieve the purpose, and employ an appropriate style. Understanding these conventions will help you decipher most nonfiction texts. Indeed, understanding the conventions will help sharpen your critical eye.

Reading for Purpose

Writers know that readers expect to understand the purpose behind an essay. Purpose gives an essay direction. It provides a destination. It keeps a reader on the track. Some writers, especially when the primary intent is to convey information, at once state a purpose: "My purpose is to explain the ways in which human beings have decorated their bodies through the ages: by tattooing, by scarring, and by reshaping bone structure." Other writers, especially those writing personal narration and description, do not state a purpose as directly, thus encouraging the reader to become more deeply involved in interpretation. You must then formulate the purpose in your own way: "The writer narrates an early childhood experience to show how important imaginative play is." When an essay is rich enough to invite interpretation, much like a careful reading of an intricate poem or short story, then all that you have heard, tasted, touched, smelled, seen, and thought; all your knowledge of people, books, music, art, culture, and language; literally everything you have lived through, is the raw material at your disposal. Drawing on that rich resource, you apply your knowledge to interpret the essayist's purpose.

Consider a short passage from Norman Mailer's *Fire on the Moon,* a work in which he concentrates on America's space program. In this passage astronauts Neil Armstrong and Buzz Aldrin have completed their historic moon walk on the Sea of Tranquility. The event takes place at the end of their first day on the moon.

> It was about three-thirty in the morning when the astronauts finally prepared for sleep. They pulled down the shades and Aldrin stretched out on the floor, his nose near the moon dust. Armstrong sat on the cover of the ascent engine, his back leaning against one of the walls, his legs supported in a strap he had tied around a vertical bar. In front of his face was the eyepiece of the telescope. The earth was in its field of view, and the earth "like a big blue eyeball" stared back at him. They could not sleep. Like the eye of a victim just murdered, the earth stared back at him.

One clear purpose is to describe the astronauts' preparations for sleep, but toward the end of the passage, Mailer compares the earth to a murder victim. Moreover, he suggests that Armstrong is haunted by the image of the earth "like the eye of a victim" staring at him. Is the comparison merely a dramatic flourish? We doubt it. The description will lead a sensitive reader to explore the deeper purpose in Mailer's comparison. Mailer does not spell out what the passage means. Instead he invites the reader to interpret it. That puts the reader in an interesting spot, for just as Mailer has drawn on his knowledge and experience to create the image, readers must draw on theirs to interpret it, to find a meaning.

The meaning may vary from reader to reader, depending on each one's knowledge and experience. One reader may recall Edgar Allan Poe's macabre tale of murder, "The Tell-Tale Heart." In

Poe's story the murder victim's eye—"a pale blue eye"—haunted the murderer, as the blue earth seems to haunt Armstrong. Does the image suggest, therefore, that the earth has been abandoned like a corpse by astronauts who seek other worlds?

Another reader may explore technological associations. The 1969 Apollo II flight was history's most advanced scientific achievement. But at what price? Isn't the human thirst for scientific achievement and the technology it generates sapping mother earth's natural resources? In a metaphorical sense, therefore, isn't technology killing the earth? And couldn't Mailer be using the moon landing to suggest that "ecological crime"? Who, then, are the perpetrators? Perhaps all humankind, represented by the astronaut who, Mailer suggests, feels accused by the "big blue eyeball" staring at him.

Not all essays invite a careful interpretation of purpose, but the many that do are rich in detail and express a personal vision.

Reading for Strategy

A writer must develop strategies to execute the purpose. The writer might first develop a sense of the audience and a strategy for addressing them: To whom is the essay directed? How much do they know about the subject? How much time are they likely to spend with the essay? Will they want a straightforward treatment of the subject or an exploration through richly textured prose? Answering questions such as these will give a writer a sense of the audience, a feel for the person sitting at a desk or in an easy chair reading the essay.

Having acquired a sense of the audience, the writer may next develop a strategy for the essay's structure, knowing that readers want essays to have clear organization. Usually writers choose a dominant rhetorical pattern to organize their work, such as development by narration, description, examples, comparison and contrast, or definition. Rhetorical patterns are not formulas. They don't offer a magic recipe for success in writing. Moreover, professional writers seldom stick to any one pattern, choosing instead to use several within a dominant structure. We suggest you see rhetorical patterns as a tool to guide your writing and to provide an effective way of fulfilling a reader's desire for structure.

To see how rhetorical patterns can work, imagine that you are a film critic and want to compare and contrast two movies. You pick thrillers and narrow your subject to plot structure. You decide to explain the similarities and differences in each director's way of hooking an audience, generating suspense, building to a climax, and constructing the resolution. Thorough knowledge of comparison-and-contrast patterns will help you balance the similarities and differences in your analysis.

While composing your essay, however, you find yourself bringing the plot of a third movie into the discussion, one that represents still another structure. A warning light flashes in the back of your mind. You pause to think through what you're doing. Your knowledge of rhetorical patterns helps you realize you're drifting into classification, which is a pattern different from comparison and contrast, perhaps one best avoided for this writing situation. You stop. You return to your original strategy or reconsider, and in fact move to classification.

At still another stage, you drift into discussing the effects of thriller plots on an audience. It makes sense—an exciting plot does affect an audience, right? Of course it does. But you would be employing yet another rhetorical pattern, cause and effect. After some thought, though, you may decide to explore the effect on the audience, but you will do it in another section of your paper, and you will arrange it according to cause-and-effect technique.

Our point is quite simple: Knowledge of rhetorical patterns helps writers organize their work. These aren't cookie-cutter patterns that writers press into the dough of their thought. They are effective strategies that writers use to organize their material and guide a reader through an essay. They also help writers remain flexible, shifting smoothly from pattern to pattern according to the demands of the subject. The best way we know for you to build knowledge of rhetorical patterns is to examine how professional writers use them—that is, to read with a critical eye.

Reading for Style

People usually think of style as appearance. Imagine a punk rocker walking across your campus. To what kinds of things are you referring when you speak of his or her "style"? Perhaps it's the black leather jacket and silver studs; the hair dyed black, swept into a peak, and shaved at the sides; the defiant swagger; even the throaty voice, rasping across the quad—all these details, and more, create the image, the "style" this person generates.

Writing also embodies many details that work together to generate a "style." To identify a writer's style, you might begin by examining word selection. Are the words abstract or concrete? Do the words lull you into inattention like the speech of a politician trying to obscure past transgressions, or do they catch your attention like pebbles pinging against a window? Are the words common, found in everyone's vocabulary? Or are they scholarly, obscure words used by specialists? Or does the writer mix common with scholarly language?

You might also study a writer's sentences. Notice how the writer builds sentences and varies their structure. We have no simple rules for this technique. Writers learn a feel for sentences, as potters develop a feel for clay. They shape them. They vary their length. They alter their rhythm to increase or slow the pace of reading for emphasis.

Writers use sentences to create figures of speech, the bits and pieces of colorful language sparkling through the essay. A writer may use figurative language to compare two things that are essentially different but alike in some way. With a crisp simile, Flannery O'Connor compares a woman's determination to a truck: Mrs. Freeman's "forward expression was steady and driving like the advance of a heavy truck." In another memorable simile,

Ralph Waldo Emerson offers a fresh way to see a child: "A sleeping child gives me the impression of a traveler in a very far country." With figurative language, writers not only help their readers understand what is being said but also add vigor to their prose.

Word choice, sentence variety, and figurative language combine to create another element of style—tone. Begin to think of tone as an expression of a writer's attitude, much as tone of voice may reflect a speaker's attitude. Imagine, for a moment, that you have given a speech. The next day you receive this note:

> That was an effective speech. You carefully covered the main points. We all thank you.

A straightforward compliment? We think so, don't you? But with a few word substitutions and additions and by altering emphasis, the tone changes dramatically:

> That was . . . *some* speech. You *lingered* on all the points—at least three times each. Thanks a lot.

The message no longer expresses appreciation. It now expresses snide criticism. In other words, the tone has changed.

Some kinds of writing are dominated by well-defined tones. News reporters seem to share a tone, an objective presentation of events—just the facts, please. Thriller and romance writers seem to favor a breathless, frenzied tone. Essayists, however, struggle to find the exact tone to fit the subject, audience, and attitude. The same writer may use one tone for one subject and another tone for another subject. The tone may be formal, informal, flippant, conversational, intimate, solemn, playful, or ironic. The tone may even reveal the writer's awe of the subject. Consider the opening lines from Richard Selzer's essay on skin:

> I sing of skin, layered fine as baklava, whose colors shame the dawn, at once the scabbard upon which is writ our only signature, and the instrument by which we are thrilled, protected, and kept constant in our natural place.

Selzer brings to his essay years of experience as a surgeon and medical-school teacher. A reader with knowledge of Selzer's background might expect him to treat the skin in a matter-of-fact way, as merely a thin barrier that must be sliced through to reach the vital organs. But this is clearly not his attitude. He writes rhapsodically, "I sing of skin"; he makes a rich comparison, "layered fine as baklava"; and he claims its "colors shame the dawn." The sentence is a tribute to skin, and the tone expresses his sense of awe.

Style is difficult territory to explore, no doubt about it. If you devote time to reading for style, you will achieve a *feel* for it. Study a writer's words and you will learn to choose the right words. Study a writer's sentences and you will learn to shape your sentences. Study a writer's figurative language and you will soon be writing colorfully. Study a writer's tone and soon a voice will rise from your pages.

Five Tips for a First Reading

When reading to improve your writing, you cannot sweep through an essay and then set it aside. You should be prepared to read it several times. The first reading may be quick, designed to give you a view of the content, a sense of the purpose, and a feeling for the style. When you begin the first reading, we suggest you keep five tips in mind.

1. Know the Writer

Whatever you learn about an author will help you anticipate his or her biases. If the author is identified as a liberal politician and the subject is poverty, then you might anticipate an argument supporting government aid to the poor. If the author is an environmentalist and the subject is the greenhouse effect, then you might expect a plea to save the world's rain forests. Many periodicals and essay anthologies include information about an author, usually on the first page of the essay or in a section often titled "Notes on Contributors." In this collection, each essay is introduced by a headnote, which includes an author profile and brief comments on the essay. Read each profile with care; it will prepare you for your first reading of the essay.

2. *Consider the Place and Year of Publication*

Knowing where the essay was first published is necessary in establishing a writer's credentials. An essay titled "Bigfoot: Hoax or Hysteria?" would have more credibility if published in *Media, Culture, and Society,* a highly respected periodical for people interested in the influence exerted by newspaper, television, and film on readers' and viewers' perceptions, than it would if published in *The National Enquirer,* a popular tabloid known for its sensationalism. Knowing when an essay was first published will also give you clues about the social environment it was written in. Certainly an essay on civil liberty written in the early 1960s is going to display different assumptions from those in one written in the late 1980s.

3. *Examine the Title*

Sounds obvious, right? Well, you would be surprised at how many readers mistakenly believe an essay begins with its first line. It doesn't. It begins with a title.

A title can help you anticipate what is to follow. It may announce the writer's subject, suggest the dominant rhetorical pattern, or hint at the writer's attitude. The title "A Hanging" lets you know you won't be going to a tea party. It makes sense to anticipate an essay about an execution, which will not be a pretty experience. The title "Cyclone! Rising to the Fall" is a little more ambiguous. Does "cyclone" refer to the destructive natural phenomenon? Or does it mean a roller coaster? Or could "Cyclone" be the name of a bronco? Anyway, you probably expect a description of a thrilling, or even frightening, experience: get a tight grip on the book. "I Want a Wife" seems like a straightforward title.

But reading the headnotes, you learn that feminist author Judy Syfers wrote the essay. Thus, you may expect an ironic tone.

4. *Take Quick Notes*

Always read with a pencil in hand. Don't just chew on the eraser: star key passages, underline startling images, bracket shifts in thought, and scribble notes in the margins. Roughly trace your reactions to the text, questions that come to mind, even disagreements with the writer. Ah yes, circle words you don't know so that you can refer to a dictionary for their meaning before the second reading.

Why go to all this trouble for a first reading? We don't suggest that you linger on any page for very long, but a first reading is like traveling in new territory. Much like markings on a map, markings on an essay will help your exploration during the return visit.

5. *Record Your First Impression*

We urge you to record your first impressions after the first reading and before going on to a second reading. Write down what you think the writer was trying to achieve—the purpose. Identify the dominant strategies. Describe the audience. Jot down your thoughts on style. Record any impressions you have.

Now let's look at an essay, Michelle Huneven's "Living Well Is the Best Revenge—Just Ask the Urban Coyote."

Huneven is a rising writer who concentrates on southern California's transformation from a "suburban dream" in the 1950s to an "urban nightmare" in the 1990s. Her essay conveys preoccupation with adapting in an urban world, not just human adaptation but also that of wild creatures.

Before reading Huneven's essay, you should know that several coyote attacks on children had been reported in southern California at about this time. These were not attacks in the wilderness as you might expect but attacks on front lawns and at the edges of vacant lots. Huneven also draws on common knowledge of the coyote, information that can be found in any encyclopedia, such as this excerpt from *World Book Encyclopedia:*

> **Coyote**, *KY oht* or *ky OH tee,* is a wild member of the dog family. It is known for its eerie howl, usually heard during the evening, night, or early morning.
>
> Coyotes once lived only in western North America. However, they now inhabit much of the United States, Canada, and Mexico, and even parts of Central America. The coyote lives in a variety of environments, including deserts, mountains, and prairies. It is sometimes called the *prairie wolf* or *brush wolf.*
>
> Adult coyotes vary in color from light yellow or yellowish-gray to brownish-yellow. Their fur may be tipped with black. The coyote has large, pointed ears and a bushy tail. An adult coyote measures about 4 feet (1.2 meters) long, including its 11- to 16-inch (28- to 41-centimeter) tail. It stands about 2 feet (0.6 meter) high and weighs from 25 to 30 pounds (11 to 14 kilograms). Most coyotes live alone or in pairs, but some form groups of three or more.
>
> Coyotes eat more kinds of food than do many other animals. They feed chiefly on rabbits and such rodents as gophers, mice, prairie dogs, rats, and squirrels. Coyotes also prey on antelope, goats, sheep, and other animals. The coyote eats various insects and reptiles as well. During the winter, many coyotes in northern regions feed on the remains of large dead animals, such as cattle, deer, and elk. In some areas, coyotes eat juniper berries, mesquite beans, watermelons, and other fruits for a few weeks of the year.
>
> Some ranchers dislike coyotes because the animals kill cattle, sheep, and other livestock. Other people, however, think coyotes help keep rodent populations under control and are valuable for that reason. Some people hunt and trap coyotes for sport. Coyote pelts are used to make coats and to trim parkas or other clothing.

You probably noticed that the purpose of the *World Book* entry is clear—the writer gives you the bare-bones facts about coyotes in general. This is the kind of writing you would read strictly for information. Huneven's purpose is different. She takes the information, limits her focus to coyotes living in urban areas, and writes in a style that lifts her subject well above the facts.

Huneven's essay is also annotated according to the suggestions in "Five Tips for a First Reading." Glance at the annotations to see how one writer recorded questions and impressions while reading the essay for the first time.

🍎 Michelle Huneven 🍎

Living Well Is the Best Revenge—
Just Ask the Urban Coyote

Canis latrans, God's dog, the song dog of the west, the trickster. The coyote is a wild canid, larger and more brazen than the fox, smaller and less social than the wolf. He's easy to spot in any pack of dogs; he's the one with the guilty look and sidling gait. Over the past hundred years or so he's acquired a bad reputation by raiding henhouses and rustling sheep. He ruined so many ranchers and gorged on so many wooly innocents that he became the target of the largest and longest predator-control program in history. He survived, of course. Proved himself indestructible. And refused to be banished into the wilderness. Even as cities encroach on his territory, he holds his ground, adapts and, frankly, flourishes. The new urban coyote is strong, healthy and busy compounding his bad reputation by plundering Southern California towns for garbage, house pets and, recently, a small child. (Brother Coyote) can't help himself; he *likes* man—maybe not to talk to or play with, but definitely to live next door to. And exploit.

(Professionally) the coyote is both scavenger and predator, sanitation engineer

15

Handwritten annotations:

Associations:

1. Cliché: Once saw a "Yuppie" Poster that featured a Rolls Royce with this phrase.

2. "Urban Coyote": Is this a metaphor for humans? "Urban Cowboy" comes to mind.

3. Coyotes run undocumented workers across Mexican border.

Huneven describes an actual coyote— a new kind of coyote that exploits people. Ironic? Because people "exploit" the natural world.

Purpose: to describe a new breed of coyote.

Coyote described as a professional, with a job.

Why Brother Coyote?

and rodent-control specialist. (His job) is to eat anything that needs to be eaten and to check any exploding population of smaller animals. He's designed to consume; form follows function. It's impossible to see a coyote without thinking of hunger. Mark Twain dubbed him "a living, breathing allegory of Want."

He looks like a German shepherd—a starving German shepherd with a long family history of malnutrition. Standing 20 to 24 inches tall at the shoulder, the coyote matches a German shepherd in height, but his average 20 to 30 pounds ranks him among beagles in weight. His long-limbed skeleton creates the illusion of greater size, but his hide seems shrunken over his frame in such a way that his nose appears unusually pinched and pointed, his ears and eyes and tail disproportionately large. He's grayish red, his forehead and feet a darker cinnamon or rust color. For a few months in the winter his fur can look quite respectable, with the soft, woolly undercoat thick and luxurious beneath longer, coarse, water-repellent hair. The rest of the year he's fading, molting, growing in, plagued by fleas and mange and, in general, a scruffy, sorry exterior. His long, black-tipped tail is always fluffy and could be his crowning glory, if only he'd untuck it from between his legs. If he ever did unfurl that tail he'd measure four feet from its tip to his nose.

Begins physical description

Huneven compares coyotes to familiar animals.

Vivid description

Tales of enormous, 50-, 60-, 80-pound coyotes abound—the creature seems to have a curious, expansive effect on the human imagination—but the largest coyote on record (a New Yorker) weighed around 50 pounds, and the largest Southern California specimen tipped the scales at 34 pounds. The standard female urban coyote weighs about 20 pounds, the male 5 pounds more.

The coyote's eyes are slanted, black-lidded, amber-colored, though they're said to glow greenish gold at night. Homeowners in L.A. County have complained of coyotes staring through front windows with their large yellow eyes, glaring at poodles or house cats. His eyes and ears are fine, sensitive instruments, but the coyote relies on his nose, takes his cues from and acts upon olfactory information; he often will not flee danger until he gets the enemy's scent.

The coyote's hardworking mouth holds 42 specialized teeth. Small nibblers up front are perfect for currying fleas, lice and ticks from his fur, uncaking mud, pulling foxtails from between his toes and scraping every last shred of meat from a bone. The sharp tusks that lend the lurid aspect to his smile do the heavy work of snagging and holding prey. Midmandible, the coyote's top and bottom teeth just meet for easy cutting and still more holding power. (In ranching country a coyote will grab a sheep by the throat and hang on for thirteen minutes until the animal suffocates; house pets are fast food by comparison.) His rear teeth are "scissor" teeth; they pass each other close to the jaw muscle and are ideal for shredding gristle, pulverizing big bones and, when necessary, chewing through PVC pipe to get

Strategy— Huneven moves from the general to the particular — coyote's nose, mouth, teeth …

House pets as fast food!!!

Urban hunt?

to water. The only teeth the coyote lacks are close-set, wide, chunky teeth like our own molars, teeth that grind grain and break down vegetable matter. But don't worry, the coyote gets his fiber and complex carbohydrates. He eats his fruits and vegetables whole—just gulps them down. This practice indirectly gives him yet another ecological function: scatterer of seeds. Not only are fruit seeds dispersed in his scat, the seeds' pericarp dissolves in his digestive tract, increasing the chance of germination by 85 percent.

No molars— an interesting detail: a meat eater.

A coyote's breath is rumored to be so rank he can stun his prey with it.

A memorable image — UGH! Why a separate paragraph? Drama?

Most people may never see a coyote— especially if they go looking for one—but everyone can hear them at night. They're most vocal from December to February, during mating season. The famous racket consists of eleven different calls: the growl, the huff, the whine, the yelp, the woof, the bark, the bark-yip, the lone howl, group howl, group howl-up and the greeting song. The lone howl is the cry of an individual separated from mate or chums; the greeting song, soft and quavering, is produced when a lesser male appears near more dominant males. Coyotes sing to declare their territory and because they love to sing— alone or with friends. A single coyote can make several noises at once and achieve all kinds of ventriloquistic effects in the process. Often what sounds like several song-dog armies scattered in the foothills is one or two coyotes really cutting loose. A passing siren triggers a spirited response.

Effective transition — *Huneven shifts to coyote's voice.*

Urban hunt —

Most animals are specialized in their eating habits: cougars as carnivores, rodents as vegetarians. Coyotes are "specialized generalists," i.e., specialized to eat *everything*. Coyotes have no problem recognizing dinner—they'll eat anything from grasshoppers to grapefruit, coleslaw to carrion, mice to Minute Rice.

Shifts to eating habits

A coyote also eats avocados, oranges, melons, berries, chickens, small dogs, livestock and fowl with relish. The rare but rising number of attacks on small children indicates that once certain coyotes overcome their inherent fear of man, very young human specimens also look like food. And if his own offspring or mate is killed, he might well snack off the carcass. A meal's a meal.

Grim humor— "young human specimens" sounds scientific but seems ironic.

To Brother Coyote, it's truly a dog-eat-dog world.

"A meal's a meal"— nice touch. This urban coyote is a real survivor.

Coyotes, it was discovered, are so intelligent they can learn from their own mistakes and the mistakes of fellow coyotes. Remarkably, they also teach their young to avoid those mistakes.

Shifts to coyote intelligence

Ultimately, man learned a few things, too. He learned coyotes step up their reproduction to compensate for losses in population—when they are threatened, litter size doubles and females breed at an earlier age. A community of coyotes can lose 70 percent of its number and replenish itself *within one year*. Killing millions of coyotes merely culled the species—the whole predator-control program effected an accelerated exercise in evolution in which the fittest survived, and reproduced.

A new housing tract in the hills initially may disorient and disturb coyotes displaced by the construction, but within a year they relax and learn to appreciate the urban development for what it is: coyote paradise. In Southern California, ground squirrels and gophers flourish in disturbed, developing environments. This profusion of rodents delights indigenous coyotes; imagine snoozing in the shade all day, then, come evening, nipping down to town for drinks and dinner. It's a wild dog's life.

H uneven picks up adaptation theme— coyotes adjust.

There's such a concentration and diversity of food available in suburban neighborhoods that the opportunistic coyote no longer has to spend long hours ranging over great distances to meet his dietary requirements. The urban coyote finds he has much more leisure time on his hands. Having yet to develop a taste for television, movies or alcohol, the coyote is still very much a family dog. He uses the extra hours in his day for courtship, mating and playing with his children. Since much of this play is instructional, each new generation of urban coyote is better educated and craftier than the last.

Irony increases: coyote becomes more human.

Human characteristics ironic. One thought: like coyotes, humans came from the wilderness and settled in cities... Strange parallel.

Over the years homeowners have complained of coyotes drinking from swimming pools, eating from outdoor pet bowls, of a big mangy coyote routinely sleeping on a back-porch chaise lounge, a coyote chasing a small dog through a doggy door and around the kitchen, a coyote tightrope walking down a

Coyotes have bad manners. An unwanted house guest.

fence rail, coyotes living in freeway landscaping, a coyote eating a poodle in public.

Small domestic animals can't protect themselves from a coyote because it attacks so swiftly. When confronted by a stalking coyote, a pet rarely takes constructive action; a cat will bunch up and hiss, a poodle may snarl or charge. Pets don't think like wild animals. When they see a coyote coming they think: uh-oh, there's going to be a fight. The coyote thinks: lunch.

Conclusion — Humans and their domesticated pets are no match for the urban coyote.

{ Is this the end? Very abrupt.

FINAL NOTES———

Purpose: Huneven gives the reader a new slant on coyotes. No longer creatures hunting in the distant hills, they are city dwellers; coyotes flourish in urban areas.

Strategy: Mostly a description, but not a scientific description — it's lively, full of fun, yet full of facts. Huneven begins with an overview of the coyote, then moves to the parts.

Style: The tone is ironic and witty. Huneven's coyote, a wily creature, seems to be the opposite of the coyote in the *Road Runner* cartoons — a survivor, not a victim. Her style suggests a cartoon — well detailed, rich in images, dark humor.

After the first reading you should be familiar with the essay's content and purpose. You should have a sense of the strategies and the tone. You also should have jotted down general impressions and responses to the essay. In other words, you've left your markings. Now you're ready to return to the territory.

Five Tips for Rereading

Before reading the essay, review your notes and reconsider the title: Did it accurately reflect the content or purpose of the essay? Did it embody the tone? If not, how does it function? Then you're ready to begin. Once again you should read with a pencil in hand, ready to expand or change your previous observations and make new ones. Remember, too, that you're attempting to read like a writer examining another writer's techniques—that is, you're reading with a critical eye.

1. *Review the Beginning and End*

The beginning and end are critical sections. The opening paragraphs usually will, directly or indirectly, establish the purpose of the essay. Sometimes the purpose will be immediately clear, as it is in Huneven's "Living Well Is the Best Revenge—Just Ask the Urban Coyote." Clearly, her purpose is to describe "a new breed" of coyote, one that thrives in urban and suburban environments. The end will often restate, or in a narrative, dramatize the purpose. Huneven's essay ends abruptly, but the end reinforces her primary purpose: People provide a very good living for the urban coyote.

2. *Read with the Purpose in Mind*

The purpose can serve as a beacon that will guide you as you read through the essay. Knowing the purpose will clarify the strategies the writer uses to achieve that purpose. Huneven's dominant rhetorical pattern is description. She begins with a general description of the coyote, then follows with a series of paragraphs concentrated on parts of the coyote—the eyes, the jaws and teeth, the howl. After the physical description, she shifts to what coyotes eat (everything, it seems), their intelligence, their ability to adapt. As you reread, mark the transitional points and underline topic sentences. Gradually the essay's skeleton will appear, much as an x-ray reveals human bone structure.

3. Examine the Style

You'll already have a sense of the style from the first reading. Now's the time to pin it down. Notice the selection of words. Pay close attention to the shapes and rhythms of sentences. Underline phrases that embody the tone. Huneven uses words that are common in almost everyone's vocabulary. Perhaps only two—*pericarp* and *trickster*—would send you to the dictionary. *Pericarp,* from botany, refers to the three layers that surround the seed in ripe fruit. *Trickster* has a special meaning in folklore: a supernatural figure that appears in many guises and engages in mischievous activities, usually considered a culture hero. In other words, it is adaptable and tough to control.

Huneven's language is crisp and vivid, but many of the sentences are lengthy:

> Over the years homeowners have complained of coyotes drinking from swimming pools, eating from outdoor pet bowls, of a big mangy coyote routinely sleeping on a backporch chaise lounge, a coyote chasing a small dog through a doggy door and around the kitchen, a coyote tightrope walking down a fence rail, coyotes living in freeway landscaping, a coyote eating a poodle in public.

She expects her readers to concentrate, demanding that they exert the patience to follow the twists and turns of sentences that often seem as unpredictable as the coyote itself.

Huneven uses humor and irony, both hard to miss. She seems to draw a great deal of pleasure from knowing that an uncontrollable creature lives at the heart of our civilization. She personifies the coyote; that is, she gives it human qualities—it has a profession; it likes its leisure, using its "extra hours for courtship, mating and playing with his children." At times she suggests that the urban coyote leads a comfortable life similar to that of a 1980s Yuppie, a young, ambitious, and well-educated city dweller with a professional career and an affluent life-style. But she also gleefully reports that this Yuppie coyote will violate social decorum by "eating a poodle in public"—a nasty *hombre,* after all.

4. *Linger on Interesting Passages*

Stop your reading to examine passages that catch your attention. What's an interesting passage? That's a judgment call. Perhaps the passage will be rich in figurative language. Perhaps it will be an interestingly structured paragraph or series of paragraphs. Later, you might want to use it as a model to emulate in your writing practice.

In one passage that deserves some attention Huneven makes use of contrast and of hyperbole, the technique of dramatic exaggeration with which writers make a point.

> Most animals are specialized in their eating habits: cougars as carnivores, rodents as vegetarians. Coyotes are "specialized generalists," i.e., specialized to eat *everything.* Coyotes have no problem recognizing dinner—they'll eat anything from grasshoppers to grapefruit, coleslaw to carrion, mice to Minute Rice.

One writer who bracketed this passage used it as a model for practicing style. The result is the following paragraph:

> Most appointed officials specialize in one area of government: the Secretary of Defense on weapons, the Attorney General on law. Elected officials are "specialized generalists"; that is, specialized to speak on any subject. Senators and members of Congress are quick to pounce on all controver-

sial issues—they'll speak on anything from abortion to prayer, peace to war, human rights to animal rights.

Of course, using passages from professional writers as models for practice comes later, after you've finished reading the essay.

5. *Record Your Closing Impressions*

Your impressions may be related to purpose, strategy, and style. They may also include your associations with the essay: Does it bring to mind any experiences you've had? Do you associate it with something you've learned or something you've seen or heard about? Does it stir a specific meaning in you? And, perhaps most important, does it call to mind any ideas you might like to explore in writing?

1

Narration

Relating Events

The Method

Once upon a time is the phrase that begins countless childhood narratives. *To narrate* is to tell a story. Our lives are full of stories, some exciting, some dull. These stories might be as brief as an anecdote—"A funny thing happened to me today while dissecting a frog in biology." They might seem as simple as a fairy tale, such as "Little Red Riding Hood," or as complex as a novel, such as James Joyce's *Ulysses*.

Narratives are so common in human experience that some psychologists have claimed that their patterns are etched on the human psyche, that people actually *need* stories. Absurd? It is difficult to imagine that some people might require stories in the same way as they require affection. One fact, though, is certain: effective narratives embody a few known characteristics, and good writers keep this fact in mind when composing their stories.

The most common of these characteristics is the **narrative effect,** or, as some writers call it, the "payoff." Readers want a payoff—a moral, an insight, a message, a point, or just good entertainment. Often the narrative effect will be subtle, nothing more than getting the reader to utter a soft "Aha!" Consider this narrative, a teaching tale from Zen Buddhist lore. At first glance, it may seem to lack a narrative effect.

> A man traveling across a field encountered a tiger. He fled, the tiger after him. Coming to a precipice, he caught hold of the root of a wild vine and swung himself down over the edge. The tiger sniffed at him from above. Trembling, the man looked down to where, far below, another tiger was waiting to eat him. Only the vine sustained him.
>
> Two mice, one white and one black, little by little started to gnaw away the vine. The man saw a luscious strawberry near him. Grasping the vine with one hand, he plucked the strawberry with the other. How sweet it tasted!

What is the payoff? is a fair question that every reader has the right to ask. Clearly the narrative effect the storyteller might wish to achieve is not spelled out; the story reveals no thesis. But it certainly has something to do with being involved in the present and, perhaps, not worrying about what can't be controlled. One student suggests that fear of the past (represented by the first tiger pacing above the man, who is a monk) or fear of the future (the second tiger pacing below the monk) should not interfere with our enjoyment of the present (the strawberry). But what about the mice? They're a detail that needs to be considered in any interpretation. Soon they will gnaw through the vine, sending the monk to his death. Perhaps the tale suggests that when death is imminent, life becomes inordinately sweet.

Why create a story to illustrate a point, you might ask, even one as brief as this Zen tale? Why not just hold up a finger, smile sagely, and directly state a purpose? "Do not let fear of the past or present interfere with your enjoyment of the moment" or "Enjoy life now, for death may be near." In other words, "Why all the mystery?"

Not all narratives are packed with hidden meanings or intended to provoke emotional responses. Many are factual reports, such as news reports or police reports, which simply recount events as they unfold, but narrative essays often deal with subjects that go beyond the limits of a report. Like the treasures in many children's tales, the purpose in many narratives—especially works of fiction such as tales, short stories, and novels—is therefore buried. In this way, the narrative essay offers its readers the opportunity to experience anything the storyteller has experienced—love, anger, fear, hate, prejudice, outrage, confusion, hope, disappointment—all the emotional states we encounter in life. The events, therefore, must be dramatized, not explained, thus re-creating, rather than reporting, events: first you live through a string of related experiences and then you get the meaning—well, maybe you get the meaning.

Strategies

Because of the nature of narrative essays, the relationship between you and the storyteller is complex. Storytellers will entice you to use your imagination to re-create the story. You should join, not resist, a writer in this effort. If the effort fails, then you will not make the creative leap that allows a narrative essay to achieve its emotional effect. Even if the purpose behind a narrative essay seems murky after a first reading, trust that the writer who chooses narration as a dominant essay pattern will always keep an eye on the purpose, usually dramatizing rather than stating it.

Narrative Structure

Every storyteller knows that readers crave order, a sense of direction, movement. To meet this need, many narrative essays are divided in three parts:

1. The **opening**. The beginning sentences usually arouse your interest without giving away the outcome. The opening may suggest the purpose of the story about to unfold, but not reveal it.
2. The **body.** The story moves forward through scenes that dramatize the events, without explaining them, using such devices as description, dialogue, conflict, and suspense.
3. The **climax**. All stories should end with a memorable conclusion. Here in the story the purpose usually lurks just beneath the surface. An effective climax may send you back to the story so that you can study how all the parts fit together.

You will find that most effective narrative essays follow this loose pattern. You can usually count on a storyteller to establish a story's situation in the opening by providing information that answers these questions: Who? What? Where? and When? They will suggest a **conflict** as well. Consider this opening from Martin Gansberg's "Thirty-eight Who Saw Murder Didn't Call the Police."

> For more than half an hour thirty-eight respectable, law-abiding citizens in Queens watched a killer stalk and stab a woman in three separate attacks in Kew Gardens.
> Twice their chatter and the sudden glow of their bedroom lights interrupted him and frightened him off. Each time he returned, sought her out, and stabbed her again. Not one person telephoned the police during the assault; one witness called after the woman was dead.
> That was two weeks ago today.

Whom does the situation involve? A murder victim, the murderer, and, most important, the "thirty-eight respectable, law-abiding citizens" who didn't call the police. What does the situation involve? Crime in the streets. Where did it take place? An area in Queens, a New York City borough. When did it happen? Two weeks before the date of the newspaper narrative. And the conflict? Gansberg clearly suggests a conflict related to social obligation—the indifference of the thirty-eight bystanders who fail to meet their legal and moral responsibility.

Point of View

Also in the opening of narrative essays, writers establish the **point of view**—that is, they reveal who is telling the story. As generally used in narrative essays, point of view is easy to understand. Stories are told either by a participant in the events (first-person point of view) or by a nonparticipant—third-person point of view.

Most often readers associate stories with the first-person point of view, which seems to give narrative essays authenticity: "I swear this is true—I was there! I lived it!" Often the events have directly affected the first-person storyteller in some emotional or intellectual way. At other times, the storyteller acts as a spectator, reporting events he or she saw others experience. In either case, first-person narratives usually are more subjective than third-person narratives. They embody the storyteller's attitudes throughout the essay, directly in overt statements or indirectly in style. Writers almost always establish the point of view in the first paragraph. Consider the opening paragraph in Flannery O'Connor's essay, "The King of Birds."

> When I was five, I had an experience that marked me for life. Pathé News sent a photographer from New York to Savannah to take a picture of a chicken of mine. This chicken, a buff Cochin Bantam, had the distinction of being able to walk either forward or backward. Her fame had spread through the press, and by the time she reached the

attention of Pathé News, I suppose there was nowhere left for her to go—forward or backward. Shortly after that she died, as now seems fitting.

O'Connor's opening paragraph illustrates one more bit of advice we can give you when reading first-person narratives: watch for the storyteller's own perspective. Notice that O'Connor begins by relating the emotional effect of an event that took place when she was five, but the first and last sentences clearly indicate that she is writing from an adult's perspective, not a five-year-old's, thus adding complexity, perhaps even irony, to the tone.

A writer who uses the third-person point of view usually relates events as accurately, and sometimes objectively, as possible. As a nonparticipant, the third-person narrator develops the story from reports by others, much as a journalist collects information for a story. This approach doesn't mean a third-person narration lacks power or drama. It merely means that the storyteller is not part of the action. Consider the opening paragraph in Maxine Hong Kingston's brief narrative "The Wild Man of the Green Swamp."

> For eight months in 1975, residents on the edge of Green Swamp, Florida, had been reporting to the police that they had seen a Wild Man. When they stepped toward him, he made strange noises as in a foreign language and ran back into the saw grass. At first, authorities said the Wild Man was a mass hallucination. Maneating animals lived in the swamp, and a human being could hardly find a place to rest without sinking. Perhaps it was some kind of a bear the children had seen.

Kingston's point of view is clearly **objective**, even dispassionate. We don't want to leave you with the impression, though, that third-person narrations are always objective and dispassionate. Review the opening from Gansberg's "Thirty-eight Who Saw Murder Didn't Call the Police," presented above. Gansberg's attitude toward the "thirty-eight respectable, law-abiding citizens" who watched a killer stalk his victim is clearly **subjective** and very passionate.

Chronological and Psychological Time

Because narratives unfold in time, storytellers must arrange the events so that the connections between them are clear. As you begin to read a narrative, notice the writer's narrative arrangement: Are the events arranged according to **chronological time**; that is, in sequence as they happened, step by step? Or are they arranged according to **psychological time**; that is, the way in which events might be connected in memory, shifting back and forth in time while keeping a sense of forward movement?

The decision a writer makes about the arrangement of a narrative essay is often determined by the subject. A historical essay, such as a narrative about a battle, usually marches along in chronological time. But if the subject comes from personal experience then the essay may be arranged in psychological time, beginning *in medias res,* "in the middle of things," with an event that comes near the end of the actual chronology. This opening event can be highly dramatic, designed to keep you in suspense until the essay closes, when its purpose becomes clear.

Whichever arrangement the writer chooses, he or she is obliged to guide you through the story. While reading with a critical eye, you should, therefore, watch for transitions in time. They may be complete sentences designed to smooth your way from one event to another: "My social life began to crumble into pieces like a stale oatmeal cookie after we settled in Santa Fe." They may take the form of brief phrases: "Two weeks later," "Only one year ago," "Soon I was to learn." Or they may be single words that help a writer cut through time: "Now, Then," "Before, Today." Identifying the transitional tactics will help you follow the most complex narrative.

Scene and Summary

While crafting a narrative essay, the storyteller has two methods to use in presenting the events: **scene** and **summary**. You'll recognize scene because it directly portrays an event on the page. Like a scene in film or drama, a narrative-essay scene is played before your eyes. Summary is a synopsis of an event. It relates the high points but leaves out much of the specific detail that a scene usually includes. Many narratives include both scene and summary, with summary serving as the glue that holds the scenes together. It might help if you think of scene and summary as showing and telling: scene shows, summary tells. Consider this scene from a student's narrative that shows the writer's battle with fear:

> I stood paralyzed on the dock, my hands clenched and my knees locked tight. Bobby was flailing at the water, trying to pull himself to the overturned boat. He shouted for help, his voice rising to a shrill pitch and carrying beyond the boathouse and into the empty woods.
>
> I wanted to plunge into the lake, but my body would not unlock, and the horrible, empty spot in my mind threatened me like a black pit I might fall into. It was the water and all it symbolized—darkness, suffocation, a murky death.

The narrator presents this dramatic moment as if it were taking place before your eyes. He is showing it to you. Now compare this scene to a summarized version:

> When my brother Bobby overturned the rowboat and fell into the lake, I panicked. You see, I had almost drowned once in this very lake. The experience left me with the deep, irrational fear that if I ever swam in it again, I would be swallowed up. Although I knew he needed help, seeing Bobby flailing in the water paralyzed me.

Here the writer tells about the event. This summary lacks the immediacy of the scenic version, yet it, too, is effective. Whether a writer uses scene or summary, or both, depends on the effect he or she wishes to create. Often narrative essayists present the dramatic moments in scenes and use summary to move from scene to scene.

Narration in College Writing

Informal narration based on personal experience is a frequent assignment in college courses. In cultural anthropology or social psychology you may be assigned a narrative report that requires your own observations. In history you may be asked to write from imagination a narrative about a historical event from a historical figure's point of view. In English you may be assigned an informal narrative essay based on a personal experience that brought you some insight. More often, college writers work brief narrative passages into an essay with other dominant patterns. In such papers, narrative passages may be used to create an interesting opening or to illustrate a point. In either case, the narrative must have a clear structural purpose to justify its use, the events must be carefully arranged, and the point of view must be clear.

The following four paragraphs function as an introduction to an essay exploring the psychological implications of living in a hostile urban environment. Raymond Luu, who grew up in San Francisco, uses personal experience to develop his subject. He opens with this narrative passage to establish the essay's psychological **mood** and to suggest his purpose:

Opening sentence states Luu's purpose—his life is "dominated by need for security." It also sets the point of view—first person.

Luu clearly marks the transitions from one narrative point to another: "My day begins," "before I leave for work," and "When I walk to my car."

I am beginning to feel as if my life is dominated by a need for security. I am not talking about the kind of security most people hope to achieve by retirement or the kind that comes from a trusting relationship. I am talking about the kind that comes from living in a dangerous world. My day begins at the bathroom sink. When I open a new bottle of mouthwash, I must pry loose a tight plastic shrink-wrap seal. This nuisance takes some time, but the seal is necessary so that a psychopath does not poison my mouthwash and kill me as I gargle.

Before I leave for work I switch on the burglar-alarm system that lets out a loud klaxon before informing the police whenever anyone passes through the perimeter of my house. The alarm is absolutely necessary because homes in my neighborhood have become piggy banks for drug addicts.

When I walk up to my car, I must deactivate the alarm system or it will shriek and the lights will begin to blink. If I did not have the alarm system, thieves would smash in the window and make off with my radio and CD player that cost me a week's pay.

He ends by driving home the narrative effect—there's no escape; he even dreams of security measures.

It is only 7:30 A.M., yet preoccupation with security measures has been at the center of my thought. This absorption will continue through the rest of the day, into the night, and even manifest itself in my dreams.

Luu's narrative passage is simple and direct. He concentrates on three moments in his morning to dramatize his need for security. He could have included a great deal more in this passage— rising from bed, showering, brushing his teeth, eating breakfast, and so on—but he selected only the details he needed to achieve the narrative effect: There is no escape from the dangers of a hostile world, not even in sleep.

Now read the narrative essays that follow. Apply the information you have acquired in this introduction. Identify each essay's structure: the opening, the body, and the climax. Is the essay arranged according to chronological or psychological time? What is the point of view, first person or third person? Mark the passages in which the author uses summary and scene. Remember, you are reading as a writer reads; you are reading to learn the craft of writing.

❦ Maya Angelou ❦

Maya Angelou's talents and accomplishments span many fields, but she is perhaps best known as the author of I Know Why the Caged Bird Sings *(1970), the first volume in her five-part autobiography, in which she recounts her childhood years living with her grandmother in Stamps, Arkansas. Born Marguerita Johnson in 1928, Angelou surmounted the hardships and disadvantages of her youth—raped at age eight, unwed mother at sixteen—to write a joyful account of her own life and to achieve distinction as a dancer, actress, director, poet, script-writer, civil-rights activist, and television writer and producer. She acted in the television series "Roots," and has written several television specials, including a BBC–TV documentary called* Trying to Make It Home *(1988). She has received numerous awards and honorary degrees for her accomplishments and her continued service to the cause of civil rights.*

Finishing School

This story describes a brief time in Maya Angelou's childhood in Arkansas, where she was sent to work in a white woman's house to learn "mid-Victorian values" as a black woman was supposed to know them. In the story, taken from I Know Why the Caged Bird Sings, *the author mixes chronological and psychological narrative to relate her growing awareness of the subtleties in white domination.*

Recently a white woman from Texas, who would quickly describe herself as a liberal, asked me about my hometown. When I told her that in Stamps my grandmother had owned the only Negro general merchandise store since the turn of the century, she exclaimed, "Why, you were a debutante." Ridiculous and even ludicrous. But Negro girls in small Southern towns, whether poverty-stricken or just munching along on a few of life's necessities, were given as extensive and irrelevant preparations for adulthood

One possible lead-in to assigning this selection is to briefly discuss how much personal names matter: How do we feel when people mispronounce or forget our names? Do some names suggest personality or character traits? Do our names influence our behavior? Do the names parents select for children suggest (at least to the parents) qualities the parents want their children to have? Why are names so important? Such a discussion should help prepare students for reading Maya Angelou's narrative.

After students have read the story, discussion might turn to structure. Have students notice the careful and thorough attention the narrator gives to presenting background information: first, about herself in paragraphs 1 and 2, and then about Mrs. Cullinan, her house, and her family in paragraphs 3 through 12. After setting up this background, the narrator presents three brief incidents: the speckled-faced woman's suggestion that "Margaret" be shortened to "Mary," Mrs. Cullinan's first use of the name "Mary," and the climactic incident of Marguerita's breaking the china. Have students discuss the purposes of each. Finally, have them discuss how effective the last two paragraphs are.

MARGINAL NOTES

Paragraphs 1 and 2 set the stage for the narration by contrasting early training of white girls with that of black girls.

"munching along": just getting by

as rich white girls shown in magazines. Admittedly the training was not the same. While white girls learned to waltz and sit gracefully with a tea cup balanced on their knees, we were lagging behind, learning the mid-Victorian values with very little money to indulge them. . . .

"mid-Victorian values": values of middle-class respectability, which would include a high degree of class consciousness.

We were required to embroider and I had trunkfuls of colorful dishtowels, pillowcases, runners and handkerchiefs to my credit. I mastered the art of crocheting and tatting, and there was a lifetime's supply of dainty doilies that would never be used in sacheted dresser drawers. It went without saying that all girls could iron and wash, but the finer touches around the home, like setting a table with real silver, baking roasts and cooking vegetables without meat, had to be learned elsewhere. Usually at the source of those habits. During my tenth year, a white woman's kitchen became my finishing school.

The physical description of Mrs. Cullinan, though brief, allows the reader to picture her quite accurately.

Mrs. Viola Cullinan was a plump woman who lived in a three-bedroom house somewhere behind the post office. She was singularly unattractive until she smiled, and then the lines around her eyes and mouth which made her look perpetually dirty disappeared, and her face looked like the mask of an impish elf. She usually rested her smile until late afternoon when her women friends dropped in and Miss Glory, the cook, served them cold drinks on the closed-in porch.

Students should notice the value attached to things and their names at Mrs. Cullinan's house, an ironic contrast to the way in which names of the servants are changed for convenience.

The exactness of her house was inhuman. This glass went here and only here. That cup had its place and it was an act of impudent rebellion to place it anywhere else. At twelve o'clock the table was set. At 12:15 Mrs. Cullinan sat down to dinner (whether her husband had arrived or not). At 12:16 Miss Glory brought out the food.

It took me a week to learn the difference between a salad plate, a bread plate and a dessert plate.

Mrs. Cullinan kept up the tradition of her wealthy parents. She was from Virginia. Miss Glory, who was a descendant of slaves that had worked for the Cullinans, told me her history. She had married beneath her (according to Miss Glory). Her husband's family hadn't had their money very long and what they had "didn't 'mount to much."

As ugly as she was, I thought privately, she was lucky to get a husband above or beneath her station. But Miss Glory wouldn't let me say a thing against her mistress. She was very patient with me, however, over the housework. She explained the dishware, silverware and servants' bells. The large round bowl in which soup was served wasn't a soup bowl, it was a tureen. There were goblets, sherbet glasses, ice-cream glasses, wine glasses, green glass coffee cups with matching saucers, and water glasses. I had a glass to drink from, and it sat with Miss Glory's on a separate shelf from the others. Soup spoons, gravy boat, butter knives, salad forks and carving platter were additions to my vocabulary and in fact almost represented a new language. I was fascinated with the novelty, with the fluttering Mrs. Cullinan and her Alice-in-Wonderland house.

Her husband remains, in my memory, undefined. I lumped him with all the other white men that I had ever seen and tried not to see.

On our way home one evening, Miss Glory told me that Mrs. Cullinan couldn't have children. She said that she was too delicate-boned. It was hard to imagine bones at all under those layers of fat. Miss Glory went on to say that the doctor had taken out all her lady organs. I reasoned that a pig's organs included the lungs, heart, and liver, so if Mrs. Cullinan was walking around without those essentials, it explained why she drank alcohol out of unmarked bottles. She was keeping herself embalmed.

When I spoke to Bailey about it, he agreed that I was right, but he also informed me that Mr. Cullinan had two daughters by a colored lady and that I knew them very well. He added that the girls were the spitting image of their father. I was unable to remember what he looked like, although I had just left him a few hours before, but I thought of the Coleman girls. They were very light-skinned and certainly didn't look very much like their mother (no one ever mentioned Mr. Coleman).

My pity for Mrs. Cullinan preceded me the next morning like the Cheshire cat's smile. Those girls, who could have been her daughters, were beautiful. They didn't have to straighten their hair. Even when they were caught in the rain, their braids still

7

8 All mentions of Mr. Cullinan remark on his insignificance to the girl and even to Mrs. Cullinan.

9 The next few paragraphs establish the girl's consideration and loyalty until Mrs. Cullinan does the unforgivable.

10

11

hung down straight like tamed snakes. Their mouths were pouty little cupid's bows. Mrs. Cullinan didn't know what she missed. Or maybe she did. Poor Mrs. Cullinan.

For weeks after, I arrived early, left late and tried very hard to make up for her barrenness. If she had her own children, she wouldn't have had to ask me to run a thousand errands from her back door to the back door of her friends. Poor old Mrs. Cullinan.   12

The suggestion of a name change in this incident is the turning point in the girl's sympathy for Mrs. Cullinan.

Then one evening Miss Glory told me to serve the ladies on the porch. After I set the tray down and turned toward the kitchen, one of the women asked, "What's your name, girl?" It was the speckled-faced one. Mrs. Cullinan said, "She doesn't talk much. Her name's Margaret."   13

"Is she dumb?"   14

"No. As I understand it, she can talk when she wants to but she's usually quiet as a little mouse. Aren't you, Margaret?"   15

I smiled at her. Poor thing. No organs and couldn't even pronounce my name correctly.   16

"She's a sweet little thing, though."   17

"Well, that may be, but the name's too long. I'd never bother myself. I'd call her Mary if I was you."   18

I fumed into the kitchen. That horrible woman would never have the chance to call me Mary because if I was starving I'd never work for her. . . .   19

That evening I decided to write a poem on being white, fat, old and without children. It was going to be a tragic ballad. I would have to watch her carefully to capture the essence of her loneliness and pain.   20

This incident illustrates Mrs. Cullinan's thoughtfulness about her white neighbors and her casual disregard of her black servants.

The very next day, she called me by the wrong name. Miss Glory and I were washing up the lunch dishes when Mrs. Cullinan came to the doorway. "Mary?"   21

Miss Glory asked, "Who?"   22

Mrs. Cullinan, sagging a little, knew and I knew. "I want Mary to go down to Mrs. Randall's and take her some soup. She's not been feeling well for a few days."   23

Miss Glory's face was a wonder to see. "You mean Margaret, ma'am. Her name's Margaret."   24

"That's too long. She's Mary from now on. Heat that soup   25
from last night and put it in the china tureen and, Mary, I want
you to carry it carefully."

Every person I knew had a hellish horror of being "called out   26
of his name." It was a dangerous practice to call a Negro anything
that could be loosely construed as insulting because of the centuries of their having been called niggers, jigs, dinges, blackbirds,
crows, boots and spooks.

Miss Glory had a fleeting second of feeling sorry for me. Then   27
as she handed me the hot tureen she said, "Don't mind, don't pay
that no mind. Sticks and stones may break your bones, but words
. . . You know, I been working for her for twenty years."

She held the back door open for me. "Twenty years. I wasn't   28
much older than you. My name used to be Hallelujah. That's what
Ma named me, but my mistress give me 'Glory,' and it stuck. I
likes it better too."

I was in the little path that ran behind the houses when Miss   29
Glory shouted, "It's shorter too."

For a few seconds it was a tossup over whether I would laugh   30
(imagine being named Hallelujah) or cry (imagine letting some
white woman rename you for her convenience). My anger saved
me from either outburst. I had to quit the job, but the problem
was going to be how to do it. Momma wouldn't allow me to quit
for just any reason.

"She's a peach. That woman is a real peach." Mrs. Randall's   31
maid was talking as she took the soup from me, and I wondered
what her name used to be and what she answered to now.

For a week I looked into Mrs. Cullinan's face as she called me   32
Mary. She ignored my coming late and leaving early. Miss Glory
was a little annoyed because I had begun to leave egg yolk on the
dishes and wasn't putting much heart in polishing the silver. I
hoped that she would complain to our boss, but she didn't.

Then Bailey solved my dilemma. He had me describe the   33
contents of the cupboard and the particular plates she liked best.
Her favorite piece was a casserole shaped like a fish and the green
glass coffee cups. I kept his instructions in mind, so on the next

This paragraph emphasizes how greatly names affect a sense of personal dignity.

Miss Glory's acceptance of her name change represents the older ways of accommodation. In contrast, the girl finds the name change intolerable and resolves to leave.

Two paragraphs of transition lead to the last incident.

The final incident, the result of a deliberate plan to get fired, once again reveals Mrs. Cullinan's values. It also illustrates Bailey's wise understanding of how vulnerable these values are.

The two short, last paragraphs, 39 and 40, close the narrative on a defiant and triumphant note.

POSSIBLE ANSWERS

Meaning and Purpose

1. Give students time to explore their experiences of being angered or humiliated when treated unfairly. Did they feel powerless? Did they seek revenge? Be sure they compare their experiences with Angelou's.

2. Before Mrs. Cullinan calls her Mary, Marguerita is critical but cooperative, and even sympathetic, about her inability to have children ("For weeks after I arrived early, left late and tried very hard to make up for her barrenness" [12]). After Mrs. Cullinan calls her Mary, Marguerita is justifiably angry and deliberately breaks precious dishes to take revenge and get herself fired.

3. Angelou wants readers to feel as she feels about Mrs. Cullinan. Angelou also gives information about how a young black girl was expected to be trained and what she had to deal with in the world of privileged whites.

4. Angelou's audience could be people of all colors who want to hear about her experiences and perhaps be made to think about how blacks were—and are—treated. They are people who want to understand why Angelou writes what she writes. Her readers are educated and aware.

5. Angelou says that blacks "had a hellish horror" of not being called by their correct names because of the abusive names they have been called for centuries. Even in calling her Margaret, Mrs. Cullinan doesn't use Angelou's correct name.

day when Miss Glory was hanging out clothes and I had again been told to serve the old biddies on the porch, I dropped the empty serving tray. When I heard Mrs. Cullinan scream, "Mary!" I picked up the casserole and two of the green glass cups in readiness. As she rounded the kitchen door I let them fall on the tiled floor.

I could never absolutely describe to Bailey what happened next, because each time I got to the part where she fell on the floor and screwed up her ugly face to cry, we burst out laughing. She actually wobbled around on the floor and picked up shards of the cups and cried, "Oh, Momma. Oh, dear Gawd. It's Mamma's china from Virginia. Oh, Momma, I sorry." 34

Miss Glory came running in from the yard and the women from the porch crowded around. Miss Glory was almost as broken up as her mistress. "You mean to say she broke our Virginia dishes? What we gone do?" 35

Mrs. Cullinan cried louder. "That clumsy nigger. Clumsy little black nigger." 36

Old speckled-face leaned down and asked, "Who did it, Viola? Was it Mary? Who did it?" 37

Everything was happening so fast, I can't remember whether her action preceded her words, but I know that Mrs. Cullinan said, "Her name's Margaret, goddamn it, her name's Margaret." And she threw a wedge of broken plate at me. It could have been the hysteria which put her aim off, but the flying crockery caught Miss Glory right over her ear and she started screaming. 38

I left the front door wide open so all the neighbors could hear. 39

Mrs. Cullinan was right about one thing. My name wasn't Mary. 40

Meaning and Purpose

1. The message you take from this selection will be influenced by your own experiences and attitudes. Think of an experience from

your life, a movie or television program, reading, or knowledge of others' experiences, which in some way parallels Marguerita's experience. In what ways was this experience similar and different?

2. How would you describe Marguerita's feelings about Mrs. Cullinan before Mrs. Cullinan calls her Mary, and then after? What actions or events does Angelou use in her narrative to show those feelings?

3. Do you think Angelou's primary purpose is to give information or to evoke emotion? Examine your own response to this selection as you decide. What words and sentences convince you of your choice?

4. How would you describe Angelou's intended audience? Does she expect that audience to be empathetic with the young black girl? How do you know?

5. What does Angelou reveal about the significance of being "called out of [one's] name" (paragraph 26)?

6. Why do you think Angelou included the story about Hallelujah's name being changed to "Glory"?

Strategy

1. What is the payoff in this narrative essay—that is, the moral, point, or message?

2. The first two paragraphs in this selection serve as introduction to the narrative, which begins in the third paragraph. How does this introduction prepare you for the narrative?

3. In the last scene, how does Angelou's telling you she has trouble remembering exactly what happened affect the credibility of the narrative? How does this admission help establish point of view?

4. The entire narrative covers several weeks. List some of the transitional phrases that Angelou uses to help her readers follow the passage of time.

5. What significance has the last sentence? How does it pull the essay together and conclude it?

6. Glory accepted and even preferred having her name changed by whites, just as most blacks then were docile and submissive. Marguerita rebelled against being called Mary and would not accept the role Glory accepted. The contrast between the two women emphasizes Angelou's point about names.

Strategy

1. The payoff for the reader is the lesson in how prejudice affects one young black girl, and, by extension, all minorities. The moral is that prejudice is evil and should be rebelled against.

2. The introduction recounts for readers first how Angelou gets into the story she tells (a white woman asked Angelou about her hometown and then made the remark about a "debutante" [1]). Then Angelou gives general information about the differences between how white and black girls were trained in domestic arts. The second paragraph has some details about what black girls learned and then gets Angelou into the setting of her narrative. After reading these two paragraphs, readers know something about the larger context for the story that begins in paragraph 3.

3. Obviously Angelou is telling this story from the perspective of an adult looking back on herself at age ten. Her memory is perhaps fuzzy because the events happened a long time ago, and they happened fast. Her credibility is not in question because an adult is usually a more reliable narrator than a child. Rather, her saying she can't remember exactly what happened is honest, and true to her adult perspective.

4. Some transitional phrases are "On our way home one evening" (9); "For weeks after" (12); "That evening I decided" (20); "Then Bailey solved my dilemma" (33). These and others keep the story flowing through its chronological order.

5. The last sentence emphasizes that Mrs. Cullinan is in fact not right in most things she says about her young black servant, including

her correct name, which is not Margaret. Mrs. Cullinan does not understand her own actions and Marguerita's feelings. The one thing she finally does understand—that Marguerita's name is not going to be Mary—is a victory for Marguerita. This sentence reminds readers of the differences in training between white and black girls that Angelou talks about in her first two paragraphs.

Style

1. Paragraph 30 is a good example of Angelou's telling us Marguerita's thoughts. They reveal that Marguerita understands, even at age ten, the abuse and unfairness in Glory's not being called by her given name. And the thoughts show that Marguerita plans to get out of her job for good cause. Marguerita is shrewd and smarter than her employer.
2. a. The irony is that the white woman's kitchen could never teach Marguerita how to be a "debutante"; she also makes sure she is "finished" with this finishing school.
   b. Marguerita would not expect to have a home herself in which she would use such fancy china and utensils or live the life-style that goes with them.
   c. Mrs. Cullinan is melodramatic about her situation, and in fact is probably not lonely and in pain. Marguerita's sympathy is misdirected toward someone who cannot sympathize with her not wanting to be called Mary.
   d. Mrs. Cullinan doesn't get the point at all about the broken dishes. She is disturbed only about losing something she valued that Marguerita scorned.
3. In paragraph 9, "She was keeping herself embalmed" refers, in a humorous and sad way, to Mrs. Cullinan's drinking habit. Marguerita's explanation of the habit fits the perspective of a ten-year-old. Paragraph 11 is a humorous description of what Marguerita thinks Mr. Cullinan's daughters must look like—beautiful and with straight hair, unlike herself. That Marguerita says "Poor Mrs. Cullinan" shows her naiveté, and the reader gets the benefit of the humor.

Style

1. Several times Angelou presents the thoughts of the young girl. In paragraph 16, after being called Margaret instead of Marguerita, the girl thinks "Poor thing. No organs and couldn't even pronounce my name correctly." Find other examples of Marguerita's thoughts and discuss what they tell us about her.
2. Irony describes our recognizing a reality different from the one that appears to us. It can be expressed in words that actually mean the opposite of what they say. Explain the irony in these items:
   a. "During my tenth year, a white woman's kitchen became my finishing school."
   b. The careful attention to lists of names Marguerita had to learn (soup spoons, gravy boat, butter knives, and so on).
   c. "I would have to watch her carefully to capture the essence of her loneliness and pain."
   d. Mrs. Cullinan's reaction to Marguerita's breaking the dishes.
   Can you find other ironies in the selection?
3. How does humor work in this essay? Find examples.

Writing Tasks

1. Consider whether you think Mrs. Cullinan has learned a lesson from Marguerita's actions at the end of the selection. Write a narrative essay about an event in which the "payoff" (moral, point) involves a subordinate or "weaker" person's taking revenge on an authority figure or "stronger" person. End your narrative so that the person in authority either learns a lesson or not, according to whether or not you think Mrs. Cullinan does.
2. Write an essay expressing your feelings about the way in which Marguerita deals with prejudice. Before writing, consider these questions and others of your own: What choices do you think Marguerita had? Was she naive to empathize with Mrs. Cullinan's lack of children? Is Mrs. Cullinan merely a product of her culture's attitudes toward blacks? What responsibility do you think she has for what happens in the final scene?

❦ George Orwell ❦

George Orwell is the pen name of Eric Arthur Blair, who was born in Bengal, India, the son of a British civil servant. At age four, he was sent to England, where he attended prestigious schools, but before finishing his university education he returned to India to serve in the British Imperial Police in Burma. Already scornful of British high society, he was soon disillusioned with imperialism as well. He returned to Europe in 1927 to spend several impoverished years in Paris and London before his writing began to bring him financial and critical rewards. His experience living among and writing about the poor workers and coal miners in urban northwest England confirmed his political stand as a socialist, which led him to fight in the Spanish Civil War against the fascists. Many of his essays and his nonfiction works relate in narrative form the first-hand experiences that shaped his political views, and in his best-known novels, Animal Farm *(1945) and* 1984 *(1949), he uses fiction to elaborate the dangers of totalitarianism.*

A Hanging

In "A Hanging," Orwell uses a simple story to examine the complexity of his personal involvement in the British imperialistic occupation of India early in the twentieth century. Taken from the collection, Shooting an Elephant and Other Essays *(1950), it is a straight chronological narrative that conveys Orwell's deep sympathy for the oppressed in society.*

It was in Burma, a sodden morning of the rains. A sickly light, like yellow tinfoil, was slanting over the high walls into the jail yard. We were waiting outside the condemned cells, a row of sheds fronted with double bars, like small animal cages. Each cell measured about ten feet by ten and was quite bare within except for a plank bed and a pot for drinking water. In some of them brown, silent men were squatting at the inner bars, with their

1

45

blankets draped round them. These were the condemned men, due to be hanged within the next week or two.

One prisoner had been brought out of his cell. He was a Hindu, a puny wisp of a man, with a shaven head and vague liquid eyes. He had a thick, sprouting mustache, absurdly too big for his body, rather like the mustache of a comic man on the films. Six tall Indian warders were guarding him and getting him ready for the gallows. Two of them stood by with rifles and fixed bayonets, while the others handcuffed him, passed a chain through his handcuffs and fixed it to their belts, and lashed his arms tight to his sides. They crowded very close about him, with their hands always on him in a careful, caressing grip, as though all the while feeling him to make sure he was there. It was like men handling a fish which is still alive and may jump back into the water. But he stood quite unresisting, yielding his arms limply to the ropes, as though he hardly noticed what was happening.

Eight o'clock struck and a bugle call, desolately thin in the wet air, floated from the distant barracks. The superintendent of the jail, who was standing apart from the rest of us, moodily prodding the gravel with his stick, raised his head at the sound. He was an army doctor, with a grey toothbrush mustache and a gruff voice. "For God's sake, hurry up, Francis," he said irritably. "The man ought to have been dead by this time. Aren't you ready yet?"

Francis, the head jailer, a fat Dravidian in a white drill suit and gold spectacles, waved his black hand. "Yes sir, yes sir," he bubbled. "All iss satisfactorily prepared. The hangman iss waiting. We shall proceed."

"Well, quick march, then. The prisoners can't get their breakfast till this job's over."

We set out for the gallows. Two warders marched on either side of the prisoner, with their rifles at the slope; two others marched close against him, gripping him by arm and shoulder, as though at once pushing and supporting him. The rest of us, magistrates and the like, followed behind. Suddenly, when we had gone ten yards, the procession stopped short without any order or warning. A dreadful thing had happened—a dog, come goodness

The bugle call and the superintendent's voice get the narration under way.

"Dravidian": a speaker of one of a family of languages used in southern India.

knows whence, had appeared in the yard. It came bounding among us with a loud volley of barks and leapt around us wagging its whole body, wild with glee at finding so many human beings together. It was a large woolly dog, half Airedale, half pariah. For a moment it pranced around us, and then, before anyone could stop it, it had made a dash for the prisoner, and jumping up tried to lick his face. Everybody stood aghast, too taken aback even to grab the dog.

"Who let that bloody brute in here?" said the superintendent angrily. "Catch it, someone!"

A warder detached from the escort, charged clumsily after the dog, but it danced and gambolled just out of his reach, taking everything as part of the game. A young Eurasian jailer picked up a handful of gravel and tried to stone the dog away, but it dodged the stones and came after us again. Its yaps echoed from the jail walls. The prisoner, in the grasp of the two warders, looked on incuriously, as though this was another formality of the hanging. It was several minutes before someone managed to catch the dog. Then we put my handkerchief through its collar and moved off once more, with the dog still straining and whimpering.

It was about forty yards to the gallows. I watched the bare brown back of the prisoner marching in front of me. He walked clumsily with his bound arms, but quite steadily, with that bobbing gait of the Indian who never straightens his knees. At each step his muscles slid neatly into place, the lock of hair on his scalp danced up and down, his feet printed themselves on the wet gravel. And once, in spite of the men who gripped him by each shoulder, he stepped lightly aside to avoid a puddle on the path.

It is curious; but till that moment I had never realized what it means to destroy a healthy, conscious man. When I saw the prisoner step aside to avoid the puddle, I saw the mystery, the unspeakable wrongness, of cutting a life short when it is in full tide. This man was not dying, he was alive just as we are alive. All the organs of his body were working—bowels digesting food, skin renewing itself, nails growing, tissues forming—all toiling away in solemn foolery. His nails would still be growing when he stood on the drop, when he was falling through the air with a

7

8

9

10

The dog's natural behavior contrasts sharply with the official military solemnity of the march to the gallows. His picking the prisoner for a special greeting links the man and the dog and reminds all of the prisoner's human worth.

"pariah": literally a drum beater; now a member of any oppressed social class, particularly in India. The dog is of mixed breed, probably unkempt, perhaps a stray.

The prisoner's natural movements and his sidestepping the puddle lead the narrator to thoughts on the wrongness of taking a human life.

tenth-of-a-second to live. His eyes saw the yellow gravel and the grey walls, and his brain still remembered, foresaw, reasoned—even about puddles. He and we were a party of men walking together, seeing, hearing, feeling, understanding the same world; and in two minutes, with a sudden snap, one of us would be gone—one mind less, one world less.

Orwell returns to objective description following the meditative thoughts in the preceding paragraph.

The gallows stood in a small yard, separate from the main   11
grounds of the prison, and overgrown with tall prickly weeds. It was a brick erection like three sides of a shed, with planking on top, and above that two beams and a crossbar with the rope dangling. The hangman, a greyhaired convict in the white uniform of the prison, was waiting beside his machine. He greeted us with a servile crouch as we entered. At a word from Francis the two warders, gripping the prisoner more closely than ever, half led, half pushed him to the gallows and helped him clumsily up the ladder. Then the hangman climbed up and fixed the rope around the prisoner's neck.

We stood waiting, five yards away. The warders had formed   12
in a rough circle round the gallows. And then, when the noose was fixed, the prisoner began crying out to his god. It was a high, reiterated cry of "Ram! Ram! Ram! Ram!" not urgent and fearful

"Ram": Rama, an incarnation of the Hindu god Vishnu, the Preserver.

like a prayer or cry for help, but steady, rhythmical, almost like the tolling of a bell. The dog answered the sound with a whine. The hangman, still standing on the gallows, produced a small cotton bag like a flour bag and drew it down over the prisoner's face. But the sound, muffled by the cloth, still persisted, over and over again: "Ram! Ram! Ram! Ram! Ram!"

The hangman climbed down and stood ready, holding the   13
lever. Minutes seemed to pass. The steady, muffled crying from the prisoner went on and on, "Ram! Ram! Ram!" never faltering for an instant. The superintendent, his head on his chest, was slowly poking the ground with his stick; perhaps he was counting the cries, allowing the prisoner a fixed number—fifty, perhaps, or a hundred. Everyone had changed colour. The Indians had gone grey like bad coffee, and one or two of the bayonets were wavering. We looked at the lashed, hooded man on the drop, and

listened to his cries—each cry another second of life; the same thought was in all our minds; oh, kill him quickly, get it over, stop that abominable noise!

Suddenly the superintendent made up his mind. Throwing up his head he made a swift motion with his stick. "Chalo!" he shouted almost fiercely.

"Chalo": Hindu; a command to let the prisoner drop through the gallows.

There was a clanking noise, and then dead silence. The prisoner had vanished, and the rope was twisting on itself. I let go of the dog, and it galloped immediately to the back of the gallows; but when it got there it stopped short, barked, and then retreated into a corner of the yard, where it stood among the weeds, looking timorously out at us. We went round the gallows to inspect the prisoner's body. He was dangling with his toes pointed straight downwards, very slowly revolving, as dead as a stone.

The superintendent reached out with his stick and poked the bare brown body; it oscillated slightly. "*He's* all right," said the superintendent. He backed out from under the gallows, and blew out a deep breath. The moody look had gone out of his face quite suddenly. He glanced at his wrist-watch. "Eight minutes past eight. Well, that's all for this morning, thank God."

The warders unfixed bayonets and marched away. The dog, sobered and conscious of having misbehaved itself, slipped after them. We walked out of the gallows yard, past the condemned cells with their waiting prisoners, into the big central yard of the prison. The convicts, under the command of warders armed with lathis, were already receiving their breakfast. They squatted in long rows, each man holding a tin pannikin, while two warders with buckets marched around ladling out rice; it seemed quite a homely, jolly scene, after the hanging. An enormous relief had come upon us now that the job was done. One felt an impulse to sing, to break into a run, to snigger. All at once everyone began chattering gaily.

The execution completed, the men turn to other activities, with exaggerated alacrity to relieve the tension.

"lathis": wooden police sticks.
"pannikin": a metal cup or dish.

The Eurasian boy walking beside me nodded towards the way we had come, with a knowing smile: "Do you know, sir, our friend (he meant the dead man) when he heard his appeal had been dismissed, he pissed on the floor of his cell. From fright. Kindly "boxwallah": a jewelry-box merchant.

take one of my cigarettes, sir. Do you not admire my new silver case, sir? From the boxwallah, two rupees eight annas. Classy European style."

Several people laughed—at what, nobody seemed certain.   19

Francis was walking by the superintendent, talking gar-   20
rulously: "Well, sir, all has passed off with the utmost satisfac-
toriness. It was all finished—flick! Like that. It iss not always
so—oah, no! I have known cases where the doctor was obliged to
go beneath the gallows and pull the prissoner's legs to ensure
decease. Most disagreeable!"

"Wriggling about, eh? That's bad," said the superintendent.   21

"Arch, sir, it iss worse when they become refractory! One   22
man, I recall, clung to the bars of hiss cage when we went to take
him out. You will scarcely credit, sir, that it took six warders to
dislodge him, three pulling at each leg. We reasoned with him,
'My dear fellow,' we said, 'think of all the pain and trouble you
are causing to us!' But no, he would not listen! Ach, he wass very
troublesome!"

I found that I was laughing quite loudly. Everyone was laugh-   23
ing. Even the superintendent grinned in a tolerant way. "You'd
better all come out and have a drink," he said quite genially. "I've
got a bottle of whisky in the car. We could do with it."

We went through the big double gates of the prison into the   24
road. "Pulling at his legs!" exclaimed a Burmese magistrate suddenly, and burst into a loud chuckling. We all began laughing
again. At that moment Francis' anecdote seemed extraordinarily
funny. We all had a drink together, native and European alike,
quite amicably. The dead man was a hundred yards away.

The matter-of-fact last sentence is more effective than a moralistic caution against cruelty would be.

Meaning and Purpose

1. Orwell titles his essay simply "A Hanging." How effective is
    this title? Is it different in meaning from "*the* hanging"?
    Would a more descriptive title, such as "A Horrible Experience

in Burma" or "The Cruelty of Capital Punishment," be better? Why or why not?

2. Why do you think the narrator describes the sudden presence of the dog as a "dreadful thing"?
3. Why does the condemned man's sidestepping a puddle make the narrator realize "what it means to destroy a healthy, conscious man"?
4. How would you characterize the behavior of the men after "the job was done"? How do you explain the behavior?
5. What is the purpose of Orwell's essay? Is it just a riveting story, or does it have a larger meaning?

Strategy

1. What is the point of view in this essay, and how well does it work?
2. What time order does Orwell use in telling his story? Does he depart from this order anywhere?
3. Why do you think Orwell doesn't tell us the crime the man is being hanged for? Does it matter? Why or why not?

Style

1. How would you describe the tone established in the first paragraph? What words create it? Is this tone sustained throughout the essay, or does it change? Explain.
2. Understatement is a form of irony that represents something as less than it actually is. Find some sentences that are examples of understatement. How does this technique serve Orwell's purpose?
3. Explain the irony in the last two sentences.

POSSIBLE ANSWERS

Meaning and Purpose

1. The simple title is effective because it fits the solemn, matter-of-fact tone and the lack of emotion in the descriptions. The title implies no judgment, as the essayist makes no explicit judgment. "*The* Hanging" is specific, but "A Hanging" says this is one of many similar hangings—unremarkable. He wants readers to figure out his point themselves.
2. The leaping, barking dog is too painful and sharp a contrast to the subdued prisoner, and the somber observers, to be comfortable.
3. The narrator sees clearly that the prisoner has a life "in full tide" (10) when he avoids the puddle. The narrator feels a connection among all the men there, "together, seeing, hearing, feeling, understanding the same world." And the death of one would mean "one mind less, one world less." The narrator sees the condemned man as an individual and understands that taking his life will demean us all.
4. After the hanging, the men are relieved and even jubilant, chattering and laughing. They are suddenly past the burden of anticipating and carrying out the execution or of taking moral responsibility for it. They need to distance themselves emotionally from it.
5. Orwell questions the morality of capital punishment and the colonial rule that imposed it, as well as the small value placed on one Indian life. His specific story illustrates how Indians were oppressed under British rule and his sympathy for them.

Strategy

1. Orwell uses first person and refers to the group of men he is with as "we." Because he and the others are spectators, the first-person voice has an objective and detached sound. Orwell is participant and spectator at the same time. This voice understates the situation and makes it all the more stark.

2. Orwell uses chronological order, beginning with his "waiting outside the condemned cells" (1), right through the hanging, and having a drink afterward. In paragraph 10 Orwell briefly stops the forward movement to reflect on "what it means to destroy a healthy, conscious man."

3. The crime is unimportant because, under British rule, the Indians had little or no value as individuals. The hanged man is simply one example of an execution. That his identity and specific crime make no difference expresses Orwell's point about injustice.

Style

1. The tone is somber and solemn, even depressing. Words such as "sodden morning of the rains," "sickly light," and "brown, silent men" establish the mood. Later in the essay, "desolately thin" (3), and "The Indians had gone grey like bad coffee" (13) carry this tone through the hanging. Then the words change to describe the men's elation and laughter, beginning in paragraph 17. But the somber mood lurks under the gaiety. Orwell's emotionless descriptions maintain the original tone.

2. The sentence, "We set out for the gallows" in paragraph 6 is understatement because it carries no emotion, yet suggests a somber and horrible journey. And, "The superintendent reached out with his stick and poked the bare brown body; it oscillated slightly" in paragraph 16 is also understatement. Orwell shows the lack of feeling in this scene, and emphasizes the emotional and moral detachment.

3. The next-to-last sentence describes the men drinking together "amicably," "native and European alike," when the reality is that one group rules the other and considers them of little value as people. In fact, the British have just executed one of them, and yet they drink together. The last sentence heightens starkly the contrast between the execution and the moral detachment of the men that allows them to be jolly.

Writing Tasks

1. In "A Hanging," Orwell uses narrative to communicate ideas without stating them directly. Write a brief narrative in which you make a point without explicitly stating it. Tell the story of an event that illustrates your point, such as how a stylish wedding shows that we care too much about money and appearance, or how a charismatic speaker shows that we are easily persuaded to believe something.

2. Write a first-person narrative in which you tell about an exciting or moving event in a detached, dispassionate voice. Let understatement emphasize the excitement or other emotion in the story.

🍎 Richard Selzer 🍎

Richard Selzer is a surgeon who writes essays and stories, aimed at a general audience, about the practice of medicine. Born in New York state in 1928, he studied at Union College and Albany Medical School and later at Yale University. He subsequently taught writing at Yale and both taught and practiced surgery at the Yale University Medical School. His articles, for which he received the National Magazine Award in 1975 and an American Medical Writer's Award in 1985, have appeared in Harper's, Esquire, *and* Redbook. *He has published a book of short stories,* Rituals of Surgery *(1975), and a collection of autobiographical essays,* Mortal Lessons: Notes on the Art of Surgery *(1976), in addition to his collections of essays about the medical profession. His most recent book is* Taking the World in for Repairs *(1986).*

The Masked Marvel's Last Toehold

Told in the first person, this narrative reveals the anguish of a patient through the eyes of his doctor, Richard Selzer. Selzer finds himself treating a man he had seen fight in a wrestling match many years earlier, when he was a boy. The author's perspective changes as he moves from the present to the childhood memory and back again to the present. The essay is from Selzer's The Confessions of a Knife *(1979).*

On the fifth floor of the hospital, in the west wing, I know that a man is sitting up in his bed, waiting for me. Elihu Koontz is seventy-five, and he is diabetic. It is two weeks since I amputated his left leg just below the knee. I walk down the corridor, but I do not go straight into his room. Instead, I pause in the doorway. He is not yet aware of my presence, but gazes down at the place in the bed where his leg used to be, and where now there is the collapsed leg of his pajamas. He is totally absorbed, like an athlete appraising the details of his body. What is he

TEACHING SUGGESTIONS

Profitable areas of discussion for this selection might concentrate on Selzer's way of blending description and action and his tying the three sections of the essay together by repeating phrases and images. His skill as a writer is evident in both techniques. A third possibility is a discussion of figurative language and irony.

In some ways, this essay is a shocker. It allows us to see the same man at two stages in his life—once vigorous and successful and somewhat famous, at the end he is anonymous, diabetic, and facing amputation of his second leg. These are the changes that time has wrought. Students may not be old enough to have witnessed such changes in those they know, but perhaps they saw the equally shocking juxtaposition of pictures of Greta Garbo as a young actress and as she appeared months before her death. At any rate, Selzer's essay will work on their imagination.

MARGINAL NOTES

The first paragraph establishes the setting and the series of questions establishes an empathy that the narrator maintains throughout the essay.

53

thinking? I wonder. Is he dreaming the outline of his toes? Does he see there his foot's incandescent ghost? Could he be angry? Feel that I have taken from him something for which he yearns now with all his heart? Has he forgotten so soon the pain? It was a pain so great as to set him apart from all other men, in a red-hot place where he had no kith or kin. What of those black gorilla toes and the soupy mess that was his heel? I watch him from the doorway. It is a kind of spying, I know.

Save for a white fringe open at the front, Elihu Koontz is bald. The hair has grown too long and is wilted. He wears it as one would wear a day-old laurel wreath. He is naked to the waist, so that I can see his breasts. They are the breasts of Buddha, inverted triangles from which the nipples swing, dark as garnets.   2

I have seen enough. I step into the room, and he sees that I am there.   3

"How did the night go, Elihu?"   4

He looks at me for a long moment. "Shut the door," he says.   5

I do, and move to the side of the bed. He takes my left hand in both of his, gazes at it, turns it over, then back, fondling, at last holding it up to his cheek. I do not withdraw from this loving. After a while he relinquishes my hand, and looks up at me.   6

"How is the pain?" I ask.   7

He does not answer, but continues to look at me in silence. I know at once that he has made a decision.   8

"Ever hear of The Masked Marvel?" He says this in a low voice, almost a whisper.   9

"What?"   10

"The Masked Marvel," he says. "You never heard of him?"   11

"No."   12

He clucks his tongue. He is exasperated.   13

All at once there is a recollection. It is dim, distant, but coming near.   14

"Do you mean the wrestler?"   15

Eagerly, he nods, and the breasts bob. How gnomish he looks, oval as the huge helpless egg of some outlandish lizard. He has very long arms, which, now and then, he unfurls to reach for   16

The conversation between doctor and patient reveals who the patient is (or has been) and, in effect, answers the questions in the first paragraph. Ehihu has been thinking proudly about his past as a contrast to the present.

things—a carafe of water, a get-well card. He gazes up at me, urging. He *wants* me to remember.

"Well, . . . yes," I say. I am straining backward in time. "I saw   17
him wrestle in Toronto long ago."

"Ha!" He smiles. "You saw *me*." And his index finger, held   18
rigid and upright, bounces in the air.

The man has said something shocking, unacceptable. It must   19
be challenged.

"You?" I am trying to smile.   20

Again that jab of the finger. "You saw *me*."   21

"No," I say. But even then, something about Elihu Koontz,   22
those prolonged arms, the shape of his head, the sudden agility
with which he leans from his bed to get a large brown envelope
from his nightstand, something is forcing me toward a memory.
He rummages through his papers, old newspaper clippings, photographs, and I remember . . .

It is almost forty years ago. I am ten years old. I have been   23
sent to Toronto to spend the summer with relatives. Uncle Max
has bought two tickets to the wrestling match. He is taking me
that night.

"He isn't allowed," says Aunt Sarah to me. Uncle Max has   24
angina.

"He gets too excited," she says.   25

"I wish you wouldn't go, Max," she says.   26

"You mind your own business," he says.   27

And we go. Out into the warm Canadian evening. I am not   28
only abroad, I am abroad in the *evening*! I have never been taken
out in the evening. I am terribly excited. The trolleys, the lights,
the horns. It is a bazaar. At the Maple Leaf Gardens, we sit high
and near the center. The vast arena is dark except for the brilliance
of the ring at the bottom.

It begins.   29

The wrestlers circle. They grapple. They are all haunch and   30
paunch. I am shocked by their ugliness, but I do not show it.
Uncle Max is exhilarated. He leans forward, his eyes unblinking,

The essay's long middle section recaptures an evening of wrestling from the doctor's child-hood. Seen through the boy's eyes, it is mar-velous and full of excitement. The memories of that evening heighten Elihu's plight now as his identity is revealed.

on his face a look of enormous happiness. One after the other, a pair of wrestlers enter the ring. The two men join, twist, jerk, tug, bend, yank, and throw. Then they leave and are replaced by another pair. At last it is the main event. "The Angel vs. The Masked Marvel."

On the cover of the program notes, there is a picture of The Angel hanging from the limb of a tree, a noose of thick rope around his neck. The Angel hangs just so for an hour every day, it is explained, to strengthen his neck. The Masked Marvel's trademark is a black stocking cap with holes for the eyes and mouth. He is never seen without it, states the program. No one knows who The Masked Marvel really is!   31

"Good," says Uncle Max. "Now you'll see something." He is fidgeting, waiting for them to appear. They come down separate aisles, climb into the ring from opposite sides. I have never seen anything like them. It is The Angel's neck that first captures the eye. The shaved nape rises in twin columns to puff into the white hood of a sloped and bosselated skull that is too small. As though strangled by the sinews of that neck, the skull had long since withered and shrunk. The thing about The Angel is the absence of any mystery in his body. It is simply *there*. A monosyllabic announcement. A grunt. One looks and knows everything at once, the fat thighs, the gigantic buttocks, the great spine from which hang knotted ropes and pale aprons of beef. And that prehistoric head. He is all of a single hideous piece, The Angel is. No detachables.   32

The Masked Marvel seems dwarfish. His fingers dangle kneeward. His short legs are slightly bowed as if under the weight of the cask they are forced to heft about. He has breasts that swing when he moves! I have never seen such breasts on a man before.   33

There is a sudden ungraceful movement, and they close upon one another. The Angel stoops and hugs The Marvel about the waist, locking his hands behind The Marvel's back. Now he straightens and lifts The Marvel as though he were uprooting a tree. Thus he holds him, then stoops again, thrusts one hand through The Marvel's crotch, and with the other grabs him by the neck. He rears and . . . The Marvel is aloft! For a long moment,   34

"bosselated": characterized by lumps and protuberances.

Have students notice how some phrases in this section echo phrases in the first section. The same thing will occur in the third section, closely binding the three though they take place years apart.

Selzer blends physical description and action to create an exciting narrative.

The Angel stands as though deciding where to make the toss. Then throws. Was that board or bone that splintered there? Again and again, The Angel hurls himself upon the body of The Masked Marvel.

Now The Angel rises over the fallen Marvel, picks up one foot   35
in both of his hands, and twists the toes downward. It is far beyond the tensile strength of mere ligament, mere cartilage. The Masked Marvel does not hide his agony, but pounds and slaps the floor with his hand, now and then reaching up toward The Angel in an attitude of supplication. I have never seen such suffering. And all the while his black mask rolls from side to side, the mouth pulled to a tight slit through which issues an endless hiss that I can hear from where I sit. All at once, I hear a shouting close by.

"Break it off! Tear off a leg and throw it up here!"   36

It is Uncle Max. Even in the darkness I can see that he is gray.   37
A band of sweat stands upon his upper lip. He is on his feet now, panting, one fist pressed at his chest, the other raised warlike toward the ring. For the first time I begin to think that something terrible might happen here. Aunt Sarah was right.

"Sit down, Uncle Max," I say. "Take a pill, please."   38

He reaches for the pillbox, gropes, and swallows without tak-   39
ing his gaze from the wrestlers. I wait for him to sit down.

"That's not fair," I say, "twisting his toes like that."   40

"It's the toehold," he explains.   41

"But it's not *fair*," I say again. The whole of the evil is laid   42
open for me to perceive. I am trembling.

And now The Angel does something unspeakable. Holding   43
the foot of The Marvel at full twist with one hand, he bends and grasps the mask where it clings to the back of The Marvel's head. And he pulls. He is going to strip it off! Lay bare an ultimate carnal mystery! Suddenly it is beyond mere physical violence. Now I am on my feet, shouting into the Maple Leaf Gardens.

"Watch out," I scream. "Stop him. Please, somebody, stop   44
him."

Next to me, Uncle Max is chuckling   45

Yet The Masked Marvel hears me, I know it. And rallies from   46
his bed of pain. Thrusting with his free heel, he strikes The Angel

"carnal": of the natural as opposed to the spiritual world.

at the back of the knee. The Angel falls. The Masked Marvel is on top of him, pinning his shoulders to the mat. One! Two! Three! And it is over. Uncle Max is strangely still. I am gasping for breath. All this I remember as I stand at the bedside of Elihu Koontz.

The short third section is especially full of echoes from the second section that heighten our perception of the irony in Elihu's fate.

Once again, I am in the operating room. It is two years since I amputated the left leg of Elihu Koontz. Now it is his right leg which is gangrenous. I have already scrubbed. I stand to one side wearing my gown and gloves. And . . . *I am masked.* Upon the table lies Elihu Koontz, pinned in a fierce white light. Spinal anesthesia has been administered. One of his arms is taped to a board placed at a right angle to his body. Into this arm, a needle has been placed. Fluid drips here from a bottle overhead. With his other hand, Elihu Koontz beats feebly at the side of the operating table. His head rolls from side to side. His mouth is pulled into weeping. It seems to me that I have never seen such misery. 47

An orderly stands at the foot of the table, holding Elihu Koontz's leg aloft by the toes so that the intern can scrub the limb with antiseptic solutions. The intern paints the foot, ankle, leg, and thigh, both front and back, three times. From a corner of the room where I wait, I look down as from an amphitheater. Then I think of Uncle Max yelling, "Tear off a leg. Throw it up here." And I think that forty years later I am making the catch. 48

"It's not fair," I say aloud. But no one hears me. I step forward to break The Masked Marvel's last toehold. 49

POSSIBLE ANSWERS

Meaning and Purpose

1. Without either leg, The Masked Marvel can't be held in a toehold. The title is made significant because the doctor breaks the last toehold by amputating the second leg. Elihu Koontz has lost his hold on what he was—a wrestler.
2. This essay is about loss and pain. Selzer relates a memory that connects him to a patient. He dramatizes, with narrative, who Elihu Koontz once was, and how the surgeon has come to appreciate his role in the former wrestler's life. If the memory of The Masked Marvel can be alive in the surgeon's mind, then Koontz will always be the wrestler the boy was in awe of. He won't really lose what he was.
3. This sentence describes the pain during the wrestling match: "The Masked Marvel does not hide his agony, but pounds and slaps the floor with his hand, now and then reaching up toward the Angel in an attitude of supplication" (35). As a patient, Elihu Koontz had "pain so great as to set him apart from all other men, in a red-hot place where he had no kith or kin." (1). The wrestler's pain sounds fake compared to the pain of gangrene. The surgeon is keenly aware of how his patient suffers and

Meaning and Purpose

1. The last sentence in this essay includes the words of the title. How does that sentence help you interpret the title? In what sense does the doctor "break The Masked Marvel's last toehold"?
2. What is Selzer's purpose in telling the story of The Masked Marvel? How do you interpret the meaning of the essay?

3. How does the surgeon describe the pain he believes Elihu Koontz experiences during the wrestling match, and as a patient? How does the surgeon's awareness of pain help you understand him (the surgeon)?
4. The boy and his uncle have different reactions to the evening of wrestling. Discuss how this contrast enriches the essay.
5. In the last three paragraphs, the surgeon takes on the role of wrestler. What details tell you so, and how effective are they in unifying the essay?

Strategy

1. Selzer departs from strict chronological order in this narrative. What order does he put the events in, and how does it affect the story?
2. Each of the three sections gives us a piece of The Masked Marvel's story, making a natural connection among them. But Selzer has taken pains to further connect the sections by repeating details from section one in section two and details from section two in section three. Examine these parallels. How do they affect your reading of the essay?
3. How does Selzer use transitions to let you know when the time order changes? Are the transitions clear and effective?
4. Though the surgeon narrates the whole essay, his perspective, or point of view, changes in each section. What picture do you have of his character because of these three perspectives?

Style

1. What does dialogue do for the story? How effective do you think the story would be without dialogue?
2. Authors don't always tell of past events in the past tense. Look at the tense used in each section. How does Selzer's choice of

was sensitive to the look of pain even as a boy.
4. Uncle Max gets so excited at the wrestling match, shouting for a leg, that he turns gray and has to take a pill. He chuckles at the boy's fear for The Masked Marvel. The boy, future doctor that he is, is solicitous of his uncle and tells him to take a pill. And the boy takes the wrestling match seriously and doesn't see it as a performance, as the uncle does. The contrast in their reactions shows the point of view of the adult looking back and emphasizes the irony in the essay.
5. The surgeon says, *"I am masked"* (47), "And I think that forty years later I am making the catch" (48), and "I step forward to break The Masked Marvel's last toehold" (49). These details put the surgeon in the wrestler's place and unify the essay by bringing readers back to the scene at the match, by recalling Koontz's identifying himself as The Masked Marvel, and by restating the title.

Strategy

1. The first section takes place two years before the last section, and the middle section takes place forty years before the first, when the narrator was a boy. Selzer makes the most of putting readers in a situation, going back in time to a memory that connects to that situation, then making the story both ironic and poignant in the end. Chronological order would diminish the effect of the irony, at least.
2. The repeated details in section two are about The Masked Marvel's breasts (33), and his "bed of pain" (46). In section three the repeated details are: *"I am masked,"* "Elihu Koontz pinned," "beats feebly at the side of the operating table," "Tear off a leg. Throw it up here," "It's not fair," and "to break The Masked Marvel's last toehold." The repetition unifies the language and makes the essay rich in irony, especially in the last section, where the surgeon becomes like the wrestler who subdued The Masked Marvel.

3. In paragraph 22, Koontz is going through old photographs and clippings, and Selzer says, "and I remember." Then comes a space break, and he begins the memory, "It is almost forty years ago" (23). At the end of the second section, Selzer pulls us back to the first section with, "All this I remember as I stand at the bedside of Elihu Koontz" (46). Section three begins after a space break, "Once again I am in the operating room" (47), and it is two years after the opening scene. These transitions make the time order clear. The reader is always in the "present" of his narrator.

4. As a surgeon in the first section, the narrator is compassionate and patient: "I do not withdraw from this loving" (6), and "He *wants* me to remember" (16). As a boy he is sympathetic and aware of the wrestler's pain and his uncle's state of health: "I have never seen such suffering" (35); " 'Sit down, Uncle Max,' I say, 'Take a pill please' " (38); and " 'Stop him. Please, somebody, stop him' " (44). The last section shows the surgeon observant and aware of the painful irony: "It seems to me that I have never seen such misery" (47), and "It's not fair" (49).

Style

1. The dialogue makes scenes immediate and dramatic and puts readers in the scenes. Without dialogue, the essay would be full of exposition and probably dull. Selzer would be telling, not showing.

2. Each section is written in present tense, making the scenes vivid and real. Because transitions to the different times are so clear, readers easily distinguish the times, even though each is in present tense.

3. In the final section, the surgeon is in the operating room and imagines it as an amphitheater. He hears Uncle Max yelling for a leg and realizes that he, the boy who was awed by The Masked Marvel, is now the surgeon who will literally tear a leg off.

tense influence your experience of the events in the narrative and your understanding of the chronology?

3. In paragraph 36, when Uncle Max yells, "Tear off a leg and throw it up here!" you already know Elihu Koontz has lost a leg to diabetes. How is this irony sustained in the final section?

Writing Tasks

1. Think of a person or event that impressed you as a child and has some significant connection to your later life. Write a narrative about it, using the same tense to describe both the past and the present, but also clearly separating past from present.

2. Write a narrative, incorporating somewhere in the story the exact words of the title you give it. How can you make the title significant?

❦ Art Harris ❦

Art Harris is an award-winning journalist based in Atlanta. After graduating from Duke University, he began his journalism career with the Atlanta Constitution. *He later worked for the* San Francisco Examiner *before joining the staff of the* Washington Post, *the paper for which he has since covered the South. His articles have appeared in* Reader's Digest, GQ, Esquire, *and* Rolling Stone. *Harris covered the downfall of evangelical preacher Jimmy Swaggart for the* Washington Post *and wrote the well-known article about Swaggart's demise for* Penthouse *magazine. He has won two National Headliner Awards for outstanding feature writing. He is on the staff at CNN news as a contributing correspondent for their investigative unit.*

Trapped in Another Life

This newspaper article, from the Los Angeles Times, *February 23, 1989, tells the story of a woman who led two distinctly separate lives, one as a drug-abusing prostitute with a criminal record and the other as a model wife and mother. Because of the remarkable turnaround in this woman's life, the story raises questions about justice and punishment.*

JESSUP, MD.   She stares out the window past twin 12-foot fences topped with razor wire, watchtowers manned by armed guards, steel electronic gates, past the stand of hardwoods, the nearby men's prison and up the road.

It's dusting snow, cold, bleak. Just over the hill, a 10-minute drive if she could just drive out of here, and she would be home in her split-level house with a devoted but baffled brood: her husband, Ray, two teen-age sons.

Kay Smith was the very model of a Severn, Md., housewife and working mother, so perfect that no one around here can

61

TEACHING SUGGESTIONS

Students will find this story of Pamela Rodgers's two lives engrossing. Undoubtedly, they will have differing opinions about the proper disposition of the case. After discussing the content and the law-enforcement dilemma, you may wish to have students examine the way in which Harris uses different rhetorical patterns—comparison and contrast, cause and effect, description, and chronological narration—to tell Pamela's story. It is a good time to emphasize that essays are not usually written in one "pure" rhetorical pattern. In any one essay a writer may use many patterns as they become appropriate.

1   **MARGINAL NOTES**

Harris begins with a contrast between prison life and life outside and between Kay and her former self.

2

3

believe she was once a hard-drinking, pill-popping criminal with a gun.

Dark Secrets Come to Light

Beginning here, Harris goes to the more distant past, then relates her recent past in paragraphs 5–9.

But for a decade, until her capture last spring, she was a fugitive from a South Carolina mill town. She had been imprisoned for a string of armed robberies until she walked away from work release and disappeared. Her first husband was a convicted killer. 4

These were secrets Kay Smith buried deep as she recast her life. Over the years, she had become a doting mom to her two boys and foster daughters. She ferried her sons to school and sports, took courses at Anne Arundel Community College. As a real estate agent for Gary Hart Realty in Glen Burnie, she sold house after house—$1 million in sales last year. 5

Who could have suspected that she really was an outlaw named Pamela Rodgers? 6

Kay Smith wore subdued suits and slacks, a bare wisp of Max Factor. In her home, she warned her sons about drinking. She spurned even a glass of wine, and politely insisted that friends take half-empty bottles home after parties. 7

"I can't imagine for the life of me how this woman could do anything remotely resembling what happened," says Bill Cashman, who coached her sons in track at Old Mill High. "She'd ask me what I thought about her sons' grades, their sports performance, the people they hung around with. Her family was always first." 8

Somehow, she managed to keep it together as she lived in fear and hid her past, even from her husband. "I just wanted to get my boys through school," she says, "then I was going to straighten it all out." 9

Continuing the chronological sequence, Harris relates the most immediate past and describes her present situation.

But detectives disrupted her plan last May. And when they came for her, she had run so long and hard, she barely knew the woman, handcuffed and under arrest. All at once, she again was Pamela Rodgers—the woman she thought she had left behind. In three months, she was on her way back to prison in South Carolina. 10

Just before Christmas, a routine interstate swap allowed her   11
to serve out the rest of her 12-year sentence for armed robbery
near home. She found herself in this stark red-brick campus, the
Maryland Correctional Institute for Women.

"At least I don't have to carry that terrible secret any more,"   12
she says, wrapping a sweater about her to ward off the chill.
Suddenly she looks panicked. "Oh, God, I'm so sorry my sons
were cheated."

She wears a purple prison jumpsuit, works in the prison   13
library, clips recipes and frets about her family. Figuring "someday
they'll want honest answers," she writes letters she never mails.

Based on her record of violent crime and escape, Kay Smith   14
was classified by Maryland prison officials as a security risk. So
she awaits the outcome of early release pleas—by her reckoning
she could be here until March, 1993, unless authorities grant an
unlikely pardon, premature parole or work release.

Family and friends have canvassed the community, collecting   15
at least 3,000 signatures petitioning South Carolina's Pardon and
Parole Board for leniency.

"I'm not saying she ought to get a medal, but she's paid her   16
debt to society," argues John Hassett, a former prosecutor, who
took her case for expenses only.

The next four paragraphs contrast two views about her possible pardon.

In South Carolina, former prosecutor Dick Harpootlian took   17
up her cause too saying, "I take other cases for money. Kay's case
is among those I take because I believe in the folks."

But sniffs Jim Anders, the South Carolina prosecutor who put   18
Kay Smith back in jail: "Don't make me cry. If we cut slack for
her, we encourage people to escape."

Jean Gilbert, Kay Smith's mother, says of her daughter in a   19
telephone interview from Greenville, S.C.: "If people could just
understand what brought her to this point. She was just a woman
desperate to have her kids, who was terrorized by bad men."

Kay Smith was born Pamela Annette Gilbert on Oct. 1, 1951,   20
the second of six children raised by a trucker and a gro-
cer's daughter in the Blue Ridge foothills of Greenville, S.C.
She remembers her father's belt, his guns, his whiskey, his
temper.

Returning to the chronological, Harris now goes to the far distant past, relating her background up to her committing criminal acts, using a cause-and-effect pattern.

Her father declines to discuss the past, but other family mem- 21
bers confirm her memories; her mother recalls stepping in to take
"many of those licks."

"I watched him whip her . . . when she was just 15 months 22
old," says her grandmother, Mary Hinton, 83.

Kay says of her father: "He just didn't know how to show 23
affection. I can't remember ever hearing him say 'I love you.' "

When Kay was a 10th-grader, she dropped out and took a job 24
at a convenience store, where she met stock boy Danny Rodgers,
another dropout.

"I knew I didn't love Danny," Kay reflects. "I married him to 25
get out. I thought I could make it work."

She was 16. 26

Bouncing between Rodgers' modest family farm in Cullman, 27
Ala., and her hometown in Greenville, they moved into a dinky
Greenville trailer.

"First time I ever saw him slap her," Kay's mother says, "I 28
hit him back. He said, 'You hit me,' and I said, 'You hit my daughter.' So he informed me, 'It's not your daughter any more; it's my
wife.' "

They moved to Florida, where Danny found construction 29
work at Disney World, but preferred hanging out. Danny Jr. was
born Dec. 17, 1969, as Pam was learning fast about her mercurial
husband, who relished "playing with guns and knives, very nice
one day and the next day beating the heck out of you."

Six months later, out of work, he ran off with a neighbor's 30
wife, she says. So Pam headed home again, hired on the midnight
shift as a cotton mill weaver. Danny returned, but she refused to
make up.

Then, one night, when she was at work, he snatched the baby 31
and ran, a tactic he repeatedly used to keep her in line. And it
worked: She kept going back to him. "It was the only way to keep
my baby," she says. Another son, James, was born in September,
1972, but life was only getting worse.

Kay moved home to Greenville, and in 1973 won temporary 32
custody of the boys. Rodgers stalked her, she says, and one day
showed up and fired a pistol into the roof of her trailer. Days later,

he snatched the boys again. Only this time Pam couldn't find them.

"She had dreams he'd drowned them because he swore he'd do it before he'd let her have them," her mother says. "She woke up at night screaming and fell into drugs and alcohol."

33

She boxed up their toys, reminders of her "failure," and dumped them at Goodwill. She reported her husband to the police, but no one offered any hope.

34

She found a kind of solace at the Little Darling, a Greenville bar that drew hustlers such as Arthur Broome Jr., a distant cousin.

35

She was 22.

36

Broome was 43, owned a tile company, but never seemed to work. He promised to help track her boys, and she moved into his trailer—a place police say attracted the local criminal fringe. Broome, she says, had money, and drugs to kill her pain.

37

Life was going badly for her. During the 1974 Masters golf tournament, she drove to Augusta, Ga., to hang out with a bar mate—a former hooker, she says. A man approached them at a local restaurant. They began flirting. Suddenly, she says, she was under arrest for possessing amphetamines and soliciting an undercover cop for prostitution. Police records suggest that case was never prosecuted.

38

Meanwhile, back home, Broome was teaching her how to use a gun—and everything a country girl needed to know about stick-ups. Together they held up stores in the Greenville area.

39

"I didn't really care if I got caught," she says. "I thought if I got in enough trouble, Danny would tell me where the boys were. I wasn't thinking straight."

40

On Sept. 14, 1974, they hit Paces Jewelers just before closing. Pulling a pistol from a large black bag, she ordered customers to the floor and grabbed 18 watches and $400 in cash.

41

Because witnesses had caught her license plate numbers, police easily tracked her to Broome's trailer, where both were arrested. But she got out on bail, and, high on uppers, hit a liquor store alone. Later, she drove the rolling countryside for hours, realizing she would never get her sons back now. She

42

Paragraphs 34–39 continue the cause-and-effect pattern leading up to her jail sentence and her escape.

went home and gobbled pills to end it all, then raced to find her mother.

"She said, 'Mama, I took a handful of pills and I'm gonna die,'" her mother recalls. "I called an ambulance, they pumped her stomach and took her to the state hospital." 43

Rodgers got the news at his California apartment, where he had taken the boys. He phoned, invited his wife to join him and try again. Ignoring bail rules against leaving the state, her mother put her on a plane. "I had to do it to save her," she says. 44

But it didn't work out. 45

Danny began knocking her around, but for the first time, she fought back. When she called the police for help, Danny told them his wife was a bail jumper from South Carolina. 46

Detectives flew her home, where she pleaded guilty in state court to five armed robberies. In October, 1975, she drew a 12½-year sentence. Broome got 25 years; Kay wound up in Columbia's women's prison. 47

Rodgers filed for divorce and won permanent custody of the children, but in March, 1977, he shot a man in California, for which he was convicted of second-degree murder and sentenced to five years in prison. The boys, 6 and 8, were dispatched to live with his family in Alabama. 48

Pam, who was told Danny was in a hospital, was being a model inmate. After 18 months, she made work release and labored in a printing plant. But she fell off the wagon on the job—using pills and whiskey, she says. And she feared further setbacks would let Danny keep her children forever. There was only one way out: Take a walk. 49

This next section, to paragraph 69, details the recent past and her new life.

With six or so months left to serve, in January, 1978, she hitched as far as Glen Burnie, Md., rented a room, took a job as a waitress in a Greek diner. To avoid confusion with a waitress named Pam, she became Kay Smith. Days later, just after midnight, a short, balding trucker plopped down, spied the sad-eyed brunette in a white apron and fell in love. 50

She was crying. A cook was screaming at her. The trucker asked her name. 51

"Ray and Kay," Ray Smith joked. "Pretty neat. We ought to get along fine. We got the same names." 52

He was gentle, optimistic. He told her he had two daughters by a woman he never had married, that he was lonely on the road and looking for a co-pilot. At quitting time, she threw down her apron and climbed aboard his snorting '74 Peterbilt. 53

High in the cab, hauling steel and furniture over the next three months, they became friends. Ray talked of a hardscrabble life, raised by grandparents in the West Virginia hollows. She was amazed. He had suffered, yet was so happy. Kay hedged about her past. 54

After three months on the road, he proposed marriage at the Truck Stop of America in Knoxville. Her dilemma was right out of some country song: How could she let someone she loved marry an outlaw with a fake name? She had forged a birth certificate, gotten a Social Security card and a Maryland driver's license. "There was no right answer," she says. "So I just decided to block out the past." 55

On July 1, 1978, Ray's family and drinking buddies, about 500 in all, crowded into a Pasadena, Md., church, and went from there to a dance hall. "I was happier than anyone could be," he says. "I knew she loved me." 56

Kay was determined to change her life. That Christmas, gambling on her former in-laws to keep her secret, she drove to Alabama with Ray to see her boys. 57

Studying on the road, she passed a high school equivalency exam, enrolled in Anne Arundel Community College, began driving on her own. 58

In 1980, the Smiths bought a three-bedroom house in Severn, outfitting bedrooms for the boys. Life without them still drove her into the bedroom with a bottle. 59

When Ray drew the line over her drinking, she found a therapist in Baltimore, and her story tumbled out for the first time. She looked inside, read Norman Vincent Peale, tried biofeedback and stopped drinking. 60

She made friends, becoming close to neighbor Cathy Moore, a divorced mother who once rescued her dog. When Moore's 61 daughter left to live with her father in Wyoming, Kay "reassured me," she says. "I wondered, 'How comes she's so smart about life?' "

On one visit to Alabama, she learned her former husband was in prison. But she knew there was nothing she could do to get her boys back without giving herself away. 62

And there was nothing she could do when Danny got out, remarried, reclaimed the boys and resettled in his new wife's hometown, Boise, Idaho. 63

But she stayed in touch, sent money, opened local charge accounts for the boys, saw them at Boise's Flying J truck stop on trips west. 64

Meanwhile, she hired a Baltimore attorney to square her past. But he reported there was no record, raising her hopes. Only later did she discover her name had been misspelled in the search. 65

She grew more concerned for her sons. They had told her that Danny had recruited them to steal from the Salvation Army to furnish his yard sales. Then, in January, 1985, James attempted suicide; young Dan got into a fight with his father. One night, James sneaked out for a ride with a teen-ager who wrapped his car around a telephone pole, killing the driver. 66

Rodgers threw in the towel. "Come get them," he told his former wife. "They're yours." 67

She flew west the next day to claim them before he changed his mind. Back in Severn, the boys made friends quickly, reveled in their rooms, Reeboks and new jeans. When Ray wheeled in, they sat grinning at the kitchen table. For the first time, he saw Kay was happy. Curfews were set; grades improved. It was a "Leave It to Beaver" home, they liked to say. 68

She seized on real estate as a way to sock away money for college. 69

Paragraphs 70–78 report the events leading to her arrest again.

But she remained haunted by the past and present. In 1987, her former husband was charged again with murder for shooting a 21-year-old Boise man over a drug deal, chopping him into 13 pieces and dumping them into a reservoir. Now he was calling 70 collect from jail; he wanted to see the boys, afraid he might get the chair.

After Rodgers was convicted last March, an Idaho pre- 71 sentencing investigator ran a routine computer check of his former wife, discovered she was a fugitive and alerted South Carolina.

But the investigator, puzzling over an unlisted Maryland 72 phone number in the killer's wallet, dialed it. He reached James, who confirmed his mother's maiden name and her hometown without knowing what he had done.

Now police had the tip they had been after. The phone rang 73 and when she answered, it was Danny. "I guess we're in the same boat," he said. "They know about you."

She was numb, near hysterics. 74

Without alarming the boys, she hinted she "might have to go 75 away for a little while" and phoned her attorney, who suggested she find a criminal lawyer. She found Hassett.

Then, on May 10, 1988, a patrolman knocked on her door. 76 After her arrest, with handcuffs on, she turned white, broke into tears. "It's been 10½ years," she said. "Why now?"

Ray was loading in New Jersey when he got the word. The 77 boys were in school. The next day, out on $25,000 bail, she told the boys the rest of the story, then sat down with Ray, alone.

"She told me everything," he says. "She was crying. She said, 78 'I hope this doesn't break us up. I love you so much.'"

Now the house feels empty. Danny, a well-mannered 6-footer 79 who has briefly curtailed college to work in a hospital billing department, cheers on James, who takes his anger out on a punching bag and works to stay afloat at Old Mill. Most Saturdays, they visit their mother for an hour in a communal room at the prison.

With Ray on the road, working double time to pay the bills, 80 friends like Pam McLane, an Old Mill senior, drop by to fix dinner, help clean up and remember Kay.

As for Kay herself, "there wasn't any freedom for the last 10 81 years, not for anyone with a conscience," she reflects on this bleak Maryland winter day. "You overcome depression, drinking and

The final section relates the present situation as she and her family await word of a possible parole.

POSSIBLE ANSWERS

Meaning and Purpose

1. Crime doesn't pay, but neither is our justice system always fair. Even though Kay seemed to have left her criminal life behind, the law caught up with her. Harris's purpose is to show her struggle to live a decent life after her misguided early life and to question the justice of her returning to prison. Perhaps Harris hopes that telling Kay's story sympathetically in the newspaper will rally support for her release and pardon.

2. Though Kay changed her life when she married Ray, she "remained haunted by the past and present" (70). Back in prison, she says, "There wasn't any freedom for the last ten years, not for anyone with a conscience" (81). The two lives she had were starkly different, and her earlier life kept her trapped.

3. Harris draws a sympathetic portrait of Kay in the first fifteen paragraphs and so leads readers to favor Hassett's statement. Harris describes Kay's exemplary life and quotes a person who says how conscientious she was. Being taken back to prison seems wrenching and unfair after these descriptions.

4. Max Factor is a cosmetics company. The phrase refers to makeup and how little Kay wore. Harris equates her use of little makeup with her new life of decency and moral uprightness.

5. Each description sounds like fiction, a stereotype. They contrast sharply, and readers will feel disbelief that both could describe the same person, will feel intrigued, even skeptical, and will want to know more.

Strategy

1. Paragraphs 1–3 describe a scene and place readers in it. Enough mystery hovers about the scene ("a devoted but baffled brood") to arouse interest. Not calling Kay by name till paragraph 3 delays this necessary information and gives Harris time to create an impression before readers know who she is. The contrasting descriptions of her in paragraph 3 have readers interested enough to read on.

2. This is a newspaper article and readers want information fast. A survey of Kay's life lets readers know the gist, then they can read on for details. If Harris had begun with her early life, readers would have a harder time sympathizing with her, and Harris's points would not be as effectively—and dramatically—made.

3. The essay is mostly a summary of events,

negative forces, but you're not free. I was 21 when it happened. I made a terrible, terrible mistake. I feel horrible about it. . . ."

But, she adds, "I am not Pam Rodgers any more. I just don't want my children destroyed. That's my sense of urgency. Why destroy a family when it's on the verge of changing the cycle?"

Meaning and Purpose

1. Taking the entire article into consideration and paying close attention to the last section (paragraphs 79–82), what do you think Harris's purpose is in this article?
2. How does the title relate to the story?
3. Examine the statements by John Hassett in paragraph 16 and Jim Anders in paragraph 18. Which statement more closely agrees with your thinking about reformed criminals in general? About Kay Smith-Pamela Rodgers in particular? Has Harris led you to a specific view? If so, how?
4. What does Harris mean by "a bare wisp of Max Factor" in paragraph 7?
5. What is the emotional effect of describing Kay as both "the very model of a Severn, Md., housewife and working mother," and "a hard-drinking, pill-popping criminal with a gun" in the same paragraph (3)?

Strategy

1. How do the first three paragraphs pull the reader into Kay Smith's story?
2. Harris summarizes Kay's life in paragraphs 4–19, then begins her story again at an earlier time and in more detail, starting with paragraph 20. Why does he choose this order of events? Why doesn't he begin the article with "Kay Smith was born Pamela Annette Gilbert on Oct. 1, 1951 . . . " (20)?

3. Does Harris use the scene or summary method to present the events of the story? Give examples to support your answer.
4. Harris alternates between present and past tense in this essay. What logic do you think he uses in choosing tenses?

Style

1. What is Harris's attitude toward Kay's situation? How does he establish this attitude in the tone of the essay?
2. What do words in paragraphs 53–56 such as "co-pilot," "snorting," and "hardscrabble" tell you about Harris's intended audience? This article originally appeared in a mass-circulation newspaper. Does that background explain his choice of words?
3. This essay is a news article, and most news writers try to claim objectivity in reporting. Does Harris care about objectivity? How do you know?

Writing Tasks

1. The Kay Smith-Pamela Rodgers article begins in the present and then goes back in time to retrace her history. Write a narrative beginning with a description of a present situation as Harris does. Then go back to record the events leading to that situation. At the end of your narrative, return to the present.
2. Write an essay in which you compare style and effectiveness of the opening situations in this chapter's first four selections. Ask yourself how well each author grabs readers, establishes a situation and a conflict, and begins to create a mood. If necessary, read the chapter introduction again for some elements of narrative openings.

giving highlights and leaving out a lot of details. The two sentences, "She remembers her father's belt, his guns, his whiskey, his temper" (20), and "With six or so months left to serve, in January, 1978, she hitched as far as Glen Burnie, Maryland, rented a room, took a job as a waitress in a Greek diner" (50) summarize events but do not dramatize them in a scene.

4. Harris is careful to put present events in the present tense, as in the opening scene in prison. He tells of her past life in past tense ("Somehow she managed to keep it together as she lived in fear and hid her past, even from her husband" [9]), but he again intersperses the present tense for her present life ("She wears a purple prison jumpsuit" [13] and "Family and friends have canvassed the community" [17]). The direct quotations are in present tense ("Kay says of her father" [23]).

Style

1. Harris sympathizes with Kay from the start when he paints a stark, lonely picture of her in prison. He highlights events that show her a victim, as in paragraph 28 when Danny slaps her, and in paragraph 31. When Harris describes her reformed life, he tells of good and generous things she did. The tipoff to her identity as a fugitive is inadvertently given by her son—she did nothing to draw the attention of the law. All these details arouse sympathy in readers and question the justice of putting Kay back in prison.

2. Though these words are fairly understandable in context, they are jargon, and Harris's audience might be readers familiar with trucking. But any audience could understand this essay.

3. The language is concise and fast-paced, but Harris doesn't care about being objective. He portrays Kay as victimized in her young life, now trying to live a decent life, and recently yanked away from her family and thrust back into prison. Harris intends readers to see the irony when he reports that Kay "was classified by Maryland prison officials as a security risk" (14). Clearly, Harris thinks she should be released and pardoned, and his article is like a plea for this action.

❦ Richard Rodriguez ❦

Teaching Suggestions

This selection is a good example of narrative used as a springboard to serious thoughts. A summer job serves as a growth experience for the narrator because he is aware of his own thoughts and emotions. Have students notice how much self-examination Rodriguez includes in this piece. It begins in the first paragraph and continues throughout. But it is not self-absorption. He is always aware of the others and his relationship to them.

The narrative covers a long time (an unspecified number of years), but the heart of the experience is in a few awkward moments Rodriguez spent attempting to converse with a group of Mexican alien workers. The narrator carries those moments with him as he examines his life since that summer.

Richard Rodriguez was born in San Francisco in 1944 to Mexican-American parents who spoke only Spanish at home. Rodriguez nonetheless mastered the English language and went on to study at Stanford, Columbia, and the University of California at Berkeley, where he earned a Ph.D. in English literature. He also received a Fulbright fellowship to study English literature in London. In spite of several offers for teaching positions, Rodriguez made writing and journalism his profession. In The Hunger of Memory *(1982), a collection of autobiographical essays, he examines the American educational system from the point of view of an immigrant who has gone all the way through it, and he strongly opposes bilingual education.*

Los Pobres

In this autobiographical essay from The Hunger of Memory, *Rodriguez describes his first experience of working at hard labor. The summer after he graduates from Stanford University, he takes a construction job that leads him to a vital insight about his relationship to the Mexican immigrant community he "left behind" because of his education.*

Marginal Notes

The first paragraph introduces the narrator and his situation. The narrator pictures himself as a nontypical student in some characteristics: almost an outsider, not quite as sophisticated as his classmates.

I went to college at Stanford, attracted partly by its academic reputation, partly because it was the school rich people went to. I found myself on a campus with golden children of western America's upper middle class. Many were students both ambitious for academic success *and* accustomed to leisured life in the sun. In the afternoon, they lay spread out, sunbathing in front of the library, reading Swift or Engels or Beckett. Others went by in convertibles, off to play tennis or ride horses or sail. Beach boys dressed in tank-tops and shorts were my classmates in undergraduate seminars. Tall tan girls wearing white strapless dresses sat

72

directly in front of me in lecture rooms. I'd study them, their physical confidence. I was still recognizably kin to the boy I had been. Less tortured perhaps. But still kin. At Stanford, it's true, I began to have something like a conventional sexual life. I don't think, however, that I really believed that the women I knew found me physically appealing. I continued to stay out of the sun. I didn't linger in mirrors. And I was the student at Stanford who remembered to notice the Mexican-American janitors and gardeners working on campus.

It was at Stanford, one day near the end of my senior year, that a friend told me about a summer construction job he knew was available. I was quickly alert. Desire uncoiled within me. My friend said that he knew I had been looking for summer employment. He knew I needed some money. Almost apologetically he explained: It was something I probably wouldn't be interested in, but a friend of his, a contractor, needed someone for the summer to do menial jobs. There would be lots of shoveling and raking and sweeping. Nothing too hard. But nothing more interesting either. Still, the pay would be good. Did I want it? Or did I know someone who did? 2

I did. Yes, I said, surprised to hear myself say it. 3

In the weeks following, friends cautioned that I had no idea how hard physical labor really is. ("You only *think* you know what it is like to shovel for eight hours straight.") Their objections seemed to me challenges. They resolved the issue. I became happy with my plan. I decided, however, not to tell my parents. I wouldn't tell my mother because I could guess her worried reaction. I would tell my father only after the summer was over, when I could announce that, after all, I did know what "real work" is like. 4

The day I met the contractor (a Princeton graduate, it turned out), he asked me whether I had done any physical labor before. "In high school, during the summer," I lied. And although he seemed to regard me with skepticism, he decided to give me a try. Several days later, expectant, I arrived at my first construction site. I would take off my shirt to the sun. And at last grasp desired sensation. No longer afraid. At last become like a *bracero*. "We 5 need those tree stumps out of here by tomorrow," the contractor said. I started to work.

I labored with excitement that first morning—and all the days after. The work was harder than I could have expected. But it was never as tedious as my friends had warned me it would be. There was too much physical pleasure in the labor. Especially early in the day, I would be most alert to the sensations of movement and straining. Beginning around seven each morning (when the air was still damp but the scent of weeds and dry earth anticipated the heat of the sun), I would feel my body resist the first thrusts of the shovel. My arms, tightened by sleep, would gradually loosen; after only several minutes, sweat would gather in beads on my forehead and then—a short while later—I would feel my chest silky with sweat in the breeze. I would return to my work. A nervous spark of pain would fly up my arm and settle to burn like an ember in the thick of my shoulder. An hour, two passed. Three. My whole body would assume regular movements; my shoveling would be described by identical, even movements. Even later in the day, my enthusiasm for primitive sensation would survive the heat and the dust and the insects pricking my back. I would strain wildly for sensation as the day came to a close. At three-thirty, quitting time, I would stand upright and slowly let my head fall back, luxuriating in the feeling of tightness relieved.

Some of the men working nearby would watch me and laugh. Two or three of the older men took the trouble to teach me the right way to use a pick, the correct way to shovel. "You're doing it wrong, too fucking hard," one man scolded. Then proceeded to show me—what persons who work with their bodies all their lives quickly learn—the most economical way to use one's body in labor.

"Don't make your back do so much work," he instructed. I stood impatiently listening, half listening, vaguely watching, then noticed his work-thickened fingers clutching the shovel. I was annoyed. I wanted to tell him that I enjoyed shoveling the wrong way. And I didn't want to learn the right way. I wasn't afraid of back pain. I liked the way my body felt sore at the end of the day.

6

7

8

This passage is required for the reader's understanding that it is not distaste for manual labor that separates the narrator from *los pobres*.

The brief incident recalled in paragraphs 7, 8, and 9 gives the narrator the insight that a summer job will not really admit him to the world of the laborer and prepares the reader for the larger insight that follows in paragraphs 20–24.

I was about to, but, as it turned out, I didn't say a thing. 　9
Rather it was at that moment I realized that I was fooling myself
if I expected a few weeks of labor to gain me admission to the
world of the laborer. I would not learn in three months what my
father had meant by "real work." I was not bound to this job; I
could imagine its rapid conclusion. For me the sensations of ex-
ertion and fatigue could be savored. For my father or uncle, working at comparable jobs when they were my age, such sensations
were to be feared. Fatigue took a different toll on their bodies—
and minds.

It was, I know, a simple insight. But it was with this realiza- 　10
tion that I took my first step that summer toward realizing something even more important about the "worker." In the company of
carpenters, electricians, plumbers, and painters at lunch, I would
often sit quietly, observant. I was not shy in such company. I felt
easy, pleased by the knowledge that I was casually accepted, my
presence taken for granted by men (exotics) who worked with
their hands. Some days the younger men would talk and talk
about sex, and they would howl at women who drove by in cars.
Other days the talk at lunchtime was subdued; men gathered in
separate groups. It depended on who was around. There were
rough, good-natured workers. Others were quiet. The more I remember that summer, the more I realize that there was no single
type of worker. I am embarrassed to say I had not expected such
diversity. I certainly had not expected to meet, for example, a
plumber who was an abstract painter in his off hours and admired
the work of Mark Rothko. Nor did I expect to meet so many
workers with college diplomas. (There were the ones who were
not surprised that I intended to enter graduate school in the fall.)
I suppose what I really want to say here is painfully obvious, but
I must say it nevertheless: The men of that summer were middle-
class Americans. They certainly didn't constitute an oppressed
society. Carefully completing their work sheets; talking about the
fortunes of local football teams; planning Las Vegas vacations;
comparing the gas mileage of various makes of campers—they
were not *los pobres* my mother had spoken about.

The narrator discovers the diversity among
American workers and finds himself at ease in
their company. The comfort contrasts with the
coming description of his uneasiness in addressing the Mexican aliens.

On two occasions, the contractor hired a group of Mexican   11
aliens. They were employed to cut down some trees and haul off
debris. In all, there were six men of varying age. The youngest in
his twenties, the oldest (his father?) perhaps sixty years old. They
came and they left in a single old truck. Anonymous men. They
were never introduced to the other men at the site. Immediately
upon their arrival, they would follow the contractor's directions,
start working—rarely resting—seemingly driven by a fatalistic
sense that work which had to be done was best done as quickly
as possible

I watched them sometimes. Perhaps they watched me. The   12
only time I saw them pay me much notice was one day at lunchtime when I was laughing with the other men. The Mexicans sat
apart when they ate, just as they worked by themselves. Quiet. I
rarely heard them say much to each other. All I could hear were
their voices calling out sharply to one another, giving directions.
Otherwise, when they stood briefly resting, they talked among
themselves in voices too hard to overhear.

The contractor knew enough Spanish, and the Mexicans—or   13
at least the oldest of them, their spokesman—seemed to know
enough English to communicate. But because I was around, the
contractor decided one day to make me his translator. (He assumed I could speak Spanish.) I did what I was told. Shyly I went
over to tell the Mexicans that the *patrón* wanted them to do
something else before they left for the day. As I started to speak, I
was afraid with my old fear that I would be unable to pronounce
Spanish words. But it was a simple instruction I had to convey. I
could say it in phrases.

The dark sweating faces turned toward me as I spoke. They   14
stopped their work to hear me. Each nodded in response. I stood
there. I wanted to say something more. But what could I say in
Spanish, even if I could have pronounced the words right? Perhaps
I just wanted to engage them in small talk, to be assured of their
confidence, our familiarity. I thought for a moment to ask them
where in Mexico they were from. Something like that. And maybe
I wanted to tell them (a lie, if need be) that my parents were from
the same part of Mexico.

I stood there.   15

Their faces watched me. The eyes of the man directly in front of me moved slowly over my shoulder, and I turned to follow his glance toward *el patrón* some distance away. For a moment I felt swept up by that glance into the Mexicans' company. But then I heard one of them returning to work. And then the others went back to work. I left them without saying anything more.

16   The man's glance over the narrator's shoulder toward *el patrón* tells the narrator that he is seen only as a messenger from the boss and dashes his hopes for a bond between him and the Mexican workers.

When they had finished, the contractor went over to pay them   17
in cash. (He later told me that he paid them collectively—"for the job"—though he wouldn't tell me their wages. He said something quickly about the good rate of exchange "in their own country.") I can still hear the loudly confident voice he used with the Mexicans. It was the sound of the *gringo* I had heard as a very young boy. And I can still hear the quiet, indistinct sounds of the Mexican, the oldest, who replied. At hearing that voice I was sad for the Mexicans. Depressed by their vulnerability. Angry at myself. The adventure of the summer seemed suddenly ludicrous. I would not shorten the distance I felt from *los pobres* with a few weeks of physical labor. I would not become like them. They were different from me.

After that summer, a great deal—and not very much really—   18
changed in my life. The curse of physical shame was broken by the sun; I was no longer ashamed of my body. No longer would I deny myself the pleasing sensations of my maleness. During those years when middle-class Black Americans began to assert with pride, "Black is beautiful," I was able to regard my complexion without shame. I am today darker than I ever was as a boy. I have taken up the middle-class sport of long-distance running. Nearly every day now I run ten or fifteen miles, barely clothed, my skin exposed to the California winter rain and wind or the summer sun of late afternoon. The torso, the soccer player's calves and thighs, the arms of the twenty-year-old I never was, I possess now in my thirties. I study the youthful parody shape in the mirror: the stomach lipped tight by muscle; the shoulders rounded by chin-ups; the arms veined strong. This man. A man. I meet him. He laughs to see me, what I have become.

18   These paragraphs take us to a more recent past and confirm the narrator's acceptance of his membership in a privileged class.

The dandy. I wear double-breasted Italian suits and custom-made English shoes. I resemble no one so much as my father—the man pictured in those honeymoon photos. At that point in life when he abandoned the dandy's posture, I assume it. At the point when my parents would not consider going on vacation, I register at the Hotel Carlyle in New York and the Plaza Athénée in Paris. I am as taken by the symbols of leisure and wealth as they were. For my parents, however, those symbols became taunts, reminders of all they could not achieve in one lifetime. For me those same symbols are reassuring reminders of public success. I tempt vulgarity to be reassured. I am filled with the gaudy delight, the monstrous grace of the *nouveau riche*.   19

The final paragraphs sum up his understanding of what the earlier experience means. The fundamental distinction between the narrator and *los pobres* is an attitude that grows from different experiences.

In recent years I have had occasion to lecture in ghetto high schools. There I see students of remarkable style and physical grace. (One can see more dandies in such schools than one ever will find in middle-class high schools.) There is not the look of casual assurance I saw students at Stanford display. Ghetto girls mimic high-fashion models. Their dresses are of bold, forceful color; their figures elegant, long; the stance theatrical. Boys wear shirts that grip at their overdeveloped muscular bodies. (Against a powerless future, they engage images of strength.) Bad nutrition does not yet tell. Great disappointment, fatal to youth, awaits them still. For the moment, movements in school hallways are dance-like, a procession of postures in a sexual masque. Watching them, I feel a kind of envy. I wonder how different my adolescence would have been had I been free. . . . But no, it is my parents I see—their optimism during those years when they were entertained by Italian grand opera.   20

The registration clerk in London wonders if I have just been to Switzerland. And the man who carries my luggage in New York guesses the Caribbean. My complexion becomes a mark of my leisure. Yet no one would regard my complexion the same way if I entered such hotels through the service entrance. That is only to say that my complexion assumes its significance from the context of my life. My skin, in itself, means nothing. I stress the point because I know there are people who would label me "disadvan-   21 taged" because of my color. They make the same mistake I made as a boy, when I thought a disadvantaged life was circumscribed by particular occupations. That summer I worked in the sun may have made me physically indistinguishable from the Mexicans working nearby. (My skin was actually darker because, unlike them, I worked without wearing a shirt. By late August my hands were probably as tough as theirs.) But I was not one of *los pobres*. What made me different from them was an attitude of *mind*, my imagination of myself.

I do not blame my mother for warning me away from the sun when I was young. In a world where her brother had become an old man in his twenties because he was dark, my complexion was something to worry about. "Don't run in the sun," she warns me today. I run. In the end, my father was right—though perhaps he did not know how right or why—to say that I would never know what real work is. I will never know what he felt at his last factory job. If tomorrow I worked at some kind of factory, it would go differently for me. My long education would favor me. I could act as a public person—able to defend my interests, to unionize, to petition, to speak up—to challenge and demand. (I will never know what real work is.) I will never know what the Mexicans knew, gathering their shovels and ladders and saws.

Their silence stays with me now. The wages those Mexicans received for their labor were only a measure of their disadvantaged condition. Their silence is more telling. They lack a public identity. They remain profoundly alien. Persons apart. People lacking a union obviously, people without grounds. They depend upon the relative good will or fairness of their employers each day. For such people, lacking a better alternative, it is not such an unreasonable risk.

Their silence stays with me. I have taken these many words to describe its impact. Only: the quiet. Something uncanny about it. Its compliance. Vulnerability. Pathos. As I heard their truck rumbling away, I shuddered, my face mirrored with sweat. I had finally come face to face with *los pobres*.

22

23 Beginning the last two paragraphs with the same sentence emphasizes the Mexican workers' compliance and vulnerability and leaves us with wonder at the chasm between the classes.

POSSIBLE ANSWERS

24 ### *Meaning and Purpose*

1. Rodriguez is observant of his fellow students and believes they are wealthier and more privileged than he. He feels inferior, more kin to the Mexican-American janitors and gardeners, and he is sensitive about his dark skin. He doesn't think he is appealing physically: he "didn't linger in mirrors" (1).

2. Rodriguez had never done hard physical labor, as his father had. Wanting to rise above the working class, he was surprised when "desire uncoiled" (2) in him for the construction job. Challenged by physical labor, he didn't want his parents to think he'd taken a job beneath him, or that he had no ambition.
3. Rodriguez's main point is realizing what makes people *los pobres*. In paragraph 22 he says, "What made me different from them was an attitude of *mind*, my imagination of myself." He worked with white laborers who had college degrees and with Mexican laborers who were silent, compliant, and vulnerable (24). It was not occupation but his perception of himself, and the voice his education had given him, which would keep him from ever being one of *los pobres* (21).
4. The insight is that Rodriguez cannot "gain admission to the world of the laborer" (9) just by working at a summer construction job. He was not bound to the job and could savor the sensation of fatigue. The connection with "But I was not one of *los pobres*" (21) is that his body might be capable of physical labor and his hands as "tough as theirs" (21), but his "attitude of *mind*" (21) and his education keep him from being poor.
5. Being paid as a group eliminates their individuality as men. The contractor takes advantage of their alien status and their inability to bargain for themselves.
6. The Mexican workers are silent because they have no union, no grounds, no "public identity" (23). They depend on others' good will. Finally their silence brings Rodriguez "face to face with *los pobres*."

Strategy

1. The order is chronological, so that Rodriguez can show his early naiveté about class and life-style, then his later sophistication and ability to understand his summer.
2. The summer job, core of the narrative, requires details to make the point about Rodriguez's realizing what it means to be poor. Sections two and three compress time and

Meaning and Purpose

1. What picture of Rodriguez do you get from the first paragraph? How does he see himself?
2. Why is he surprised to hear himself say yes (paragraph 3) to the offer of a summer job at manual labor? What is his motive for taking the job? Why doesn't he tell his parents?
3. Rodriguez talks about many things in this essay: being a student at Stanford, physical labor, the Italian suits he wears, and ghetto high-school students. What do you think his main point is, and where does he state it?
4. Paragraph 10 begins with "It was, I know, a simple insight." What is the insight and what triggers it? How does this insight connect with his later statement, "But I was not one of *los pobres*"?
5. Is it significant that the Mexican workers were paid as a group rather than individually? Explain.
6. Rodriguez begins paragraphs 23 and 24 with the words, "Their silence stays with me." What does the silence signify?

Strategy

1. Rodriguez's narrative begins with one summer while he is a student at Stanford, then jumps to the vague time frame of "After that summer" (18), then to "In recent years" (20). Why does he choose to arrange the events and skip to the periods that he does?
2. Why does Rodriguez draw out details of his summer construction job and compress the details of the longer periods in sections 2 and 3?
3. Does Rodriguez use summary or scene to tell his story? Give examples.
4. What is Rodriguez's point of view? Give evidence from the essay of how effective it is.

Style

1. Locate the words *los pobres, bracero, patrón,* and *gringo* in the text. Can you define them using only the context of the narrative?
2. Rodriguez occasionally uses sentence fragments purposely. Find at least three in the first two paragraphs and explain how they affect the tone of the introduction.
3. A good narrative re-creates life. Does "Los Pobres" do so? Explain.

Writing Tasks

1. At some time in your life you have undoubtedly been an "outsider." It may have been in another country or at a new school, in a new neighborhood, or on a new job. Write a narrative about that time. As Rodriguez does in "Los Pobres," blend the details of the situation with your thoughts and insights from a later perspective.
2. Choose an event to narrate, and write it in two ways. In one version, use the scene method to dramatize the event and make it immediate. In the other version, use summary to tell more than show. Which version is more effective?

summarize the life-style he later lived and now lives. These two sections don't describe just one event but show Rodriguez looking back through postcollege experiences that help him understand that summer.

3. Rodriguez uses both summary and scene. The summer job is presented more as scene, a drama acted out with characters and dialogue. (" 'Don't make your back do so much work,' he instructed. I stood patiently listening" [8]). But some of it is summarized: "I labored with excitement the first morning—and all the days after" (6). Section two is summary about his physical condition and the clothes he wears (18–19). And in section three, he also summarizes (20). The summary parts have little or no dialogue and no scenes are acted out.

4. Rodriguez uses first person to tell his own story, but he is looking back from his thirties on the summer job in college. With this point of view he can show how he came to understand what it is to be poor. Examples that show this effectiveness are: "The more I remember that summer, the more I realize that there was no single *type* of work" (10); "And I can still hear the quiet, indistinct sounds of the Mexican, the oldest, who replied . . ." (17).

Style

1. In the last sentence of paragraph 10, *los pobres* is what the middle-class construction workers just described are not. A *bracero* (5) is "no longer afraid," but a strong worker. The *patrón* (13), or the contractor, gives orders to the Mexicans. *Gringo* (17) comes right after the description of how the contractor pays the Mexicans, and how "loudly confident" his voice is. *Gringo* is a disparaging name for whites.

2. Three fragments in the first two paragraphs are "Less tortured perhaps"; "But still kin"; "Nothing too hard." These fragments create the informal, conversational tone of the opening, and they are emphatic in their brevity.

3. Rodriguez re-creates life, especially in describing the Mexican workers, who seem immediate and real, even in their anonymity.

❦ Deborah Salazar ❦

Deborah Salazar was born in Ecuador and grew up in Denham Springs, Louisiana. She received her Master of Fine Arts degree from Louisiana State University. Her poetry has been published in a number of feminist magazines and small literary journals, including Exquisite Corpse *and* New Delta Review. *In 1988 she was the challenger for the World Heavyweight Poetry Championship in Taos, New Mexico, an unusual poetry competition in which the competitors engage in "bouts" of poetry reading and improvisation in front of an audience.*

TEACHING SUGGESTIONS

One of our currently volatile topics, abortion has strong enemies and strong supporters, many of whom have not read a first-person narrative written by a woman who has had an abortion.

A congenial way to begin a discussion is by asking students whether the United States is a one-religion country or whether it separates religion and state. Then ask whether it is possible to have a personally high ethical standard without subscribing to a specific religion. And then ask which is more important: the rights of the individual or the rights of the state. Under what circumstances should the rights of the individual (or of the state) take precedence?

You will probably find that the discussion ends on the moot "It all depends." Depends on what?

The point of the discussion is to cause the students to wonder whether laws should be passed that satisfy one group but restrict another, only because the first group has seemingly stronger ethical reasons for its position, be it "right to life" or "pro-choice."

Their wondering puts them into an excellent state of mind for reading this essay.

MARGINAL NOTES

Salazar interests her readers by beginning with a small mystery. Readers will continue reading this essay to discover *why* the procedure was the easiest part.

My Abortion

Though this essay is a first-person account of a woman's first-hand experience of abortion, the author does not insert opinions or draw conclusions, but rather leaves those up to the reader. Salazar's use of straightforward narrative leaves this volatile subject open for "discussion." The article was first published in Exquisite Corpse, *a small literary journal, and later reprinted in* Harper's, *in April 1990.*

The procedure itself was the easiest part. A friend had told me to close my eyes and think about anything, think about Donald Duck—sweet and useless advice, I thought at the time—but when I heard the machine come on and the doctor say, "The cervix is slanted at a right angle, this could be a problem; okay, honey, *relax*," I thought, Donald Duck, Donald Duck, Donald Duck, Donald Duck. I will never be able to watch another Donald Duck cartoon without thinking about my abortion, but I went through the experience feeling pretty calm and entitled. Twenty-seven years old and pregnant for the first time in my life. God bless America, I thought, I sure as hell want a cheap, legal, safe abortion.

1

After I learned that I was pregnant, I started practicing a necessary detachment. The Supreme Court was due to hand down its *Webster* decision any day, and the usual mobs of protesters around women's clinics were doubling in size. I got up before dawn on the fifteenth of June and packed a paper bag with a sweater and socks (because the receptionist said it would be cold inside the clinic) and maxi pads. I wanted to get there as soon as the doors opened, before most of the cross-waving, sign-carrying, chanting, singing protesters showed up. When I pulled into the clinic parking lot with my friend Beth, I saw only two people standing on the curb: a woman, dressed all in black, and a man. As we got closer, I saw that the woman was about my age, with straight black hair and pale eyes turned skyward. She was moaning the words, "Don't kill me, Mommy, don't kill me."

The man and the woman followed our car until it stopped at the door. I stepped out, and the man stood in front of me. He was tall, wearing a suit and tie and singing, "Jesus loves the little children." I laughed in his face. Strange. Three years ago I had worked as a volunteer escort at this very clinic, and I'd always been so solemn with these people. I never would've expected to laugh today. The man obviously hadn't expected me to laugh either. He got angry. "Lesbian!" he called after me as I walked into the clinic. "You're a lesbian. That's why you hate babies!" A tall young man wearing an official clinic-escort T-shirt was standing at the threshold. "Sorry about this," he muttered as I passed by. I was still laughing. "I wish I were a lesbian," I said a little hysterically. "I wouldn't be pregnant." And then I was inside the clinic.

I knew the routine. I took my forms and my plastic cup. I went directly to the bathroom. I could hear the protesters while I was in the bathroom. I could hear them the whole time I was in the clinic. The chanting was discontinuous, but it was louder every time it started up. "Murderers! Murderers!" I could hear them in the dressing room, in the weigh-in room, in counseling, in recovery, although I don't remember if I heard them in the procedure room itself. I was told later that my encounter with the protesters had been relatively undramatic; one escort said that

2

"*Webster*": The "Webster decision," later handed down, gives the states greater powers to restrict abortions than they have had since *Roe vs. Wade* (1973), which says that state antiabortion laws are unconstitutional, except as they apply to the last trimester of pregnancy.

Notice the imagery, with the black-haired woman "dressed in all black," coupled with her moaning message. The narrative gains interest because of the way in which Salazar describes her "characters."

3

Here Salazar leaves chronology to recall the irony that she is being helped much as she herself helped others in the past.

The man resorts to name-calling instead of reasoning. This highly emotional way won't convert anyone to his views about whether or not to have an abortion.

Salazar turns the word "lesbian" against the name-caller. The tension in such an encounter is tangible, even though the narrator has practiced detachment.

4

Having worked in the clinic, Salazar knew the routine. The irony is that she herself is now being led through it and also that the routine, designed to be understanding and supportive, is nearly as much an ordeal as coping with the protesters outside.

Notice that the narrative does not follow a strictly chronological sequence.

these days he was seeing protesters trying to hold car doors shut while women fought to get out.

After I turned in my urine cup, I sat back in the waiting room and started filling out forms. One of them was a personal questionnaire that included the question, "What method of birth control were you using at the time you got pregnant?" I thought about lying for a second before I checked the box beside "none." One of the protesters outside had started playing a tape of a baby crying. I signed my name over and over. Yes, I understand the risks involved, yes, I understand that the alternatives to abortion are birth and adoption. I wanted to do more—I wanted to fill out a page or so explaining why I had chosen to do this. I wanted to explain to someone that I was a responsible person; you see, ladies and gentlemen, I never had sex without condoms unless I was having my period; I got pregnant during my period, isn't there something I could sign swearing to that? I had a three-day affair with a friend, I'm broke and unemployed, I can't give up a baby for adoption, I can't afford to be pregnant while I look for a job.

In counseling, I was asked why I'd gone off the pill, and I didn't hesitate to respond, "I can get rid of an accidental pregnancy. I can't get rid of cancer." In the lounge room where I sat in my dressing gown before going in to see the doctor, there was a tiny television (Pee-wee Herman was on) and a table with magazines (*Cosmopolitan, Vogue, American Baby*). The room was already filled to capacity, all twelve chairs taken, when the little bowhead came in. She couldn't have been more than seventeen, wearing only her gown and a very big white satin bow in her hair. She was a beauty. She looked like she belonged on a homecoming float. She had been crying. "I hate them," she announced, dropping her shopping bag of clothes on the floor. "They don't have to say the things they say. Makes me want to go out there and shoot them with a gun."

"You can't hear them that well in here, honey," one of the older women said. "You can watch the cartoons."

"You know what one of them called my mama?" the beauty said. "Called her a slut, an unchristian woman. My mama yelled

5

6

7

8

Salazar recounts the events leading up to the abortion, wishing that she had a way to explain more fully, both for the audience who will read the personal questionnaire and for us, the reading audience. Real situations are often more complex than laws, forms, and moral positions make them appear.

Notice the symbolism in the magazine titles: *Cosmopolitan* often publishes articles about women's rights and individuality; *Vogue*, about women's styles. Is *American Baby* there by accident, or is its presence intended to discourage abortion?

Salazar shows that she is not the only one—or the only "type"—to have an abortion. She describes physically and psychologically a girl far different from her, except for being pregnant. This anecdote also gives Salazar a chance to remind the readers of the anti-abortion crowd outside the clinic.

back that I got raped by a priest, that's how come I'm here." Stares. The bowhead picked up her shopping bag and leaned against the wall. She spoke again in a quieter voice. "I didn't really get raped by a priest. My mama just said that."

The doctor was late that morning. Outside, the chants were getting louder, competing with Pee-wee Herman, who was on full blast. The protesters were singing a hymn when my name was called. I walked down a short hallway in my bare feet, and then liquid Valium injected directly into my left arm made everything after that feel like it was taking place on another planet. I remember that the doctor was wearing a dark red surgical outfit and that it looked pretty gruesome—I wished he'd worn the traditional pale blue or green. I remember that the Valium made me want to laugh and I didn't want to laugh because I was afraid I'd wiggle, and I'd been warned *not* to wiggle unless I wanted my uterus perforated. I'd been at the clinic six hours already, preparing for this little operation that would take only five minutes. I remember that after the machine came on, it seemed like less than five minutes. I remember that it hurt and that I was amazed at how empty, relieved, and not pregnant I felt as soon as it was over. The cramps that followed were painful but not terribly so; I could feel my uterus contracting, trying to collapse back to its former size. I was led by a nurse into a dark room, where I sat on a soft mat in a soft chair and bled for a while. I closed my eyes. The woman in the next seat was sobbing softly. I knew it was the blond with the white bow in her hair. I reached over and took her hand in mine. The Valium made me feel as though we were both wearing gloves. Her hand was so still I wondered if she knew I was there, but the sobbing grew softer and softer and eventually it just stopped.

9   Notice the juxtaposition for the sake of irony: Salazar is called just as the crowd begins its hymn.

Valium is benzodiazepine, used to treat anxiety.

Salazar does not clinically describe the abortion. Why? Because the purpose of the narrative is to recount the experience of dealing with the situation both outside and inside the clinic. She has already told us "the procedure itself was the easiest part."

"her hand": Salazar and the woman join hands. Notice that the woman had been described earlier as "little bowhead," a girl about seventeen years old. Here they are both women, joined by a common bond.

Meaning and Purpose

1. Why do you think Salazar wants to tell the story of her abortion? What is her purpose?

Possible Answers

Meaning and Purpose

1. Salazar seems to want to tell what her abortion was like honestly, without condemning or romanticizing it. She explains her reasons for having an abortion and shows how the pro-life demonstrators affect the people in the clinic. She shows that, for her, having an abortion is not the crime some think it is, and that women in abortion clinics should be treated with respect and understanding.

2. If students never protested against anything, encourage them to imagine doing so and speculate about what their feelings might be.

3. Pro-life people probably would not care to hear Salazar's story. She undoubtedly wants to reach people who are undecided about their stand on abortion, women considering abortion, and women who have had similar experiences.

4. Salazar considers herself a responsible, moral person who had the bad luck to get pregnant during her period. The clinic is a place for honesty.

5. Salazar imagines she faces a box of jurors about to pass judgment on her, and she wants to vindicate herself.

Strategy

1. Salazar chooses small but significant details to make the story real, such as thinking about Donald Duck (1), "I saw that the woman was about my age, with straight black hair and pale eyes turned skyward" (2), and "The Valium made me feel as though we were both wearing gloves" (9). She also reveals her personal thoughts (in paragraph 5, where she talks about the circumstances of getting pregnant), which brings readers closer to her experience.

2. Salazar uses psychological order, the sequence in which events might appear in memory. She begins in the room where the abortion is performed, then skips back to preparing to go to the clinic that morning, then to the arrival at the clinic, then back to how she got pregnant, then uses chronological order to the end. The sense of movement is always forward. Opening with the abortion itself grabs readers, and then giving background information is necessary. The rest unfolds at a steady pace, as

2. Have you ever demonstrated against something? What did the experience feel like? Did you think about how your protests might sound to those who didn't share your views?

3. Whom is Salazar addressing in her essay? Do you think she knows a group with which she wants to share her experience?

4. Why do you think Salazar tells the truth on the questionnaire about not having used a birth-control method?

5. Whom is Salazar addressing in this sentence and for what reason: "you see, ladies and gentlemen, I never had sex without condoms unless I was having my period" (5)?

Strategy

1. How effectively does Salazar make you as a reader experience what she experienced? Give examples from the essay to support your answer.

2. Discuss the order of events and how that order works in the story.

3. How does Salazar use the descriptions of the protesters to tell you her opinion of them and how they make her feel?

Style

1. Salazar notices details in the clinic, such as *American Baby* magazine, the girl with the bow in her hair, and the doctor's red surgical suit. How do these details add to the effect of the story?

2. In paragraph 4, Salazar describes hearing the protesters as she goes through preparations. How does the language of this description create a feeling?

3. The story ends rather abruptly as the girl's sobbing stops. Why does Salazar end it in this way and not tell about leaving the clinic?

Writing Tasks

1. Have you ever gone through with a difficult decision over some-one's objections? Write a narrative in which you dramatize the experience and describe how the protests or objections affected you. Use the order of events that you think best suits an effective telling of the story.

2. Write the story of any event or experience from two points of view, first in the first person, and then in the third, more objec-tive person. Which voice do you think tells the better story?

it happened, to imitate the course of action Salazar set out on.

3. Salazar wants to avoid the protesters and first refers to them critically as "cross-waving, sign-carrying, chanting, singing" (2). She re-marks that the woman was "dressed all in black" and that she was "moaning" (2). Salazar laughs at the man, an act of jeering and a re-lease of her tense feelings. The protesters make her feel anxious and angry. It's ironic that she had earlier been an escort there, protecting women like herself from protesters (3).

Style

1. These details seem out of place in an abor-tion clinic: *American Baby* magazine in a place where women end unwanted pregnancies; a girl with a bow who looks like a child herself; red surgical clothes that suggest blood and car-nage to Salazar, who already feels scared about having an abortion.

2. The chanting escalates as Salazar's anxious feelings escalate, and she can't shut it out of her mind. The parallel structure of repeating "I could hear them" and of "in the dressing room, in the weigh-in room, in counseling, in recovery" mimics the chanting outside and gives the paragraph a tense feeling.

3. Salazar ends her story with a touching con-nection between herself and the young girl. After Salazar has described the dreaded protesters, the grim procedure, and tried to defend her choice of abortion, realizing that a small gesture of caring and understanding can make a difference is significant. This ending, like the rest of the story, evokes sympathy for women who choose abortion.

❦ *Additional Writing Tasks* ❦
Narration

1. All of us have had experiences that can be retold in narrative form. Often these experiences stay with us much longer than impersonal events we have merely observed. For this writing task, select an incident from your early years that involves a simple action that you can recall clearly and vividly. The incident does not have to be exceptionally dramatic, but it should be interesting enough to move from the opening through the body to the climax—the major components of narrative. The incident may involve you alone or it may involve others as well. It must have enough action with connected events to be developed as a narration.

   Because this is to be an incident from your early years, you might begin by setting aside time to explore your past. Begin by spontaneously jotting down memories from your early past as a way to begin the selection procedure. Make a list by devoting no more than three or four sentences to each experience you recall. These three entries are from one student's memory list:

   > I remember walking home from school one June morning. Hot. Humid. A man with a Bible and wearing a black suit stopped me and asked, "Have you been saved, Sonny?" I was frightened.

   > When I was ten I visited my grandfather in the hospital. He was very ill, dying. I recalled all the wonderful and all the horrible fishing trips we took together.

   > Why was my dog shot? The killer was never found. I remember searching the faces of strangers for looks of guilt.

   Each writer, of course, will have his or her own memories: an automobile accident, a mystery, a sudden appearance, a victory, a defeat, a meeting with a famous person, and so on.

   Once you have compiled a list, select one of the memories, perhaps the one that stirs the most emotion in you when you recall it, and use it as the basis for your narration. Before starting your first draft, take at least an uninterrupted hour to compose a rough sketch of the incident, capturing the movement of events and the people. Then you will be prepared to start the first draft. Begin by arranging the material in dramatic order to serve as a loose outline.

2.   Select an incident to narrate that you have not directly experienced yourself. The incident may come from what you have seen, heard, or read. Perhaps you will select an incident from a television show, film, short story, news article, or friend's experience. If you select a newspaper article as your source, you may want to retell it as though you had witnessed the incident. If you want to convey a friend's story, you may add observations of your own. If you select an incident from a film or short story, you may want to concentrate on an incident involving one character and rearrange the events to suit your purpose. Keep in mind, though, that your task is not to merely summarize the story line; your task is to select material for your own narrative.

2

Description
Capturing Sensory Details

The Method

To describe is to picture in words—the people we meet, the places we visit, the conversations we hear, the infinite number of things we encounter. Description, like narration, is often associated with imaginative literature: children's tales, short stories, and novels. In fiction, narrative events provide a story's bones; description adds flesh to the skeletal structure, helping a reader to imagine the narrative events: "The wind rattled the windows . . . a tall figure wearing a cape emerged from the darkness . . . a pasty white face . . . black hair plastered like a swimmer's cap to his head . . . red lips curled in a sneer . . . the air smelling of rotting meat. . . ." For a descriptive passage to be effective, fiction writers know they must involve their readers' senses to create a reaction to the words. This requirement also applies to essayists who use description as a dominant essay pattern. They, too, must involve a reader's senses—that is, make their readers see, hear, smell, feel, and taste.

Sight

The streets boiled with shoppers . . .
His sunburned face looked grim, heavily lined, and ringed with a gray beard . . .
Flames lashed the sky . . .

Sound

The breath rasped from his lungs . . .
Water trickled from the faucet in a steady beat . . .
The silence was broken by clicks of forks against plates and the crunching of lettuce . . .
The soft lilt of Asian voices carried across the river . . .

Smell

The streets smelled of ripe fruit and straw . . .
The aroma of curry floated above the cooking pots . . .
The perfume was full of musk . . .
His breath, laced with garlic and onions, could stop a bloodhound . . .

Touch

The fur, soft and silky, touched my skin . . .
Sharp pebbles covered the path . . .
The cold shower felt like a gust of Arctic air . . .
His fingers said the wound was gaping . . .

Taste

The potion had a sharp, coppery flavor . . .
She held the bite of sweet melon in her mouth, then began to chew, the juice, like rich syrup, trickling down her throat . . .

Beyond the specific senses is a source that writers also use to involve their readers in a descriptive passage. It might be called a writer's "impression" of an experience, his or her own reaction or perception. Or more simply, a writer's *feelings*.

Feelings

The air was fresh, cool, and clean, as I walked up the trail, feeling as if I had been reborn . . .
Around and around the park the motorcyclists buzzed like deadly black bees, and I was afraid to move . . .
I feel happy when I am curled up in bed with a good book . . .

Strategies

When reading with a critical eye, study the techniques writers use to involve your senses. Remember that serious writers calculate each detail in a descriptive passage, shaping the words to touch a circuit in your imagination. Study this passage from "In the Jungle" by naturalist and essayist Annie Dillard. Dillard describes a jungle encampment by appealing to our senses of sight, touch, sound, and smell. She closes by expressing her feelings about the site.

It was February, the middle of summer. Green fireflies spattered lights across the air and illuminated for seconds, now here, now there, the pale trunks of enormous, solitary trees. Beneath us the brown Napo River was rising, in all silence; it coiled up the sandy bank and tangled its foam in vines that trailed from the forest and roots that looped the shore.

Each breath of night smelled sweet, more moistened and sweet than any kitchen, or garden, or cradle. Each star in Orion seemed to tremble and stir with my breath. All at once, in the thatch house across the clearing behind us, one of the village's Jesuit priests began playing an alto recorder, playing a wordless lyric, in a minor key, that twined over the village clearing, that caught in the big trees' canopies, muted our talk on the bankside, and wandered over the river, dissolving downstream.

This will do, I thought. This will do, for a weekend, or a season, or a home.

Dillard describes a concrete scene full of details directly perceived by the senses. But writers don't limit their descriptive passages to that which can be perceived. Often they describe abstract experiences, such as love, hate, joy, or anger. But to fire a reader's imagination, they must describe the abstract in concrete words. Anger might be described as "a fire in the blood." In this passage from *Dispatches*, a collection of essays about the Vietnam War, Michael Herr captures the fear that comes when an enemy-filled jungle suddenly goes silent. Notice how Herr uses concrete words to describe the abstract and weaves his feelings and earlier experiences into the descriptive fabric.

There were times during the night when all the jungle sounds would stop at once. There was no dwindling down or falling away, it was all gone in a single instant as though some signal had been transmitted out to the life; bats, birds, snakes, monkeys, insects, picking up on a frequency that a thousand years in the jungle might condition you to receive, but leaving you as it was to wonder what you weren't hearing now, straining for sound, one piece of information. I had heard it before in other jungles, the Amazon and the Philippines, but those jungles were "secure," there wasn't much chance that hundreds of Viet Cong were coming and going, moving and waiting, living out there just to do you harm.

The thought of that one could turn any sudden silence into a space that you'd fill with everything you thought was quiet in you, it could even put you on the approach to clairvoyance. You thought you heard impossible things: damp roots breathing, fruit sweating, fervid bug action, the heartbeat of tiny animals.

Subjective and Objective Description

Descriptive writing is likely to be either subjective or objective. The passage above from Herr's *Dispatches* is subjective. Herr describes a personal encounter with fear, trying to picture his response to the threat an utterly silent jungle foreshadows in a war zone. Objective description, by contrast, is factual, impersonal, thoroughly scrubbed of the writer's impressions. An objective report on yesterday's weather might read like this:

> Westerly ten-mile-an-hour winds blew across the beach. The swells reached fifteen feet.

Rewritten from a subjective angle—that is, with a writer's impressions coloring the facts—the description might read like this:

> Kicked up by ten-mile-an-hour winds, waves rose to mountainous crests before crashing like an avalanche of water onto body surfers.

Purely objective writing is rare in essays with description as the dominant pattern. It is mainly found in scientific reports and encyclopedias. Of course, we find degrees of subjectivity and objectivity. Most descriptive essays, as your reading will confirm, fall somewhere between the extremes.

Dominant Impression

To create an effective description, you might think writers do nothing more than record all they perceive. They do much more.

As a critical reader, keep in mind that descriptive writing is not a haphazard activity. With so much detail available for any description, writers must select descriptive details with care and shape them with precision to achieve a **dominant impression.**

In subjective description, selecting detail to create a dominant impression is even more critical than in objective description. Writers must not only select but also embellish descriptive details to create the impression they want. When describing a desert, a writer might want to show that the land is hostile: "the harsh sunlight reflecting from the bleached sand like needles plunging into the hiker's eyes." Describing a politician, a writer might want to show him to be untrustworthy: "his face heavily lined from years of calculating behind closed doors, his eyes skipping around the crowd like those of a criminal about to be exposed." Writers seldom directly state the dominant impression they wish to create; they suggest it.

Consider this passage from Gretel Ehrlich's "A Season of Portraits." Ehrlich, who is an essayist, a novelist, and a Wyoming rancher, describes the dry summer of 1988, when raging fires consumed much of Yellowstone National Park forests. In this passage she concentrates on the wind, suggesting that it is a wind from hell, savage and ghostly, perhaps even isolating her as souls are isolated in a mythical underworld.

> A breeze stiffens. Gusts are clocked at forty-five, sixty, eighty-five miles per hour. Rainless thunderclouds crack above, shaking pine pollen down. *La bufera infernale*—that's what Dante calls winds that lashed at sinners in hell. I decide to go out in the infernal storm. "This is hell," a herder moving his sheep across the mountain says, grinning, then clears his parched throat and rides away. Wind carries me back and forth, twisting, punching me down.
>
> I'm alone here for much of the summer, these hot winds my only dancing partner. The sheep and their herder vanish over the ridge. I close my eyes, and the planet is auditory only: tree branches twist into tubas and saxes, are caught by large hands that press down valves, and everywhere on this

ranch I hear feral music—ghostly tunes made not by animals gone wild but by grasses, sagebrush, and fence wire singing.

Once writers decide on a dominant impression and select the appropriate details to suggest it, they must arrange the details in an effective order. Often a structure will become visible during the writing and revision, one that will be unique for that passage. Ehrlich arranges the passage above in two parts: the world she sees and the world she hears, which are clearly separated when she writes, "I closed my eyes." She continues by suggesting that the wind plays the branches of trees like musical instruments and creates ghostly music by rushing through grasses, sagebrush, fence wire. By shutting her eyes, and yours as a sensitive reader, she transforms the world into a mysterious place.

Arrangement of Details

But you will find no strict formulas for arranging descriptive details; writers do, however, follow some general principles. In visual description, a writer will usually structure the details in the way that the eye would record them; that is, by spatial arrangement—from left to right, right to left, near to far, far to near, center outward. A writer might begin with a broad picture and narrow to the particulars, like a film opening with a panoramic view of a landscape or city and gradually moving into the scene, finally focusing on one specific image.

To describe a person, a writer might begin with a general descriptive statement: "She looked as if she had stepped from the pages of *Vogue,* a stylish woman," and then moved downward from head to toe, "Her hair was the color of straw and cropped short; her neck seemed carved from ivory. . . ." Or this writer might begin by describing an unusual physical feature and work from there: "Her nose didn't fit her stylish appearance: it was a bit long and bent slightly to the left, as if it had stopped a boxer's left cross. Otherwise, she was unflawed. . . ." As you read descriptive passages, keep in mind that writers have many ways in which to organize a description. Critical readers examine writers' varied ways of structuring descriptive details and applying the techniques.

Description in College Writing

Vivid description is embedded in all but the most scientifically objective papers, bringing life to reports, arguments, explanations, even essay examinations. Often you may want to use a descriptive passage to add color and drama to an essay that is developed around a dominant pattern other than description. The principles of description for such a passage still apply. Above all, you must establish a clear purpose for such a passage and clearly understand your audience to determine how much descriptive detail to include in the passage.

This descriptive passage begins an extended student essay analyzing the ways in which people use their physical appearance to communicate a message. Debra Carlson wrote twelve paragraphs to complete the project, but only the first two paragraphs are pure description. The third brief paragraph here establishes the purpose of the descriptive passage.

Carlson's opening sentences suggest the purpose—Tom's appearance is clearly not in the "mainstream." She begins the description at Tom's head and moves to his feet, following a clear structure. She selects her details carefully to reinforce her purpose. It might help to imagine what she has excluded—color of Tom's

At first glance, Tom does not look like a typical teenager in advertisements for the Gap and Polo. In fact, his appearance contrasts sharply with the image of the typical upper-middle-class teen splashed on the pages of mainstream magazines. His hair is twisted into finger-sized dreadlocks and hangs in long strands below his shoulders, like the hair of Jamaican musicians. He wears an earring, sometimes a gold post that twinkles in the light, at other times a peace symbol that dangles from the end of a chain. He wears "tie-dyed" shirts, a popular sixties style that comes in bright oranges, greens, reds, *hair and eyes, his physical size, and so on. She doesn't need these details to achieve the dominant impression she wants to create.*

purples, and yellows, with psychedelic patterns. His trousers are usually faded jeans with threadbare knees and strategically placed rips held together with safety pins, "A carryover from punk days," he says. When he is not wearing hiking boots, well worn and split on the sides, he wears sandals.

Carlson opens paragraph 2 by responding to Tom's appearance, defining it for the reader.

His appearance might be described as "scruffy" today; twenty-five years ago, it would have been described as "counterculture." But on closer examination, it is clear that Tom's earring is not gold plated, it is fourteen karat, his T-shirt did not come from the local thrift shop, it came from a unisex boutique with high price tags, and his jeans were not made by Levi, they were made by a high-fashion designer company. His appearance might suggest he lives in a low-rent apartment, but in reality he lives in an expensive suburb, attends a private high school, and has a straight A grade average. Although he listens to reggae music while his peers listen to rock, he is quick to set aside his Sony Walkman and discuss his recent spiritual conversion.

She reviews some of the details she had recorded, recasting them, suggesting that Tom is not what he appears to be.

This paragraph clearly sets the purpose of the passage and leads to the discussion that follows.

What explains Tom's appearance? Why is his dress so dramatically different though his behavior reflects conservative middle-class values? Tom's appearance is sending a message that says, "I'm different, I'm unique." Appearance—or style— always communicates a message.

Carlson has applied the principles of description effectively. She has carefully selected the details to create the impression she wants. She arranges the details in a sensible structure and sticks to it. She achieves what description should achieve when used with another dominant essay pattern—she invigorates her essay by adding color to a passage that might have been a colorless analysis.

Most of us share senses—sight, sound, smell, touch, taste—and we have feelings. Professional writers know that by evoking sensory experience and feelings in their readers' minds, they will enrich the reading experience. Read the essays in this section. See how the authors evoke the senses; analyze their selection of descriptive details; and examine how they shape descriptive passages to achieve a dominant impression. Take notes as you read, mark an interesting passage, underline a vivid phrase. When you write your own descriptive passages, apply the principles you've learned from reading as a writer. Don't be timid about using a professional writer's passage for a model. The techniques of effective description are universal—available for everyone to use. Professional writers are challenged by the demands of description; certainly you, the beginning writer, should also feel challenged.

❦ Maxine Hong Kingston ❦

Maxine Hong Kingston was born and raised in a Chinese-American community in Stockton, California, where her parents ran a laundry. She grew up listening to stories about China from her parents and relatives, who were first-generation immigrants. She attended the University of California at Berkeley and currently teaches creative writing at the University of Hawaii. Her stories, essays, and poems have been published in Ms., The New Yorker, *and* American Heritage. The Woman Warrior: Memoirs of a Girlhood among Ghosts *(1975), Kingston's award-winning autobiography, describes her memories and retells the stories she heard as a child. Her second book,* China Men *(1980), won the National Book Award.*

Photographs of My Parents

In this selection from The Woman Warrior, *Kingston looks at much more than photographs. Her searching descriptions of mundane objects reveal some of the deep differences between the culture she grew up in and the China her parents left. In writing of both the familiarity and the strangeness in the photographs of her parents, she reaches into the past to better understand the present.*

Once in a long while, four times so far for me, my mother brings out the metal tube that holds her medical diploma. On the tube are gold circles crossed with seven red lines each—"joy" ideographs in abstract. There are also little flowers that look like gears for a gold machine. According to the scraps of labels with Chinese and American addresses, stamps, and postmarks, the family airmailed the can from Hong Kong in 1950. It got crushed in the middle, and whoever tried to peel the labels off stopped because the red and gold paint came off too, leaving silver scratches that rust. Somebody tried to pry the end off before discovering that the tube pulls apart. When I open it, the smell of

101

In China, the bat is emblematic of happiness and long life.

Kingston mentions four predominantly Chinese regions in the Far East, each having its distinct politics and customs; all are Chinese, nonetheless.

The National Republic of China, under Chiang Kai-Shek, was formally recognized by the United States in 1928.

The stork-brings-the-baby myth can be traced to an Old Norse legend. To account for the mother's bed rest after giving birth, children were told that the stork bit the mother just before he departed. The stork has long been a symbol of filial devotion: The Romans enforced *Lex Ciconaria*, the "Stork's Law," compelling children to care for their aged parents. "Ex-assistant étranger . . .": literally, "Former foreign teacher (ex-assistant) at the surgical and maternity clinic of the University of Lyons." *Chop* is from Hindi *chap*, "impression, stamp." A chop is an official stamp or seal; also, a person's "signature stamp," used in many parts of Asia.

The small mystery about the mother's true age heightens interest in this descriptive passage.

China flies out, a thousand-year-old bat flying heavy-headed out of the Chinese caverns where bats are as white as dust, a smell that comes from long ago, far back in the brain. Crates from Canton, Hong Kong, Singapore, and Taiwan have that smell too, only stronger because they are more recently come from the Chinese.

Inside the can are three scrolls, one inside another. The largest says that in the twenty-third year of the National Republic, the To Keung School of Midwifery, where she has had two years of instruction and Hospital Practice, awards its Diploma to my mother, who has shown through oral and written examination her Proficiency in Midwifery, Pediatrics, Gynecology, "Medecine," "Surgary," Therapeutics, Ophthalmology, Bacteriology, Dermatology, Nursing and Bandage. This document has eight stamps on it: one, the school's English and Chinese names embossed together in a circle; one, as the Chinese enumerate, a stork and a big baby in lavender ink; one, the school's Chinese seal; one, an orangish paper stamp pasted in the border design; one, the red seal of Dr. Wu Pak-liang, M.D., Lyon, Berlin, president and "Ex-assistant étranger à la clinique chirugicale et d'accouchement de l'université de Lyon"; one, the red seal of Dean Woo Yin-kam, M.D.; one, my mother's seal, her chop mark larger than the president's and the dean's; and one, the number 1279 on the back. Dean Woo's signature is followed by "(Hackett)." I read in a history book that Hackett Medical College for Women at Canton was founded in the nineteenth century by European women doctors.

The school seal has been pressed over a photograph of my mother at the age of thirty-seven. The diploma gives her age as twenty-seven. She looks younger than I do, her eyebrows are thicker, her lips fuller. Her naturally curly hair is parted on the left, one wavy wisp tendrilling off to the right. She wears a scholar's white gown, and she is not thinking about her appearance. She stares straight ahead as if she could see me and past me to her grandchildren and grandchildren's grandchildren. She has spacy eyes, as all people recently from Asia have. Her eyes do not focus on the camera. My mother is not smiling; Chinese do not smile for photographs. Their faces command relatives in foreign lands—"Send money"—and posterity forever—"Put food in front of this picture." My mother does not understand Chinese-American snapshots. "What are you laughing at?" she asks.

The second scroll is a long narrow photograph of the graduating class with the school officials seated in front. I picked out my mother immediately. Her face is exactly her own, though forty years younger. She is so familiar, I can only tell whether or not she is pretty or happy or smart by comparing her to the other women. For this formal group picture she straightened her hair with oil to make a chinlength bob like the others'. On the other women, strangers, I can recognize a curled lip, a sidelong glance, pinched shoulders. My mother is not soft; the girl with the small nose and dimpled underlip is soft. My mother is not humorous, not like the girl at the end who lifts her mocking chin to pose like Girl Graduate. My mother does not have smiling eyes; the old woman teacher (Dean Woo?) in front crinkles happily, and the one faculty member in the western suit smiles westernly. Most of the graduates are girls whose faces have not yet formed; my mother's face will not change anymore, except to age. She is intelligent, alert, pretty. I can't tell if she's happy.

The graduates seem to have been looking elsewhere when they pinned the rose, zinnia, or chrysanthemum on their precise black dresses. One thin girl wears hers in the middle of her chest. A few have a flower over a left or right nipple. My mother put hers, a chrysanthemum, below her left breast. Chinese dresses at that time were dartless, cut as if women did not have breasts; these young doctors, unaccustomed to decorations, may have seen their chests as black expanses with no reference points for flowers. Perhaps they couldn't shorten that far gaze that lasts only a few years after a Chinese emigrates. In this picture too my mother's eyes are big with what they held—reaches of oceans beyond China, land beyond oceans. Most emigrants learn the barbarians' directness—how to gather themselves and stare rudely into talking faces as if trying to catch lies. In America my mother has eyes as strong as boulders, never once skittering off a face, but she has not learned to place decorations and phonograph needles, nor has she stopped seeing land on the other side of the oceans. Now her

4

5

The white chrysanthemum has a long and fabled history in both China and Japan. The famous haiku poet Basho wrote that the white chrysanthemum "remains immaculate," even under intense scrutiny.

In tailoring, a dart is a short, stitched fold meant to make a garment fit closely while conforming to the natural shape of the body.

Earlier, Kingston's mother had "spacy eyes, as all people recently from Asia have." Now the eyes have become "accustomed" to America, and the description gives Kingston a chance to comment obliquely on her mother's life.

eyes include the relatives in China, as they once included my father smiling and smiling in his many western outfits, a different one for each photograph that he sent from America.

The beginning of a *flashback*, a device with which writers present a scene or incident that happened before some preceding scene or incident in the work.

He and his friends took pictures of one another in bathing suits at Coney Island beach, the salt wind from the Atlantic blowing their hair. He's the one in the middle with his arms about the necks of his buddies. They pose in the cockpit of a biplane, on a motorcycle, and on a lawn beside the "Keep Off the Grass" sign. They are always laughing. My father, white shirt sleeves rolled up, smiles in front of a wall of clean laundry. In the spring he wears a new straw hat, cocked at a Fred Astaire angle. He steps out, dancing down the stairs, one foot forward, one back, a hand in his pocket. He wrote to her about the American custom of stomping on straw hats come fall. "If you want to save your hat for next year," he said, "you have to put it away early, or else when you're riding the subway or walking along Fifth Avenue, any stranger can snatch it off your head and put his foot through it. That's the way they celebrate the change of seasons here." In the winter he wears a gray felt hat with his gray overcoat. He is sitting on a rock in Central Park. In one snapshot he is not smiling; someone took it when he was studying, blurred in the glare of the desk lamp. 6

Fred Astaire (1899–1987) starred in such musical comedies as *Top Hat* (1935) and *Shall We Dance?* (1937). His graceful and original tap dancing was famous.

There are no snapshots of my mother. In two small portraits, however, there is a black thumbprint on her forehead, as if someone had inked in bangs, as if someone had marked her. 7

"Mother, did bangs come into fashion after you had the picture taken?" One time she said yes. Another time when I asked, "Why do you have fingerprints on your forehead?" she said, "Your First Uncle did that." I disliked the unsureness in her voice. 8

The photographs are described as if they were ordinary identification or passport photos.

The last scroll has columns of Chinese words. The only English is "Department of Health, Canton," imprinted on my mother's face, the same photograph as on the diploma. I keep looking to see whether she was afraid. Year after year my father did not come home or send for her. Their two children had been dead for ten years. If he did not return soon, there would be no more children. ("They were three and two years old, a boy and a girl. They could talk already.") My father did send money regularly, 9 though, and she had nobody to spend it on but herself. She bought good clothes and shoes. Then she decided to use the money for becoming a doctor. She did not leave for Canton immediately after the children died. In China there was time to complete feelings. As my father had done, my mother left the village by ship. There was a sea bird painted on the ship to protect it against shipwreck and winds. She was in luck. The following ship was boarded by river pirates, who kidnapped every passenger, even old ladies. "Sixty dollars for an old lady" was what the bandits used to say. "I sailed alone," she says, "to the capital of the entire province." She took a brown leather suitcase and a seabag stuffed with two quilts.

A sea bird painted on a ship's bow may be a traditional emblem of protection, but it is also interesting that a bird, according to Jungian theory, is a beneficent creature representing spirits or angels, supernatural aid, or thoughts and flights of fancy.

Notice that Kingston's mother took one quilt for each of them.

Meaning and Purpose

1. Have you ever looked through old photographs of your parents or grandparents? What feelings did you have when you looked at them? What questions did you ask? What do the photographs tell you about yourself?
2. What are the contrasts between Chinese and Chinese-American photographs and what do these contrasts suggest about the meaning of "Photographs of My Parents"?
3. In paragraph 3, Kingston writes that "the school seal has been pressed over a photograph of my mother"; in paragraph 7, Kingston describes a small portrait of her mother, "there is a black thumbprint on her forehead . . . as if someone had marked her"; and in paragraph 9, she reports that another photograph has the English words, "Department of Health, Canton," printed over her face. How do these descriptive details work in the essay?
4. What does paragraph 6 reveal about Kingston's father?
5. Discuss the significance of flowers pinned awkwardly on the graduates' dresses.
6. In the first paragraph, what does the "thousand-year-old bat" signify?

POSSIBLE ANSWERS

Meaning and Purpose

1. Encourage students to discuss how they feel about old photographs. Ask them to describe some photographs in as much detail as Kingston does.
2. The Chinese in the photographs are nearly expressionless because "Chinese do not smile for photographs" (3), and Kingston "can't tell if [her mother] is happy" (4). The Chinese-Americans in the photographs are "always laughing" (6), and they pose as westerners do.
3. The seals and words over the photographs of Kingston's mother show that the photographs were official. They are not taken for pleasure, or to capture fun or happiness, as those of Kingston's father are.
4. Kingston's father is happy-go-lucky in some photographs. He works in a laundry, watches American movies, adapts an American custom about "stomping on straw hats" (6), and pursues a course of study. He seems to combine fun, work, and ambition.
5. The women were unaccustomed to decoration, and the dresses did not conform to the female figure. The flowers therefore seem out of place, and were pinned on awkwardly.
6. The bat is a symbol of happiness and long life in China.

Strategy

1. Kingston organizes her essay as the contents of the metal tube are organized: she describes the three scrolls as they appear, one inside another. The transitions from one section to the next are the second sentence in paragraph 2, and the first sentences in paragraphs 4 and 9.

2. Some examples of sensory details are: *smell*—"The smell of China flies out, a thousand-year-old bat . . . brain" (1) (metaphor); *sight*—"Her naturally curly hair is parted on the left, one wavy wisp tendrilling off to the right" (3) (image); and "flowers that look like gears for a gold machine" (1) (simile). Examples of *impression* or *feeling* are: "Most of the graduates are girls whose faces have not yet formed . . . happy" (4), and "She wears a scholar's white gown and she is not thinking about her appearance" (3).

3. This is a subjective essay, told from the author's point of view.

4. Kingston describes the tube in careful details that evoke China: the "joy" ideographs, the flowers, and the stamps. The tube was damaged in the mail but still carries the smell of China. These details already suggest a contrast between East and West and prepare readers for the depth of detail that follows.

Style

1. Kingston is nostalgic about the China of her mother's younger life when she describes, in paragraph 1, the smell flying out of the tube, and in paragraph 9, "In China, there was time to complete feelings." She describes her mother with affectionate detail.

2. Kingston's mother embodies the essence of China, as the tube does. She is rigid and contained, and her Chinese customs are "damaged" by life in the West, like the tube.

3. *Ophthalmology*, specialty in eyes; *pediatrics*, specialty in children's medicine; *gynecology*, specialty in women's medicine; *dermatology*, specialty in the skin; *therapeutics*, specialty in remedies.

Strategy

1. What is Kingston's general organizational strategy for description? Where are the three transition points at which Kingston moves from one section to another?
2. Identify some descriptions that involve the senses, and some that evoke impressions or feelings. What kinds of figures of speech are they—metaphor, simile, personification, descriptive image?
3. Is this descriptive essay subjective or objective, and how do you know?
4. What impression does Kingston give of the metal tube in the first paragraph? How does her description prepare you for the rest of the essay?

Style

1. How would you describe the tone of the essay or the narrator's feelings about the contents of the metal tube?
2. Consider the metal tube to be a symbol for Kingston's mother. What qualities does it suggest about her?
3. Kingston uses some medical terms. Be sure you know their meanings: *ophthalmology, pediatrics, gynecology, dermatology, therapeutics* (paragraph 2).

Writing Tasks

1. Study Kingston's essay to see how she uses photographs to reveal bits and pieces of her parents' history. Then select photographs of two friends or relatives who have both similar and opposing character traits. Use the photographs to write a description that reveals their character traits without stating them directly.
2. Describe a significant possession of someone you know, and show how it characterizes the person.

🐛 E. B. White 🐛

Born in Mount Vernon, New York, in 1899, Elwyn Brooks White is considered one of America's finest essayists. At Cornell University he studied English composition with Edmund Strunk, and years later revised Strunk's concise book of writing guidance, now known as Strunk and White's Elements of Style. *He was for many years a staff writer at* The New Yorker, *where he first earned his reputation as a master essayist. He also wrote a regular column for* Harper's *magazine for several years. His essay collections include* One Man's Meat *(1944),* The Second Tree from the Corner *(1953), and* The Essays of E. B. White *(1977). Two of his books—*Stuart Little *(1945) and* Charlotte's Web *(1952)—have become classics of children's literature. He died in 1985 at his farm in coastal Maine, to which he had retired in 1957.*

Once More to the Lake

In this essay, first published in Harper's in 1941 and collected in One Man's Meat (1944), White uses the force of reminiscence to enhance a meticulous description of a recent event. On a fishing trip to a lake in Maine with his young son, the author recalls his own childhood summers at the same lake. He inevitably begins to see himself in his son and is jolted into awareness of his own mortality.

August 1941

One summer, along about 1904, my father rented a camp on a lake in Maine and took us all there for the month of August. We all got ringworm from some kittens and had to rub Pond's Extract on our arms and legs night and morning, and my father rolled over in a canoe with all his clothes on; but outside of that the vacation was a success and from then on none of us ever

TEACHING SUGGESTIONS

This evocative essay deals with time: its delightful past, its pleasant present, and its tragic future—when the author finally acknowledges its passing.

The subject intrigues students, mainly because it has not often been taken seriously: time is now, to many of us. Only as our days close do we realize that time is not constantly on the sidelines. It's here and we are its products. Hemingway said to Lillian Ross, "Time is the least thing we have of."

Instructors have energized a conversation on time by asking students, "How old is *old*?" Experience suggests that answers will vary, from "Five years older than I am right now," to "Forty." These answers will help to establish the chronological climate in which students approach this essay, which was written when White was about forty-one, about the age that is still considered a time for reflection.

After students have discussed age well enough to establish that no one has a definitive answer, instructors have asked, "How far back can you remember?" Again, answers range from five years to whenever, depending on how long students think about their answers.

The third and fourth questions lead in to White's essay: "How far back can you remember a pleasant experience that has *meaning* for you now?" followed quickly by "Has the meaning of the experience changed for you, over the years?" These two questions are not lightly answered, for they require much memory-searching, which one student calls "scratching the bottom of the database barrel."

When White visited the lake as a boy, the experience had no meaning for him except as a trigger: Lake = joy. No more. With age, however, his experience took on hitherto unsuspected meaning. Students often see that the past event, plus time, equals a new meaning for the event—after they have thought over their class discussion about time.

Born in 1899, White would have been about five years old at the time of the earlier excursion.

Here, nostalgia, a longing for former happy times, is White's stimulus to return to the lake to "revisit old haunts," after almost forty years.

White combines light tension and reverie in this paragraph. First, he worries about how the lake might have been changed by encroaching civilization. Next, he recounts memories of his early days on the lake.
  White reminds us that we can remember our calm moments of joy if we allow ourselves to pursue the mental paths of least resistance, letting one memory softly lead into another.

Notice White's combining an image of nature (the lake) with a symbol of religion.

thought there was any place in the world like that lake in Maine. We returned summer after summer—always on August 1 for one month. I have since become a salt-water man, but sometimes in summer there are days when the restlessness of the tides and the fearful cold of the sea water and the incessant wind that blows across the afternoon and into the evening make me wish for the placidity of a lake in the woods. A few weeks ago this feeling got so strong I bought myself a couple of bass hooks and a spinner and returned to the lake where we used to go, for a week's fishing and to revisit old haunts.

I took along my son, who had never had any fresh water up his nose and who had seen lily pads only from train windows. On the journey over to the lake I began to wonder what it would be like. I wondered how time would have marred this unique, this holy spot—the coves and streams, the hills that the sun set behind, the camps and the paths behind the camps. I was sure that the tarred road would have found it out, and I wondered in what other ways it would be desolated. It is strange how much you can remember about places like that once you allow your mind to return into the grooves that lead back. You remember one thing, and that suddenly reminds you of another thing. I guess I remembered clearest of all the early mornings, when the lake was cool and motionless, remembered how the bedroom smelled of the lumber it was made of and of the wet woods whose scent entered through the screen. The partitions in the camp were thin and did not extend clear to the top of the rooms, and as I was always the first up I would dress softly so as not to wake the others, and sneak out into the sweet outdoors and start out in the canoe, keeping close along the shore in the long shadows of the pines. I remembered being very careful never to rub my paddle against the gunwale for fear of disturbing the stillness of the cathedral.

The lake had never been what you would call a wild lake. There were cottages sprinkled around the shores, and it was in farming country although the shores of the lake were quite heavily wooded. Some of the cottages were owned by nearby farmers, and you would live at the shore and eat your meals at the farmhouse. That's what our family did. But although it wasn't wild, it was a fairly large and undisturbed lake and there were places in it that, to a child at least, seemed infinitely remote and primeval.

I was right about the tar; it led to within half a mile of the shore. But when I got back there, with my boy, and we settled into a camp near a farmhouse and into the kind of summertime I had known, I could tell that it was going to be pretty much the same as it had been before—I knew it, lying in bed the first morning, smelling the bedroom and hearing the boy sneak quietly out and go off along the shore in a boat. I began to sustain the illusion that he was I, and therefore, by simple transposition, that I was my father. This sensation persisted, kept cropping up all the time we were there. It was not an entirely new feeling, but in this setting it grew much stronger. I seemed to be living a dual existence. I would be in the middle of some simple act, I would be picking up a bait box or laying down a table fork, or I would be saying something, and suddenly it would be not I but my father who was saying the words or making the gesture. It gave me a creepy sensation.

We went fishing the first morning. I felt the same damp moss covering the worms in the bait can, and saw the dragonfly alight on the tip of my rod as it hovered a few inches from the surface of the water. It was the arrival of this fly that convinced me beyond any doubt that everything was as it always had been, that the years were a mirage and that there had been no years. The small waves were the same, chucking the rowboat under the chin as we fished at anchor, and the boat was the same boat, the same color green and the ribs broken in the same places, and under the floorboards the same fresh-water leavings and débris—the dead hellgrammite, the wisps of moss, the rusty discarded fishhook, the dried blood from yesterday's catch. We stared silently at the tips of our rods, at the dragonflies that came and went. I lowered the tip of mine into the water, tentatively, pensively dislodging the fly, which darted two feet away, poised, darted two feet back, and came to rest again a little farther up the rod. There had been no years between the ducking of this dragonfly and the other one—

4   White gives us the larger picture of the lake, pointing out its general virtues, and then he mentions how those virtues appear through the eyes of a child—as "primeval"; that is, "of the earliest times or ages."

Throughout the essay, the boy is never clearly described; he is never identified beyond mere "boy." William Wordsworth's lines from *My Heart Leaps Up* (1807) are worth reviving here, as capturing the essence of White's "boy":

The child is father of the man;
And I could wish my days to be
Bound each to each by natural piety.

White approaches an almost instinctual, innate need to see himself as the boy.

5   The beginning of the adventure, the reliving of White's childhood. His years fall away, he becomes the boy again, and the water remains as when he had first seen it.

Water as symbol has a venerable history. Limitless and immortal in the eyes of the ancients, water is the beginning of all life. Homer, in book IV of *The Iliad,* speaks of "Ocean, who is the source of all." Modern psychology sees water as symbolizing the unconscious: the nonformal, dynamic, motivating, female side of the personality.

To enchant is "to cast a spell over," "to charm greatly," and more. An enchantment is a reduction to an inferior state, as in a person changing into an animal, for which see the story of Circe, as told in *The Odyssey*. White's "sea" enchants; that is, in mysterious ways the lake itself has its effect on White, causing him in a way to "be" his childhood self.

A cult is a system of ritual. White's passing comment is that some things never change. We will always have the pseudo-cultists of nature with us, who despoil nature by using it, this time to bathe with scum-producing soap.

White is no longer in 1904 or thereabout. Horse-drawn wagons produce three tracks, the middle one made by the horse. Now that the automobile has replaced the horse, the middle track has disappeared. For that matter, middle alternatives in people's lives also disappear with passing time, White suggests, but life itself goes on, "there having been no passage of time, only the illusion of it."

the one that was part of memory. I looked at the boy, who was silently watching his fly, and it was my hands that held his rod, my eyes watching. I felt dizzy and didn't know which rod I was at the end of.

We caught two bass, hauling them in briskly as though they were mackerel, pulling them over the side of the boat in a businesslike manner without any landing net, and stunning them with a blow on the back of the head. When we got back for a swim before lunch, the lake was exactly where we had left it, the same number of inches from the dock, and there was only the merest suggestion of a breeze. This seemed an utterly enchanted sea, this lake you could leave to its own devices for a few hours and come back to, and find it had not stirred, this constant and trustworthy body of water. In the shallows, the dark, water-soaked sticks and twigs, smooth and old, were undulating in clusters on the bottom against the clean ribbed sand, and the track of the mussel was plain. A school of minnows swam by, each minnow with its small individual shadow, doubling the attendance, so clear and sharp in the sunlight. Some of the other campers were in swimming, along the shore, one of them with a cake of soap, and the water felt thin and clear and unsubstantial. Over the years there had been this person with the cake of soap, this cultist, and here he was. There had been no years.

Up to the farmhouse to dinner through the teeming, dusty field, the road under our sneakers was only a two-track road. The middle track was missing, the one with the marks of the hooves and the splotches of dried, flaky manure. There had always been three tracks to choose from in choosing which track to walk in; now the choice was narrowed down to two. For a moment I missed terribly the middle alternative. But the way led past the tennis court, and something about the way it lay there in the sun reassured me; the tape had loosened along the backline, the alleys were green with plantains and other weeds, and the net (installed in June and removed in September) sagged in the dry noon, and the whole place steamed with midday heat and hunger and emptiness. There was a choice of pie for dessert, and one was blueberry and one was apple, and the waitresses were the same country girls, there having been no passage of time, only the illusion of it as in a dropped curtain—the waitresses were still fifteen; their hair had been washed, that was the only difference— they had been to the movies and seen the pretty girls with the clean hair.

Summertime, oh summertime, pattern of life indelible, the fade-proof lake, the woods unshatterable, the pasture with the sweetfern and the juniper forever and ever, summer without end; this was the background, and the life along the shore was the design, their tiny docks with the flagpole and the American flag floating against the white clouds in the blue sky, the little paths over the roots of the trees leading from camp to camp and the paths leading back to the outhouses and the can of lime for sprinkling, and at the souvenir counters at the store the miniature birch-bark canoes and the postcards that showed things looking a little better than they looked. This was the American family at play, escaping the city heat, wondering whether the newcomers in the camp at the head of the cove were "common" or "nice," wondering whether it was true that the people who drove up for Sunday dinner at the farmhouse were turned away because there wasn't enough chicken.

It seemed to me, as I kept remembering all this, that those times and those summers had been infinitely precious and worth saving. There had been jollity and peace and goodness. The arriving (at the beginning of August) had been so big a business in itself, at the railway station the farm wagon drawn up, the first smell of the pine-laden air, the first glimpse of the smiling farmer, and the great importance of the trunks and your father's enormous authority in such matters, and the feel of the wagon under you for the long ten-mile haul, and at the top of the last long hill catching the first view of the lake after eleven months of not seeing this cherished body of water. The shouts and cries of the other campers when they saw you, and the trunks to be unpacked, to give up their rich burden. (Arriving was less exciting nowadays, when you sneaked up in your car and parked it under a tree near

8   In ancient Greece, a paean was a hymn of thanksgiving to the gods, especially to Apollo, the god of music, poetry, prophecy, and medicine, represented as exemplifying manly youth and beauty. In this paragraph of unrestrained and timeless joy, White has written his own modern paean.

9   The less frequently we see something, the less likely we are to recognize it because of familiarity alone. In this paragraph, White dwells on the sheer excitement a boy feels (or felt) at the moment when the family arrived at the lake. These times were worth saving in the storehouse of his memory, from which other times have long since faded. (Nothing nowadays is as exciting as memories of past excitement.)

the camp and took out the bags and in five minutes it was all over, no fuss, no loud wonderful fuss about trunks.)

The paragraph begins with a complaint: the new outboard motors are too loud. Then it drifts into the past, when the older motors were comparatively silent and depended more on the operator. White as a boy had more control over machines; he could tinker with them, experiment, attain complete mastery. The man could control more of his life when he and machines were young.

Peace and goodness and jollity. The only thing that was wrong now, really, was the sound of the place, an unfamiliar nervous sound of the outboard motors. This was the note that jarred, the one thing that would sometimes break the illusion and set the years moving. In those other summertimes all the motors were inboard; and when they were at a little distance, the noise they made was a sedative, an ingredient of summer sleep. They were one-cylinder and two-cylinder engines, and some were make-and-break and some were jump-spark, but they all made a sleepy sound across the lake. The one-lungers throbbed and fluttered, and the twin-cylinder ones purred and purred, and that was a quiet sound, too. But now the campers all had outboards. In the daytime, in the hot mornings, these motors made a petulant, irritable sound; at night, in the still evening when the afterglow lit the water, they whined about one's ears like mosquitoes. My boy loved our rented outboard, and his great desire was to achieve single-handed mastery over it, and authority, and he soon learned the trick of choking it a little (but not too much), and the adjustment of the needle valve. Watching him I would remember the things you could do with the old one-cylinder engine with the heavy flywheel, how you could have it eating out of your hand if you got really close to it spiritually. Motorboats in those days didn't have clutches, and you would make a landing by shutting off the motor at the proper time and coasting in with a dead rudder. But there was a way of reversing them, if you learned the trick, by cutting the switch and putting it on again exactly on the final dying revolution of the flywheel, so that it would kick back against the compression and begin reversing. Approaching a dock in a strong following breeze, it was difficult to slow up sufficiently by the ordinary coasting method, and if a boy felt he had complete mastery over his motor, he was tempted to keep it running beyond its time and then reverse it a few feet from the dock. It took a cool nerve, because if you threw the switch a twentieth of a second too soon you would catch the flywheel when it still had speed enough to go up past center, and the boat would leap ahead, charging bull-fashion at the dock.

We had a good week at camp. The bass were biting well and the sun shown endlessly, day after day. We would be tired at night and lie down in the accumulated heat of the little bedrooms after the long hot day and the breeze would stir almost imperceptibly outside and the smell of the swamp drift in through the rusty screens. Sleep would come easily and in the morning the red squirrel would be on the roof, tapping out his gay routine. I kept remembering everything, lying in bed in the mornings—the small steamboat that had a long rounded stern like the lip of a Ubangi, and how quietly she ran on the moonlight sails, when the older boys played their mandolins and the girls sang and we ate doughnuts dipped in sugar, and how sweet the music was on the water in the shining night, and what it had felt like to think about girls then. After breakfast we would go up to the store and the things were in the same place—the minnows in a bottle, the plugs and spinners disarranged and pawed over by the youngsters from the boys' camp, the Fig Newtons and the Beeman's gum. Outside, the road was tarred and cars stood in front of the store. Inside, all was just as it had always been, except there was more Coca-Cola and not so much Moxie and root beer and birch beer and sarsaparilla. We would walk out with the bottle of pop apiece and sometimes the pop would backfire up our noses and hurt. We explored the streams, quietly, where the turtles slid off the sunny logs and dug their way into the soft bottom; and we lay on the town wharf and fed worms to the tame bass. Everywhere we went I had trouble making out which I was, the one walking at my side, the one walking in my pants.

One afternoon while we were there at that lake a thunderstorm came up. It was like the revival of an old melodrama that I had seen long ago with childish awe. The second-act climax of the drama of the electrical disturbance over a lake in America had not changed in any important respect. This was the big scene, still the big scene. The whole thing was so familiar, the first feeling of oppression and heat and a general air around camp of

11 As he does with the other paragraphs in this essay, White is playing with time. Halfway through this paragraph, he abruptly shifts from past to present, from "what it had felt like to think about girls then" to "After breakfast we [he and his boy] would go up to the store." This strategy reinforces his earlier claim that things remain the same, timeless in his eyes, a point that he makes clear in the last line of this paragraph, where the boy and he become indivisible.

12 Typically, a melodrama ended happily, after the second-act *climax*, which describes the intensity of interest in the audience. White remains with the "timelessness motif," saying that "The whole thing was so familiar." The storm itself is indeed timeless: It is melodramatic, with its kettle, snare, and bass drums, and ancient Greece with its "gods grinning and

licking their chops." It ends with the eternal comedian, who is out of place yet strangely appropriate—the two conditions of comedy.

The shock of recognition. White suddenly realizes that time in fact passes, and that he will pass with time as part of his life—his boy—goes on. No stores of imagination or memory can erase the knowledge that sooner or later one reaches the point of no return.

not wanting to go very far away. In mid-afternoon (it was all the same) a curious darkening of the sky, and a lull in everything that had made life tick; and then the way the boats suddenly swung the other way at their moorings with the coming of a breeze out of the new quarter, and the premonitory rumble. Then the kettle drum, then the snare, then the bass drum and cymbals, then crackling light against the dark, and the gods grinning and licking their chops in the hills. Afterward the calm, the rain steadily rustling in the calm lake, the return of light and hope and spirits, and the campers running out in joy and relief to go swimming in the rain, their bright cries perpetuating the deathless joke about how they were getting simply drenched, and the children screaming with delight at the new sensation of bathing in the rain, and the joke about getting drenched linking the generations in a strong indestructible chain. And the comedian who waded in carrying an umbrella.

When the others went swimming, my son said he was going in, too. He pulled his dripping trunks from the line where they had hung all through the shower and wrung them out. Languidly, and with no thought of going in, I watched him, his hard little body, skinny and bare, saw him wince slightly as he pulled up around his vitals the small, soggy, icy garment. As he buckled the swollen belt, suddenly my groin felt the chill of death.

13

POSSIBLE ANSWERS

Meaning and Purpose

1. Let students share experiences about places for which they feel nostalgia. Ask them how they look at the changes time has made in the place and in themselves, and how their feelings compare to White's.
2. White states that he wants to return to the lake to fish and "revisit old haunts" (1). He longs for "the placidity of a lake in the woods" (1), and to reconnect with his youth. This paragraph sets the scene for the return.
3. The title has a poetic ring that suits White's

Meaning and Purpose

1. Have you a special place about which you feel nostalgic that you've visited recently? If so, has anything changed? If not, what are you afraid might have changed? Do any of White's descriptions remind you of this place?
2. As you read the opening paragraph of "Once More to the Lake," what do you understand White's purpose to be?
3. How does the title relate to the essay? After you've read the essay, does the title become more significant?

4. What do you think White comes to understand about time and change during his visit to the lake?
5. In the closing paragraph, White describes his son pulling on his wet swimming trunks. At that moment, White says he feels "the chill of death." What do you believe he means? Has anything in the essay prepared you for this conclusion?

Strategy

1. What is the dominant impression that White creates in paragraph 12? How does he use language to create it?
2. White mixes description of his recent trip to the lake with details from past trips. How does he avoid confusion? What transitions does he use to go back and forth in time?
3. Could White's essay have significance for you even if you have never been to Maine, or camped by a lake, or fished? Does the essay transcend its subject? If so, how does White accomplish this feat? Does the lake have a larger meaning?
4. Why does White call his son his "boy" and not name him or give him strong identifying characteristics?

Style

1. Identify in the opening three paragraphs the words that White uses to describe the lake. What impressions do they create? How does the closing sentence in paragraph 3 reinforce this impression?
2. White's essay is clearly subjective, amply mixing descriptive details about the lake with his personal thoughts. How would you describe the essay's tone? What frame of mind does White seem to be in?
3. If necessary, check the dictionary for the meaning of these words: *gunwale* (paragraph 2); *primeval* (paragraph 3); *transposition* (paragraph 4); *hellgrammite* (paragraph 5); *undulating*

descriptions of nature. The words "Once More" are not final and suggest that this may not be White's last visit to the lake.

4. White understands that time at the lake has stood still because so many things are the same as when he was a boy—"The small waves were the same, chucking the rowboat under the chin as we fished at anchor, and the boat was the same boat, the same color green and the ribs broken in the same places . . ." (5). He even confuses his identity with his son's in paragraph 4. At the same time, White notices changes all around him—"The middle track was missing, the one with the marks of the hooves and the splotches of dried, flaky manure" (7)—and understands that change is inevitable.

5. White is suddenly confronted with his own death and the relentless march of time. Readers are prepared only in little ways as White records each change he sees.

Strategy

1. In paragraph 12, White creates the impression of a storm as a natural drama played out. First it is oppressive, then percussive, then calm. White manipulates language to create impressions. "It was like the revival of an old melodrama"—a simile. The approach of the storm creates a "feeling of oppression," "a curious darkening of the sky," and a "lull in everything." Comparing the storm to the sound of drums is a metaphor. The language that describes the lake after the storm is quite different: "return of light and hope and spirits," "joy and relief," and "bright cries."

2. White uses many transitions to avoid confusion about time. In paragraph 2, thinking about returning to the lake with his son, he slips into a memory: "I guess I remembered clearest of all. . . ." In paragraph 5, he describes fishing with his son and says, "There had been no years between the ducking of this dragonfly and the other one—the one that was part of memory." Another shift to memory occurs in paragraph 9 with, "It seemed to me, as I kept remembering all this, that those times and those summers had been infinitely precious and worth saving." Let students find other transitions between past and present.

3. The more specific the writing, the more nearly universal the meaning. Most students will have had some experience to help them identify with White's lake. But he goes beyond the specific, as in paragraph 8, when he talks about "summer without end" and "the American family at play," and also in paragraph 9, "There had been jollity and peace and goodness." White offers his lake as a symbol of natural goodness and American family values, the necessary retreat from the ills of the city.

4. White's "boy" becomes himself as White remembers his boyhood summers at the lake (5). If he had given the boy a more specific identity, it would have been harder for White to sustain the illusion that he becomes the boy.

Style

1. Some of the descriptive words about the lake are "Placidity" (1); in paragraph 2, "holy spot," "cool and motionless," "sweet outdoors," "the stillness of a cathedral." These words show the lake as a sacred place, undisturbed and natural, respected and held in awe, almost in a religious way. In paragraph 3, "remote and primeval" reinforces these impressions, as if to say the lake is prehistoric, without the imprint of people.

2. The essay is nostalgic and affectionate in tone, a little sad, and peaceful, like a reverie. White seems to need reconnecting with the lake before it's too late, before he, too, passes on. He delights in what he finds on his return: "I could tell it was going to be pretty much the same as it had been before" (4). And he feels sad and "jarred" by some changes (see sentences 2 and 3 of paragraph 10).

3. *Gunwale,* the upper edge of a ship's or boat's side; *primeval,* existing from the beginning; *transposition,* a changing of the normal order; *helgramite* (also *hellgrammite*), the dark brown aquatic larva of a fly, used as fish bait; *undulating,* moving in a wavy or flowing manner; *petulant,* rude, or capriciously ill-humored; *premonitory,* giving warning; *languidly,* sluggishly or listlessly. White expects his audience to be fairly well educated.

(paragraph 6); *petulant* (paragraph 10); *premonitory* (paragraph 12); *languidly* (paragraph 13). What do these words reveal about White's intended audience?

Writing Tasks

1. Describe a place such as a camp, a farm home, a relative's house, or a childhood haunt, to which you returned after long absence. Structure your description so that it captures how the place appears in your memory and how it appears now. Select the descriptive details carefully and include your subjective thoughts.

2. Write a short descriptive essay (about any subject) in which you appeal to all five senses.

❦ George Simpson ❦

Born in Virginia in 1950, George Simpson studied journalism at the University of North Carolina. He wrote for the Carolina Financial Times *in North Carolina and for the* News-Gazette *in Virginia before joining the staff at* Newsweek *in 1972. In 1978 he was appointed* Newsweek's *director of public affairs. For a series of articles about the football program at the University of North Carolina, he won the Sigma Delta Chi Best Feature Writing Award in 1972. He has contributed stories to* The New York Times, Sport, Glamour, *and other major publications.*

The War Room at Bellevue

In this essay, first published in New York *magazine in 1983, George Simpson uses objective description of events during one night at Bellevue Hospital to achieve immediacy. Arranging the emergency-room scenes in strict (by-the-clock) chronological order creates the impression of a minute-by-minute account and contributes to the power of the description.*

TEACHING SUGGESTIONS

Reportorial description, the "see-it, write-it" detached yet energetic prose of the experienced observer, appeals to the reader's imagination because it displays little of the writer's own imaginative commentary, allowing readers to explore freely their own reactions. The fewer the writer's remarks about descriptions, the more readers can conjure their own remarks, a vital force behind all "appearance-versus-reality" prose.

Sometimes we look, but we do not see. Instructors can take advantage when introducing the article by asking students to look around, to *see* the classroom itself, often for the first time. How would the room seem to the outside observer?

Students often reply that the room is no more than "just a room." "Yes," you can reply, "and to medical personnel experienced in trauma, a battered woman is just a battered woman, a corpse is just a corpse, and a gunshot wound or a stabbing is just that. No more." To illustrate your point, you can then introduce this essay.

Bellevue. The name conjures up images of an indoor war zone: the wounded and bleeding lining the halls, screaming for help while harried doctors in blood-stained smocks rush from stretcher to stretcher, fighting a losing battle against exhaustion and the crushing number of injured. "What's worse," says a long-time Bellevue nurse, "is that we have this image of being a hospital only for . . ." She pauses, then lowers her voice; "for crazy people."

Though neither battlefield nor Bedlam is a valid image, there is something extraordinary about the monstrous complex that spreads for five blocks along First Avenue in Manhattan. It is said best by the head nurse in Adult Emergency Service: "If you have any chance for survival, you have it here." Survival—that is why they come. Why do injured cops drive by a half-dozen other

1 **MARGINAL NOTES**

The author lists the word's *connotations,* the implications or emotional surroundings that words in context carry, as distinguished from their denotative or lexical meanings. Simpson reinforces the connotations by quoting a nurse about Bellevue's rumored reputation.

2 In London, an old insane asylum, later a hospital for the mentally ill.

Bellevue has a world-class reputation for its trauma center.

117

A "typical" Friday night in Bellevue begins and all is routine, down to deciding who will go for coffee.

Simpson foreshadows events by showing the shock and seriousness of what has already happened.

A stiletto's blade is slender and tapering, designed for use as a weapon.

In trauma-care jargon, *emergent* means "sudden, or unforeseen."

A tube passed through the body for evacuating or injecting fluids from or into body cavities. This paragraph mirrors the standard operating procedure for trauma victims, which includes first aid for shock, test for blood type, and quick evaluation of internal organs.

Medically, shivers are slight tremors of the skin, as from cold or fear. To a nonmedical person like Simpson, perhaps it suggests shock, which is marked by paleness of skin.

hospitals to be treated at Bellevue? They've seen the Bellevue emergency team in action.

9:00 P.M. It is a Friday night in the Bellevue emergency room. The after-work crush is over (those who've suffered through the day, only to come for help after the five-o'clock whistle has blown) and it is nearly silent except for the mutter of voices at the admitting desk, where administrative personnel discuss who will go for coffee. Across the spotless white-walled lobby, ten people sit quietly, passively, in pastel plastic chairs, waiting for word of relatives or to see doctors. In the past 24 hours, 300 people have come to the Bellevue Adult Emergency Service. Fewer than 10 percent were true emergencies. One man sleeps fitfully in the emergency ward while his heartbeat, respiration, and blood pressure are monitored by control consoles mounted over his bed. Each heartbeat trips a tiny bleep in the monitor, which attending nurses can hear across the ward. A half hour ago, doctors in the trauma room withdrew a six-inch stiletto blade from his back. When he is stabilized, the patient will be moved upstairs to the twelve-bed Surgical Intensive Care Unit.

9:05 P.M. An ambulance backs into the receiving bay, its red and yellow lights flashing in and out of the lobby. A split second later, the glass doors burst open as a nurse and an attendant roll a mobile stretcher into the lobby. When the nurse screams, "Emergent!" the lobby explodes with activity as the way is cleared to the trauma room. Doctors appear from nowhere and transfer the bloodied body of a black man to the treatment table. Within seconds his clothes are stripped away, revealing a tiny stab wound in his left side. Three doctors and three nurses rush around the victim, each performing a task necessary to begin treatment. Intravenous needles are inserted into his arms and groin. A doctor draws blood for the lab, in case surgery is necessary. A nurse begins inserting a catheter into the victim's penis and continues to feed in tubing until the catheter reaches the bladder. Urine flows through the tube into a plastic bag. Doctors are glad not to see blood in the urine. Another nurse records pulse and blood pressure.

The victim is in good shape. He shivers slightly, although the trauma room is exceedingly warm. His face is bloodied, but shows

3

4

5

no major lacerations. A third nurse, her elbow propped on the treatment table, asks the man a series of questions, trying to quickly outline his medical history. He answers abruptly. He is drunk. His left side is swabbed with yellow disinfectant and a doctor injects a local anesthetic. After a few seconds another doctor inserts his finger into the wound. It sinks in all the way to the knuckle. He begins to rotate his finger like a child trying to get a marble out of a milk bottle. The patient screams bloody murder and tries to struggle free.

The doctor tries to determine the depth of the wound and its nearness to bone, nerves, and other parts or systems of the human body. The yellow disinfectant probably is a tincture of iodine.

Meanwhile in the lobby, a security guard is ejecting a derelict who has begun to drink from a bottle hidden in his coat pocket. "He's a regular, was in here just two days ago," says a nurse. "We checked him pretty close then, so he's probably okay now. Can you believe those were clean clothes we gave him?" The old man, blackened by filth, leaves quietly.

6 Juxtaposing the wounded man and the derelict suggests the spectrum of patients treated by Bellevue's staff.

9:15 P.M. A young Hispanic man interrupts, saying his pregnant girl friend, sitting outside in his car, is bleeding heavily from her vagina. She is rushed into an examination room, treated behind closed doors, and rolled into the observation ward, where, much later in the night, a gynecologist will treat her in a special room—the same one used to examine rape victims. Nearby, behind curtains, the neurologist examines an old white woman to determine if her headaches are due to head injury. They are not.

7 Again, coupling examination of the Hispanic girl with that of the old white woman helps illustrate the kinds of patients who go to Bellevue. Notice that each woman is attended by a specialist.

9:45 P.M. The trauma room has been cleared and cleaned mercilessly. The examination rooms are three-quarters full—another overdose, two asthmatics, a young woman with abdominal pains. In the hallway, a derelict who has been sleeping it off urinates all over the stretcher. He sleeps on while attendants change his clothes. An ambulance—one of four that patrol Manhattan for Bellevue from 42nd Street to Houston, river to river—delivers a middle-aged white woman and two cops, the three of them soaking wet. The woman has escaped from the psychiatric floor of a nearby hospital and tried to drown herself in the East River. The cops fished her out. She lies on a stretcher shivering beneath white blankets. Her eyes stare at the ceiling. She speaks clearly when an administrative worker begins routine questioning. The cops are given hospital gowns and wait to receive tetanus shots and gamma globulin—a hedge against infection from the

8

Despite one's condition, one is treated carefully.

Tetanus is an acute infectious disease that causes painful muscle spasms. Because its first sign is stiffness of the jaw, it is sometimes called "lockjaw." It is usually, but not always, fatal. Gamma globulin is a protein formed in the blood; it and other proteins, concentrated, resist infection.

Methadone hydrochloride is a habit-forming, synthetic, analgesic drug with potency equal to that of morphine, but with weaker narcotic action. Under careful supervision, methadone hydrochloride is used to treat people who are dependent on drugs derived from opium, such as heroin.

In hospital jargon, a person who has overdosed on drugs is an "O.D."

Notice that "alleged perpetrator" is used to describe a crime suspect. This jargon expression has become standard in police work.

The story of the suicide continues. Simpson shows that Bellevue becomes one setting for the drama of many people's lives.

befouled river water. They will hang around the E.R. for another two hours, telling their story to as many as six other policemen who show up to hear it. The woman is rolled into an examination room, where a male nurse speaks gently: "They tell me you fell into the river." "No," says the woman, "I jumped. I have to commit suicide." "Why?" asks the nurse. "Because I'm insane and I can't help [it]. I have to die." The nurse gradually discovers the woman has a history of psychological problems. She is given dry bedclothes and placed under guard in the hallway. She lies on her side, staring at the wall.

The pace continues to increase. Several more overdose victims 9 arrive by ambulance. One, a young black woman, had done a striptease on the street just before passing out. A second black woman is semiconscious and spends the better part of her time at Bellevue alternately cursing it and pleading with the doctors. Attendants find a plastic bottle coated with methadone in the pocket of a Hispanic O.D. The treatment is routinely the same, and sooner or later involves vomiting. Just after doctors begin to treat the O.D., he vomits great quantities of wine and methadone in all directions. "Lovely business, huh?" laments one of the doctors. A young nurse confides that if there were other true emergencies, the overdose victims would be given lower priority. "You can't help thinking they did it to themselves," she says, "while the others are accident victims."

10:30 P.M. A policeman who twisted his knee struggling with 10 an "alleged perpetrator" is examined and released. By 10:30, the lobby is jammed with friends and relatives of patients in various stages of treatment and recovery. The attendant who also functions as a translator for Hispanic patients adds chairs to accommodate the overflow. The medical walk-in rate stays steady—between eight and ten patients waiting. A pair of derelicts, each with battered eyes, appear at the admitting desk. One has a dramatically swollen face laced with black stitches.

11:00 P.M. The husband of the attempted suicide arrives. He 11 thanks the police for saving his wife's life, then talks at length with doctors about her condition. She continues to stare into the void and does not react when her husband approaches her stretcher.

Meanwhile, patients arrive in the lobby at a steady pace. A young G.I. on leave has lower-back pains; a Hispanic man complains of pain in his side; occasionally parents hurry through the adult E.R. carrying children into the pediatric E.R. A white woman of about 50 marches into the lobby from the walk-in entrance. Dried blood covers her right eyebrow and upper lip. She begins to perform. "I was assaulted on 28th and Lexington, I was," she says grandly, "and I don't have to take it *anymore*. I was a bride 21 years ago, and, God, I was beautiful then." She has captured the attention of all present. "I was there when the boys came home—on Memorial Day—and I don't have to take this kind of treatment."

12

Emergency room. Simpson's descriptions of people include a representative spectrum from military personnel to members of minority groups to children to battered women.

As midnight approaches, the nurses prepare for the shift change. They must brief the incoming staff and make sure all reports are up-to-date. One young brunet says, "Christ, I'm gonna go home and take a shower—I smell like vomit."

13

While preparing for a shift change, the conversations are normal. No one recounts a specific incident that happened during her shift. The implication is that no matter what happens, it is "normal" for Bellevue.

11:50 P.M. The triage nurse is questioning an old black man about chest pains, and a Hispanic woman is having an asthma attack, when an ambulance, its sirens screaming full tilt, roars into the receiving bay. There is a split-second pause as everyone drops what he or she is doing and looks up. Then all hell breaks loose. Doctors and nurses are suddenly sprinting full-out toward the trauma room. The glass doors burst open and the occupied stretcher is literally run past me. Cops follow. It is as if a comet has whooshed by. In the trauma room it all becomes clear. A half-dozen doctors and nurses surround the lifeless form of a Hispanic man with a shotgun hole in his neck the size of your fist. Blood pours from a second gaping wound in his chest. A respirator is slammed over his face, making his chest rise and fall as if he were breathing. "No pulse," reports one doctor. A nurse jumps on a stool and, leaning over the man, begins to pump his chest with her palms. "No blood pressure," screams another nurse. The ambulance driver appears shaken. "I never thought I'd get here in time," he stutters. More doctors from the trauma team upstairs arrive. Wrappings from syringes and gauze pads fly through the air. The victim's eyes are open yet devoid of life. His body takes on a yellow tinge. A male nurse winces at the gunshot wound. "This guy really pissed off somebody," he says. This is no ordinary

14

A triage nurse screens and classifies sick and injured people to determine the most efficient way of using medical and nursing personnel, equipment, and facilities. In emergency rooms, the triage nurse ranks patients in order of importance for treatment.

This paragraph illustrates how Bellevue has earned its high reputation as a trauma center. Despite the man's condition, no medical person gives up treating him until his death is clinically determined.

Intravenous infusions. Solutions such as those containing saline, dextrose, or potassium chloride are injected into veins in an attempt to produce immediate results, when treating hemorrhage, shock, or collapse.

This casual comment is not to be taken as a cold, unfeeling statement. People who work daily in trauma centers have learned to mask their feelings. The alternative is to destroy their careers by becoming psychologically involved with their work.

An appearance-versus-reality paragraph. The midnight episode quickly reminds other patients that their problems, in the harsh, comparative light of reality, may not be so serious after all.

Another appearance-versus-reality paragraph, this time comparing patients' view of the various emergencies with the Bellevue staffers' view of them.

shooting. It is an execution. IV's are jammed into the body in the groin and arms. One doctor has been plugging in an electrocardiograph and asks everyone to stop for a second so he can get a reading. "Forget it," shouts the doctor in charge. "No time." "Take it easy, Jimmy," someone yells at the head physician. It is apparent by now that the man is dead, but the doctors keep trying injections and finally they slit open the chest and reach inside almost up to their elbows. They feel the extent of the damage and suddenly it is all over. "I told 'em he was dead," says one nurse, withdrawing. "They didn't listen." The room is very still. The doctors are momentarily disgusted, then go on about their business. The room clears quickly. Finally there is only a male nurse and the still-warm body, now waxy-yellow, with huge ribs exposed on both sides of the chest and giant holes in both sides of the neck. The nurse speculates that this is yet another murder in a Hispanic political struggle that has brought many such victims to Bellevue. He marvels at the extent of the wounds and repeats, "This guy was really blown away."

Midnight. A hysterical woman is hustled through the lobby into an examination room. It is the dead man's wife, and she is nearly delirious. "I know he's dead, I know he's dead," she screams over and over. Within moments the lobby is filled with anxious relatives of the victim, waiting for word on his condition. The police are everywhere asking questions, but most people say they saw nothing. One young woman says she heard six shots, two louder than the other four. At some point, word is passed that the man is, in fact, dead. Another woman breaks down in hysterics; everywhere young Hispanics are crying and comforting each other. Plainclothes detectives make a quick examination of the body, check on the time of pronouncement of death, and begin to ask questions, but the bereaved are too stunned to talk. The rest of the uninvolved people in the lobby stare dumbly, their injuries suddenly paling in light of a death. 15

12:30 A.M. A black man appears at the admission desk and says he drank poison by mistake. He is told to have a seat. The ambulance brings in a young white woman, her head wrapped in white gauze. She is wailing terribly. A girl friend stands over her, 16 crying, and a boyfriend clutches the injured woman's hands, saying, "I'm here, don't worry, I'm here." The victim has fallen downstairs at a friend's house. Attendants park her stretcher against the wall to wait for an examination room to clear. There are eight examination rooms and only three doctors. Unless you are truly an emergency, you will wait. One doctor is stitching up the elbow of a drunk who's been punched out. The friends of the woman who fell down the stairs glance up at the doctors anxiously, wondering why their friend isn't being treated faster.

1:10 A.M. A car pulls into the bay and a young Hispanic asks if a shooting victim has been brought here. The security guard blurts out, "He's dead." The young man is stunned. He peels his tires leaving the bay.

1:20 A.M. The young woman of the stairs is getting stitches in a small gash over her left eye when the same ambulance driver who brought in the gunshot victim delivers a man who has been stabbed in the back on East 3rd Street. Once again the trauma room goes from 0 to 60 in five seconds. The patient is drunk, which helps him endure the pain of having the catheter inserted through his penis into his bladder. Still he yells, "That hurts like a bastard," then adds sheepishly, "Excuse me, ladies." But he is not prepared for what comes next. An X-ray reveals a collapsed right lung. After just a shot of local anesthetic, the doctor slices open his side and inserts a long plastic tube. Internal bleeding had kept the lung pressed down and prevented it from reinflating. The tube releases the pressure. The ambulance driver says the cops grabbed the guy who ran the eight-inch blade into the victim's back. "That's not the one," says the man. "They got the wrong guy." A nurse reports that there is not much of the victim's type blood available at the hospital. One of the doctors says that's okay, he won't need surgery. Meanwhile blood pours from the man's knife wound and the tube in his side. As the nurses work, they chat about personal matters, yet they respond immediately to orders from either doctor. "How ya doin'?" the doctor asks the patient. "Okay," he says. His blood spatters on the floor.

So it goes into the morning hours. A Valium overdose, a woman who fainted, a man who went through the windshield of

17   Just as the drama of the suicide had a follow-up paragraph earlier, the murder drama has its follow-up—Simpson's method of showing that life goes on, desperately or otherwise, despite the deaths at Bellevue.

18

Simpson compares the quickness of the Bellevue trauma staff with that of an automobile that can accelerate from 0 to 60 miles an hour in five seconds, which is remarkably fast.

Although normal in a fetus, a collapsed lung in a mature adult is serious, often caused (though not in this case) by the rupture of a bleb (an "internal blister") on the pleural (membrane) surface of the lung, which then becomes airless or nearly so.

Again, the nurses deal realistically with their lives while treating the lives of others. This healthy way of handling a job that could be emotionally painful distinguishes expert trauma-center personnel from those who do not last long as employees there.

19   The last paragraph strongly reinforces what Simpson has been describing and commenting about all along: Although unnerving for lay visitors, emergencies are routine for the medical experts at a trauma center, particularly at Bellevue.

POSSIBLE ANSWERS

Meaning and Purpose

1. Give students a chance to relate their own experiences in hospital emergency rooms and compare theirs to those Simpson describes.
2. Simpson's purpose is to expose a vital feature of Manhattan representing its people, violence, and trauma. He also wants to praise the emergency team by showing them in action.
3. At Bellevue injured people have a good chance for survival (2). Bellevue is a "monstrous complex" (2) like an "indoor war zone" (1). Some think it's only "for crazy people" (1). The emergency staff are highly trained and efficient. Simpson's details of the varied cases that come to them illustrate their expertise. " 'This is nothing, about normal, I'd say,' concludes the head nurse. 'No big deal' " (19).
4. From the emergency ward Manhattan looks like a violent, harsh city with a wide racial and ethnic mixture. "A policeman . . . twisted his knee struggling with an 'alleged perpetrator.' " (10). "A Hispanic man complains of pains in his side." (12).
5. "Bedlam" is capitalized because it is a variant of "Bethlehem"—the Hospital of St. Mary of Bethlehem, an old insane asylum in London. Bedlam: a state of uproar and confusion, a wild and frantic condition.

Strategy

1. Two introductory paragraphs set the scene and describe the hospital's reputation. Paragraphs 3–18 describe the typical activity of the emergency room from 9:00 P.M. Friday to 1:20 A.M. Saturday. The suicide story (8) has a follow-up in paragraph 11, and the gunshot victim (14–15) in paragraph 17. The final paragraph telescopes the activity till morning. This structure is clear and easy to follow. The sections by time suggest the methodical and orderly running of the emergency room.
2. Other stimulus-response patterns: the gun-

his car. More overdoses. More drunks with split eyebrows and chins. The doctors and nurses work without complaint. "This is nothing, about normal, I'd say," concludes the head nurse. "No big deal."

Meaning and Purpose

1. Have you ever been in a hospital emergency room? How would you describe the experience? Were you aware of the attitude of the doctors and nurses? Of the people waiting with the patients? Do any of Simpson's descriptions compare to what you saw?
2. What do you believe to be Simpson's purpose in "The War Room at Bellevue"?
3. What impressions of the hospital and its staff grow from the description? What details give you that impression?
4. Although Simpson does not describe the city that surrounds the hospital, what impression of the city does he leave you with? Support your answer with detail from the essay.
5. Why does Simpson capitalize "Bedlam" in paragraph 2? What are the denotation and connotation of the word?

Strategy

1. What is the structure of this descriptive essay?
2. Many internal workings of "The War Room at Bellevue" are constructed on a "stimulus-response" pattern—that is, an event takes place and people respond. You'll find a stimulus-response pattern in paragraph 4: it opens with the arrival of an ambulance; a patient is rolled into the lobby on a mobile stretcher; a nurse screams "Emergent!" and the scene explodes with action. Find a stimulus-response pattern in other passages of the essay.
3. Often Simpson has to describe simultaneous events—that is, separate actions that take place at the same time. Find at least

four overt transitions at the beginning of paragraphs that capture the sense of simultaneous action.

4. Simpson describes the Bellevue emergency room in the present tense. What is the effect of using this tense?
5. Comment on the spatial arrangement of some of the descriptions. Is it broad to narrow? near to far? center outward? Give examples.

Style

1. How would you describe the narrator of "The War Room at Bellevue"? Is the material presented objectively or subjectively?
2. What words and images help create the sense of a battle in the first two paragraphs?
3. How does the tone of the final paragraph differ from the tone Simpson creates through most of the essay?
4. Identify phrases that help create the sense of sound in paragraph 3. Find words that create a dominant sense impression in one or two other paragraphs.

Writing Tasks

1. Describe a scene in which a great deal of action takes place—a sports event, a shopping mall, an intersection, a park, or a school yard. Keep your description objective, carefully selecting the details to create, without emotion or judgment, a dominant impression.
2. Compare the subjective description in "Once More to the Lake" with the objective description in "The War Room at Bellevue." What words make the essays predominantly subjective or objective? What is the overall effectiveness of each strategy and its suitability to the subject? Could each essay be told from the other point of view?

shot victim arrives (14), and the stab victim arrives (18).
3. Transitions indicating simultaneous action: "Meanwhile in the lobby" (6); "A Young Hispanic man interrupts" (7); "The pace continues to increase" (9); and "Meanwhile, patients arrive in the lobby" (12).
4. The present tense creates an immediacy that conveys the quick action and intensity of the emergency room.
5. A panoramic view of admitting desk, waiting room, and emergency room, where "one man sleeps fitfully" (3). A far-to-near arrangement shows when the ambulance arrives, the "glass doors burst open," and a man is put on the treatment table (4). Another visual sweep takes the eye from trauma room to examination rooms to hallway (8).

Style

1. The intense emergency-room activity shows in the depth of detail—"After a few seconds another doctor inserts his finger into the wound. It sinks in all the way to the knuckles" (5). Simpson is objective and detached; "Another woman breaks down in hysterics; everywhere young Hispanics are crying and comforting each other" (15), and "The young woman of the stairs is getting stitches in a small gash over her left eye" (18).
2. Words suggestive of battle are "war zone," "wounded and bleeding," "harried doctors," "rush from stretcher to stretcher," "crushing number of injured," "battlefield," and "survival."
3. The closing paragraph quickly surveys the time from 1:20 A.M. to "the morning hours." Simpson catalogues the cases even more dispassionately, not even specifying who has which injuries. This activity is routine. The tone conveys a less harried, less immediate, less alarming atmosphere. The narrator has pulled back from the situation.
4. The sound words are "whistle has blown," "mutter of voices," "sit quietly," "tiny bleep," and "nurses can hear." Paragraph 4 has mostly touch words, and paragraph 14, sound words.

TEACHING SUGGESTIONS

Call it "optional fright": All of us at one time or another have voluntarily frightened ourselves—in short, we have dipped into our childhood from time to time. But few of us have been as affected by rides as Peter Schjeldahl by his adventure on Cyclone. Or at least few of us have bothered to tell how we have been affected.

Often, instructors introduce this essay with a reminiscence about deliberately becoming involved in a frightening situation, just for the thrill. One instructor described her first parachute jump, and how it determined her to jump and jump again. Another instructor shouted at a police officer, when he was ten, just to see if he could outrun the law. (He couldn't.)

Such quick descriptions may relax the class enough so that some want to volunteer their own memorable events. Stimulate descriptions with questions: When did it happen? How did you look? Why did you do it, *really*? How did your stomach feel? Did you have friendly witnesses? Were you with others?

MARGINAL NOTES

Loosely defined, a cyclone—from the Greek *kykloein*, "to circle around; to whirl"—is a windstorm with a violently whirling movement: a tornado or a hurricane.

A play on "art for art's sake": art is its own excuse for being.

The Cyclone is a wooden roller coaster.

The Cyclone is on Brooklyn's Coney Island, a peninsula at the southwest end of Long Island.

The outline enclosing the words or thoughts of a character in a cartoon.

❦ Peter Schjeldahl ❦

Peter Schjeldahl was born in North Dakota in 1942. He has published several collections of poetry, including White Country *(1968),* An Adventure of the Thought Police *(1971), and* Dreams *(1973), and in 1964 he cofounded the poetry magazine,* Mother. *He has also been an art critic for* Art News *and for the* Village Voice. *His book* Samaras Pastels *was published by the Denver Art Museum in 1981.*

Cyclone!
Rising to the Fall

This short essay, first published in Harper's in 1988, is written with a poet's eye for detail. Telling comparisons add to this vivid description of riding a famous roller coaster at Coney Island. Schjeldahl describes the sheer fun of the experience, gives each section of the track a name, and takes the reader for a ride that turns out to be as memorable as the one he took.

The Cyclone is art, sex, God, the greatest. It is the most fun you can have without risking bad ethics. I rode the Cyclone seven times one afternoon last summer, and I am here to tell everybody that it is fun for fun's sake, the pure abstract heart of the human capacity for getting a kick out of anything. Yes, it may be anguishing initially. (I promise to tell the truth.) Terrifying, even, the first time or two the train is hauled upward with groans and creaks and with you in it. At the top then—where there is sudden strange quiet but for the fluttering of two tattered flags, and you have a poignantly brief view of Brooklyn, and of ships far out on the Atlantic—you may feel very lonely and that you have made a serious mistake, cursing yourself in the last gleam of the reflective consciousness you are about, abruptly, to leave up there between the flags like an abandoned thought-balloon. To keep yourself company by screaming may help, and no one is noticing: try it. After a couple of rides, panic abates, and after four or five you aren't even frightened, exactly, but *stimulated,* blissed, sent. The squirt of adrenaline you will never cease to have at the top as the train lumbers, wobbling slightly, into the plunge, finally fuels just happy wonderment because you can't, and never will, *believe* what is going to happen.

Every roller coaster has that first, immense drop. In practical terms, it provides the oomph for the entire ride, which is of course impelled by nothing but ecologically sound gravity, momentum, and the odd slingshot of centrifugal force. The coaster is basically an ornate means of falling and a poem about physics in parts of stanzas, with jokes. The special quality of the Cyclone is how different, how *articulated,* all the components of its poem are, the whole of which lasts a minute and thirty-some seconds—exactly the right length, composed of distinct and perfect moments. By my fifth ride, my heart was leaping at the onset of each segment as at the approach of a dear old friend, and melting with instantaneous nostalgia for each at its finish.

I think every part of the Cyclone should have a name, the better to be recalled and accurately esteemed. In my mind, the big drop is Kismet—fate, destiny. I can't think of what to call the second, a mystery drop commenced in a jiffy after we have been whipped around, but good, coming out of Kismet. (Someday soon I will devote particular attention to the huge and violent but elusive second drop.) I do know that the third drop's name can only be Pasha. It is so round and generous, rich and powerful, looking like a killer going in but then actually like a crash landing in feathers that allows, for the first time in the ride, an instant for luxuriating in one's endorphin rush. . . .

Rolling up out of Pasha, we enter the part of the Cyclone that won't quit laughing. First there's the whoop of a whipping hairpin curve, which, if someone is sitting with you, Siamese-twins you. (Having tried different cars in different company, I prefer being alone at the very front—call me a classicist.) The ensuing dips, humps, dives, and shimmies that roar, chortle, cackle, and snort continue just long enough to suggest that they may go on

2   Anticipatory behavior once allowed people to avoid danger before disaster. We have now "evolved" into placing ourselves into a position of imaginary danger for the sake of fun.

The force pulling a thing outward when it is rotating rapidly around a center.

"articulated": A play on words: "having parts connected by joints," as in roller-coaster construction; also, "made of distinct syllables or words," as in poetic constructions.

3   An oxymoron, yoking two contradictory words. The word *nostalgia* refers to longing for something far away or long ago, not ordinarily associated with *instantaneous.*

Turkish, *qismet,* from the arabic *qismah,* akin to *qasama,* "to divide," alluding to philosophical differences between free will and determinism.

In Turkey, the title of rank or honor formerly placed after the name of a high civil or military official.

4   Endorphins: chemical substances produced in the brain that act as opiates producing analgesia, absence of a normal sense of pain. The "rush" is a momentary feeling of euphoria, exaggerated high spirits.

That is, pushes you both together in such a way that you feel you have become physically attached, joined like Siamese twins.

"Irene": An ironic name for this sharp drop. In classical mythology, the Horae are the goddesses of the seasons, of cyclical death and rebirth. Usually three, they are Dikē (justice), Eunomia (order), and Irēnē (peace).

"banal": Dull or stale; commonplace.

In Belgium, the scene of Napoleon's final defeat, Waterloo refers to any loosely defined disaster.

Aversion training: applying or showing frightening or disturbing situations or objects to a person, to ease phobias by gradually increasing familiarity with those objects or situations. The author wants to learn how to flee "Irene types," rather than to learn how to tolerate them.

The author relives his passage to maturity at every pass through this part of Cyclone.

Part of the author's infatuation with Cyclone is its age. Wear and tear over the years have produced a unique roller coaster, on which no two rides are exactly the same.

The author learns at Coney Island what the cowboy learns in Wyoming. One prevents fear by facing that which could cause fear.

forever—as worrisome as the thought, when you're laughing hard, that maybe you can never stop—and then it's hello, Irene. Why do I think Irene is the name of the very sharp drop, not deep but savage, that wipes the grin off the laughing part of the Cyclone? (Special about it is a crosspiece, low over the track at the bottom, that you swear is going to fetch you square in the eyebrows.) Irene is always the name—or kind of name, slightly unusual but banal—of the ordinary-seeming girl whom a young man may pursue idly, in a bored time, and then *wham!* fall horribly in love with, blasted in love with this person he never bothered to even particularly look at and now it's too late, she's his universe, Waterloo, *personal* Kismet. This is one good reason I can think of for growing older: learning an aversion reflex for girls named something like Irene. In this smallish but vicious, sobering drop, abstract shapes of my own youthful romantic sorrows do not fail to flash before my inner eye . . . but then, with a jarring zoom up and around, I am once more grown-up, wised-up me, and the rest of the ride is rejoicing.

The Cyclone differs from other roller coasters in being (a) a work of art and (b) old, and not only old but odd-looking, decrepit, rusting in its metal parts and peeling in its more numerous wooden parts, filthy throughout and jammed into a wire (Cyclone!) fence abutting cracked sidewalks of the Third World sinkhole that Coney Island is, intoxicatingly. Nor is it to be denied or concealed that the Cyclone, unlike newer coasters, tends to run *rough,* though each ride is unique and some are inexplicably velvety. One time the vibration, with the wheels shrieking and the cars threatening to explode with strain, made me think, "This is *no fun at all!*" It was an awful moment, with a sickening sense of betrayal and icy-fingered doubt: was my love malign?

That was my worst ride, which left me with a painfully yanked muscle in my shoulder, but I am glad to say it wasn't my last. I got back on like a thrown cowboy and discovered that the secret of handling the rough rides is indeed like riding a horse, at trot or gallop—not tensing against it, as I had, but posting and rolling. It's all in the thighs and rear end, as I especially realized when— what the hell—I joined pimpled teenagers in the arms-raised *no hands!* trick. I should mention that a heavy, cushioned restraining bar locks down snugly into your lap and is very reassuring, although, like everything upholstered in the cars, it may be cracked or slashed and leaking tufts of stuffing from under swatches of gray gaffer's tape. One thing consistently disquieting is how, under stress, a car's wooden sides may *give* a bit. I wish they wouldn't do that, or that my imagination were less vivid. If a side did happen to fail on a curve, one would depart like toothpaste from a stomped-on tube.

I was proud of braving the *no hands!* posture—as trusting in the restraining bar as a devout child in his heavenly Father— particularly the first time I did it, while emerging from the slinging return that succeeds Irene into the long, long careen that bottoms out at absolute ground level a few feet from the fence where pedestrians invariably gather to watch, transfixed. I call this swift, showy glide Celebrity: the ride's almost over, and afflatus swells the chest. But going *no hands!* soon feels as cheap and callow as it looks, blocking with vulgar self-centeredness the wahoo-glimmering-away-of-personality-in-compulsive-Nirvana that is the Cyclone's essence. A righteous ride is hands on, though lightly, like grace. The payoff is intimacy in the sweet diminuendo, the jiggling and chuckling smart little bumps and dandling dips that brings us to a quick, pillowy deceleration in the shed, smelling of dirty machine oil, where we began and will begin again. It is a warm debriefing, this last part: "Wasn't that *great?*" it says. "Want to go again?"

Of course, I do, but first there is the final stage of absorption, when you squeeze out (it's easy to bang a knee then, so watch it) to stand wobbly but weightless, euphoric, and then to enjoy the sensation of walking as if it were a neat thing you had just invented. Out on the sidewalk, the object of curious gazes, you see that they see that you see them, earthlings, in a diminishing perspective, through the wrong end of the telescope of your pleasure, and your heart is pitying. You nod, smiling, to convey that yes, they should ride, and no, they won't regret it.

"upholstered": Again, the very age of Cyclone provides some of its grandest thrills.

In entertainment-business jargon, a gaffer is the head electrician on a movie or television set. "Gaffer's tape" is electrical tape, known to stick to almost anything, often used for quick nonelectrical repairs that are usually temporary.

7

Partly because of television, many celebrities are now famous merely for being well known; they are swift and showy, like Cyclone's Celebrity. The term *afflatus* refers to an artist's or poet's powerful impulse or inspiration. "Nirvana": In Buddhism, state of perfect blessedness achieved when individual existence ends and the soul is absorbed into the supreme spirit, after desires and passions are extinguished.

"diminuendo": In music, a gradual decrease in loudness or intensity.

8

The author wrote earlier of an "endorphin rush." Here, quite soon after the ride, the "rush" is still upon him, affecting his perspective, making the ride worthwhile all over again.

Meaning and Purpose

1. Most students will think at least some of Schjeldahl's descriptions are successful. The first paragraph has such expressions as "anguishing initially," "terrifying, even," "screaming may help," "the squirt of adrenaline," and "into the plunge," which describe most people's experiences on roller coasters.

2. Some students may know this roller coaster by name. For some, "I rode the Cyclone" may give it away, or "the train is hauled upward."

3. The dominant impression is that riding the Cyclone is exhilarating and scary—unadulterated fun. Schjeldahl says you are "*stimulated, blissed, sent*" (1).

4. "Fun for fun's sake" is a play on "art for art's sake"; that is, art—or fun—is its own excuse for being.

5. This sentence refers to nirvana, the Buddhist state of selfless blessedness and union with the supreme spirit, and the blocking of this state by the conscious effort of riding *no hands!* The bliss of riding the Cyclone is exaggerated in a humorous way.

Strategy

1. The impressions of feelings are dominant in these passages: "The squirt of adrenaline you will never cease to have at the top . . . what is going to happen" (1); "By my fifth ride, my heart was leaping at the onset of each segment . . . at its finish" (2); and "Out on the sidewalk, the object of curious gazes . . . pitying" (8).

2. The first two paragraphs describe the Cyclone as the author sees it; paragraph 3 begins the discussion of the Cyclone's parts, and Schjeldahl names the first and third parts; paragraph 4 names the fourth part; paragraphs 5 and 6 describe the roughness of the ride; paragraph 7 calls the last part Celebrity; and the last paragraph ends the ride out on the sidewalk. Schjeldahl has so much to say about the Cyclone that dividing the ride into parts and naming them organizes his description in a manageable way and helps readers experience the ride—and all it means to him—with him.

Meaning and Purpose

1. Schjeldahl intends to re-create the experience of riding a roller coaster—the Cyclone at Coney Island, New York. Is his description successful for you? Why or why not?

2. Schjeldahl doesn't mention the name roller coaster until paragraph 2. When did you know that he was describing a roller coaster?

3. What dominant impression of riding the Cyclone does Schjeldahl's description leave you with?

4. What does "fun for fun's sake" in paragraph 1 signify?

5. In paragraph 7, what does Schjeldahl mean by "blocking with vulgar self-centeredness the wahoo-glimmering-away-of-personality-in-convulsive-Nirvana that is the Cyclone's essence"?

Strategy

1. How does Schjeldahl use impressions or perceptions to convey the feeling of riding the Cyclone? Give examples of passages that convey feelings.

2. Outline briefly the structure Schjeldahl uses to organize his descriptions. What is the overall effect of structuring the essay as he does?

3. A digression is material, unrelated or distantly related to the subject, which is inserted into a work. Paragraphs 5 and 6 make up a digression from the subject of naming the parts of the ride. Why do you think Schjeldahl digresses here? Does the digression fit? Is it effective?

4. "Embellish" means to enhance, or to add ornamental details, to create a desired impression. Do you think Schjeldahl embellishes his descriptions of the Cyclone? If so, give examples. Does the embellishment make the essay better? How?

Style

1. Identify the metaphors in paragraphs 2 and 6 and explain why they are appropriate or inappropriate.
2. Why is the phrase "it's easy to bang a knee," in paragraph 8, ironic?
3. Explain these words and phrases as they are used in the essay: *instantaneous nostalgia* (2); *Siamese-twins you* (4); *Waterloo* (4); *gaffer's tape* (6); *earthlings* (8).
4. Do you agree that the final paragraph captures Schjeldahl's attitude toward riding the Cyclone and embodies the tone of the whole essay? If so, how does the final paragraph do these things?

Writing Tasks

1. Write a descriptive passage about an exhilarating ride you've had—perhaps a carnival ride, a ski or toboggan run, or a motorcycle sprint—whatever you feel lends itself to a description similar to Schjeldahl's. Describe the experience in detail while trying to create a dominant impression. Be generous with figures of speech, such as simile or metaphor.
2. In a descriptive paragraph about a place, focus on the order in spatial arrangement and describe your subject from near to far, right to left, center outward, top to bottom, and so on, as you want your reader's eyes to see the place.

3. In paragraph 4, Schjeldahl has just talked about youthful romance, then being "once more grown up" after a "jarring zoom up and around." The jarring suggests roughness, which he describes in the digression, and growing up out of youth ties in with the Cyclone's being "old" (5). These are the transitions into a discussion of the effect of old age on the Cyclone. The digression fits here also because it comes right before the description of the ride's end.

4. Schjeldahl embellishes his descriptions to match his enthusiasm and pleasure in riding the Cyclone. The embellishment is necessary to convey Schjeldahl's excitement, thrill, and awe.

Style

1. In paragraph 2, Schjeldahl compares the Cyclone to a "poem about physics." This metaphor fits because he holds the Cyclone up as a work of art and says it is "the right length, composed." A poem suggests something carefully constructed, beautiful beyond the ordinary. In paragraph 6 the cyclone is like a bucking bronco, and Schjeldahl like a cowboy riding it. This description is appropriate to the discussion of how rough the ride is.

2. This phrase is ironic because, after nearly risking his life on a ride, Schjeldahl cautions about a little thing like a banged knee.

3. "Instantaneous nostalgia" is an oxymoron, an expression joining two contradictory terms. The effect is exaggerated humor about how eagerly Schjeldahl anticipates each part of the ride. "Siamese-twins you" means that, if two people are in the seat, they are pushed together so forcefully that they feel physically attached. "Waterloo" is the scene in Belgium of Napoleon's final defeat, and now the word can refer to any disaster. "Gaffer's tape" is electrical tape used for temporary repairs by a gaffer, the head electrician on a movie or television set. "Earthlings" refers to people who have not ridden the Cyclone; those who have ridden it see them as if through the eyes of aliens.

4. The final paragraph has words that summarize Schjeldahl's feelings about riding the Cyclone. The tone here is of elation, otherworldliness, satisfaction—as it is throughout the essay.

Are all gestures symbolic—does every movement we make have a meaning all its own? We hear a great deal about "body language": How you move may partially determine what you really mean when you say something. Folding your arms tightly across your chest while talking, for example, is often taken as a symbol of belligerence or hostility.

Instructors have had great fun when introducing this essay. They ask their students to arrange the desks or chairs so that each student is facing another. Then, after everyone has taken a seat and is in a state of relative calm, they shout something like "Okay! Don't move! *Freeze just as you are!*"

After everyone is "frozen," the instructor quickly examines the nearest student and describes the student's posture, arm position, foot position, and so on, interspersing among the descriptive remarks comments on the symbolic meaning derived from studying the student's overall physical attitude. Does the student look intelligent? How can the instructor tell? Are the arms resting lightly on the desk, eyes alert, head up, posture straight? Or, does the student look bored? How do you know? Are the arms resting in the lap, legs sprawled straight out in front, chin resting on a shoulder? And so on.

Following your exercise in judging a person by frozen body movements, ask each student to frame an opinion (symbolically, of course) about the person sitting opposite, based on how they are "frozen." After demonstrating the worth of studying gestures as a form of meaning, the class is ready to read Whyte's essay.

MARGINAL NOTES

In the social sciences, a *hypothesis* is an assertion that can be tested, or a statement or proposition about relations between two or more

❦ William H. Whyte ❦

Born in Pennsylvania in 1917, graduated from Princeton University, William Whyte is best known for his books about urban America and American business, especially The Organization Man *(1956). He has also worked extensively on conservation problems and has written several books about conservation and urban areas, including* The Exploding Metropolis *(1958),* Cluster Development *(1964), and* The Last Landscape *(1968). He has been a writer for* Fortune *magazine, where he was also assistant managing editor from 1953 to 1958, and has contributed articles to other national publications, including* Harper's *and* Life. *His latest work,* City: Rediscovering Its Center *(1989), is a study of street life in cities.*

The Social Life of the Streets

Excerpted from City: Rediscovering Its Center, *this essay was produced by many hours of people-watching. Close observation, both first-hand and second-hand (with time-lapse photography) reveals startling truths about the everyday behavior of people on city streets. Whyte describes in great detail the daily social rituals that city dwellers take utterly for granted.*

It was a dandy hypothesis. How far, I had wondered, would people move out of the pedestrian flow to have a conversation? My hypothesis was that they would gravitate to the unused foot or so of buffer space along the building walls. It was a matter of simple common sense. 1

We focused time-lapse cameras on several street corners and recorded the activity for two weeks. On maps of the corners we plotted the location of each conversation and how long it lasted. To screen out people who were only waiting for the light to change, we noted only those conversations lasting a minute or longer. 2

132

The activity was not as expected. To our surprise, the people who stopped to talk did not move out of the main pedestrian flow; and if they had been out of it, they moved into it. The great bulk of the conversations were smack in the middle of the pedestrian flow—the 100 percent location, to borrow the real estate term. In subsequent studies we were to find the same impulse to the center in traveling conversations—the kind in which two people move about a lot but don't go very far. There is much apparent motion, but if you plot the orbits, you will find that they are centered around the 100 percent location.

What attracts people most, in sum, is other people. If I labor the point, it is because many urban spaces are being designed as though the opposite were true and as though what people like best are the places they stay away from. People themselves often talk along such lines, and that is why their responses to questionnaires can be so misleading. How many people would say they like to sit in the middle of a crowd? Instead, they speak of getting away from it all, and they use terms like "oasis," "retreat," and "escape." I am very glad my hypothesis blew up in my face. It has forced me to look at what people do.

The best places to look are street corners. As a general rule, 100 percent conversations are spotted most often at the busiest crossroads locations. Fifth Avenue at Fiftieth Street is one such. The heaviest pedestrian flows are at the entrance to Saks department store and at the street corner. It is at these two places that the greatest number of conversations are clustered, with relatively few in the space between the corner and the entrance. Of 133 conversations we mapped over several days, 57 percent were concentrated in the highest-traffic locations. While there were no significant differences between men and women, men did tend to talk somewhat longer than women: 50 percent of male groups talked five minutes or longer, compared to 45 percent of female groups.

People waiting for people are interesting to observe, particularly so a few minutes after the hour. But most interesting of all are people who meet people they did not expect to. When I

3 phenomena. As defined by A. J. Ayre in *Language, Truth and Logic* (1936), "Empirical propositions are one and all hypotheses which may be confirmed or discredited in actual sense experience." Social scientists disagree among themselves about formulating an empirical hypothesis so that it can be immediately tested or using relatively abstract constructs in the formulation.

Whyte's empirical hypothesis was formulated to be immediately tested, and the results of his study were counterintuitive—things did not

4 work out as Whyte's "common sense" told him they would.

Although urban planners plan for open space, in fact people may not prefer such space, even though they speak of yearning for it. Perhaps the open space they yearn for is not space that is really confined, set aside by fences, hedges, and so on, but the open space of the mind, the attitude that allows them freedom to move with safety, even in a crowd.

5 Fifth Avenue at Fiftieth Street is an extraordinarily busy corner in New York City.

Whyte describes in a general way his methodology, his practice, and the resulting statistics. Neither men nor women preferred either open or concentrated spaces, but men talked longer.

6

Whyte moves from his professional side into his personal side, observing people as an ordinary person, not as a social scientist.

How one dresses reflects one's station in life. Whyte determines people's station in life from their apparel and age.

Whyte moves into an even more personal connection with his audience, beginning with, "It's a little like the people who hover in office doorways." He cautions readers not to be fooled by someone's glancing at his or her watch, almost as if he is giving advice to a friend.

started observing street behavior, it was the high incidence of these chance meetings that struck me. But when you come to think of it, it is not chance at all. With about three thousand people an hour streaming past a spot, there is an actuarial probability that someone will see a friend, an acquaintance, or the familiar stranger you can almost place but not quite. The probability may be higher yet when you take shifts into account.

7   The postlunch groups heading back to the office around one o'clock look like junior and middle management people. The people you see around two are older, more expensively dressed, and apparently not in a hurry.

8   Of the street conversations we tracked, about 30 percent appear to have been unplanned. Some encounters were too brief to develop into a conversation—a quick hello and a wave of the hand. Some were awkwardly tentative, with neither party quite sure whether it would be right to pass on or stop. But many went on for three minutes or more. If one of the persons was with a group, the encounter sometimes involved a full round of introductions and handshakes.

9   Most goodbyes are brief: a fast "ciao," "take care," a wave, and they're off. But a number are protracted, particularly so when they are an extension of a failed goodbye. It's a little like the people who hover in office doorways, forever on the verge of leaving, but never doing so. If people go through the motions of a goodbye and stop short at the point of consummation, a momentum is set up that can lead to progressively more emphatic goodbyes, up to the final resolving goodbye. It is fascinating to watch these three- and four-wave goodbyes and try to distinguish the real goodbye from the false ones. Don't be fooled by the glance at the watch. It is only premonitory. I have a wonderful film record of two men gripped in indecision in front of Saks Fifth Avenue. They just can't bring themselves to part. There are several rounds of goodbyes and looks at the watch, but it's not until a third party comes along that they finally break out of their impasse.

10   Best to watch are the postlunch goodbyes of the senior executives. Sometimes there is a note of irresolution about the leave-taking, as if the real business the lunch was supposed to have

been about has not yet been broached. Finally, someone brings it up. The deal? The contract? Yes, yes, of course. How could they have forgotten? They now proceed to the business and as they do, their foot and arm movements tend to become reciprocal. This is an indication of people obliging one another, and soon the matter will be completed.

One of the most notable social rituals is schmoozing. In New York's garment district on Seventh Avenue, you will see groups of men lined up along the curb, facing inward. There are often so many of them that you have to go out into the street along with the handcart pushers if you want to make any headway. Sometimes the vehicular traffic slows to a near halt for all the gabbing.

"Schmoozing" is a Yiddish term for which there is no precise definition. But basically it means "nothing talk"—idle gossip, political opinions, sports talk, but not, so they say, business talk. But groups do tend to form up along occupational lines; salesmen, for example, tend to schmooze with other salesmen, and pattern-makers, with other patternmakers. Some of the schmoozers are retirees who like to come back around midday to keep in touch. Almost all garment district schmoozers are men.

Physically, it's an awful place. It is without trees or graces, it is noisy and fume-ridden, and the traffic is so bad even cyclists try to give the place a wide berth. If you ask the schmoozers if they wouldn't prefer the plazas and open spaces further uptown, they will look at you as though you are crazy. Those other places: people don't *work* there. Kid stuff. This is the center of things.

In one respect, it most certainly is: in few places will you see such a clear demonstration of the relation between centrality and word of mouth communication. The schmoozing groups are anything but static. Some will last only ten minutes or so, dissolve, and then be replaced by a new group. Other groups will constantly renew themselves, with newcomers joining as others leave. Then there are the people who roam. These are often senior men, to judge by the deference paid them. They work the block, stopping friends to chat for a moment or so, checking in briefly with the standing group. One man that we tracked talked with eighteen separate groups. He accosted them with a look of urgency, and

11

12

13

14

The author imagines a complete scenario, filling in gaps in the "script" with his own descriptive imagination, as if he were shooting a contrived scene rather than simply recording chance meetings.

The slang word *schmooze* is from the Yiddish *shmuesn,* from the Hebrew *shemuoth,* "items reported; gossip."

The garment district bears out Whyte's statement that some people like to congregate with other people, regardless of surroundings, so long as the surroundings look busy.

Notice the men's roaming, clustering, and roaming again, reminiscent of small herds of other gregarious animals, eager to communicate, whether the communication is important or not.

they listened with interest. Whatever it was he was communicating, it was multiplied almost geometrically—and it wasn't "nothing talk" either.

Schmoozing is now to be seen all over, uptown and downtown, and while the intensity cannot match that of the garment district, the basic patterns are similar. Banks and corporations with large clerical staffs tend to have lots of schmoozers. These are also the kind of places that provide in-house cafeterias, recreation facilities, TV rooms, hobby clubs, and the like. But schmoozers want to get outside. They won't do much when they get there; generally they will form up abreast in a line. This is the most functional way to watch people go by. The schmoozers will sometimes exchange remarks on the passersby, but sometimes simply watch, bound in an amiable silence.

Schmoozers are fairly consistent in choosing locations. They show a liking for well-defined places—the edge of the curb, for example, or a ledge. They are also very pillar-tropic, obeying perhaps a primeval instinct for something at their backs. Rarely will they stand for long in the middle of large spaces.

Schmoozers are also consistent in the duration of their sessions, which will be either fairly brief or fairly long—fifteen minutes or even more. Some groups, as on Seventh Avenue, are of the semipermanent floating kind, and many last the whole lunch hour. The stayers dominate. If you add up the minutes spent by each schmoozer over an hour's time, you will find that the great majority of the total schmoozing minutes will be accounted for by the long-term schmoozers.

The most common form that street conversation takes is that of straight man and principal. For a while, one man dominates, while the other cooperates by remaining still and listening. Then there will be a shift—the onlooker can sense it coming—and the active man becomes the passive one.

Or should. Sometimes people will violate the tacit compact and keep on talking and gesturing beyond their time. Conversely, the straight man may fail to respect the pause during the principal's turn and jump in prematurely. When there are such failures of accommodation, there is a lack of symmetry in their move-

15

16

17

18

19

Whyte has moved from examining his original hypothesis to examining and describing all the characteristics of schmoozing, as if he were infected with the whole social notion of this form of communication.

Conversations are "supposed to be" reciprocal: First, it's my turn, and then it's your turn. When one person breaks this social contract, the other person shows her or his lack of interest in interesting ways.

ments. I have a film sequence of a long conversation on Fifty-seventh Street that is a catalog of discords. A cigar-smoking man has been long overextending his turn. This begins to be reflected in the gestures of the listener. He begins to look this way and that, as if for help and brushes lint off his lapels. He rocks up and down on his heels and then stops abruptly. He wheels to leave. The other man, still talking, grabs him by the sleeve and then finally releases him.

Soapboxers display cooperative antagonism in heightened form. About 1 P.M. they gather at Broad and Wall streets. Most are regulars; some are Henry George single-tax people, some specialize in world affairs, many concentrate on religion, interpretation of the Bible in particular. The proceedings will be highly adversarial, and that is why the soapboxers come—to dispute and be disputed. Some structure their discourse to be heckled and may be discomfited if they are not.

The classic form of their encounters is thrust and counter-thrust. With a jabbing finger punctuating each point, one man advances on his adversary, who gives way at the same pace. After a climactic flourish, the first man stops, and his hands go limp. What more could possibly be said? The other man jabs out his finger. How could that be squared with Genesis? He advances on the other man, who gives way. The whole preceding scene is now acted out in reverse. Other soapboxers may egg them on. A man who is known as the Logician, a man with a spade beard and an incongruous tweed hat, may top off the session. Both men have missed the point.

Gestures reinforce the speech and the pauses. A person may pause for effect and then add an "uh" or an "um" to signal that he's going to go on again. As he does he may signal the same message with a move of the hand. Gestures are especially important when one speaker does not play the game, jumping a pause, for example, or talking well beyond his turn. At such times, gestures are apt to be touching gestures—a hand on the other's sleeve, for example, as if to say, "I'm not finished yet."

Most touching gestures are friendly; the arm around another's shoulders is one of the more common ones. But the purpose is often a measure of control. The one who does the touching is

20   An American economist (1839–1897) born in Philadelphia, George argued that the entire tax burden should be based on land ownership, freeing industry from taxation and equalizing opportunity by destroying the advantages of monopolies.

21   The soapboxers argue in the lexical sense of *argument,* albeit with added verve. As opposed to quarrelers, arguers attempt to sway other people to their position by offering reasons for that position.

22   Gestures are used to show that some behavior is a matter of stimulus-response, and therefore does not involve exchanging ideas.

23

dominant—at that particular moment, at least—or seeking to be. When a man who is talking reaches out and touches another's arm, he is giving a command: Don't start talking again now, because I'm not finished yet. A more-open coercion is the grasping of another's arm to stay a departure.

Some of the most interesting gestures are unseen by the other party. The man who's doing the gesturing often does it with his hands behind his back, out of the sight of the person for whom they're presumably intended. If you follow a traveling conversation, you will note that very often one of the group will have his hands joined behind his back and will show all sorts of finger and thumb movement, sometimes at variance with the placid mien he's showing his companion. 24

Whatever the function of the gestures and movements, the street is a congenial place for the expression of them. They tend to be more expansive there than in internal spaces. You may see orbiting conversations in a building lobby, but out on the street they may cover far more space. Is there more room on the street? Not really; the highest incidence of encounters is in the most-crowded locations. 25

The street is a stage, and the sense that an audience is watching pervades the gestures and movements of the players on it. 26

Animals employ gestures in a stimulus-response pattern. Monkeys gesture back and forth, as do some species of birds. But people are singular in adding and sharing meanings of ideas that lie behind their gestures; people alone employ significant gestures, a part of meaning in language.

See Shakespeare's *As You Like It* (II, vii): "All the world's a stage, / And all the men and women merely players: / They have their exits and their entrances. . . ."

Meaning and Purpose

1. Does the title give you clues about the content of Whyte's essay? How is the title effective, or how is it not?
2. What is a hypothesis?
3. How did Whyte's hypothesis, which "blew up in [his] face," lead him to another focus?
4. In paragraph 21, what does Whyte mean by "How could that be squared with Genesis?"
5. In the last paragraph, what is "the street is a stage" an allusion to?

POSSIBLE ANSWERS

Meaning and Purpose

1. The title is nonspecific and could refer to a number of kinds of socializing on the streets, such as teenagers hanging out together, or street performers. It suggests to readers only that the setting is the street, and the general subject some kind of socializing there. The title is unimaginative but benign.
2. A hypothesis is a tentative assertion or

6. What is Whyte's main point, the meaning of his essay? Where does he state it?

Strategy

1. Whyte's first four paragraphs serve as the introduction, providing background and direction for the essay. Review the introduction and identify what he achieves in each paragraph. In paragraph 1, for instance, he establishes the purpose underlying his study. What are the functions of paragraphs 2, 3, and 4?
2. After the introduction, the essay could be divided into four sections, each with a clear focus. Identify each section and its focus, and create an appropriate title for each.
3. Whyte's conclusion is brief, only one sentence. Do you feel it is appropriate for the essay? Does it capture the dominant impression Whyte gives of his street people? Explain your response.
4. Look at the many descriptions of anonymous people in "The War Room at Bellevue" and compare them to Whyte's descriptions of street people. How does each author create impressions of people in action? of types of people? of the ways in which they communicate? of the setting's effects on behavior? Give examples from each essay.

Style

1. Whyte's descriptions generally reflect "typical" behavior that he observed. In several places he does describe "specific" behavior. Identify three examples of "specific" behavior and tell how they affect the description.
2. Study the language that Whyte uses to create a tone. Is it formal? friendly? authoritative? confrontational? humorous? Give examples to support your answers. Judging by the tone, what audience do you think Whyte addresses?
3. What is the metaphor in paragraph 21, and how does it serve Whyte's purpose in this paragraph?

proposition that can be tested for its validity or truth.

3. Whyte first assumed that people would move into less crowded or empty spaces on the street to converse, but he discovered just the opposite. His observations led him to look more closely at people's behavior and gestures during conversations on the street.

4. In the preceding paragraph, Whyte has talked about "soapboxers," who "concentrate on religion." As he describes their gestures, he imagines that one asks of the other the question about Genesis, which is the book in the Old Testament that tells the story of creation.

5. This statement alludes to Hamlet's words: "All the world's a stage, / And all the men and women merely players" (*As You Like It*, II, vii).

6. Whyte's point is that the street is a congenial place for people to converse, and they prefer the most crowded spaces in which to do so. The first and last sentences of paragraph 25 state this main idea.

Strategy

1. Paragraph 2 describes how Whyte collected his data. Paragraph 3 interprets the data and shows that the hypothesis is suspect. Paragraph 4 states Whyte's conclusion that "What attracts people most, in sum, is other people," and shifts the focus from the original hypothesis to looking at how people behave when they converse.

2. Of the four sections following the introduction, the first consists of paragraphs 5–10, and could be called "Fifth Avenue and Fiftieth Street." Whyte discusses the behavior of different kinds of people encountering one another. Section two, paragraphs 11–17, is focused on "schmoozing," which word could also be its title. The third section is paragraphs 18–21—"Power Conversations"—and here Whyte talks about dominant and passive roles in street conversation. The fourth is paragraphs 22–26, which could be titled "Gestures," for those are the focus.

3. Whyte observes people on the street

throughout the essay, as if they are on a stage and he is the audience. His final sentence makes this relationship visual from his point of view; however, he has not made it clear that the people behave as they do because they think they are being observed.

4. Ask students to reread Simpson's essay and make careful comparisons, citing passages to illustrate their points, between the descriptions of people in his and Whyte's essays. Afterward, ask them if they think the descriptions in each essay suit the essayist's purpose.

Style

1. Examples of specific behavior are "One man that we tracked talked with eighteen separate groups" (14); "A cigar-smoking man has been long overextending his turn" (19); "one man advances on his adversary" (20). These specific descriptions support the general assertions in the paragraph about behavior.

2. Whyte's tone is mostly friendly, not overly formal, and detached from emotional involvement in the behavior he describes. It is not the typical academic tone of a social-science essay. Examples of the tone are "It was a dandy hypothesis" (1); "But when you come to think of it, it is not chance at all" (6); and "It's a little like the people who hover in office doorways, forever on the verge of leaving, but never doing so" (9). Whyte's audience is the well-educated lay reader.

3. Whyte compares the soapboxers' conversations to fencing moves ("thrust and counterthrust," "advances," "gives way," "flourish"). The description is much more visual with this metaphor, and it helps Whyte make his point about the "cooperative antagonism" (20) that he says soapboxers display.

Writing Tasks

1. Describe the typical behavior of people in an ordinary scene you might encounter daily—people boarding buses, riding elevators, standing in lines, waiting at stoplights, or children in a playground. Remain objective and describe at least three typical behaviors people exhibit in this scene.

2. Take the part of a person in the scene you described in task 1. Combining narration and description, write an essay in which you create the scene subjectively, as a participant. How does this description differ from the first, objective one?

❦ Barry Lopez ❦

Barry Lopez, born in New York state in 1945, spent most of his childhood in Southern California. He studied at the University of Notre Dame and the University of Oregon and has been a full-time writer since 1970. An authority on natural history and the environment, he has contributed numerous articles and essays to anthologies and national publications. He also writes short stories, which have been collected in two volumes. His best-known nonfiction works are Of Wolves and Men *(1978), a book that grew out of an article assignment for* Smithsonian, *and* Arctic Dreams: Imagination and Desire in a Northern Landscape *(1986), for which he received the National Book Award. His latest book is a collection of essays,* Crossing Open Ground *(1988).*

The Stone Horse

Lopez is known for the moral and philosophical messages he draws from his observations of nature. In this selection, which is Part II of the essay "The Stone Horse," from Crossing Open Ground, *Lopez brings a naturalist's powers of observation to bear in studying an archaeological artifact. Describing his visit to the "stone horse," however, his thoughts run to history, language, and the pace of modern life.*

TEACHING SUGGESTIONS

This essay densely compacts the Spanish history of the Americas, and includes sidelights on other historical facts. Spurred by the sight of the horse, Lopez contemplates time as it is mirrored in art—in this essay, the "primitive" art of a sophisticated culture.

His descriptions trigger his vast historical knowledge, and as he traces the lines of the horse, a line of history unfolds in his reverie. He demonstrates that a description of art can also describe culture, depending on the observer's experience.

You might begin by wondering aloud if some facsimile of an artifact like the one Lopez describes best represents part of this country's modern history, since about 1970. Do we have a piece of art, a building, or a site in this community, this county or parish, this state, or somewhere else in this country, which captures a part of our history in the last twenty years or so?

After students select three or four "artifacts," ask how they react imaginatively to history as it is represented by their chosen objects. What do our modern monuments suggest about us? After discussing that question for a while, they begin to see how reality can provoke imagination. Then they are ready to see how far Lopez can carry this notion.

A BLM archaeologist told me, with understandable reluctance, where to find the intaglio. I spread my Automobile Club of Southern California map of Imperial County out on his desk, and he traced the route with a pink felt-tip pen. The line crossed Interstate 8 and then turned west along the Mexican border.

"You can't drive any farther than about here," he said, marking a small X. "There's boulders in the wash. You walk up past them."

On a separate piece of paper he drew a route in a smaller scale that would take me up the arroyo to a certain point where I

1

MARGINAL NOTES

The Bureau of Land Management (BLM) is part of the U.S. Department of the Interior.

2   In archeology, an intaglio is an emblem, a figure, or a design that is carved or engraved into hard material so that it is below the surface.

3   In southern California, Imperial County borders Arizona on the east and Mexico on the south.

141

"arroyo": A dry gully that turns into a rivulet or stream after a substantial rain.

With a population of 24,000, this town in Imperial County is about ten miles from the Mexican border.

Many who study symbols historically have long been aware that the horse had an important part in many ancient rites. More recently, the psychologist Jung asserted that the horse expresses "the mother within us"; that is, intuitive understanding.

Lopez himself alludes to intuition in this paragraph.

was to cross back east, to another arroyo. At its head, on higher ground just to the north, I would find the horse.

"It's tough to spot unless you know it's there. Once you pick it up . . ." He shook his head slowly, in a gesture of wonder at its existence. 4

I waited until I held his eye. I assured him I would not tell anyone else how to get there. He looked at me with stoical despair, like a man who had been robbed twice, whose belief in human beings was offered without conviction. 5

I did not go until the following day because I wanted to see it at dawn. I ate breakfast at four A.M. in El Centro and then drove south. The route was easy to follow, though the last section of road proved difficult, broken and drifted over with sand in some spots. I came to the barricade of boulders and parked. It was light enough by then to find my way over the ground with little trouble. The contours of the landscape were stark, without any masking vegetation. I worried only about rattlesnakes. 6

I traversed the stone plain as directed, but, in spite of the frankness of the land, I came on the horse unawares. In the first moment of recognition I was without feeling. I recalled later being startled, and that I held my breath. It was laid out on the ground with its head to the east, three times life size. As I took in its outline I felt a growing concentration of all my senses, as though my attentiveness to the pale rose color of the morning sky and other peripheral images had now ceased to be important. I was aware that I was straining for sound in the windless air, and I felt the uneven pressure of the earth hard against my feet. The horse, outlined in a standing profile on the dark ground, was as vivid before me as a bed of tulips. 7

I've come upon animals suddenly before, and felt a similar tension, a precipitate heightening of the senses. And I have felt the inexplicable but sharply boosted intensity of a wild moment in the bush, where it is not until some minutes later that you discover the source of electricity—the warm remains of a grizzly bear kill, or the still moist tracks of a wolverine. 8

But this was slightly different. I felt I had stepped into an unoccupied corridor. I had no familiar sense of history, the 9 temporal structure in which to think: this horse was made by Quechan people three hundred years ago. I felt instead a headlong rush of images: people hunting wild horses with spears on the Pleistocene veld of southern California; Cortés riding across the causeway into Montezuma's Tenochtitlán; a short-legged Comanche, astride his horse like some sort of ferret, slashing through cavalry lines of young men who rode like farmers; a hoof exploding past my face one morning in a corral in Wyoming. These images had the weight and silence of stone.

When I released my breath, the images softened. My initial feeling, of facing a wild animal in a remote region, was replaced with a calm sense of antiquity. It was then that I became conscious, like an ordinary tourist, of what was before me, and thought: this horse was probably laid out by Quechan people. But when? I wondered. The first horses they saw, I knew, might have been those that came north from Mexico in 1692 with Father Eusebio Kino. But Cocopa people, I recalled, also came this far north on occasion, to fight with their neighbors, the Quechan. And *they* could have seen horses with Melchior Díaz, at the mouth of the Colorado River in the fall of 1540. So, it could be four hundred years old. (No one in fact knows.)

I still had not moved. I took my eyes off the horse for a moment to look south over the desert plain into Mexico, to look east past its head at the brightening sunrise, to situate myself. Then, finally, I brought my trailing foot slowly forward and stood erect. Sunlight was running like a thin sheet of water over the stony ground and it threw the horse into relief. It looked as though no hand had ever disturbed the stones that gave it its form.

The horse had been brought to life on ground called desert pavement, a tight, flat matrix of small cobbles blasted smooth by sand-laden winds. The uniform, monochromatic blackness of the stones, a patina of iron and magnesium oxides called desert varnish, is caused by long-term exposure to the sun. To make this type of low-relief ground glyph, or intaglio, the artist either selectively turns individual stones over to their lighter side or removes areas of stone to expose the lighter soil underneath, creating a negative image. This horse, about eighteen feet from brow to rump

10

11

12

Possibly related to South American Indian tribes dominant in the former Inca Empire, which flourished 1438–1538.

During the Pleistocene Era, great glaciers covered much of northern North America. Modern human beings are said to have appeared late in the Pleistocene, from 600,000 to 12,000 years ago.

Hernando Cortés (1485–1547) was the Spaniard who conquered Mexico. He held Montezuma hostage. After Montezuma died in 1520, Cortés led his soldiers and allies out of the city following severe fighting.

Montezuma II (1480?–1520) was Aztec emperor at the time of the Spanish conquest. Tenochtitlán was his capital, on the site of today's Mexico City.

The Comanche were UtoAztecan American Indians, who ranged from Nebraska's Platte River to the Mexican border.

Father Eusebio Kino (1645?–1711) was a Jesuit missionary to Indians in land that is now northern Mexico and southern Arizona (1687–1711).

The Colorado River separates southern California's Imperial County and Arizona's Yuma County.

A glyph is a pictograph or other symbolic character, especially when it is cut into a surface or carved in relief.

and eight feet from withers to hoof, had been made in the latter way, and its outline was bermed at certain points with low ridges of stone a few inches high to enhance its three-dimensional qualities. (The left side of the horse was in full profile; each leg was extended at 90 degrees to the body and fully visible, as though seen in three-quarter profile.)

A berm is an edge or a shoulder, most commonly along paved roads.

I was not eager to move. The moment I did I would be back 13 in the flow of time, the horse no longer quivering in the same way before me. I did not want to feel again the sequence of quotidian events—to be drawn off into deliberation and analysis. A human being, a four-footed animal, the open land. That was all that was present—and a "thoughtless" understanding of the very old desires bearing on this particular animal: to hunt it, to render it, to fathom it, to subjugate it, to honor it, to take it as a companion.

Events that are ordinary, normal, and recurring. Lopez wants to remain where he is, musing on wide swaths of history, instead of returning to the logical, analytical world of the archeologist.

What finally made me move was the light. The sun now filled 14 the shallow basin of the horse's body. The weighted line of the stone berm created the illusion of a mane and the distinctive roundness of an equine belly. The change in definition impelled me. I moved to the left, circling past its rump, to see how the light might flesh the horse out from various points of view. I circled it completely before squatting on my haunches. Ten or fifteen minutes later I chose another view. The third time I moved, to a point near the rear hooves, I spotted a stone tool at my feet. I stared at it a long while, more in awe than disbelief, before reaching out to pick it up. I turned it over in my left palm and took it between my fingers to feel its cutting edge. It is always difficult, especially with something so portable, to rechannel the desire to steal.

Lopez studies the horse carefully from every angle. He finds the ancient stone tool and decides it is ethical to leave it at the site.

I spent several hours with the horse. As I changed positions 15 and as the angle of the light continued to change I noticed a number of things. The angle at which the pastern carried the hoof away from the ankle was perfect. Also, stones had been placed within the image to suggest at precisely the right spot the left shoulder above the foreleg. The line that joined thigh and hock was similarly accurate. The muzzle alone seemed distorted—but perhaps these stones had been moved by a later hand. It was an admirably accurate representation, but not what a breeder would

"pastern": The part of a horse's foot just above the hoof.

"hock": The joint in the hind leg of a horse, which bends backward.

call perfect conformation. There was the suggestion of a bowed neck and an undershot jaw, and the tail, as full as a winter coyote's, did not appear to be precisely to scale.

The more I thought about it, the more I felt I was looking at an individual horse, a unique combination of generic and specific detail. It was easy to imagine one of Kino's horses as a model, or a horse that ran off from one of Coronado's columns. What kind of horses would these have been? I wondered. In the sixteenth century the most sought-after horses in Europe were Spanish, the offspring of Arabian stock and Barbary horses that the Moors brought to Iberia and bred to the older, eastern European strains brought in by the Romans. The model for this horse, I speculated, could easily have been a palomino, or a descendant of horses trained for lion hunting in North Africa.

A few generations ago, cowboys, cavalry quartermasters, and draymen would have taken this horse before me under consideration and not let up their scrutiny until they had its heritage fixed to their satisfaction. Today, the distinction between draft and harness horses is arcane knowledge, and no image may come to mind for a blue roan or a claybank horse. The loss of such refinement in everyday conversation leaves me unsettled. People praise the Eskimo's ability to distinguish among forty types of snow but forget the skill of others who routinely differentiate between overo and tobiano pintos. Such distinctions are made for the same reason. You have to do it to be able to talk clearly about the world.

For parts of two years I worked as a horse wrangler and packer in Wyoming. It is dim knowledge now; I would have to think to remember if a buckskin was a kind of dun horse. And I couldn't throw a double-diamond hitch over a set of panniers— the packer's basic tie-down—without guidance. As I squatted there in the desert, however, these more personal memories seemed tenuous in comparison with the sweep of this animal in human time. My memories had no depth. I thought of the Hittite cavalry riding against the Syrians 3,500 years ago. And the first of the Chinese emperors, Ch'in Shih Huang, buried in Shensi Province in 210 B.C. with thousands of life-size horses and soldiers, a terra-cotta guardian army. What could I know of what was in the mind of whoever made this horse? Was there some

16

17

18

The Barbary Coast is the coastal region between Egypt and the Atlantic Ocean, inhabited chiefly by Berbers, the Muslim people of North Africa. The so-called Barbary Moors are Muslims of mixed Arab and Berber descent, living in Northwest Africa. Muslims settled in Spain, beginning in A.D. eighth century. The Iberian Peninsula comprises Spain and Portugal.

"distinction": Lopez makes the interesting point that differentiations help us to think clearly. Reflects the Whorfian hypothesis, after Benjamin Whorf, who maintained that the language a culture uses determines its perception of the world.

"panniers": Basketlike containers hung across the back of a donkey or horse.

The Hittites rode through Mesopotamia, an ancient country, now a part of Iraq, between the lower Tigris and Euphrates rivers. Horses were known there as early as the twenty-first century B.C. The Hittite cavalry horses were often clad in mail.

"Ch'in Shih Huang": This Chinese emperor was buried in full battle regalia and with a retinue of thousands. His magnificent burial ground was discovered and excavated in the 1980s.

A Spanish explorer (1735–1788) born in Fronteras, Mexico, who founded San Francisco in 1776; also governed New Mexico, 1777–1788. "Sinaloa" is a Mexican state along the Gulf of California. "Alta California" covers approximately modern San Diego to San Francisco."El Camino Real" is "The Royal (or regal) Road," from Mexico through northern California, marked at intervals by old Spanish Catholic missions. *Los primitivos* are, literally, "the primitive [people]."

Ponce de León (1527–1591), Spanish governor of Puerto Rico, discovered Florida on Easter Sunday, 1513. The Spanish word *Florida* means "flowery Easter," or "feast of flowers."

"bajada": An alluvial plain at the base of a mountain; results from gradual depositing of sand or clay by moving water.

"ocotillo": A spiny, woody shrub having a tight cluster of red flowers at the tip of each branch.

racial memory of it as an animal that had once fed the artist's ancestors and then disappeared from North America? And then returned in this strange alliance with another race of men?

Certainly, whoever it was, the artist had observed the animal very closely. Certainly the animal's speed had impressed him. Among the first things the Quechan would have learned from an encounter with Kino's horses was that their own long-distance runners—men who could run down mule deer—were no match for this animal.

From where I squatted I could look far out over the Mexican plain. Juan Bautista de Anza passed this way in 1774, extending El Camino Real into Alta California from Sinaloa. He was followed by others, all of them astride the magical horse: *gente de razón,* the people of reason, coming into the country of *los primitivos.* The horse, like the stone animals of Egypt, urged these memories upon me. And as I drew them up from some forgotten corner of my mind—huge horses carved in the white chalk downs of southern England by an Iron Age people; Spanish horses rearing and wheeling in fear before alligators in Florida—the images seemed tethered before me. With this sense of proportion, a memory of my own—the morning I almost lost my face to a horse's hoof—now had somewhere to fit.

I rose up and began to walk slowly around the horse again. I had taken the first long measure of it and was now looking for a way to depart, a new angle of light, a fading of the image itself before the rising sun, that would break its hold on me. As I circled, feeling both heady and serene at the encounter, I realized again how strangely vivid it was. It had been created on a barren bajada between two arroyos, as nondescript a place as one could imagine. The only plant life here was a few wands of ocotillo cactus. The ground beneath my shoes was so hard it wouldn't take the print of a heavy animal even after a rain. The only sounds I heard were the voices of quail.

The archaeologist had been correct. For all its forcefulness, the horse is inconspicuous. If you don't care to see it you can walk right past it. That pleases him, I think. Unmarked on this bleak shoulder of the plain, the site signals to no one; so he wants no protective fences here, no informative plaque, to act as beacons. He would rather take a chance that no motorcyclist, no aimless wanderer with a flair for violence and a depth of ignorance, will ever find his way here.

The archaeologist had given me something before I left his office that now seemed peculiar—an aerial photograph of the horse. It is widely believed that an aerial view of an intaglio provides a fair and accurate depiction. It does not. In the photograph the horse looks somewhat crudely constructed; from the ground it appears far more deftly rendered. The photograph is of a single moment, and in that split second the horse seems vaguely impotent. I watched light pool in the intaglio at dawn; I imagine you could watch it withdraw at dusk and sense the same animation I did. In those prolonged moments its shape and so, too, its general character changed—noticeably. The living quality of the image, its immediacy to the eye, was brought out by the light-in-time, not, at least here, in the camera's frozen instant.

Intaglios, I thought, were never meant to be seen by gods in the sky above. They were meant to be seen by people on the ground, over a long period of shifting light. This could even be true of the huge figures on the Plain of Nazca in Peru, where people could walk for the length of a day beside them. It is our own impatience that leads us to think otherwise.

This process of abstraction, almost unintentional, drew me gradually away from the horse. I came to a position of attention at the edge of the sphere of its influence. With a slight bow I paid my respects to the horse, its maker, and the history of us all, and departed.

23 Ecologists of this region in southern California often voice alarm about motorcyclists' races through the desert, upsetting its delicate ecological balance. Deserts are fragile even though they look formidable.

Lopez remarks that photographs freeze time, but imagination causes time to flow. Images change in the mind as well as in reality, as the sun passes slowly over the land.

24 The Plain of Nazca, in southwestern Peru, had many remarkable, gigantic figures, of which only fragments remain. They were formed by pre-Incan people; that is, well before the fifteenth century.

25 Lopez turns from musing on the histories of various peoples, the result of his being with the horse, to face his own future.

Meaning and Purpose

1. Lopez mixes his description of the stone horse with history and personal experience. What dominant impression does the mixture create?

POSSIBLE ANSWERS

Meaning and Purpose

1. Lopez is in awe of the stone horse as a work of art (12, 15), and sees it as a connection between himself as an individual and the history of settlement in the area (9). The dominant impression is that the horse captures the past and the "sweep of this animal in human time" (18). Another impression is that Lopez knows a lot about horses and the history of the Southwest.

2. Lopez "came on the horse unawares" (7) and so wasn't prepared to react. He takes in the shape of the horse as his senses respond gradually. It's as if he froze for a moment before the horse "was as vivid before me as a bed of tulips" (7).

3. Lopez means that art is meant to be experienced close up, not observed from a perspective that the artist could not have considered when creating it. Lopez thinks we are too impatient to bother with first-hand experience of art, and so we find easy ways, such as taking aerial photos.

4. Lopez tells readers that there are rattlesnakes in the desert (7); the ground under the horse was "desert pavement" (12); the only plant life "was a few wands of ocotillo cactus" on "a barren bajada between two arroyos"; the ground wouldn't take a heavy imprint even when wet (21); and motorcyclists sometimes disturb and destroy the desert (22).

5. The vocabulary describes art, the desert, and horses. Lopez assumes his readers are somewhat knowledgeable about these subjects, or that they can infer meanings from context.

6. Lopez leaves the stone tool there because he respects its antiquity and realizes that it is an inseparable part of the horse and the setting.

Strategy

1. The first five paragraphs locate the stone horse exactly and tell a little about the landscape—"There's boulders in the wash" (2). They also create a little mystery that heightens readers' interest about what Lopez is planning to do.

2. Lopez takes the reader on a visual tour of the horse that is easy to follow.

3. Some words that indicate the passage of seconds are "In the first moment of recognition" (7); "I felt . . . a headlong rush of images" (9);

2. Why do you think Lopez "was without feeling" (7) when he first saw the horse?

3. Reread paragraphs 24 and 25 with the assumption that Lopez is making an indirect comment on experience. What does Lopez mean? If the intaglio of the horse cannot be fully appreciated by looking at a photograph, can an actual horse be appreciated by looking at the intaglio?

4. What have you learned about the desert by reading "The Stone Horse"?

5. Judging from the vocabulary, what audience do you think Lopez is writing to?

6. Why doesn't Lopez take the stone tool (14)?

Strategy

1. Lopez recounts his conversation with the archeologist in the first five paragraphs. Why does he begin there, instead of with the beginning of his journey in paragraph 6?

2. Describe the spatial arrangement, or the order of details, in the descriptions in paragraphs 12 and 15. How easy is it for your eyes to follow the descriptions?

3. Paragraphs 6–14 take place in a moment. What are the phrases and sentences that indicate only seconds have passed?

4. This essay is a narrative as well as a description. How does Lopez weave the two together? Give examples of passages that illustrate both rhetorical strategies.

Style

1. Describe Lopez's tone. Find some passages that illustrate the tone.

2. Identify some similes and metaphors in the essay.

3. If necessary, check a dictionary for the meaning of these words: *intaglio* (1); *arroyo* (3); *stoical* (5); *peripheral* (7); *veld, ferret* (9);

glyph (12); *quotidian* (13); *arcane* (17); *tenuous* (18); *bajada* (22).

Writing Tasks

1. Write a passage describing a painting, photograph, or sculpture. First study the work carefully, making notes on its appearance and your responses. Then describe the work, choosing an order for the eye to follow and expressing the range of your responses to it.

2. Using figures of speech and visual images, describe an abstraction such as love, or respect, or humiliation, in a paragraph.

"When I released my breath" (10); "I still had not moved" (11); "I was not eager to move" (17); "What finally made me move" (14).

4. Lopez keeps a sense of forward movement in his narrative even as he stops to describe what he sees and thinks. Some examples of the mixed narration and description: he talks to the archeologist and describes the area at the same time (1–5); he moves around the horse to describe it (14); he recalls his years as a "horse wrangler," and keeps the narrative moving with "as I squatted there in the desert" (18); he describes the horse and the desert in a different light and says, "I rose up and began to walk slowly around the horse again" (21).

Style

1. The tone is one of respect—"The more I thought about it, the more I felt I was looking at an individual horse, a unique combination of generic and specific detail" (16)—and wonder—"I felt I had stepped into an unoccupied corridor. I had no familiar sense of history, the temporal structure in which to think: this horse was made by Quechan people three hundred years ago" (9).

2. One metaphor is "These images had the weight and silence of stone" (9). Some similes are: "like a man who had been robbed twice" (5); "as vivid before me as a bed of tulips" (7); "a short-legged Comanche, astride his horse like some kind of ferret" (9); and "Sunlight was running like a thin sheet of water" (11).

3. The definitions are *intaglio,* in archeology, an emblem, figure, or design carved or engraved into hard material beneath a surface; *arroyo,* a dry gully that turns into a rivulet or stream after a rain; *stoical,* firmly restraining a response; *peripheral,* the outer part of a field of vision; *veld,* a grassland; *ferret,* an active and persistent searcher; *glyph,* a pictograph or symbolic character cut or carved into a surface; *quotidian,* occurring every day; *arcane,* mysterious; *tenuous,* flimsy or weak; *bajada,* an alluvial plain (resulting from gradual depositing of sand or clay by moving water) at the base of a mountain.

❦ Additional Writing Tasks ❦
Description

1. Recall a spot you visited when younger, not far from your home. It should be a place you remember well but not one you visit constantly. Once you have selected the spot, draw upon your strength of recollection: visualize yourself in this place, seeing the physical features, hearing the sounds, and smelling the odors and aromas. Jot down your memories. What details do you recall, and in what order of importance? Record your memories just as the place was at that time in your life. How would you tell what you saw if you were describing the scene for a stranger? Which details would create images in this stranger's mind? Try to write this part of the description from a child's perspective.

    Once you have described the place as you recall it, write a description of how the place appears now, after years have passed. This part of the description should be done from an adult's perspective. Perhaps the place has not held up under time's pressure. Perhaps your view of it has changed. Perhaps you colored this place with romantic illusions.

    Once the second rough description is completed, begin the first draft. Develop a structure that shifts between past and present, revealing both the child's and the adult's attitude.

2. Select several photographs that represent milestones in your life. Describe them as if you were a reporter relating the events that are taking place in the photo. Keep your description objective but vivid. Or, if you wish, use several magazine ads as the basis for a description. Here, too, describe the events in the advertisement objectively, merely reporting the image you see on the page, not interpreting it.

3. Describe an animal you have encountered, perhaps a wild animal such as a coyote, wolf, deer, bear, or whale. Begin with a description of the animal from folklore, which will probably require a visit to the library. Then follow with a description of the animal as you experienced it. Seek a connection between the two elements in this description.

150

4. Do something slightly out of the ordinary and describe the experience. Perhaps you will climb a tree and sit among the branches. Maybe you will sit in a closed closet for half an hour. You might roller skate, stand on your head, dance a waltz, lie on the grass and stare at the clouds—the possibilities are endless. Once you have had the experience, describe it in detail.

5. Select a physical event and describe it in detail: the fog rolling through the woods or city streets; a storm gathering in the distance and sweeping toward you; a cloudburst; wind roaring through the trees and rattling the windows; an earthquake. In your description capture a sense of motion, sound, and smell, as well as visual detail.

6. Describe people at work in various settings:

    A supermarket
    A fast-food restaurant
    A newsstand
    A factory
    A car wash
    A pizza parlor

In your description create a dominant impression.

3

Examples

Illustrating Ideas

The Method

Examples bring the vague and abstract down to earth. They clarify the historian's lectures. They make concrete the philosopher's abstractions. They electrify the politician's arguments. By using examples effectively you will not only help your readers understand your point, but you will also improve your chances of holding their attention because vivid, concrete examples can make your writing more interesting to read.

Examples are much used, even in everyday conversation. If someone claims that advertisers use fear of rejection to manipulate consumers, you might say, "Show me."

Examples such as these would follow: "What about those mouthwash commercials? One actually shows a salesman rejected because he has bad breath. And then after a quick rinse, Presto! he makes the sale, and the customer drives away smiling. And what about the commercial that shows a young female banker passed over for a promotion? A wiser, older colleague whispers in her ear. In the next scene she is scrubbing her head with the advertiser's shampoo, and the commercial closes with the smiling banker now managing her own department."

The speaker is using examples to clarify the general observation that advertisers use fear of rejection to manipulate consumers into buying their products. Writers use examples with the same intent—to illustrate a generalization; that is, to select one thing from many to represent the *whole*. In fact, the word *example* derives from the Latin *exemplum,* which refers to "one thing selected from the many." Examples used to represent ideas are essential to clear communication because they give readers something concrete to visualize. It might be difficult for a reader to understand what social critic Jack Solomon means by this statement:

> No matter how you look at it, in the scant space of some forty years, television has revolutionized our lives. First introduced as a novelty alternative to radio, television has rapidly evolved into the most profound invention of the age. Nothing is immune from its influence.

For the sake of clarity, Solomon immediately provides several examples to illustrate his idea for the reader:

> Politicians play for the cameras, and so do international terrorists. Physicians call news conferences, and judges host courtroom dramas. Television, through its hyping of the Olympic Games, has transformed sport into politics and

politics into sport, treating everything from presidential elections to military conflicts as prime-time entertainment. What is not televised is hardly thought of at all in a world in which television creates reality as much as it records.

These examples add clarity to Solomon's statement. Without them the reader would have only a vague understanding of Solomon's point in this paragraph, which would amount to a slip in communication.

Strategies

Professional writers use three kinds of examples—specific, typical, and hypothetical—to support their ideas. They can be used in any combination and are often mixed within one paragraph.

Specific Examples

Specific examples capture an experience, event, incident, or fact. Banesh Hoffman, in "My Friend, Albert Einstein," uses a specific example (an **anecdote**) to support the general comment that the essence of Einstein's personality was simplicity.

> He was one of the greatest scientists the world has ever known, yet if I had to convey the essence of Albert Einstein in a single word, I would choose *simplicity*. Perhaps an anecdote will help. Once, caught in a downpour, he took off his hat and held it under his coat. Asked why, he explained, with admirable logic, that the rain would damage the hat, but his hair would be none the worse for its wetting. This knack for going instinctively to the heart of the matter was the secret of his major scientific discoveries.

Hoffman selects this specific example with a clear purpose in mind. He wants to make concrete the generalization in the topic sentence. The example is vivid and interesting, capturing Einstein's essence.

Hoffman's specific example illustrating Einstein's simplicity is a short narrative, but writers often shape examples in other ways. Sometimes the writer will use several specific examples in one paragraph. A series of brief examples might function like verbal snapshots, freezing in time several events or experiences. In this paragraph, naturalist Jane van Lawick-Goodall uses seven short visual examples to illustrate social behavior among the chimpanzees she studied in Tanzania.

> While many details of their [the chimpanzees'] social behavior were hidden from me by the foliage, I did get occasional fascinating glimpses. I saw one female, newly arrived in a group, hurry up to a big male and hold her hand toward him. Almost regally he reached out, clasped her hand in his, drew it toward him, and kissed it with his lips. I saw two adult males embrace each other in greeting. I saw youngsters having wild games through treetops, chasing around after each other or jumping again and again, one after the other, from a branch to a springy bough below. I watched small infants dangling happily by themselves for minutes on end, patting at their toes with one hand, rotating gently from side to side. Once two tiny infants pulled on opposite ends of a twig in a gentle tug-of-war. Often during the heat of midday or after a long spell of feeding, I saw two or more adults grooming each other, carefully looking through the hair of their companions.

Sometimes writers will create a *list* or a *catalogue* of specific examples to illustrate their observations. In this paragraph from *The Distant Mirror,* historian Barbara Tuchman catalogues how people in fourteenth-century England might imagine the distant places they had heard of but never seen.

> Faraway lands, however—India, Persia, and beyond— were seen through a gauze of fabulous fairy tales revealing

an occasional nugget of reality: forests so high they touch the clouds, horned pygmies who move in herds and grow old in seven years, brahmins who kill themselves on funeral pyres, men with dogs' heads and six toes, "cyclopeans" with only one eye and one foot who move as fast as the wind, the "monoceros" which can be caught only when it sleeps in the lap of a virgin, Amazons whose tears are of silver, panthers who practice the caesarean operation with their own claws, trees whose leaves supply wool, snakes 300 feet long, snakes with precious stones for eyes, snakes who so love music that for prudence they stop up one ear with their tail.

Tuchman's and Goodall's paragraphs also illustrate another point: examples can come from various sources. Tuchman finds her specific examples by researching historical documents; Goodall gets hers by observing chimpanzees in their natural habitat. Both writers use their examples for the same purpose, however: to illustrate a general observation.

Typical Examples

In contrast to specific examples, writers compose **typical examples** by generalizing from many experiences, events, incidents, or facts. Consider this paragraph from Jonathan Kozol's essay "The Human Cost of an Illiterate Society." Kozol uses a typical example to develop the point that illiterates, people who cannot read, lead a precarious existence, even when they are in the care of professionals trained to provide for their health. As you read Kozol's paragraph, keep in mind that this typical example represents the experience of many people, not that of one specific person.

Illiterates live, in more than literal ways, an uninsured existence. They cannot understand written details on a health insurance form. They cannot read the waivers that they sign preceding surgical procedures. Several women

I have known in Boston have entered a slum hospital with the intention of obtaining a tubal ligation and have emerged a few days later after having been subjected to a hysterectomy. Unaware of their rights, incognizant of jargon, intimidated by the unfamiliar air of fear and atmosphere of ether that so many of us find oppressive in the confines even of the most attractive and expensive medical facilities, they have signed their names to documents they could not read and which nobody, in the hectic situation that prevails so often in those overcrowded hospitals that serve the urban poor, had even bothered to explain.

Kozol begins with a general statement that establishes the dangers illiterate patients face. He follows with two sentences of background: illiterate patients cannot understand insurance forms or the legal documents that give away their rights during surgery. He then supports his general statement with an extended typical example, thus illustrating, even dramatizing, the result of being unable to read: several illiterate Boston women signed papers permitting hysterectomies when they wanted tubal ligations.

Typical examples, as Kozol's illustrates, are composites of many experiences. They are not rooted in specific times but compiled after many observations over an extended period. In the next paragraph cultural anthropologist Edward T. Hall uses typical examples developed after extended observation to illustrate how people react when their sense of space is violated:

People are very sensitive to any intrusion into their spatial bubble. If someone stands too close to you, your first instinct is to back up. If that's not possible, you lean away and pull yourself in, tensing your muscles. If an intruder doesn't respond to these body signals, you may then try to protect yourself, using a briefcase, umbrella, or raincoat. Women—especially when traveling alone—often plant their pocketbook in such a way that no one can get very close to them. As a last resort, you may move to another spot and position yourself behind a desk or a chair that provides screening. Everyone tries to adjust the space around himself in a way that's comfortable for him; most often, he does this unconsciously.

Hypothetical Examples

Sometimes writers create **hypothetical examples** from their imagination. Hypothetical examples are similar to typical examples, usually composed from bits and pieces of experience or information. Often a writer will use a hypothetical example where something concrete is needed to tie down an abstraction and no *actual* example is available. In the opening paragraph of *The White Album*, essayist and novelist Joan Didion uses hypothetical examples to illustrate why stories are important in life.

> We *tell* ourselves stories in order to live. The princess is caged in a consulate. The man with candy will lead the children to the sea. The naked woman on the ledge outside the window on the sixteenth floor is a victim of *accidie,* or the naked woman is an exhibitionist, and it would be "interesting" to know which. We *tell* ourselves that it makes some difference whether the naked woman is about to commit a mortal sin or is about to register a political protest or is about to be, the Aristophanic view, snatched back to the human condition by the fireman in priest's clothing just visible in the window behind her, the one smiling at the telephoto lens. We *look* for the sermon in the suicide, for the social or moral lesson in the murder of five. We *interpret* what we see, select the most workable of the multiple choices. We *live* entirely, especially if we are writers, by the imposition of a narrative line upon disparate images, by the "ideas" with which we have learned to freeze the shifting phantasmagoria which is our actual experience.

Didion has clearly drawn these brief examples from her imagination, yet they are effective because they make her observation more concrete. With these conjectures, she hopes to stir her readers' interest by appealing to typical experiences they might have encountered in fairy tales and newspapers, the mysterious experiences for which many seek explanations.

Mixing Examples

When studying professional writing, you'll notice that writers use different strategies to develop their examples. You'll find specific, typical, and hypothetical examples mixed, and you'll notice that sometimes examples illustrating one point will be presented in several paragraphs. In this passage from *No House Calls,* Peter Gott, a practicing physician and medical columnist, develops his point in several paragraphs and mixes examples with explanation to reveal the scientific facts behind the commercial claims of mouthwash and disinfectant companies.

> With people's increasing knowledge about bacteria, it was inevitable that some companies would, with success, try to play upon the fear that we have all developed about "bacterial infection." For instance, Listerine and Lysol are currently being advertised to produce "clean breath" and a clean environment, respectively, as a result of their bacteria-killing properties. While it is true that these compounds do, in fact, kill bacteria, the consumer would do well to demand more precision in evaluating their claims.
>
> As an example, the mouth contains billions of harmless bacteria. Some forms of bad breath are caused by bacterial decomposition of food between teeth. Listerine—and many other mouthwashes—will kill millions of bacteria on contact, but only a tiny proportion of the *total.* Furthermore, as soon as the Listerine has been spit out, billions of bacteria are reintroduced into the mouth during breathing and eating. So while the consumer's mouth will feel "fresh," in fact the bacterial count rapidly rises to "pretreatment" levels; essentially, nothing has been accomplished.
>
> Lysol spray when applied to surfaces will kill some bacteria, but most of these are nonpathogens and would do us no harm anyway. Bacteria that cause venereal disease die

quickly outside the body and would be unlikely to reside on public toilet seats long enough for the spray to make any difference. The Lysol spray will scent the air, however, and that seems to be the important consideration. Somehow, if we don't see or smell the germs, we assume they're all gone. The room must be safe. The evil has been repelled. We can take a shower.

Peter Gott's passage establishes an important principle to keep in mind: every writer, whether a professional writer or a student writer, must develop an eye for examples. The most effective way we know of developing that eye is to read critically; that is, read as a writer reads. Study how professional writers shape their examples. Study how their examples relate to their generalizations. And study the kinds of examples they develop.

Examples in College Writing

Examples are so effective in clarifying an idea that you will probably use them in every college essay you write. The following passage is from an essay written for a course on law and society. Rick Yocum, the student writer, illustrates how fans menace not only the "rich and famous" but also community leaders. In these three paragraphs, a significant part of the essay's discussion, Yocum uses varied examples to support his observations.

Yocum opens this passage by clearly stating his general observation.

He develops the paragraph with specific examples that remind readers of past attacks by fans on celebrities.

When increased public attention is placed on the lives of celebrities, disturbed fans often become dangerous menaces. For example, in 1980 Mark Chapman, a disturbed fan, murdered the former Beatle John Lennon; in 1981 John W. Hinckley Jr. stalked actress Jodie Foster before he tried to kill President Reagan; in 1988 a woman falsely claimed to be talk-show-host David Letterman's wife and kept trying to move into his home; in 1989 a delusional fan murdered Rebecca Schaeffer, star of the television series "My Sister Sam."

He opens the second paragraph by rephrasing his general observation and supporting it with one extended specific example.

Even more menacing were a fan's delusions involving actress Theresa Saldana. The man had traveled from Scotland under the belief that the two of them shared a common destiny and had to be "united." When he finally met the actress, he attacked her with a knife. She survived, and he was arrested and jailed. Even in prison his delusions continued. When he was about to be paroled, Saldana objected and prosecutors kept him in custody by filing new charges that he had threatened her from jail.

He opens this paragraph by shifting focus from "the rich and famous" to local leaders. With an extended hypothetical example he gives the reader an impression of how a typical case might develop.

People need not be among the very famous to be a target of such delusions. Typically, they could be local elected officials, such as county supervisors, council members, or aldermen. They could be teachers, community activists, or prominent business people. A typical case might develop as follows: Mr. Smith meets a well-known female attorney over a business matter. Although the meeting concentrates on his business concerns, Mr. Smith decides that she has fallen in love with him and he is in love with her. To recognize her love and declare his, he besieges her with telephone calls, love letters, and flowers. She is stunned, of course, and denies any interest in Mr. Smith, finally filing harassment charges with the police. He interprets her reactions as a "test of love." He soon leaves his wife and abandons his business to pursue the lawyer. When she continues to rebuff his advances, he sends threatening letters and

> demands to see her. The next step is diffi-
> cult to predict: he could become violent, or
> he could be committed to psychiatric care.
> From any angle, the situation is menacing.

Yocum has carefully selected and mixed his examples to represent his general observation—a series of brief examples that catalogue recent assaults by fans on celebrities, an extended example about a highly dramatic attack, and an extended hypothetical example that illustrates a typical situation a local celebrity might face. He has met one of his primary obligations as a writer: his examples clearly represent his general observation. These examples also take away any confusion a reader might have about his meaning and they add interest to his essay. Why does Yocum use a hypothetical example instead of a victim's actual experience as he does with celebrities? If you think about the subject, you will realize that fewer assaults on local leaders than on celebrities are recorded. Yocum must therefore create a hypothetical example from reports to nail down his general observation. Yocum's use of examples is very effective: they will probably convince the reader that he knows what he's talking about.

As you read the essays in this section, you will see that there is no one way of developing examples. Sometimes a writer will use a single extended example. At other times, a writer will combine short and extended examples, specific and typical examples, and include personal observations and background information.

Sometimes examples will serve as the dominant pattern of development, but, like narration and description, examples also function in essays with other dominant patterns, such as comparison and contrast, cause and effect, classification, and argumentation. Always, however, writers use examples with one fundamental purpose in mind: *to make the general more specific and the abstract more concrete.*

❦ Lewis Thomas ❦

Lewis Thomas, born in 1913, studied at Princeton University and Harvard Medical School. He has had a distinguished career as research pathologist, medical doctor, biologist, professor, and writer, but is best known for his collections of essays, many of which first appeared in the New England Journal of Medicine. *He has been a professor of pathology and medicine at the Cornell University Medical School and has served as both president and chief executive officer of the Memorial Sloan-Kettering Cancer Center in New York City. His first collection,* Notes of a Biology Watcher: The Lives of a Cell *(1975), won the National Book Award and was followed by* More Notes of a Biology Watcher: The Medusa and the Snail *(1979).*

On Natural Death

In this short essay from The Medusa and the Snail, *Lewis Thomas invites the reader to consider a new way of thinking about death. His examples are taken from his own observations and from medical research, from the professional realm as well as the personal, from the extraordinary and the mundane.*

There are so many new books about dying that there are now special shelves set aside for them in bookshops, along with the health-diet and home-repair paperbacks and the sex manuals. Some of them are so packed with detailed information and step-by-step instructions for performing the function that you'd think this was a new sort of skill which all of us are now required to learn. The strongest impression the casual reader gets, leafing through, is that proper dying has become an extraordinary, even an exotic experience, something only the specially trained get to do.

1

164

Also, you could be led to believe that we are the only creatures capable of the awareness of death, that when all the rest of nature is being cycled through dying, one generation after another, it is a different kind of process, done automatically and trivially, more "natural," as we say.

An elm in our backyard caught the blight this summer and dropped stone dead, leafless, almost overnight. One weekend it was a normal-looking elm, maybe a little bare in spots but nothing alarming, and the next weekend it was gone, passed over, departed, taken. Taken is right, for the tree surgeon came by yesterday with his crew of young helpers and their cherry picker, and took it down branch by branch and carted it off in the back of a red truck, everyone singing.

The dying of a field mouse, at the jaws of an amiable household cat, is a spectacle I have beheld many times. It used to make me wince. Early in life I gave up throwing sticks at the cat to make him drop the mouse, because the dropped mouse regularly went ahead and died anyway, but I always shouted unaffections at the cat to let him know the sort of animal he had become. Nature, I thought, was an abomination.

Recently I've done some thinking about that mouse, and I wonder if his dying is necessarily all that different from the passing of our elm. The main difference, if there is one, would be in the matter of pain. I do not believe that an elm tree has pain receptors, and even so, the blight seems to me a relatively painless way to go even if there were nerve endings in a tree, which there are not. But the mouse dangling tail-down from the teeth of a gray cat is something else again, with pain beyond bearing, you'd think, all over his small body.

There are now some plausible reasons for thinking it is not like that at all, and you can make up an entirely different story about the mouse and his dying if you like. At the instant of being trapped and penetrated by teeth, peptide hormones are released by cells in the hypothalamus and the pituitary gland; instantly these substances, called endorphins, are attached to the surface of other cells responsible for pain perception; the hormones have

2   Thomas points out that we consider deaths of people to be "special" but deaths in nature "natural," part of a recycling. You might ask your students if nature has "special" deaths. Remind them that we have pet cemeteries, which suggest that we value some animals more than others.

3   A specific example. Thomas's elm tree was "taken" in two senses. "Taken" is a euphemism for "died," and in the literal sense the tree was "carted off." This might be a good time to ask students to think of other expressions we use to describe death, such as "passed away" and "moved on." Ask why we don't simply say "They died," when we talk about people we knew.

4   A typical example comparing the death of an animal to that of a tree. Because the mouse, unlike the tree, has pain receptors, it must feel pain before it dies (but maybe not *just* before it dies, as the author explains in paragraph 6). The death of an animal seems horrid, compared to that of a tree. This comparison prepares us for later discussion of human deaths.

5

6   Thomas uses clinical words to explain the mouse's absence of pain. He elevates (or reduces) the immediate pain before death to a scientific description. This cold, clinical analysis lacks emotional appeal. Then Thomas shifts abruptly to the mouse, who would "shrug" if he could, bringing us back to the warmth of emotion. Your students might want

to give some thought to this question: If we knew absolutely that we were going to die, would we "shrug" if we could?

A specific example. Montaigne's view of death connects with the speculation about the final peacefulness of the mouse's death (paragraph 6). Inspired by the Latin classics, especially Plutarch, Montaigne's essays reflect his skeptical spirit.

the pharmacologic properties of opium; there is no pain. Thus it is that the mouse seems always to dangle so languidly from the jaws, lies there so quietly when dropped, dies of his injuries without a struggle. If a mouse could shrug, he'd shrug.

I do not know if this is true or not, nor do I know how to prove it if it is true. Maybe if you could get in there quickly enough and administer naloxone, a specific morphine antagonist, you could turn off the endorphins and observe the restoration of pain, but this is not something I would care to do or see. I think I will leave it there, as a good guess about the dying of a cat-chewed mouse, perhaps about dying in general. 7

Montaigne had a hunch about dying, based on his own close call in a riding accident. He was so badly injured as to be believed dead by his companions, and was carried home with lamentations, "all bloody, stained all over with the blood I had thrown up." He remembers the entire episode, despite having been "dead, for two full hours," with wonderment: 8

> It seemed to me that my life was hanging only by the tip of my lips. I closed my eyes in order, it seemed to me, to help push it out, and took pleasure in growing languid and letting myself go. It was an idea that was only floating on the surface of my soul, as delicate and feeble as all the rest, but in truth not only free from distress but mingled with that sweet feeling that people have who have let themselves slide into sleep. I believe that this is the same state in which people find themselves whom we see fainting in the agony of death, and I maintain that we pity them without cause. . . . In order to get used to the idea of death, I find there is nothing like coming close to it.

Later, in another essay, Montaigne returns to it:

> If you know not how to die, never trouble yourself: Nature will in a moment fully and sufficiently instruct you; she will exactly do that business for you; take you no care for it.

The worst accident I've ever seen was on Okinawa, in the early days of the invasion, when a jeep ran into a troop carrier and was crushed nearly flat. Inside were two young MPs, trapped in bent steel, both mortally hurt, with only their hands and shoulders visible. We had a conversation while people with the right tools were prying them free. Sorry about the accident, they said. No, they said, they felt fine. Is everyone else okay, one of them said. Well, the other one said, no hurry now. And then they died.

Pain is useful for avoidance, for getting away when there's time to get away, but when it is end game, and no way back, pain is likely to be turned off, and the mechanisms for this are wonderfully precise and quick. If I had to design an ecosystem in which creatures had to live off each other and in which dying was an indispensable part of living, I could not think of a better way to manage.

9   Thomas talks about "the early days of the invasion." Some students need to be told that Thomas refers to an action during World War II, and that "MPs" means "military police." This paragraph brings us to Thomas's personal credibility: he witnessed deaths that share the natural features of the mouse's death in paragraphs 4 and 5. In a sense, the MPs "shrugged."

10   In his conclusion, Thomas expresses admiration for nature's way of handling death. He no longer sees it as an abomination, as he mentions in paragraph 4, but as an "indispensable part of living," handled efficiently.

Meaning and Purpose

1. The first paragraph may make readers think they are going to read an essay about "books on dying." What is the topic of the essay, and where does it first appear?
2. In the second paragraph, Thomas suggests that most of us think the deaths of things or creatures other than human beings are "natural," or trivial. How does Thomas use the example of a mouse's death to turn that notion around? Is nature necessarily trivial?
3. What kind or kinds of examples does Thomas use—specific, typical, hypothetical, or a combination of these—to support his ideas? Explain.
4. What does Thomas tell you that is important for you to know about death? Do you agree with him?

POSSIBLE ANSWERS

Meaning and Purpose

1. The reader discovers the topic of the essay in sentence 1, paragraph 3, suddenly, as the elm dies almost overnight. This sudden shift leads the reader into the topic of "natural death," also mentioned in the title of the work.
2. Thomas describes the sophisticated—and rather beautiful—mechanism that shuts down pain; it sets in naturally when a creature is mortally injured. He therefore suggests that the natural process of death is not trivial but something to be admired, even to be in awe of.
3. He uses the specific examples of a tree stricken with blight, a mouse caught in a cat's jaws, and soldiers crushed in a jeep. These are

all individual events or experiences. Thomas does say that he doesn't know if his "story" about the mouse's dying without pain is true. This story part of the example has hypothetical elements.

4. Students might respond by saying something about how important it is to know that dying is natural, even painless. Some may mention that they had never before thought about the actual experience of dying, but only about the prelude and the aftermath.

5. This quotation is important because the essayist deals with the knowledge that nature knows how to handle death. This mildly sarcastic quotation says much the same thing.

Strategy

1. Everyone sings to show that life itself goes on, oblivious to the natural death of an elm tree. It is "natural" to sing while one works. The dead elm tree is now a thing to be removed, a job.

2. Thomas begins with the lesser life form to emphasize his point that "natural"—and all the sophistication it implies—is not necessarily trivial. By the time we read about the soldiers' deaths, we can easily apply Thomas's thesis and see the connection death makes among all living things.

3. This light humor, mostly in the first paragraph and in the author's way of describing his relationship with the cat in paragraph 4, helps hold the reader's interest in a potentially morbid subject. This touch generates interest in a topic that readers often avoid.

4. In this personal essay that deals with a universal topic the author uses "I" throughout, comments personally on death, and concludes with another personal reference. Students might comment on his various uses of the first person.

Style

1. The word *amiable* suggest the connotative qualities that constitute friendliness. Cats are not by nature overly friendly, but they have

5. The author quotes Montaigne, who says elsewhere, "Let us give Nature a chance; she knows her business better than we do." How is this quotation important to the essay?

Strategy

1. In the last sentence of paragraph 3, why does everyone sing?
2. Why do you think Thomas devotes four paragraphs to his thoughts about details in the mouse's death, and only one to the soldiers' deaths? How does the former example set you up for the latter?
3. Despite the topic, this essay has some humor. How is this humor appropriate to the essay?
4. Would you call this a "personal" essay? Which specific sentences in the essay support your answer?

Style

1. Reread the first sentence in paragraph 4. The author uses the word "amiable" instead of "friendly," "spectacle" instead of "sight," and "beheld" instead of "seen." How are these words more appropriate than their synonyms? Look up the words in a good dictionary before you answer this question.
2. The first sentence in paragraph 8 is written in an informal style. Reread the sentence and then tell how a reader would know that it is informal.
3. The final paragraph includes the chess expression "end game," which means "the final stage of a game, usually after the exchange of queens and the serious reduction of forces." How is this phrase appropriate to the paragraph and to the essay?

Writing Tasks

1. Your views on death may be strengthened or changed by this essay, even if only a little. In an essay, discuss your views on death and then tell how Thomas's essay has strengthened those views or changed them. If you believe that death is "normal" to all things, including human beings, what do you mean by "normal"? If you believe that human beings somehow die differently, what do you think makes their deaths different from those of other creatures?

2. Think of something—an experience, a situation—which at first appears unpleasant or distressing, but which actually has redeeming or beneficial features. Write an essay exploring these ideas and use examples to support your statements. Decide whether to use specific, typical, or hypothetical examples, or a mixture.

natural "amiable" qualities that make people like them. The word "beheld" suggests the regal quality often associated with feline demeanor. "Spectacle" connotes drama, consistent with the many small dramas witnessed by the author.

2. "Had a hunch" and "close call" are trite phrases inappropriate to a formal sentence.

3. "End game" compares the finality of death to the end of a chess game.

TEACHING SUGGESTIONS

If you are so inclined, this brief excerpt can be used as a springboard to larger issues. The message here is simple enough: the frontier myth is produced by "Hollywood hype" and self-aggrandizement by individuals and places. Historical figures apparently have been idealized in all cultures at all times. Cultures need heroes and much idealizing of the past is benign and even salutary when achieved by natural folk-telling over a long period. When hype is applied in a conscious effort by a group to distort the reality of current people and events, though, the implication is more ominous.

Have students consider the ways in which modern institutions and individuals distort facts about a situation or event. Do they see danger in the "image making" done by governments, institutions, corporations, and individuals today? What about the media?

This selection can easily be paired with "Future Shlock" (pp. 188–198) and the discussion of how *Peter the Great* was filmed may be especially relevant.

MARGINAL NOTES

Shenkman relies heavily on these books: W. Eugene Hallon, *Frontier Violence: Another Look* (1974); Raymond F. Adams, *More Burrs under the Saddle* (1970); Dixon Wecter, *The Hero in America* (1941).

The two films that critics most acclaimed romanticizing the OK Corral shoot-out between the Earp and Clanton families. They are *Gunfight at the OK Corral* (1957), with Burt Lancaster and Kirk Douglas as Wyatt Earp and Doc Holliday, and *My Darling Clementine* (1946), with Henry Fonda as Earp and Walter Brennan as the villainous head of the Clanton gang.

❦ Richard Shenkman ❦

Richard Shenkman was born in New York City. He studied history at Vassar College and in the History of American Civilization Program at Harvard, and he worked as a researcher on the Andrew Jackson Papers Project. In 1981 he began working as a television news reporter. His first book, One Night Stands with American History *(1980) (written with Kurt Reiger) includes some examples of fabricated history, and his second book,* Legends, Lies, and Cherished Myths of American History *(1988) is devoted to that subject.*

The Frontier

This essay is from Richard Shenkman's Legends, Lies, and Cherished Myths of American History. *Shenkman looks at the ways in which Hollywood "hype" and other lies have contributed to the distorted image Americans have of their own history. He uses little-known historical facts to refute the frontier "myths" immortalized in literature and on film.*

The popular image of the frontier as a place of violence is only partly due to the fact that the place often was violent. Most of it is due to hype, particularly Hollywood hype. The truth is many more people have died in Hollywood westerns than ever died on the real frontier (Indian wars considered apart). In the real Dodge City, for instance, there were just five killings in 1878, the most homicidal year in the little town's frontier history—scarcely enough to sustain a typical two-hour movie. In the most violent year in Deadwood, South Dakota, only four people were killed. In the worst year in Tombstone, home of the shoot-out at the OK Corral, only five people were killed. The only reason the OK Corral shoot-out even became famous was that town boosters deliberately overplayed the drama to attract new settlers. "They eventually cashed in on the tourist boom," historian W. Eugene

1

Hollon says, "by inventing a myth about a town too tough to die."

The most notorious cow towns in Kansas—Abilene, Dodge City, Ellsworth, Wichita, and Caldwell—did see comparatively more violence than similar size small towns elsewhere but probably not as much violence as is believed. Records indicate that between 1870 and 1885 just forty-five murders occurred in the towns.

Most surprisingly, there is no evidence anyone was ever killed in a frontier shoot-out at high noon.

In fact, few of those who are famous for shooting people shot as many people as is commonly thought. Billy the Kid was a "psychopathic murderer," but he hadn't killed twenty-one people by the time he was twenty-one. Hollon says authorities "can only account for three men he killed for sure, and there were probably no more than three or four more."

Bat Masterson is another overrated killer. He's been credited, says Hollon, with killing between twenty and thirty men; "the actual number was only three."

Wild Bill Hickok, the Abilene marshal, claimed to have killed six Kansas outlaws and secessionists in the incident that first made him famous. He lied. He killed just three—all unarmed. And he never killed anybody for violating the ordinance against firing guns within town limits.

Bill Cody's reputation as a gunslinger often seemed like pure fiction, and was. For it was only in dime novels, which he himself had a hand in writing, that Cody resorted so often to gunfire. As he acknowledged in a letter to his publisher, he didn't care much for the truth. "I am sorry to have to lie so outrageously in this yarn. . . . If you think the revolver and the bowie-knife are used too freely, you may cut out a fatal shot or stab wherever you deem it wise." Cody was a good shot and is said to have proved it repeatedly at the bison-killing contests where he earned the nickname Buffalo Bill. But he didn't kill many Indians, and when he was old his estranged wife revealed he had been wounded in combat with Indians only once, not 137 times as he claimed.

2

3

4

5

6

7

The allusion, of course, is to the classic western, *High Noon* (1952), in which Gary Cooper, on his wedding day, must face vengeance claimed by an outlaw gang due to arrive in town at noon. When he turns to his fellow townspeople for help, no one comes forward and he must face the gang alone.

After refuting the violent reputations ascribed to towns, Shenkman here narrows his focus to the reputations ascribed to famous frontiersmen.

Wyatt Earp tells the story that after Bat Masterson had retired and was living in New York, he was pestered by a rapacious collector of souvenirs for the six-gun he had used on the frontier. To get rid of the man, Masterson bought a gun at a pawnshop (he wouldn't part with his own), and as a joke carved twenty-two "credits" into its handle before giving it to him. The collector asked if he had indeed killed twenty-two men. " 'I didn't tell him yes, and I didn't tell him no,' Bat said, 'and I didn't exactly lie to him. I simply said I hadn't counted either Mexicans or Indians, and he went away tickled to death.' " Soon afterward, stories of Masterson having killed twenty-two men crept into print (B. A. Botkin, ed., *A Treasury of Western Folklore,* 1951).

Here the author again broadens his vision to all American frontiers and uses the myth John Smith created about himself as his first example.

The first sentence in the paragraph serves as a transition from the preceding paragraph and then leads to the topic sentence.

POSSIBLE ANSWERS

Meaning and Purpose

1. The purpose of this essay should be evident to the student: to argue that a substantial difference separates the popular image of the American frontier from the realities of its towns and characters; that the image is a myth propagated by Hollywood and often originated by the self-serving towns and characters themselves.

2. Even a most superficial survey of movie and television westerns will reveal numerous myths that have little basis in fact. Almost all of John Wayne's westerns depict the rugged individualist who conquered over all odds. Cowherders led adventurous and constantly interesting lives. (Larry McMurty's *Lonesome Dove* and the television miniseries based on the novel play on the myth but edge it a bit closer to the tedious reality.)

The truth is, few frontiersmen who are remembered for anything are remembered accurately. That's true no matter which frontier era they're from. Of all our frontier heroes, the most confusion may surround the hero who appeared first, John Smith, of Jamestown fame. Even the story about Pocahontas's saving Smith's life is a matter of dispute. Smith first related the story ten years after it had supposedly happened. When he did, no one stepped forward to corroborate the tale. Furthermore, he told it at a suspiciously opportune moment in 1616, when Pocahontas, then the celebrated wife of Virginia planter John Rolfe, was being courted by the British royal family. Even Smith's defenders admit he probably brought the story up in order to ingratiate himself with the crown. When Pocahontas appeared at court, Smith sent the queen a little book explaining how the young Indian had "hazarded the beating out of her own brains to save mine." 8

At least John Smith was responsible for most of the myths about John Smith. Most of the myths about Davy Crockett were created not by Crockett but by his political supporters, the Whigs. The politicians published ghostwritten autobiographies to improve Crockett's standing as a frontier hero and as a possible successor to Democrat Andrew Jackson. In one book, recounting his first trip to Washington, Crockett is asked to identify himself. He does so—in his own inimitable way. Why, I'm Davy Crockett, he says. "I'm that same David Crockett, fresh from the backwoods, half-horse, half-alligator, a little touched with the snapping-turtle; can wade the Mississippi, leap the Ohio, ride upon a streak of lightning, and slip without a scratch down a honey locust; can whip my weight in wild cats—and if any gentleman pleases, for a ten-dollar bill, he may throw in a panther." 9

The true Davy Crockett was neither like the figure in the autobiographies nor like the clean-shaven, soft-talking, bath-taking hero portrayed by Fess Parker in the 1954–55 television series. He wasn't universally popular, he wasn't respectable, and he wasn't the perfect role model for children. When he ran for reelection to Congress in 1835, he was defeated. When he grew disenchanted with his wife, he deserted her. As a child he was a juvenile delinquent. He always had plenty of friends, but he was 10 known as something of an ignoramus. When he claimed to have shot more than a hundred bears, friends reportedly joked that couldn't be. Davy couldn't count that high.

Meaning and Purpose

1. What is Shenkman's purpose in "The Frontier"?
2. The author claims in the first paragraph that "Hollywood hype" is mainly responsible for the myths of violence that pervade popular imagings about the American frontier. Can you think of other myths about the West that have been created by film and television?
3. What, other than "Hollywood hype," seems to have both generated and perpetuated the romanticized versions we have of historical characters? Is the same system at work today?
4. If you didn't understand the allusion to the 1940s movie about the OK Corral, and if you'd never heard of either the old Davy Crockett television series or dime novels, would this information still be meaningful to you? Why or why not?

Strategy

1. Paragraphs 2–6 include examples and are relatively short compared to those in the rest of the essay. What kind of examples are they—specific, typical, or hypothetical—and what effect do the short paragraphs create?
2. What is the function of the break between paragraphs 7 and 8?
3. What is the structure of paragraphs 4–7? How does this structure contribute to the author's purpose?
4. The author employs several examples in a rather short essay. How does he avoid making the piece sound like a laundry list? How does he achieve coherence among all these examples?
5. How does his use of examples in the last paragraph serve as a clincher for the author's argument?

3. Many of the myths were created by the principals themselves for self-serving reasons: a kind of chamber-of-commerce effort promoted an adventurous reputation for Tombstone, Arizona, to attract settlers; Bill Cody helped write the fiction that glorified his own life; John Smith embellished his story with Pocahontas "to ingratiate himself with the [English] crown"; Davy Crockett and his supporters exaggerated his career for political reasons. Today, self-aggrandizement in public life abounds. Lee Iacocca, Donald Trump, and Oliver North come immediately to mind.

4. Most students will probably think the information is meaningful in context. The "OK Corral" sounds significant because the words are capitalized and Shenkman tells us the shoot-out is famous. He describes how Davy Crockett was portrayed by Fess Parker, so that we find meaning here in context. The "dime novel" is probably self-explanatory or at least suggestive to students.

Strategy

1. After the introduction, Shenkman gives us a quick list of examples to illustrate his thesis. All the examples are specific: they describe events and give facts. The paragraphs create a staccato effect that establishes validity for his position before he pursues his point in a more sustained way.

2. The first seven paragraphs illustrate with examples that popular perceptions of violence in frontier life differ from reality. The second part of the essay expands Shenkman's vision to all American frontiers, and gives two more extended examples of his thesis.

3. Each paragraph begins with a topic sentence that contradicts common views and then validates that statement by citing examples. Each of the paragraphs mirrors the author's argument in miniature.

4. Shenkman's examples become enriched by detail, rather than growing into a mere long list. The similarities among the examples give the essay coherence, and the opening sentence in nearly every paragraph serves as a skillful transition from one example to another.

5. The final paragraph is constructed like all the others in the essay—a topic sentence that contradicts a common view followed by short examples that demonstrate the author's point. Here, though, the examples are increasingly derisive. The short final sentence focuses so closely on Davy Crockett's intellectual insufficiencies that the exaggerations of his reputation are made to look absurd.

Style

1. No one seems to agree on an etymology for the word "hype," but all the derivations emphasize exaggeration, deception, and falsity. One source suggests the word might be a shortening of "hyperbole," "hyper" being a prefix in loan words from Greek, meaning over, excess, or exaggeration. The word may have been influenced by "hypocrisy." It also means artificial or phony "high" from drug stimulation. Repeating the word emphasizes its denotation and connotations; connecting it with Tinsel Town emphasizes its falsity.

2. Because a dime novel was a cheap, sensational, and melodramatic paperback enormously popular between 1850 and 1920, the life of Bill Cody portrayed in such a novel had to be "pure fiction," playing to the public's lowest common denominator.

3. In this context, "myth" means a story that is simply untrue. This myth was created by "politicians," a notably untrustworthy breed, who concocted a fictitious reputation for Crockett to further their own nefarious schemes.

4. Crockett uses tall-tale language, characterizing himself as a comic demigod capable of superhuman deeds. The description is full of imagination and humor and in another context could be full of fun, even self-deprecating fun. Here it becomes another example of fiction passing itself off as reality.

Style

1. In the first paragraph the author says that the reputation of the western frontier as a violent place "is due to hype, particularly Hollywood hype." What is the derivation of "hype," and how does the word affect the passage's meaning and tone? What effect is created by repeating the word in the same sentence and by connecting it with "Hollywood"?

2. The author claims that Bill Cody's reputation is "pure fiction" popularized in "dime novels." How does this diction further the essayist's main purpose? What is a dime novel?

3. In paragraph 9 the author uses the word "myth" twice, once in each of the first two sentences. In the third sentence he says that "politicians published ghostwritten autobiographies [of Davy Crockett] to improve Crockett's standing as a frontier hero. . . ." How does this language further the author's purpose?

4. At the conclusion of paragraph 9, the author quotes Davy Crockett himself. How would you describe Crockett's language? Considering the context, how is the quotation supposed to affect the reader?

Writing Tasks

1. "The Frontier" illustrates the differences between our common belief about the frontier and its actuality. Write an essay in which you examine the differences between what is real and what is commonly perceived in incidents you know about, and use examples to support your ideas. You might choose a historical or political situation, a public figure, or even yourself. Choose carefully the kinds of examples you use.

2. What popular images do advertisers try to build for a product such as sugar-coated cereal, perfume, or blue jeans, and what is the reality of the product? Use specific or typical examples to explain your assertions.

❦ Joan Didion ❦

A Californian by birth, educated at the University of California at Berkeley, descended from pioneers, Joan Didion has written extensively about contemporary life in the western United States. From 1956 to 1963 she was an associate feature editor at Vogue *magazine, and during that time published widely in prominent national magazines. Her first book of essays,* Slouching Towards Bethlehem *(1968), compiles many of those early essays and is focused on America in the 1960s, particularly San Francisco. She has written four novels, including* Play It as It Lays *(1970) and* Book of Common Prayer *(1977), and has collaborated with her husband on several screenplays. She is known for her incisive reflections and unique vision of American life-styles.*

Marrying Absurd

From Slouching Towards Bethlehem, *this passage describes the wedding "business" of Las Vegas, Nevada. Didion's loosely structured essay relies primarily on description and specific examples to achieve her purpose of objective social commentary. The author's opinion, however, is not far from the surface, and is revealed in her choice of examples.*

To be married in Las Vegas, Clark County, Nevada, a bride   1
must swear that she is eighteen or has parental permission and a bridegroom that he is twenty-one or has parental permission. Someone must put up five dollars for the license. (On Sundays and holidays, fifteen dollars. The Clark County Courthouse issues marriage licenses at any time of the day or night except between noon and one in the afternoon, between eight and nine in the evening, and between four and five in the morning.) Nothing else is required. The State of Nevada, alone among these United States, demands neither a premarital blood test nor a waiting period

TEACHING SUGGESTIONS

Examples lend emphasis to statements. In "Marrying Absurd," Didion claims that some kinds of people are at the mercy of appearances. She presents innumerable examples of how Las Vegas appears and what those appearances suggest about the Las Vegas attitude toward marriages. They are good for business; that's it.

Showing the difference between appearance and reality is one of the oldest strategies in rhetoric, going back at least to Socrates. But making appearance replace reality in the eye of the beholder is a relatively recent strategy, an advertiser's gimmick to encourage consumers to buy before they think, much as brides and grooms "buy" a Las Vegas marriage.

Is this strategy used elsewhere?

Ask students whether they have seen evidence of appearance being used to replace reality, for advertising purposes. What of pictures that are part of advertisements for new homes? Has any member of the class seen the real home after having seen its picture? Do they compare favorably? What about the advertised automobile versus the automobile "in person"? What about an advertisement for a movie? Was it better than the movie itself? And on and on.

After the class grasps the notion that modern advertising is done to supplant reality rather than to describe reality, they are prepared to read Didion's "Marrying Absurd," which deals with people who cannot see the difference between a Las Vegas wedding and a "real" wedding.

MARGINAL NOTES

Notice the repetition of the *s* sound in the "moonscape" phrase. The desert looks as barren as the moon. Mesquite is thorny small trees or shrubs, the pods of which are used for fodder.

The examples of weddings later in this essay have miragelike qualities. They seem to be real, but they don't seem to resemble marriages elsewhere in the country.

The phrases "wedding industry" and "peak operational efficiency" suggest a production line more than a ceremony uniting people in matrimony.

The 171 couples were married according to Clark County and the state of Nevada. Traditional references to God are omitted.

The accidental irony in Mr. Brennan's remark is inescapable. Didion lets her character speak for himself, emphasizing an example of absurdity.

The word "allegorical," with its moral and biblical overtones, and the word "venality," which means "to prostitute talents for money," combine with "mobsters" and "call girls" to exemplify Las Vegas as a city bent on enjoying itself without giving a thought to possible consequences.

About half as long as a cigarette, these "poppers" are used for anginal pain, which is often associated with heart attacks.

Las Vegas is pictured as imaginary, a mirage. It has no reason for being; it just *is*.

before or after the issuance of a marriage license. Driving in across the Mojave from Los Angeles, one sees the signs way out on the desert, looming up from that moonscape of rattlesnakes and mesquite, even before the Las Vegas lights appear like a mirage on the horizon: "GETTING MARRIED? Free License Information First Strip Exit." Perhaps the Las Vegas wedding industry achieved its peak operational efficiency between 9:00 P.M. and midnight of August 26, 1965, an otherwise unremarkable Thursday which happened to be, by Presidential order, the last day on which anyone could improve his draft status merely by getting married. One hundred and seventy-one couples were pronounced man and wife in the name of Clark County and the State of Nevada that night, sixty-seven of them by a single justice of the peace, Mr. James A. Brennan. Mr. Brennan did one wedding at the Dunes and the other sixty-six in his office, and charged each couple eight dollars. One bride lent her veil to six others. "I got it down from five to three minutes," Mr. Brennan said later of his feat. "I could've married them *en masse,* but they're people, not cattle. People expect more when they get married."

What people who get married in Las Vegas actually do expect—what, in the largest sense, their "expectations" are—strikes one as a curious and self-contradictory business. Las Vegas is the most extreme and allegorical of American settlements, bizarre and beautiful in its venality and in its devotion to immediate gratification, a place the tone of which is set by mobsters and call girls and ladies' room attendants with amyl nitrate poppers in their uniform pockets. Almost everyone notes that there is no "time" in Las Vegas, no night and no day and no past and no future (no Las Vegas Casino, however, has taken the obliteration of the ordinary time sense quite so far as Harold's Club in Reno, which for a while issued, at odd intervals in the day and night, mimeographed "bulletins" carrying news from the world outside); neither is there any logical sense of where one is. One is standing on a highway in the middle of a vast hostile desert looking at an eighty-foot sign which blinks "STARDUST" or "CAESAR'S PALACE." Yes, but what does that explain? This geographical implausibility reinforces the sense that what happens here has no connection with "real" life; Nevada cities like Reno and Carson are ranch

2

towns, Western towns, places behind which there is some historical imperative. But Las Vegas seems to exist only in the eye of the beholder. All of which makes it an extraordinarily stimulating and interesting place, but an odd one in which to want to wear a candlelight satin Priscilla of Boston wedding dress with Chantilly lace inserts, tapered sleeves and a detachable modified train.

And yet the Las Vegas wedding business seems to appeal to precisely that impulse. "Sincere and Dignified Since 1954," one wedding chapel advertises. There are nineteen such wedding chapels in Las Vegas, intensely competitive, each offering better, faster, and, by implication, more sincere services than the next: Our Photos Best Anywhere, Your Wedding on a Phonograph Record, Candlelight with Your Ceremony, Honeymoon Accommodations, Free Transportation from Your Motel to Courthouse to Chapel and Return to Motel, Religious or Civil Ceremonies, Dressing Rooms, Flowers, Rings, Announcements, Witnesses Available, and Ample Parking. All of these services, like most others in Las Vegas (sauna baths, payroll-check cashing, chinchilla coats for sale or rent) are offered twenty-four hours a day, seven days a week, presumably on the premise that marriage, like craps, is a game to be played when the table seems hot.

But what strikes one most about the Strip chapels, with their wishing wells and stained-glass paper windows and their artificial bouvardia, is that so much of their business is by no means a matter of simple convenience, of late-night liaisons between show girls and baby Crosbys. Of course there is some of that. (One night about eleven o'clock in Las Vegas I watched a bride in an orange minidress and masses of flame-colored hair stumble from a Strip chapel on the arm of her bridegroom, who looked the part of the expendable nephew in movies like *Miami Syndicate*. "I gotta get the kids," the bride whimpered. "I gotta pick up the sitter, I gotta get to the midnight show." "What you gotta get," the bridegroom said, opening the door of a Cadillac Coupe de Ville and watching her crumble on the seat, "is sober.") But Las Vegas seems to offer something other than "convenience"; it is merchandising "niceness," the facsimile of proper ritual, to children who do not know how else to find it, how to make the arrangements, how to do it "right." All day and evening long on the Strip, one sees

3

Often attributed to Shakespeare or Pope, the line "Beauty is in the eye of the beholder" was written by Margaret Wolfe Hungerford (1855–1897). It appears in *Molly Bawn* (1878).

The catalog of advertisements for quick and easy marital bliss has a wealth of irony, ending with marriage compared to shooting craps "when the table seems hot." The suggestion is that one is playing a game on impulse, not reason, hoping that the marriage will be lucky.

4

A genus of plants cultivated for their showy flowers, bouvardia are often used in brides' bouquets. The wishing wells and the paper stained-glass windows add to the scene's artificiality.

The anecdote about the "bride in an orange minidress" heightens the contrast between the examples of artificiality and this real example of a marriage truly in the Las Vegas style.

Las Vegas caters to the imagination, not to reality. Such catering becomes apparent to Didion when she examines the wedding ritual. The "children" who know no better believe that the Las Vegas facsimile *is* the "proper ritual." They cannot see through the neon advertising to the shoddy Las Vegas production of a marriage.

Refers to the Bridal Chorus from Richard Wagner's 1848 opera, *Lohengrin.*

Notice that the mother and *step*father are present.

"One moment please—Wedding": This sign carries a signal message, but also might be seen as a comment on the relative duration of this kind of marriage.

After Dr. Pangloss, a foolish optimist in Voltaire's *Candide.* An unreasonably optimistic atmosphere or person.

The example of the after-wedding scene seems sad to the reader, with the "bored waiter," the off-color joke by the bride's father, and the greatly pregnant bride, too young to sip her own wedding champagne.

Sadly, the party's over, the champagne's no longer free. The bride exemplifies, with her sobbing statement, Didion's claim that Las Vegas is so successful at merchandising imitation "niceness" to a specific kind of people that they remain ignorant of reality and devoid of taste.

actual wedding parties, waiting under the harsh lights at a crosswalk, standing uneasily in the parking lot of the Frontier while the photographer hired by The Little Church of the West ("Wedding Place of the Stars") certifies the occasion, takes the picture: the bride in a veil and white satin pumps, the bridegroom usually in a white dinner jacket, and even an attendant or two, a sister or a best friend in hot-pink *peau de soie,* a flirtation veil, a carnation nosegay. "When I Fall in Love It Will Be Forever," the organist plays, and then a few bars of Lohengrin. The mother cries; the stepfather, awkward in his role, invites the chapel hostess to join them for a drink at the Sands. The hostess declines with a professional smile; she has already transferred her interest to the group waiting outside. One bride out, another in, and again the sign goes up on the chapel door: "One moment please—Wedding."

I sat next to one such wedding party in a Strip restaurant the last time I was in Las Vegas. The marriage had just taken place; the bride still wore her dress, the mother her corsage. A bored waiter poured out a few swallows of pink champagne ("on the house") for everyone but the bride, who was too young to be served. "You'll need something with more kick than that," the bride's father said with heavy jocularity to his new son-in-law; the ritual jokes about the wedding night had a certain Panglossian character, since the bride was clearly several months pregnant. Another round of pink champagne, this time not on the house, and the bride began to cry. "It was just as nice," she sobbed, "as I hoped and dreamed it would be."

Meaning and Purpose

1. What is the meaning of *absurd* as used in the title "Marrying Absurd"?
2. Two examples of artificiality in this essay are "stained-glass paper windows and artificial bouvardia." What is another example?

3. What does the example of the wedding in paragraph 4 suggest to you about marrying in Las Vegas?
4. Unlike Harold's Club in Reno, Las Vegas casinos never issued "bulletins" with news from the outside. Why not, do you think?

Strategy

1. One hundred and seventy-one couples were married in Las Vegas, on August 26, 1965. What is the probable reason that most of them wanted to get married on that day?
2. The waiter mentioned in the last paragraph of the essay is "bored." Why?
3. Which of the advertisements in paragraph 3 strikes you as least desirable for a wedding chapel? Why?
4. In paragraph 4, what is a "baby Crosby"?

Style

1. The author says that Las Vegas is both "bizarre and beautiful." What does *bizarre* mean?
2. In paragraph 4, why does the author use *actual* in the sentence that includes "one sees *actual* wedding parties"?
3. In paragraph 5, the author mentions *peau de soie*. What is it?
4. Some readers believe that the author is being sarcastic in mentioning the song "When I Fall in Love It Will Be Forever" in paragraph 4 of this essay. Why would they believe that?

Writing Tasks

1. This essay exhibits no examples of anything that is included in what we call "the modern wedding." The author mentions only facsimiles of such inclusions.

POSSIBLE ANSWERS

Meaning and Purpose

1. As used in the title, the word *absurd* denotes a specific way of marrying: marrying so unreasonably or so ridiculously as to make the ceremony laughable.
2. Answers vary and might include the professional smile of the hostess in paragraph 4, the "masses of flame-colored hair" in paragraph 4, or the "wedding night" as described in paragraph 5.
3. The marriage suggests a match conceived impulsively. The bride is drunk and the groom is compared to a petty hoodlum in a movie.
4. Las Vegas casinos do nothing to remind people of time, as the author says in paragraph 2.

Strategy

1. The couples probably married to keep the groom from being drafted, which is not a substantial reason for something as important as marriage.
2. The waiter has seen so many newly married couples that he is not impressed by one more bride and groom.
3. Opinions vary, of course, but a number of students choose "Free Transportation from Your Motel to Courthouse to Chapel and Return to Motel," saying that the advertisement makes a marriage seem like a "round-trip ticket to a bedroom," as one student put it.
4. A recent American biographical dictionary will tell students that Bing Crosby was an immensely popular singer from the 1930s through the 1950s.

Style

1. The word *bizarre* means "odd, grotesque; marked by extreme contrasts of color, design, or style."

2. So much of what Didion describes is mirage-like, artificial, or sham, that she exaggerates the truth of the description here with the adjective *actual.*

3. The phrase *peau de soie,* literally "skin of silk" in French, refers to rich silk or rayon cloth with a dull, satiny finish.

4. Readers notice the irony or sarcasm of including a song title that promises "love forever" in an essay that almost totally suggests the opposite in a Las Vegas style marriage.

After reading this essay, however, the reader gains some general understanding of what Didion thinks a wedding should involve. Using your imagination, discuss, with clear examples, a bride, groom, and a modern wedding of which you think Didion would approve.

2. At one time or another, all of us have looked forward to an event—a party, a dance, a purchase, or a special date, for example—with great anticipation. The event may not, however, have turned out nearly so successfully as we had anticipated.

Describe such an event in your life. Using examples, show how the event did not live up to your expectations.

❧ Phyllis Rose ❧

*Phyllis Rose was born in 1926 in New Jersey and attended Connect-
icut College, Duke University, and the University of Wisconsin,
where she earned her Ph.D. in English. She has been a professor of
English at the University of Hawaii and a member of the board of
several Hawaiian councils for the arts and humanities. She has
published two works of biography*—Woman of Letters: A Life of
Virginia Woolf *and* Parallel Lives: Five Victorian Marriages—*and
a collection of essays,* Writing of Women. *She wrote the "Hers"
column for* The New York Times *for ten weeks and has contributed
to numerous national publications, including* The Atlantic, Vogue,
and The Nation. *She is an English professor at Wesleyan University.*

Tools of Torture

In this work, first published in The Atlantic *in 1968, Phyllis Rose
takes an uncompromising look at the social and psychological
sources of and rationalizations for torture. She uses specific examples from an exhibit in Paris of torture instruments to draw conclusions about the relation of pleasure to pain.*

In a gallery off the rue Dauphine, near the *parfumerie* where
I get my massage, I happened upon an exhibit of medieval torture
instruments. It made me think that pain must be as great a challenge to the human imagination as pleasure. Otherwise there's no
accounting for the number of torture instruments. One would be
quite enough. The simple pincer, let's say, which rips out flesh.
Or the head crusher, which breaks first your tooth sockets, then
your skull. But in addition I saw tongs, thumbscrews, a rack, a
ladder, ropes and pulleys, a grill, a garrote, a Spanish horse, a
Judas cradle, an iron maiden, a cage, a gag, a strappado, a stretching table, a saw, a wheel, a twisting stork, an inquisitor's chair,
a breast breaker, and a scourge. You don't need complicated

one of the tortures devised to further this end, as were most of the other devices described in the essay. That is the reasoning behind the claim in paragraph 6 that human torture has been instituted, condoned, and "vetted" hand in hand by church and state.

machinery to cause incredible pain. If you want to saw your victim down the middle, for example, all you need is a slightly bigger than usual saw. If you hold the victim upside down so the blood stays in his head, hold his legs apart, and start sawing at the groin, you can get as far as the navel before he loses consciousness.

Even in the Middle Ages, before electricity, there were many things you could do to torment a person. You could tie him up in an iron belt that held the arms and legs up to the chest and left no point of rest, so that all his muscles went into spasm within minutes and he was driven mad within hours. This was the twisting stork, a benign-looking object. You could stretch him out backward over a thin piece of wood so that his whole body weight rested on his spine, which pressed against the sharp wood. Then you could stop up his nostrils and force water into his stomach through his mouth. Then, if you wanted to finish him off, you and your helper could jump on his stomach, causing internal hemorrhage. This torture was called the rack. If you wanted to burn someone to death without hearing him scream, you could use a tongue lock, a metal rod between the jaw and collarbone that prevented him from opening his mouth. You could put a person in a chair with spikes on the seat and arms, tie him down against the spikes, and beat him, so that every time he flinched from the beating he drove his own flesh deeper onto the spikes. This was the inquisitor's chair. If you wanted to make it worse, you could heat the spikes. You could suspend a person over a pointed wooden pyramid and whenever he started to fall asleep, you could drop him onto the point. If you were Ippolito Marsili, the inventor of this torture, known as the Judas cradle, you could tell yourself you had invented something humane, a torture that worked without burning flesh or breaking bones. For the torture here was supposed to be sleep deprivation.

The secret of torture, like the secret of French cuisine, is that nothing is unthinkable. The human body is like a foodstuff, to be grilled, pounded, filleted. Every opening exists to be stuffed, all flesh to be carved off the bone. You take an ordinary wheel, a heavy wooden wheel with spokes. You lay the victim on the ground with blocks of wood at strategic points under his shoulders, legs, and arms. You use the wheel to break every bone in his body. Next you tie his body onto the wheel. With all its bones broken, it will be pliable. However, the victim will not be dead. If you want to kill him, you hoist the wheel aloft on the end of a pole and leave him to starve. Who would have thought to do this with a man and a wheel? But, then, who would have thought to take the disgusting snail, force it to render its ooze, stuff it in its own shell with garlic butter, bake it, and eat it?

Not long ago I had a facial—only in part because I thought I needed one. It was research into the nature and function of pleasure. In a dark booth at the back of the beauty salon, the aesthetician put me on a table and applied a series of ointments to my face, some cool, some warmed. After a while she put something into my hand, cold and metallic. "Don't be afraid, madame," she said. "It is an electrode. It will not hurt you. The other end is attached to two metal cylinders, which I roll over your face. They break down the electricity barrier on your skin and allow the moisturizers to penetrate deeply." I didn't believe this hocus-pocus. I didn't believe in the electricity barrier or in the ability of these rollers to break it down. But it all felt very good. The cold metal on my face was a pleasant change from the soft warmth of the aesthetician's fingers. Still, since Algeria it's hard to hear the word "electrode" without fear. So when she left me for a few minutes with a moist, refreshing cheesecloth over my face, I thought, What if the goal of her expertise had been pain, not moisture? What if the electrodes had been electrodes in the Algerian sense? What if the cheesecloth mask were dipped in acid?

4

In Paris, where the body is so pampered, torture seems particularly sinister, not because it's hard to understand but because—as the dark side of sensuality—it seems so easy. Beauty care is among the glories of Paris. *Soins esthétiques* include makeup, facials, massages (both relaxing and reducing), depilations (partial and complete), manicures, pedicures, and tanning, in addition to the usual run of *soins* for the hair: cutting, brushing, setting, waving, styling, blowing, coloring, and streaking. In Paris the state of your skin, hair, and nerves is taken

5

The French colonized Algeria in 1830. The native Muslim Algerians, like all conquered peoples, continually smarted under foreign rule and finally rebelled, attaining independence in 1962. In the last convulsions of the revolution, the French tortured Algerians with electrodes and other devices to elicit information. Having ruled Algeria for so long, the French involved in the atrocities considered their acts both patriotic and necessary.

seriously, and there is little of the puritanical thinking that tries to persuade us that beauty comes from within. Nor do the French think, as Americans do, that beauty should be offhand and low-maintenance. Spending time and money on *soins esthétiques* is appropriate and necessary, not self-indulgent. Should that loving attention to the body turn malevolent, you have torture. You have the procedure—the aesthetic, as it were—of torture, the explanation for the rich diversity of torture instruments, but you do not have the cause.

After explaining why so many instruments of torture are to be found, the author proposes to move to the even more important question of why they were invented in the first place.

Historically torture has been a tool of legal systems, used to 6 get information needed for a trial or, more directly, to determine guilt or innocence. In the Middle Ages confession was considered the best of all proofs, and torture was the way to produce a confession. In other words, torture didn't come into existence to give vent to human sadism. It is not always private and perverse but sometimes social and institutional, vetted by the government and, of course, the Church. (There have been few bigger fans of torture than Christianity and Islam.) Righteousness, as much as viciousness, produces torture. There aren't squads of sadists beating down the doors to the torture chambers begging for jobs. Rather, as a recent book on torture by Edward Peters says, the institution of torture creates sadists: the weight of a culture, Peters suggests, is necessary to recruit torturers. You have to convince people that they are working for a great goal in order to get them to overcome their repugnance to the task of causing physical pain to another person. Usually the great goal is the preservation of society, and the victim is presented to the torturer as being in some way out to destroy it.

Milgram's experiments reinforce the idea that sadists are not responsible for institutionalized human cruelty. On the contrary, ordinary people can be convinced that the pain they inflict is for some higher cause, this time for scientific learning. Milgram also cites Hannah Arendt's 1963 book, *Eichmann in Jerusalem.* She contends that the prosecution's assertion

From another point of view, what's horrifying is how easily 7 you can persuade someone that he is working for the common good. Perhaps the most appalling psychological experiment of modern times, by Stanley Milgram, showed that ordinary, decent people in New Haven, Connecticut, could be brought to the point of inflicting (as they thought) severe electric shocks on other people in obedience to an authority and in pursuit of a goal, the advancement of knowledge, of which they approved. Milgram used—some would say abused—the prestige of science and the university to make his point, but his point is chilling nonetheless.

We can cluck over torture, but the evidence at least suggests that with intelligent handling most of us could be brought to do it ourselves.

In the Middle Ages, Milgram's experiment would have had no point. It would have shocked no one that people were capable of cruelty in the interest of something they believed in. That was as it should be. Only recently in the history of human thought has the avoidance of cruelty moved to the forefront of ethics. "Putting cruelty first," as Judith Shklar says in *Ordinary Vices,* is comparatively new. The belief that the "pursuit of happiness" is one of man's inalienable rights, the idea that "cruel and unusual punishment" is an evil in itself, the Benthamite notion that behavior should be guided by what will produce the greatest happiness for the greatest number—all these principles are only two centuries old. They were born with the eighteenth-century democratic revolutions. And in two hundred years they have not been universally accepted. Wherever people believe strongly in some cause, they will justify torture—not just the Nazis, but the French in Algeria.

Many people who wouldn't hurt a fly have annexed to fashion the imagery of torture—the thongs and spikes and metal studs—hence reducing it to the frivolous and transitory. Because torture has been in the mainstream and not on the margins of history, nothing could be healthier. For torture to be merely kinky would be a big advance. Exhibitions like the one I saw in Paris, which presented itself as educational, may be guilty of pandering to the tastes they deplore. Solemnity may be the wrong tone. If taking one's goals too seriously is the danger, the best discouragement of torture may be a radical hedonism that denies that any goal is worth the means, that refuses to allow the nobly abstract to seduce us from the sweetness of the concrete. Give people a good croissant and a good cup of coffee in the morning. Give them an occasional facial and a plate of escargots. Marie Antoinette picked a bad moment to say "Let them eat cake," but I've often thought she was on the right track.

All of which brings me back to Paris, for Paris exists in the imagination of much of the world as the capital of pleasure—of fun, food, art, folly, seduction, gallantry, and beauty. Paris is

8   that the Nazi Eichmann was a sadist monster, responsible for the murder of thousands of Jews, was wrong. Rather, she claims, he came closer to being a dull bureaucrat who simply sat at his desk and followed orders (Stanley Milgram, *Obedience to Authority,* 1974).

Jeremy Bentham (1748–1832) was an English philosopher who promoted utilitarianism, the ethical doctrine that asserted actions are right or good in proportion to their usefulness or as they tend to promote happiness. The doctrine claimed that the end and criterion of public action is the greatest happiness of the greatest number. Thus, human happiness becomes the one and only measure of right and wrong.

9

Marie Antoinette (1755–1793), queen of France, was the wife of Louis XVI, whom she married when she was fifteen. As daughter of Maria Theresa of Austria, she sought Austria's aid against French revolutionaries. In 1791 she counseled Louis to flee from France, an attempt that ended in their imprisonment. They were regarded as traitors and Marie Antoinette was guillotined on October 16, 1793. Her personal charm, her naive ignorance of practical life, her extravagance, and her frank and courageous honesty contributed to her unpopularity both at court and with the French masses.

10 When she was told that a revolution was threatening because the people had no bread, she is said to have replied, "Let them eat cake."

Meaning and Purpose

1. Paragraph 1, sentences 2–4.

2. Rose gluts her readers with names and descriptions of torture devices, much as her eyes may have been glutted with them in the exhibit she mentions. The list of examples also elaborates her topic immediately and leaves the reader under no illusion that she will deal with the topic gently. Students may or may not think this opening a good one, depending on their responses to the topic.

3. When connected with food, the word "unthinkable" is positive, indicating imaginative power dedicated to gustatory pleasure. Connected with torture, however, the word's severe negative connotations come into play: when the power of the imagination is applied to evil, the results are too horrible.

4. Legal, social, and religious institutions working in unison create torture in order to perpetuate themselves (6). Feeling the need to belong, people become convinced that their actions against others, normally considered morally abhorrent, contribute to society's greater good. Torture thus becomes a patriotic duty (6). Rose cites the French torture of Algerians (4), the Nazis and the French again (8), and the Milgram experiments (7).

5. Because allegiance to abstract ideals leads people to torture, its precise opposite, the absolute pursuit of sensual pleasure, is torture's natural antidote (9).

Strategy

1. Electricity vastly expands the potential for human torture, but even without it the fertility of the human imagination applied to torture is impressive.

2. One specific example is Milgram's experiment (7). It supports the topic (first) sentence of paragraph 1 and is concrete: it actually happened. In one typical example, Rose describes how a person might have been tortured on the wheel (3). The example is effective because it suggests that this torture was used many times on nameless, and helpless, victims.

civilization's reminder to itself that nothing leads you less wrong than your awareness of your own pleasure and a genial desire to spread it around. In that sense the myth of Paris constitutes a moral touchstone, standing for the selfish frivolity that helps keep priorities straight.

Meaning and Purpose

1. What is the thesis of the essay and where is it explicitly stated?
2. Rose gives a long list of garish torture devices in the first paragraph. What do you think her purpose is in using examples in this way? Do you feel that they overwhelm and discourage the reader, or hook the reader?
3. In paragraph 3, the author says "The secret of torture, like the secret of French cuisine, is that nothing is unthinkable." How is this statement both a compliment and a condemnation?
4. According to the author, what is the primary cause of human torture? What does this idea imply about social values and human nature? What examples does the author give to demonstrate that those social and psychological tendencies are still with us?
5. In the last two paragraphs the author argues that hedonistic, selfish frivolity is just the thing to keep our moral priorities straight. Why?

Strategy

1. The author says in the opening sentence of paragraph 2 that even before electricity many ways had been devised to torture a person. Why does the author bring in the idea of electricity?
2. Can you point out one specific and one typical example in the essay? How effective is each?
3. Reread paragraphs 7, 8, and 9. Describe the focus of each paragraph and the logic of moving from one to the other.
4. In informative (some might say academic) essays like this one, writers use examples "to make the general more specific and the

abstract more concrete" (chapter introduction [page 163]). What effect overall does Rose accomplish with her graphic examples of torture? Read as a writer and assess how her examples affect tone and the reader's senses.

Style

1. Two French expressions go untranslated: *parfumerie* (paragraph 1) and *soins esthétiques* (paragraph 5). Presumably, the author thinks their meanings should be evident from the context. Are they? What effect is created by leaving the words in the original French?
2. In the final paragraph, Rose generalizes when she uses Paris as *the* example of a place of pleasure, a "moral touchstone." How does this general paragraph, following as it does many paragraphs of specific and even graphic examples and facts, serve to close the essay?
3. Explain how the expression "puritanical thinking" is used in paragraph 5.
4. If necessary, check a dictionary for the meaning of these words: *benign* (paragraph 1); *aesthetician* (paragraph 4); *malevolent* (paragraph 5); *vetted* (paragraph 6); *inalienable* (paragraph 8); *transitory* (paragraph 9); *touchstone* (paragraph 10).

Writing Tasks

1. In "Tools of Torture," Rose uses an event in her life to generate a thesis. Can you think of an event or incident in your life that you can expand into an essay? Make the essay informative, developing your thesis with specific, concrete examples; you may have to do some research.
2. In a few paragraphs, write about a typical example of something—that is, a composite. You might write about a typical day at the beach, a typical American traveler overseas, a typical pet, a typical birthday, and so on.

3. Paragraph 7 is focused on the Milgram experiments. Rose reminds us that cruelty was accepted before the enlightenment; thus, Milgram's experiments would have been meaningless at that time (8). Recent history suggests, however, that the enlightenment's ideals have not really taken hold. She considers the possibility that cruelty may have drifted to the margins of society, leading to her conclusion that radical hedonism may be the cure for abstract idealism (9).

4. Some readers might consider the graphic examples an assault on the senses. Rose does not back away from her topic and make torture seem less terrible than it is or was. This honest tone gives her argument strength and her voice as a writer credibility.

Style

1. Because one of Rose's themes is that the French have a unique talent for creating ways to give "loving attention to the body," it is appropriate to use the French rather than English word in order to capture the French flavor. *Parfumerie* means perfume store (the author gets her massage in one). *Soins esthétiques* means beauty care.

2. The final paragraph sums up Rose's belief that Paris can be considered the "capital of pleasure." She has already given specific examples (4, 5). Ending the essay with her thoughts on the pleasures of modern Paris is a neat connection to her having begun with thoughts on the opposite sensation (pain) in medieval Paris.

3. Because the Puritans shunned the flesh, the idea that beauty radiates from the inner self must be puritanical. The French, according to the author, will have none of that thinking.

4. *benign*: showing or expressive of gentleness or kindness; *aesthetician*: a person who is versed in aesthetics, the branch of philosophy dealing with such notions as the beautiful, the ugly, the sublime, and the comic as applicable to the fine arts; *malevolent*: evil, harmful, injurious; *vetted*: to have appraised, verified, or checked for accuracy, authenticity, validity, and so on; *inalienable*: not transferable to another or capable of being repudiated; *transitory*: not lasting, enduring, permanent, or eternal; *touchstone*: a test or criterion for the quality of a thing.

❧ Neil Postman ❧

Neil Postman has written widely on education, often examining how language relates to education and calling for radical reform in the field. His books include Crazy Talk, Stupid Talk: How We Defeat Ourselves by the Way We Talk and What to Do about It *(1976),* Teaching as a Conserving Activity *(1980),* The Disappearance of Childhood *(1982), and* Amusing Ourselves to Death: Public Discourses in the Age of Show Business *(1985). He is also coauthor of several books on educational reform, including* Linguisitics: A Revolution in Teaching *(1966) and* Teaching as a Subversive Activity *(1969). He was born in 1931 and has been a professor of media ecology at New York University. His articles have appeared in major periodicals, including* The Atlantic *and* The Nation.

Future Shlock

In "Future Shlock," from his Conscientious Objections: Stirring up Trouble about Language, Technology and Education *(1988), Postman uses a string of examples—from politics, religion, film, and literature—to illustrate the dangers of eroding intelligence in a society hooked on entertainment. He mentions in particular the danger of television, which presents everything, from news reports to religion, as entertainment.*

TEACHING SUGGESTIONS

Postman is provocative, though easy to understand. His remarks about the show-business mentality in politics, religion, education, and news programs should elicit strong responses from students. Some will think he exaggerates. Others will be eager to provide additional examples. A good beginning is a discussion of student responses to the overall message.

Don't miss the opportunity to discuss the strategies Postman employs to keep the reader interested and to present his challenging views as reasonable.

MARGINAL NOTES

The first three sentences plunge us directly into the subject. If you assign this essay as outside reading, it might be useful to read these sentences aloud in class first and ask if students are inclined to agree or disagree at first thought.

The long example of Germany prior to World War II may need amplification, briefly identifying the men listed:

Human intelligence is among the most fragile things in nature. It doesn't take much to distract it, suppress it, or even annihilate it. In this century, we have had some lethal examples of how easily and quickly intelligence can be defeated by any one of its several nemeses: ignorance, superstition, moral fervor, cruelty, cowardice, neglect. In the late 1920s, for example, Germany was, by any measure, the most literate, cultured nation in the world. Its legendary seats of learning attracted scholars from every corner. Its philosophers, social critics, and scientists were of the

1

first rank; its humane traditions an inspiration to less favored nations. But by the mid-1930s—that is, in less than ten years—this cathedral of human reason had been transformed into a cesspool of barbaric irrationality. Many of the most intelligent products of German culture were forced to flee—for example, Einstein, Freud, Karl Jaspers, Thomas Mann, and Stefan Zweig. Even worse, those who remained were either forced to submit their minds to the sovereignty of primitive superstition, or—worse still—willingly did so: Konrad Lorenz, Werner Heisenberg, Martin Heidegger, Gerhardt Hauptmann. On May 10, 1933, a huge bonfire was kindled in Berlin and the books of Marcel Proust, André Gide, Emile Zola, Jack London, Upton Sinclair, and a hundred others were committed to the flames, amid shouts of idiot delight. By 1936, Joseph Paul Goebbels, Germany's Minister of Propaganda, was issuing a proclamation which began with the following words: "Because this year has not brought an improvement in art criticism, I forbid once and for all the continuance of art criticism in its past form, effective as of today." By 1936, there was no one left in Germany who had the brains or courage to object.

Exactly why the Germans banished intelligence is a vast and largely unanswered question. I have never been persuaded that the desperate economic depression that afflicted Germany in the 1920s adequately explains what happened. To quote Aristotle: Men do not become tyrants in order to keep warm. Neither do they become stupid—at least not *that* stupid. But the matter need not trouble us here. I offer the German case only as the most striking example of the fragility of human intelligence. My focus here is the United States in our own time, and I wish to worry you about the rapid erosion of our own intelligence. If you are confident that such a thing cannot happen, your confidence is misplaced, I believe, but it is understandable.

After all, the United States is one of the few countries in the world founded by intellectuals—men of wide learning, of extraordinary rhetorical powers, of deep faith in reason. And although we have had our moods of anti-intellectualism, few people have been more generous in support of intelligence and learning than

---

Albert Einstein (1879–1955). Physicist; theory of relativity. Nobel Prize, 1921. Became United States citizen in 1940.

Sigmund Freud (1856–1939). Founder of modern psychoanalysis.

Thomas Mann (1875–1955). Novelist and critic. Nobel Prize, 1929. Came to United States in 1937.

Stefan Zweig (1881–1942). Austrian dramatist, critic, novelist.

Konrad Lorenz (born 1903). Ethologist. Nobel Prize, 1973.

Werner Heisenberg (1901–1976). Physicist. Nobel Prize, 1932.

Martin Heidegger (1889–1976). Philosopher and writer.

Gerhardt Hauptmann (1862–1946). Dramatist, novelist, poet. Nobel Prize, 1912.

Marcel Proust (1871–1922). French novelist.

André Gide (1869–1951). French novelist, poet, critic. Nobel Prize, 1947.

Emile Zola (1840–1902). French novelist.

Jack London (1876–1916). United States novelist and short-story writer.

Upton Sinclair (1878–1968). United States novelist.

2 The paragraph ends with an emphatic clincher sentence. Postman often uses this device to drive a point home or to look ahead to the next paragraph. See 2–4, 11, 14, 15, 19, and 24.

3 Having evoked the memory of pre–World War II Germany, an easy-to-accept example, Postman challenges his readers by saying that a similar erosion of intelligence could happen in the United States. This contrast between America's past and Postman's perception of its present condition gives his readers a measure of how much he feels has been lost.

The Land Grant Act of 1862 was a federal-government act that financed the establishment of state colleges.

Henry Steele Commager (born 1902). United States historian and author.

Shlock—of inferior quality, cheap, junk (also spelled *schlock*).

The first sentence is a fairly direct statement of Postman's thesis. (A fuller statement is at the end of paragraph 11.)

For readers who are saying to themselves that the United States is different from Germany, Postman accepts the objection, but argues that similar methodology is not necessary. He picks up this contrast later in discussing Orwell's *1984* and Huxley's *Brave New World*.

Have students comment on the effectiveness of the three sentences that begin with "a culture" and the shock value of the word "stupidity" in the last sentence.

Americans. It was the United States that initiated the experiment in mass education that is, even today, the envy of the world. It was America's churches that laid the foundation of our admirable system of higher education; it was the Land-Grant Act of 1862 that made possible our great state universities; and it is to America that scholars and writers have fled when freedom of the intellect became impossible in their own nations. This is why the great historian of American civilization Henry Steele Commager called America "the Empire of Reason." But Commager was referring to the United States of the eighteenth and nineteenth centuries. What term he would use for America today, I cannot say. Yet he has observed, as others have, a change, a precipitous decline in our valuation of intelligence, in our uses of language, in the disciplines of logic and reason, in our capacity to attend to complexity. Perhaps he would agree with me that the Empire of Reason is, in fact, gone, and that the most apt term for America today is the Empire of Shlock.

In any case, this is what I wish to call to your notice: the frightening displacement of serious, intelligent public discourse in American culture by the imagery and triviality of what may be called show business. I do not see the decline of intelligent discourse in America leading to the barbarisms that flourished in Germany, of course. No scholars, I believe, will ever need to flee America. There will be no bonfires to burn books. And I cannot imagine any proclamations forbidding once and for all art criticism, or any other kind of criticism. But this is not a cause for complacency, let alone celebration. A culture does not have to force scholars to flee to render them impotent. A culture does not have to burn books to assure that they will not be read. And a culture does not need a Minister of Propaganda issuing proclamations to silence criticism. There are other ways to achieve stupidity, and it appears that, as in so many other things, there is a distinctly American way.

To explain what I am getting at, I find it helpful to refer to two films, which taken together embody the main lines of my argument. The first film is of recent vintage and is called *The Gods Must Be Crazy*. It is about a tribal people who live in the Kalahari Desert plains of southern Africa, and what happens to their culture when it is invaded by an empty Coca-Cola bottle tossed from the window of a small plane passing overhead. The bottle lands in the middle of the village and is construed by these gentle people to be a gift from the gods, for they not only have never seen a bottle before but have never seen glass either. The people are almost immediately charmed by the gift, and not only because of its novelty. The bottle, it turns out, has multiple uses, chief among them the intriguing music it makes when one blows into it.

But gradually a change takes place in the tribe. The bottle becomes an irresistible preoccupation. Looking at it, holding it, thinking of things to do with it displace other activities once thought essential. But more than this, the Coke bottle is the only thing these people have ever seen of which there is only one of its kind. And so those who do not have it try to get it from the one who does. And the one who does refuses to give it up. Jealousy, greed, and even violence enter the scene, and come very close to destroying the harmony that has characterized their culture for a thousand years. The people begin to love their bottle more than they love themselves, and are saved only when the leader of the tribe, convinced that the gods must be crazy, returns the bottle to the gods by throwing it off the top of a mountain.

The film is great fun and it is also wise, mainly because it is about a subject as relevant to people in Chicago or Los Angeles or New York as it is to those of the Kalahari Desert. It raises two questions of extreme importance to our situation: How does a culture change when new technologies are introduced to it? And is it always desirable for a culture to accommodate itself to the demands of new technologies? The leader of the Kalahari tribe is forced to confront these questions in a way that Americans have refused to do. And because his vision is not obstructed by a belief in what Americans call "technological progress," he is able with minimal discomfort to decide that the songs of the Coke bottle are not so alluring that they are worth admitting envy, egotism, and greed to a serene culture.

The second film relevant to my argument was made in 1967. It is Mel Brooks's first film, *The Producers*. *The Producers* is a rather raucous comedy that has at its center a painful joke: An

Many students will be familiar with this film, first shown in the United States in 1984 and frequently offered on cable. In paragraph 5, he presents the situation in the movie, and in paragraph 6, he explains the bottle's disrupting effect: "The people begin to love their bottle more than they love themselves."

6

7   Before moving to the second movie example, you may want to make sure that students understand Postman's point: A new technology should be examined carefully and rejected if necessary.

8   The second movie example illustrates a different point: We are in danger of so trivializing dignified, serious, and important aspects of life that they will become mere entertainment.

unscrupulous theatrical producer has figured out that it is relatively easy to turn a buck by producing a play that fails. All one
has to do is induce dozens of backers to invest in the play by
promising them exorbitant percentages of its profits. When the
play fails, there being no profits to disperse, the producer walks
away with thousands of dollars that can never be claimed. Of
course, the central problem he must solve is to make sure that his
play is a disastrous failure. And so he hits upon an excellent idea:
he will take the most tragic and grotesque story of our century—
the rise of Adolf Hitler—and make it into a musical.

Because the producer is only a crook and not a fool, he as-   9
sumes that the stupidity of making a musical on this theme will
be immediately grasped by audiences and that they will leave the
theater in dumbfounded rage. So he calls his play *Springtime for
Hitler,* which is also the name of its most important song. The
song begins with the words:

> Springtime for Hitler and Germany;
> Winter for Poland and France.

The melody is catchy, and when the song is sung it is accom-   10
panied by a happy chorus line. (One must understand, of course,
that *Springtime for Hitler* is no spoof of Hitler, as was, for example, Charlie Chaplin's *The Great Dictator*. The play is instead a
kind of denial of Hitler in song and dance; as if to say, it was all
in fun.)

The ending of the movie is predictable. The audience loves   11
the play and leaves the theater humming *Springtime for Hitler*. The
musical becomes a great hit. The producer ends up in jail, his
joke having turned back on him. But Brooks's point is that the
joke is on us. Although the film was made years before a movie
actor became President of the United States, Brooks was making
a kind of prophecy about that—namely, that the producers of
American culture will increasingly turn our history, politics, religion, commerce, and education into forms of entertainment, and
that we will become as a result a trivial people, incapable of
coping with complexity, ambiguity, uncertainty, perhaps even

reality. We will become, in a phrase, a people amused into stupidity.

For those readers who are not inclined to take Mel Brooks as seriously as I do, let me remind you that the prophecy I attribute here to Brooks was, in fact, made many years before by a more formidable social critic than he. I refer to Aldous Huxley, who wrote *Brave New World* at the time that the modern monuments to intellectual stupidity were taking shape: Nazism in Germany, fascism in Italy, communism in Russia. But Huxley was not concerned in his book with such naked and crude forms of intellectual suicide. He saw beyond them, and mostly, I must add, he saw America. To be more specific, he foresaw that the greatest threat to the intelligence and humane creativity of our culture would not come from Big Brother and Ministries of Propaganda, or gulags and concentration camps. He prophesied, if I may put it this way, that there is tyranny lurking in a Coca-Cola bottle; that we could be ruined not by what we fear and hate but by what we welcome and love, by what we construe to be a gift from the gods.

And in case anyone missed his point in 1932, Huxley wrote *Brave New World Revisited* twenty years later. By then, George Orwell's *1984* had been published, and it was inevitable that Huxley would compare Orwell's book with his own. The difference, he said, is that in Orwell's book people are controlled by inflicting pain. In *Brave New World,* they are controlled by inflicting pleasure.

The Coke bottle that has fallen in our midst is a corporation of dazzling technologies whose forms turn all serious public business into a kind of *Springtime for Hitler* musical. Television is the principal instrument of this disaster, in part because it is the medium Americans most dearly love, and in part because it has become the command center of our culture. Americans turn to television not only for their light entertainment but for their news, their weather, their politics, their religion, their history—all of which may be said to be their serious entertainment. The light entertainment is not the problem. The least dangerous things on television are its junk. What I am talking about is television's preemption of our culture's most serious business. It would be

12

13

14

Aldous Huxley (1894–1963). English novelist and critic.

"Big Brother" (the television image in Orwell's *1984*), "Ministries of Propaganda," "gulags," and "concentration camps" represent the tyranny of force.

The Coca-Cola bottle is used as a symbol of new technologies.

George Orwell [Eric Blair] (1903–1950). English novelist and essayist.

Paragraph 14 marks the culmination of Postman's interpretation of the current situation. His examples thus far have pointed to the insufficiently examined power of show business (particularly, but not exclusively, television) to trivialize serious discourse.

merely banal to say that television presents us with entertaining subject matter. It is quite another thing to say that on television all subject matter is presented as entertaining. And that is how television brings ruin to any intelligent understanding of public affairs.

Political campaigns, for example, are now conducted largely   15
in the form of television commercials. Candidates forgo precision, complexity, substance—in some cases, language itself—for the arts of show business: music, imagery, celebrities, theatrics. Indeed, political figures have become so good at this, and so accustomed to it, that they do television commercials even when they are not campaigning, as, for example, Geraldine Ferraro for Diet Pepsi and former Vice-Presidential candidate William Miller and the late Senator Sam Ervin for American Express. Even worse, political figures appear on variety shows, soap operas, and sitcoms. George McGovern, Ralph Nader, Ed Koch, and Jesse Jackson have all hosted "Saturday Night Live." Henry Kissinger and former President Gerald Ford have done cameo roles on "Dynasty." Tip O'Neill and Governor Michael Dukakis have appeared on "Cheers." Richard Nixon did a short stint on "Laugh-In." The late Senator from Illinois, Everett Dirksen, was on "What's My Line?" a prophetic question if ever there was one. What *is* the line of these people? Or, more precisely, *where* is the line that one ought to be able to draw between politics and entertainment? I would suggest that television has annihilated it.

It is significant, I think, that although our [then] current   16
President, a former Hollywood movie actor, rarely speaks accurately and never precisely, he is known as the Great Communicator; his telegenic charm appears to be his major asset, and that seems to be quite good enough in an entertainment-oriented politics. But lest you think his election to two terms is a mere aberration, I must remind you that, as I write [1988], Charlton Heston is being mentioned as a possible candidate for the Republican nomination in 1988. Should this happen, what alternative would the Democrats have but to nominate Gregory Peck? Two idols of the silver screen going one on one. Could even the fertile imagination of Mel Brooks have foreseen this? Heston giving us intimations of Moses as he accepts the nomination; Peck re-creating

Beginning with paragraph 15, Postman turns to examples of this trivialization in politics, religion, education, news, and history in the next six paragraphs. This section will probably stimulate most discussion. Some students will undoubtedly be delighted with Postman's examples and want to add some of their own. Others may feel that he overstates his position and succumbs to the very disease he warns us of. With the following examples he attempts to show the scope of the influence:

Geraldine Ferraro (born 1935). First woman vice-presidential nominee, 1984.
William Miller (born 1914). Republican candidate for vice president in 1964.
Sam Ervin (1896–1985). U.S. Senator, chairman of Senate Watergate investigation committee.
George McGovern (born 1922). Democratic presidential candidate, 1972.
Ralph Nader (born 1934). Consumer advocate, lawyer, writer.
Ed Koch (born 1924). Former mayor of New York City, 1977–1989.
Jesse Jackson (born 1941). Civil-rights activist, minister, presidential hopeful.
Henry Kissinger (born 1923). Secretary of State, 1973–1977. Nobel Prize, 1973.
Gerald Ford (born 1913). President of United States, 1974–1977.
Tip O'Neill (born 1912). Speaker of the House, 1977–1987.
Michael Dukakis (born 1933). Democratic candidate for president, 1988.
Richard Nixon (born 1913). President of United States, 1969–1974.
Everett Dirksen (1896–1969). U.S. Senator.

the courage of his biblical David as he accepts the challenge of running against a modern Goliath. Heston going on the stump as Michelangelo; Peck countering with Douglas MacArthur. Heston accusing Peck of insanity because of *The Boys from Brazil*. Peck replying with the charge that Heston blew the world up in *Return to Planet of the Apes*. *Springtime for Hitler* could be closer than you think.

But politics is only one arena in which serious language has been displaced by the arts of show business. We have all seen how religion is packaged on television, as a kind of Las Vegas stage show, devoid of ritual, sacrality, and tradition. Today's electronic preachers are in no way like America's evangelicals of the past. Men like Jonathan Edwards, Charles Finney, and George Whitefield were preachers of theological depth, authentic learning, and great expository power. Electronic preachers such as Jimmy Swaggart, Jim Bakker, and Jerry Falwell are merely performers who exploit television's visual power and their own charisma for the greater glory of themselves.

17   Jonathan Edwards (1703–1758). Clergyman and theologian.
Charles Finney (1792–1875). Clergyman and educator.
George Whitefield (1714–1770). Methodist revivalist.
Jimmy Swaggart (born 1935). Television evangelist.
Jim Bakker (born 1948). Former television evangelist.
Jerry Falwell (born 1933). Television evangelist.

We have also seen "Sesame Street" and other educational shows in which the demands of entertainment take precedence over the rigors of learning. And we well know how American businessmen, working under the assumption that potential customers require amusement rather than facts, use music, dance, comedy, cartoons, and celebrities to sell their products.

18

Even our daily news, which for most Americans means television news, is packaged as a kind of show, featuring handsome news readers, exciting music, and dynamic film footage. Most especially, film footage. When there is no film footage, there is no story. Stranger still, commercials may appear anywhere in a news story—before, after, or in the middle. This reduces all events to trivialities, sources of public entertainment and little more. After all, how serious can a bombing in Lebanon be if it is shown to us prefaced by a happy United Airlines commercial and summarized by a Calvin Klein jeans commercial? Indeed, television newscasters have added to our grammar a new part of speech—what may be called the "Now . . . this" conjunction, a conjunction that does not connect two things, but disconnects them. When newscasters say, "Now . . . this," they mean to indicate that what you

19

have just heard or seen has no relevance to what you are about to hear or see. There is no murder so brutal, no political blunder so costly, no bombing so devastating that it cannot be erased from our minds by a newscaster saying, "Now . . . this." He means that you have thought long enough on the matter (let us say, for forty seconds) and you must now give your attention to a commercial. Such a situation is not "the news." It is merely a daily version of *Springtime for Hitler,* and in my opinion accounts for the fact that Americans are among the most ill-informed people in the world. To be sure, we know *of* many things; but we know *about* very little.

To provide some verification of this, I conducted a survey a 20 few years back on the subject of the Iranian hostage crisis. I chose this subject because it was alluded to on television *every day for more than a year.* I did not ask my subjects for their opinions about the hostage situation. I am not interested in opinion polls; I am interested in knowledge polls. The questions I asked were simple and did not require deep knowledge. For example, Where is Iran? What language do the Iranians speak? Where did the Shah come from? What religion do the Iranians practice, and what are its basic tenets? What does "Ayatollah" mean? I found that almost everybody knew practically nothing about Iran. And those who did know something said they had learned it from *Newsweek* or *Time* or *The New York Times.* Television, in other words, is not the great information machine. It is the great disinformation machine. A most nerve-wracking confirmation of this came some time ago during an interview with the producer and the writer of the TV mini-series *Peter the Great.* Defending the historical inaccuracies in the drama—which included a fabricated meeting between Peter and Sir Isaac Newton—the producer said that no one would watch a dry, historically faithful biography. The writer added that it is better for audiences to learn something that is untrue, if it is entertaining, than not to learn anything at all. And just to put some icing on the cake, the actor who played Peter, Maximilian Schell, remarked that he does not believe in historical truth and therefore sees no reason to pursue it.

I do not mean to say that the trivialization of American public 21 discourse is all accomplished on television. Rather, television is

How do your students take to the accusation leveled here against all of us?

Similar "polls" appear regularly in the press. Students may want to discuss others they have heard about, or question how accurate they are and what conclusions they justify.

Ayatollah: a highly advanced scholar of Islamic law and religion (Shi'ite title).

Peter the Great (1672–1725). Peter I, czar of Russia, 1682–1725.

Sir Isaac Newton (1642–1727). English philosopher and mathematician. Formulated the law of gravitation.

the paradigm for all our attempts at public communication. It conditions our minds to apprehend the world through fragmented pictures and forces other media to orient themselves in that direction. You know the standard question we put to people who have difficulty understanding even simple language: we ask them impatiently, "Do I have to draw a picture for you?" Well, it appears that, like it or not, our culture will draw pictures for us, will explain the world to us in pictures. As a medium for conducting public business, language had receded in importance; it has been moved to the periphery of culture and has been replaced at the center by the entertaining visual image.

Please understand that I am making no criticism of the visual arts in general. That criticism is made by God, not by me. You will remember that in His Second Commandment, God explicitly states that "Thou shalt not make unto thee any graven image, nor any likeness of anything that is in Heaven above, or that is in the earth beneath, or the waters beneath the earth." I have always felt that God was taking a rather extreme position on this, as is His way. As for myself, I am arguing from the standpoint of a symbolic relativist. Forms of communication are neither good nor bad in themselves. They become good or bad depending on their relationship to other symbols and on the functions they are made to serve within a social order. When a culture becomes overloaded with pictures; when logic and rhetoric lose their binding authority; when historical truth becomes irrelevant; when the spoken or written word is distrusted or makes demands on our attention that we are incapable of giving; when our politics, history, education, religion, public information, and commerce are expressed largely in visual imagery rather than words, then a culture is in serious jeopardy.

Neither do I make a complaint against entertainment. As an old song has it, life is not a highway strewn with flowers. The sight of a few blossoms here and there may make our journey a trifle more endurable. But in America, the least amusing people are our professional entertainers. In our present situation, our preachers, entrepreneurs, politicians, teachers, and journalists are committed to entertaining us through media that do not lend themselves to serious, complex discourse. But these producers of

22

23

In three paragraphs (21, 22, 23), Postman tells us he is not blaming television alone, nor is he attacking the visual arts or entertainment in themselves.

In paragraph 23, he restates his belief that "entertainment" has permeated the serious aspects of our culture and reminds us, using the words "the gods must be crazy," about the message of that film: The effects of new technology must be examined carefully.

In the concluding paragraph he reminds us again that America seems to have chosen the Huxleyan rather than the Orwellian road.

Postman offers no specific way out of the situation he describes. In fact, paragraph 23 ends with a discouraging note: "there is no mountaintop from which we can return what is dangerous to us."

POSSIBLE ANSWERS

Meaning and Purpose

1. Postman's purpose is to warn us about the "rapid erosion of our own intelligence" as a result of the trivialization of serious matters: politics, education, religion, and news. He simply informs us; he does not offer solutions. The last sentences in paragraphs 22–24 discourage hope. Students should be able to support their opinions about whether or not the purpose succeeds.
2. Paragraph 11 includes the statement that seems most nearly complete.
3. *The Gods Must Be Crazy* example shows that new technologies profoundly affect cultures, and they should be examined and discarded if necessary. *The Producers* example shows how serious matters can be trivialized.
4. The Reagan example is fairly well explained, and Postman shows that Reagan's style is "good enough in an entertainment-oriented politics." (Some students may disagree with Postman's opinion of Reagan; encourage discussion.) *Sesame Street* is mentioned briefly and criticized for placing learning second to entertainment. Postman does not offer support for this opinion, so that the example does not demonstrate his meaning as clearly as the other does. (Some students may have watched *Sesame Street* as children and may have an opinion different from Postman's.) Encourage them to evaluate other examples for their contributions to meaning.
5. Perhaps only a few students will agree with

our culture are not to be blamed. They, like the rest of us, believe in the supremacy of technological progress. It has never occurred to us that the gods might be crazy. And even if it did, there is no mountaintop from which we can return what is dangerous to us.

We would do well to keep in mind that there are two ways in which the spirit of a culture may be degraded. In the first—the Orwellian—culture becomes a prison. This was the way of the Nazis, and it appears to be the way of the Russians. In the second—the Huxleyan—culture becomes a burlesque. This appears to be the way of the Americans. What Huxley teaches is that in the Age of Advanced Technology, spiritual devastation is more likely to come from an enemy with a smiling countenance than from one whose face exudes suspicion and hate. In the Huxleyan prophecy, Big Brother does not watch us, by his choice; we watch him, by ours. When a culture becomes distracted by trivia; when political and social life are redefined as a perpetual round of entertainments; when public conversation becomes a form of baby talk; when a people become, in short, an audience and their public business a vaudeville act, then—Huxley argued—a nation finds itself at risk and culture-death is a clear possibility. I agree. 24

Meaning and Purpose

1. The purpose of an essay is like a goal that the writer sets. The writer has to keep the reader reminded of the purpose and pointed in the right direction. What do you think Postman's purpose is in "Future Shlock," and does he achieve it? How does he do so, and if he doesn't, why does he fail?
2. Postman states his general thesis in a number of ways. Paragraphs 2, 3, 4, 11, and 12 have sentences that sound like thesis statements. Reread these paragraphs and find the statement that you think best summarizes the essay as a whole.
3. What is the main point in *The Gods Must Be Crazy* example? in *The Producers* example?

4. Choose any two examples (such as, Reagan as an example of the blurred distinction between politics and entertainment [paragraph 6]; Sesame Street as an example of the needs of entertainment overriding the "rigors of learning" [paragraph 18]), and discuss whether or not these choices help elucidate Postman's meaning. Are they effective in their immediate contexts?

5. How convincing is Postman? Does his view of our culture coincide with yours? In what ways? Do you disagree with portions of his argument?

Strategy

1. Postman often ends paragraphs with strong statements. See paragraphs 1, 2, and 3. Find other strong statements that end paragraphs and discuss the purpose they serve.

2. Why does Postman begin with a pre-World War II German example in an essay about the United States? Why does he turn away from the example without examining its causes?

3. Whom do you think Postman had in mind as his audience when he wrote "Future Shlock"? What kind of reader does he appeal to? Do you think he wants to provoke readers with his criticisms of television and American culture and intelligence? Discuss.

4. Trace the use of examples in the essay. Are they specific or typical? extended or brief? Are different types of examples put to different uses?

Style

1. In Postman's opening example, Germany, he says, "this cathedral of human reason had been transformed into a cesspool of barbaric irrationality." Comment on the effectiveness of this metaphor, especially the words "cathedral," "cesspool," and "barbaric."

2. The Coca-Cola bottle so vital to Postman's discussion of *The Gods Must Be Crazy* is used as a metaphor for what? Comment

Postman completely. Some may feel he exaggerates; others will strongly resist his intensely critical message.

Strategy

1. This sentence—"We will become, in a phrase, a people amused into stupidity"—summarizes the lengthy sentence preceding it and provides shock value with the word "stupidity."

"And that is how television brings ruin. . . ." The uncompromising harshness of "ruin" conveys the seriousness of his charge in the preceding sentence (14).

"I would suggest that television has annihilated it." The word "annihilated" means total erasure of the line, thus conveying Postman's contention that politics has become entertainment (15).

"To be sure, we know *of* many things; but we know *about* very little." The parallelism used here to contrast *of* and *about* creates a memorable phrasing, reinforcing his point that television news is not really educating people (19).

"I agree." Coming after a long (sixty-word) sentence developed with parallel structure, the punchiness of this two-word sentence is emphatic (24).

2. Germany is, first, a notorious example of unexplained "madness." Therefore, it is easy for a reader to accept the example and the conclusion. When he moves in the next paragraph to the United States example, the reader has already, at least in part, accepted his credibility.

3. Postman appeals to an intelligent, aware audience that can understand many of his historical references, or know how to look them up. Yet he probably knows that some of his readers get most of their information from television, even though he criticizes this habit. He surely intends to be provocative and make readers think and perhaps reevaluate.

4. In the first half of the essay (through paragraph 13), he uses specific, extended examples: Germany, the United States, *The Gods Must Be Crazy, The Producers,* and *Brave New World,* as well as a brief mention of *1984.*

In the second half of the essay the examples are brief and both specific and typical (see paragraph 19 for a good illustration), though he gives one extended example of a hypothetical Heston versus Peck political campaign.

Style

1. "Cathedral" may be loosely applied to any large church. The connotation here is of spiritual authority, suggesting dedication, piety, learning, reverence, love, aspiration—the best human qualities.

A "cesspool" is a drainage hole for sewage. It brings to mind filth, foul smells, disease, and waste.

"Barbarian" originally meant anyone who belonged to a group outside one's own culture, and "barbaric" denoted such a person's behavior, whatever it might be. Now the word commonly indicates lack of learning, lack of restraint, wild, uneducated, uncivilized, and uncultured—a person living without reasonable values and behaviors.

The metaphor moves from the lofty to the debased and characterizes the change as a retreat to less than civilized behavior.

2. The Coca-Cola bottle is a metaphor for new technologies. The quotations, in turn, mean a new technology can become tyrannical, recall the bottle's effect on the tribe, connect television with the Coke bottle, and restate the original metaphor.

3. *Shlock:* shoddy; *nemeses:* (plural of nemesis) a powerful rival, one who inflicts destruction; *rhetorical:* use of words for persuasion; *precipitous:* steep; *preemption:* acquisition or appropriation of something beforehand; *banal:* predictable, trite; *intimations:* declarations; *sacrality:* religious rites; *Ayatollah:* Islamic scholar of high rank; *paradigm:* a model; *countenance:* appearance.

on the connection between these statements and the original metaphor:

> ". . . there is tyranny lurking in a Coca-Cola bottle." (paragraph 12).

> ". . . we could be ruined . . . by what we welcome and love." (paragraph 12)

> "The Coke bottle that has fallen in our midst is a corporation of dazzling technologies." (paragraph 14)

> "Television . . . is the medium Americans most dearly love." (paragraph 14)

3. If necessary, check a dictionary for the meaning of these words: *shlock; nemeses* (paragraph 1); *rhetorical* (paragraph 3); *precipitous* (paragraph 3); *preemption* (paragraph 14); *banal* (paragraph 14); *intimations* (paragraph 16); *sacrality* (paragraph 17); *Ayatollah* (paragraph 20); *paradigm* (paragraph 21); *countenance* (paragraph 24).

Writing Tasks

1. In paragraph 1, Postman says, "In this century, we have had some lethal examples of how easily and quickly intelligence can be defeated by any one of its several nemeses: ignorance, superstition, moral fervor, cruelty, cowardice, neglect." Have you ever seen these forces at work in your studies or in your own experience? Consider your own behavior, your friends' behavior, the workings of your city or community, national or international affairs, your college, your clubs and organizations. Write an essay about one of these forces as you have seen it at work in one or more situations. Develop your essay with either typical or specific examples.

2. Postman argues that "serious matters of public concern" have been turned into entertainment. Write an essay in which you agree or disagree with his view in relation to one serious matter of public concern. Use one or more specific, extended examples to support your assertions.

❦ Alleen Pace Nilsen ❦

Alleen Pace Nilsen was born in 1936 and attended Brigham Young University as an undergraduate and American University as a masters student. She received her doctorate from the University of Iowa, where she studied linguistic sexism in children's literature. She is coauthor, with her husband, of two books: Pronunciation Contrasts in English *(1971) and* Semantic Theory: A Linguistic Perspective *(1975). Continuing her work in linguistic sexism and children's literature, she has coedited a book of essays,* Sexism and Language *(1977), and a textbook,* Literature for Today's Young Adults *(1980). Currently she is a professor of English and assistant vice president for academic affairs at Arizona State University.*

Sexism in English:
A 1990s Update

In an essay written in the early 1970s, Nilsen examined the sexist biases inherent in numerous words of the English language. The article was published as part of a series sponsored by the Modern Language Association's Commission on the Status of Women. Nilsen wrote this following essay, in which she looks at how language use has changed since then, and adds new examples to her old list. "A 1990s Update" first appeared in Language Awareness, *a composition anthology.*

Twenty years ago I embarked on a study of the sexism inherent in American English. I had just returned to Ann Arbor, Michigan, after living for two years (1967–69) in Kabul, Afghanistan, where I had begun to look critically at the role society assigned to women. The Afghan version of the *chaderi* prescribed for Moslem women was particularly confining. Few women attended the American-built Kabul University where my husband was teaching linguistics because there were no women's

201

TEACHING SUGGESTIONS

How we label the things around us determines how we view them. What of the school mascot? If it had been the Teddy bear, how would our athletic teams feel about themselves? What if automobiles had names like Plymouth Rock or Chrysler Banana or Cadillac El Desperfecto (which means "the flaw")?

Younger students in the 1990s occasionally do not realize how the feminist movement has affected their lives. For that matter, they sometimes are not aware that discrimination still pervades our culture. A lively discussion grows from the question, "Why is it that we have never had a woman president of the United States?" The usual quick answer is that no woman has applied for the job. But wait a minute: *Why* has no woman applied? Is it because she has no chance of winning? If she has no chance of winning, then *why* does she have no chance of winning? Do men completely control politics in this country, so that "women need not apply"?

The real question, though not so dramatic, runs deep: Have we, consciously or not, used language in such a way for so many years that women have been perceived as "the weaker sex," the "sexy" gender, the "passive" gender, the "second sex"—only because of our language usage and without reason or logic? Are we not aware that the language can operate against our notions of equality?

MARGINAL NOTES

Sometimes, people are fortunate enough to travel to other countries where they can better see the merits and demerits of their own country by objective comparison. Being in another country and not knowing its culture and customs, they see in a way that the natives do not see—by comparing their own ways with the way of the Afghans, in this example.

dormitories, which meant that the only females who could attend were those whose families happened to live in the capital city. Afghan jokes and folklore were blatantly sexist, for example this proverb, "If you see an old man, sit down and take a lesson; if you see an old woman, throw a stone."

Nilsen compares the roles of Afghan women with those of American women, particularly those in Kabul. She gives examples of how women are treated in Kabul, which open her eyes to the ways in which women in general are treated.

But it wasn't only the native culture that made me question women's roles; it was also the American community. Nearly six hundred Americans lived in Kabul, mostly supported by U.S. taxpayers. The single women were career secretaries, school teachers, or nurses. The three women who had jobs comparable to the American men's jobs were textbook editors with the assignment of developing reading books in Dari (Afghan Persian) for young children. They worked at the Ministry of Education, a large building in the center of the city. There were no women's restrooms, so during their two-year assignment whenever they needed to go to the bathroom they had to walk across the street and down the block to the Kabul Hotel.

Removed from their own culture, the American women in Kabul take up ways of life that are unusual for them. Nilsen gives examples of how the American women's activities in Kabul changed her way of thinking about women's roles in general.

The rest of the American women were like myself—wives and mothers whose husbands were either career diplomats, employees of USAID, or college professors who had been recruited to work on various contract teams including an education team from Teachers College, Columbia University and an agricultural team from the University of Wyoming. These were the women who were most influential in changing my way of thinking. We were suddenly bereft of our traditional roles; some of us became alcoholics; others got very good at bridge, while others searched desperately for ways to contribute either to our families or to the Afghans. The local economy provided few jobs for women and certainly none for foreigners; we were isolated from former friends and the social goals we had grown up with. Most of us had three servants (they worked for $1.00 a day) because the cook refused to wash dishes and the dishwasher refused to water the lawn or sweep the sidewalks—it was their form of unionization. Occasionally, someone would try to get along without servants, but it was impossible because the houses were huge and we didn't have the mechanical aids we had at home. Drinking water had to be brought from the deep well at the American Embassy, and kerosene and wood stoves had to be stocked and lit. The servants were all males, the highest-paid one being the cook who could usually speak some English. Our days revolved around supervising these servants. One woman's husband got so tired of hearing her complain about such annoyances as the *bacha* (the housekeeper) stealing kerosene and needles and batteries, and about the cook putting chili powder instead of paprika on the deviled eggs, and about the gardener subcontracting his work and expecting her to pay all his friends that he scheduled an hour a week for listening to complaints. The rest of the time he wanted to keep his mind clear to focus on his important work with his Afghan counterparts and with the president of the university and the Minister of Education. What he was doing in this country was going to make a difference! In the great eternal scheme of things, of what possible importance could be his wife's trivial troubles with the servants?

Notice the hint of imitation here. The American man seems to be imitating what he sees as a facet of Afghan culture. He takes "valuable" time out from his "important work"—an hour a week—to listen to his wife's complaints. The rhetorical question that concludes this paragraph is meant to reflect sarcastically the man's inflated view of his job.

These were the thoughts in my mind when we finished our contract and returned in the fall of 1969 to the University of Michigan in Ann Arbor. I was surprised to find that many other women were also questioning the expectations that they had grown up with. In the spring of 1970, a women's conference was announced. I hired a babysitter and attended, but I returned home more troubled than ever. Now that I knew housework was worth only a dollar a day, I couldn't take it seriously, but I wasn't angry in the same way these women were. Their militancy frightened me. Since I wasn't ready for a revolution, I decided I would have my own feminist movement. I would study the English language and see what it could tell me about sexism. I started reading a desk dictionary and making notecards on every entry that seemed to tell something about male and female. I soon had a dog-eared dictionary, along with a collection of notecards filling two shoe boxes.

4 Nilsen decides to take up academic involvement in the feminist movement, rather than an overtly political part. Not being ready for a revolution, she instead decides to study the ways in which language affects people's attitudes.

Ironically, I started reading the dictionary because I wanted to avoid getting involved in social issues, but what happened was that my notecards brought me right back to looking at society. Language and society are as intertwined as a chicken and an egg. The language that a culture uses is telltale evidence of the values and beliefs of that culture. And because there is a lag in how fast

5

Briefly, the "Whorfian hypothesis" (after Benjamin Lee Whorf) says that the language a culture uses determines its perceptions of the world. The popularity of this view has waned because we seem to have no way to prove that different groups of languages reflect different thought processes. Nilsen is not dealing with *language* linguistically defined, however; she is dealing with words and how those words can tell us something about ourselves, which is part of the semantic component of language.

a language changes—new words can easily be introduced, but it takes a long time for old words and usages to disappear—a careful look at English will reveal the attitudes that our ancestors held and that we as a culture are therefore predisposed to hold. My notecards revealed three main points. Friends have offered the opinion that I didn't need to read the dictionary to learn such obvious facts. Nevertheless, it was interesting to have linguistic evidence of sociological observations.

Women Are Sexy; Men Are Successful

First, in American culture a woman is valued for the attractiveness and sexiness of her body, while a man is valued for his physical strength and accomplishments. A woman is sexy. A man is successful. 6

The writer offers general arguments based on examination of the evidence, then moves from general arguments to particular examples that support those arguments. "A women is sexy" is a general argument, as is "A man is successful." Nilsen sets out to prove both general arguments by offering the wealth of examples that she found to support them.

A persuasive piece of evidence supporting this view are the eponyms—words that have come from someone's name—found in English. I had a two-and-a-half-inch stack of cards taken from men's names, but less than a half-inch stack from women's names, and most of those came from Greek mythology. In the words that came into American English since we separated from Britain, there are many eponyms based on the names of famous American men: bartlett pear, boysenberry, diesel engine, franklin stove, ferris wheel, gattling gun, mason jar, sideburns, sousaphone, schick test, and winchester rifle. The only common eponyms taken from American women's names are *Alice blue* (after Alice Roosevelt Longworth), *bloomers* (after Amelia Jenks Bloomer), and *Mae West jacket* (after the buxom actress). Two out of the three feminine eponyms relate closely to a woman's physical anatomy, while the masculine eponyms (except for *sideburns* after General Burnsides) have nothing to do with the namesake's body, but instead honor the man for an accomplishment of some kind. 7

Although in Greek mythology women played a bigger role than they did in the biblical stories of the Judeo-Christian cultures and so the names of goddesses are accepted parts of the language in such place names as Pomona from the goddess of fruit and Athens from Athena and in such common words as *cereal* 8 from Ceres, *psychology* from Psyche, and *arachnoid* from Arachne, the same tendency to think of women in relation to sexuality is seen in the eponyms *aphrodisiac* from Aphrodite, the Greek name for the goddess of love and beauty, and *venereal disease,* from Venus, the Roman name for Aphrodite.

Another interesting word from Greek mythology is *Amazon.*   9
According to Greek folk etymology, the *a* means "without" as in *atypical,* or *amoral* while *mazon* comes from *mazos,* meaning *breast* as still seen in *mastectomy.* In the Greek legend, Amazon women cut off their right breasts so that they could better shoot their bows. Apparently, the storytellers had a feeling that for women to play the active, "masculine" role that the Amazons adopted for themselves, they had to trade in part of their femininity.

This preoccupation with women's breasts is not limited to   10
ancient stories. As a volunteer for the University of Wisconsin's *Dictionary of American Regional English (DARE),* I read a western trapper's diary from the 1830s. I was to make notes of any unusual usages or language patterns. My most interesting finding was that he referred to a range of mountains as *The Teats,* a metaphor based on the similarity between the shapes of the mountains and women's breasts. Because today we use the French wording, *The Grand Tetons,* the metaphor isn't as obvious, but I wrote to the mapmakers and found the following listings: *Nippletop* and *Little Nipple Top* near Mt. Marcy in the Adirondacks, *Nipple Mountain* in Archuleta County, Colorado, *Nipple Peak* in Coke County, Texas, *Nipple Butte* in Pennington, South Dakota, *Squaw Peak* in Placer County, California (and many other locations), *Maiden's Peak* and *Squaw Tit* (they're the same mountain) in the Cascade Range in Oregon, *Mary's Nipple* near Salt Lake City, Utah, and *Jane Russell Peaks* near Stark, New Hampshire.

Except for the movie star Jane Russell, the women being   11
referred to are anonymous—it's only a sexual part of their body that is mentioned. When topographical features are named after men, it's probably not going to be to draw attention to a sexual part of their bodies but instead to honor individuals for an accomplishment. For example, no one thinks of a part of the male body

Moving from examples in Greek mythology to examples in American regional English, Nilsen shows that our own language is stocked with examples to prove her argument that "Women are sexy."

This is a good time to remind students that *connotation* refers to the meaning "surrounding" a term or word. They may have a friend who is "mildly obese" (a positive connotation) though someone they do not particularly like is "fat" (a negative connotation).

In this paragraph, she discusses some words historically, showing how they change (or are changed) in meaning as time passes. Students are interested to learn that the best source in which to study how words change meaning is the *Oxford English Dictionary*.

when hearing a reference to Pike's Peak, Colorado, or Jackson Hole, Wyoming.

Going back to what I learned from my dictionary cards, I was surprised to realize how many pairs of words we have in which the feminine word has acquired sexual connotations while the masculine word retains a serious businesslike aura. For example, a *callboy* is the person who calls actors when it is time for them to go on stage, but a *callgirl* is a prostitute. Compare *sir* and *madam*. *Sir* is a term of respect while *madam* has acquired the specialized meaning of a brothel manager. Something similar has happened to *master* and *mistress*. Would you rather have a painting by *an old master* or *an old mistress*? 12

It's because the word *woman* had sexual connotations, as in "She's his woman," that people began avoiding its use, hence such terminology as *ladies' room, lady of the house,* and *girls' school* or *school for young ladies.* Feminists, who ask that people use the term *woman* rather than *girl* or *lady,* are rejecting the idea that *woman* is primarily a sexual term. They have been at least partially successful in that today *woman* is commonly used to communicate gender without intending implications about sexuality. 13

I found two hundred pairs of words with masculine and feminine forms, e.g., *heir–heiress, hero–heroine, steward–stewardess, usher–usherette,* etc. In nearly all such pairs, the masculine word is considered the base with some kind of a feminine suffix being added. The masculine form is the one from which compounds are made, e.g., from *king–queen* comes *kingdom* but not *queendom,* from *sportsman–sportslady* comes *sportsmanship* but not *sportsladyship*. There is one—and only one—semantic area in which the masculine word is not the base or more powerful word. This is in the area dealing with sex and marriage. When someone refers to a *virgin,* a listener will probably think of a female unless the speaker specifies *male* or uses a masculine pronoun. The same is true for *prostitute.* 14

In relation to marriage, there is much linguistic evidence showing that weddings are more important to women than to men. A woman cherishes the wedding and is considered a bride for a whole year, but a man is referred to as a groom only on the 15 day of the wedding. The word *bride* appears in *bridal attendant, bridal gown, bridesmaid, bridal shower,* and even *bridegroom. Groom* comes from the Middle English *grom,* meaning "man," and in this sense is seldom used outside of a wedding. With most pairs of male/female words, people habitually put the masculine word first—*Mr. and Mrs., his and hers, boys and girls, men and women, kings and queens, brothers and sisters, guys and dolls,* and *host and hostess*—but it is the *bride and groom* who are talked about, not the *groom and bride.*

The importance of marriage to a woman is also shown by the fact that when a marriage ends in death, the woman gets the title of *widow.* A man gets the derived title of *widower.* This term is not used in other phrases or contexts, but *widow* is seen in *widowhood, widow's peak,* and *widow's walk.* A *widow* in a card game is an extra hand of cards, while in typesetting it is an extra line of type.

How changing cultural ideas bring changes to language is clearly visible in this semantic area. The feminist movement has caused the differences between the sexes to be downplayed, and since I did my dictionary study two decades ago, the word *singles* has largely replaced such sex-specific and value-laden terms as *bachelor, old maid, spinster, divorcee, widow,* and *widower.* And in 1970 I wrote that when a man is called *a professional* he is thought to be a doctor or a lawyer, but when people hear a woman referred to as *a professional* they are likely to think of a prostitute. That's not as true today because so many women have become doctors and lawyers that it's no longer incongruous to think of women in those professional roles.

Another change that has taken place is in wedding announcements. They used to be sent out from the bride's parents and did not even give the name of the groom's parents. Today, most couples choose to list either all or none of the parents' names. Also it is now much more likely that both the bride and groom's picture will be in the newspaper, while a decade ago only the bride's picture was published on the "Women's" or the "Society" page. Even the traditional wording of the wedding ceremony is being changed. Many officials now pronounce the couple "husband and wife" instead of the old "man and wife," and they ask the bride if

First cited from evidence in the twelfth century, Middle English *grom* means "young man" or "boy." The Middle English *guma,* "man," is the original suffix in "bridegroom." The "bride and groom" are talked about in that order, just as many people still begin speeches with "Ladies and Gentlemen."

16 The *widow's peak* is the point formed by hair that grows down in the middle of a forehead. At one time it was believed to signal early widowhood. A *widow's walk* is a roof platform built on some New England coastal homes, so that one could observe ships at sea.

17

In the relatively few years since Nilsen's first in-depth study of words and sexism, cultural ideas have helped to change the connotations of some words. Notice that every time Nilsen offers a general argument, she follows it with examples that show her argument's worth.

18 As words have changed, so also have customs and attitudes. Younger students often do not realize how many changes have occurred in such a short time, resulting in comparatively diminished sexist attitudes.

she promises "to love, honor, and cherish," instead of "to love, honor, and obey."

Women Are Passive; Men Are Active

The transition from the preceding subtopic is structurally smooth, moving from the wedding-ceremony examples to roles in general, considered historically and currently.

The wording of the wedding ceremony also relates to the second point that my cards showed, which is that women are expected to play a passive or weak role while men play an active or strong role. In the traditional ceremony, the official asks, "Who gives the bride away?" and the father answers, "I do." Some fathers answer, "Her mother and I do," but that doesn't solve the problem inherent in the question. The idea that a bride is something to be handed over from one man to another bothers people because it goes back to the days when a man's servants, his children and his wife were all considered to be his property. They were known by his name because they belonged to him and he was responsible for their actions and their debts. [19]

"grammar": In some regions of the country, the verb form *to wed* has been replaced by the nonsexist verb form *to marry*. That is, a woman can "marry" a man, and a man can "marry" a woman.

The grammar used in talking or writing about weddings as well as other sexual relationships shows the expectation of men playing the active role. Men *wed* women while women *become* brides of men. A man *possesses* a woman; he *deflowers* her; he *performs;* he *scores;* he *takes away* her virginity. Although a woman can *seduce* a man, she cannot offer him her virginity. When talking about virginity, the only way to make the woman the actor in the sentence is to say that "She lost her virginity," but people lose things by accident rather than by purposeful actions, and so she's only the grammatical, not the real-life, actor. [20]

Ms. first came into use in the 1950s as a title before a woman's surname when her marital status was unknown or irrelevant. In the early 1970s, the women's movement encouraged *Ms.,* reasoning that if *Mr.* does not indicate a man's marital status, then we have no reason to indicate a woman's marital status.

The reason that women tried to bring the term *Ms.* into the language to replace *Miss* and *Mrs.* relates to this point. Married women resented being identified only under their husband's names. For example, when Susan Glascoe did something newsworthy, she would be identified in the newspaper only as Mrs. John Glascoe. The dictionary cards showed what appeared to be an attitude on the part of editors that it was almost indecent to let a respectable woman's name march unaccompanied across the pages of a dictionary. Women were listed with male names whether or not the male contributed to the woman's reason for [21] being in the dictionary or in his own right was as famous as the woman. For example, Charlotte Brontë was identified as Mrs. Arthur B. Nicholls, Amelia Earhart as Mrs. George Palmer Putnam, Helen Hayes as Mrs. Charles MacArthur, Jenny Lind as Mme. Otto Goldschmit, Cornelia Otis Skinner as the daughter of Otis Skinner, Harriet Beecher Stowe as the sister of Henry Ward Beecher, and Edith Sitwell as the sister of Osbert and Sacheverell. A very small number of women got into the dictionary without the benefit of a masculine escort. They were rebels and crusaders: temperance leaders Frances Elizabeth Caroline Willard and Carry Nation, women's rights leaders Carrie Chapman Catt and Elizabeth Cady Stanton, birth control educator Margaret Sanger, religious leader Mary Baker Eddy, and slaves Harriet Tubman and Phyllis Wheatley.

Etiquette books used to teach that if a woman had *Mrs.* in front of her name then the husband's name should follow because *Mrs.* is an abbreviated form of *Mistress* and a woman couldn't be a mistress of herself. As with many arguments about "correct" language usage, this isn't very logical because *Miss* is also an abbreviation of *Mistress.* Feminists hoped to simplify matters by introducing *Ms.* as an alternative to both *Mrs.* and *Miss,* but what happened is that *Ms.* largely replaced *Miss* to become a catch-all business title for women. Many married women still prefer the title *Mrs.,* and some resent being addressed with the term *Ms.* As one frustrated newspaper reporter complained, "Before I can write about a woman, I have to know not only her marital status but also her political philosophy." The result of such complications may contribute to the demise of titles which are already being ignored by many computer programmers who find it more efficient to simply use names; for example in a business letter: "Dear Joan Garcia," instead of "Dear Mrs. Joan Garcia," "Dear Ms. Garcia," or "Dear Mrs. Louis Garcia."

The titles given to royalty provide an example of how males can be disadvantaged by the assumption that they are always to play the more powerful role. In British royalty, when a male holds a title, his wife is automatically given the feminine equivalent. But the reverse is not true. For example, a *count* is a high

22   *Mrs.*, first recorded in the seventeenth century, was originally synonymous with *Miss.;* both were abbreviations for *mistress.*

From her earlier examples, the writer forecasts how titles will be handled in the near future. They might well disappear.

23

Traced from its Germanic roots, *king* probably means in its basic sense "head of a kin" or "son of noble kin." The word *queen* comes from the Gothic *qens,* "woman." The husband of a queen who rules in her own right is the *prince consort,* to distinguish him from other princes of the royal family.

political officer with a *countess* being his wife. The same is true for a *duke* and a *duchess* and a *king* and a *queen.* But when a female holds the royal title, the man she marries does not automatically acquire the matching title. For example, Queen Elizabeth's husband has the title of *prince* rather than *king,* but if Prince Charles should become king while he is still married to Lady or Princess Diana, she will be known as the queen. The reasoning appears to be that since masculine words are stronger, they are reserved for true heirs and withheld from males coming into the royal family by marriage. If Prince Phillip were called *King Phillip,* it would be much easier for British subjects to forget where the true power lies.

The names that people give their children show the hopes and   24
dreams they have for them, and when we look at the differences between male and female names in a culture we can see the cumulative expectations of that culture. In our culture girls often have names taken from small, aesthetically pleasing items, e.g., *Ruby, Jewel,* and *Pearl. Esther* and *Stella* mean "star." *Ada* means "ornament," and *Vanessa* means "butterfly." Boys are more likely to be given names with meanings of power and strength, e.g., *Neil* means "champion," *Martin* is from Mars, the god of war, *Raymond* means "wise protection," *Harold* means "chief of the army," *Ira* means "vigilant," *Rex* means "king," and *Richard* means "strong king."

Some would suggest that the names *Ruby, Jewel,* and *Pearl* connote wealth, and the great worth that parents place on their daughters.

We see similar differences in food metaphors. Food is a pas-   25
sive substance just sitting there waiting to be eaten. Many people have recognized this and so no longer feel comfortable describing women as "delectable morsels." However, when I was a teenager, it was considered a compliment to refer to a girl (we didn't call anyone a *woman* until she was middle-aged) as *a cute tomato, a peach, a dish, a cookie, honey, sugar,* or *sweetie-pie.* When being affectionate, women will occasionally call a man *honey* or *sweetie,* but in general, food metaphors are used much less often with men than with women. If a man is called *a fruit,* his masculinity is being questioned. But it's perfectly acceptable to use a food metaphor if the food is heavier and more substantive than that used for women. For example, pinup pictures of women have long been

This paragraph illustrates inductive reasoning: The writer moves from a series of examples to her conclusion, that the gender line is dimming.

known as *cheesecake,* but when Burt Reynolds posed for a nude centerfold, the picture was immediately dubbed *beefcake,* c.f. *a hunk of meat.* That such sexual references to men have come into the general language is another reflection of how society is beginning to lessen the differences between their attitudes toward men and women.

Something similar to the *fruit* metaphor happens with references to plants. We insult a man by calling him *a pansy,* but it wasn't considered particularly insulting to talk about a girl being a *wallflower,* a *clinging vine,* or a *shrinking violet,* or to give girls such names as *Ivy, Rose, Lily, Iris, Daisy, Camellia, Heather,* and *Flora.* A plant metaphor can be used with a man if the plant is big and strong, for example Andrew Jackson's nickname of *Old Hickory.* Also, the phrases *blooming idiots* and *budding geniuses* can be used with either sex, but notice how they are based on the most active thing a plant can do which is to bloom or bud.

26

Students occasionally point out that in their experience, boys refer to girls as "wallflowers" and the like, but girls do not apply these descriptions to other girls. What are your students' observations?

Animal metaphors also illustrate the different expectations for males and females. Men are referred to as *studs, bucks,* and *wolves* while women are referred to with such metaphors as *kitten, bunny, beaver, bird, chick,* and *lamb.* In the 1950s we said that boys went *tomcatting,* but today it's just *catting around* and both boys and girls do it. When the term *foxy,* meaning that someone was sexy, first became popular, it was used only for girls, but now someone of either sex can be described as *a fox.* Some animal metaphors that are used predominantly with men have negative connotations based on the size and/or strength of the animals, e.g., *beast, bull-headed, jackass, rat, loanshark,* and *vulture.* Negative metaphors used with women are based on smaller animals, e.g., *social butterfly, mousy, catty,* and *vixen.* The feminine terms connote action, but not the same kind of large-scale action as with the masculine terms.

27

A metaphor is an implied analogy that suggestively identifies one object with another, here particular animals with particular people, depending on their sex and on their actions and personal characteristics.

Women are Connected with Negative Connotations, Men with Positive Connotations

The final point that my notecards illustrated was how many positive connotations are associated with the concept of

28

Connotation refers to the meanings or implications "surrounding" a word, as distinguished from *denotation,* which refers to the lexical definition of a word.

masculine, while there are either trivial or negative connotations connected with the corresponding feminine concept. An example from the animal metaphors makes a good illustration. The word *shrew* taken from the name of a small but especially vicious animal was defined in my dictionary as "an ill-tempered scolding woman," but the word *shrewd* taken from the same root was defined as "marked by clever, discerning awareness" and was illustrated with the phrase "a shrewd businessman."

Early in life, children are conditioned to the superiority of the masculine role. As child psychologists point out, little girls have much more freedom to experiment with sex roles than do little boys. If a little girl acts like a *tomboy,* most parents have mixed feelings, being at least partially proud. But if their little boy acts like a *sissy* (derived from *sister*), they call a psychologist. It's perfectly acceptable for a little girl to sleep in the crib that was purchased for her brother, to wear his hand-me-down jeans and shirts, and to ride the bicycle that he has outgrown. But few parents would put a boy baby in a white and gold crib decorated with frills and lace, and virtually no parents would have their little boy wear his sister's hand-me-down dresses, nor would they have their son ride a girl's pink bicycle with a flower-bedecked basket. The proper names given to girls and boys show this same attitude. Girls can have "boy" names—*Cris, Craig, Jo, Kelly, Shawn, Teri, Toni,* and *Sam*—but it doesn't work the other way around. A couple of generations ago, *Beverley, Frances, Hazel, Marion,* and *Shirley* were common boys' names. As parents gave these names to more and more girls, they fell into disuse for males, and some older men who have these names prefer to go by their initials or by such abbreviated forms as *Haze* or *Shirl.* 29

When a little girl is told to *be a lady,* she is being told to sit with her knees together and to be quiet and dainty. But when a little boy is told to *be a man,* he is being told to be noble, strong, and virtuous—to have all the qualities that the speaker looks on as desirable. The concept of manliness has such positive connotations that it used to be a compliment to call someone a *he-man,* to say that he was doubly a man. Today many people are more 30

We rarely examine masculine names, feminine names, and crossover names, all at the same time. The class might consider names other than those in this paragraph, such as Sydney, Jamie, Sandy, Wendy, and Merle, and nicknames, such as Curly, Red, Happy, Shorty, and Smiley. Which in the preceding list are absolutely masculine names, according to your class? Which are absolutely feminine names?

ambivalent about this term and respond to it much as they do to the word *macho*. But calling someone a *manly man* or a *virile man* is nearly always meant as a compliment. *Virile* comes from the Indo-European *vir* meaning "man," which is also the basis of *virtuous*. Contrast the positive connotations of both *virile* and *virtuous* with the negative connotations of *hysterical*. The Greeks took this latter word from their name for *uterus* (as still seen in *hysterectomy*). They thought that women were the only ones who experienced uncontrolled emotional outbursts and so the condition must have something to do with a part of the body that only women have.

Differences between positive male and negative female connotations can be seen in several pairs of words which differ denotatively only in the matter of sex. *Bachelor* as compared to *spinster* or *old maid* has such positive connotations that women try to adopt them by using the term *bachelor-girl* or *bachelorette*. *Old maid* is so negative that it's the basis for metaphors: pretentious and fussy old men are called *old maids*, as are the leftover kernels of unpopped popcorn and the last card in a popular children's game.

Patron and *matron* (Middle English for *father* and *mother*) have such different levels of prestige that women try to borrow the more positive masculine connotations with the word *patroness*, literally "female father." Such a peculiar term came about because of the high prestige attached to *patron* in such phrases as *a patron of the arts* or *a patron saint*. *Matron* is more apt to be used in talking about a woman in charge of a jail or a public restroom.

When men are doing jobs that women often do, we apparently try to pay the men extra by giving them fancy titles; for example, a male cook is more likely to be called a *chef*, while a male seamstress will get the title of *tailor*. The armed forces have a special problem in that they recruit under such slogans as "The Marine Corps Builds Men!" and "Join the Army! Become a Man." Once the recruits are enlisted, they find themselves doing much of the work that has been traditionally thought of as "woman's work." The solution to getting the work done and not

Students are interested to learn that the Latin *vir*, "man," is akin to the Old English *wer*, the "man" in *werewolf*.

31

32 The word *patron*, from Latin *patronus*, "legal protector or advocate," is derived from *pater*, "father." The word *matron* is from Latin *mater*, "mother."

33

Here, point out that in the armed services, a registered nurse is a commissioned officer, but a corpsman or a medic is an enlisted person.

insulting anyone's masculinity was to change the titles as shown below:

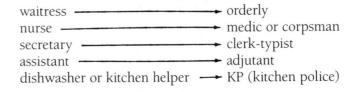

waitress ⟶ orderly
nurse ⟶ medic or corpsman
secretary ⟶ clerk-typist
assistant ⟶ adjutant
dishwasher or kitchen helper ⟶ KP (kitchen police)

Compare *brave* and *squaw*. Early settlers in America truly admired Indian men and hence named them with a word that carried connotations of youth, vigor, and courage. But they used the Algonquin's name for "woman," and over the years it developed almost opposite connotations to those of *brave*. *Wizard* and *witch* contrast almost as much. The masculine *wizard* implies skill and wisdom combined with magic, while the feminine *witch* implies evil intentions combined with magic. Part of the unattractiveness of both *witch* and *squaw* is that they have been used so often to refer to old women, something with which our culture is particularly uncomfortable, just as the Afghans were. Imagine my surprise when I ran across the phrases *grandfatherly advice* and *old wives' tales* and realized that the underlying implication is the same as the Afghan proverb about old men being worth listening to while old women talk only foolishness. 34

Other terms which show how negatively we view old women as compared to young women are *old nag* as compared to *filly, old crow* or *old bat* as compared to *bird,* and being *catty* as compared to being *kittenish*. There is no matching set of metaphors for men. The chicken metaphor tells the whole story of a woman's life. In her youth she is a *chick*. Then she marries and begins *feathering her nest*. Soon she begins feeling *cooped up,* so she goes to *hen parties* where she *cackles* with her friends. Then she has her *brood*, begins to *henpeck* her husband, and finally turns into *an old biddy*. 35

I embarked on my study of the dictionary not with the intention of prescribing language change but simply to see what the language would tell me about sexism. Nevertheless I have been both surprised and pleased as I've watched the changes that have 36

Students are interested to learn that *warlock* refers to the male equivalent of *witch*. Also, some students have pointed out that colloquially, *wizard* can refer to anyone who does something quite well, as in the sentence, "Shirley is a math wizard."

Nilsen comes full circle here, mentioning that the Afghan proverb and some English phrases share some features.

A filly is a young female horse. Interestingly, in horse-racing jargon, a "maiden" is *any* horse that has never won a race.

In some American-English dialects, "old dog" refers to an old man, and "young whelp," albeit redundant, refers to a young man.

A biddy is a chicken and, by extension, a fussy old woman.

occurred over the past two decades. I'm one of those linguists who believes that new language customs will cause a new generation of speakers to grow up with different expectations. This is why I'm happy about people's efforts to use inclusive language, to say *he or she* or *they* when speaking about individuals whose names they do not know. I'm glad that leading publishers have developed guidelines to help writers use language that is fair to both sexes, and I'm glad that most newspapers and magazines list women by their own names instead of only by their husbands' names and that educated and thoughtful people no longer begin their business letters with "Dear Sir" or "Gentlemen," but instead use a memo form or begin with such salutations as "Dear Colleagues," "Dear Reader," or "Dear Committee Members." I'm also glad that such words as *poetess, authoress, conductress,* and *aviatrix* now sound quaint and old fashioned and that *chairman* is giving way to *chair* or *head, mailman* to *mail carrier, clergyman* to *clergy,* and *stewardess* to *flight attendant.* I was also pleased when the National Oceanic and Atmospheric Administration bowed to feminist complaints and in the late '70s began to alternate men's and women's names for hurricanes. However, I wasn't so pleased to discover that the change did not immediately erase sexist thoughts from everyone's mind as shown by a headline about Hurricane David in a 1979 New York tabloid, "David Rapes Virgin Islands." More recently a similar metaphor appeared in a headline in the *Arizona Republic* about Hurricane Charlie: "Charlie Quits Carolinas, Flirts with Virginia."

What these incidents show is that sexism is not something existing independently in American English or in the particular dictionary that I happened to read. Rather, it exists in people's minds. Language is like an x-ray in providing visible evidence of invisible thoughts. The best thing about people being interested in and discussing sexist language is that as they make conscious decisions about what pronouns they will use, what jokes they will tell or laugh at, how they will write their names, or how they will begin their letters, they are forced to think about the underlying issue of sexism. This is good, because as a problem that begins in people's assumptions and expectations, it's a problem that will be

37   Nilsen ends her essay positively, pointing out that our language is changing for the better, socially and politically. And she reminds us that our speaking and writing determine our way of viewing our world.

solved only when a great many people have given it a great deal of thought.

POSSIBLE ANSWERS

Meaning and Purpose

1. Encourage students to examine their own experiences with sexism in language and compare those experiences with some of Nilsen's information.

2. The author argues for examining the words that we use to describe the genders so that we may see what we mean when we use them. She argues against using any words that demean people, especially women. Several sentences could be cited, including the "for" sentence, "I'm one of those linguists who believes that new language customs will cause a new generation of speakers to grow up with different expectations" (paragraph 36); and the "against" sentence, the last in paragraph 28.

3. Nilsen's main point is stated in paragraph 5, when she says, "The language that a culture uses is telltale evidence of the values and beliefs of that culture." Each of the sections has a main point, or thesis, which is a more specific example of the main thesis. The first sentence in each section is the main point of that section.

4. These experiences are included because they pushed the author into awareness of how another culture treated its females, and made her question sexism in our own culture.

5. Some students will be overwhelmed with the examples. Others will say they are necessary to show the reader just what Nilsen means, and will not feel overwhelmed because each example is brief.

Strategy

1. Nilsen's examples are specific—they are all words and their meanings and connotations.

Meaning and Purpose

1. What is your first response to Nilsen's essay? Are you aware of sexist language? Explain.
2. An argument is a reason or reasons stated for or against something. What is the author arguing for? What is she arguing against? Find one sentence from the essay that shows each position.
3. Where does Nilsen state her purpose in this essay? What is her point in each of the three sections, and how are these points related to the thesis?
4. The first three paragraphs tell about Nilsen's experiences in another culture. Why are those experiences included in this essay?
5. Nilsen fills her essay with examples of words and phrases that support her assertions about language. As a reader, how do you react to her using so many examples? Do you feel overwhelmed with information, or does she need the many examples to make her meaning clear?

Strategy

1. Does Nilsen use specific, typical, or hypothetical examples? How effective is her choice?
2. Paragraph 33 lists examples of the differences in job descriptions between the jobs women hold in civilian life and those men hold in the armed services. What role do you believe Nilsen thinks the language of these examples has in people's attitudes toward the jobs?
3. How does Nilsen use her final paragraph in the structure of the essay?

Style

1. How do you characterize this essayist's tone? Is she angry? Is she informative? Is she calm? Is the tone neutral? Show evidence of Nilsen's tone from the essay.
2. How does her use of many short examples affect the pace of the essay, or your way of reading it?
3. Why does Nilsen use subtitles and divide her essay into sections? How effective are the subtitles?

Writing Tasks

1. What is your opinion of the way in which women are portrayed in sitcoms? In an essay, develop a thesis and use specific examples of television shows to support it. (You could also write this essay about the way in which men are portrayed in sitcoms.)
2. In a few paragraphs for each person, draw two hypothetical examples—one male and one female—illustrating the abstractions of masculinity and femininity.

Her study requires specific examples to support her assertions about sexism in language.
2. Nilsen suggests that the language fools no one but is necessary for image. She refers to the military job titles as "fancy titles."
3. Nilsen ends with some examples of how language is changing to eliminate sexism. In her final paragraph she refines her thesis to say, "[Sexism] exists in people's minds. Language is like an x-ray in providing visible evidence of invisible thoughts." She uses this paragraph to express her opinion that people will begin thinking consciously about the language they use. This positive statement somewhat balances all the examples of sexism still in force that she has given in the essay.

Style

1. Nilsen is calm and informative. She intends to expose sexism in language for what it is without being militantly feminist. One example of this tone is the sentence, "When topographical features are named after men, it's probably not going to be to draw attention to a sexual part of their bodies but instead to honor individuals for an accomplishment" (paragraph 11).
2. The reading pace is fast because each example is short and gives way quickly to the next. Readers have one interesting bit of information to read after another.
3. The three sections set off the three large areas in which Nilsen found sexist language. These sections are necessary for clarity and readability in an essay that is so long and full of facts. They help guide the reading.

Examples

1. Write an essay on one of the general statements listed here or on a general statement you compose. Throughout your essay use examples to illustrate your main idea or thesis. Your discussion should include a mixture of typical and specific examples. Remember: you are not bound by any of these statements; you may rewrite them to reflect your interests, or you may compose your own.
   a. People must assume responsibility for their actions.
   b. Success comes from 5 percent talent and 95 percent hard work.
   c. Vandals control the night in local neighborhoods.
   d. Teenagers can learn both positive and negative lessons about economic survival from part-time jobs.
   e. Graffiti scrawled on walls throughout the city carry psychological messages about human behavior.
   f. Books I have read have taught me a great deal about life.
   g. Bumper stickers reveal a person's values.
   h. Public obscenity is objectionable.
   i. Life in the fast lane leads to head-on collisions.
2. Write a full essay related to one of these situations. Be sure examples serve as the dominant essay pattern of development.
   a. Some contemporary political figures have demonstrated courage in office. Using examples from recent history, write an essay illustrating how important political courage is.
   b. Society seems to require more and more cooperation among individuals and groups to function effectively. Write an essay illustrating how cooperation is needed for success.
   c. Although society seems to require more and more cooperation among individuals and groups, the values of the "rugged individualist" are still required for success. Write an essay illustrating how much "rugged individualism" helps in becoming successful.

d. Often the better moments in life go unnoticed. Recollect some of your better moments and write an essay making use of them to illustrate what they have taught you.

e. Magazine advertisers attempt to entice customers to buy products not by high quality but by associating the products with selected "life-styles." Write an essay illustrating that some magazine advertisements encourage consumers to buy products for the wrong reasons.

3. Read this paragraph from Jack Solomon's *The Signs of Our Time,* in which he generally concentrates on the messages that clothing communicates in American society.

> The complexity of the dress code in America, the astonishing range of styles that are available to us in our choice of clothing designs, directly reflects the cultural diversity of our country. Americans are differentiated by ethnic, regional, religious, and racial differences that are all expressed in the clothing they wear. Age differences, political differences, class differences, and differences in personal taste further divide us into finer and finer subcultures that maintain, and even assert, their sense of distinct identity through their characteristic clothing. From the severe black suits of the Amish to the safety-pinned T-shirts and chains of punk culture, Americans tell one another who they are through the articles of their dress.

Write an essay, with examples as the dominant method of development, illustrating Solomon's general observation that "Americans tell one another who they are through the articles of their dress."

4

Comparison and Contrast

Presenting Similarities and Differences

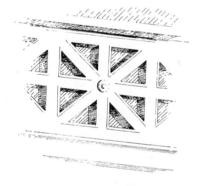

The Method

In conversation we often hear comments that could lead to **comparison and contrast**:

"I eat vegetables, fruits, grains, nuts, and dairy products. It is a lot healthier than a diet that includes red meat, fowl, and even fish."

"Strip away the rhetoric and compare their economic platforms; you will see few differences between Republicans and Democrats."

"The effects of marijuana are no more harmful than those of alcohol. In fact they may be less harmful."

No doubt in class discussions, at family gatherings, or during arguments at the local pizza parlor you have heard similar comments. How such comparisons are developed in conversation probably depends on the group's mood and analytical talent. Nevertheless, a fundamental principle is at work: We all make decisions by comparing and contrasting our options.

To compare is to point out similarities; to contrast is to point out differences. Poems and song lyrics are often similar in some ways: both often rhyme; they are constructed on rhythmic patterns; sometimes they repeat key lines. They also have one major difference: poems are written to be spoken; songs are written to be sung to music. Presenting similarities and differences is a common technique not only in conversation but also in all forms of writing, including essays, research papers, reports, and examinations.

Commonly, writers include informal comparisons that are merely incidental to the dominant essay pattern. Often such brief comparisons are implied rather than fully developed, merely suggesting a comparison. This paragraph opens an essay explaining the causes directing new trends in city planning.

> In southern California, historically known for its suburban sprawl, city planning seems to have come full circle. Using the concept of the traditional village, planners are designing new urban villages that feature a main street and a mix of stores, offices, town halls, and parks. They are trying to re-create the traditional village by designing neighborhoods where thousands of residents can live and work, where they can walk to shopping and stroll to places of entertainment.

The writer, Jack Scott, does not intend to compare traditional with contemporary city design; he alludes to traditional design merely to place his reader in familiar territory.

When writers use comparison and contrast as a dominant essay pattern, they explore their subjects in detail, applying several principles to guide the composition. To sharpen your critical eye and read as a writer reads, be aware of these general principles.

Strategies

Professional writers know they need a basis for the comparison: any subjects they choose to compare must belong to the same general category. If the subjects do not belong to that category, the writers have no logical reason to enumerate the similarities and differences. Usually, but not always, the general categories are obvious. For such a discussion, consider hammerhead sharks, great white sharks, chimpanzees, and dolphins.

Comparing and contrasting a hammerhead with a great white shark is clearly logical because although they are similar, they differ in several distinctive ways. But to compare and contrast a chimpanzee to a great white shark is clearly illogical. Yes, they belong to a category we might call "living creatures," but do you see any other basis for a comparison? The chimpanzee is a mammal, the great white shark a fish. One lives on land, the other in the sea. One is a hunter, the other a forager. To compare and contrast them just would not make much sense.

To compare and contrast a dolphin and a great white shark, however, does make sense. Even though the dolphin is a mammal, it is a marine mammal. The dolphin and the great white shark are also shaped roughly alike, but with significant differences. Perhaps most important, both the dolphin and the great white shark are significant in sea lore. In fact, Hollywood films featuring a dolphin and a great white shark have been box-office hits, as in *Flipper* and *Jaws*.

What about comparing a dolphin and a chimpanzee? Although they are not obvious selections, both are categorized as mammals. A writer might ask if their both being mammals makes them subjects worth comparing and contrasting. What else do they have in common? Close examination reveals that scientists are studying communication patterns of both chimpanzees and dolphins. Perhaps they are in the limited category of animals that communicate with human beings. Taking up this similarity, a writer might explore the possibility of comparing chimpanzees and dolphins.

Now we must consider an exception to the principle that subjects should belong to the same general category if they are to be logically compared. This figurative comparison is called **analogy**. Writers use analogy to explain something difficult to understand by describing it as if it were something familiar. A writer might choose to explain life by comparing it with a river, watching a situation comedy with taking a narcotic, or being in love with riding a roller coaster. Writers of analogy are interested only in using one subject to explain another; they are not out to explain the major similarities and differences of both subjects equally as they would be when writing a typical comparison-and-contrast passage.

In this following paragraph, humorist James Thurber develops an analogy by comparing his editor Harold Ross to a skilled auto mechanic.

Having a manuscript under Ross's scrutiny was like putting your car in the hands of a skilled mechanic, not an automotive engineer with a bachelor of science degree, but a guy who knows what makes a motor go, and sputter, and wheeze, and sometimes come to a dead stop; a man with an ear for the faintest body squeak as well as the loudest engine rattle. When you first gazed, appalled, upon an uncorrected proof of one of your stories or articles, each margin had a thicket of queries and complaints—one writer got a hundred and forty-four on one profile. It was as though you beheld the works of your car spread all over the garage floor, and the job of getting the thing together again and making it work seemed impossible. Then you realized that Ross was trying to make your Model T or old Stutz Bearcat into a Cadillac or Rolls-Royce. He was at work with the tools of his unflagging perfectionism, and, after an exchange of growls or snarls, you set to work to join him in his enterprise.

Clearly, Thurber has stuck to the principle of analogy: he uses the familiar work of an auto mechanic to explain the unfamiliar work of a magazine editor.

Professional writers are always wary of confusing their readers. Well, because comparisons involve at least two subjects, writers become even more cautious when writing them. As you study comparison-and-contrast essays, notice how writers immediately orient their readers by informing them that a comparison and contrast follows.

Read the opening paragraph in Russell Baker's "From Song to Sound: Elvis and Bing." Baker quickly establishes that he will compare two eras and the popular singers who represent them.

> The grieving for Elvis Presley and the commercial exploitation of his death were still not ended when we heard of Bing Crosby's death the other day. Here is a generational puzzle. Those of an age to mourn Elvis must marvel that their elders could really have cared about Bing, just as the Crosby generation a few weeks ago wondered what all the to-do was about when Elvis died.

Baker's opening paragraph gives a clear idea that the essay is headed into comparison and contrast. Most professional writers do likewise, thus keeping their readers on the track.

Professional writers also use clear—and we stress that word—stylistic techniques to keep their readers from becoming confused. Sometimes they use parallel structure to balance the similarities and differences of their subjects. They also use such transitional words and phrases as *on the one hand, on the other hand, in contrast, like,* and *unlike,* words with which they delineate similarities and differences.

In a paragraph from an essay contrasting crows and ravens, Barry Lopez applies both transitional phrases and parallel structures.

> The raven is larger than the crow and has a beard of black feathers at his throat. He is careful to kill only what he needs. Crows, on the other hand, will search out the great horned owl, kick and punch him awake, and then for roosting too close to their nests, they will kill him. They will come out of the sky on a fat, hot afternoon and slam into the head of a dozing rabbit and go away laughing. They will tear out a whole row of planted corn and eat only a few kernels. They will defecate on scarecrows and go home and sleep with 200,000 of their friends in an atmosphere of congratulation. Again, it is only a game; this should not be taken to mean that they are evil.

In his paragraph Lopez concentrates primarily on the crow's destructive behavior, contrasting it sharply to the raven in the two sentences describing that black bird. Usually, writers will develop both subjects in more detail. They generally employ one of two organizational strategies when comparing and contrasting: **subject-by-subject** development or **point-by-point** development.

Subject-by-Subject Development

Developing a subject-by-subject comparison is quite simple: all the details of one side of the comparison or contrast are presented first, followed by all the details of the other side. Anthropologist Edward T. Hall uses subject-by-subject development to contrast Arab and American attitudes in a paragraph from *The Hidden Dimension.*

> Another silent source of friction between Americans and Arabs is in an area that Americans treat very informally—the manners and rights of the road. In general, in the United States we tend to defer to the vehicle that is bigger, more

powerful, faster, and heavily laden. While a pedestrian walking along a road may feel annoyed he will not think it unusual to step aside for a fast-moving automobile. He knows that because he is moving he does not have the right to the space around him that he has when he is standing still. It appears that the reverse is true with the Arabs who apparently *take on rights to space as they move.* For someone else to move into a space an Arab is also moving into is a violation of his rights. It is infuriating to an Arab to have someone else cut in front of him on the highway. It is the American's cavalier treatment of moving space that makes the Arab call him aggressive and pushy.

Hall contrasts these subjects in one paragraph, but sometimes a writer will divide the subjects into separate contrasting paragraphs, as Noel Perrin does in these two discussion paragraphs from his essay "The Two Faces of Vermont."

On the one hand, it's to the interest of everyone in the tourist trade to keep Vermont (their motels, ski resorts, chambers of commerce, etc., excepted) as old-fashioned as possible. After all, it's weathered red barns with shingle roofs the tourists want to photograph, not concrete-block barns with sheet aluminum on top. Ideally, from the tourist point of view, there should be a man and two boys inside, milking by hand, not a lot of milking machinery pumping directly into a bulk tank. Out back, someone should be turning a grindstone to sharpen an ax—making a last stand, so to speak, against the chainsaw.

On the other hand, the average farmer can hardly wait to modernize. He wants a bulk tank, a couple of arc lights, an automated silo, and a new aluminum roof. Or in a sense he wants these things. Actually, he may like last-stand farming as well as any tourist does, but he can't make a living at it. In my town it's often said that a generation ago a man could raise and educate three children on fifteen cows and still put a little money in the bank. Now his son can just barely keep going with 40 cows. With fifteen cows, hand-milking was possible, and conceivably even economic; with 40 you need all the machinery you can get. But the tourists don't want to hear it clank.

Point-by-Point Development

Subject-by-subject development is effective for an essay of a few paragraphs, but when an essay is longer the reader may lose track of the information about the first subject while reading about the second. The point-by-point development solves this short-coming by alternately presenting each point under consideration. Alison Lurie, in a paragraph from *The Language of Clothes,* uses the point-by-point method to compare and contrast boys' and girls' clothes.

> In early childhood girls' and boys' clothes are often iden-tical in cut and fabric, as if in recognition of the fact that their bodies are much alike. But the T-shirts, pull-on slacks and zip jackets intended for boys are usually made in darker colors (especially forest green, navy, red and brown) and printed with designs involving sports, transportation and cute wild animals. Girls' clothes are made in paler colors (especially pink, yellow and green) and decorated with flow-ers and cute domestic animals. The suggestion is that the boy will play vigorously and travel over long distances; the girl will stay home and nurture plants and small mammals. Alternatively, these designs may symbolize their wearers: the boy is a cuddly bear or a smiling tiger, the girl a flower or a kitten. There is also a tendency for boys' clothes to be full-est at the shoulders and girls' at the hips, anticipating their adult figures. Boys' and men's garments also emphasize the shoulders with horizontal stripes, epaulets or yokes of con-trasting color. Girls' and women's garments emphasize the hips and rear through the strategic placement of gathers and trimmings.

Lurie's strategy is quite simple. She organizes the discussion around three points: the different colors in girls' and boys' clothes;

the different designs that decorate them; and the different cut. She presents the details point by point, carefully balancing one with the other.

Comparison and Contrast in College Writing

When you compare the similarities and differences of two subjects, carefully follow the principles that govern this pattern: be sure to select subjects from the same general category (unless, of course, you are developing an analogy); be especially careful to guide your reader through a comparison with stylistic techniques such as overt transitions and parallel structure; and select the appropriate structural strategies, whether block method, point-by-point method, or a combination.

You must also consider your purpose in using comparison. Generally, in college writing, you will compare the similarities and differences of your subjects for one of two reasons: to describe two subjects in order to clarify them or to evaluate two subjects in order to determine which is better. For either comparison, you must consider the outstanding features of each subject, and when the purpose is evaluation, you must carefully delineate both positive and negative aspects of the subjects.

For an assignment in American literature, Jim Cartozian compares and contrasts Ernest Hemingway and William Faulkner. In this four-paragraph passage from his essay, Cartozian develops his subjects by using both subject-by-subject and point-by-point development. He even develops an analogy.

Opening establishes Hemingway and Faulkner as the subjects.

If Ernest Hemingway and William Faulkner were to attend the same party, both would command attention for different reasons. Hemingway was a big bear of a man, seemed gregarious, and liked to hold the center of attention. He was handsome, and some have said he prided him-

Subject-by-subject development contrasts the physical and social differences between the subjects.

self on being a lady's man. Faulkner was slight of build, soft-spoken, and tended to be reclusive. He would not seek the attention Hemingway seemed to thrive on, but would probably find a mantel to lean on. Speaking in a gentle, lilting voice, he would tell a story about the rural South while holding the attention of everyone within earshot.

Point-by-point is more effective than subject-by-subject development here because similarities and differences are so numerous.

No modern American writers have gained as much worldwide critical recognition as Ernest Hemingway and William Faulkner, and no two could be more different. Both did win the coveted Nobel Prize for literature, but when the mild-mannered Faulkner won first, Hemingway is said to have lost his temper and then sulked. Both were publishing at a young age, but Hemingway attracted popular attention early in his career while Faulkner worked in near obscurity. Hemingway became America's first modern literary media star. Magazines featured spreads of his war exploits, his African safaris, and his bullfighting adventures. Faulkner, in contrast, was never a media celebrity. Instead, he seemed to embody the lifestyle of small-town Southern gentry, spending most of his quiet life in Oxford, Mississippi. Hemingway's novels and stories were often set in exotic locales like France, Spain, and Cuba; Faulkner set his works in the South, in the mythical Yoknapatawpha County. Each dealt with very different visions: Hemingway's work displays psychologically wounded characters struggling to establish a personal code of values in an absurd world. Faulkner's work displays characters who are victims of history, suffering because of the sins of their ancestors, the men who wrenched the land from Native Americans and enslaved Native Africans. In 1961 Hemingway died violently by his own hand; in 1962 Faulkner died peacefully.

Final paragraphs develop an analogy exploring similarities in both writers' ways of working. As in paragraph 1, subject-by-subject development is used.

Whatever quality made such different men successful novelists is difficult to identify. No doubt their success came from determination and hard work, for both men were dedicated craftsmen. But another quality—inspiration—must be figured into the equation. Inspiration that comes from pursuing the creative process is perhaps similar to the spiritual insight that comes from participating in a mystical practice. A mystical practice, such as meditation, is usually performed daily in psychological isolation. Most successful novelists pursue their creative inspiration by isolating themselves, too. Faulkner and Hemingway were no different. Both created special spaces to write in. When Faulkner wrote he isolated himself in an upstairs bedroom located in the family house. Although Hemingway was more nomadic than Faulkner, he still created a "space apart" to write in no matter where he was living, the most famous one in a tower at his Cuban hacienda.

Too often spiritual insight and creative inspiration are thought to arrive like a bolt of lightning. But mystics claim insight comes from the relentless pursuit of routines. As writers, Faulkner and Hemingway ritualistically pursued their routines. Hemingway would rise at first light and spend the morning writing with a hand-sharpened pencil while standing at a high desk or bookcase top. Faulkner

would also rise early, but he would sit at a
desk and plunk away at an old typewriter.
The routines seldom varied, but perhaps it
was routine pursued with the fervor of a
mystic that generated their inspiration
and led to their recognition.

In Cartozian's passage the principles of comparison and contrast
are clearly at work. Hemingway and Faulkner are both members
of the same logical category of critically acclaimed American writers, and so Cartozian had no trouble selecting his subjects. In the
opening sentences he establishes that the two writers will be his
subjects, thus preparing his reader for comparison and contrast.
Finally, he combines organizational strategies. In the opening paragraphs Cartozian contrasts Hemingway's and Faulkner's physical
and social characteristics with subject-by-subject development. In
paragraph 2, he presents both similarities and differences with
point-by-point development. In the last two paragraphs he
stresses the novelists' similarities by concentrating on their work
habits with analogy. Cartozian's purpose is also clear: he is not
judging these authors, he is clarifying who they are and what they
achieved; consequently, he carefully balances his points.

The most effective way to develop skill in comparison and
contrast is to study the professionals. Analyze their choices. Ask
yourself why one writer chooses point-by-point development over
subject-by-subject development for a passage. Notice how another
mixes the two types of development. Study the kinds of transitional techniques they use. This kind of careful reading—that is,
reading with a critical eye—will prepare you to write your own
comparisons.

❦ Bruce Catton ❦

Bruce Catton (pronounced Cayton) was one of those rare historians who could bring the past to life. Born in Michigan in 1899, he grew up hearing Civil War stories from the many Civil War veterans in his small midwestern town. After attending Oberlin College he was a reporter for newspapers in Boston and Cleveland, served as director of information for government agencies in Washington, D.C., and finally accepted a position as full-time editor and writer for American Heritage *magazine, which he kept until his death in 1978. Considered one of the foremost authorities on the American Civil War era, he published many books on the subject. The most popular of those books is* A Stillness at Appomattox *(1953), which won both the Pulitzer Prize for history and, in 1954, the National Book Award.*

Grant and Lee:
A Study in Contrasts

In this essay, first published in The American Story, *an anthology of essays by noted historians, Catton describes the similarities and differences in style and character between the opposing Civil War generals. It was their coming together and their ability to put aside their extreme differences that marked the end of the war and a turning point in American history.*

When Ulysses S. Grant and Robert E. Lee met in the parlor of a modest house at Appomattox Court House, Virginia, on April 9, 1865, to work out the terms for the surrender of Lee's Army of Northern Virginia, a great chapter in American life came to a close, and a great new chapter began.

These men were bringing the Civil War to its virtual finish. To be sure, other armies had yet to surrender, and for a few days the fugitive Confederate government would struggle desperately

233

1

2

TEACHING SUGGESTIONS

You might want to start by discussing how some current civil conflicts (Lebanon, Northern Ireland, and El Salvador, perhaps) resemble our Civil War and how they differ. Outlining these similarities and differences can lead to discussion of the essay's structure: the first three paragraphs as introduction; paragraphs 4–6 describing the attributes of Robert E. Lee and the society he represented; paragraphs 7–9 describing Ulysses S. Grant and the values he represented; paragraphs 10 and 11 paired against each other; point-by-point contrast in paragraph 12; paragraph 13 a transition moving from contrast to comparison; and paragraphs 14, 15, and 16 showing the similarities of the two men, moving from the least important to the most important.

From there you might ask students to evaluate the contrary social ideals the two men represented.

MARGINAL NOTES

The contrast between the closing of "a great chapter in American history" taking place in "the parlor of a modest house" emphasizes the enormity of the occasion.

After students have looked up *poignant,* you might discuss why it is such a fitting word here, why it is better than *teary, sad,* or *touching,* for instance.

Not only does this sentence serve as the essay's thesis, but it also has a metaphor that emphasizes the strength of the two men's personalities and characters and the power of the two societies they represented; that is, they were "two conflicting currents" so powerful that when they met the "collision" was "final." Paragraph 4 leads to a discussion of Lee and the society and ideal he represented. It also is a kind of mini-thesis that controls the essay's next section (5 and 6).

It was the Virginia tidewater where the very first permanent English settlers landed and founded Jamestown, well before *Mayflower* (1620). Ironically, in fact, *Mayflower* was headed there but veered off course and landed at Plymouth instead. These first settlers brought with them medieval English ideals (chivalry and all the aristocratic and ritualistic courtesies that went with it, including idealization of women) and a feudal social structure, described in the rest of the paragraph.

The implication here seems to be that as the war wore on to an end and it became more and more apparent that the Confederacy itself would fall, the Confederate soldier found it psychologically necessary to personify his ideals in a living man. Lee, thus ironically, became a symbol, an abstraction.

and vainly, trying to find some way to go on living now that its chief support was gone. But in effect it was all over when Grant and Lee signed the papers. And the little room where they wrote out the terms was the scene of one of the poignant, dramatic contrasts in American history.

They were two strong men, these oddly different generals, and they represented the strengths of two conflicting currents that, through them, had come to final collision. 3

Back of Robert E. Lee was the notion that the old aristocratic concept might somehow survive and be dominant in American life. 4

Lee was tidewater Virginia, and in his background were family, culture, and tradition . . . the age of chivalry transplanted to a New World which was making its own legends and its own myths. He embodied a way of life that had come down through the age of knighthood and the English country squire. America was a land that was beginning all over again, dedicated to nothing much more complicated than the rather hazy belief that all men had equal rights and should have an equal chance in the world. In such a land Lee stood for the feeling that it was somehow of advantage to human society to have a pronounced inequality in the social structure. There should be a leisure class, backed by ownership of land; in turn, society itself should be keyed to the land as the chief source of wealth and influence. It would bring forth (according to this ideal) a class of men with a strong sense of obligation to the community; men who lived not to gain advantage for themselves, but to meet the solemn obligations which had been laid on them by the very fact that they were privileged. From them the country would get its leadership; to them it could look for the higher values—of thought, of conduct, or personal deportment—to give it strength and virtue. 5

Lee embodied the noblest elements of this aristocratic ideal. Through him, the landed nobility justified itself. For four years, the Southern states had fought a desperate war to uphold the ideals for which Lee stood. In the end, it almost seemed as if the Confederacy fought for Lee; as if he himself was the Confederacy . . . the best thing that the way of life for which the Con- 6 federacy stood could ever have to offer. He had passed into legend before Appomattox. Thousands of tired, underfed, poorly clothed Confederate soldiers, long since past the simple enthusiasm of the early days of the struggle, somehow considered Lee the symbol of everything for which they had been willing to die. But they could not quite put this feeling into words. If the Lost Cause, sanctified by so much heroism and so many deaths, had a living justification, its justification was General Lee.

Grant, the son of a tanner on the Western frontier, was everything Lee was not. He had come up the hard way and embodied nothing in particular except the eternal toughness and sinewy fiber of the men who grew up beyond the mountains. He was one of a body of men who owed reverence and obeisance to no one, who were self-reliant to a fault, who cared hardly anything for the past but who had a sharp eye for the future.

These frontier men were the precise opposites of the tidewater aristocrats. Back of them, in the great surge that had taken people over the Alleghenies and into the opening Western country, there was a deep, implicit dissatisfaction with a past that had settled into grooves. They stood for democracy, not from any reasoned conclusion about the proper ordering of human society, but simply because they had grown up in the middle of democracy and knew how it worked. Their society might have privileges, but they would be privileges each man had won for himself. Forms and patterns meant nothing. No man was born to anything, except perhaps to a chance to show how far he could rise. Life was competition.

Yet along with this feeling had come a deep sense of belonging to a national community. The Westerner who developed a farm, opened a shop, or set up in business as a trader could hope to prosper only as his own community prospered—and his community ran from the Atlantic to the Pacific and from Canada down to Mexico. If the land was settled, with towns and highways and accessible markets, he could better himself. He saw his fate in terms of the nation's own destiny. As its horizons expanded, so did his. He had, in other words, an acute dollars-and-cents stake in the continued growth and development of his country.

7   The first sentence in paragraph 7, the topic sentence, immediately draws the distinctions between Lee and Grant. Grant, a product of the frontier rather than the settled and aristocratic East Coast, differed from Lee in everything. The rest of the paragraph lists some primary differences.

8

9

And that, perhaps, is where the contrast between Grant and 10
Lee becomes most striking. The Virginia aristocrat, inevitably, saw
himself in relation to his own region. He lived in a static society
which could endure almost anything except change. Instinctively,
his first loyalty would go to the locality in which that society
existed. He would fight to the limit of endurance to defend it,
because in defending it he was defending everything that gave his
own life its deepest meaning.

The Westerner, on the other hand, would fight with an equal 11
tenacity for the broader concept of society. He fought so because
everything he lived by was tied to growth, expansion, and a
constantly widening horizon. What he lived by would survive or
fall with the nation itself. He could not possibly stand by un-
moved in the face of an attempt to destroy the Union. He would
combat it with everything he had, because he could only see it as
an effort to cut the ground out from under his feet.

So Grant and Lee were in complete contrast, representing two 12
diametrically opposed elements in American life. Grant was the
modern man emerging; beyond him, ready to come on the stage,
was the great age of steel and machinery, of crowded cities and a
restless burgeoning vitality. Lee might have ridden down from the
old age of chivalry, lance in hand, silken banner fluttering over
his head. Each man was the perfect champion of his cause, drawing both his strengths and his weaknesses from the people he led.

Yet it was not all contrast, after all. Different as they were—in 13
background, in personality, in underlying aspiration—these two
great soldiers had much in common. Under everything else, they
were marvelous fighters. Furthermore, their fighting qualities
were really very much alike.

Each man had, to begin with, the great virtue of utter tenacity 14
and fidelity. Grant fought his way down the Mississippi Valley in
spite of acute personal discouragement and profound military
handicaps. Lee hung on in the trenches at Petersburg after hope
itself had died. In each man there was an indomitable quality . . .
the born fighter's refusal to give up as long as he can still remain
on his feet and lift his two fists.

Whereas Lee's commitment to community was local and insular, Grant's was national and even expansionist.

Paragraph 13 serves as a transition, carrying the reader from the differences between the two men to a comparison of their likenesses.

The topic sentence cites their first similarity and is followed by examples.

Daring and resourcefulness they had, too: the ability to think faster and move faster than the enemy. These were the qualities which gave Lee the dazzling campaigns of Second Manassas and Chancellorsville and won Vicksburg for Grant.

Lastly, and perhaps greatest of all, there was the ability, at the end, to turn quickly from war to peace once the fighting was over. Out of the way these two men behaved at Appomattox came the possibility of a peace of reconciliation. It was a possibility not wholly realized, in the years to come, but which did, in the end, help the two sections to become one nation again . . . after a war whose bitterness might have seemed to make such a reunion wholly impossible. No part of either man's life became him more than the part he played in their brief meeting in the McLean house at Appomattox. Their behavior there put all succeeding generations of Americans in their debt. Two great Americans, Grant and Lee—very different, yet under everything very much alike. Their encounter at Appomattox was one of the great moments of American history.

15

16 After citing the qualities that made them great warriors, Catton points out that their greatest virtue was their ability to be men of peace after the fighting was over.

Catton's phrasing of the last two sentences recalls that of the thesis sentence in paragraph 3, thus bringing the essay to a satisfying close.

POSSIBLE ANSWERS

Meaning and Purpose

1. Recall some of the economic and social differences between the North and South that Catton cites as the cause of the United States Civil War. Lead students to discuss in detail the major differences between the Civil War and modern conflicts in other regions. Currently, civil strife seems endless in Lebanon, Northern Ireland, and El Salvador.
2. In paragraph 5, Catton describes a social system in which privilege was based on land ownership, inspiring a strong sense of obligation to the community. Lee, embodying "the noblest elements of this aristocratic ideal" (paragraph 6), became a symbol of that ideal for the soldiers who had been willing to die to preserve it.
3. Throughout history, wars have been fought for emotional attachment to ideals rather than intellectual understanding of realities. Ask students for examples of this tendency (the Crusades, Vietnam). Even poor southerners saw Lee as a hero who could save the integrity of the southern way of life. The romance in backing such a cause was stronger, for many, than the fear of deprivation and death.
4. Grant represented a society with great hope for the future and disregard for the past. He stood for democracy, with privilege based on

Meaning and Purpose

1. The essay begins with a brief description of the negotiations at Appomattox that led to the end of the Civil War. Can you think of any countries today so torn by civil strife and bitterness that reunion and reconciliation seem difficult or nearly impossible? What are the differences between their condition now and that of the United States at the time of the Civil War?
2. Describe the social structure of the Confederacy that Lee defended. The author claims that Lee was also a symbol of that social order (paragraph 6). In what way was he such a symbol?
3. In paragraph 5, Catton states, "Lee stood for the feeling that it was somehow of advantage to human society to have a pronounced inequality in the social structure." Apparently, one

what a man did for himself, not on landed birthright (paragraph 8).

5. Both Lee and Grant had virtues that made them great soldiers, such as "tenacity," "fidelity," and the "ability to think" (paragraphs 14 and 15). Greatest among these virtues was their ability to become men of peace after the war (paragraph 16). Their pivotal difference was the kind of society each represented: Grant stood for a modern, expanding one; Lee an established, stagnant one.

6. The expression "tidewater Virginia" refers to the tidal flats, up to the Piedmont Plateau, where all the rivers met. Here grew the quintessential southern plantations where slavery began, and where the Virginia aristocracy was founded.

Strategy

1. The first three paragraphs form the introduction, which ends with the thesis (paragraph 3); the next paragraph begins the body of the essay with a discussion of Lee. The rest of the essay is structured as a comparison and contrast; the introduction is not. In the introduction, Catton gives background facts about the meeting between the two generals at the close of the Civil War, and sets the basis for comparison.

2. The first and second sentences tell us that Lee and Grant, "these men" (the transition from the preceding paragraph), have brought the war to a virtual end, the key word being virtual. The third confirms that the war is essentially over, and the fourth, which concludes the paragraph, points forward to the body of the essay, the contrasts between the two men and the societies they represented.

3. Catton uses paragraph 13 as a transition from contrasting the differences between the two men to comparing their likenesses.

4. The first sentence in each paragraph uses a clear transition that tightly connects it with the preceding paragraph, thus giving the entire essay solid coherence.

5. Catton uses the subject-by-subject method in paragraphs 4 to 11. Paragraph 12 begins point-by-point comparison of similarities between the two men until the conclusion in paragraph 16. The subject-by-subject structure gives, uninterrupted, all the background on

underclass in that society consisted of the "Thousands of tired, underfed, poorly clothed Confederate soldiers, long since past the simple enthusiasm of the early days of the struggle," but who, nonetheless, "somehow considered Lee the symbol of everything for which they had been willing to die" (paragraph 6). Discuss the apparent contradictions in this situation.

4. Describe the social structure that Grant represented.

5. How were the two men the same? What was their most important similarity? What was their key difference?

6. What is the meaning of "tidewater Virginia" (paragraph 5), and what is its significance in this essay?

Strategy

1. Identify the introduction in Catton's essay and state his thesis. How do you know where the introduction ends? How does the information in the introduction differ from that in the rest of the essay; in other words, what characterizes Catton's introductory remarks?

2. Paragraph 2 consists of four sentences. Describe the function of each.

3. What new rhetorical technique does Catton begin to apply in paragraph 13?

4. Examine the first sentence in each paragraph. What transitional devices does the author use in each? What effect do these devices have?

5. Study Catton's method or methods of comparison and contrast in the essay. Does he use the subject-by-subject method, the point-by-point method, or a combination of the two? Discuss the effectiveness of his rhetorical structure.

Style

1. In paragraph 1, Catton uses a metaphor comparing the negotiations to end the Civil War to a concluding chapter in the larger

book of American life. How effective is that metaphor? What are its implications?

2. In paragraph 12, the author says that "Lee might have ridden down from the old age of chivalry, lance in hand, silken banner fluttering over his head." What effect does this language have? Is it satirical?

3. Check the dictionary for the meaning of these words: *virtual, poignant, chivalry, legends, myths, embodied, deportment, obeisance, static, tenacity, fidelity, indomitable.*

4. In the final paragraph, Catton brings the reader back to the setting he describes in the opening paragraph. What is the stylistic effect of this technique?

5. What is Catton's attitude toward Lee and Grant? How is this attitude shown?

Writing Tasks

1. Write an essay in which you compare and contrast two historical or literary characters who represent two ways of life or value systems. The structure of your essay should include an introduction in which you set the scene for the two people you will discuss; that is, put them in the same category or on the same basis. Choose the subject-by-subject method, point-by-point method, or a combination to set up your comparison and contrast. Pay attention to transitions. Conclude your essay by bringing the two characters together again.

2. Write a brief dialogue between the two characters you chose for the assignment above, or any other two people you want to compare and contrast. Put them in a scene and let their conversation illustrate clearly the differences and similarities between them. You might enjoy presenting this exercise as a dramatic reading with fellow students.

each man that Catton needs to make his point-by-point comparisons in the second half.

Style

1. The metaphor suggests that the unfolding history of the United States is a story—a narrative that could be written and read—and that the close of the Civil War is a natural ending to one chapter and beginning of another. The metaphor is effective because Catton goes on to tell the "story" of Lee and Grant.

2. Lee, as a knight in shining armor, may represent a lost cause and a social ideal that has been bypassed by history, but to interpret such a description satirically would miss the tone of the essay, which is entirely laudatory.

3. *Virtual:* being in effect, though not actually or expressly; *poignant:* keenly distressing to the feelings; *chivalry:* the medieval institution and principles of knighthood, the ideal qualities of which include courage, generosity, and courtesy; *legends:* nonhistorical or unverifiable stories handed down by tradition from earlier times and popularly accepted as historic; *myths:* stories or beliefs that are attempts to explain basic truths; *embodied:* given a concrete form; *deportment:* demeanor, conduct, behavior; *obeisance:* a movement of the body expressing deep respect or deferential courtesy, as before a superior; *static:* pertaining to or characterized by a fixed or stationary condition; *tenacity:* holding fast; *fidelity:* loyalty; *indomitable:* unable to be subdued or overcome.

4. Ending the essay in the same place as it began brings it full circle and reconnects the reader to the situation described in the first paragraph. This technique is structurally satisfying because in the body of the essay Catton has given background on and expanded the meaning of the scene in the Court House.

5. Though Lee and Grant represent two entirely different social ideals, Catton admires them both. Both were, in their own ways, admirable. Even when the author contrasts them, he always does so on positive terms. When comparing them, he speaks only of virtues: tenacity and faithfulness (14); daring, resourcefulness, and the ability to think quickly (15); and, ultimately, the capacity to be men of peace (16).

❦ Gloria Steinem ❦

TEACHING SUGGESTIONS

One way to approach the essay is to have your students not only read it but also look up the origins and definitions of *erotica, pornography,* and *obscenity* before they come to class for discussion. This exercise might help the students understand the distinctions Steinem is making. The essay can be a springboard for getting your students to rationally examine their own attitudes toward the subject, attitudes that are not usually rationally examined.

We think the essay is also worthy of being analyzed structurally. Steinem's reasoning is careful and her use of comparing and contrasting is sophisticated. A paragraph-by-paragraph examination might help your students get at her thinking.

Gloria Steinem is one of the most prominent organizers of the American feminist movement. She was born in Toledo, Ohio, in 1934 and studied at Smith College. She did graduate work in India, at the University of Delhi and the University of Calcutta, where she developed sensitivity to the plight of the underclasses. She began her career in journalism in the 1960s as a freelance writer and quickly gained respect among her mostly male colleagues in the field, but that respect began to wane as she focused more and more on controversial women's issues. In 1972 she cofounded Ms. *magazine, of which she was also editor from 1972 to 1987. She has contributed to leading periodicals and has published various books, including* Marilyn: Norma Jean *(1986), about Marilyn Monroe, and, most recently, the* Bedside Book of Self-Esteem *(1989).*

Erotica and Pornography

Gloria Steinem compares erotica and pornography in an attempt to untangle the differences between the two. By separating one from the other, she helps the reader judge more clearly their positive and negative aspects. This essay is an excerpt from her Outrageous Acts and Everyday Rebellions *(1983).*

MARGINAL NOTES

The one-sentence opening paragraph captures attention with a fact distinguishing human beings from all other animals.

Steinem further shows that, precisely because sex is not tied to human reproduction, it can and does satisfy other complex and subtle human needs for communication. Human sexuality is evolutionarily advanced.

Human beings are the only animals that experience the same sex drive at times when we can—and cannot—conceive. 1

Just as we developed uniquely human capacities for language, planning, memory, and invention along our evolutionary path, we also developed sexuality as a form of expression; a way of communicating that is separable from our need for sex as a way of perpetuating ourselves. For humans alone, sexuality can be and often is primarily a way of bonding, of giving and receiving pleasure, bridging differentness, discovering sameness, and communicating emotion. 2

We developed this and other human gifts through our ability to change our environment, adapt physically, and in the long run, to affect our own evolution. But as an emotional result of this spiraling path away from other animals, we seem to alternate between periods of exploring our unique abilities to change new boundaries, and feelings of loneliness in the unknown that we ourselves have created; a fear that sometimes sends us back to the comfort of the animal world by encouraging us to exaggerate our sameness.

The separation of "play" from "work," for instance, is a problem only in the human world. So is the difference between art and nature, or an intellectual accomplishment and a physical one. As a result, we celebrate play, art, and invention as leaps into the unknown; but any imbalance can send us back to nostalgia for our primate past and the conviction that the basics of work, nature, and physical labor are somehow more worthwhile or even moral.

In the same way, we have explored our sexuality as separable from conception: a pleasurable, empathetic bridge to strangers of the same species. We have even invented contraception—a skill that has probably existed in some form since our ancestors figured out the process of birth—in order to extend this uniquely human difference. Yet we also have times of atavistic suspicion that sex is not complete—or even legal or intended-by-god—if it cannot end in conception.

No wonder the concepts of "erotica" and "pornography" can be so crucially different, and yet so confused. Both assume that sexuality can be separated from conception, and therefore can be used to carry a personal message. That's a major reason why, even in our current culture, both may be called equally "shocking" or legally "obscene," a word whose Latin derivative means "dirty, containing filth." This gross condemnation of all sexuality that isn't harnessed to childbirth and marriage has been increased by the current backlash against women's progress. Out of fear that the whole patriarchal structure might be upset if women really had the autonomous power to decide our reproductive futures (that is, if we controlled the most basic means of production),

3   The paragraph is developed by contrasting our evolutionary advance with the fear of that advance that makes some of us deny it.

4   Sentences 1 and 2 have two examples illustrating the idea from the preceding paragraph. Sentence 3 shows effects of those causes, and its two halves compare and contrast with sentences 1 and 2.

5

Steinem's attitude toward the idea that only procreative sex is good shows in her calling it "atavistic."

6   Steinem states the essay's thesis in sentence 1. The confusion she describes, she argues, gets the Women's Movement called "obscene." Her job here is to clarify the confusion.

right-wing groups are not only denouncing prochoice abortion literature as "pornographic," but are trying to stop the sending of all contraceptive information through the mails by invoking obscenity laws. In fact, Phyllis Schlafly recently denounced the entire Women's Movement as "obscene."

Not surprisingly, this religious, visceral backlash has a secular, intellectual counterpart that relies heavily on applying the "natural" behavior of the animal world to humans. That is questionable in itself, but these Lionel Tiger-ish studies make their political purpose even more clear in the particular animals they select and the habits they choose to emphasize. The message is that females should accept their "destiny" of being sexually dependent and devote themselves to bearing and rearing their young.   7

Defending against such reaction in turn leads to another temptation: to merely reverse the terms, and declare that *all* non-procreative sex is good. In fact, however, this human activity can be as constructive as destructive, moral or immoral, as any other. Sex as communication can send messages as different as life and death; even the origins of "erotica" and "pornography" reflect that fact. After all, "erotica" is rooted in *eros* or passionate love, and thus in the idea of positive choice, free will, the yearning for a particular person. (Interestingly, the definition of erotica leaves open the question of gender.) "Pornography" begins with a root meaning "prostitution" or "female captives," thus letting us know that the subject is not mutual love, or love at all, but domination and violence against women. (Though, of course, homosexual pornography may imitate this violence by putting a man in the "feminine" role of victim.) It ends with a root meaning "writing about" or "description of" which puts still more distance between subject and object, and replaces a spontaneous yearning for closeness with objectification and a voyeur.   8

The difference is clear in the words. It becomes even more so by example.   9

Look at any photo or film of people making love; really making love. The images may be diverse, but there is usually a sensuality and touch and warmth, an acceptance of bodies and nerve   10

Lionel Tiger (born 1937), a Canadian-born sociologist and anthropologist teaching at Rutgers University has experimentally compared human behavior with that of other animals.

Steinem begins by defining her terms, tracing the origins of the two words.

She now illustrates erotica but doesn't label it.

endings. There is always a spontaneous sense of people who are there because they *want* to be, out of shared pleasure.

Now look at any depiction of sex in which there is clear force, or an unequal power that spells coercion. It may be very blatant, with weapons or torture or bondage, wounds and bruises, some clear humiliation, or an adult's sexual power being used over a child. It may be much more subtle: a physical attitude of conqueror and victim, the use of race or class difference to imply the same thing, perhaps a very unequal nudity, with one person exposed and vulnerable while the other is clothed. In either case, there is no sense of equal choice or equal power.

11   Illustrating pornography, she contrasts it with erotica in the preceding paragraph.

The first is erotic: a mutually pleasurable, sexual expression between people who have enough power to be there by positive choice. It may or may not strike a sense-memory in the viewer, or be creative enough to make the unknown seem real; but it doesn't require us to identify with a conqueror or a victim. It is truly sensuous, and may give us a contagion of pleasure.

12   Steinem labels her example in paragraph 10 erotic: it always involves mutual pleasure and choice.

The second is pornographic: its message is violence, dominance, and conquest. It is sex being used to reinforce some inequality, or to create one, or to tell us the lie that pain and humiliation (ours or someone else's) are really the same as pleasure. If we are to feel anything, we must identify with conqueror or victim. That means we can only experience pleasure through the adoption of some degree of sadism or masochism. It also means that we may feel diminished by the role of conqueror, or enraged, humiliated, and vengeful by sharing identity with the victim.

13   In contrast to the preceding paragraph, she now labels the example in paragraph 11 pornographic, which always involves inequality and humiliation.

Perhaps one could simply say that erotica is about sexuality, but pornography is about power and sex-as-weapon—in the same way we have come to understand that rape is about violence, and not really about sexuality at all.

14   A one-sentence paragraph further contrasts erotica and pornography.

Yes, it's true that there are women who have been forced by violent families and dominating men to confuse love with pain; so much so that they have become masochists. (A fact that in no way excuses those who administer such pain.) But the truth is that, for most women—and for men with enough humanity to

15   The next two paragraphs account for the differences in the things that various people consider erotic.

imagine themselves into the predicament of women—true pornography could serve as aversion therapy for sex.

Of course, there will always be personal differences about what is and is not erotic, and there may be cultural differences for a long time to come. Many women feel that sex makes them vulnerable and therefore may continue to need more sense of personal connection and safety before allowing any erotic feelings. We now find competence and expertise erotic in men, but that may pass as we develop those qualities in ourselves. Men, on the other hand, may continue to feel less vulnerable, and therefore more open to such potential danger as sex with strangers. As some men replace the need for submission from childlike women with the pleasure of cooperation from equals, they may find a partner's competence to be erotic, too.

Steinem now paints the ideal that human sexuality might become.

Such group changes plus individual differences will continue to be reflected in sexual love between people of the same gender, as well as between women and men. The point is not to dictate sameness, but to discover ourselves and each other through sexuality that is an exploring, pleasurable, empathetic part of our lives; a human sexuality that is unchained both from unwanted pregnancies and from violence.

She immediately contrasts the ideal with current reality.

But that is a hope, not a reality. At the moment, fear of change is increasing both the indiscriminate repression of all nonprocreative sex in the religious and "conservative" male world, and the pornographic vengeance against women's sexuality in the secular world of "liberal" and "radical" men. It's almost futuristic to debate what is and is not truly erotic, when many women are again being forced into compulsory motherhood, and the number of pornographic murders, tortures, and woman-hating images are on the increase in both popular culture and real life.

It's a familiar division: wife or whore, "good" woman who is constantly vulnerable to pregnancy or "bad" woman who is unprotected from violence. *Both* roles would be upset if we were to control our own sexuality. And that's exactly what we must do.

In spite of all our atavistic suspicions and training for the "natural" role of motherhood, we took up the complicated battle for reproductive freedom. Our bodies had borne the health burden of endless birth and poor abortions, and we had a greater motive for separating sexuality and conception.

Now we have to take up the equally complex burden of explaining that all nonprocreative sex is *not* alike. We have a motive: our right to a uniquely human sexuality, and sometimes even to survival. As it is, our bodies have too rarely been enough our own to develop erotica in our own lives, much less in art and literature. And our bodies have too often been the objects of pornography and the woman-hating, violent practice that it preaches. Consider also our spirits that break a little each time we see ourselves in chains or full labial display for the conquering male viewer, bruised or on our knees, screaming a real or pretended pain to delight the sadist, pretending to enjoy what we don't enjoy, to be blind to the images of our sisters that really haunt us—humiliated often enough ourselves by the truly obscene idea that sex and the domination of women must be combined.

Sexuality *is* human, free, separate—and so are we.

But until we untangle the lethal confusion of sex with violence, there will be more pornography and less erotica. There will be little murders in our beds—and very little love.

21

22

23

Meaning and Purpose

1. What do you think Steinem's purpose is in this essay? Where does she most clearly state it?
2. In what sense does Steinem think we are the same as other animals?
3. Who does Steinem think are the enemies of women's progress and the separation of sex from violence?
4. Who is Steinem's primary audience? How do you know?
5. Why does Steinem call the confusion of sex with violence "lethal" in the last paragraph? Has she supported this contention in the essay? Explain.

Steinem concludes by stating what women have already done and what they still must do to gain the ideal.

POSSIBLE ANSWERS

Meaning and Purpose

1. Steinem intends to distinguish between erotica and pornography (6). Paragraph 14 is one sentence asserting this difference.
2. We are the same as other animals when we revert to the belief that "the basics of work, nature, and physical labor are somehow more worthwhile or even moral" (4) than celebrating play, art, and invention, and when we think sex is not complete unless it ends in conception.
3. The enemies of women's progress are right-wing groups who are against choice in abortion, and who try to suppress contraceptive information (6). Other enemies do not separate sex from the dominance of women by men (18).
4. Steinem speaks to those who confuse sex with violence or dominance as well as to those who agree with her—her essay would confirm their beliefs and perhaps rouse them to action against pornography.
5. Lethal means deadly, and Steinem has described pornography as "sex-as-weapon" (14) throughout. The word is reinforced by "little murders."

Strategy

1. Paragraphs 1–5 establish the difference between human beings and other animals that she will need when talking about differences between erotica and pornography. She makes assertions about "sexuality as a form of expression" (1), and about how we revert to "our primate past" (4) in our confusion over higher human pursuits and animalistic tendencies. Now she can compare erotica and pornography as in the same category.

2. Steinem uses both subject-by-subject and point-by-point methods to compare and contrast erotica and pornography: point by point about root words in each expression and their meanings (8); subject-by-subject method, each characterizing one word in detail (12, 13). She alternates and combines these methods throughout the essay.

3. Effective transitions: "Defending against such reaction" (8); "Such group changes plus individual differences" (17); and "But that is a hope, not a reality" (18). Each transition is connected to the last thought in the preceding paragraph.

Style

1. The tone is authoritative (as in the essay's first sentence), and at times persuasive and almost strident (20). Steinem feels strongly that pornography is immoral (13), and describes erotica (11). She has little tolerance for the extreme right wing (6).

2. Paragraph 9 follows the paragraph about the roots of each term, and precedes the first paragraph of examples of what each expression is and is not. Paragraph 9 therefore is an emphatic transition between the two. Paragraph 22 brings together the points Steinem has made about sexuality—human or animal, free or chained, tied to conception or separate—in one concise statement.

3. "Atavistic": recurrence of a "form typical of ancestors; a throwback." Steinem means that human suspicions come from an animalistic source.

Strategy

1. Steinem does not mention either erotica or pornography until paragraph 6. What is the importance of the first five paragraphs?
2. How is Steinem's essay structured for comparison and contrast? Does she use the block or point-by-point method of discussion? Give examples to support your answer.
3. What are some effective transitions in the essay to get readers from one point to the next?

Style

1. What is the tone of this essay? How does Steinem feel about her subject?
2. Paragraphs 9 and 22 are extremely short. Why are these statements set apart?
3. What does "atavistic" mean in paragraphs 5 and 20?

Writing Tasks

1. In an essay, compare and contrast two aspects of one thing, such as the discipline and fun of dance, or the joys and risks of falling in love. Choose either the subject-by-subject or the point-by-point method of discussion.
2. Write about the same subject you chose for number 1, but change the method; that is, if you used subject-by-subject structure, this time use point-by-point. Which method is better for your subject?

❦ Phil Donahue ❦

Born in Cleveland, Ohio, in 1935, Phil Donahue began his broadcasting career while still at the University of Notre Dame when he took a job at the school's radio station. Since then he has worked at numerous radio and television stations across the country. In 1963 he became the co-anchor of a popular phone-in radio talk show, which led to an offer to host a television show of similar format in 1967. The show, now called "Donahue," focused on one guest or controversial topic each week and became a forum for discussion of changing values in America. He has won several Emmy awards as host of this sometimes controversial show. He ardently supports the civil-rights and feminist movements and is a member of the National Organization for Women (NOW). His autobiography, Donahue: My Own Story *(1980), includes observations about contemporary life in the United States.*

Beauty and the Beast

This essay is from Phil Donahue's The Human Animal *(1985). Comparing the two sides of human nature—"noble and petty, sublime and savage, beauty and beast"—Donahue raises questions about contemporary attitudes toward the dark side of the human animal.*

Compared to the animals around us, there's no doubt we are a remarkable phenomenon. Someone once referred to us as the "superdeluxe model": we walk, we talk, we smell, we taste, we touch, we think. All this in a relatively small and attractive package. We're also very good with our hands. In the comparatively brief time we've been available in the current form—about 50,000 years—we've invented the wheel, the alphabet, the clock, the reciprocating machine, the cyclotron, and everything in between. When we weren't busy making progress, we invented more

By contrasting our realities with our ideals, Donahue's essay shows that humankind contains the beauty of humanity and the beast of the jungle. He compares our great works of art with our great destructive wars. The cathedral of Chartres, the symbol of great art that came from love and devotion, contrasts sharply with the Crusades, the symbol of great destruction, ironically also said to have come from love and devotion.

Before discussing the essay in depth, you might want to offer the class two concepts, the concept of hypocrisy and the concept of rationalization. *Hypocrisy* as used to discuss this essay means pretense. Some people pretend to have virtuous characters and strong moral beliefs or principles, but do not really possess them. In twentieth-century psychology, *rationalization* ascribes our opinions and acts to causes that seem reasonable but are in fact not related to true, possibly unconscious, causes.

Some students might complain that Donahue makes his case with only limited evidence. Ask the class for other evidence that supports or refutes Donahue's contention that our actions contradict our beliefs.

MARGINAL NOTES

A blithely optimistic tone permeates the first paragraph. Human beings are masters of the universe! (Soon, Donahue brings us back to earth.) Albert Einstein (1875–1955): Awarded 1921 Nobel Prize for physics; deprived of German citizenship and property confiscated by the Nazi government (1934); member, Institute for Advanced Study, Princeton, New Jersey (1933–1945). Developed a unified field theory designed to include in one mathematical formula the laws of electromagnetism and gravitation.

playful things like music, art, baseball, and bridge. Over the years, we've demonstrated an admirable willingness to cooperate with each other. We assemble in big groups to form towns and cities; we get together in twos to discover love. We've also shown a lot of individual spunk. The wheel wasn't invented by a committee, and Albert Einstein, by himself, revolutionized our understanding of the universe.

Of course, most of our uniquely human accomplishments are the result of a combination of cooperation and individual achievement. Even Charles Lindbergh had a ground crew. Beethoven composed the *Ninth Symphony* in the solitude of deafness, but scores of musicians are needed to bring it to life. Neil Armstrong had to have personal courage to step out on the surface of the moon, knowing that he might sink into 15 feet of "moondust," but he had an army of people to help put him there and bring him back.

We can only imagine what it must have felt like to stand on the moon; look back at the earth, suspended like a blue-and-white marble in space; and think how far we humans have come in such a short time. That feeling itself—the tightening in the throat, the tingle up the spine, the tear of pride—is unique to the human animal. Throughout most of our history, that feeling belonged exclusively to religion. When most people's lives were "solitary, poor, nasty, brutish, and short," religion was the only thing that made them feel dignified, special, proud of being human.

The peasants who gazed for the first time at the stained glass in the cathedral at Chartres undoubtedly experienced that same feeling—the most human of emotions—wonder. Most of them had never been inside anything bigger than a thatched hut and never seen anything more colorful than a piece of dyed cloth. Even today, the sight of this huge, arched space with those luminous windows suspended high in the darkness is almost enough to make a believer of even the most skeptical. In 1260, when the church was consecrated, the peasants who shuffled through those doors must have thought they had died and gone to heaven.

The optimism stresses our collaborative successes. Charles Lindbergh (1902–1974): First solo nonstop transatlantic flight, New York to Paris, 1927. Ludwig von Beethoven (1770–1827): German composer of Flemish descent; became totally deaf, c. 1819; composed Ninth Symphony, 1823. Neil Armstrong (born 1930): First man to stand on the moon, 1969.

Thomas Hobbes (1588–1679) says in *Leviathan* (1651) that human beings in a state of nature, without religion, have "No arts; no letters; no society; and which is worst of all, continual fear and danger of violent death; and the life of man, solitary, poor, nasty, brutish, and short."

In fact, Chartres cathedral, like dozens of other cathedrals built in the same period, is the medieval equivalent of the modern effort to put a man on the moon. Both represent the perfect combination of individual achievement and group cooperation in the pursuit of something beautiful and lasting. The space program would never have gotten off the ground if Wernher von Braun hadn't made his discoveries in the field of jet propulsion, and the arches of Chartres would never have soared if an anonymous French architect hadn't devised a system of buttresses to support a two-ton block of stone 120 feet in the air and keep it there for a thousand years. But there would have been no stones to support if the wealthier townspeople hadn't dug deep into their pockets and come up with the money needed for construction. The glass in the openings would be clear instead of stained if merchant guilds, members of the nobility, and even the French king hadn't contributed money for the windows. And all the money would have been worthless if legions of craftsmen hadn't been willing to dedicate their skills and often their lives to making this not just another building, but a monument to human achievement.

Bees get together and build hives, termites build mounds, beavers build dams, and spiders spin webs, but what other animal can change stone and glass into poetry? Other animals can alter their environment at the margins, but only we can transform our environment so completely that we reshape our destiny. Alone in the animal kingdom, we can set goals for ourselves and then pursue them. The dream of the medieval craftsmen who built Chartres was to secure a place for themselves in heaven. By lavishing love on this stone and glass, they glorified God and hoped to be rewarded in the next life. But in the process, they changed this life, made it more beautiful and more worth living.

A place like Chartres makes us proud to be human. We can stand tall and hold our heads high. Certainly no other creature could conceive and create something of such sublime beauty. Case closed? Hardly. There is, unfortunately, another side to the human animal that's nothing to be proud of. At places like Chartres, it's easy—and tempting—to overlook this other side, the ugly side,

5 The author draws historical parallels between thirteenth-century and twentieth-century cooperative efforts. So far, the discussion of human achievements has moved from the earliest of times to the present, and then back, to show our emotional and cooperative continuum. Wernher von Braun (1912–1977): Developed German World War II rockets. Came to America (1945); worked on United States space program. He lived at about the same time as Lindbergh. We have gone from the first solo transatlantic flight to the moon, in one lifetime. The French king is Louis IX (1214–1270), canonized in 1297. The writer views the church as a monument to "human achievement" as well as to God.

6 Humanity plans and shapes its own future; "other animals" are controlled only by natural laws. The writer says that striving to be rewarded in the future can inspire beauty and worth in the present.

7 The transitional paragraph, introducing the reason for presenting new evidence in "the case": to show the duality of human nature. Beauty contrasts with beast. We were "compared with animals" in paragraph 1; now we have become "the human animal."

of our nature. But we can't begin to understand the human animal without it. Surely there's beauty inside us—but there's also a beast, a part of us that we'd like to deny but can't, a part that gives us a knot in the stomach instead of a lump in the throat.

Even the God-loving people who fashioned the soaring vaults   8
and delicate windows of Chartres had murder on their minds. Some of the workers may well have been veterans of the First Crusade, an expedition to save the Holy Land from the infidel Muslims that was part religious frenzy, part military adventure, and part social fad. On that excursion, begun four years after work on Chartres began, the Crusaders slaughtered thousands of noncombatants, leveled whole communities, and finally "saved" the holy city of Jerusalem by massacring all its inhabitants—men, women, children, Muslims, Jews: everybody. Muslims, after all, were only infidels, not humans, so it wasn't like killing your next-door neighbor.

After the shrines of Christianity were in "safe" hands, many   9
Crusaders returned home and turned their attention to other things, like the cathedral at Chartres.

How could the same hands that carved these stones and   10
stained this glass have wielded swords and butchered women and children? How could so much beauty and so much brutality exist side by side? This is the great contradiction of the human animal. We can be both noble and petty, sublime and savage, beauty and beast. We can pray one minute and kill the next, create one minute and destroy the next, even love and hate simultaneously. We like to think that our erratic behavior is a thing of the past, that we've outgrown the excesses of the Crusades. But nothing could be further from the truth. There are people in Belfast today who will repeat the catechism, then go toss a bomb into a crowded pub; people who grieve for the victims of crime, then pay good money to see it reenacted on a movie screen. The same technological wizardry, individual bravery, and group effort that put us on the moon have also given us weapons that can blow our whole planet into permanent winter.

Far from having disappeared with the last Crusade, the hu-   11
man animal's strange capacity for contradictory behavior still af-

---

Notice the irony in this paragraph. The First Crusade, launched by Pope Urban II in 1095, "saved" the holy city by killing thousands of people. Yet some of those who fought in the crusade may have returned to work on Chartres, a monument to the love of God. Similarly, an American officer in Vietnam was quoted as saying, "It became necessary to destroy the town [Ben Tre] to save it."

The rhetorical questions begin the ironical comparison between the two parts of each person: the beauty and the beast. We are compared and contrasted within ourselves. Belfast is the capital of Northern Ireland, which is predominantly Protestant. Since the eighteenth century attempts have been made to forge Ireland into one country. Some scientists believe that a nuclear war could cause a cloud cover, reducing the temperature of the planet disastrously.

fects our daily lives. As parents, we desperately want our kids to grow up emotionally healthy, able to love and be loved; then our culture teaches them that sex is dirty and they should be ashamed of their sexual desires. Women say they want to marry a nice person who will respect them and communicate with them; then they melt for *machismo* and fall for the strong, silent type. They want a man who will share the housework and feed the baby at three in the morning, but they live in a society in which few bosses grant time off to men who want to share parenting. Cops throw drunken drivers in jail while television sells beer as though it were an American entitlement. The message to teenage males: "You're not a man without a beer can in your hand." But there are millions of teenage drivers and thousands of cloverleaves out there, and the phone rings every day, in homes across America, and it's the hospital calling—or the morgue.

We cannot complacently claim that "the past is past." We strangely contradict ourselves daily. What we want contrasts with what we have. What we do contrasts with what we believe should be done. The tension builds between the ideal and the real.

Why do we do the things we do? Why, after thousands of years of personal tragedies and group catastrophes, do we continue to make the same mistakes? Why do we persist in the same contradictory behavior day after day, century after century, alternating between Chartres and the Crusades, between grief and gore, between moonwalks and megatons?

12 This series of provocative rhetorical questions directly addresses readers.

These questions aren't just for the historians and the sociologists. They're for everyone who wrestles with these contradictory drives in his or her own life. The impulse that sends a society back to war, despite the knowledge that children will die and mothers will grieve, is the same impulse that leads you to light up another cigarette or have "one more for the road," despite the knowledge that it may kill you. We live with contradictions in our own behavior—and the behavior of others—every day. It's about time we tried to understand those contradictions. Are they a permanent part of the human condition, or can we do something about them?

13 *They* (historians and sociologists), *you*, and *we* are addressed here, in the writer's plea that everyone try to understand humanity's contradictions. The final either-or question leads to another question: *If* contradictions are part of the human condition, can we ever have a world of peace and beauty? This question and the ones in the paragraph could stimulate lively classroom discussion.

Meaning and Purpose

1. Encourage students to explore and make specific connections between the text and their responses.

2. Readers may recall the classic story: a beautiful woman falls in love with a grotesque beast, only to find he is a handsome man whom she has released from a spell. The larger connotation of the words "beauty and the beast" includes a two-sided nature, or the capacity for both good and evil. Donahue talks about beauty and brutality existing side by side in human undertakings. The title helps keep the reader aware of this duality as Donahue's theme.

3. Donahue's purpose is to make readers think about human dual nature and why we allow "the beauty and the beast" contradiction to persist. His thesis is best stated in paragraph 10.

4. Henry Adams's *Mont-Saint-Michel and Chartres* is an excellent aesthetic study of the cathedral. Adams ends the book with this final assessment of and tribute to Gothic architecture:

> Perhaps the best proof of [the style of the great cathedrals is its] apparent instability. Of all the elaborate symbolism which has been suggested for the gothic Cathedral, the most vital and most perfect may be that the slender *nervure,* the springing motion of the broken arch, the leap downwards of the flying buttress,—the visible effort to throw off a visible strain,—never lets us forget that Faith alone supports it, and that, if Faith fails, Heaven is lost.

5. Students might mention athletes, former presidents, artists, or even fictional characters.

Strategy

1. Donahue compares the heights human beings can achieve with the "ugly side of our

Meaning and Purpose

1. Does Donahue's essay make you think of contradictions or dualities in your own life? What specific statements in the essay apply in some way to you?

2. The title is usually the first thing you read in an essay. Does Donahue's title set you up for what he has to say? Does it guide your reading of the essay? Who is the beauty and who is the beast?

3. What is Donahue's purpose in this essay and where does he state it?

4. Throughout his discussion of the heights human beings can achieve, Donahue uses the cathedral at Chartres as a metaphor for the good side of our nature. What do you know about this cathedral, and why do you think Donahue chose it?

5. Albert Einstein greatly affected our lives. Name three other people who have affected our lives profoundly in the past thirty years and tell why you chose them.

Strategy

1. What is Donahue comparing and contrasting in this essay? Analyze the method he uses. Is it subject-by-subject, point-by-point, or a combination? Support your answers with statements in the text.

2. According to paragraph 8, why did the Crusaders call Muslims "infidels"?

3. What kind of language does Donahue use to appeal to his readers and try to gain their agreement with his assertions?

4. In the last two paragraphs, Donahue asks several questions that he leaves unanswered. To whom does he direct the questions? How does ending with unanswered questions affect you as a reader?

Style

1. In paragraph 8, why is *saved* in quotation marks?
2. In paragraph 4, Donahue says that "the most human of emotions" is wonder, which is surprise, admiration, and awe caused by something strange, unexpected, or incredible. The word *wonderful* means "that which causes wonder." Find an advertisement in a newspaper or magazine that uses *wonder* or *wonderful*. In no more than five sentences, tell why the word is or is not appropriately used in the advertisement. Attach a copy of the advertisement to your paper.
3. According to the essayist, our message to teenage males is "You're not a man without a beer can in your hand." Who sends this message? How is it sent? What kind of teenage males believe the message?
4. In paragraph 11, Donahue says that women "melt for machismo." What does that word mean to you? Name two television or film characters and describe the qualities that make them conventional macho males.

Writing Tasks

1. Think about someone you know well and write an essay about the duality of that person's nature. Compare two of his or her exemplary deeds or character traits with two mean deeds or character traits. Can you explain the apparent contradiction? Set up your comparison and contrast in subject-by-subject form, point-by-point form, or a combination.
2. Compare and contrast the Catton essay in this chapter with Donahue's on these points: purpose, appeal to audience, structure of comparison and contrast, and style of language (tone). Choose carefully and deliberately the structure for your own comparison and contrast in this essay.

nature." With the subject-by-subject method he discusses our achievements (through 6), then our depravities (through 11). Let students find any statements that illustrate one side or the other of human nature. The second portion (on the ugly side) has some point-by-point technique (such as 10).

2. Calling the Muslims "infidels" made it easier to murder them. The (hypocritical) reason for which Muslims and Jews were massacred is that they did not believe in God in the way that the Crusaders did.

3. From the first sentence, Donahue makes generous use of "we" and "us" to include the reader in his thinking. He invites readers to identify with both the good and evil sides of human nature even as he challenges them to explain this duality.

4. Donahue directs the questions to the reader, as well as to himself. By the time he poses them, he hopes to have left his reader as puzzled as he is about why "we do the things we do," and so the questions are the very ones the reader too would raise.

Style

1. The word *saved,* used ironically, describes rescuing Jerusalem by murdering all its citizens. "Saving" the city destroyed it.

2. Your students' answers will almost always effectively compare the wonder of Donahue's examples, such as Chartres and the Ninth Symphony, with such meaningless wonders as bread, automobiles, and television sets, showing that the word is trivialized in advertisements.

3. Answers will vary, including advertisers in general, billboards, television commercials, radio commercials, movies, endorsements by sports celebrities, and so on. Students often point out that the teenage males most affected by this kind of advertising are those interested in projecting a particular kind of image.

4. "Machismo" means "a strong sense of male pride; an exaggerated awareness and assertion of masculinity." John Wayne (swaggering bravado) and James Bond (sexy daring) are two macho characters.

P. S. Wood

Born in New York City in 1930, and a graduate of Hamilton College, P. S. Wood writes primarily about sports and the outdoors. After college he worked for a while at The New Yorker *and later was a staff writer for* Time-Life Books, *a job he kept until 1975. Since then, he has worked as a freelance writer, contributing articles to such periodicals as* The New Yorker, Smithsonian, *and* The New York Times Magazine. *He has also published several books, including* The Book of Squash, The Caribbean Isles, Running the Rivers of North America, *and* The Spanish Main.

Female Athletes:
They've Come a Long, Long Way, Baby

This essay originally appeared in The New York Times *in 1980 as "Sex Difference in Sports." Wood compares women athletes with men athletes by examining social attitudes and stating pertinent facts and statistics on their athletic performance and abilities. His comparison reveals the advances women had made in sports by 1980.*

TEACHING SUGGESTIONS

All of us are guilty, to one degree or another, of the intellectually lazy and often damaging habit of stereotyping. It is this mindless habit that Wood attacks in his essay. Women, he shows, are not athletically inferior to men. They are simply different—not as big or as strong as men, perhaps, but probably more durable. You might lead into the essay by exploring the stereotypes of men and women perpetuated by our society. The discussion could be quite lively, with some students staunchly defending stereotypes and others just as staunchly denying them. This dispute could lead not only to provocative subjects for potential papers, but also to a discussion of how Wood controls his subject by carefully comparing and contrasting his information paragraph by paragraph.

MARGINAL NOTES

Four paragraphs launch the essay and offer statistics to support the subtitle, "They've Come a Long, Long Way, Baby."

There has been an explosion in women's competitive sports. If women have not yet achieved equal time on the playing fields of America, or equal space in the halls of fame, they have come a long way, and are moving up fast. For example: 1

• Thirty-three percent of all high school athletes are female, a six-fold increase since the early 1970s, according to figures supplied by the Women's Sports Foundation. In colleges, the figure is 30 percent, an increase in ten years of 250 percent. 2

• Since 1970, the number of women tennis players in the country has jumped from about 3 million to 11 million, the number of golfers from less than a half million to more than 5 3 million. According to one survey, of the nation's 17.1 million joggers, well over one-third are women—in 1970, there were too few to count.

• In 1980, according to six sports federations (tennis, golf, bowling, skiing, racquetball, basketball), financial rewards for female athletes topped more than $16 million, up from less than $1 million a decade ago.

As women rush into athletic competition, certain questions are being raised: How good are women as athletes? How do they compare with men? Are women's bodies strong enough, tough enough, to take the battles?

New research on the physical and athletic differences between men and women shows that in some respects women may be at least as tough as men. Some evidence suggests that women's endurance may be equal or perhaps even superior to men's. Women's bodies are constructed so that certain crucial organs are better guarded from injury; ovaries, for instance, lie inside the pelvic cavity, far better placed for protection than the testicles.

Furthermore, the folk wisdom that other elements of the female anatomy make women athletes more vulnerable seems incorrect. The suspicion that severe bruises cause breast cancer is not borne out; breasts are less susceptible to injury than knees or elbows, whether male or female. And the old idea that, at certain times of the month, women do not operate at peak performance is generally not true for athletes. World and Olympic records have been set by women in all stages of their menstrual cycles. Moreover, at certain intense levels of training, menstruation conveniently turns off for many women, a phenomenon that has been linked in some studies to a reduction in body fat, in other studies to physical and emotional stress.

The point is that, if concern for safety is a determining factor, women should have the same opportunities to participate in competitive athletics as men. And, by and large, they have the same reasons for wanting to do so. Says tennis star Billie Jean King: "Athletics are an essential part of education for both sexes. Girls and boys are going to grow up easier in each other's company."

4

5   Three questions set the boundaries of the coming discussion.

6   This paragraph points to new research comparing men and women on toughness, endurance, and susceptibility to injury.

7   Wood contrasts folk wisdom about female anatomy with the previously mentioned new research and dismisses safety as a problem in women's participation in sports.

8

The next nine paragraphs compare and contrast the physical development and attributes of men and women and discuss their implications for specific athletic activities.

No one suggests now that equal experience is going to lead to   9
equal performance in all things athletic. Men are bigger and
stronger, can run faster, throw and jump farther. But the fact that
women are genetically ordained through most of life to compete
with less powerful bodies, far from tarnishing their performance,
makes it more worthy.

Actually, boys and girls start out with nearly identical equip-   10
ment so far as fitness for sports goes. If anything, girls, because
they mature faster, may have an edge, as youth soccer-league
coaches, for example, are finding out.

At puberty, the situation abruptly changes. Estrogen levels   11
begin to build in the female body. There is a growth spurt which
peaks at about 12 years, then tapers off by 14 or 15. Most boys
begin to mature sexually a year and a half to two years later than
girls, and then keep on developing much longer, in some cases up
to six years longer.

On the average, men end up ten percent bigger. They have   12
longer bones, providing better leverage; wider shoulders—
the foundation for a significant advantage in upper-body
strength—and bigger hearts and lungs. In addition, while the
body of the female adolescent is preparing for childbirth by storing up fat reserves, the male body is growing muscle. And this
occurs quite apart from exercise. Exercise adds strength and endurance, and increases the size of the muscles. But on average,
men have more muscle fibers than women; and they have an
added advantage in the hormone testosterone, which adds bulk to
those fibers.

When the Army first accepted women at West Point in 1976,   13
it found it necessary to quantify the strength differences of the
incoming plebes. The upshot of numerous tests indicated that
women had approximately one-third the strength of men in the
upper body and two-thirds the strength of men in the legs, and
about the same amount of strength as men in the abdomen. The
implications are obvious for those American games that have
dominated the sports pages for years: women are no match for
men in football, baseball and basketball, all of which place a
high premium on upper-body strength. Tennis, too, illustrates the

female disadvantage. Tracy Austin has mastered the basic strokes of the game every bit as well as most of the top male players. But she simply cannot match them in the serve, which demands upper-arm strength and happens to be the key stroke of the game.

Sometimes the special combination of female traits works to women's advantage. Ever since Gertrude Ederle swam the English Channel in 1926, two hours faster than any man had ever done it, women have dominated the sport of long-distance swimming. Women generally have ten percent more fat than men. This appears not only in the characteristic deposits on the thighs, buttocks and breasts, but in an overall layer of subcutaneous fat. The result is that women are more buoyant than men and better insulated against cold. An added edge is their narrower shoulders, which offers less resistance through the water.

14

Another advantage long-distance swimmers may share with other well-trained female athletes is the ability to call on reserves of energy perhaps unavailable to men. Running the marathon, women get tired, but few report "hitting the wall," an expression for the sudden pain and debilitating weakness that strike many male runners after about two hours, when most of the glycogen that fuels their muscles is gone. The training necessary to run the marathon conditions the body to call directly on fats after the glycogen is used up. One controversial theory is that women, because of hormonal differences, utilize their fat more efficiently than men. Another is that, since women have more stored fat than men, their staying power is greater.

15

Beyond physical characteristics, past social attitudes have had a substantial influence on the sex factor in athletics. The old attitude was epitomized in the expression "throwing like a girl." At first glance there does appear to be a certain innate awkwardness in the way girls throw a ball. But Prof. Jack Wilmore of the University of Arizona, in researching female and male relative athletic ability, had a number of right-handed men throw lefty: the men proved equally awkward. Wilmore said it seemed apparent from his studies that throwing is an acquired trait. The broader shoulders and bigger muscles of men give them an advantage in speed or distance, but not, innately, in grace.

16

In the final section Wood traces the changes in attitude that have taken place in this century.

The effect of such subtle forces on women's competitive athletics seems clear. A coach at an Ivy League university says, "Women have taken up athletics so recently that they don't understand what it takes to be good. They are greener and they lack competitive experience. Beyond that, and the greater strength and speed of men, there is no fundamental difference. Girls make the same mistakes boys do—and have the same youthful enthusiasm. It will just take time." 17

It already has taken time, but the first step may have been the hardest: shucking the encumbering skirts and petticoats in which Western women had been trapped. Another early milestone was the introduction around 1900 of the "safety bicycle," the basic two-wheeler used today. It is credited with getting women actively out on their own in large numbers for the first time. Then came World War II and the opportunity for Rosie the Riveter and her sisters to prove themselves. 18

Shortly thereafter, the communist world began to score propaganda points in the Olympics with the formidable showing of its female athletes. Eastern-bloc sports factories turned out such superior goods that when at Rome, in 1960, a hitherto unknown American sprinter named Wilma Rudolph ran off with three gold medals, she became an instant national hero. The vehicle that carried Rudolph to her fame was television—and from that year on, the upstart medium, with its voracious appetite for sporting events, would find ample fare in women's sports. 19

In the past decade, more milestones went by. In 1972, Congress passed Title IX of the Education Amendments of 1972, providing that "no person in the United States shall, on the basis of sex, be excluded from participation in any education program or activity receiving federal financial assistance." It took most of the remainder of the '70s for the Department of Health, Education and Welfare to define the law, and for schools across the country to begin to comply. 20

In 1973, New Jersey ruled that qualified girls must be allowed to play Little League baseball. Male coaches across the country screamed that the sky was falling. The following year, Little League changed its bylaws to include girls. 21

Even so, as the '80s begin, Donna Loplano, director of women's athletics at the University of Texas at Austin, assesses women athletes as still ten years from realizing their potential. "The kids we think are super now," she says, "are going to be the rule, not the exception. We are just starting to get kids who are good already, who have received coaching from the age of 15."

Some believe the day is coming when women will compete head to head with men in more and more sports events, particularly in track and swimming events of longer distance. Australian scientist K. F. Dyer sees the difference between some men's and women's track and swimming records closing so fast he expects it to disappear altogether in the not too distant future.

There are predictions, too, that women will eventually surpass men in the super-marathons—those of 50 miles or more. Lyn Lemaire, a 29-year-old Harvard law student, proved that last year when she joined a field of 15 for the Iron Man Triathlon, a 140.6-mile non-stop race around the Hawaiian Island of Oahu, combining swimming, cycling, and a final, conventional 26-mile marathon. Of the 12 finishers, Lyn Lemaire placed fifth. The event may have to be renamed.

22   Wood ends with predictions for the future and an ironic last sentence that punches home the message.

23

24

Meaning and Purpose

1. What do you think Wood's purpose is in this essay, and to whom is he speaking? Where does he state his main point?
2. To what does the essay's subtitle refer? How does it contribute to the author's purpose?
3. What myths about women athletes has Wood dispelled?
4. Where in the essay does Wood begin comparing male and female athletic abilities? Do any of his facts surprise you? Do you doubt any of his assertions?

POSSIBLE ANSWERS

1. Wood seems to want to bring to light recent information about women's physical and athletic ability and dispel some wrong notions. He shows how and why women have advanced as athletes and speculates on how much further they may go. Wood could be addressing more than one audience: men (or women) who believe the myth that women are weak and vulnerable in competitive sports; and women or men who are interested in knowing the facts. Wood's main point is in the questions (5), and also in sentence 1 (8).
2. The essay's subtitle refers to the catchy and familiar advertising slogan used by Virginia Slims cigarettes. The ads themselves juxtapose

contemporary, "liberated" women with their earlier counterparts who were bound by their "encumbering skirts and petticoats" (18).

3. That women are anatomically more vulnerable, or that they are athletically hampered by menstruation, are dubious ideas.

4. Wood introduces his comparison in paragraph 9 (when he says that equal experience does not mean equal performance in athletics), and begins it in paragraph 10. Encourage students to talk about their own opinions about women in athletics and look critically at Wood's.

5. Because men have been taught from infancy that they are bigger, stronger, and more athletic than women, many could easily fear, consciously or unconsciously, being beaten by a woman. But women's strength and size could be a real factor in, say, their playing basketball or soccer against men.

Strategy

1. Students may say they trust him because of the "official-sounding" tone an essay full of facts has. Some students may doubt some of Wood's assertions. Encourage them to be critical. Lead them to see some of his strategies for gaining readers' trust and for putting authority in his voice: he immediately throws statistics at the reader.

2. After clearly demonstrating the "explosion in women's competitive sports" (paragraph 1) in paragraphs 2–4, Wood uses paragraph 5 as a transition from irrefutable statistics to his own assertions. The questions, which Wood answers in the rest of the essay, direct readers to begin thinking about the things he wants them to think about.

3. The main comparison and contrast is in the middle of the essay (paragraphs 10–16), where Wood uses a point-by-point structure. On the first and last pages, Wood does not use comparison and contrast but gives supporting information about the history of women in sports and speculates about their future.

4. In the latter part of the essay (17–21) Wood

5. Consider the prospect of men and women competing against each other in recreational sports, not professionally. Might there be psychological as well as athletic and physical barriers? If so, why?

Strategy

1. Like any other writer, Wood wants you to believe all he is telling you. Do you trust him as a narrator? Why or why not? What strategies does he use to try to gain your trust?

2. What function does paragraph 5 serve in the essay? Why does Wood ask these questions?

3. How does Wood structure his comparison and contrast, and is that structure effective for his purpose? Why or why not?

4. How strong is Wood's final paragraph? How appropriate is the example he gives and how effective is his final sentence?

Style

1. Look at the language of the last sentence in paragraph 9 and the quotation in paragraph 17. Do you think these are telling statements about Wood's attitude toward women in athletics? Explain.

2. Consider the subtitle and the placement in the essay of Wood's information about the brief history of women in athletics (beginning in paragraph 18) and how far women have come. Why do you think Wood puts this information near the end rather than the beginning of the essay?

3. If necessary, check a dictionary for the meaning of these words: *susceptible* (7); *estrogen* (11); *testosterone, plebes* (13); *subcutaneous, buoyant* (14); *glycogen* (15); *epitomized* (16); *shucking, encumbering, milestone* (18); *upstart, voracious* (19).

Writing Tasks

1. Choose something in your first-hand experience to compare and contrast, such as an area you once lived in and the place you live in now, the first day of high school and the first day of college, winning an academic versus a nonacademic award. Will you compare and contrast your points in a subject-by-subject or a point-by-point structure?

2. Write an essay in which you compare and contrast a stereotype to a reality, or an ideal to a reality. Some possibilities are: the stereotype of the female athlete to a real person, the stereotype of the male athlete to a real person, the ideal vacation compared to a real one, or the ideal date compared to a real one (or several real ones). Use the subject-by-subject method and write first about the stereotype, then the reality, or the reverse. Your introduction should set up the subject and include your thesis. In your conclusion you should make some evaluation or judgment. Don't be afraid to use humor if it is appropriate in treating your subject.

cites "milestones" of athletic achievement that women have recently passed and then cites some optimistic predictions (22–23), making it seem entirely appropriate for him to state the prediction he does in the concluding paragraph's first sentence.

Style

1. Some readers might think the statement in paragraph 9 is condescending toward women, suggesting that they must always be compared to men for their strengths and abilities and will always be found only "worthy." Some readers might think these statements not condescending but encouraging.

2. Wood could have begun his essay with the chronology on women in athletics, but his opening is more riveting, with statistics and questions that spur readers to think about their own stand on the subject. The bit of history is stronger, coming as it does toward the end, and nicely fills in with some background that supports and gives all Wood's facts and assertions greater meaning in a larger context.

3. *Susceptible:* liable or subject to some influence; *estrogen:* any of several female sex hormones capable of inducing and maintaining secondary female sex characteristics; *testosterone:* the sex hormone secreted by the testes that stimulates the development of male sex organs, secondary sexual traits, and sperm; *plebes:* members of the freshman class at U.S. Military and Naval academies—short for *plebeians,* belonging or pertaining to the common people; *subcutaneous:* situated or lying under the skin; *buoyant:* having the power to float or rise in a fluid; *glycogen:* the principal carbohydrate storage material in animals, occurring chiefly in the liver and muscles; *epitomized:* served as a typical example of; *shucking:* removing or discarding; *encumbering:* impeding or hindering; *milestone:* a significant event; *upstart:* having suddenly risen from a humble position to a position of consequence; *voracious:* craving or consuming large quantities of food.

TEACHING SUGGESTIONS

This essay extends an analogy, like tentacles, into several allied topics, but the body of the analogy remains clear. Our modern battles are usually no more important, though just as exciting to an objective observer, as the battle of the ants. Students occasionally need reminding that each recent generation has had a war: World War II in the '40s, the Korean War in the '50s, the Vietnam War in the late '60s and early '70s. What about the '80s and the new '90s? For openers, we have the war on drugs and the war on illiteracy, internal wars.

Thoreau's ants mirror the actions of two peoples at war. Thoreau's ants are fighting for a principle, the author remarks sarcastically. No war, at least according to propaganda, was ever fought except for a principle. But some of the principles are as trivial as that which caused the Trojan War, the kidnaping of one person.

Students like to brainstorm principles. List several words on the chalk board and then discuss whether those words in fact name principles. Truth? Honesty? Art? Ethics? The discussion invariably leads to analogies, for students will use analogies to explain their thinking about each "principle."

MARGINAL NOTES

Thoreau, a legendary master of diction, using words precisely, did not "see" the ants; he "observed" them. The analogy between ants and soldiers becomes obvious in description in sentence 1: the ants are not "fighting"; they are "fiercely contending." This strategy of *personification*, writing about something as if it were human, permeates the essay.

The chips are left over from Thoreau's chopping wood. A *duellum* is a duel; a *bellum* is a

When he was twenty-eight years old, Henry David Thoreau built a cabin in the woods by Walden Pond, Massachusetts, and lived there alone for two years. His best-known book, Walden *(1854), is about that experience. Born in nearby Concord, Massachusetts, in 1817, Thoreau was educated at Harvard University and was influenced by the American essayist, poet, and philosopher Ralph Waldo Emerson, who was also a close friend. Thoreau believed in the citizens' duty to act on their conscience and once spent a night in jail for refusing to pay a poll tax on the grounds that he objected to United States involvement in war with Mexico. In his famed essay, "Civil Disobedience" (1849), he outlines his philosophy of passive resistance and has often been cited in support of the American civil-rights movement.*

The Battle of the Ants

In this extended analogy from Walden, *Thoreau compares a battle between red ants and black ants that he witnessed on his woodpile, to the wars men have waged all through history. While elevating the ants by comparing them to men, Thoreau diminishes the glory of human wars by comparing them to battles among insects.*

One day when I went out to my wood-pile, or rather my pile of stumps, I observed two large ants, the one red, the other much larger, nearly half an inch long, and black, fiercely contending with one another. Having once got hold they never let go, but struggled and wrestled and rolled on the chips incessantly. Looking farther, I was surprised to find that the chips were covered with such combatants, that it was not a *duellum*, but a *bellum*, a war between two races of ants, the red always pitted against the black, and frequently two red ants to one black. The legions of these Myrmidons covered all the hills and vales in my wood-yard, 1

262

and the ground was already strewn with the dead and dying, both red and black. It was the only battle which I have ever witnessed, the only battle-field I ever trod while the battle was raging; internecine war; the red republicans on the one hand, and the black imperialists on the other. On every side they were engaged in deadly combat, yet without any noise that I could hear, and human soldiers never fought so resolutely. I watched a couple that were fast locked in each other's embraces, in a little sunny valley amid the chips, now at noonday prepared to fight till the sun went down, or life went out. The smaller red champion had fastened himself like a vise to his adversary's front, and through all the tumblings on that field never for an instant ceased to gnaw at one of his feelers near the root, having already caused the other to go by the board; while the stronger black one dashed him from side to side, and, as I saw on looking nearer, had already divested him of several of his members. They fought with more pertinacity than bulldogs. Neither manifested the least disposition to retreat. It was evident that their battle-cry was "Conquer or die." In the meanwhile there came along a single red ant on the hillside of this valley, evidently full of excitement, who either had dispatched his foe, or had not yet taken part in the battle; probably the latter, for he had lost none of his limbs; whose mother had charged him to return with his shield or upon it. Or perchance he was some Achilles, who had nourished his wrath apart, and had now come to avenge or rescue his Patroclus. He saw this unequal combat from afar—for the blacks were nearly twice the size of the red—he drew near with rapid pace till he stood on his guard within half an inch of the combatants; then, watching his opportunity, he sprang upon the black warrior, and commenced his operations near the root of his right foreleg, leaving the foe to select among his own members; and so there were three united for life, as if a new kind of attraction had been invented which put all other locks and cements to shame. I should not have wondered by this time to find that they had their respective musical bands stationed on some eminent chip, and playing their national airs the while, to excite the slow and cheer the dying combatants. I was myself excited somewhat even as if they had been men. The more you

war. The "races" of ants remind us that Thoreau's America was militantly divided over slavery, and Thoreau was strongly against it.

The Myrmidons were ants, changed into warriors by Zeus, supreme deity of the ancient Greeks. They accompanied Achilles to the Trojan War.

The soldier ants "fast locked in each other's embraces" remind students that lovers, not warriors, are usually so described. The next sentence heightens that ironic comparison by moving us from lovers' to warriors' language.

The writer's almost microscopic view of ants in battle alludes to the notion that all wars are petty and that nature itself carries on benignly.

Notice Thoreau's euphemism here, substituting inoffensive words for some that could be distasteful. Contrasts with the brutal reality of "tore off his legs."

A Roman motto, *aut vincere aut mori,* literally "either to conquer or to die," intended to inspire soldiers going into battle.

Notice the personification, the human qualities of the red ant.

The mothers of Sparta, an ancient Greek city-state, told their sons, "Return with your shield or [carried] upon it," literally, "Win or die trying."

Achilles was a Greek hero in the Trojan Wars; Patroclus was his friend slain in those wars. From Homer's *Iliad.*

The writer's internal transition, moving the reader from ant wars to human wars, reinforcing the analogy.

Two bloody battles won in the early 1800s by Napoleon's armies.

The Battle of Concord Bridge, 1775, involved few soldiers (including "Davis and Hosmer") but became famous in American history.

A reference to the Boston Tea Party, December 16, 1773, when the colonists defied the English crown. The British won the battle of Bunker Hill, fought in June 1775, but suffered enormous casualties. Notice how this battle compares with those won with great loss of men by Napoleon's armies.

Notice the calm, objective curiosity here, contrasted with the furious life-and-death battle being studied. The description that follows depicts graphically and minutely the thirty-minute struggle.

A home for old soldiers, in Paris, and the actual tomb of Napoleon I, as well.

think of it, the less the difference. And certainly there is not the fight recorded in Concord history, at least, if in the history of America, that will bear a moment's comparison with this, whether for the numbers engaged in it, or for the patriotism and heroism displayed. For numbers and for carnage it was an Austerlitz or Dresden. Concord Fight! Two killed on the patriots' side, and Luther Blanchard wounded! Why here every ant was a Buttrick—"Fire! for God's sake fire!"—and thousands shared the fate of Davis and Hosmer. There was not one hireling there. I have no doubt that it was a principle they fought for, as much as our ancestors, and not to avoid a three-penny tax on their tea; and the results of this battle will be as important and memorable to those whom it concerns as those of the battle of Bunker Hill, at least.

I took up the chip on which the three I have particularly described were struggling, carried it into my house, and placed it under a tumbler on my window-sill, in order to see the issue. Holding a microscope to the first-mentioned red ant, I saw that, though he was assiduously gnawing at the near foreleg of his enemy, having severed his remaining feeler, his own breast was all torn away, exposing what vitals he had there to the jaws of the black warrior, whose breastplate was apparently too thick for him to pierce; and the dark carbuncles of the sufferer's eyes shone with ferocity such as war only could excite. They struggled half an hour longer under the tumbler, and when I looked again the black soldier had severed the heads of his foes from their bodies, and the still living heads were hanging on either side of him like ghastly trophies at his saddle-bow, still apparently as firmly fastened as ever, and he was endeavoring with feeble struggles, being without feelers, and with only the remnant of a leg, and I know not how many other wounds, to divest himself of them, which at length, after half an hour more, he accomplished. I raised the glass, and he went off over the window-sill in that crippled state. Whether he finally survived that combat, and spent the remainder of his days in some Hôtel des Invalides, I do not know; but I thought that his industry would not be worth much thereafter. I never learned which party was victorious, nor the cause of the war, but I felt for the rest of that day as if I had my feelings excited and harrowed by witnessing the struggle, the ferocity and carnage, of a human battle before my door.

Kirby and Spence tell us that the battles of ants have long been celebrated and the date of them recorded, though they say that Huber is the only modern author who appears to have witnessed them. "Aeneas Sylvius," say they, "after giving a very circumstantial account of one contested with great obstinacy by a great and small species on the trunk of a pear tree," adds that " 'this action was fought in the pontificate of Eugenius the Fourth, in the presence of Nicholas Pistoriensis, an eminent lawyer, who related the whole history of the battle with the greatest fidelity.' A similar engagement between great and small ants is recorded by Olaus Magnus, in which the small ones, being victorious, are said to have buried the bodies of their own soldiers, but left those of their giant enemies a prey to the birds. This event happened previous to the expulsion of the tyrant Christian the Second from Sweden." The battle which I witnessed took place in the Presidency of Polk, five years before the passage of Webster's Fugitive-Slave Bill.

3 Kirby, Spence, and Huber were three leading specialists in the study of insects.

(1383–1447) Pope from 1431 to 1447.

(1490–1558) Swedish Roman Catholic ecclesiastic and historian who wrote a Swedish history that was long accepted in Europe as authoritative.

(1481–1559) called "The Cruel." King of Denmark and Norway, 1513–1523. Showed extreme cruelty against the Swedes, massacring their nobility (1520). Imprisoned for life in 1532.

James Knox Polk (1795–1849) was eleventh president of the United States (1845–1849). Thoreau published his first book, *A Week on the Concord and Merrimac Rivers,* in 1849.

The Fugitive-Slave Bill required that slaves who escaped to the North be captured and returned to their owners in the South.

Meaning and Purpose

1. Have you ever stopped to observe and perhaps become fascinated by small things in nature? Explain. What in Thoreau's essay reminds you of your own experience?
2. What was Thoreau's opinion of war? Use evidence from the essay for your answer.
3. Can you find a statement or statements of Thoreau's main point, or thesis?
4. Thoreau mentions Greek heroes, great historical battles, a pope, and a president of the United States. What is his purpose in these widely different references?

Meaning and Purpose

1. Encourage students to explore first their personal responses to Thoreau's essay. Ask them to be specific in connecting their responses to statements or ideas in the essay.

2. Thoreau considered war a far from noble pursuit, beneath human dignity, to be fought by ants if fought at all. This extended analogy between ants and soldiers is evidence of this opinion, as are his numerous and satiric examples of wars fought throughout history.

3. Thoreau buries his thesis statements well into the first paragraph: "I was myself excited somewhat even as if they had been men. The more you think of it, the less the difference." The next sentence might also be considered part of his main point.

4. Thoreau's commentary is timeless. With mockery, he raises the battle of the ants to such "heights" as comparing it to an ancient Greek war and a patriotic American war. Of course, he is mocking our seeing wars as glorious, serving his purpose (satire), and extending his analogy.

5. Thoreau wrote mostly for an educated male readership. Most who could then read were well-educated men, many holding authority in government or church. Thoreau used this essay to mock the very thing most learned men admired, and to point out to them the folly in their thinking.

6. Thoreau extends the analogy through history by showing that such battles have been noteworthy for centuries. With great mocking, Thoreau raises the battle of the ants to the level of recorded human history and compares it to other ant battles celebrated in writing. He ends the extended analogy by poking fun at academic historians, whose style he mocks here.

Strategy

1. Ants and men in this essay share cruelty, tenacity, courage, bravery, and other qualities associated with combat.

5. Think of the time in which Thoreau lived. What audience do you think he is addressing?
6. Although the last paragraph in the essay seems to drift into other topics, in fact, it serves an important purpose. What is that purpose?

Strategy

1. The body of this essay is an extended analogy that parallels some activities of ants and men. What are two qualities that ants and men share in this essay? Give examples from specific sentences.
2. Midway through the first paragraph, Thoreau says, "The more you think of it, the less the difference." What is he comparing? What "difference" is he talking about?
3. Toward the end of paragraph 2, Thoreau wonders whether a crippled ant survived to spend the rest of his days "in some Hôtel des Invalides." What is the analogy here?
4. Thoreau makes generous use of satire as a strategy in his analogy. What is satire and how is it effective here?
5. Overall, how effective do you judge Thoreau's extended analogy is in comparing human battles with those of ants? Without this analogy, how might Thoreau have talked about the folly of war, and do you think his message would have been as forceful?

Style

1. Early in the essay, Thoreau says that he witnessed an "internecine war." Define that kind of war.
2. The first paragraph in the essay includes "Concord Fight!" and "Two killed on the patriots' side, and Luther Blanchard wounded!" Where do these kinds of exclamations often appear? Who might Luther Blanchard be?
3. The second paragraph in the essay includes this description: "the dark carbuncles of the sufferer's eyes shone with ferocity such as

war only could excite." Is this description realistic, or is it factual? Support your answer with your own opinions.

4. Thoreau says that the soldier-ants "fought with more pertinacity than bulldogs." Look up *pertinacity*. The word has at least two meanings. Which meaning compares ants with men? Which meaning compares ants with bulldogs?

Writing Tasks

1. In the essay, Thoreau says, "I have no doubt that it was a principle they fought for, as much as our ancestors. . . ." Can you think of a principle many people believe in that you feel is not worth fighting or working for? Write an essay in which you use an analogy and compare that principle to something familiar to readers in order to show why it is not worth the struggle.
2. There are other analogies for war besides the battle of the ants. Finish the statement "War is like . . . ," listing three things to compare war to. Write a few paragraphs of analogy for each comparison you choose.

2. The comparison is between soldiers and ants. He has been personifying ants and talking about them as if they were men. He realizes that he is as excited as if they were human and that the ant–human differences are less than he thought. Of course Thoreau is making fun here.

3. The analogy is between a wounded ant and a wounded soldier who spends his days in a home for old soldiers, trying to keep the glory of the war alive. Of course, the analogy is factually weak, but it is ironic.

4. Satire is a literary technique or style that combines humor and wit with a critical attitude for the purpose of improving human institutions or actions. The satirist pokes fun not so much to tear down as to inspire remodeling of the subject being satirized. Jonathan Swift's famous "A Modest Proposal" is a good example of satire to place alongside Thoreau's essay.

5. Students should evaluate Thoreau's use of satire on his subject. Without the analogy's mockery, Thoreau might have written a more formal, pedantic, or sermonlike treatise on war and principles and how thinly they disguise petty human squabbles. Such a hypothetical essay probably would have been boring by comparison, not as attention-getting, amusing, or successful in making his points.

Style

1. An internecine war is mutually destructive, full of slaughter, with enormous casualties on both sides. It is a "no-win" war.

2. These kinds of exclamations appear in newspaper headlines. Luther Blanchard, in the headline's context, is an American who fought at Concord.

3. This could have been a factual description of a man-soldier, but not an ant-soldier. Ants do not have the eyes described here, or the kind of body that permits a carbuncle. By analogy, however, it is a realistic description imaginatively comparing ant with man.

4. *Pertinacity* means "the quality of holding firmly to a belief or purpose," and "the quality of being hard to get rid of, physically." The first meaning compares ants with men, the second with bulldogs.

A graduate of Williams College and the Wharton School of Economics, University of Pennsylvania, Robert W. Keidel is a senior fellow at the Wharton Applied Research Center. As director of a management consulting firm, he advises several large companies and corporations. His writings and essays, geared to both a professional and a popular audience, are published widely in magazines, newspapers, and journals. He has also published two books: Game Plans: Sports Strategies for Business *(1985), and* Corporate Players: Designs for Working and Winning Together *(1988).*

A New Game for Managers to Play

This essay first appeared in The New York Times, *December 5, 1985. Here Keidel compares and contrasts the games of football and basketball, using them as metaphors for different approaches to business management. In Keidel's view, football and basketball might also be seen as metaphors for different approaches to life.*

TEACHING SUGGESTIONS

This brief, timely comparison-and-contrast essay illustrates extended analogies. A discussion might begin by considering the differences between basketball games and football games. Who is in charge on the field? On the court? How many times is the ball passed in basketball compared to football? How does the quarterback on a football team compare to the center on a basketball team? Then move to a discussion of a specialist versus a generalist. Is a basketball player more of a generalist than a football player? In what ways? Then you might want to move the discussion into the workplace. Some students have jobs in which they are generalists; others are specialists. A person working in a small yogurt shop serves customers, makes change, cleans the mirrors, sweeps the shop, makes the yogurt, cleans the storeroom, and so forth. A person working as a librarian's assistant might have only one responsibility—shelving books. The first person determines how and when to do each duty; the second person does one job. Which one is more like a basketball player? Which is more like a football player? Then move into a discussion of the analogies in Keidel's essay.

MARGINAL NOTES

The writer sets up his comparison and contrast and also introduces an essay that will become an extended analogy, comparing business management to athletic coaching.

Paragraphs 3–8 develop the football portion of the analogy and its implications.

1   As the football season gradually gives way to basketball, corporate managers would do well to consider the differences between these games. For just as football mirrors industrial structures of the past, basketball points the way to the corporate structure of the future.

2   It's the difference between the former chief executive officer of I.T.T., Harold Geneen, the master football coach who dictates his players' roles and actions, and Donald Burr, the People Express Airlines chief executive officer, who puts his players on the floor and lets them manage themselves.

3   Football is, metaphorically, a way of life in work today—the corporate sport. This is reflected in the language many managers use:

"It's taken my staff and me a sizable chunk of time, but we now have a solid game plan for the XYZ job. Jack, I want you to quarterback this thing all the way into the end zone. Of course, a lot of it will be making the proper assignments—getting the right people to run interference and the right ones to run with the ball. But my main concern is that we avoid mistakes. No fumbles, no interceptions, no sacks, no penalties. I don't want us to have to play catch-up; no two-minute drills at the end. I want the game plan executed exactly the way it's drawn. When we're done we want to look back with pride at a win—and not have to Monday-morning-quarterback a loss." 4

Does this football language represent more than just a convenient shorthand? Almost certainly it does, because the metaphors we use routinely are the means by which we structure experience. Thus, football metaphors may well reflect—and reinforce—underlying organizational dynamics. But football, despite its pervasiveness, is the wrong model for most corporations. 5

Consider the scenario above. Planning has been neatly separated from implementation; those expected to carry out the game plan had no part in creating it. Also, the communication flow is one-way: from the head coach (speaker) to the quarterback (Jack)—and, presumably, from the quarterback to the other players. And the thrust of the message is risk-averse; the real name of the game is control—minimizing mistakes. But perhaps most significant is the assumption of stability—that nothing will change to invalidate the corporate game plan. "No surprises!" as Mr. Geneen likes to say. 6

Stability is a realistic assumption in football, even given the sport's enormous complexity, because of the time available to coaches—between games and between plays. A pro football game can very nearly be programmed. Carl Peterson, formerly with the Philadelphia Eagles and now president of the United States Football League's champions, the Baltimore Stars, has estimated that managing a game is 75 percent preparation and only 25 percent adjustment. 7

Thus, football truly is the realm of the coach—the head coach, he who calls the shots. (Most pro quarterbacks do not call 8 their own plays.) As Bum Phillips has said in tribute to the head coach of the Miami Dolphins, Don Shula, "He can take his'n and beat your'n, or he can take your'n and beat his'n."

But football is not an appropriate model for most businesses 9
precisely because instability is an overwhelming fact of life. Market competition grows ever more spastic, product life-cycles shrink unimaginably and technology courses on paths of its own.

In this milieu, corporate "players" simply cannot perform 10
effectively if they must wait for each play to be called for them, and remain in fixed positions—or in narrowly defined roles—like football players; increasingly, they need to deploy themselves flexibly, in novel combinations.

Thirty years ago it may have been possible to regard core 11
business functions—R&D, manufacturing and marketing—as separate worlds, with little need for interaction. R&D would design the product and then lob it over the wall to manufacturing; manufacturing would make the product and lob it over another wall to the customer.

No need to worry about problems that do not fit neatly into 12
the standard departments; these are inconsequential and infrequent. And when they do arise, they are simply bumped up the hierarchy to senior management—the head coach and his staff.

In effect, performance is roughly the sum of the functions— 13
just as a football team's performance is the sum of the performances of its platoons—offense, defense and special teams. Clearly, this view of the corporation is anachronistic. Yet it remains all too common.

Business's "season" is changing, and a new metaphor is 14
needed. While football will continue to be a useful model for pursuing machinelike efficiency and consistency—that is, for minimizing redundancies, bottlenecks and errors—this design favors stability at the expense of change. Since now more than ever businesses must continuously innovate and adapt, a more promising model is basketball.

To begin with, basketball is too dynamic a sport to permit the 15
rigid separation of planning and execution that characterizes football. Unlike football teams, basketball teams do not pause and

---

In paragraphs 9–13 he argues that football is no longer an appropriate model for business.

This paragraph serves as a transition to the basketball portion of the analogy.

The remaining paragraphs develop the basketball portion of the analogy and argue for its adoption as the new metaphor for successful companies.

regroup after each play. As the former star player and coach Bill Russell has noted, "Your game plan may be wiped out by what happens in the first minute of play." Success in basketball depends on the ability of the coach and players to plan and adjust while in motion. Such behavior requires all-around communication—just as basketball demands all-around passing, as opposed to football's linear sequence of "forward," one-way passing.

Basketball also puts a premium on generalist skills. Although different players will assume somewhat different roles on the court, all must be able to dribble, pass, shoot, rebound and play defense. Everyone handles the ball—a far cry from what happens on the gridiron. Indeed, basketball is much more player-oriented than football—a sport in which players tend to be viewed as interchangeable parts. 16

If football is a risk-averse game, basketball is risk-accepting. In basketball, change is seen as normal, not exceptional; hence, change is regarded more as the source of opportunities than of threats. Mr. Geneen has claimed that "Ninety-nine percent of all surprises in business are negative." 17

Mr. Geneen's perspective is classic football and is tenable in stable, "controllable" environments. But such environments are becoming rare. The future increasingly belongs to managers like Mr. Burr or James Treybig, the founder of Tandem Computers, who thrive on change rather than flee from it. 18

We need fewer head coaches and more player-coaches, less scripted teamwork and more spontaneous teamwork. We need to integrate planning and doing—managing and working—far more than we have to date. Are you playing yesterday's game—or tomorrow's? 19

19   In the conclusion he pleads for a change of direction and asks businessmen to question their own styles of management.

POSSIBLE ANSWERS

Meaning and Purpose

1. The new game is basketball, the old game is football. Keidel's view of football is described in paragraphs 6–8, of basketball in 15–17.
2. Keidel states his purpose at the beginning: "Corporate managers would do well to consider the differences between these games."
3. "Solid game plan"; "Quarterback . . . into the end zone"; "getting the right people to run interference and the right ones to run with the ball"; "No fumbles, no interceptions, no sacks, no penalties"; "to play catch-up"; "no two-minute drills at the end"; "the game plan executed"; "Monday-morning-quarterback."
4. Keidel states, "Business's 'season' is changing, and a new metaphor is needed. . . . Since now more than ever businesses must continuously innovate and adapt, a more promising model is basketball" (14). He says "basketball is risk-accepting. In basketball, change is seen as normal, not exceptional. . ." (17).
5. Keidel cites a former football coach's statement that "managing a game is 75 percent preparation and only 25 percent adjustment" (7). He says that basketball is "too dynamic a sport to permit the rigid separation of planning and execution that characterizes football. . . . Success in basketball depends on the ability of the coach and players to plan and adjust while in motion" (15).

Strategy

1. Keidel's primary audience is corporate managers. In sentence 1, he asks that they "consider the differences between these games" and goes on throughout to draw comparisons between coaches and corporate managers. In the last sentence, he uses second person to address these managers directly: "Are *you* playing yesterday's game—or tomorrow's?"
2. Information is most easily digested when broken into short units. Busy corporate man-

Meaning and Purpose

1. What is the "new game" for managers to play? What is the "old game"? How do the games differ?
2. Where in the essay does Keidel establish his purpose?
3. In paragraph 5, Keidel says, "the metaphors we use routinely are the means by which we structure experience." What are the metaphors in paragraph 4 that "structure experience" in the language of a manager?
4. Explain why Keidel argues that basketball is a more appropriate metaphor for businesses today.
5. How does Keidel differentiate the coach's role in the two sports?

Strategy

1. Who is the primary audience in this essay? Offer support for your answer.
2. Most paragraphs in this essay are unusually short. How does this strategy help Keidel's readers?
3. Where in the essay does Keidel make the transition between his football and basketball analogies?
4. At what time of year was this essay written? Why do you think Keidel chooses that time of year?
5. Is Keidel's conclusion effective? Explain.

Style

1. Paragraph 12 can be described as sarcastic in tone. Why?
2. How does Keidel's diction in talking about basketball make that game more attractive to his audience?
3. Keidel uses the word "anachronistic" to describe one view of corporate management. Why does he use this word rather than "dated" or "old-fashioned"?

Writing Tasks

1. Draw a comparison between a career you might pursue and the rules of a game. Consider whether this profession will have set rules, like those in chess or mathematics, or negotiable rules, like those in sandlot baseball or art.

2. Keidel states that modern business managers need to be generalists. In an essay, explain why you agree or disagree with this statement. Contrast the advantages and disadvantages of such a generalist background.

agers, Keidel's audience, are used to receiving new ideas in bite-sized chunks. His essay can be likened to a newspaper format. His short paragraphs are succinct and helpful for a busy reader.

3. The transition is "a new metaphor is needed" (14).

4. The first words of the essay indicate that it is the beginning of winter. At this time in the seasonal cycle, corporate managers are looking toward the new calendar year, a natural time for businesses to reassess their policies.

5. Keidel sums up his comparisons of the two games in one concise sentence here. His next sentence makes clear that he has been comparing the two sports so that business managers will consider the comparison as it reflects their own policies. In the last sentence he directly addresses managers.

Style

1. In this paragraph he says that if a problem doesn't "fit neatly," then by definition it must be "inconsequential and infrequent." Of course, their very being keeps problems from fitting neatly into a corporate hierarchy—that's why they are problems. Keidel uses irony here to emphasize that the "football" approach to management is less than ideal.

2. The words he uses to describe basketball are more appropriate to today's business climate. Phrases such as, "too dynamic"; "plan and adjust while in motion"; "all-around communication"; "generalist skills"; "more player-oriented"; and "interchangeable parts" all appeal to more progressive managers (15, 16).

3. "Anachronistic" is more appropriate because it describes something that occurs at a time other than its proper one. The management style that Keidel implicitly criticizes is still widely used today, but because it is not suitable to the current business climate, Keidel's word choice indicates that it should have been abandoned. "Dated" and "old-fashioned" refer to past practices.

❦ *Additional Writing Tasks* ❦

Comparison and Contrast

1. Using comparison and contrast as the dominant pattern, write an essay on one of these tasks or one you compose for yourself. Keep in mind that you may modify any of the tasks to fit your interests.

    a. At the library find two advertisements for the same product, one published in the 1950s and one published within the last year. Write an essay presenting the similarities and differences in these advertisements.

    b. Select two fairy tales that have similar patterns and characters, such as children journeying into a forest, an encounter with death, the appearance of a mysterious creature, a magical transformation. Identify at least three significant elements the tales have in common and three significant elements that are different. Write an essay comparing and contrasting the similarities and differences in these two tales.

    c. Collect several advertisements for two brands of the same product type that direct their advertising campaigns toward men and women, such as Marlboro cigarettes (men) and Virginia Slims (women). After examining the advertisements, write an essay comparing and contrasting how these advertisements appeal to male consumers and how they appeal to female consumers.

    d. Accurately and fairly, compare and contrast the arguments on both sides of a controversial issue, such as abortion, capital punishment, pornography, or gun control.

    e. Most people hold important social or political beliefs that are opposed by people close to them. Select a belief you hold and in an essay contrast your attitude to the opposing attitude of one of your parents, a brother, a sister, or a close friend.

    f. Select two classes you have attended, two jobs you have held, or two vacations you have taken. Write a comparison-and-contrast essay discussing the similarities and differences of your subjects.

g. Compare and contrast a past experience with a current experience. You might compare how you once viewed a holiday, such as Thanksgiving, Christmas, or Chanukah, with your view of it today. Or you might compare how you once viewed a special place, such as a vacation site, a fun zone, or even your bedroom, with your current view.

h. Compare and contrast how two people from different cultures, economic situations, or age groups might perceive the same experience.

i. Select two public figures with opposing views on one controversial issue. After familiarizing yourself with their positions, write an essay contrasting their attitudes.

j. Select two campus groups that hold opposing social values. In an essay, compare and contrast their views and behavior.

2. Write an essay with comparison and contrast as the dominant pattern on one of these general subjects or on a subject of your own choice. By the end of your essay, the reader should know why you prefer one thing to the other.

a. two people who embrace different life-styles
b. a national news program and a local news program
c. two methods for losing weight
d. female and male consumers
e. children's games yesterday and today
f. two characters from film or fiction
g. a film created from a novel
h. watching a movie on television and watching it in the cinema
i. coverage of a news event by television and by a newspaper
j. two classic films: horror, western, mystery, or romance

3. Read this quotation from social critic Morton Hunt:

> The record of man's inhumanity to man is horrifying, when one compiles it—enslavement, castration, torture, rape, mass slaughter in war after war. But who has compiled the record of man's kindness to man—the

trillions of acts of gentleness and goodness, the helping hands, smiles, shared meals, kisses, gifts, healings, rescues? If we were no more than murderous predators, with a freakish lack of inhibition against slaughtering our own species, we would have been at a terrible competitive disadvantage compared with other animals; if this were the central truth of our nature, we would scarcely have survived, multiplied and become the dominant species on earth. Man does have an aggressive instinct, but it is not naturally or inevitably directed to killing his own kind. He is a beast and perhaps at times the cruelest beast of all—but sometimes he is also the kindest beast of all. He is not all good and not perfectible, but he is not all bad and not wholly unchangeable or unimprovable. That is the only basis on which one can hope for him; but it is enough.

Hunt stresses humanity's dual nature. Write an essay with comparison and contrast as the dominant pattern that makes Hunt's general observation specific.

5

Cause and Effect

Identifying Reasons and Results

The Method

When you explain why something happened or the consequences of that happening, you are engaged in an intellectual activity that seems to be at the core of human curiosity—that is, the search for **causes and effects**.

In their simplest form cause-and-effect relationships appear as a series of escalating events, one triggering another like a chain reaction. Consider the children's song in which a woman swallows a fly. The lively fly causes her to swallow a spider to catch the fly. She then swallows a bird to catch the spider;

then a cat to catch the bird; then a dog to catch the cat; then a goat; then a cow; and finally, a horse. The effect? She dies, of course.

In a more complex form, cause and effect is often at work in thrillers and mysteries. A wealthy politician falls dead during a banquet. He had been in excellent health. There seems to be no clear cause of death. Could he have been murdered in some mysterious way? The question triggers the appearance of a supersleuth who begins the investigation. The detective discovers clues, each of which reveals a new suspect. After an exhaustive exploration of the many reasons suspects had for wanting the victim dead, the murderer is unmasked, the mysterious murder method explained, and the dark reasons for the murder revealed.

Of course, mystery fans aren't consciously seeking cause or effect patterns. They're probably trying to beat the writer at his or her own game by figuring out "Whodunit?" before the final scene. But that question is not much different from, What caused it?

If you think of causes as **reasons** and effects as **results,** you might better understand cause-and-effect patterns. Like a detective you can begin with questions: Why did something happen? What are the consequences of something's happening? When you answer the Why, you are giving reasons; that is, causes. When you answer the What, you are giving results; that is, effects. Professional writers observe this distinction when exploring the causes or effects behind any event. Generally, the distinction keeps them on the track.

Consider this question: "Why did the women's liberation movement bloom in the 1960s?" The question would lead a writer to seek reasons—that is, causes.

But the question, "What were the consequences of the women's liberation movement on college campuses during the 1970s?" would lead a writer to seek results—that is, effects.

And the compound question, "Why did the women's liberation movement falter in the 1980s, and what will be the consequences in the 1990s?" would lead a writer to explain the reasons and the results—that is, both causes and effects.

Strategies

When you begin analyzing the cause or effect relationships in a complex subject, you may feel somewhat like a detective unraveling a mystery. You must be prepared for the false starts and deceptive clues that will send you down the wrong path, but don't lose heart: you can learn by studying professional writers, who often approach cause-and-effect analysis from several angles, depending on the characteristics of their subjects. First, they may narrow their effort by concentrating only on the causes. Second, they may concentrate only on the effects. And third, they may choose to concentrate on both causes and effects. If you understand cause-and-effect development patterns and apply your knowledge critically as you read, you'll soon master the technique of analyzing cause-and-effect relationships in your own writing.

Identifying Causes

When effects are clear, writers will concentrate on causes. In 1948, Harry Truman upset Thomas Dewey, Governor of New York, for the presidency. Dewey was predicted to win by a landslide. In fact, one newspaper prematurely printed headlines announcing Dewey's victory. The political pundits were wrong: Truman won. A writer who asked, "Why did Truman win?" would not have to establish the result (Truman's victory), but he or she would concentrate on the reasons—that is, the causes—behind Truman's victory. Did his "underdog" image generate sympathy among voters? Did a last-minute whistlestop campaign through America's heartland swing the election his way? Was it a well-oiled Democratic machine that kept the party faithful in line? These and other causes would have to be explored in any analysis of the election.

In *Redoing America,* Robert Faltermayer discusses the interwoven character of American cities. In the following paragraph, Faltermayer concentrates on causes. He opens with the common assumption that the automobile has had a destructive effect on the "close-knit fabric" of cities. He then presents the reasons for this phenomenon:

> The close knit fabric was blown apart by the automobile, and by the postwar middle-class exodus to suburbia which the mass-ownership of automobiles made possible. The automobile itself was not to blame for this development, nor was the desire for suburban living, which is obviously a genuine aspiration of many Americans. The fault lay in our failure, right up to the present time, to fashion new policies to minimize the disruptive effects of the automobile revolution. We have failed not only to tame the automobile itself, but to overhaul a property-tax system that tends to foster automotive-age sprawl and to institute coordinated planning in the politically fragmented suburbs that have caught the brunt of the postwar building boom.

In the opening sentence Faltermayer establishes a relationship between automobiles and the changing character of cities and sprawling suburbs. In the next sentence he refines his focus by dismissing two possible causes, the automobile itself and the desire for suburban living. In the remainder of the paragraph he explains what he believes to be the true cause, the failure to fashion public policies that would have controlled the automobile and the building boom.

Identifying Effects

When writers select subjects with very clear causes, they will then concentrate on effects. For instance, drug merchants are expanding their operations into rural communities. Crack houses are springing up in small towns where drugs had previously been scarce. This fact has been substantiated by law-enforcement agencies across the nation. A writer who asked, "What are the consequences of increased drug use in rural communities?" would spend very little time establishing the existence of increased drug activity in small-town America because it is widely known. He or she would, however, concentrate on the effects this trend might have on rural communities. What, for instance, are the consequences for families? What will be the effects on undertrained and underbudgeted law-enforcement agencies, on social services, and on schools?

In this paragraph from *Anatomy of an Illness,* Norman Cousins uses this pattern. He quickly establishes the cause, a hypothetical injury, and then concentrates on exploring effects of pain suppressants on injured professional athletes.

> Professional athletes are sometimes severely disadvantaged by trainers whose job it is to keep them in action. The more famous the athlete, the greater the risk that he or she may be subjected to extreme medical measures when injury strikes. The star baseball pitcher whose arm is sore because of a torn muscle or tissue damage may need sustained rest more than anything else. But this team is battling for a place in the World Series; so the trainer or team doctor, called upon to work his magic, reaches for a strong dose of butazolidine or other powerful pain suppressants. Presto, the pain disappears! The pitcher takes his place on the mound and does superbly. That could be the last game, however, in which he is able to throw the ball with full strength. The drugs didn't repair the torn muscle or cause the damaged tissue to heal. What they did was to mask the pain, enabling the pitcher to throw hard, further damaging the torn muscle. Little wonder that so many star athletes are cut down in their prime, more the victims of overzealous treatment of their injuries than of the injuries themselves.

Cousins opens by establishing the direction the paragraph will take. He then states the cause of the effects that will follow—a hypothetical injury to a star baseball pitcher's throwing arm. Next, he develops the effects of the injury—under pressure to win, a trainer or team doctor prescribes a pain killer; the pitcher plays as if he had no injury; and the ultimate effect, a career cut short, not by injury but by the mistreatment of injury.

Identifying Causes and Effects

Writers are always cautious about assuming that readers know the causes or effects of an event, especially when exploring a complex subject that is not part of common knowledge. When such a subject is discussed, they usually explain both causes and effects. Often they will alternate causes and effects in one paragraph.

Victor C. Cline uses this pattern in a paragraph from "How TV Violence Damages Your Children."

> Much of the research that has led to the conclusion that TV and movie violence could cause aggressive behavior in some children has stemmed from the work in the area of imitative learning or modeling which, reduced to its simplest expression, might be termed "monkey see, monkey do." Research by Stanford psychologist Albert Bandura has shown that even brief exposure to novel aggressive behavior on a *one-time basis* can be repeated in free play by as high as 88 percent of the young chidren seeing it on TV. Dr. Bandura also demonstrated that even a single viewing of a novel aggressive act could be recalled and produced by children six months later, without any intervening exposure. Earlier studies have estimated that the average child between the ages of 5 and 15 will witness, during this 10-year period, the violent destruction of more than 13,400 fellow humans. This means that through several hours of TV-watching, a child may see more violence than the average adult experiences in a lifetime. Killing is as common as taking a walk, a gun more natural than an umbrella. Children are thus taught to take pride in force and violence and to feel ashamed of ordinary sympathy.

Cline's first sentence establishes that children learn aggressive behavior from television through modeling, or, as Cline phrases it, "monkey see, monkey do." In the second sentence he presents his first cause and first effect—even *brief exposure* to aggressive behavior (cause) can lead to children's repeating it in free play (effect). In the third sentence, he presents the second cause and its effect—a *single viewing* of an aggressive act (cause) can be recalled by children six months later (effect). The next three sentences detail the violence a typical child might see over ten years, thus establishing a very dramatic cause. In his final sentence, Cline states the ultimate effect: television teaches children to take pride in violence and to be ashamed of sympathy.

Rather than alternate causes and effects in individual paragraphs, writers will sometimes divide them into separate paragraphs. The following two paragraphs are from Frank Trippett's humorous essay, "The Great American Cooling Machine." In the first paragraph, Trippett establishes that air conditioning has been overlooked as a major cause for change in American society. In the second paragraph he presents three effects of air conditioning on society.

> Neither scholars nor pop sociologists have really got around to charting and diagnosing all the changes brought about by air conditioning. Professional observers have for years been preoccupied with the social implications of the automobile and television. Mere glancing analysis suggests that the car and TV, in their most decisive influences on American habits, have been powerfully aided and abetted by air conditioning. The car may have created all those shopping centers in the boondocks, but only air conditioning has made them attractive to mass clienteles. Similarly, the artificial cooling of the living room undoubtedly helped turn the typical American into a year-round TV addict. Without air conditioning, how many viewers would endure reruns (or even Johnny Carson) on one of those pestilential summer nights that used to send people out to collapse on the lawn or to sleep on the roof?

> Many of the side effects of air conditioning are far from being fully pinned down. It is a reasonable suspicion, though, that controlled climate, by inducing Congress to stay in Washington longer than it used to during the swelter season, thus presumably passing more laws, has contributed to bloated government. One can only speculate that the

advent of the supercooled bedroom may be linked to the carnal adventurism associated with the mid-century sexual revolution. Surely it is a fact—if restaurant complaints about raised thermostats are to be believed—that air conditioning induces at least expense-account diners to eat and drink more; if so, it must be credited with adding to the national fat problem.

Identifying Immediate and Ultimate Causes

Careful writers usually distinguish between immediate and ultimate causes; that is, those which are most apparent and those which underlie them. In the example above, Trippett, in his humorous way, presents the ultimate effects of air conditioning: bloated government, the sexual revolution, and the national fat problem. The depth to which a writer analyzes causes or effects depends upon the subject and the purpose. Exploring the ultimate causes or effects requires more effort than getting to the immediate ones because a writer must establish a foundation for the analysis.

In *The Seasons of a Man's Life,* Daniel J. Levenson studies the psychological development of men. In these two paragraphs, after establishing a solid foundation for his conclusions, he presents the ultimate effects of middle age on a man's relationships with young adults.

At around 40 a man is deeply involved in the Young/ Old polarity. This developmental process has a powerful effect upon his relationships with his offspring and with young adults generally. When his own aging weighs heavily upon him, their exuberant vitality is more likely to arouse his envy and resentment than his delight and forbearance. He may be preoccupied with grievances against his own parents for damage, real or imagined, that they have inflicted upon him at different ages. These preoccupations make him less appreciative of the (often similar) grievances his offspring direct toward him.

If he feels he has lost or betrayed his own early Dream, he may find it hard to give his wholehearted support and blessing to the Dreams of young adults. When his offspring show signs of failure or confusion in pursuing their adult goals, he is afraid that their lives will turn out as badly as his own. Yet, when they do well, he may resent their success. Anxiety and guilt may undermine his efforts to be helpful and lead him instead to be nagging and vindictive.

Levenson's analysis probes deeply into the nagging relationship some middle-aged men might have with young adults. He exposes the ultimate cause and its effects—anxiety over aging, failure, and competition.

In this paragraph from *The Faces of the Enemy,* Sam Keen explores the ultimate cause of war, not the politicians who start wars or the generals who carry them out, but the "good people" who allow their leaders to act out community neuroses by waging war.

The major responsibility for war lies not with villains and evil men but with reasonably good citizens. Any depth understanding of the social function of war leads to the conclusion that it was the "good" Germans who created the social ecology that nurtured the Nazis. Lincoln said, "War is much too important to be left to the generals." But the psychological truth is much more disturbing. The generals are the (largely unconscious) agents of a (largely unconscious) civilian population. The good people send out armies as symbolic representatives to act out their repressed shadows, denied hostilities, unspoken cruelties, unacceptable greed, unimagined lust for revenge against punitive parents and authorities, uncivil sexual sadism, denied animality, in a purifying blood ritual that confirms their claim to goodness before the approving eyes of history or God. Warfare is the political equivalent of the individual process of seeking "vindictive triumph," which Karen Horney described as the essence of neurosis.

Writers keep two cautions in mind when exploring cause-and-effect relationships; be aware of them. First, writers avoid confusing process patterns with cause-and-effect patterns. The analysis of a process usually stems from a question of How? not Why? or What? *How* did Ronald Reagan get elected to the presidency? sends a writer into process analysis. *Why* was Ronald Reagan elected to the presidency? sends a writer into an examination of the causes—that is, the reasons. *What* were the consequences of Ronald Reagan's presidency? sends a writer to examine the effects—that is, the results.

Second, they avoid the *post hoc, ergo propter hoc* fallacy; that is, "after this, therefore because of this" or "false-cause," fallacy. Writers commit this fallacy (argument from a false inference) by jumping to conclusions based on insufficient information. That former president Ronald Reagan was elected when the electorate's average life expectancy was increasing does not mean an older voting population will elect older presidents.

In a variation of the false-cause fallacy, an event is identified as triggering a series of events in a cause-and-effect chain reaction, or *causal chain*. This kind of reasoning was at work in the arguments of politicians who supported the United States military action in Vietnam during the 1960s and 1970s. They maintained that if North Vietnam was successful in its efforts to take over South Vietnam, then the nearby Southeast Asian countries would soon be taken over by Communist regimes one at a time, like a file of falling dominoes triggered by the first domino toppling into the second. History, of course, has shown that these events did not happen. But keep in mind that causes of complicated events are seldom simple or obvious, and that predicting the future with cause-and-effect reasoning is a chancy business.

Cause and Effect in College Writing

Essays exploring causes or effects are common assignments in academic writing. In history you might be asked to discuss the causes of racial discrimination following the Civil War. In economics you might be asked to explain the international effects of the massive United States budget deficit. In psychology you might be asked to discuss the causes of clinical depression and its effects on personality. When responding to a cause-and-effect question, decide if you need to explore both causes and effects, or simply causes *or* effects. Also be sure to select the most important causes or effects to emphasize; weigh them carefully to avoid becoming mired in the obvious and trivial.

The next paragraphs are part of a student essay responding to an assignment in mass communications: Discuss the influence of television on politics. The writer, Nancy Pringle, decided to concentrate on the influence of television and related technology in totalitarian countries, specifically the Communist-controlled East European countries that gained independence during 1989. These three paragraphs begin her essay.

Pringle's opening announces cause and effect. Both Orwell and Huxley are pertinent to her point: they represent general views of the ways in which governments might use television to control their people.

George Orwell's 1984 and Aldous Huxley's Brave New World, both anti-utopian novels, warn of the effect communication technology might have on society. Orwell warns that governments might use it to control society by inflicting pain; Huxley warns that governments might use it to control society by stimulating pleasure. The ultimate effect would be the same: Dictators would stay in power by controlling history's most powerful medium—television. Recent events, however, seem to prove both authors wrong. Television and related technology, rather than being a tool of repression, seems to be a tool of liberation.

In Europe's communist-bloc countries, television fueled the 1989 desire for liberty. Although Communist governments controlled their own broadcast

She presents the effect of television entertainment and news: they provided information and stimulated discontent.

systems, their citizens still had access to western entertainment programs and films. These programs indirectly showed that West Europeans had more freedom and were more affluent than East Europeans, all of which inspired discontent. Moreover, many Soviet-bloc countries saw news broadcasts that spilled over from neighboring countries. East Berliners would watch West German news broadcasts. Communist-controlled Hungarians watched Austrian news broadcasts. People throughout the Soviet Union, East Germany, and Czechoslovakia watched liberalized Polish news broadcasts. Nightly reports of political victories against Communist governments filled the airwaves. Soon a domino effect began: victories in Poland inspired Hungarians, Hungarian victories inspired East Germans, and the East Germans inspired the Czechoslovaks.

Here she presents a series of causes and effects.

Pringle shifts to related technology—video cameras and playback systems—presenting their effects.

Inexpensive video cameras and playback systems also dramatically affected liberation politics. Solidarity, the workers union that spearheaded the Polish revolution, spread its message with crude "home-movies" reproduced by the thousands and played in homes throughout Poland. The message was quite simple—there is an alternative to Communist-party rule—and had the effect of keeping the freedom movement alive. In Czechoslovakia, when the government-controlled television stations suppressed reports of uprisings put down by government troops, students used video cameras to film the events, copied the cassettes, and distributed them throughout the country, thus revealing to an entire nation the secret actions of its repressive government.

In the first sentence, Pringle indicates that she will be seeking effects. Clearly the cause, the reason for the discussion—television and related technology—is pervasive in the West, and so she does not need to establish its existence. Then, referring to the works of two internationally known novelists, she points out that television's influence might not be what many people expected. In the second paragraph, she concentrates on the specific effects: television stimulated the desire for liberty in Soviet-bloc countries by showing that westerners had more freedom and wealth and by reporting the gains made in other Communist-controlled countries, thus creating a domino effect. In the third paragraph, Pringle turns to the effects of video cameras and playback systems. Their use kept an alternative point of view alive in Poland and captured events the government wanted to suppress in Czechoslovakia. Throughout the passage Pringle keeps her eye on the task by effectively discussing the effects of television on totalitarian governments.

One way to introduce students to the ideas of this essay is to ask, "What responsibilities go with material wealth?" The answers will be mixed, many students saying that materially wealthy people should care for the homeless and the hungry, others saying that the affluent have few responsibilities beyond caring for themselves and their own families. The follow-up question is, "Does material wealth cause a restriction of one's freedom?" Usually, students reply, "No," almost in unison.

But wait! Many materially wealthy people must wear specific kinds of clothing; otherwise, they will risk being outcasts from their own society. How about cars? Don't materially wealthy people have to drive expected makes and models? What about friends? Can materially wealthy people afford to have poor friends? What about bodyguards? Security gates? Special places in which to live?

After students see that one effect of material wealth is lack of social freedom, they are better able to grasp the points made in Forster's essay.

MARGINAL NOTES

The British have been in India since 1600. India became independent in 1947, after many years of strife. Forster's *A Passage to India* chronicles life among the British in India before its independence. Mention the British and American English differences: Many American dialects have "woods" for *wood*, and Americans spell *cheque* "check." Notice the simple cause-and-effect statement in the first paragraph. Forster's check allows him to buy the wood. The interjection "blast it" is Forster's momentary opinion of the public footpath in his wood. The paragraph's last sentence introduces the psychological cause-and-effect topic of the essay.

❦ E. M. Forster ❦

Edward Morgan Forster was born in London in 1879 and attended King's College, Cambridge, where he studied classics and history and developed a strong interest in foreign cultures. From a family of bankers, he had no interest in business, and after finishing his education traveled to India, Greece, and Italy. He later settled in London to pursue a career as a writer. His travels in India (in 1912 and again in 1921) inspired his best-known novel, A Passage to India *(1924). His other books include the novels,* A Room with a View *(1908) and* Howard's End *(1910), two collections of essays, and a collection of short stories. Forster died in 1970.*

My Wood

This selection is from Forster's Abinger Harvest *(1936), a collection of essays. He opens with a reference to his novel* A Passage to India, *and uses his experience in buying a piece of land to examine the effects of property ownership. He distinguishes between the unavoidable materialism of "life on earth" and the problematic desire for ownership.*

A few years ago I wrote a book which dealt in part with the difficulties of the English in India. Feeling that they would have had no difficulties in India themselves, the Americans read the book freely. The more they read it the better it made them feel, and a cheque to the author was the result. I bought a wood with the cheque. It is not a large wood—it contains scarcely any trees, and it is intersected, blast it, by a public footpath. Still, it is the first property that I have owned, so it is right that other people should participate in my shame, and should ask themselves, in accents that will vary in horror, this very important question: What is the effect of property upon the character? Don't let's touch economics; the effect of private ownership upon the community as a whole is another question—a more important question, perhaps, but another one. Let's keep to psychology. If you own things, what's their effect on you? What's the effect on me of my wood?

In the first place, it makes me feel heavy. Property does have this effect. Property produces men of weight, and it was a man of weight who failed to get into the Kingdom of Heaven. He was not wicked, that unfortunate millionaire in the parable, he was only stout; he stuck out in front, not to mention behind, and as he wedged himself this way and that in the crystalline entrance and bruised his well-fed flanks, he saw beneath him a comparatively slim camel passing through the eye of a needle and being woven into the robe of God. The Gospels all through couple stoutness and slowness. They point out what is perfectly obvious, yet seldom realized: that if you have a lot of things you cannot move about a lot, that furniture requires dusting, dusters require servants, servants require insurance stamps, and the whole tangle of them makes you think twice before you accept an invitation to dinner or go for a bathe in the Jordan. Sometimes the Gospels proceed further and say with Tolstoy that property is sinful; they approach the difficult ground of asceticism here, where I cannot follow them. But as to the immediate effects of property on people, they just show straightforward logic. It produces men of weight. Men of weight cannot, by definition, move like the lightning from the East unto the West, and the ascent of a fourteen-stone bishop into a pulpit is thus the exact antithesis of the coming of the Son of Man. My wood makes me feel heavy.

In the second place, it makes me feel it ought to be larger.

The other day I heard a twig snap in it. I was annoyed at first, for I thought that someone was blackberrying, and depreciating the value of the undergrowth. On coming nearer, I saw it was not a man who had trodden on the twig and snapped it, but a bird, and I felt pleased. My bird. The bird was not equally pleased. Ignoring the relation between us, it took fright as soon as it saw the shape of my face, and flew straight over the boundary hedge into a field, the property of Mrs. Henessy, where it sat down with a loud squawk. It had become Mrs. Henessy's bird. Something

2   See New Testament, Matthew 19:24: "It is easier for a camel to go through the eye of a needle, than for a rich man to enter into the kingdom of God." Forster follows that verse with a coupling of the religious and secular cause-and-effect possibilities. Leo Tolstoy (1828–1910), social and moral philosopher and Russian mystic, wrote *War and Peace* (1865–1869), among other great works. He emancipated his serfs in 1861. *Stone:* a unit of weight in Great Britain equal to 14 pounds. The stout bishop weighs 196 pounds.

The first and last lines of the paragraph end with the same four words, for effective emphasis: "makes me feel heavy." Forster, too, feels stout.

3   "In the second place" is the clearest kind of transition, as the author moves from the psychological effect of weight, caused by owning his property, to that of size. The property Forster acquired has caused him to want more.

4   "The other day" begins Forster's example displaying how the psychological effect of wanting more property has caused him to view his surroundings—greedily. King Ahab in the Old Testament, the seventh king of Israel (c. 875–853 B.C.), greatly expanded his territories, especially by marrying Jezebel, daughter of the king of Sidon. In Herman Melville's *Moby-Dick*, Captain Ahab's obsession was to find and kill the white whale, at whatever cost. Forster discusses his growing obsession for getting

more land. Canute II of Denmark (994?–1035), subject of many legends, conquered England and was chosen king in 1017 by the witan, the king's council of Anglo-Saxons. Alexander the Great (356–323 B.C.), said to have wept after he had no more worlds to conquer, directed enormously successful campaigns in Greece, Persia, northern India, Syria, and Egypt, among others. Sirius, the Dog Star, is the brightest star in the constellation Canis Major. Forster's imaginary domain is boundless, a cause of sadness when he compares it with his real, limited domain. The bird reminds us of nature's "definition" of property. We "own" only ourselves.

Owning property causes us to want to change it, to make it clearly ours. This psychology of ownership—nothing really belongs to us until we change it, pseudo-creatively—deeply bothers Forster. We want to mold our property into an extension of our personality, but without a creative motive. Shakespeare's Sonnet 129 begins, "The expense of spirit in a waste of shame / Is lust in action. . . ." The "internal defect" is our inability to accept ourselves as we are, just as we are unable to accept our property for what it is. As Forster uses *carnal*, the word relates to the body as the seat of physical appetites, without intellectual or moral influence. Our life on earth should be carnal and material, yet managed by the intellect and morality. Ironically, however, our desire for ownership manages our intellect and morality. Dante Alighieri (1265–1321) wrote *The Divine Comedy*.

seemed grossly amiss here, something that would not have occurred had the wood been larger. I could not afford to buy Mrs. Henessy out, I dared not murder her, and limitations of this sort beset me on every side. Ahab did not want that vineyard—he only needed it to round off his property, preparatory to plotting a new curve—and all the land around my wood has become necessary to me in order to round off the wood. A boundary protects. But—poor little thing—the boundary ought in its turn to be protected. Noises on the edge of it. Children throw stones. A little more, and then a little more, until we reach the sea. Happy Canute! Happier Alexander! And after all, why should even the world be the limit of possession? A rocket containing a Union Jack, will, it is hoped, be shortly fired at the moon. Mars. Sirius. Beyond which . . . But these immensities ended by saddening me. I could not suppose that my wood was the destined nucleus of universal dominion—it is so very small and contains no mineral wealth beyond the blackberries. Nor was I comforted when Mrs. Henessy's bird took alarm for the second time and flew clean away from us all, under the belief that it belonged to itself.

In the third place, property makes its owner feel that he ought to do something to it. Yet he isn't sure what. A restlessness comes over him, a vague sense that he has a personality to express—the same sense which, without any vagueness, leads the artist to an act of creation. Sometimes I think I will cut down such trees as remain in the wood, at other times I want to fill up the gaps between them with new trees. Both impulses are pretentious and empty. They are not honest movements towards money-making or beauty. They spring from a foolish desire to express myself and from an inability to enjoy what I have got. Creation, property, enjoyment form a sinister trinity in the human mind. Creation and enjoyment are both very, very good, yet they are often unattainable without a material basis, and at such moments property pushes itself in as a substitute, saying, "Accept me instead—I'm good enough for all three." It is not enough. It is, as Shakespeare said of lust, "The expense of spirit in a waste of shame": it is "Before, a joy proposed; behind, a dream." Yet we don't know how to shun it. It is forced on us by our economic system as the alternative to starvation. It is also forced on us by an internal defect in the soul, by the feeling that in property may lie the germs of self-development and of exquisite or heroic deeds. Our life on earth is, and ought to be, material and carnal. But we have not yet learned to manage our materialism and carnality properly; they are still entangled with the desire for ownership, where (in the words of Dante) "Possession is one with loss."

And this brings us to our fourth and final point: the blackberries.

Blackberries are not plentiful in this meagre grove, but they are easily seen from the public footpath which traverses it, and all too easily gathered. Foxgloves, too—people will pull up the foxgloves, and ladies of an educational tendency even grub for toadstools to show them on the Monday in class. Other ladies, less educated, roll down the bracken in the arms of their gentlemen friends. There is paper, there are tins. Pray, does my wood belong to me or doesn't it? And, if it does, should I not own it best by allowing no one else to walk there? There is a wood near Lyme Regis, also cursed by a public footpath, where the owner has not hesitated on this point. He had built high stone walls each side of the path, and has spanned it by bridges, so that the public circulate like termites when he gorges on the blackberries unseen. He really does own his wood, this able chap. Dives in Hell did pretty well, but the gulf dividing him from Lazarus could be traversed by vision, and nothing traverses it here. And perhaps I shall come to this in time. I shall wall in and fence out until I really taste the sweets of property. Enormously stout, endlessly avaricious, pseudo-creative, intensely selfish, I shall weave upon my forehead the quadruple crown of possession until those nasty Bolshies come and take it off again and thrust me aside into the outer darkness.

6 Forster's homely transition detaches us from his deeply philosophical paragraph.

7 The natural products of Forster's wood attract people. Foxgloves have long spikes of thimble-like flowers. A medicine made from their leaves (digitalis) is used as a heart stimulant. Bracken are large, coarse, weedy ferns. All the public activity causes Forster to question the definition of ownership. Does the owner own the property, or does the property own the owner? For Dives, see the parable of the selfish rich man, Luke 16:19–31; Lazarus is the poor diseased man in the same parable.

To make his "quadruple crown of possession," Forster weaves together the four subtopics in this essay: worldly wealth, greed, false creativity, and selfishness. "[N]asty Bolshies": Bolsheviks are Communists or, loosely used, any radicals.

Possible Answers

Meaning and Purpose

1. Forster intends to explore the questions he poses in the first paragraph: "What is the effect of property upon the character?" and "What's the effect on me of my wood?" These two sentences are his thesis in question form; he is asserting that ownership *does* affect a person.

2. Encourage students to share their stories about things they have owned and done something to. Be sure they account for clear causes and effects, such as "I painted an American flag on my leather jacket because I want people to know that I am patriotic."

3. Students are free to select their own allusions. Occasionally reading and discussing the better papers in class is an exercise that helps students realize this essay's depth.

4. The author's freedom is restricted by his imagined obligations to himself and his possession, which stem from his owning the wood in the first place. Now that he has the wood, he feels obliged to enlarge it, improve it, and protect it.

5. The interjection "blast it" sums up his opinion of the wood's being publicly and easily accessible by the footpath. This is the first clue that Forster will feel possessive about his wood.

Strategy

1. Forster gives the cause in paragraph 1: the acquiring of money that enabled him to buy the wood. In subsequent paragraphs, he develops one effect at a time. This structure is effective because it is clear and makes his reasoning easy to follow. Giving one long paragraph to each effect allows him to single it out and explore it in depth.

2. The statement quoted is an example of a causal chain, or a series of things, one triggering the next, in chronological order. This tech-

Meaning and Purpose

1. What is Forster's purpose in "My Wood," and where does he most clearly state it?

2. In paragraph 5, he says "property makes its owner feel that he ought to do something to it." What do you own that you have done something to, just because you owned it? A pair of shoes? a jacket? a car? Briefly describe the ways in which you changed it and your reasons for changing it.

3. An allusion often refers to a historical or literary figure, event, or object. Choose one allusion from this essay and learn more about it. If you chose "Canute," you might look it up in an unabridged dictionary, an encyclopedia, or other reference works. Select an allusion other than "Canute" and describe it briefly.

4. In paragraph 2, Forster says that owning many things restricts one's freedom. How does owning the wood restrict the author's freedom?

5. The first paragraph includes the words "blast it." Why does the author use that interjection?

Strategy

1. Study the cause-and-effect structure of the essay. Does Forster alternate cause and effect in each paragraph, or develop them one at a time in separate paragraphs? Explain the effectiveness of the structure.

2. In the middle of paragraph 2 is the statement, "if you have a lot of things you cannot move about a lot, that furniture requires dusting, dusters require servants, servants require insurance stamps, and the whole tangle of them makes you think twice before you accept an invitation to dinner or go for a bathe in the Jordan." What is the cause-and-effect structure of this sentence called, and how is it used here?

3. The last paragraph in this essay says that the owner of a wood near Lyme Regis "really does own his wood." What caused that ownership? What is the effect of that kind of ownership?

4. In paragraph 6, he says that the fourth and final point in the essay is blackberries. But it is not. What is the fourth and final point, and why does the author tell us it is blackberries?

Style

1. What is the occupation of the "ladies of an educational tendency," in paragraph 7, and why do you think the author describes them as he does?

2. In paragraph 4, the author says, "A little more, and then a little more, until we reach the sea." What is the author describing in this sentence?

3. Look at paragraphs 3 and 6. Why do you think each has only one sentence?

Writing Tasks

1. The American writer Henry David Thoreau said, "A man is rich in proportion to the number of things which he can afford to let alone." E. M. Forster's essay "My Wood" has much in common with Thoreau's statement. In your paper, consider being rich a cause and discuss what you think are some of its effects. Develop each effect in a paragraph.

2. Here is a list of causes. Write about one effect of each. Develop at least one causal chain.
   Teenager watching MTV
   Landfill overflowing
   Apple trees blossoming
   Car breaking down in the fast lane during rush hour

nique here exaggerates Forster's point that owning property is heavy or cumbersome. He imagines that ownership will cause slowness, having things "you cannot move about," until you'd better think twice before you "bathe in the Jordan." Forster is using humor to stress one danger of ownership.

3. The ownership was caused by the high stone walls that the owner built on both sides of the path. The effect is that those walls have imprisoned the owner.

4. The fourth and final point is selfishness. Forster means that blackberries lure people in until he is tempted to "wall in and fence out . . . property. [acts that are] Enormously . . . selfish" (paragraph 7).

Style

1. The ladies are probably elementary school teachers, and the author thinks little of them for "grubbing" in his wood just to show the children toadstools.

2. Forster extends his need to enlarge the boundary of his wood all the way to the sea to keep out noise and children. This exaggeration stresses his point that once he is an owner, his greed will know no bounds.

3. These two paragraphs are transitions from discussion of one effect to the next. They are clear statements of Forster's chronology in presenting his points. And they are stylistically effective because they are short and rather abrupt between two long paragraphs. They catch attention and bring the reader back on track.

TEACHING SUGGESTIONS

Four distinct but complementary approaches may prove profitable in teaching this brief but provocative essay. First, discuss differences and effects of inductive versus deductive methods. Many writers state the thesis first and follow with examples to demonstrate its validity. Miller begins by vividly describing an actual experience and then lists examples that are more and more hypothetical until he reaches his speculative conclusion.

Second, Miller deals with cause and effect. The "severing of the human connection" in each example is immediately caused by "chiselers." He then speculates about the ultimate cause. Are people incorrigibly dishonest? But people behave as they are expected to, and we have a different ultimate cause: our collective paranoia, which causes us to overreact to the chiselers, creating more chiselers, who force us to react even more.

Thirdly, even the most speculative examples are rooted in the most concrete language. Linguistic analysis of each paragraph easily demonstrates that concrete language is more effective than vague and abstract words. Miller offers us no abstractions (1). He precedes the more abstract "thievery" and "violence" with a list of vivid things to demonstrate meaning (6). Instead of reflecting on an abstract, vague "future," he says we are on a dark and descending road.

Finally, discussing Miller's ideas could prove provocative. His conclusion is pessimistic: he admits to intellectual understanding of the problem, but cannot accept it emotionally. Students will take sides; show that they must accumulate evidence, facts, to convince someone that their reactions are valid.

MARGINAL NOTES

Miller uses a striking turn of phrase ("these days of expensive gas and cut-rate ethics") to describe his attitude toward the social situation that has created the atrocity he describes in paragraph 1.

❦ H. Bruce Miller ❦

Bruce Miller was born in New Jersey in 1946 and studied at Princeton University. He received his master's degree in journalism from Columbia University, after which he began his journalistic career at the Trentonian *in Trenton, New Jersey. He has also worked at* Newsday *in Los Angeles and the* San Jose Mercury News, *where he was first an editorial writer for several years and then a columnist. He is currently managing editor of the* Bulletin *in Bend, Oregon.*

Severing the Human Connection

In this short essay from the San Jose Mercury News *(August 4, 1981), Miller laments the widespread distrust in American society. Beginning by describing a specific result of this self-protective distrust, the pay-before-you-pump gas station, he gradually moves toward a consideration of possible causes.*

Went down to the local self-serve gas station the other morning to fill up. The sullen cashier was sitting inside a dark, glassed-in, burglar-proof, bullet-proof, probably grenade-proof cubicle covered with cheerful notices. "No Checks." "No Credit." "No Bills Over $50 Accepted." "Cashier Has No Small Change." And the biggest one of all: "Pay Before Pumping Gas." A gleaming steel box slid out of the wall and gaped open. I dropped in a $20 bill. "Going to fill 'er up with no-lead on Number 6," I said. The cashier nodded. The steel box swallowed my money and retracted into the cubicle. I walked back to the car to pump the gas, trying not to slink or skulk. I felt like I ought to be wearing striped overalls with a number on the breast pocket. 1

The pay-before-you-pump gas station (those in the trade call it a "pre-pay") is a response to a real problem in these days of expensive gas and cut-rate ethics: people who fill their tanks and then tear out of the station without paying. Those in the business 2

296

call them "drive-offs." The head of one area gasoline dealers' association says drive-offs cost some dealers $500 to $600 a month. With a profit margin of only about a nickel a gallon, a dealer has to sell a lot of gallons to make up that kind of loss. The police aren't much help. Even if the attendant manages to get a license plate number and description of the car, the cops have better things to do than tracking down a guy who stole $15 worth of gas. So the dealers adopt the pre-pay system.

Intellectually, I understand all of this, yet I am angry and resentful. Emotionally I cannot accept the situation. I understand the dealers' position, I understand the cops' position. But I cannot understand why I should be made to feel like John Dillinger every time I buy a tank of gasoline. It's the same story everywhere. You go to a department store and try to pay for a $10.99 item with a check and you have to pull out a driver's license, two or three credit cards and a character reference from the pope—and then stand around for 15 minutes to get the manager's approval. Try to pay with a credit card and you have to wait while the cashier phones the central computer bank to make sure you're not a deadbeat or the Son of Sam or something. It's not that we don't trust you, they smile. It's just that we have to protect ourselves.

Right. We all have to protect ourselves these days. Little old ladies with attack dogs and Mace and 12-gauges, shopkeepers with closed-circuit TVs and electronic sensors to nab shoplifters, survivalists storing up ammo and dehydrated foods in hope of riding out Armageddon, gas station owners with pay-before-you-pump signs and impenetrable cashiers' cages—all protecting themselves. From what? From each other. It strikes me that we are expending so much time, energy and anguish on protecting ourselves that we are depleting our stock of mental and emotional capital for living. It also strikes me that the harder we try to protect ourselves, the less we succeed. With all the home burglar alarms and guard dogs and heavy armament, the crime rate keeps going up. With all the electronic surveillance devices, the shoplifters' take keeps climbing. The gas chiselers haven't figured out a way to beat the pre-pay system yet, but they will.

This is the only place in the essay where Miller actually uses facts.

3 The topic sentence has a strong transition ("I understand all of this") and creates the organizational pattern for the paragraph, comparison and contrast: his intellectual understanding of the situation and his emotional inability to accept it.

John Dillinger (1902–1934) was an American bank robber and murderer.

David Berkowitz was arrested in 1977 for a 1976–1977 series of murders with satanic overtones in New York City. He often left notes with his victims calling himself Son of Sam.

4

Armageddon was the name given in "The Revelation of St. John the Divine" (Rev. 16:16) to the site of the last great battle between good and evil before the Day of Judgment; hence, any great final struggle or conflict.

Our efforts to protect ourselves have not had the desired effect. Crime keeps going on.

Miller begins the sentence with a question that he will answer in the last two sentences of the same paragraph. The "glue" mentioned here that he claims holds society together connects with the title and the clause in the concluding paragraph that "The human connection is severed. . . ." An affirmative answer to these questions would suggest the ultimate causes of our perceived need for protection. Neither accepting nor rejecting these causes, Miller says that if the answer is "yes" the cause is even closer to the ultimate: our collective paranoia.

POSSIBLE ANSWERS

Meaning and Purpose

1. Miller states his thesis at the end of the essay, that sometime during his life we have changed from "A society which assumes its members are honest and humane" to one that "treats everyone like a criminal. . . ." In the opening paragraph he vividly describes a commonplace in our society that insulates us from one another and, for Miller, is emblematic of a society that has become "harsh, unfeeling, punitive, paranoid" (7). The "glue of integrity and mutual respect" that has held our society together has dissolved (5) so that now "The human connection is severed . . ." (7).
2. The prepay gas station is an effect, and Miller draws out the description in cold details to stress the inhumanity of it. The cause behind such a gas station is a world in which people feel they have to protect themselves and treat everyone like criminals.
3. Miller shows that ordinary people can be made to feel like criminals in their everyday business transactions (1, 3). The more we do to protect ourselves against crime, the more crime is created (4). If that hypothesis can be borne out by fact, then so can the opposite.
4. Miller implies that a society forcing many citizens to feel guilty is innately inhumane (3).

Is it that the people are simply incorrigibly dishonest, that the glue of integrity and mutual respect that holds society together is finally dissolving? I don't know, but I suspect that if something like this really is going on, our collective paranoia contributes to the process. People, after all, tend to behave pretty much the way other people expect them to behave. If the prevailing assumption of a society is that people are honest, by and large they will be honest. If the prevailing assumption is that people are crooks, more and more of them will be crooks. 5

What kind of message does a kid get from an environment where uniformed guards stand at the entrance of every store, where every piece of merchandise has an anti-shoplifting tag stapled to it, where every house has a burglar alarm and a .38, where the gas station cashiers huddle in glass cages and pass your change out through a metal chute? What can he conclude but that thievery and violence are normal, common, expected behaviors? 6

A society which assumes its members are honest is humane, comfortable, habitable. A society which treats everyone like a criminal becomes harsh, unfeeling, punitive, paranoid. The human connection is severed; fear of detection and punishment becomes the only deterrent to crime, and it's a very ineffective one. Somehow, sometime—I don't know when, but it was within my lifetime—we changed from the first type of society to the second. Maybe it's too late to go back again, but the road we are now on is a dark and descending one. 7

Meaning and Purpose

1. What is Miller's thesis and where is it stated? What does his title mean and how does it relate to his thesis?
2. Is the "pre-pay" gas station described in the first paragraph a cause or an effect? Explain.

3. Reread the last two sentences of paragraph 5. Do you feel that the author's conclusion is valid? Why or why not? How well does the author prepare us for that conclusion?
4. Have you had experiences that made you feel as Miller does in paragraph 3? What do you think might be the causes of the situations you describe in your experiences?
5. In paragraph 3, the author mentions John Dillinger and Son of Sam. Even if you do not know who they were, what conclusions can you draw about them by examining the context in which they are mentioned?

Strategy

1. How does Miller develop his cause-and-effect strategy, by alternating each in the same paragraph, or by exploring each in separate paragraphs? Give examples.
2. Critique paragraph 2 for its structure and function in the essay.
3. Would you say that "little old ladies with attack dogs and Mace and 12-gauges" (paragraph 4) are an immediate or ultimate effect? Give reasons for your answer.
4. In the last paragraph, Miller claims that during his lifetime, society changed from being humane to being inhumane. He ends pessimistically. What do you think is the effect on the reader of his bleak pronouncements? Does he present enough evidence for his conclusions?

Style

1. Examine paragraph 1, sentence by sentence, paying close attention to the author's use of concrete language. How does each sentence work stylistically? What tone is created by this language?
2. After describing situations in which he is made to feel guilty for transacting everyday business in paragraph 3, the author

Encourage students to differentiate cause from effect in the experiences.

5. In each case, the author has been made to feel that he is under suspicion, potentially criminal. Logically, the two men must be examples of criminals.

Strategy

1. Miller generally gives whole paragraphs to either causes or effects. Paragraphs 1 and 2 are effects. He explains how these effects of a paranoid society make him feel (3). Cause dominates paragraph 4, about how people protect themselves; the effect is not less crime but more inhumanity. He gives possible causes that can result in prepay gas stations (5, 6). In the last paragraph Miller states what he thinks is the final effect: we will behave as we expect each other to behave.

2. The topic sentence states why the absurd and inhumane incident in paragraph 1 can occur. He explains why the incident is not an anomaly, and why it has, in fact, become typical. The author understands the problem and establishes his authority to fight it.

3. That little old ladies are protecting themselves is an immediate effect of society's paranoia about self-protection. Other immediate effects are in paragraph 4, and prepay gas stations in the first part of the essay. By contrast, ultimate effects are that more and more people will be crooks (paragraph 5), that kids will believe "thievery and violence are normal" (paragraph 6), and that society will become "harsh, unfeeling, punitive, paranoid" (7).

4. Miller successfully portrays himself as a victim of society's attempts to make him feel guilty and criminal (paragraph 3 makes this feeling clearest). He gives examples of alienation from human interchange that readers probably have in their own experience, the effects caused by the need for self-protection. He gives no strong evidence that all this change occurred in Miller's lifetime; that is just his perception. The effect on the reader of Miller's pessimism might be awareness of the situation that could lead to the reader's taking some action to turn the situation around. "Maybe it's too late" in the last paragraph could be taken as a challenge.

1. The paragraph is a marvel of vivid concrete language that grabs the reader and creates the essay's pervading tone of shocked disbelief and disenchantment.

In sentence 1 he uses informal language that creates the normalcy of the situation, with the author going down to the "local self-serve" station one morning to "fill up."

The tone suddenly changes with the "sullen cashier" sitting in a dark cubicle entirely cut off and protected from the outside world (2). The cashier is further cut off by the "cheerful notices" plastered on his cubicle.

The notices are made emphatic by their capitalization (3).

The "gleaming steel box" further separates human being from human being while it becomes an inhuman mouth that "gaped" (4) for money (5).

The common—and cryptic—language between narrator and attendant. The physical setup of the station discourages either from acknowledging the other's humanity (6, 7).

That inhuman steel mouth "swallowed" the author's money and immediately "retracted into the cubicle," emphasizing separation (8).

"Slink" is to move in a furtive abject manner, as from fear, cowardice, or shame, and "skulk" is to move in a stealthy way (9). The author walks back to his car "trying" not to walk in these ways. Miller feels like a convict in the last sentence.

2. Miller has prepared us for the disdainful tone of paragraph 4 by the examples he cites in paragraph 3. If we are continually scrutinized and made to feel guilty, the last two sentences in paragraph 4 sound not only hypocritical but dishonest. Opening the next paragraph with "Right," therefore, he creates a tone of sarcastic disbelief. This sarcasm is then confirmed by the absurd list that follows.

3. Miller asks the reader these questions directly. His tone is despairing, yet pleading, as if he wants his readers to say no to the first question, agree with him on the last—and then do something about the condition. Questions usually draw the reader into direct participation in the dialogue.

concludes that he is told: " 'It's not that we don't trust you,' they smile. 'It's just that we have to protect ourselves.' " What tone does he create by beginning the next paragraph with the word "Right"?

3. Miller asks questions in paragraphs 5 and 6. How do these questions work stylistically? Are they effective?

Writing Tasks

1. In a short essay, explain either the causes or effects of one of the following. Decide how far back to go for ultimate causes or effects.

> Pass-fail grading policy
> Installation of front-seat air bags in all cars
> Proliferation of McDonald's restaurants worldwide
> A serious disagreement with your parents or roommate
> Popularity of a rock group or singer
> Benefit concerts by artists
> The need for doctors to have malpractice insurance

2. Consider your own attitudes about the ways in which people treat each other in our society. Assuming your attitudes can be considered effects, what are the causes of your attitudes? Explore these causes in an essay in which you first give concrete evidence of your attitudes.

❧ Arlene B. Hirschfelder ❧

Arlene Hirschfelder was born in Chicago in 1943. She attended Brandeis University and did graduate work in American history and education at the University of Chicago and at Columbia University. She has been involved in Indian Affairs since 1965 and attributes this long commitment to having attended college at a time when civil-rights passion was high and to the social-justice philosophy of reform Judaism. She has been on the staff of the Association on American Indian Affairs since 1969 and is also currently a freelance education consultant in Indian affairs. Her book, Happily May I Walk: American Indians and Alaska Natives *(1986), won the Carter G. Woodson Book Award and a Western Heritage Book Award. She has also published five scholarly books and many articles about Indian affairs. Her articles have appeared in* Ms., *the* Los Angeles Times, Social Studies, *and* Indian Affairs, *among other periodicals.*

It Is Time to Stop Playing Indians

Hirschfelder argues that stereotypical images of American Indians, or Native Americans, trivialize their culture in the popular view and romanticize their plight, when in fact they are often faced with poverty, discrimination, and injustice. Her essay was first published in the Los Angeles Times *in 1987.*

It is predictable. At Halloween, thousands of children trick-or-treat in Indian costumes. At Thanksgiving, thousands of children parade in school pageants wearing plastic headdresses and pseudo-buckskin clothing. Thousands of card shops stock Thanksgiving greeting cards with images of cartoon animals wearing feathered headbands. Thousands of teachers and librarians trim bulletin boards with Anglo-featured, feathered Indian boys and girls. Thousands of gift shops load their shelves with Indian figurines and jewelry.

TEACHING SUGGESTIONS

This is a good time to reminisce about costumes. What costumes have members of the class worn? For what occasions were they worn? What caused them to select the costumes they wore? What effects were they trying to achieve? Have any students ever dressed in Indian costumes? Can they describe those costumes?

Many students have not read about the origin of Thanksgiving since they were in elementary school. They may have forgotten that the Pilgrims probably would not have survived their first two years at Plymouth (1620–1621), had it not been for an English-speaking Pawtuxet Indian named Squanto, who helped them build sturdy houses and plant corn and barley. How did Squanto learn English? As a boy he had been captured by explorers and sold into slavery in Spain. After escaping to England, he spent several years working for a wealthy merchant. He had returned to his native Indian village just six months before the Pilgrims landed.

1

MARGINAL NOTES

The first sentence refers to all that follows in the two introductory paragraphs. A weak traditional topic sentence, it is used here as a strategy to engage the reader by causing curiosity. The Anglo-featured Indians on the bulletin boards are actually white Americans in stereotypical costume. Even the pictures are not realistic.

301

The examples expand to imitation-Indian motifs seen by "hundreds of thousands" throughout the country, throughout the year. The author catalogs evidence in the first two paragraphs.

The effects: "Tens of thousands" of American Indians are offended by their cultures' being trivialized; "millions of us" are prevented from understanding those cultures. The image of the comic, commercialized Indian has replaced the real, cultural Indian.

The author expands her "Halloween sentence" of the first paragraph. People hide themselves in Halloween costumes, and the costumes themselves hide people from the realities of Indian life.

The author expands her "Thanksgiving sentence" of the first paragraph. "Giving," to many of the seventeenth-century immigrants, for many Indians now marks the historical beginning of "taking from."

After partially expanding her sports comments of the second paragraph, the writer shows the effects of stereotyping by suggesting how toy-Indian products cause children to imagine real Indians and how their imaginations cause children to fear real Indians.

2 Fall and winter are also the seasons when hundreds of thousands of sports fans root for professional, college and public school teams with names that summon up Indians—"Braves," "Redskins," "Chiefs." (In New York State, one out of eight junior and senior high school teams call themselves "Indians," "Tomahawks" and the like.) War-whooping team mascots are imprinted on school uniforms, postcards, notebooks, tote bags and car floor mats.

3 All of this seems innocuous; why make a fuss about it? Because these trappings and holiday symbols offend tens of thousands of other Americans—the Native American people. Because these invented images prevent millions of us from understanding the authentic Indian America, both long ago and today. Because this image-making prevents Indians from being a relevant part of the nation's social fabric.

4 Halloween costumes mask the reality of high mortality rates, high diabetes rates, high unemployment rates. They hide low average life spans, low per capita incomes and low educational levels. Plastic war bonnets and ersatz buckskin deprive people from knowing the complexity of Native American heritage—that Indians belong to hundreds of nations that have intricate social organizations, governments, languages, religions and sacred rituals, ancient stories, unique arts and music forms.

5 Thanksgiving school units and plays mask history. They do not tell how Europeans mistreated Wampanoags and other East Coast Indian peoples during the 17th century. Social studies units don't mention that, to many Indians, Thanksgiving is a day of mourning, the beginning of broken promises, land theft, near extinction of their religions and languages at the hands of invading Europeans.

6 Athletic team nicknames and mascots disguise real people. Warpainted, buckskin-clad, feathered characters keep the fictitious Indian circulating on decals, pennants and team clothing. Toy companies mask Indian identity and trivialize sacred beliefs by manufacturing Indian costumes and headdresses, peace pipes and trick-arrow-through-the-head gags that equate Indianness with playtime. Indian figures equipped with arrows, guns and

tomahawks give youngsters the harmful message that Indians favor mayhem. Many Indian people can tell about children screaming in fear after being introduced to them.

It is time to consider how these images impede the efforts of Indian parents and communities to raise their children with positive information about their heritage. It is time to get rid of stereotypes that, whether deliberately or inadvertently, denigrate Indian cultures and people.

It is time to bury the Halloween costumes, trick arrows, bulletin-board pin-ups, headdresses and mascots. It has been done before. In the 1970s, after student protests, Marquette University dropped its "Willie Wampum," Stanford University retired its mascot, "Prince Lightfoot," and Eastern Michigan University and Florida State modified their savage-looking mascots to reduce criticism.

It is time to stop playing Indians. It is time to abolish Indian images that sell merchandise. It is time to stop offending Indian people whose lives are all too often filled with economic deprivation, powerlessness, discrimination and gross injustice. This time next year, let's find more appropriate symbols for the holiday and sports seasons.

7 In these three short paragraphs, the same clause begins six sentences: "It is time." Each repetition introduces the reader to something else that we must do, which will help eliminate the causes and effects of stereotyping and otherwise diminishing the dignity of American Indians. She mentions that some steps, because of student protests, have already been 8 taken. In the last sentence she pleads directly for specific changes.

9

Meaning and Purpose

1. Does the title suggest anything to you about the subject or tone of the essay?
2. Where does the author state her purpose, or main point?
3. According to paragraph 9, Indian images sell merchandise, yet the writer wants to abolish those images. Why? What is the effect of those images?
4. In the last paragraph, Hirschfelder calls for an end to playing Indians, and for an end to using Indian images to sell merchandise. What do you think some of the effects of these changes would be?

POSSIBLE ANSWERS

Meaning and Purpose

1. The "It's Time to Stop" in the title suggests that an admonishing or scolding tone will follow. "Playing Indians" announces the subject of Indians represented in forms of "play." This title gives a good indication, in general, of what may follow.
2. In paragraph 3, Hirschfelder makes her strongest points, beginning with "Because these trappings offend . . ." and ending with the paragraph. The rest of the essay supports these assertions.

3. Those images demean Indians. For moral or ethical reasons, no one should try to make a profit by sacrificing the dignity of an ethnic group.

4. Banning Indian images would certainly affect the tourist industry in areas where Indian themes and trading posts are found. Not playing Indians would affect Thanksgiving celebrations and school art projects. Families and teachers would have to find substitutes for Indian decorations and construction-paper headdresses. Some schools would have to find new symbols and mascots and team uniforms—certainly an expense. But people's awareness of the integrity of native Americans would be another, and positive, effect of banning images. Surely the economy would survive, as it did when images like the old black mammy and Sambo became unacceptable.

5. Students are free to select their own symbols. They might select religious icons, foods, plants, Indians truer to history than the ones in the essay, Pilgrim leaders—any symbols that they can offer with cause.

Strategy

1. This is a rhetorical question, seemingly addressed to the reader but not requiring a reply. It is used for effect, to provoke interest. Readers know the question is not asked of them because the author gives her own answer to it immediately following.

2. The first two paragraphs list how Indian images are used in play and in the economy. These are causes. Paragraph 3 states the effects of using Indian images. These three paragraphs summarize the main information and the main points for Hirschfelder's argument. Paragraphs 4–6 expand this information with specific examples of effects. The last three paragraphs, as the conclusion, call for awareness and change.

3. The rhetorical device of repetition is used strategically for emphasis, adding force and clarity to the statements that follow.

4. The first sentence is brief and, in fact, weak,

5. The writer says that by this time next year, we should find more appropriate symbols for the holiday and sports seasons. What effective new symbols would you suggest for Thanksgiving? What would those symbols cause us to think about Thanksgiving?

Strategy

1. Paragraph 2 includes the question, "Why make a fuss about it?" To whom is this question addressed? How do you know?

2. What is the cause-and-effect structure of the first three paragraphs? How are these paragraphs related to the rest of the essay?

3. Paragraphs 7–9 all begin with "It is time." Why does the writer use this strategy?

4. What is the effect of the first sentence in the essay?

Style

1. In paragraph 1, why does the writer use "plastic headdresses and pseudo-buckskin clothing"? Why not simply use "headdresses and buckskin clothing"?

2. Some Indians object to being called "Indian," preferring the name "Native American." In paragraph 3 the author calls them "the Native American people." Using an unabridged dictionary, discover why we use the name "Indian" to describe Native Americans. How can you better understand what this essayist argues against if you know the American history of the word *Indian*?

3. The author says in paragraph 5 that "Thanksgiving school units and plays *mask* history." Why does the author choose the word *mask* instead of another word such as *conceal* or *hide*?

Writing Tasks

1. If you were invited to a costume party and told to wear a costume that would help undo a current negative stereotype, what would that costume be? Write a dramatic scene in which you describe your costume and, with action and dialogue, show how the costume affects the other partygoers.

2. Think of being taught a stereotypical characterization of an ethnic or racial group from the time you were a child. Write a short essay in which you speculate about a causal chain, or series of causes and effects, which being taught this stereotype might set off in a person's life.

because the pronoun "It" doesn't refer to anything. But the sentence gets readers' attention because of its brevity and because it makes them curious about what "it" is and why it is predictable.

Style

1. The modifiers "plastic" and "pseudo-" emphasize the cheapness of the costumes and the falsity of the images.

2. Columbus called the natives of the Caribbean island on which he had landed "Indians," thinking he had landed on an island off the coast of India. The name stuck, but because it came from ignorance, some Americans believe it should be replaced by the more appropriate "native American," which describes the tribes who were here before the Europeans arrived.

3. The term *mask* is most appropriate because it refers not only to masks that hide history but also to masks that hide faces of children who pretend to be Indians.

Teaching Suggestions

In one sense, Hamill's essay is easy to deal with. First, his attitude is always clear. From the very first he calls his real subject, the 1980s, odious. And because we all have just lived through the times he describes, students should be at least generally familiar with the particulars he cites.

It might be helpful to start by getting the students to look at the essay as a whole before considering its specifics. That is, if they can see that Hamill's purpose is to show that the self-centered greed he describes is essentially antisocial and ultimately exacerbates the social evils he describes in the latter paragraphs, it might then be easier to go back and look at the particulars more closely.

Some students may have problems understanding the subtlety of his language, Hamill's ability to concentrate meaning. Reading some of those difficult passages closely will help.

Marginal Notes

The essay's title alludes to *Tea and Sympathy* (1956), a film about a troubled schoolboy's affair with a teacher's wife. The film is based on a successful Broadway play by Robert Anderson. Here, "T." is Donald Trump, a New York millionaire known for his real-estate deals and other entrepreneurial activities.

Contras were rebels trained and paid by the United States to attack the Nicaraguan government during the Reagan administration. Deconstructionism: A philosophical movement that questions the ability of language to describe reality, saying that words refer only to other words. Haig: Secretary of State in the first Reagan administration and former member of Joint Chiefs of Staff. University of Southern California economist Arthur Laffer graphed the "trickle-down" theory of economics, emblematic of "Reaganomics."

❦ Pete Hamill ❦

Born in 1935 in Brooklyn, New York, Pete Hamill was educated at the Pratt Institute and Mexico City College. He began his writing career as a journalist but went on to write a number of novels as well as several screenplays and musical scripts. He has been a reporter for the New York Post *and the* Saturday Evening Post *and a columnist for* Newsday, New York Daily News, *and* Village Voice. *In 1966 he was a war correspondent in Vietnam. He has won awards for his journalistic writing but is best known for his novels. Two of them,* The Gift *(1973) and* Flesh and Blood *(1977), have been adapted for television. Hamill has contributed to many national periodicals, including* Cosmopolitan, Life, Playboy, Village Voice, *and* Reader's Digest.

T. Without Sympathy

This essay, from the December 1989 issue of Esquire, *is a disparaging look at the decade Hamill calls the "Odious '80s." Using an unnamed public figure as an example, Hamill examines the possible cause-and-effect relationship between society's problems and the values of the individuals who make up that society.*

All across the Odious '80s, the name and character of T. insisted upon entrance to my mind and imagination. So many other phenomena arrived and departed: the contras, deconstruction theory, Al Haig, the Laffer Curve. All vanished down a black hole. But T. didn't go away. T. endured, T. overpowered all efforts of the will to resist him. He was like some crazy spirochete, attacking the mind with such remorseless insistence that I cannot now even type his name.

I first met him in the mid-'70s, in one of those rich men's houses in the Hamptons that are the permanent legacy of Jay Gatsby. T. was downy-faced then, a rich man's son just making

306

his moves out of the grinding tedium of collecting rents for his builder father in the obscure wastes of Brooklyn and Queens. He was pleasant. He was polite to his elders. And I don't remember a a goddamned thing he said.

But I soon began to notice T.'s name everywhere. After Ronald Reagan issued his license to steal, it was mentioned with respect—and then a kind of awe. Greed, after all, was the creed. Men still young enough to be lyric poets nattered away about LBOs and junk bonds and hostile takeovers and . . . T. Young men who had ducked Vietnam talked tough, and T. was the model for the style. The Reaganistas flourished. Infamy was piled upon infamy, and I would walk down Rodeo Drive or Madison Avenue, or hide on some southern island, and a new chant followed me everywhere. It had only one word: *more. More,* shouted the boys and girls of the '80s, we want *more, more, more.* Not gruel, of course. Ferraris and houses and dope and sex and money, yeah, *bucks,* yeah, and the biggest, greatest, most aphrodisiacal thing that money could buy, pal: *power!*

And the collective face of these boys and girls seemed to merge into one: the Golden Goy. T.

He owned the '80s. And he established his ownership by profoundly understanding the era. From the beginning, T. knew better than most that American journalism had degenerated into a fixation on nouns. I had been nurtured by a journalism of verbs: COP SHOT or PLANE CRASHES. After Vietnam and Watergate, nouns were usually enough. Proper nouns. What a person did was far less important than who he or she was. So T. applied himself to transforming himself into a brand name. He showered the gossip columns with factlets, staging those nonevents that brought out the noun photographers.

And, of course, he threw in a few verbs. He built some buildings. He bought others. He made them shine as brightly as newly borrowed coins. And he slapped his name on everything he owned: the T. Tower, the T. Parc, the T. Plaza, the T. Castle, and later, even the T. Shuttle. The crowd cheered. I must admit that in some peculiar way, I was one of them. When friends arrived from out of town, I always took them first to the lobby of the Tower.

The mysterious main character in F. Scott Fitzgerald's novel *The Great Gatsby* (1925), lived in a luxurious mansion on the wealthy Long Island shore, entertained hundreds of guests at lavish parties that had become legend on the island, and had accumulated enormous wealth by shady transactions.

As the contras were financed by the United States government, the "Reaganistas" had been given government license to maraud the economy. LBOs are leveraged buy-outs.

[""]

Pink marble! An eighty-foot indoor *waterfall!* The first truly American cathedral, dedicated to luxury, to a great blinding opulence, to . . . mammon! If T. hadn't existed, Tom Wolfe would have had to invent him.

And T. soon made clear he was only beginning. As the decade rolled on, he became the center of a gigantic self-created wind, the El Niño of hype, celebrating his own existence, his own absolutely delirious joy in excess. *More,* roared the crowd. I stared at his pores on the covers of *Time* and *Newsweek, New York* and *People,* trying to connect him to the nice young man I'd met in the Hamptons. I followed him through *Doonesbury.* I read about his wife, Ivana, and a few other stray relatives, desperately seeking the subjunctive, finding only nouns.

He had one immense triumph. For six baffled years, the New York City bureaucracy had managed to spend $12 million on refurbishing the Wollman skating rink in Central Park, and had failed dismally to get the job done. T. loudly offered to finish the job for the original price; he did it in three months and came in $750,000 under budget. That became a cornerstone of his reputation, a stirring example of the superiority of the genius of private enterprise over governmental incompetence. Instantly, T. became the hero of the age.

He also had his failures, of course. His USFL New Jersey Generals flopped. He couldn't get Television City, with its 150-story World's Tallest Building, to rise from Manhattan's West Side. He announced a T. Stadium for Queens, certain he could attract an NFL team; it withered away. Ah, well, the crowd sighed: you can't always get what you want.

But if you try sometime, of course, you get what you need. And T. clearly needed more. He buys a 727 for his personal use. He buys a ten-seat black Puma helicopter for commuting to his growing fiefdom in Atlantic City. He buys a 282-foot yacht; he brags he paid a measly $29 million for the boat, renames it the *T. Princess,* sails it to the Super Bowl last January, while smoke drifts through the air from the burning buildings of the Liberty City ghetto. He buys New York's venerable Plaza hotel for $390 million, says he'll put another $20 million into rehabbing it, and

Riches or material wealth, often personifying riches as an evil spirit. Tom Wolfe is an American journalist and novelist who has written much on pop culture.

Connotes falsity, exaggeration, and emptiness. Here it is a self-created ill wind, El Niño, associated with an ocean current that often causes catastrophic weather conditions. An extremely concentrated, destructive image.

names his wife president. After fixing up Mar-a-Lago, he discovers it's in the flight path of the new Palm Beach International Airport, which cost $62 million to build. His solution to the noise problem: move the airport.

Then he published The Book. I interviewed T. twice around this time. I couldn't help myself: I liked him and did not like myself for liking him. The raw need was so obvious, so authentic, so specific a fuel for his personal engine. He'd crossed the river from Queens and Brooklyn and, by Christ, he was never going back. And besides, how could you not feel some basic human pity for a man who talked about class and quality and then agreed to play himself in a John Derek movie?   11

But I had learned that pity was a most treacherous human emotion. I looked more coldly then, and listened. T. was not really the same young man I met long ago. He'd absorbed all the soul-numbing lessons of the '80s, and taught a few of his own. The Book was the essential text: "The other thing I do when I talk with reporters is to be straight. When a reporter asks me a tough question, I try to frame a positive answer, even if that means shifting the ground." I asked questions; he talked; the ground shifted. Alas, what he told me was no different from what he told *Time, Larry King Live! Today, 20/20, Donahue,* and Letterman. The art of the spiel. I never wrote the interview.   12

The Book was word-processed in the standardized plainsong of the ghostwriter, but it was faithful to the man. All over America, good novelists were wasting their writing hours teaching Am. lit. to sophomores; poets pumped gas; historians panhandled for grants. Their wares couldn't get shelf space. And in the bookstores of the country, *T.* became a roaring success. In a B. Dalton in Miami, I looked for a copy of *Moby-Dick* to give an ailing friend; there were no copies; they had more than a hundred copies of *T.*, and had already reordered. T. would not labor in the obscurity of the Custom House for thirty years. T. was a winner, in all that he touched, even the rusting American language. The Book sold over 800,000 copies in hardcover at $19.95 apiece. In its pages, T. revealed little about himself, and everything. "Deals are my art form," he said. That was the '80s. To the canvas, the symphony,   13

After pitying Trump for his vacuity, Hamill looks at him more coldly and passes harsh judgment.

Trump has become master of the spiel—high-flown language used to lure someone to buy something, often of questionable value—in this case himself.

the shelter, the novel, the sonnet, and the split-fingered fastball, T. had added The Deal. The ultimate '80s noun.

And then, the whole gaudy performance began to sicken me. 14 For a long time I'd made myself immune to the decade's porous values; I looked at the hard-eyed young people who embraced them with a mixture of irony and indifference. I was amused by T.; his shamelessness was so full of bullying joy and desperate need. But I thought that perhaps he had to go through this stage, and then, like the Robber Barons of an earlier time, he would calm down, take his clues from the Medicis, and use his wealth and name and power to Do Good. The Robber Barons, for all their ravenous appetites, left behind Carnegie Hall, the Frick Collection, the Morgan Library, and other ornaments of the culture.

Ruthlessly powerful United States capitalists and industrialists late in the nineteenth century, considered to have become wealthy by exploiting natural resources, corrupting legislatures, and using other unethical means.

The Medicis were an extremely wealthy and powerful Italian family who dominated Florence and Tuscany during the Renaissance; patrons of the arts.

But that hasn't happened with T. The royalties from The Book 15 went to charities, of course, and in some interviews he recognized that the country had problems (which could probably be solved by making T. president). But everywhere I went, the American cities were coming unraveled. A ghostly army of the homeless began emerging from the shadows. The plague of crack arrived, and the nights grew louder with Uzis. The casualties filled hospital wards and cemeteries; prisons groaned with new arrivals. While the ghettos rotted, the government sent development money to Beverly Hills. I wandered in and out of the stench of welfare hotels. I saw men eating from garbage cans.

And there was T., leading a *Time* reporter through his triplex 16 on top of the Tower, spread out over fifty rooms, with hand-carved marble columns and onyx baseboards. There was T., calling New York's Mayor Koch "a moron," claiming that "the Japs" were ripping us off, volunteering to negotiate an arms deal with Mikhail Gorbachev, bragging that he'd actually made $175 million by selling off just before the October 19, 1987, stock-market crash. There was T., easing out of real estate into the gambling rackets in Atlantic City, courting Mike Tyson.

In short, there was no growth, no maturity, no commitment 17 to use his wealth and power for the good of society. We saw only the self-assertion of a man who seemed to need, most of all, to see his name in print in order to know that he existed. And then

He Went Too Far. Last spring, when a gang of young black men assaulted and raped a young white woman jogging in New York's Central Park, the nation was horrified. Cops, politicians, sociologists, columnists, academics, and citizens all tried to understand this latest evidence of our barbarization in order to prevent its recurrence.

But T. had his own ideas. And he bought hundreds of thousands of dollars worth of advertising in the newspapers to make them known. His solution: bring back the death penalty and give the police a free hand. He did pay homage to "the fine and noble pursuit of genuine civil liberties." But then he made himself perfectly clear: 18

"Mayor Koch has stated that hate and rancor should be removed from our hearts. I do not think so. I want to hate these muggers and murderers. They should be forced to suffer and, when they kill, they should be executed for their crimes. . . . I want to hate these murderers and I always will. I am not looking to psychoanalyze or understand them, I am looking to punish them."   19

That was the perfect epitaph for the Odious '80s. Snarling and heartless and fraudulently tough, insisting on the virtues of stupidity, refusing any invitation to examine one's self, it was the epitome of blind negation. Hate was just another luxury. And T. stood naked, revealed as the spokesman for that tiny minority of Americans who lead well-defended lives. Forget poverty and its causes, forget the collapse of the manufacturing economy, forget the degradation and squalor of millions; fry them into passivity. When, a few months later, there was a notice in the gossip columns that T. was building a newer, bigger yacht to replace the *Princess,* the news had a sickening odor. I'm sure I wasn't the only American who yearned for a cold-cleansing wind to succeed the El Niño, sweeping away the whole smelly decade and all its common and proper nouns.   20

POSSIBLE ANSWERS

Meaning and Purpose

1. T. is Donald Trump, the entrepreneur extraordinaire of the 1980s. Unlike all the phenomena in the "Odious 80's" that have disappeared down a "black hole," T., the author claims, has invaded and overpowered his brain like "some crazy spirochete" (disease-producing or parasitic bacterium) so that Hamill cannot type T.'s name.

2. The essay outlines the meteoric career of Trump, his attitudes and character. But Trump serves as a symbol of the 1980s and what the decade represents to Hamill: mindless greed and self-aggrandizement.

3. Hamill wants to indict the 1980s for fostering greed and self-interest at the expense of real social needs. He uses T. as the decade's ultimate symbol of the destructive power of wealth and shameless hedonism.

4. The Reagan administration, which spanned most of the decade, deregulated much of industry, eliminating many economic constraints on big business. For Hamill and many others, deregulation ushered in a decade of privilege for the rich; making money by any means was not only legal, but chic (2).

5. The intimation in the last several paragraphs is that the rich and privileged were indulged during the 1980s while social problems grew silently and steadily.

6. Hamill is probably addressing (almost as a confession) mainly other people like himself who were taken in by T.'s success and style. He hopes to make those readers aware of the need to be more selfless and attend to poverty and homelessness and other social problems.

Strategy

1. Hamill says that "Ronald Reagan issued a license to steal," which made it trendy to be in awe of the power of T.'s money.

2. T.'s unbridled greed was an effect of a self-centered mindset in this country that the Reagan years gave rise to. Encourage students to use statements from the essay to support their opinions.

3. An immediate cause of the 1980s greed was the political and social look-out-for-yourself mentality that the Reagan years encouraged, desensitizing ourselves to those in real need and neglecting action on their behalf. Hamill explores these ultimate effects (15 to end).

4. Although earlier men of greed, the Robber Barons and the Medicis, left behind monuments of human merit (14), Trump (the 1980s) leaves behind the homeless, crack, and "men eating from garbage cans" (15). He opens up the hope (14) that some good will come from the 1980s greed, but paragraphs 15 and 16 show that the hope was in vain.

Meaning and Purpose

1. Who is T.? Why can't the author type his name (paragraph 1)?
2. Is the essay only about T., or about something else as well?
3. What is the purpose of this essay? What is the main thing Hamill wants to say?
4. In paragraph 3, Hamill claims that "Ronald Reagan issued his license to steal . . . ." What does he mean by that? How does it relate to the author's purpose?
5. Instead of wealth and privilege, crime and poverty are increasingly emphasized from paragraph 15 to the end of the essay. Why?
6. Who do you think Hamill's audience is, and why?

Strategy

1. What does Hamill give early in the essay as a cause behind T.'s rise to wealth and the respect paid him as an owner of the 1980s?
2. Decide whether you agree or disagree with the statement: T.'s brand of greed was both a cause and an effect. Then explain your position, using the essay to support it.
3. Does Hamill differentiate between immediate and ultimate causes and effects? Explain.
4. What effect does Hamill create by juxtaposing paragraphs 14 and 15?
5. Comment on the effectiveness of the final paragraph. In what ways does it summarize the sense of the rest of the essay?

Style

1. In paragraph 10, Hamill describes T.'s sailing to the Super Bowl: "while smoke drifts through the air from the burning buildings of the Liberty City ghetto." Why does Hamill include this sen-

tence in a paragraph otherwise devoted to describing wealth and luxury?

2. In your own words, explain this sentence: "He [T.] showered the gossip columns with factlets, staging those nonevents that brought out the noun photographers" (5).

3. What is Hamill's attitude toward T.? Point out some places in the essay that show this attitude.

4. How do the first three sentences in paragraph 17 set the reader up for the rest of the paragraph, as well as for paragraphs 18 and 19?

Writing Tasks

1. Hamill attempts to show what he sees as the greed and self-centeredness that epitomized the 1980s as at least a partial cause of the potentially vast social problems that will fully appear in the 1990s. Write a paper in which you concentrate on causes, as Hamill did, to show how they brought, or will bring, something into effect. But concentrate on something you know at first hand: why some of your acquaintances chose college or why others did not (or both); why some of your high-school acquaintances became involved with drugs or alcohol or why others did not (or both). Whichever you choose, make sure you describe each cause with specific, concrete examples.

2. Do you like or dislike "T. Without Sympathy"? Write a short essay in which you talk specifically about what in Hamill's essay causes your opinion of it.

5. Beginning with the statement that Trump's simplistic reaction to the assault and rape was the "perfect epitaph for the Odious 80's"(17), Hamill characterizes it as, among other things, "heartless and fraudulently tough," completely ignoring the causes of poverty, squalor, and crime. Hamill summarizes (17) the essay's whole message.

Style

1. While Trump sails his $29-million yacht to the Super Bowl (10), a fleeting whiff of reality intrudes in the form of smoke from a burning ghetto. The contrast of wealth and poverty is deliberately stark for emphasis.

2. Trump created his own fame that was no more than a glittering façade. Instead of news, there was gossip. Instead of facts, there was nonnews ("factlets"). He staged "nonevents" rather than events, attracting photographers who took pictures of glittering people (nouns) instead of news events.

3. Hamill is harshly judgmental of T. from the beginning, with the words "Odious '80s" (1) characterizing both the decade and the man. Even Hamill's being unable to type the full name is a gesture of disrespect. Hamill calls T. the "Golden Goy" (4), Yiddish for a non-Jewish person, and most often used disparagingly. The phrase then is a mean twist on "Golden Boy," which refers to a young man loaded with talent, fame, and honor. Words like "transforming himself into a brand name" (5), and "He slapped his name on everything he owned" (6), sound sarcastic. "T. loudly offered to finish the job," the "loudly" judges T. crass and self-serving (8). The first two sentences in paragraph 17 summarize T.'s character as unredeemable. In short, Hamill despises T. and all he stands for.

4. If the first three sentences of paragraph 17 are true, then Trump's reactions to the atrocity in Central Park are an empty, hollow sham.

❦ William Severini Kowinski ❦

William Kowinski grew up in Pennsylvania and attended Knox College in Illinois. He spent one semester at the University of Iowa studying fiction and poetry writing. His writing career, however, has been in nonfiction. To research his book, The Malling of America *(1985), Kowinski visited malls all over both the United States and Canada. He has been a writer and editor for the* Boston Phoenix *and for* Newsworks *of Washington, D.C., and his articles have appeared in* Esquire, The New York Times, *and the* New York Times Magazine.

Kids in the Mall:
Growing Up Controlled

Many American children grow up almost entirely in the controlled environments of home, school, and "the mall." What are the effects, Kowinski asks, of "growing up controlled"? The essay is from his book, The Malling of America: An Inside Look at the Great Consumer Paradise *(1985).*

TEACHING SUGGESTIONS

Many, if not most, of your students will have had first-hand and extensive mall experience. They can testify to the validity of Kowinski's observations, therefore, from immediate, first-hand knowledge—not always from an unbiased or critical perspective, perhaps, but from an extensive background nonetheless. Starting off by asking students to respond to the first two paragraphs can serve several purposes in getting them to evaluate the essay critically. First, because they will have personal knowledge, they will, we're sure, be able to add specific examples to the two that Kowinski gives in paragraph 1. This activity, logically enough, leads to an evaluation of his typical examples in paragraph 2. In turn, this examination could turn into a discussion of the author's strategy in the first three paragraphs to convince the reader of the importance of thinking about what spending so much time in the mall does to teenagers. Most students will probably agree with Kowinski's early observations. Many, no doubt, will object to his later, critical commentary. The question could then be asked: If his early factual observations seem on target, how does he go wrong in evaluating this behavior later on? No doubt some students will remain adamant in their uncritical acceptance of the behavior Kowinski describes. Others may start looking more objectively at his evaluation.

MARGINAL NOTES

Both specific examples the author gives are second-hand evidence, but this origin doesn't diminish their validity. On the contrary, they indicate that the author's observations are not isolated but widespread.

Butch heaved himself up and loomed over the group. "Like it was different for me," he piped. "My folks used to drop me off at the shopping mall every morning and leave me all day. It was like a big free baby-sitter, you know? One night they never came back for me. Maybe they moved away. Maybe there's some kind of a Bureau of Missing Parents I could check with." 1

—Richard Peck
Secrets of the Shopping Mall,
a novel for teenagers

From his sister at Swarthmore, I'd heard about a kid in Florida whose mother picked him up after school every day, drove him 2 straight to the mall, and left him there until it closed—all at his insistence. I'd heard about a boy in Washington who, when his family moved from one suburb to another, pedaled his bicycle five miles every day to get back to his old mall, where he once belonged.

These stories aren't unusual. The mall is a common experience for the majority of American youth; they have probably been going there all their lives. Some ran within their first large open space, saw their first fountain, bought their first toy, and read their first book in a mall. They may have smoked their first cigarette or first joint or turned them down, had their first kiss or lost their virginity in the mall parking lot. Teenagers in America now spend more time in the mall than anywhere else but home and school. Mostly it is their choice, but some of that mall time is put in as the result of two-paycheck and single-parent households, and the lack of other viable alternatives. But are these kids being harmed by the mall?

I wondered first of all what difference it makes for adolescents to experience so many important moments in the mall. They are, after all, at play in the fields of its little world and they learn its ways; they adapt to it and make it adapt to them. It's here that these kids get their street sense, only it's mall sense. They are learning the ways of a large-scale artificial environment: its subtleties and flexibilities, its particular pleasures and resonances, and the attitudes it fosters.

The presence of so many teenagers for so much time was not something mall developers planned on. In fact, it came as a big surprise. But kids became a fact of mall life very early, and the International Council of Shopping Centers found it necessary to commission a study, which they published along with a guide to mall managers on how to handle the teenage incursion.

The study found that "teenagers in suburban centers are bored and come to the shopping centers mainly as a place to go. Teenagers in suburban centers spent more time fighting, drinking, littering and walking than did their urban counterparts, but presented fewer overall problems." The report observed that "adolescents congregated in groups of two to four and predominantly

3 The first sentence serves as a transition and leads into the description of typical teenage mall activities. The examples are arranged chronologically to show typical stages in teenage development. The question at the end of the paragraph tells us that a cause-and-effect discussion will follow.

4

"Street sense" connotes hard-won practical knowledge; "mall sense" connotes a knowledge that is somehow separated and protected from the real world.

5 Paragraphs 5, 6, and 7 are grouped to show how mall developers were originally unprepared for the incursion by teenagers, how they then studied the phenomenon, and how, finally, the malls became finishing schools for kids who had already been indoctrinated into the consumer ethic.

6

at locations selected by them rather than management." This probably had something to do with the decision to install game arcades, which allow management to channel these restless adolescents into naturally contained areas away from major traffic points of adult shoppers.

The guide concluded that mall management should tolerate and even encourage the teenage presence because, in the words of the report, "The vast majority support the same set of values as does shopping center management." *The same set of values* means simply that mall kids are already preprogrammed to be consumers and that the mall can put the finishing touches to them as hard-core, lifelong shoppers just like everybody else. That, after all, is what the mall is about. So it shouldn't be surprising that in spending a lot of time there, adolescents find little that challenges the assumption that the goal of life is to make money and buy products, or that just about everything else in life is to be used to serve those ends.

Growing up in a high-consumption society already adds inestimable pressure to kids' lives. Clothes consciousness has invaded the grade schools, and popularity is linked with having the best, newest clothes in the currently acceptable styles. Even what they read has been affected. "Miss [Nancy] Drew wasn't obsessed with her wardrobe," noted *The Wall Street Journal,* "but today the mystery in teen fiction for girls is what outfit the heroine will wear next." Shopping has become a survival skill and there is certainly no better place to learn it than the mall, where its importance is powerfully reinforced and certainly never questioned.

Kowinski cites authority to demonstrate that the seemingly benevolent mall of the preceding paragraph can actually be psychologically damaging.

The mall as a university of suburban materialism, where Valley Girls and Boys from coast to coast are educated in consumption, has its other lessons in this era of change in family life and sexual mores and their economic and social ramifications. The plethora of products in the mall, plus the pressure on teens to buy them, may contribute to the phenomenon that psychologist David Elkind calls "the hurried child": kids who are exposed to too much of the adult world too quickly, and must respond with a sophistication that belies their still-tender emotional development. Certainly the adult products marketed for children—form-

7

8

9

fitting designer jeans, sexy tops for preteen girls—add to the social pressure to look like an adult, along with the home-grown need to understand adult finances (why mothers must work) and adult emotions (when parents divorce).

Kids spend so much time at the mall partly because their parents allow it and even encourage it. The mall is safe, it doesn't seem to harbor any unsavory activities, and there is adult supervision; it is, after all, a controlled environment. So the temptation, especially for working parents, is to let the mall be their babysitter. At least the kids aren't watching TV. But the mall's role as a surrogate mother may be more extensive and more profound.   10

Karen Lansky, a writer living in Los Angeles, has looked into the subject and she told me some of her conclusions about the effects on its teenaged denizens of the mall's controlled and controlling environment. "Structure is the dominant idea, since true 'mall rats' lack just that in their home lives," she said, "and adolescents about to make the big leap into growing up crave more structure than our modern society cares to acknowledge." Karen pointed out some of the elements malls supply that kids used to get from their families, like warmth (Strawberry Shortcake dolls and similar cute and cuddly merchandise), old-fashioned mothering ("We do it all for you," the fast-food slogan), and even home cooking (the "homemade" treats at the food court).   11

The problem in all this, as Karen Lansky sees it, is that while families nurture children by encouraging growth through the assumption of responsibility and then by letting them rest in the bosom of the family from the rigors of growing up, the mall as a structural mother encourages passivity and consumption, as long as the kid doesn't make trouble. Therefore all they learn about becoming adults is how to act and how to consume.   12   In this paragraph real psychological growth that involves active acceptance of responsibility is contrasted with the mall's promotion of passive consumption. This passivity is further emphasized in the opening sentence of the next paragraph.

Kids are in the mall not only in the passive role of shoppers— they also work there, especially as fast-food outlets infiltrate the mall's enclosure. There they learn how to hold a job and take responsibility, but still within the same value context. When *CBS Reports* went to Oak Park Mall in suburban Kansas City, Kansas, to tape part of their hour-long consideration of malls, "After the Dream Comes True," they interviewed a teenaged girl who   13 worked in a fast-food outlet there. In a sequence that didn't make the final program, she described the major goal of her present life, which was to perfect the curl on top of the ice-cream cones that were her store's specialty. If she could do that, she would be moved from the lowly soft-drink dispenser to the more prestigious ice-cream division, the curl on top of the status ladder at her restaurant. These are the achievements that are important at the mall.

Other benefits of such jobs may also be overrated, according 14 to Laurence D. Steinberg of the University of California at Irvine's social ecology department, who did a study on teenage employment. Their jobs, he found, are generally simple, mindlessly repetitive and boring. They don't really learn anything, and the jobs don't head anywhere. Teenagers also work primarily with other teenagers; even their supervisors are often just a little older than they are. "Kids need to spend time with adults," Steinberg told me. "Although they get benefits from peer relationships, without parents and other adults it's a one-sided socialization. They hang out with each other, have age-segregated jobs, and watch TV."

Perhaps much of this is not so terrible or even so terribly 15 different. Now that they have so much more to contend with in their lives, adolescents probably need more time to spend with other adolescents without adult impositions, just to sort things out. Though it is more concentrated in the mall (and therefore perhaps a clearer target), the value system there is really the dominant one of the whole society. Attitudes about curiosity, initiative, self-expression, empathy, and disinterested learning aren't necessarily made in the mall; they are mirrored there, perhaps a bit more intensely—as through a glass brightly.

Besides, the mall is not without its educational opportunities. 16 There are bookstores, where there is at least a short shelf of classics at great prices, and other books from which it is possible to learn more than how to do sit-ups. There are tools, from hammers to VCRs, and products, from clothes to records, that can help the young find and express themselves. There are older people with stories, and places to be alone or to talk one-on-one with a kindred spirit. And there is always the passing show.

The meaninglessness of teenage mall employment in the preceding paragraph is assaulted a second time by citing academic authority.

Because the author has already established that mall teenagers have been conditioned as consumers before they ever became mall denizens and have now completed their consumer higher education, the likelihood is slight that they will ever assimilate this list of deeper values.

A sad irony colors this entire paragraph. Though the mall has objects with educational value, they will never be bought or used by mall children. And though older people with stories are there—knowledge used to be handed down from the old to the young in stories—the stories will not be heard. Instead, teenagers will just watch the "passing show."

The mall itself may very well be an education about the future. 17
I was struck with the realization, as early as my first forays into
Greengate, that the mall is only one of a number of enclosed and
controlled environments that are part of the lives of today's young.
The mall is just an extension, say, of those large suburban
schools—only there's Karmelkorn instead of chem lab, the ice
rink instead of the gym: It's high school without the impertinence
of classes.

Growing up, moving from home to school to the mall—from 18
enclosure to enclosure, transported in cars—is a curiously continuous process, without much in the way of contrast or contact with
unenclosed reality. Places must tend to blur into one another. But
whatever differences and dangers there are in this, the skills these
adolescents are learning may turn out to be useful in their later
lives. For we seem to be moving inexorably into an age of pre-
planned and regulated environments, and this is the world they
will inherit.

Still, it might be better if they had more of a choice. One 19
teenaged girl confessed to *CBS Reports* that she sometimes felt she
was missing something by hanging out at the mall so much. "But
I'm here," she said, "and this is what I have."

Meaning and Purpose

1. What has been your experience in malls? What is your response
   to Kowinski's essay? Do you agree or disagree with him? Do you
   identify with the situations he describes?
2. What primary questions does the author attempt to answer in
   the essay? What is the thesis and where is it stated?
3. What negative effects does growing up in the mall have on
   children? Are there any positive effects?
4. Whom is Kowinski addressing in this essay? Who should hear
   his message?

POSSIBLE ANSWERS

Meaning and Purpose

1. Most students will probably have experiences to relate about shopping malls. Encourage them to compare their experiences with
the situations Kowinski talks about.
2. Kowinski asks, "Are these kids being
harmed by the mall?" (3). His thesis is the last
sentence in paragraph 4. The thesis does not
completely answer the question because he has
yet to explore the values of the mall environment and the extent of their effects on kids.
3. Kowinski points out all through the essay
that mall life hones to a fine edge kids' already
accepted false assumptions that life's primary
goal is to buy and consume (7). Probably the
most damaging effect the mall has on our kids
is serving as a surrogate nurturing mother and
family (10–12). All the mall's positive effects
are described ironically.

4. Teenagers themselves would probably have their eyes opened by some of the facts Kowinski presents. But certainly the parents of mall teenagers would benefit most from reading this article. The information, the language, and the authorities cited suggest that adults are the target audience.

5. Kowinski's values can be determined by simply inverting the values he finds disconcerting—in his title, in his discussion of consumerism, and particularly in his description of the mall serving as a surrogate family (10–12). More explicitly, he lists attitudes he finds valuable that are not made in the mall: "curiosity, initiative, self-expression, empathy, and disinterested learning" (15).

Strategy

1. Kowinski cites two specific examples, both tinged with dark humor, of kids who live at malls (2). He switches to typical examples to show how many children have gone through typical milestones of development at the mall (3). He speculates about all that important experience happening in an artificial environment and states his thesis in the final sentence (4).

2. The immediate cause is the "plethora of products in the mall, plus the pressure on teens to buy them." The effect from this cause is both immediate and ultimate—"the hurried child"—who must grow up too fast. This child learns how to shop in the short term, but in the longer term, he or she is pressured to look like an adult and to understand adult finances and emotions.

3. Superficially the two examples seem contradictory, but they are almost totally unlike. First, children are pressured to act in adult ways sexually and emotionally far beyond their own emotional development. Second, children just beginning to face responsibilities in the public work force need adult models on which to base their own behavior.

4. The cause of kids' spending time in the mall

5. Can a careful reading of the essay establish the author's values? What are they? Where are these attitudes evident?

Strategy

1. Paragraphs 2–4 serve as the essay's introduction. How does each function independently? How do they fit together to form the larger unit?

2. Does Kowinski talk about immediate or ultimate causes and effects in paragraph 9? Explain.

3. Compare paragraphs 9 and 14. In paragraph 9, Kowinski describes "the hurried child syndrome," the negative effect on a child who is too quickly exposed to the adult world and must respond with a sophistication still beyond him or her. In paragraph 14, discussing how teenagers who work in malls work mostly with other teenagers, Kowinski cites an authority who claims kids need more time in their work with adults. Do you see a contradiction here?

4. A related cause-and-effect structure is visible in paragraphs 10–12. What is it and how does it work?

5. Study the structure of paragraph 18. How does it contribute to the essayist's main purpose of showing how stultifying and controlling malls are for teenagers?

Style

1. Comment on the effects of the final sentence in paragraph 13 on the rest of the paragraph. What does it say about the mall experience as a whole?

2. What is Kowinski's attitude toward his subject? Where is this attitude manifest?

3. If necessary, look up the meanings of these words: *resonances* (4), *inclusion* (5), *plethora* (9), *denizens* (11), *impertinence* (17), *inexorably* (18).

Writing Tasks

1. Kowinski takes a rather dim view of what happens to kids when they "grow up" in a mall. Write an essay in which you either show that mall experiences do not have such dire consequences, or agree with Kowinski. Either way, draw from your own experience or that of those you know. Be sure to discuss immediate and ultimate causes and effects, either alternately in the same paragraphs, or in separate paragraphs.
2. Think of a place, other than a mall, where you spent a lot of time during your teenage years—a hangout of some sort. What do you think some of the immediate and ultimate effects were and are from your having spent time there? Answer this question in a short essay. Be specific.

is that parents allow or encourage it (10). Kids' spending time at the mall becomes a cause of the mall's role of surrogate parent, which is the effect, but then this role itself becomes a cause (11) of structure being imposed on kids and elements of family life. Because kids crave structure and family life, they are drawn to cuddly merchandise and "home cooking." These elements in turn are causes, and their effects are that kids embrace passivity and consumerism. The whole progression is a causal chain.

5. Paragraph 18 is divided into two parts. The first two sentences describe how frighteningly insulated a child's mall existence is and how, therefore, every place becomes the same place. The next two sentences project that this is actually a good preparation for the future they face. In the first part, Kowinski looks back at the essay and encapsulates the experience he has just described, and in the second he looks forward to an ominous future.

Style

1. After describing how a teenage girl's major ambition was to learn how to put the perfect swirl on an ice-cream cone in order to gain a promotion in the company she worked for, and then to call that "achievement," makes a mockery of the emptiness and vapidity of the entire mall experience. Compare that to the achievement of "attitudes" (15).

2. Kowinski seems sympathetic toward his subject. He both acknowledges and understands the problem of teenagers in malls (first sentence in 4, 8, and 10). Still, he sees the dangers and hopes for a better choice for teenagers (7, first sentence, 19).

3. *Resonances*: the states or qualities of resounding or echoing; *incursion*: a hostile entrance into or invasion of a place or territory, especially a hostile one; *plethora*: overabundance, excess; *denizens*: inhabitants, residents; *impertinence*: unmannerly intrusion or presumption, insolence; *inexorably*: unyieldingly, unalterably.

Some students "slot" people, putting scientists into their scientific slot, artists into their artistic slot, and so on, not realizing that scientists, artists, and advertisers greatly yet subtly affect our thinking, acting, and perceiving.

You might want to open a class discussion by talking about the modern automobile, a combination of artistic, scientific, and advertising pragmatics. When an automobile is designed, is it designed from an engineering standpoint or from an artistic standpoint? (Any mechanic who has worked on a recently designed automobile will assure you that nobody designs an automobile with repairs in mind.) If an automobile is designed from an artistic standpoint, does the art differ greatly from the art that went into other automobiles? If an automobile is designed from an engineering standpoint, does the engineering differ greatly from the engineering that went into other automobiles? When the automobiles are advertised, as on television, are they shown realistically? Or are they shown in beautiful surroundings or in humorous ways that effectively manipulate the viewers' minds?

The discussion that grows from the questions above helps prepare students having little knowledge of art to understand Kuh's essay, which concludes with a statement about the coalescing of contemporary art and modern science.

MARGINAL NOTES

The vocabulary in this paragraph suggests total destruction, but with artistic design. "Dissolution" suggests dissolving or termination, but "disintegration" suggests "taking apart," as opposed to "integration." Notice the play on words: "breaking up" versus "breaking down." An artist is, by definition, disciplined.

❦ Katherine Kuh ❦

Katherine Kuh was born in 1904 and attended Vassar College and the University of Chicago, where she did graduate work in fine arts. From 1936 to 1943 she directed the Katherine Kuh Gallery in Chicago, which specialized in modern art. She was curator at the Art Institute of Chicago for thirteen years and has also been the art editor for Saturday Review. *Kuh has been a visiting professor of art at the University School of Fine Arts in San Miguel, Mexico, and in 1946 she did a survey of Alaskan Indian totemic art for the U.S. Office of Indian Affairs. She has lectured on art throughout the United States and Canada since 1950 and has published extensively on art and the artist.*

Break-Up:
The Core of Modern Art

In this essay from her book by the same title (1965), Kuh examines the relation between experiments and innovations in modern art in the past century and concurrent scientific developments. She sees a correlation between the "break-up" of all aspects of art in recent history and the development of technology but ends by questioning which is cause and which effect.

The art of our century has been characterized by shattered surfaces, broken color, segmented compositions, dissolving forms and shredded images. Curiously insistent is this consistent emphasis on break-up. However, dissolution today does not necessarily mean lack of discipline. It can also mean a new kind of discipline, for disintegration is often followed by reconstruction, the artist deliberately smashing his material only to reassemble it in new and unexpected relationships. Moreover, the process of breaking up is quite different from the process of breaking down.

322

And during the last hundred years, every aspect of art has been broken up—color, light, pigment, form, line, content, space, surface and design.

In the nineteenth century, easels were moved out-of-doors and color was broken into relatively minute areas in order to approximate the reality of sunlight and to preserve on canvas nature's own fleeting atmospheric effects. Known as impressionism, this movement was the first step in a long sequence of experiments that finally banished the Renaissance emphasis on humanism, on three-dimensional form and on a traditional center of interest. Here was the beginning of a gradual but steady tendency toward diffusion in art. A few years later, Vincent Van Gogh transformed broken color into broken pigment. Less interested in realistic light than in his own highly charged emotions, he allowed smashing rhythmic brush-strokes to mirror his personal turbulence. In doing so he foretold twentieth-century Expressionism, that aptly named movement which relied on pitted surfaces, broken outlines, unpredictable color and scarred textures to intensify emotional expression. As the Impressionists were bent on freeing nature from sham, so the Expressionists hoped to liberate their own feelings from all trace of artificiality.

Perhaps the most revolutionary break-up in modern art took place a little more than fifty years ago with the advent of Cubism. It was the Cubists, Picasso, Braque, Duchamp, Picabia, Léger, Delaunay and Juan Gris, who responded to the inordinate multiplicity of present-day life by breaking up and arbitrarily rearranging transparent planes and surfaces so that all sides of an object could be seen at once. As the Cubists broke through the boundaries of conventional form to show multiple aspects simultaneously, their Italian colleagues, the Futurists, hoped to encompass the uninterrupted motion of an object at one time. This they tried to do by a series of overlapping transparent forms illustrating the path of an object as it moved through space.

With Surrealism came still another kind of break-up, the breakup of chronology. Frankly influenced by Freudian discoveries, this movement splintered time sequence with an abandon borrowed from the world of fragmented dreams. Content was

2

Impressionism, coined in 1874 after Monet's painting "Impression, sunrise," aims to capture a momentary glimpse of a subject; to reproduce the changing effects of light by applying paint to canvas in short strokes of pure color; to retain the impression the object makes on the artist.

Vincent Van Gogh (1853–1890): Dutch painter whose notable canvases are, among others, *The Potato Eaters* and *Restaurant on Montmarte*. Expressionism aims to objectify and transmit an inner experience by retaining the impression the artist makes on the object.

3

Cubism fragments the object into cubes and other geometric forms—Picasso called them "destructions"—and then rearranges them into a new and meaningful synthesis—Picasso called it "sum of destructions."

4

Surrealism aims to capture, seemingly without conscious control, the expression of the imagination as realized in dreams. Sigmund Freud (1856–1939) founded psychoanalysis. In his system, the great source of psychic energy is the unconscious, which influences all our actions. He developed a theory that dreams are an unconscious representation of repressed desires.

Abstract expressionism aims to derive meaning from the arrangement of colors and shapes, without representing objects. Abstractions are severe abridgments, in this case abridgments of artists' psychological statements to themselves and to their surroundings.

After briefly outlining the break-up of art in our century, Kuh does not ignore the obvious cause: wars and modern methods of destruction affecting our daily thinking. But she points out that the most recent cause is not necessarily the most important. We are asked to think cumulatively, instead of believing that whatever is recent is the only cause.

purposely unhinged in denial of all rational expression, allowing disconnected episodes to re-create the disturbing life of our unconscious. At the same time, perspective and distance often became severely dislocated. Denying the orderly naturalism of the Renaissance, painters today project space and distance from innumerable eye levels, intentionally segmenting their compositions into conflicting perspectives. We look from above, from below, from diverse angles, from near, from far—all at one and the same time (not an unfamiliar experience for eyes accustomed to air travel). Here again is the Cubist idea of simultaneity, the twentieth-century urge to approach a scene from many different directions in a single condensed encounter.

Finally we come to the total break-up of Abstract Expressionism, a technique that celebrates the specific act of painting (sometimes appropriately called Action Painting). Now everything is shattered—line, light, color, form, pigment, surface and design. These canvases defy all the old rules as they reveal the immediate spontaneous feelings of the artist in the process of painting. There is no one central idea, no beginning, no end—only an incessant flow and flux where lightning brushstrokes report the artist's impulsive and compulsive reactions. The pigment actually develops a life of its own, almost strong enough to hypnotize the painter. Here break-up turns into both content and form, with the impetuous paint itself telling the full story. No naturalistic image is needed to describe these artists' volatile feelings.

As one looks back over the last hundred years, the history of break-up becomes a key to the history of art. Why painters and sculptors of this period have been so involved with problems of dissolution is a question only partly answered by the obvious impact of modern scientific methods of destruction. One cannot deny that the last two devastating wars and the possibility of a still more devastating one to come do affect our daily thinking. Since the discovery of the atom bomb, science has become almost synonymous with destruction. The influence of contemporary warfare with its colossal explosions and upheavals has unquestionably had much to do with the tendency toward fragmentation in art, but there have been other and earlier causes.

From the beginning, it was science in one form or another that affected modern painting and sculpture. In nineteenth-century Europe the interest in atmospheric phenomena was not an isolated expression limited to the Impressionists. At that time, numerous scientists were experimenting with all manner of optical color laws, writing widely on the subject as they investigated the relationship of color to the human eye. Artists like Monet and Seurat were familiar with these findings and not unnaturally applied them to their paintings. It would be a grave mistake to underestimate the influence of contemporary scientific research on the development of Impressionism. The wonders of natural light became a focus for nineteenth-century artists exactly as the magic of artificial light stimulated painters of the precentury. If the earlier men were more interested in rural landscapes seen out-of-doors in the sunlight, the later artists quite reasonably concentrated on city scenes, preferably at night when man-made luminosity tends to puncture both form and space.

Other scientific investigations also exerted considerable influence on present-day painters and sculptors. Inventions like the microscope and telescope, with their capacity to enlarge, isolate and probe, offer the artist provocative new worlds to explore. These instruments, which break up structures only to examine them more fully, demonstrate how details can be magnified and separated from the whole and operate as new experiences. Repeatedly artists in recent years have exploited this idea, allowing one isolated symbol to represent an entire complex organism. Miró often needs merely part of a woman's body to describe all women, or Léger, one magnified letter of the alphabet to conjure up the numberless printed words that daily bombard us.

As scientists smash the atom, so likewise artists smash traditional forms. For how, indeed, can anyone remain immune to the new mushroom shape that haunts us day and night? The American painter, Morris Graves, put it well recently, "You simply can't keep the world out any longer. Like everyone else, I've been caught in our scientific culture." This is not to say that painters are interested in reproducing realistic scenes of atomic explosions, but rather that they are concerned with the reactions

7   Kuh puts to rest the myth that artists and their art are somehow uniquely removed from life. One cannot neatly categorize art historically. Kuh has begun her main argument, that scientific discoveries and experiments have contributed heavily to artists' works.

Monet, Claude (1840–1926): French landscape painter, recognized as one of the greatest impressionists. Seurat, Georges (1859–1891): French painter known as the founder, with Paul Signac, of neoimpressionism, a theory and practice of painting based on strict scientific application of impressionist techniques, especially pointillism, in which tiny points of pure color are used to cover a white ground systematically, the points blending when seen from a distance.

8   Expanding her argument, Kuh introduces as evidence other scientific workings and their catalytic effects on art.

Miró, Joan (1893–1983): Spanish painter, engraver, and sculptor identified with the cubists. Léger, Fernand (1881–1955): French painter identified with the cubists.

9   An expansion of paragraph 6. Notice the rhetorical question, Kuh's inferring that the effects of scientific discoveries permeate all our thinking. Artists are not disturbed about atomic explosions; rather, they worry about the effects of those explosions, the resulting atomization of their surroundings. As used

326 *Cause and Effect*

here, *intuition* refers to direct and immediate perception, arrived at without reflective thinking.

The X-ray was discovered in 1895, by Wilhelm Conrad Roentgen, a German physicist. The author here moves from her topic into a general statement of how science directs our thinking.

Modern art and popular dance might be two socially different reflections of the same causes, scientific endeavors over the centuries. *Kinetic* here means abrupt body movement and movements of specific body parts. In art, *staccato* describes works including distinct elements fragmented abruptly by space.

The speed in all our lives causes us to receive too much information too fast to interpret. Instead, we pull together fragments of information, making new information that does not always carry the original information's intended meaning.

The artist's creative mind finds new ways to use recently developed materials and tools, effectively joining science, technology, and art.

accompanying these disasters. It is just possible that, with their extra-sensitized intuition, artists may have unconsciously predicted the discovery of atomic energy long before "the bomb" became a familiar household word, for the history of break-up in art antedates the history of nuclear break-up.

Even the invention of the X-ray machine has brought us closer 10 to penetrating form. We no longer think of outer coverings as solid or final; we know they can be visually pierced merely by rendering them transparent. We have also learned from science that space penetrates everything.

The sculptor Gabo claims, "Space is a reality in all of our 11 experiences and it is present in every object. . . . That's what I've tried to show in certain of my stone carvings. When they turn, observe how their curved forms seem interpenetrated by space." For the artist today, nothing is static or permanent. The new popular dances are no more potently kinetic than the new staccato art forms that everywhere confront us.

With the dramatic development of speedier transportation 12 and swifter communication comes a visual overlapping responsible for much of contemporary art. In modern life one is simultaneously subjected to countless experiences that become fragmented, superimposed, and finally rebuilt into new experiences. Speed is a cogent part of our daily life.

How natural, then, that artists reflect this pressure by show- 13 ing all sides of an object, its entire motion, its total psychological content in one concerted impact. It is almost as if the pressures of time had necessitated a visual speed-up not unlike the industrial one associated with the assembly line and mass production. Speed with its multiple overlays transforms our surroundings into jagged, interrupted images.

Modern technology and science have produced a wealth of 14 new materials and new ways of using old materials. For the artist this means wider opportunities. There is no doubt that the limitations of materials and nature of tools both restrict and shape a man's work. Observe how the development of plastics and light metals along with new methods of welding and brazing have changed the direction of sculpture. Transparent plastic materials allow one to look through an object, to see its various sides superimposed on each other (as in Cubism or in an X ray). Today, welding is as prevalent as casting was in the past. This new method encourages open designs, often of great linear agility, where surrounding and intervening space becomes as important as form itself. In fact, it becomes a kind of negative form. While bronze casting and stone carving are techniques more readily adapted to solid volumes, welding permits perforated metal designs of extreme versatility that free sculpture from the static restrictions which for centuries have moored it to the floor.

More ambiguous than other scientific inventions familiar to modern artists, but no less influential, are the psychoanalytic studies of Freud and his followers, discoveries that have infiltrated recent art, especially Surrealism. The Surrealists, in their struggle to escape the monotony and frustrations of everyday life, claimed that dreams were the only hope. Turning to the irrational world of their unconscious, they banished all time barriers and moral judgments to combine disconnected dream experiences from the past, present and intervening psychological states. The Surrealists were concerned with overlapping emotions more than with overlapping forms. Their paintings often become segmented capsules of associative experiences. For them, obsessive and often unrelated images replaced the direct emotional messages of Expressionism. They did not need to smash pigment and texture; they went beyond this to smash the whole continuity of logical thought.

There is little doubt that contemporary art has taken much from contemporary life. In a period when science has made revolutionary strides, artists in their studios have not been unaware of scientists in their laboratories. But this has rarely been a one-way street. Painters and sculptors, though admittedly influenced by modern science, have also molded and changed our world. If break-up has been a vital part of their expression, it has not always been a symbol of destruction. Quite the contrary: it has been used to examine more fully, to penetrate more deeply, to analyze more thoroughly, to enlarge, isolate and make more familiar certain aspects of life that earlier we were apt to neglect.

15   After discovering the phenomenon of the unconscious, Freud developed a technique for analyzing dreams. He discovered narcissism and then interpreted human behavior by means of one innate drive, Eros, the force of love. Later, Freud revised his theory of instinctual drives by introducing the death instinct, Thanatos, and destructive energy.

Carl Gustav Jung (1875–1961), one of Freud's associates, wrote that the "collective unconscious" holds acquired traits and cultural patterns universally transmitted by heredity, and the "personal unconscious," different in each person, consists of subliminal perceptions; repressed, suppressed, forgotten, and ignored experiences; and personal fantasies and dreams.

16

Art preserves the history of the senses. Just as science has changed social history including art, art itself has interpreted scientific events. Art and science carry on a cyclic affair. Science influences art, and art interprets science— together they continue to organize and change our experiences.

Meaning and Purpose

1. Encourage students to tell what they know about the different kinds of art Kuh discusses. If a lot of the information is new for students, ask them to talk about the difficulty or ease of following Kuh's history and of understanding all her terminology and references.
2. The original audience already had some background in art. Kuh's essay has few definitions of its art terms.
3. The thesis is the first sentence in paragraph 6. The rest of the essay supports this statement with examples of how and why art has been broken up.
4. The word "Break-Up" in the title connects to the essay immediately in paragraph 1 with "shattered surfaces, broken color, segmented compositions, dissolving forms and shredded images." Kuh mentions break-up directly three times in this paragraph. That break-up is the "Core of Modern Art" has yet to be established, but it is asserted in the thesis.
5. Kuh states the main cause of break-up in modern art in her thesis paragraph (6) when she says that scientific methods of destruction, wars, and (7) simply "science in one form or another" all have affected modern art.

Strategy

1. In paragraphs 2–5, Kuh gives a chronological synopsis of the progression of art trends from Impressionism to Abstract Expressionism. One technique led to the next in a causal chain. In paragraphs 7–14, Kuh does the same thing with scientific advances, showing how each was the cause of some new form or material in art. This new form or material in turn led to the next innovation—and we have another causal chain. In her final paragraph she restates the cause-and-effect connection between life and art and shows art as a cause of yet another effect: it "provides rich multiple experiences so organized as not merely to reflect our world, but in fact to interpret it."

In addition, it sometimes provides rich multiple experiences so organized as not merely to reflect our world, but in fact to interpret it.

Meaning and Purpose

1. How many of the art terms in Kuh's essay were you already familiar with? Do you find much new information in this essay, and, if so, how does it affect your reading?
2. What kind of people comprised the original audience for this essay? Why do you think so?
3. Where does Kuh state her thesis?
4. When in the reading does the title become meaningful for you?
5. From reading Kuh's essay, what do you think the main cause of "break-up" in modern art has been?

Strategy

1. After another careful reading, outline briefly the cause-and-effect structure of the essay.
2. In paragraph 12, the author says that "Speed is a cogent part of our daily lives." What does "cogent" mean? In your opinion, is the author correct? Why or why not?
3. What is one clear cause-and-effect sentence in the essay? Explain how it works in its immediate and larger context.
4. In the last paragraph, Kuh says, "If break-up has been a vital part of their [painters' and sculptors'] expression, it has not always been a symbol of destruction." Review the essay and decide whether you think Kuh has established this as an effect of advances in science.

Style

1. Study this sentence from paragraph 2, about Van Gogh: "Less interested in realistic light than in his own highly charged emotions, he allowed smashing rhythmic brush-strokes to mirror his personal turbulence." What feelings and images does this sentence create for you?
2. Paragraph 6 includes the sentence "Since the discovery of the atom bomb, science has become almost synonymous with destruction." Recast the information in that sentence into a clear and obvious cause-and-effect sentence.
3. What is Kuh's attitude toward her subject? What is the tone of the essay?

Writing Tasks

1. Commercial art tries to cause a specific effect on a large, diverse audience. Scan an advertisement that uses commercial art. What effect is it supposed to cause? Is the effect immediate, ultimate, or both? Write an essay in which you explain the effects. Attach a copy of the advertisement to your paper.
2. Choose a field or subject other than art—agriculture, higher education, cable television—and trace its development and changes during a specified period. Set up your essay in a causal-chain structure where one thing causes the next, and the next, and so on. Make the transitions clear.

2. "Cogent" means "having power to compel or constrain; appealing forcibly to the mind or reason." The final sentence in paragraph 12 is its topic sentence, and those before it support it with examples. Students might or might not agree with Kuh here. Ask them for specific examples of the effects of "speed" in their lives.
3. One example is in paragraph 14: "Observe how the development of plastics. . . . "
4. Kuh shows in several places that changes in artistic techniques caused by new developments in science are not necessarily destructive. Some examples: in paragraph 8, "Inventions like the microscope and telescope, with their capacity to enlarge, isolate and probe, offer the artist provocative new worlds to explore"; in paragraph 12, "With the dramatic development of speedier transportation and swifter communication comes a visual overlapping responsible for much of contemporary art"; and in paragraph 14, "Today, welding is as prevalent as casting was in the past. This new method encourages open designs, often of great linear agility. . . ."

Style

1. The expressions "highly charged," "smashing rhythmic," and "personal turbulence" all suggest chaos, fragmentation, frenzied movement. This sentence has an unsettling feeling, and perhaps one of both destruction and innovation. The sentence is strong stylistically, dynamic and evocative.
2. One way in which the sentence could be recast is this: "The discovery of the atom bomb [cause] has made science a synonym for destruction [effect]."
3. From the breadth of information in the essay and the compact chronology, one could say that Kuh is authoritative and sure of what she says. She is convinced of a clear connection between science and art. She is knowledgeable about artistic terminology and descriptive words. The article has an academic yet readable tone. Ask students to point out some sentences that illustrate this tone, such as the last sentence in paragraph 7.

❦ Additional Writing Tasks ❦
Cause and Effect

1. Using cause and effect (or one of the two alone) as the dominant development pattern, write an essay explaining something that interests you. These general questions are offered as ways to get you started. Revise them in any way that reflects your interests and then in a well-developed essay answer them, using the principles of cause and effect or one of the two.
    a. Why do works by some artists, filmmakers, poets, or novelists affect you?
    b. Why do people need "idols," such as singers, athletes, actors, and politicians?
    c. Why does a television series—police drama, situation comedy, talk show—succeed?
    d. What are the effects of music lyrics that some political activists believe are obscene and condone violence?
    e. What are the effects of stand-up comedians who deliver monologues that critics claim are racist and sexist?
    f. Why are stories that repeat familiar formulas successful?
    g. Is common sense an effective way to solve complex problems?
    h. Is routine the great deadener or do we need it to organize experience?
    i. Is homelessness a "real" problem in America?
    j. Can government solve the national-deficit problem by printing more money?
    k. Should children be seen and not heard?
    l. What results can you expect from an education?
    m. Is deceit self-destructive?
    n. Should children be made to feel guilty as a way of controlling teenage recklessness?
    o. Why should a dieter avoid eating foods high in fat?
    p. What causes stress and what are its temporary and lasting effects?
    q. What are the effects of a mental illness?

     r.   Why does the destruction of symbols such as the American flag enrage some people?

     s.   What would happen if everyone were given the college degree of his or her choice without completing course work?

2.   Discuss one of these subjects in an essay using cause and effect (or one of the two) as the dominant pattern.

     a.   Violence has always been a major element in action-oriented entertainment, from Flash Gordon to Indiana Jones. In recent years, however, action-oriented children's television cartoons, such as "G.I. Joe" and "Rambo," have become stripped of story line of any value and of characterization. The shows present unrelenting karate chopping and related mayhem and "us versus them" worlds with little or no complexity. Currently, some experts and a growing number of parents are beginning to worry about the possible harmful effects these shows might have upon children. In a cause-and-effect (or cause or effect alone) essay, explain the influence of action-oriented cartoons on children.

     b.   David A. Goslin, Ph.D., of the American Institute for Research in Washington, D.C., which conducts behavioral and social-science research, claims, "Choices do not make life easier; they make it more difficult, for all of us. As social scientists, we know that with an increase in choices, people tend to become more anxious."

          In your experience, is Dr. Goslin's comment valid? Write a cause-and-effect (or cause or effect alone) essay discussing his point of view. You might keep in mind that Americans can choose from more than 25,000 items shelved in their supermarkets. They can tune in more than fifty television channels. They can buy more than 11,000 magazines or periodicals. They are solicited by tens of thousands of special-interest groups. Some call this opportunity "freedom of choice," but social critics and experts are beginning to believe that the marketplace may have outsmarted itself by creating all these choices.

     c.   In *The Tyranny of Malice,* Joseph H. Berke explains that "Envy is a state of exquisite tension, torment, and ill will provoked by an overwhelming sense of inferiority, impotence, and worthlessness. It begins in the eye of the beholder and is so painful to the mind that the envious person will go to almost any lengths to diminish, if not destroy, whatever or whoever may have aroused it." Basing a cause-and-effect (or cause or effect alone) essay on personal observation, discuss the sources of envy and how it might affect behavior.

d. "Think globally, act locally" was the rallying cry of environmental activism in the 1960s. This advice is as appropriate now as it was then. Just as the Greenpeace movement started more than two decades ago not with governments but at the grass roots, so today it is individuals who must occupy the front lines in protecting the environment. In a cause-and-effect (or cause or effect alone) essay discuss individual or local-government actions that have resulted from environmental activism.

e. In "The Slaughterer," a short story by Isaac Bashevis Singer, Yoineh Meir wanted to be a rabbi. Instead, the religious authorities in his community made him the ritual slaughterer. Obediently, Meir learned the laws of slaughter as found in religious texts and followed the command of authority.

"Barely three months had passed since Yoineh Meir had become a slaughterer," Singer wrote, "but the time seemed to stretch endlessly. He felt as though he were immersed in blood and lymph. His ears were beset by the squawking of hens, the crowing of roosters, the gobbling of geese, the lowing of oxen, the mooing and bleating of calves and goats; wings fluttered, claws tapped on the floor. The bodies refused to know any justification or excuse—every body resisted in its own fashion, tried to escape, and seemed to argue with the Creator to its last breath."

Yoineh Meir's life ended in madness: "The killing of every beast, great or small, caused him as much pain as though he were cutting his own throat. Of all the punishments that could have been visited upon him, slaughtering was the worst."

Although Yoineh Meir is an extreme example, many people are forced to follow the dictates of authority against their better judgment. In an essay describe a situation in which authority has been used to pressure an individual into action that seems contrary to his or her nature and discuss the related causes and effects.

6

Process Analysis
Explaining Step by Step

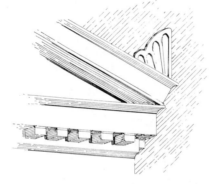

The Method

Are you, like many readers, fascinated by how things work? Are you attracted to writing that explains how to organize your life and time? You might want to understand how the stock market works or how Colombian drug producers smuggle cocaine into the United States. Perhaps your interests have to do with the mind—you might want to learn how psychotherapy works. Authors of essays or books explaining how things work use **process analysis**: they help us to better understand something by breaking it down into its components.

335

In some ways process analysis comes close to narration and cause-and-effect analysis by attending to a sequence of related events. Narration, however, is meant to tell a story, and cause-and-effect analysis deals with the reasons for and results of an event or experience. In process analysis a writer examines the way in which something works. In short, narration concentrates on *what* happened; cause and effect, on *why* it happened; and process analysis, on *how* it happened.

Strategies

Careful writers distinguish between two kinds of process analysis: **directive** and **informative.** Directive process analysis explains *how to* do something. Directive process analysis is usually a practical kind of writing based on the assumption that someone will follow the directions to complete a task. Informative process analysis emphasizes *how* something works rather than *how to* do something. Informative process analysis might explain how the brain functions, how gravity holds human beings to the face of the earth, or how food is grown, processed, and merchandised, but an informative process analysis will not offer directions for completing a task.

Directive Process Analysis

Directive process analysis can range from brief instructions on a soup-can label to a complicated plan for putting an astronaut on another planet. Keep in mind that directive process analysis has one clear purpose: to guide a reader to a predetermined goal by breaking down the steps required to get there. Consider this paragraph from Tom Cuthbertson's *Anybody's Bike Book,* setting out simple directions for checking bike tire pressure.

There's a great *curb-edge test* you can do to make sure your tires are inflated just right. Rest the wheel on the edge of a curb or stair so the bike sticks out into the street or path, perpendicular to the curb or stair edge. Get the wheel so you can push down on it at about a 45 degree angle from above the bike. Push hard on the handlebars or seat, depending on which wheel you're testing. The curb should flare the tire a bit but shouldn't push right through the tire and clunk against the rim. You want the tire to have a little give when you ride over chuckholes and rocks, in other words, but you don't want it so soft that you bottom out. If you are a hot-shot who wants tires so hard that they don't have any give, you'll have to stick to riding on cleanswept Velodrome tracks, or watch very carefully for little sharp objects on the road. Or you'll have to get used to that sudden riding-on-the-rim feeling that follows the blowout of an overblown tire.

Cuthbertson's paragraph illustrates several characteristics of directive process analysis. First, he clearly establishes his purpose: to explain how to test bike tires for proper inflation. Second, he breaks the process down into simple steps and explains the final result: "The curb should flare the tire . . . ." Third, Cuthbertson addresses his reader directly by using the second person pronoun *you,* a practice that many writers adopt in directive process analysis: "There's a great curb-edge test *you* can do to make sure *your* tires are inflated just right." A fourth frequent characteristic of directive process analysis alerts the reader to possible mistakes and their consequences. Notice that Cuthbertson states the consequences of overinflated bike tires.

Now consider this passage from *The New York Times Complete Manual of Home Repair.* Bernard Gladstone gives directions for building a fire. Notice that Gladstone's passage embodies most of the common characteristics of process analysis, but he chooses not to address the reader as "you." Instead he writes in the more impersonal passive voice, which seems to create a distance between the reader and the subject.

Though "experts" differ as to the best technique to follow when building a fire, one generally accepted method consists of first laying a generous amount of crumpled newspaper on the hearth between the andirons. Kindling wood is then spread generously over this layer of newspaper and one of the thickest logs is placed across the back of the andirons. This should be as close to the back of the fireplace as possible, but not quite touching it. A second log is then placed an inch or so in front of this, and a few additional sticks of kindling are laid across these two. A third log is then placed on top to form a sort of pyramid with air space between all logs so that flames can lick freely up between them.

A mistake frequently made is in building the fire too far forward so that the rear wall of the fireplace does not get properly heated. A heated back wall helps increase the draft and tends to suck smoke and flames rearward with less chance of sparks or smoke spurting out into the room.

Another common mistake often made by the inexperienced firetender is to try to build a fire with only one or two logs, instead of using at least three. A single log is difficult to ignite properly, and even two logs do not provide an efficient bed with adequate fuel-burning capacity.

Use of too many logs, on the other hand, is also a common fault and can prove hazardous. Building too big a fire can create more smoke and draft than the chimney can safely handle, increasing the possibility of sparks or smoke being thrown out into the room. For best results, the homeowner should start with three medium-size logs as described above, then add additional logs as needed if the fire is to be kept burning.

Like Cuthbertson, Gladstone opens by clearly stating his purpose; that is, to explain the steps necessary to build a fire in a fireplace. He then follows with a series of steps—six in all—that are clearly written and easy to follow. After devoting a paragraph to directions for building a fire, he presents three common mistakes people make when building a fire, and their consequences, with one brief paragraph devoted to each mistake. Although Gladstone's directions for building a fire are longer than Cuthbertson's for testing air pressure in a bike tire, both follow the same general pattern. They begin with a clear statement of purpose, then present the steps necessary to complete the process, and, as is often done in directive process analysis, they identify the common mistakes people make when following the procedure.

Informative Process Analysis

Instead of guiding a reader through a series of directions to complete a task as directive process analysis does, informative process analysis explains how something happens or how it works. In this paragraph from Caroline Sutton's *How Do They Do That?* she explains how stripes are put into striped toothpaste.

> Although it's intriguing to imagine the peppermint stripes neatly wound inside the tube, actually stripes don't go into the paste until it's on its way out. A small hollow tube, with slots running lengthwise, extends from the neck of the toothpaste tube back into the interior a short distance. When the toothpaste tube is filled, red paste—the striping material—is inserted first, thus filling the conical area around the hollow tube at the front. (It must not, however, reach beyond the point to which the hollow tube extends into the toothpaste tube.) The remainder of the dispenser is filled with the familiar white stuff. When you squeeze the toothpaste tube, pressure is applied to the white paste, which in turn presses on the red paste at the head of the tube. The red then passes through the slots and onto the white, which is moving through the inserted tube—and which emerges with five red stripes.

Sutton doesn't expect any of her readers to make a tube of striped toothpaste, but she does answer a common question, one that might have aroused your curiosity, too, "How do they get the stripes into the tube?"

An informative process analysis is usually arranged in chronological order and makes careful use of transitional techniques to guide a reader through the process. Sometimes the procedure is quite simple and easily organized in a step-by-step sequence. Often, however, the process is complex, such as a chemical reaction or human digestion, and challenges a writer's organizational skills, especially when the writer wishes to interrupt the explanation to add additional information or description.

For example, John McPhee in *Oranges* devotes a paragraph to describing the process oranges undergo when made into concentrated juice. As you read McPhee's paragraph, notice that he interrupts to bring in related information—first, to explain that oranges culled from the crop were once dumped in fields and eaten by cattle, thus accounting for the orangeade flavor of Florida milk; and second, to describe two kinds of juicing machines. Even though McPhee interrupts the process, he still guides the reader's attention with clear transitional techniques, especially phrases that create a sense of movement, such as, "As the fruit starts to move . . . ," "Moving up a conveyor belt . . . ," "When an orange tumbles in . . . ," and, finally, "As the jaws crush the outside . . . ."

As the fruit starts to move along a concentrate plant's assembly line, it is first culled. In what some citrus people remember as "the old fresh-fruit days," before the Second World War, about forty per cent of all oranges grown in Florida were eliminated at packinghouses and dumped in fields. Florida milk tasted like orangeade. Now, with the exception of the split and rotten fruit, all of Florida's orange crop is used. Moving up a conveyor belt, oranges are scrubbed with detergent before they roll on into juicing machines. There are several kinds of juicing machines, and they are something to see. One is called the Brown Seven Hundred. Seven hundred oranges a minute go into it and are split and reamed on the same kind of rosettes that are in the centers of ordinary kitchen reamers. The rinds that come pelting out the bottom are integral halves, just like the rinds of oranges squeezed in a kitchen. Another machine is the Food Machinery Corporation's FMC In-line Extractor. It has a shining row of aluminum jaws, upper and lower, with shining aluminum teeth. When an orange tumbles in, the upper jaw comes crunching down on it while at the same time the orange is penetrated from below by a perforated steel tube. As the jaws crush the outside, the juice goes through the perforations in the tube and down into the plumbing of the concentrate plant. All in a second, the juice has been removed and the rind has been crushed and shredded beyond recognition.

Some processes defy chronological explanation because they take place simultaneously. Here a writer must present the material in parallel stages, as McPhee does in the last three sentences of his paragraph when he describes juicing, clearly indicating with transitional markings that two or more interlocked events are taking place at once.

In a paragraph from in "The Spider and the Wasp," zoologist Alexander Petrunkevitch presents the procedure a female *Pepsis* wasp follows when paralyzing a tarantula before burying it with a wasp egg attached to its belly. The challenge Petrunkevitch faced was to show both the wasp's and the spider's simultaneous behavior.

When the grave is finished, the wasp returns to the tarantula to complete her ghastly enterprise. First, she feels it all over once more with her antennae. Then her behavior becomes more aggressive. She bends her abdomen, protruding her sting, and searches for the soft membrane at the point where the spider's legs join its body—the only spot where she can penetrate the horny skeleton. From time to time, as the exasperated spider slowly shifts ground, the wasp turns on her back and slides along with the aid of her wings, trying to get under the tarantula for a shot at the vital spot. During all this maneuvering, which can last for several minutes, the tarantula makes no move to save itself. Finally the wasp corners it against some obstruction and grasps one of its legs in her powerful jaws. Now at last the harassed spider tries a desperate but vain defense. The two contestants roll over and over on the ground. It is a terrifying sight and the outcome is always the same. The wasp finally manages to thrust her sting into the soft spot and holds it there for a few seconds while she pumps in the poison. Almost immediately the tarantula falls paralyzed on its back. Its legs stop twitching; its heart stops beating. Yet it is not dead, as is shown by the fact that if taken from the wasp it can be restored to some sensitivity by being kept in a moist chamber for several months.

Often the success of a process-analysis essay rests on clear information about the reader. The writer must estimate how much knowledge about the process the reader may already have and how much additional information must be included in the essay. If the writer's guess is wildly inaccurate, then he or she will include either too much information, which may send the reader into a fit of yawning, or too little, which may send the reader into an intellectual fog bank.

Process Analysis in College Writing

In the sciences and social sciences, process analysis is an important pattern of development. In laboratory sciences you will often use directive process analysis to write reports that communicate the procedure in an experiment or research project. Courses such as geology, biology, cultural anthropology, and social psychology concentrate on such processes as the formation of mountains, photosynthesis, initiation ceremonies, and socialization. In courses such as these, informative process analysis comes with the territory.

The following six paragraphs are part of an extended essay written for the introduction to psychology course. John Barton, a psychology major, chose to write about new techniques used in psychotherapy. After reviewing traditional therapeutic techniques in three paragraphs, he turns to a recent technique, "photoanalysis."

Barton establishes photoanalysis as his topic. He points out it might save time in therapy.

Although some critics of psychotherapy claim the field is slow to change, some new techniques are developing. One is photoanalysis. No doubt you have heard that "A photograph is worth a thousand words." Well, photoanalysists would agree, but with a slight revision, "A <u>family photo album</u> is worth a thousand words." For example, a person might be aware that he has difficulty showing affection and expressing himself. After a session with a photoanalyst, usually a certified psychiatrist or psychologist, he could become aware that the difficulty is rooted in his family history. Instead of spending hours verbally exploring his family relationships, a client working with a photoanalyst would examine a family photo album where the patterns of restraint might be documented in photographs.

This paragraph clearly indicates Barton will use process analysis, and he begins by stating the importance of using a group of photographs.

Besides being trained as a therapist, a photoanalyst should also be sensitive to visual images and the nonverbal expression they embody. But analyzing photographs to uncover family themes is not simple. The analyst should use group photographs taken over a number of years. A single photograph may whet curiosity but is no more helpful in unearthing patterns of family relationship than a crystal ball.

The process might begin by spreading the photographs on a table. Then the analyst will study the faces to determine the general "tone" of the relationships. Are the subjects looking at each other or at the camera? Are their expressions happy? Or severe? Or angry? Often a child's first impression of the world comes from parents.

*"The process might be-
gin . . ." reminds the
reader that Barton is
using process analysis
and also that the pro-
cedures are not rigid.
Throughout these three
paragraphs, notice how
he works in additional
information. His intent
is not to "train" some-
one to analyze photo-
graphs but to give an
"impression" of what is
involved in the process.*

Their expressions, captured in a series of photographs, may reveal their general perceptions.

Next, the analyst will study the body language of family members. Do they stand rigidly or are they relaxed, at ease? Do they seem to interact with each other or do they seem emotionally isolated from each other? Are they touching? Perhaps one has an arm around another's shoulder or a hand on another's leg. Is the hand open or clenched?

Finally, the analyst will also examine family members' proximity to each other. If they are close enough to rub elbows, they probably enjoy a warm relationship. If they put distance between themselves to avoid touching, they may shun intimacy with each other. What if males and females are clearly separated? Does this distance suggest that men and women play tradi-tional roles within the family? An ana-lyst will notice who takes the dominant place in the photographs. Mother? Father? A grandparent? Perhaps the children. Whoever takes a dominant place in a se-ries of photographs probably takes the dominant role at home as well. A parent who consistently gravitates toward one child in photographs might play favorites in family relationships. A person who al-ways chooses to stand at the outside of the group might feel like an outsider.

*Barton ends with an
indirect warning and
one more detail related
to interpretation.*

Throughout a photoanalysis session, the analyst should avoid narrow interpre-tations of the photographs, but should of-fer observations for the client's response. After all, the client is the one with the direct experience and therefore should have the last word in interpreting any photograph. The photoanalyst must, however, point out that a friendly smile might be masking the tension revealed by a clenched fist half hidden in a lap.

Barton's strategy is very effective. Rather than simply defining photoanalysis, he describes the general process while clearly indicating what photoanalysis involves. The opening paragraph provides a brief transition from the preceding paragraphs and introduces photoanalysis as the subject. Here Barton also shows the benefits of photoanalysis. In the next paragraph, he clearly indicates he will be using process analysis and clarifies what an analyst needs to get started. The next three paragraphs describe the process. Because an analyst would use neither a chronological nor a step-by-step procedure in photoanalysis, Barton merely suggests the chronological order to give his paragraphs structure while working additional information into his text along the way. Finally, Barton ends with a bit of advice: an analyst should avoid narrowly interpreting a photograph but instead should allow a client's responses to guide the procedure.

❧ Joan Gould ❧

Joan Gould was born in 1927 in New York City and attended Bryn Mawr College. She has written a juvenile novel and the "Hers" column in The New York Times, *and has contributed to major magazines such as* Esquire, Life, Sports Illustrated, *and* McCall's. *Many of her essays are very personal explorations of the experience of being a wife, a mother, a mother-in-law, and an adult daughter of an aging mother. Her book* Spirals: A Woman's Journey Through Family Life *(1988) is a collection of those essays.*

Binding Decisions

This essay was first printed in Memories *magazine in 1989. The author describes an event from her past, the ritual of getting ready for a blind date in 1950, which she uses to reveal social attitudes about women and men, marriage, and relationships at that time. The essay invites us to wonder how much attitudes like these have changed since then.*

I'm out of the bathtub. I'm ready to get dressed for my date tonight, which is a blind date, serious business in this year of 1950 for any girl who's over 20 and still single. I'm 22. No matter how much money I may earn in my job, I'll never be allowed to have an apartment of my own; I'll never pay an electric bill or buy a bedspread or spend a night away from home without my parents; in fact, I'll never be a grown-up so long as I remain single.

How shall I dress? I want to look sexy enough to attract this unknown man, so that he'll call and ask me for another date next week. (Needless to say, I won't call him, even if my life depends on it.) On the other hand, I don't want to hide the fact that I'm what's known as a Nice Girl, addicted to Peter Pan collars and velvet hats and white gloves, which means that I'm good wife

346

material, and also makes it clear that he'll get nothing more than a goodnight kiss from me tonight.

And so I dress carefully. Every single item that I put on not only is complicated in itself but carries an even more complicated message.

My girdle comes first. Here's the badge, the bind, the bondage of womanhood. Here's the itch of it. This is the garment that tells me I'm not a little girl anymore, who wears only underpants, but neither am I middle-aged like my mother, who wears a real corset with bones that dig into her diaphragm and leave cruel sores there. I can get away with either a panty girdle or a two-way stretch, both of which are made of Lastex with a panel of stiff satin over the abdomen. The basic difference is that a panty girdle, unlike a two-way stretch, covers the crotch, which was considered a shocking—indeed obscene—idea when first introduced. Victorian women were obliged to wear half a dozen petticoats at a time to be respectable, but never, never would they put on anything that slipped between their thighs, like a pair of pants.

But why should I be bothering with this sausage casing when I weigh a grand total of a hundred and two pounds?

I bother because being thin has nothing to do with it. A girdle is a symbolic garment, and unless I want to be regarded as a child or a slut I have to put it on. When I go out with girlfriends in the daytime I may choose to be more comfortable in only a garter belt, a device with four long, wiggly elastics that dangle down my thighs like hungry snakes lunging at my stockings. When I'm with a boy, however, it would be unthinkable—it would be downright indecent—to let him see my rear end jiggle or let him notice that it has two halves. (All males are called "boys," no matter what their age, so long as they're single.) My backside is supposed to be molded in a rigid piece that divides into two legs, like a walking clothespin.

Besides, if I don't wear a girdle every day, the older girls warn me, I'm going to "spread." Spreading is somehow related to letting my flesh hang loose, which is in turn related to the idea of the "loose" woman, and none of us wants to be considered loose. A man doesn't buy a cow if he can get milk for free, our mothers

3 The process begins: step 1. Notice that each step is descriptively, personally, and culturally explained. These paragraphs hold a wealth of information beyond the description of girdles.

4 The cultural process described here reflects the lockstep 1950s thinking in Gould's element of society. Gould fits her process to the symbolism required by each social situation because such modifications are expected by her mother and her friends, who themselves are bound to the same symbol-laden process. Gould finally compromises, but not to the point of innovation. Betty Friedan says about the generation following Gould's, in *The Feminine Mystique* (1963), "When she stopped conforming to the conventional picture of femininity, she finally began to enjoy being a woman" (chapter 14).

5

6

7

tell us in dire tones. We don't point out that we're not cows, and we don't fight against girdles, which apparently do a good job of discouraging wandering hands, since most of the single girls I know are virgins.

But which girdle should I wear? If I pick the panty girdle, I'll need 10 minutes' advance notice before going to the toilet. If I wear the two-way stretch, it will ride up and form a sausage around my waist. Either way, my flesh will be marked with welts and stripes when, at that delirious moment in my bedroom, I can strip off my clothes and scratch and scratch. 8

I pick the two-way stretch but, born compromiser that I am, put underpants over it. 9

Lana Turner and Betty Grable, voluptuous American movie stars and pinup girls during World War II, predated Twiggy, the British model thin almost to emaciation, by more than twenty years. The padded bra was first advertised in nineteenth-century Paris. The first modern bra was designed and made by socialite Mary Phelps Jacobs, in 1913. Notice the mother's warning. Some things never change.

Next comes the bra. I don't dare look at myself in the mirror as I put it on. This is the era of the pinup girl, the heyday of Lana Turner and Betty Grable, when breasts bubble and froth over the rims of C-cups and a flat chest is considered about as exciting as flat champagne. Not until Twiggy appears on the scene in the 1960's will thinness become acceptable in a girl, much less desirable—but how am I supposed to survive until then? The answer is the garment I've just put on, the confession of my disgrace—a padded bra. If I wear a strapless gown, I pin foam-rubber bust pads, which are known as "falsies," in place. Occasionally one of these breaks loose during a particularly ardent conga or mambo and rises above my dress like the rim of the sun peering over a hilltop. 10

At least the bra won't show under my silk slip. Silk is expensive, of course, and no male will see my underwear unless he marries me or I'm carried off to a hospital emergency room—but then, as all the mothers warn us, accidents do happen. 11

Nylon stockings were again available in 1950. Gould reminisces about "stockings" during World War II. The Du Pont chemical company had invented nylon in 1938 and sent spools of nylon to selected hosiery manufacturers in 1940. Chosen stores received nylon stockings only if they agreed not to sell them before May 15, 1940, "Nylon Day"; riots nearly broke out as women all over the United States rushed hosiery departments. By the end of 1940, 36 million pairs of nylons had been sold—only because no more could be had.

Stockings next. During World War II, just as I became old enough to wear them, our wonderful new nylons were snatched away from us in order to make parachutes for what was known as the "war effort." What were we girls supposed to do—go out on a date in socks, like little children? If there weren't any stockings around, we'd have to create them. And so we bought bottles of makeup base and painted stockings on our legs and drew seams up the back with eyebrow pencils, which was undoubtedly the last time my seams were ever straight. 12

My dress, oddly enough, is easy to choose. For a woman of my years, a skirt-and-sweater is out of the question on a date. The dress mustn't be too high-style or expensive, however, or else the young man will think that I'm spoiled, a fatal defect in a girl who might otherwise qualify as good wife material. Never mind that I earned the money to buy my own clothes; I still have to show that it won't cost much to support me once we marry and I quit my job. For the same reason, wherever we go—which is always at his expense, of course—I'll insist that we travel by bus or subway, never by taxi. If he invites me out to dinner (which doesn't happen often, because of cost, and never on a first date), I'll eat a sandwich at home before I leave, to make sure I won't be tempted to order an appetizer or dessert in the restaurant.

Shoes. I'd like to wear my fashionable new ones, with their ankle straps crisscrossing in back and fastening above the ankle bone, but they have 3½-inch heels, and I have no idea if I'll tower over this unknown man. If I choose low heels, on the other hand, he may think that I'm condescending. I pick the high heels but hide a low-heeled pair in the hall closet, just in case. Blind dates have their special hazards.

I still have to put on my makeup, which includes lots of lipstick, loose face power and an eyebrow pencil to extend my brow line, but no eye shadow, much less liner. I also have to do my hair, which is set with heavy lotion and rollers in the beauty parlor every week. (At night I sleep in a cotton mesh hairnet that I tie around my head, in order to preserve the set for at least a week.)

Speeding up the pace, I rush to equip my pocketbook with a monogrammed handkerchief and some "mad money," including several nickels for phone calls or a bus, obligatory for a blind date. I run to my glove drawer and hunt up a pair in white kid, since he's invited me to a concert. I won't need a hat. He'll wear one, of course.

The doorbell rings. I dab Shalimar on a tuft of cotton, which I tuck inside my bra; I check my stocking seams and move toward the door. For an instant, my hand rests on the knob, while I wonder what sort of person is breathing out there, only inches away from me but still unrevealed, unexplored. And then I open

13 Notice how Gould embodies her times. Although the man is obliged socially to pay for everything on the date, Gould is obliged to do all that society expects from a woman who "needs" to marry.

14 Her process of dressing for the occasion is consciously based on 1950s social requirements for a date.

Tell the class about this 1770 legislation in the British Parliament: "That women of whatever age, rank, or profession, whether virgins, maids, or widows, who shall seduce or betray into matrimony, by scents, paints, cosmetic washes, artificial teeth, [or] false hair, shall incur the penalty of the law as against witchcraft, and that the marriage shall stand null and void." The bill was defeated.

15

16 Her process of getting ready for the date is almost complete. In this entire essay, Gould has mentioned only two requirements for her blind date: that he pay all expenses incurred on the date and that he wear a hat, as befits the occasion.

17 Shalimar: A popular scent by Guerlain, developed in 1925. Its name is from Sanskrit, meaning "temple of love." Notice that the process is completed with the opening of the door. Her blind date, oblivious to her careful preparations for the evening, concentrates on himself

and his cold. She wears Shalimar; he carries Kleenex.

All the planning and process itself lead to the man's proposing, after the proper length of time has passed, of course. Before she gives him her answer, she injects candor, in a sense revealing part of the process.

The process works! Notice the element of small mystery in the last line.

the door, and I see his face and hear his voice, because he's already in mid-sentence. As a matter of fact, he's in mid-story, as if it's inconceivable that anyone could be less than fascinated with what he's saying, which happens to be true, or as if he's my husband already and has waited all day, or maybe all his life, to tell me about what happened to him that afternoon.

A box of Kleenex is tucked under his arm, because he has a cold, and he lays the box down on the hall table with the assurance of the rightful prince stepping into his kingdom at last. This one I'll marry or I'll marry no one, I say to myself an hour later. 18

Three dates—which means three weeks—later, he proposes. "Wait. I have to tell you something first," I declare in distress. He waits. I'm in turmoil. I'm risking everything on candor, and candor isn't a virtue in which I've had much practice. I've never said anything like this out loud before. "You have a right to know," I announced. "I wear a padded bra." 19

He says he imagines he can handle that. 20

We were married three months later. I wonder, if he hadn't proposed so promptly, how much longer it would have been before he discovered my secret for himself. 21

Possible Answers

Meaning and Purpose

1. Gould devotes several paragraphs to the subject of girdles (4–9). The "Binding" of the title relates first to what girdles do to the body (sentence 2, paragraph 4). A bra, which Gould describes choosing, is also binding. Dressing for a date in 1950 bound young women to a rigid set of behaviors and values. The word "Decisions" in the title is ironic because young women then were not free to choose not to follow the rules of dating, courtship, and marriage; they could make only decisions that

Meaning and Purpose

1. What significance does the title have for you after you read the essay?
2. In paragraph 6, Gould says that the girdle is a "symbolic garment." We still have symbolic garments. What is one of them? How is it symbolic?
3. The author makes sure that she "won't be tempted to order an appetizer or dessert" if she is invited by a date to eat in a restaurant (paragraph 13). Why?
4. What is Gould's purpose in writing about the procedure of getting ready for a blind date in 1950? From what perspective is she writing?

5. In paragraph 10, she talks about what could happen during "an ardent conga or mambo." To what do *conga* and *mambo* refer? Why is *ardent* an appropriately descriptive word?

Strategy

1. The process in this essay can be broken into specific steps. What are three of those steps?
2. Gould often interrupts the chronology of her process of dressing for a date to give explanations and related information. Where is one example of this strategy, and how does it work in the essay?
3. From the kind and detail of information in this essay, what decision would you say Gould has made about the knowledge her audience has of her subject?
4. The blind date is in "mid-story" as the author opens the door. What does this strategy of description tell you about the mental attitude of the blind date?

Style

1. The process described in this essay was carried out forty or so years ago. Why is the essay written in the present tense?
2. What is Gould's attitude toward the procedure she must go through for a date? Point out specific language that illustrates her attitude.
3. Why is the word *delirious* so appropriate, as it is used in paragraph 8?
4. In paragraph 14, she says that "Blind dates have their special hazards." What "hazards" could the author be talking about?

were ultimately insignificant and superficial, such as which girdle to wear.

2. Students may choose any symbolic garment, including white wedding gown, veil, necktie, vest, and hat. Their reasoning provides the key to judging the answer to this question.

3. She might want to show that she is "naturally" frugal, or she might want to keep down her date's expenses. Either way, she will be more appealing as a wife.

4. We know from Gould's mention of Twiggy in the 1960s (10) that Gould is looking back from more than a decade in the future of 1950. Her article captures a particular social etiquette in a particular time and intimates the values of the whole decade. This period-piece article can be useful for comparison with any current dating preparations and social values.

5. The conga originated in Latin America; the mambo in Cuba; both are energetic dances quite popular in the 1950s. *Ardent* means "warm or intense in feeling; passionate." The author feared becoming too intense during either dance, and therefore forgetful.

Strategy

1. Three of the steps are: choosing a girdle (9); putting on a padded bra (10); and "Stockings next" (11).

2. In describing her choice of a girdle, Gould begins with "My girdle comes first" (4). From here through 7, she digresses about girdles that older women wear, girdles that Victorian women wore, the girdle as a symbolic garment (6), and the consequences of not wearing a girdle (7). Gould then resumes the chronology of dressing (8).

3. Gould does not spare details about dressing for a date, or other relevant facts. She assumes her readers may be younger than herself, may not have first-hand experience with the procedure she describes, and may know little about dating and women's clothes in the 1950s. On the other hand, readers who were dating in the 1950s might be amused and carried back by her details. The information thus is not necessarily too much for an audience of Gould's peers.

4. The young man seems nervous, intent on talking to himself, and not attentive to his date.

Style

1. Written in present tense, the essay has a tone of immediacy, of excitement. The author is reliving her own past. This tone fits the essay's process—of dressing symbolically and appropriately, with anxiety, for a blind date who later becomes the author's husband.

2. Gould, even at the time of the date, is less than pleased with the rigmarole she has to go through. But her perspective from a future time also shows that she considered the ritual false and unnecessary, even humorous. Some language that illustrates her attitude: paragraph 4, "Here's the itch of it"; paragraph 5, "sausage casing"; paragraph 6, "like a walking clothespin"; and paragraph 11, "rises above my dress like the rim of the sun peering over a hilltop." Ask students for other examples.

3. The word *delirious* means, among other definitions, "wildly excited." The author is ecstatic because she can now "scratch and scratch," and be relieved of the binding girdle.

4. The word *candor* refers to "sharp honesty or frankness in expressing oneself." The author's candor serves as counterpoint to the masquerade imposed by society on her choice of clothing—particularly, here, the padded bra. Custom restricted her from using candor until now.

Writing Tasks

1. The title is quite important to this essay. The expression "binding decisions" means at least two things. Using the material in this essay, write a paper exploring two meanings of "binding decisions": as the expression describes the process in this essay, and as the expression defines the reason the author carries out that process.

2. How do you dress for a date, or for some other occasion? Write a brief essay chronicling the steps in the process. If it is relevant, give background information that places your process in a larger social context.

❦ Don Lago ❦

Don Lago, 33, has written for the Bulletin of Atomic Scientists, Science Digest, *and* Cosmic Search *magazine. In 1981 Lago received the* Cosmic Search *magazine award for young writers. Apparently fascinated by the mysterious, Lago writes about the future, space exploration, and the search for intelligent life beyond earth.*

Symbols of Mankind

From Science Digest, March 1981, *Lago's essay describes in a few paragraphs the development of written communication throughout human history. By greatly simplifying this historical process, the author leads us to consider how advanced technology has brought us full circle, back to "new beginnings."*

TEACHING SUGGESTIONS

Because students often perceive process as a continuum, and because this essay is rather short, we suggest paragraph-by-paragraph analysis to demonstrate that each paragraph is a self-contained, controlled unit. From that stylistic analysis, you might lead a discussion back to the essay's ideas and question your students about the importance of reading and writing.

Many thousands of years ago, a man quietly resting on a log reached down and picked up a stick and with it began scratching upon the sand at his feet. He moved the stick slowly back and forth and up and down, carefully guiding it through curves and straight lines. He gazed upon what he had made, and a gentle satisfaction lighted his face.

Other people noticed this man drawing on the sand. They gazed upon the figures he had made, and though they at once recognized the shapes of familiar things such as fish or birds or humans, they took a bit longer to realize what the man had meant to say by arranging these familiar shapes in this particular way. Understanding what he had done, they nodded or smiled in recognition.

This small band of humans didn't realize what they were beginning. The images these people left in the sand would soon be swept away by the wind, but their new idea would slowly grow until it had remade the human species. These people had discovered writing.

MARGINAL NOTES

1   Lago briefly but vividly describes what the first act of human writing may have been like. His focus is on the writer and his recognition that he in some way accomplished something meaningful: "a gentle satisfaction lighted his face."

2   The perspective broadens in paragraph 2 to describe the writer's audience and their recognition and understanding of the writer's accomplishment. An active interchange flows between writer and reader.

3   Lago now explains what he has just described and the enormous consequences to the human race with the invention of writing.

353

Process Analysis

To emphasize the vast potential of writing, Lago contrasts it with memory and speech.

Now Lago focuses on early written language and compares pictographs with the more sophisticated ideograms.

After a simple transition ("The next leap occurred"), Lago describes the next development of writing by comparing syllabic and alphabetic systems.

Human knowledge exploded with the development of new technologies, but those technologies could not have been born without written language.

Technology has progressed so far that we must now go back to pictographs in order to attempt to communicate with other intelligences in space.

Writing, early people would learn, could contain much more information than human memory could and contain it more accurately. It could carry thoughts much farther than mere sounds could—farther in distance and in time. Profound thoughts born in a single mind could spread and endure.

The first written messages were simply pictures relating familiar objects in some meaningful way—pictographs. Yet there were no images for much that was important in human life. What, for instance, was the image for sorrow or bravery? So from pictographs humans developed ideograms to represent more abstract ideas. An eye flowing with tears could represent sorrow, and a man with the head of a lion might be bravery.

The next leap occurred when the figures became independent of things or ideas and came to stand for spoken sounds. Written figures were free to lose all resemblance to actual objects. Some societies developed syllabic systems of writing in which several hundred signs corresponded to several hundred spoken sounds. Others discovered the much simpler alphabetic system, in which a handful of signs represented the basic sounds the human voice can make.

At first, ideas flowed only slightly faster when written than they had through speech. But as technologies evolved, humans embodied their thoughts in new ways: through the printing press, in Morse code, in electromagnetic waves bouncing through the atmosphere and in the binary language of computers.

Today, when the Earth is covered with a swarming interchange of ideas, we are even trying to send our thoughts beyond our planet to other minds in the Universe. Our first efforts at sending our thoughts beyond Earth have taken a very ancient form: pictographs. The first message, on plaques aboard Pioneer spacecraft launched in 1972 and 1973, featured a simple line drawing of two humans, one male and one female, the male holding up his hand in greeting. Behind them was an outline of the Pioneer spacecraft, from which the size of the humans could be judged. The plaque also included the "address" of the two human figures: a picture of the solar system, with a spacecraft emerging from the third planet. Most scientists believe that when other civilizations attempt to communicate with us they too will use pictures.

All the accomplishments since humans first scribbled in the sand have led us back to where we began. Written language only works when two individuals know what the symbols mean. We can only return to the simplest form of symbol available and work from there. In interstellar communication, we are at the same stage our ancestors were when they used sticks to trace a few simple images in the sand.

We still hold their sticks in our hands and draw pictures with them. But the stick is no longer made of wood; over the ages that piece of wood has been transformed into a massive radio telescope. And we no longer scratch on sand; now we write our thoughts onto the emptiness of space itself.

9

10

Meaning and Purpose

1. Why do you think Lago titles his essay "Symbols of Mankind" and not "Symbols of Communication"?
2. In paragraph 3, Lago says that the original invention of writing "would slowly grow until it had remade the human species." What does he mean by that? In what ways have people changed because of writing?
3. What function of writing is intimated in paragraph 2?
4. What process has writing gone through, according to Lago? Why do we have to go back to rather primitive pictographs in our attempt at interstellar communication?

Strategy

1. Lago traces the development of writing from its hypothetical discovery to the present. Examine each paragraph as an

Meaning and Purpose

1. "Mankind" in the title encompasses all the possibilities that the word connotes, including abilities to write, to communicate, to feel, and to share ideas. Lago means that symbolic systems of communication are unique to humanity on this planet.

2. First, by writing, man could store more information than could human memory, and could store it more accurately. Thoughts could be disseminated more widely in time and distance. By writing, the thoughts of one man "could spread and endure" (4). Thus grew knowledge and communication so that new technologies could be developed to even further expand human knowledge (5). Now, "The Earth is covered with a swarming interchange of ideas," and we are attempting to send our thoughts beyond earth (8).

3. Writing is a means of communication and thus is directed to an audience.

4. First, people drew pictures of things—pictographs—which could depict only concrete things. In order to depict emotions and abstractions, ideograms were developed (5). Then, written figures became independent of things and ideas and came to represent spoken sounds. Two such basic systems evolved: syllabic systems, in which hundreds of figures corresponded to hundreds of spoken sounds; and alphabetic systems, in which just a few figures represented the basic sounds of the human voice (6). These systems can work only when both writer and reader understand what the written symbols mean. In attempting to communicate with extraterrestrials, therefore, we must return to universal pictographs.

Strategy

1. Probably the most difficult thing for students to recognize about a process essay is that it is organized around paragraphs that are, or should be, tightly organized units, that the essay is not "this happened, and this happened, and then this happened." Lago's essay is short enough that you can examine each paragraph to demonstrate this principle.

2. Lago switches to first person plural in paragraph 8 when, after tracing the history of writing, he comes to the present, "today." By using "we" he includes all humanity in the current endeavor to "send our thoughts beyond our planet to other minds in the Universe."

3. Beginning with the solitary man making designs with a stick in the sand as a cause, a series of effects, causes, and effects follows in subsequent paragraphs. Finally, the cause of our returning to primitive pictographs is our desire to reach beyond earth to other life, and our belief that pictographs are a universal language. The structure is a causal chain.

4. Lago follows the progression from pictographs to alphabets to binary notation—and back to pictographs. But the use of pictographs at the end is of course much more sophisticated than their first use because interstellar probes carry their message into deep space. Irony lies in the contrast between this technology and the form of communication it carries. With a new species the process begins again.

Style

1. The first sentence in paragraph 10, the topic sentence, indicates that we write now very much as our ancestors did. The next two sentences contrast the past with the present, balancing the two in each sentence by using semicolons, thereby connecting them and giving equal weight to each.

2. Paragraph 2 has enough detail to make it vivid. But the situation is hypothetical and Lago includes just enough detail to make the scene plausible. Paragraph 8, on the other hand, is a present-day reality, and the extensive detail here both transmits important information and gives the passage immediacy.

3. Lago is direct and informative, yet he seems to be in awe thinking of how writing began, and how it evolved: "He gazed upon what he had made, and a gentle satisfaction lighted his face" (1); "Profound thoughts born in a single mind could spread and endure" (4); and "now we write our thoughts onto the emptiness of space itself" (10).

organizational unit that helps demonstrate that progression. What function does each paragraph serve?

2. Where does the author switch from third person to first person plural? What is the reason for this switch?

3. Sometimes process analysis is closely related to cause and effect. How could the structure of this essay be analyzed as a cause-and-effect analysis?

4. As a process analysis, the structure of Lago's essay appears to be circular because it comes back to pictographs at the end. Explain how this circular process works in the essay.

Style

1. Examine the use of punctuation in paragraph 10. Why does Lago link clauses with semicolons rather than make them separate sentences?

2. Compare Lago's use of detail in paragraphs 2 and 8. Why would he choose to use more detail in one than the other?

3. What do you think are Lago's feelings about his subject—the tone of the essay? Point to language that shows this tone.

Writing Tasks

1. Using Lago's essay as a model, write an informative process-analysis essay in which you inform your audience about a process that falls within your expert knowledge, such as how your team came to win the championship. Your essay should cover the problems and situations your readers might encounter with a process that is new to them.

2. Choose something about which you know how to give instructions, such as putting up a tent or raising golden retrievers. Write a short, directive process-analysis essay in which you guide your readers toward a goal, step by step.

❦ William Zinsser ❦

William Zinsser is best known for On Writing Well: An Informal Guide to Writing Nonfiction *(1976), a book that grew out of a writing course he developed and taught as a professor of English at Yale University. He was born in New York City in 1922 and was educated at Princeton University, after which he worked successively as feature writer, drama editor, and film critic for the* New York Herald Tribune. *He has been a columnist for* Look, Life, *and* The New York Times, *and his essays have appeared in* The New Yorker *and other major national periodicals. Of his works on American culture, the best known is* Willie and Dwike: An American Profile *(1984). In 1979 he was appointed executive editor of the* Book-of-the-Month Club.

The Act of Writing:
One Man's Method

In this excerpt from Writing with a Word Processor *(1983), Zinsser says that every writer has "a deeply personal process" of writing. Here the author discusses his own process and how using a word processor has affected it. He also gives useful suggestions for making the most of a word processor as a writing tool.*

Writing is a deeply personal process, full of mystery and surprise. No two people go about it in exactly the same way. We all have little devices to get us started, or to keep us going, or to remind us of what we think we want to say, and what works for one person may not work for anyone else. The main thing is to get something written—to get the words out of our heads. There is no "right" method. Any method that will do the job is the right method for you.

It helps to remember that writing is hard. Most non-writers don't know this; they think that writing is a natural function, like

357

TEACHING SUGGESTIONS

One approach to Zinsser's essay might be a general one, a discussion of the pros and cons of the computer age. How have computers made our lives easier? How have they made them more difficult? What are the dangers to a free society in pervasive use of computers by both private industry and government? Various conclusions could lead to topics for papers.

A different, but certainly not incompatible, approach could be a discussion of Zinsser's ideas about good writing. Most helpful here, we think, are paragraphs 11–16, where he discusses how to recognize and eliminate nonessentials. And in paragraph 17, Zinsser mentions (parenthetically) that "Passive verbs are the death of clarity and vigor." Many students, we have found, not only don't know the difference between active and passive voice, but use passive voice extensively because it sounds like the bureaucratic prose they have unthinkingly accepted as real English. This subject could serve to launch a lesson in using active voice.

1 ## MARGINAL NOTES

After establishing that the writing process must be unique to each writer, that it is painful because difficult to do, and that, because it is painful, writers establish patterns to avoid writing, Zinsser now focuses on two specific doubts he had about writing with a word processor.

2

breathing, that ought to come easy, and they're puzzled when it doesn't. If you find that writing is hard, it's because it is hard. It's one of the hardest things that people do. Among other reasons, it's hard because it requires thinking. You won't write clearly unless you keep forcing yourself to think clearly. There's no escaping the question that has to be constantly asked: What do I want to say next?

So painful is this task that writers go to remarkable lengths to postpone their daily labor. They sharpen their pencils and change their typewriter ribbon and go out to the store to buy more paper. Now these sacred rituals, as [the computer manuals] would say, have been obsoleted. 3

When I began writing this book on my word processor I didn't have any idea what would happen. Would I be able to write anything at all? Would it be any good? I was bringing to the machine what I assumed were wholly different ways of thinking about writing. The units massed in front of me looked cold and sterile. Their steady hum reminded me that they were waiting. They seemed to be waiting for information, not for writing. Maybe what I wrote would also be cold and sterile. 4

I was particularly worried about the absence of paper. I knew that I would only be able to see as many lines as the screen would hold—twenty lines. How could I review what I had already written? How could I get a sense of continuity and flow? With paper it was always possible to flick through the preceding pages to see where I was coming from—and where I ought to be going. Without paper I would have no such periodic fix. Would this be a major hardship? 5

The only way to find out was to find out. I took a last look at my unsharpened pencils and went to work. 6

My particular hang-up as a writer is that I have to get every paragraph as nearly right as possible before I go on to the next paragraph. I'm somewhat like a bricklayer: I build very slowly, not adding a new row until I feel that the foundation is solid enough to hold up the house. I'm the exact opposite of the writer who dashes off his entire first draft, not caring how sloppy it looks or how badly it's written. His only objective at this 7

After a brief, transitional paragraph, Zinsser describes his own writing habits. He contrasts his paragraph-by-paragraph approach to that of the writer who sails through a complete draft.

early stage is to let his creative motor run the full course at full speed; repairs can always be made later. I envy this writer and would like to have his metabolism. But I'm stuck with the one I've got.

I also care how my writing looks while I'm writing it. The visual arrangement is important to me: the shape of the words, of the sentences, of the paragraphs, of the page. I don't like sentences that are dense with long words, or paragraphs that never end. As I write I want to see the design that my piece will have when the reader sees it in type, and I want that design to have a rhythm and a pace that will invite the reader to keep reading. O.K., so I'm a nut. But I'm not alone; the visual component is important to a large number of people who write.

One hang-up we visual people share is that our copy must be neat. My lifelong writing method, for instance, has gone like this. I put a piece of paper in the typewriter and write the first paragraph. Then I take the paper out and edit what I've written. I mark it up horribly, crossing words out and scribbling new ones in the space between the lines. By this time the paragraph has lost its nature and shape for me as a piece of writing. It's a mishmash of typing and handwriting and arrows and balloons and other directional symbols. So I type a clean copy, incorporating the changes, and then I take that piece of paper out of the typewriter and edit it. It's better, but not much better. I go over it with my pencil again, making more changes, which again make it too messy for me to read critically, so I go back to the typewriter for round three. And round four. Not until I'm reasonably satisfied do I proceed to the next paragraph.

This can get pretty tedious, and I have often thought that there must be a better way. Now there is. The word processor is God's gift, or at least science's gift, to the tinkerers and the refiners and the neatness freaks. For me it was obviously the perfect new toy. I began playing on page 1—editing, cutting and revising—and have been on a rewriting high ever since. The burden of the years has been lifted.

Mostly I've been cutting. I would guess that I've cut at least as many words out of this article as the number that remain.

8   Zinsser cites another of his writing idiosyncracies, a taste for the visual arrangement of words on a page.

9   He cites a lifelong writing habit to demonstrate one result of his feel for the visual effect of writing—neatness.

10   He concludes that there must be a cure for such tedious revision and finds it in a word processor.

11   In paragraphs 11–25, Zinsser takes us through his process of writing with a word processor. He begins by eliminating clutter.

Probably half of those words were eliminated because I saw that they were unnecessary—the sentence worked fine without them. This is where the word processor can improve your writing to an extent that you will hardly believe. Learn to recognize what is clutter and to use the DELETE key to prune it out.

How will you know clutter when you see it? Here's a device I used when I was teaching writing at Yale that my students found helpful; it may be a help here. I would put brackets around every component in a student's paper that I didn't think was doing some kind of work. Often it was only one word—for example, the useless preposition that gets appended to so many verbs (order up, free up), or the adverb whose meaning is already in the verb (blare loudly, clench tightly), or the adjective that tells us what we already know (smooth marble, green grass). The brackets might surround the little qualifiers that dilute a writer's authority (a bit, sort of, in a sense), or the countless phrases in which the writer explains what he is about to explain (it might be pointed out, I'm tempted to say). Often my brackets would surround an entire sentence—the sentence that essentially repeats what the previous sentence has said, or tells the reader something that is implicit, or adds a detail that is irrelevant. Most people's writing is littered with phrases that do no new work whatever. Most first drafts, in fact, can be cut by fifty percent without losing anything organic. (Try it; it's a good exercise.)

By bracketing these extra words, instead of crossing them out, I was saying to the student: "I may be wrong, but I think this can go and the meaning of the sentence won't be affected in any way. But *you* decide: read the sentence without the bracketed material and see if it works." In the first half of the term, the students' papers were festooned with my brackets. Whole paragraphs got bracketed. But gradually the students learned to put mental brackets around their many different kinds of clutter, and by the end of the term I was returning papers to them that had hardly any brackets, or none. It was always a satisfying moment. Today many of those students are professional writers. "I still see your brackets," they tell me. "They're following me through life."

You can develop the same eye. Writing is clear and strong to the extent that it has no superfluous parts. (So is art and music

12

13

14

and dance and typography and design.) You will really enjoy writing on a word processor when you see your sentences growing in strength, literally before your eyes, as you get rid of the fat. Be thankful for everything that you can throw away.

I was struck by how many phrases and sentences I wrote in this book that I later found I didn't need. Many of them hammered home a point that didn't need hammering because it had already been made. This kind of overwriting happens in almost everybody's first draft, and it's perfectly natural—the act of putting down our thoughts makes us garrulous. Luckily, the act of editing follows the act of writing, and this is where the word processor will bail you out. It intercedes at the point where the game can be won or lost. With its help I cut hundreds of unnecessary words and didn't replace them.   15

Hundreds of others were discarded because I later thought of a better word—one that caught more precisely or more vividly what I was trying to express. Here, again, a word processor encourages you to play. The English language is rich in words that convey an exact shade of meaning. Don't get stuck with a word that's merely good if you can find one that takes the reader by surprise with its color or aptness or quirkiness. Root around in your dictionary of synonyms and find words that are fresh. Throw them up on the screen and see how they look.   16

Also learn to play with whole sentences. If a sentence strikes you as awkward or ponderous, move your cursor to the space after the period and write a new sentence that you think is better. Maybe you can make it shorter. Or clearer. Maybe you can make it livelier by turning it into a question or otherwise altering its rhythm. Change the passive verbs into active verbs. (Passive verbs are the death of clarity and vigor.) Try writing two or three new versions of the awkward sentence and then compare them, or write a fourth version that combines the best elements of all three. Sentences come in an infinite variety of shapes and sizes. Find one that pleases you. If it's clear, and if it pleases you and expresses who you are, trust it to please other people. Then delete all the versions that aren't as good. Your shiny new sentence will jump into position and the rest of the paragraph will rearrange itself as quickly and neatly as if you had never pulled it apart.   17

17 While eliminating clutter, he also plays with the form and structure of sentences.

Turning to the whole essay, he first checks for unity.

Another goal that the word processor will help you to achieve 18 is unity. No matter how carefully you write each sentence as you assemble a piece of writing, the final product is bound to have some ragged edges. Is the tone consistent throughout? And the point of view? And the pronoun? And the tense? How about the transitions? Do they pull the reader along, or is the piece jerky and disjointed? A good piece of writing should be harmonious from beginning to end in the voice of the writer and the flow of its logic. But the harmony usually requires some last-minute patching.

I've been writing a book by the bricklayer method, slowly and 19 carefully. That's all very well as far as it goes—at the end of every chapter the individual bricks may look fine. But what about the wall? The only way to check your piece for unity is to go over it one more time from start to finish, preferably reading it aloud. See if you have executed all the decisions that you made before you started writing.

Keeping in mind his purpose and projected audience, he checks for tone and coherence.

One such decision is in the area of tone. I decided, for in- 20 stance, that I didn't want my book to be a technical manual. I'm not a technician; I'm a writer and an editor. The book wouldn't work if I expected the reader to identify with the process of mastering a new technology. He would have to identify with me. The book would be first of all a personal journey and only par- enthetically a manual. I knew that this was a hybrid form and that its unities would never be wholly intact. Still, in going over each finished chapter I found places where the balance could be improved—where instructional detail smothered the writer and his narrative, or, conversely, where the writer intruded on the procedures he was trying to explain. With a word processor it was easy to make small repairs—perhaps just a change of pro- noun and verb—that made the balance less uneven.

The instructional portions of the book posed a problem of 21 their own—one that I had never faced before. My hope was to try to explain a technical process without the help of any diagrams or drawings. Would this be possible? It would be possible only if I kept remembering one fundamental fact: writing is linear and sequential. This may seem so obvious as to be insulting: everybody knows that writing is linear and sequential. Actually everybody doesn't know. Most people under thirty don't know. They have been reared since early childhood on television—a kaleidoscope of visual images flashed onto their brain—and it doesn't occur to them that sentence B must follow sentence A, and that sentence C must follow sentence B, or all the elegant sentences in the world won't add up to anything but confusion.

I mention this [in part] because word processors are going to   22
be widely used by people who need to impart technical information: matters of operating procedure in business and banking, science and technology, medicine and health, education and government and dozens of other specialized fields. The information will only be helpful if readers can grasp it quickly and easily. If it's muddy they will get discouraged or angry, or both, and will stop reading.

You can avoid this dreaded fate for your message, whatever it   23
is, by making sure that every sentence is a logical sequel to the one that preceded it. One way to approach this goal is to keep your sentences short. A major reason why technical prose becomes so tangled is that the writer tries to make one sentence do too many jobs. It's a natural hazard of the first draft. But the solution is simple: see that every sentence contains only one thought. The reader can accommodate only one idea at a time. Help him by giving him only one idea at a time. Let him understand A before you proceed to B.

Here and in the next two paragraphs, Zinsser asserts the value of simplifying sentence structure.

In writing this book I was eager to explain the procedures   24
that I had learned about how word processors work, and I would frequently lump several points together in one sentence. Later, editing what I had written, I asked myself if the procedure would be clear to someone who was puzzling through it for the first time—someone who hadn't struggled to figure the procedure out. Often I felt that it wouldn't be clear. I was giving the reader too much. He was being asked to picture himself taking various steps that were single and sequential, and that's how he deserved to get them.

I therefore divided all troublesome long sentences into two   25
short sentences, or even three. It always gave me great pleasure.

Not only is it the fastest way for a writer to get out of a quagmire that there seems to be no getting out of; I also like short sentences for their own sake. There's almost no more beautiful sight than a simple declarative sentence. This book is full of simple declarative sentences that have no punctuation and that carry one simple thought. Without a word processor I wouldn't have chopped as many of them down to their proper size, or done it with so little effort. This is one of the main clarifying jobs that your machine can help you to perform, especially if your writing requires you to guide the reader into territory that is new and bewildering.

Not all my experiences, of course, were rosy. The machine   26 had disadvantages as well as blessings. Often, for instance, I missed not being able to see more than twenty lines at a time— to review what I had written earlier. If I wanted to see more lines I had to "scroll" them back into view.

Zinsser anticipated lack of printed paper to be a problem in paragraph 5. But here he shows that this difference and the attendant problem of a paragraph broken at the end of the page turn out to be, really, nonproblems.

But even this wasn't as painful as I had thought it would be. I   27 found that I could hold in my head the gist of what I had written and didn't need to keep looking at it. Was this need, in fact, still another writer's hang-up that I could shed? To some extent it was. I discovered, as I had at so many other points in this journey, that various crutches I had always assumed I needed were really not necessary. I made a decision to just throw them away and found that I could still function. The only real hardship occurred when a paragraph broke at the bottom of the screen. This meant that the first lines of the paragraph were on one page and the rest were on the next page, and I had to keep flicking the two pages back and forth to read what I was writing. But again, it wasn't fatal. I learned to live with it and soon took it for granted as an occupational hazard.

The conclusion brings us back full circle to the first paragraph with the idea that any successful writing process must be personal and idiosyncratic. His statement here recalls his beginning words: "Writing is a deeply personal process, full of mystery and surprise."

The story that I've told in this chapter is personal and idio-   28 syncratic: how the word processor helped one writer to write one book. In many of its details it's everybody's story. All writers have different methods and psychological needs. . . .

Meaning and Purpose

1. Describe in detail your own writing process. What does it have in common with Zinsser's?
2. What is Zinsser's purpose in the essay?
3. What audience do you think Zinsser is addressing, and how do you know?
4. In what ways does Zinsser find a word processor both helpful and disadvantageous in his writing?
5. In paragraph 1, Zinsser says that writing is "full of mystery and surprise." What does he mean?

Strategy

1. Zinsser says in paragraph 1 that writing is a "deeply personal experience," and that there is no one "right" way to write. Yet he puts forth a process of writing in the essay. Do you see a contradiction here? Why or why not?
2. Is Zinsser's essay an example of an informative or a directive process analysis? Explain.
3. The first sentence in paragraph 10 is a smooth transition from the preceding paragraph. What other transitions help you follow Zinsser's process?

Style

1. In describing his process—how he writes—Zinsser also describes the elements of what he considers good prose. How does his own writing fit his criteria?
2. What tone does Zinsser establish in his essay, and how does he achieve it?
3. Make sure you know the meaning of these words: *festooned* (13); *garrulous* (15); *root* (16).

POSSIBLE ANSWERS

Meaning and Purpose

1. Students will probably have varied and idiosyncratic methods of writing. Ask them to be specific about how their procedures compare to Zinsser's.

2. Zinsser's ostensible purpose is to show "how the word processor helped one writer to write one book." But beyond that, he explains how composing is personal and exciting, and that a word processor can help improve prose.

3. Zinsser's main audience is people who have had little or no experience writing with a word processor. The first-person account of his learning to use one would attract readers interested in a similar undertaking. Zinsser also offers good, general advice about writing that might appeal to a broader audience.

4. In paragraph 8, Zinsser says he cares about how writing is arranged on the page, its "visual arrangement." The word processor makes it easy to be neat and to edit and revise. And because the biggest part of writing is rewriting—Zinsser demonstrates this truth well enough—the word processor can relieve one of the greatest burdens of writing.

5. Zinsser doesn't address this subject directly, but at least a partial answer can be inferred from his essay. He says (6) that he would never know the answers to his questions without just doing it. Writing is a surprise, and all good writing is a mystery in that it comes from the deepest part of ourselves. Often we learn what we really think about a subject only by writing about it.

Strategy

1. The process that Zinsser describes is only one way, and it is his. He does not claim that what he does is what all writers do. Paragraph 7 is a good example of how he sticks to his own procedure as one way of going about writing. It is easier for Zinsser to write about any method at all because the tool—here, a word processor—is shared. In the last sentence of paragraph 25, he says that this common tool can help all writers, no matter which methods they use.

2. This is an informative process analysis, though some of the directives about using a word processor are just that—directive. The essay therefore has elements of both. Zinsser explains his writing process in detail and often interrupts himself to give even more description. Zinsser breaks his writing process down and approaches its steps chronologically, as in a how-to essay. He relates those steps to what he is learning about the word processor. He guides readers toward the goal of getting something written.

3. There are some good transitions: paragraph 12 begins with a question that leads the reader further into the subject of 11—cutting words; paragraph 16's first sentence repeats the "hundreds of" in the last sentence in 15 for a smooth transition; and 20 begins, "One such decision," which is an example of "decisions" at the end of paragraph 19. More can be found.

Style

1. Zinsser's prose fits his criteria for good writing: controlled, relatively short paragraphs; each point leads logically and clearly to the next; vocabulary simple and precise; style honed to the essence of meaning.

2. The tone is friendly because Zinsser addresses readers as "you" throughout. He shares personal anecdotes and describes misgivings about his writing and about corrections he makes. All these techniques help readers identify with him as a struggling fellow writer. At the same time he sounds authoritative. He combines a friendly, informal voice with an experienced one.

3. *Festooned:* adorned with a string or chain of flowers, foliage, ribbon, and so on, suspended in a curve between two points; *garrulous:* wordy or diffuse; *root:* to poke, pry, or search, as if to find something.

Writing Tasks

1. Describe in detail your method of writing, from choosing and modifying a topic to revising your final draft. In a short essay, take your reader through your usual step-by-step process.
2. Write a directive process analysis, a how-to essay, about something you know how to do, such as repairing a bicycle, or tie-dying a shirt. Keep in mind a goal to take your reader toward, and break the process down step by step.

❧ Judith Viorst ❧

Born in Newark, New Jersey, Judith Viorst is a graduate of Rutgers University and has been a regular columnist and contributing editor at Redbook *magazine since 1968. In 1970 she wrote a series of poetic monologues for a CBS special entitled "Annie: The Women in the Life of a Man," for which she received an Emmy award. She has written children's books, both fiction and nonfiction, and several volumes of light verse, including* It's Hard to Be Hip Over Thirty and Other Tragedies of Married Life *(1968) and* How Did I Get to be Forty and Other Atrocities *(1976). Her book* Necessary Losses: The Loves, Illusions, Dependencies and Impossible Expectations That All of Us Have to Give Up in Order to Grow *(1986), reached the top of* The New York Times *bestseller list.*

TEACHING SUGGESTIONS

You might begin with a discussion of how Viorst describes heroines to represent different stages in her own maturation. What is interesting about an essay explaining the forces that shaped her life? What is not? This subject could lead into a discussion of heroes and heroines that your students have found attractive, and why they found them so. Which come from books? Are films and television now a greater source of influence?

How Books Helped Shape My Life

First published in Redbook *in 1960, this essay analyzes the ways in which literary heroines influenced the author's life. Using examples from the books of her childhood through those she read as a young woman, Viorst describes a process of growing awareness through literature.*

In books I've read since I was young I've searched for heroines who could serve as ideals, as models, as possibilities—some reflecting the secret self that dwelled inside me, others pointing to whole new ways that a woman (if only she dared!) might try to be. The person that I am today was shaped by Nancy Drew; by Jo March, Jane Eyre and Heathcliff's soul mate Cathy; and by other fictional females whose attractiveness or character or audacity for a time were the standards by which I measured myself.

I return to some of these books to see if I still understand the powerful hold that these heroines once had on me. I still understand.

1

2

MARGINAL NOTES

Viorst states her thesis in its most typical position, the last sentence in paragraph 1.

367

A series of Nancy Drew mystery novels was published under the name of Carolyn Keene. A television series based on the novels was broadcast in the 1970s.

Little Women is a widely read story by Louisa May Alcott (1832–1888). The heroine is Jo March, the tomboyish and literary member of the family, who retires to the attic when "genius burns." Meg, her older, pretty sister, marries a young tutor, John Brooke. Gentle, music-loving Beth dies young. The fashionable and artistic Amy finally marries Laurie, a high-spirited boy who had long been Jo's boon companion, but who failed to persuade her to marry him. Jo herself becomes the wife of a kindly old German professor, Mr. Bhaer.

Consider teen-aged Nancy Drew—beautiful, blond-haired, blue-eyed girl detective—who had the most terrific life that I as a ten-year-old could ever imagine. Motherless (in other words, quite free of maternal controls), she lived with her handsome indulgent lawyer father in a large brick house set back from the street with a winding tree-lined driveway on the outside and a faithful, nonintrusive housekeeper Hannah cooking yummy meals on the inside. She also had a boy friend, a convertible, nice clothes and two close girl friends—not as perfect as she, but then it seemed to me that no one could possibly be as perfect as Nancy Drew, who in dozens and dozens of books (*The Hidden Staircase, The Whispering Statue, The Clue in the Diary, The Clue of the Tapping Heels*) was resourceful and brave and intelligent as she went around solving mysteries left and right, while remaining kind to the elderly and invariably polite and absolutely completely delightfully feminine.

I mean, what else *was* there?

I soon found out what else when I encountered the four March sisters of *Little Women,* a sentimental, old-fashioned book about girls growing up in Civil War time in New England. About spoiled, vain, pretty Amy. And sickly, saintly Beth. And womanly, decent Meg. And about—most important of all—gawky, bookworm Jo. Dear Jo, who wasn't as flawless as the golden Nancy Drew but who showed me that girls like her—like *us*—could be heroines. Even if we weren't much to look at. Even if we were clumsy and socially gauche. And even if the transition into young womanhood often appeared to our dubious eye to be difficult and scary and even unwelcome.

Jo got stains on her dress and laughed when she shouldn't and lost her temper and didn't display tact or patience or restraint. Jo brought a touch of irreverence to the cultural constraints of the world she lived in. And yet her instincts were good and her heart was pure and her headstrong ways led always to virtue. And furthermore Jo—as I yearned to be—was a writer!

In the book the years go by, Beth dies, Meg and Amy marry and Jo—her fierce heart somewhat tamed—is alone. " 'An old maid, that's what I'm to be. A literary spinster, with a pen for a spouse, a family of stories for children, and twenty years hence a morsel of fame, perhaps!' . . . Jo sighed, as if the prospect was not inviting."

This worried young reader concurred—not inviting at all!   8

And so I was happy to read of Jo's nice suitor, Mr. Bhaer, not   9
handsome or rich or young or important or witty, but possessed of kindness and dignity and enough intelligence to understand that even a girl who wasn't especially pretty, who had no dazzling charms and who wanted to write might make a wonderful wife. And a wonderful mother. And live happily ever after.

What a relief!   10

What Jo and Nancy shared was active participation in life—   11
they went out and *did;* they weren't simply done to—and they taught and promised me (at a time when mommies stayed home and there was no Women's Movement) that a girl could go out and do and still get a man. Jo added the notion that brusque, ungainly girls could go out and do and still get a man. And Jane of *Jane Eyre,* whose author once said, "I will show you a heroine as small and as plain as myself," added the further idea that such women were able to "feel just as men feel" and were capable of being just as passionate.

Charlotte Brontë (1816–1855) struggled with several literary works and finally published *Jane Eyre,* which achieved spectacular success.

Orphaned Jane, a governess at stately Thornfield Hall, was a   12
no-nonsense lady, cool and self-contained, whose lonely, painful childhood had ingrained in her an impressive firmness of character, an unwillingness to charm or curry favor and a sense of herself as the equal of any man. Said Jane to Mr. Rochester, the brooding, haughty, haunted master of Thornfield: "Do you think I am an automaton?—a machine without feelings? Do you think, because I am poor, obscure, plain, and little, I am soulless and heartless? You think wrong!—I have as much soul as you, and full as much heart!"

I loved it that such hot fires burned inside so plain a Jane. I   13
loved her for her unabashed intensity. And I loved her for being so pure that when she learned of Mr. Rochester's lunatic wife, she sacrificed romance for honor and left him immediately.

For I think it's important to note that Nancy and Jo and Jane,   14
despite their independence, were basically as good as girls can be:

honest, generous, kind, sincere, reliable, respectable, possessed of absolute integrity. They didn't defy convention. They didn't challenge the rules. They did what was right, although it might cause them pain. And their virtue was always rewarded—look at Jane, rich and married at last to her Mr. Rochester. Oh, how I identified with Jane!

But then I read *Wuthering Heights,* a novel of soul-consuming 15
love on the Yorkshire moors, and Catherine Earnshaw totally captured me. And she captured me, not in spite of her dangerous, dark and violent spirit, but *because* of it.

Cathy was as wild as the moors. She lied and connived and 16
deceived. She was insolent, selfish, manipulative and cruel. And by marrying meek, weak Edgar instead of Heathcliff, her destiny, she betrayed a love she described in throbbing, unforgettable prose as . . . elemental:

"My love for Heathcliff resembles the eternal rocks beneath— 17
a source of little visible delight, but necessary. Nelly, I *am* Heathcliff—he's always, always in my mind—not as a pleasure, any more than I am always a pleasure to myself—but as my own being. . . ."

Now who, at the age of 16, could resist such quivering inten- 18
sity? Who would settle for less than elemental? Must we untamed creatures of passion—I'd muse as I lay awake in my red flannel nightie—submit ourselves to conventional morality? Or could I actually choose not to be a good girl?

Cathy Earnshaw told me that I could. And so did lost Lady 19
Brett, of *The Sun Also Rises.*

Brett Ashley was to me, at 18, free, modern, woman incar- 20
nate, and she dangled alluring new concepts before my eyes:

The value of style: "She wore a slipover jersey sweater and a 21
tweed skirt, and her hair was brushed back like a boy's. She started all that."

The glamour of having a dark and tortured past: "Finally, 22
when he got really bad, he used to tell her he'd kill her. . . . She hasn't had an absolutely happy life."

The excitement of nonconformity: "I've always done just what 23
I wanted."

Emily Brontë (1818–1848), younger sister of Charlotte, wrote the passionate and mystically intense novel *Wuthering Heights.* Wuthering Heights is the Yorkshire moorland estate where the story takes place. The adjective *wuthering* is a Yorkshire word referring to turbulent weather, and so the place and the weather reflect the psychological turbulence of the story.

The Sun Also Rises is a novel by Ernest Hemingway (1899–1961). Considered by many critics to be his finest work, it deals with the "lost generation" of Americans who fought in France during World War I and then expatriated themselves from the America of Calvin Coolidge. The story is told by Jake Barnes, rendered impotent by a war wound. Lady Brett Ashley, who is divorcing her husband, is in love with him. These two go to Spain with a group that includes Michael Campbell, whom Brett plans to marry; Bill Gorton, a friend of Jake; a Greek nobleman; and Robert Cohn, an American-Jewish writer. Brett has an affair

The importance of (understated) grace under pressure: "Brett   24
was rather good. She's always rather good."

And the thrill of unrepressed sexuality: "Brett's had affairs   25
with men before. She tells me all about everything."

Brett married lovelessly and drank too much and drifted too   26
much and had an irresponsible fling with a bullfighter. But she
also had class—and her own morality. She set her bullfighter
free—"I'd have lived with him if I hadn't seen it was bad for him."
And even though she was broke, she lied and "told him I had
scads of it. . . . I couldn't take his money, you know."

Brett's wasn't the kind of morality that my mother was teach-   27
ing me in suburban New Jersey. But maybe I wasn't meant for
suburban life. Maybe—I would muse as I carefully lined my eyes
with blue liner—maybe I'm meant for something more . . .
emancipated.

I carried Brett's image with me when, after college, I lived for   28
a while in Greenwich Village, in New York. But I couldn't achieve
her desperate gallantry. And it struck me that Brett was too lonely
and sad, and that Cathy had died too young (and that Scarlett
O'Hara got Tara but lost her Rhett), and that maybe I ought to
forget about unconventionality if the price was going to be so
painfully high. Although I enjoyed my Village fling, I had no wish
to live anguishedly ever after. I needed a heroine who, like me,
wanted just a small taste of the wild before settling down into
happy domesticity.

I found her in *War and Peace*. Her name was Natasha.   29

Natasha, the leading lady of this epic of Russian society dur-   30
ing Napoleon's time, was "poetic . . . charming . . . overflowing
with life," an enchanting girl whose sweet eagerness and passionate impulsivity were tempered by historic and private tragedies.
Betrothed to the handsome and excellent Prince Andrew, she fell
in love with a heel named Anatole, and when she was warned that
this foolish and dangerous passion would lead to her ruin, "I'll go
to my ruin . . . ," she said, "as soon as possible."

It ended badly with Anatole. Natasha tried suicide. Prince   31
Andrew died. Natasha turned pale, thin, subdued. But unlike
Brett and Cathy, her breach with convention was mended and, at

with Romero, a bullfighter whom the others
respect for his grace and control in the face of
danger; she eventually leaves him and returns
to Michael. At the end, nothing has really
changed in life for any of the characters, which
is exactly the point of the novel: for these disillusioned people, life can have no direction,
no point toward which to develop.

Scarlett O'Hara is the heroine of *Gone with the
Wind,* a historical novel by Margaret Mitchell
(1900–1949). She is a fiery southern belle,
whose love for Ashley Wilkes is frustrated
when he marries gentle Melanie Hamilton.
After being widowed twice, Scarlett marries Rhett Butler, who proves more than a
match for her. The novel also depicts, from a
southern viewpoint, the tumult and suffering
caused by the War between the States and
Reconstruction.

War and Peace, a novel by Count Leo Tolstoy
(1828–1910), is considered the author's mas-
terwork. The story covers roughly the years
between 1805 and 1820, centering on the invasion of Russia by Napoleon's army in 1812
and the Russian resistance to the invader.
More than 500 characters, all completely and
individually rendered, throng the pages of the
novel. Every social level from Napoleon himself to the peasant Platon Karatayev, is represented. Interwoven with the story of the war
are narrations on the lives of several main
characters, especially those of Natasha Ros-
tova, Prince Andrei Balkonski, and Pierre Be-
zukhov. These people are shown as they

progress from youthful uncertainties and searchings toward more mature understanding of life. Natasha exemplifies the instinctual approach to life that Tolstoy was later to preach as the way to true happiness. She is one of the most successful characters in the book and perhaps ranks as Tolstoy's greatest achievement in character creation. Everything from her girlish excitement at her first ball through her experiences of first love and her final role as wife and mother are depicted with perfect skill.

long last, she married Pierre—a decent, substantial, loving man, the kind of man all our mothers want us to marry.

In marriage Natasha grew stouter and "the old fire very rarely kindled in her face now." She became an exemplary mother, an ideal wife. "She felt that her unity with her husband was maintained not by the poetic feelings that had attracted him to her but by something else—indefinite but firm as the bond between her own body and soul." 32

It sounded—if not elemental and doomed—awfully nice. 33

I identified with Natasha when, the following year, I married and left Greenwich Village. I too was ready for domesticity. And yet . . . her husband and children became "the subject which wholly engrossed Natasha's attention." She had lost herself—and I didn't want to lose me. What I needed next was a heroine who could reconcile all the warring wants of my nature—for fire and quiet, independence and oneness, ambition and love, and marriage and family. 34

But such reconciling heroines, in novels and real life, may not yet exist. 35

Nevertheless Natasha and Jane and Jo, Cathy, Nancy and Brett—each spoke to my heart and stirred me powerfully. On my journey to young womanhood I was fortunate to have them as my companions. They were, they will always remain, a part of me. 36

Meaning and Purpose

1. What books have shaped your life so far? Name at least three and describe their heroes and heroines. Can you associate these books with specific times in your life, as Viorst does with hers?
2. What is Viorst's main point in her essay, and where does she state it?
3. Who were Viorst's heroines, and what does she find attractive about each? Why does she put them in the order she chooses?

4. Why do you think Viorst chose heroines from works of fiction rather than from real life?
5. Do Viorst's heroines always have a positive, uplifting effect on her? Explain.

Strategy

1. Viorst uses first person throughout her essay and does not address the reader directly. How does this strategy draw readers into her analysis?
2. How does Viorst organize her essay? How is the process structured?
3. Viorst uses some one- and two-sentence paragraphs (2, 4, 8, 10, 15, 19, 29, 33, 35). How does each of these function in the essay?

Style

1. From what perspective does Viorst discuss her heroines, and what is her attitude toward them and toward their influence on her? Support your answers with statements from the essay.
2. Viorst often uses dashes in her sentences. What effect do they create?
3. How does Viorst use sentence fragments? Are they effective? Why or why not?
4. If necessary, check a dictionary for the meanings of these words: *gawky, gauche* (5); *brusque* (11); *curry favor* (12); *unabashed* (13); *incarnate* (20).

fictional heroines who influenced her as a girl and show how they were a standard of measure for her.

3. Viorst lists her heroines chronologically, according to her own natural development and maturation.

4. Viorst has obviously read fiction from an early age, and purposefully at that (1). She finds in fiction characters and human situations more vividly and psychologically real than those in history. Good novelists are able to imaginatively penetrate the human psyche.

5. In paragraph 28, Viorst describes a darker side to a few of her heroines and says, "I had no wish to live anguishedly [as they did]." She ends her essay by acknowledging that "such reconciling heroines [whom she now longs for], in novels and real life, may not yet exist" (paragraph 35).

Strategy

1. Viorst can talk about her heroines in first person only because they are peculiar to her and were important at specific times in her life. She can't speak so for anyone else. But the general appeal of this first-person strategy is that readers are free to fill in their own heroes and heroines and make a similar list for themselves. The more specific writing is, the more universal its appeal.

2. In this informative process analysis, Viorst begins chronologically with Nancy Drew and ends five heroines later with Natasha of *War and Peace*. Viorst talks about how each one influenced her at the time she read them, and also relates what was important then in her own life. She makes clear her identification with each heroine (last sentence, 14; 27). Viorst paces her chronology with an explanation of each heroine's character, often with quotations from the novels, and with summaries of her fascination with the heroine. Within the order in which she read the books is Viorst's own chronology, from age ten to being "ready for domesticity" (34).

3. Each of these paragraphs serves as a transition, carrying the reader gracefully from one heroine to the next. Paragraph 2 is a transition from thesis to body of the essay.

Style

1. Viorst is looking back as a grown woman on her childhood (2). She has insight into her own maturation that she couldn't have had as a girl. Paragraph 18 illustrates this viewpoint. Viorst's attitude is fond and affectionate—and understanding—toward her fascination with girlhood heroines (sentence 1, paragraph 11), and she says, "I was fortunate to have had them as my companions" (last paragraph).
2. Dashes set off sentence elements from each other sharply and usually emphasize them. Viorst uses the dash to set off an appositive (sentence 1, paragraph 1), to set off a parenthetical element that is abrupt (sentence 1, paragraph 3), and to mark a sudden break in thought (sentence 3, paragraph 3).
3. Viorst uses fragments for emphasis and sometimes informality. With fragments she can avoid colorless or repetitious noun or verb phrases. In context, these fragments (often called "minor sentences") are clear and complete, but they are grammatically incomplete (they do not have an independent noun phrase plus verb-phrase core). Viorst's most extensive use of fragments for rhetorical purposes is in 5. The first group of minor sentences sets off each of the main characters in *Little Women*. The second group isolates characteristics that the author and fictional characters Jo and Nancy Drew have in common.

Many students are not ready to use fragments stylistically and should stick to complete sentences.
4. *Gawky:* awkward, ungainly, clumsy; *gauche:* lacking social grace, sensitivity; *brusque:* abrupt in manner, blunt, rough; *curry favor:* to seek to advance oneself by flattery or fawning; *unabashed:* unashamed; *incarnate:* embodied in flesh.

Writing Tasks

1. Using Viorst's essay as a model, write an informative process analysis showing how a series of events, situations, or people helped you grow up.
2. When Judith Viorst was a preteenager, girls read Nancy Drew and boys read the Hardy boys. What did you read when you were ten to twelve years old, and how did those books and characters reflect your values? How were they a standard of measure for you?

❦ Joan Didion ❦

A Californian by birth, educated at the University of California at Berkeley, descended from pioneers, Joan Didion has written extensively about contemporary life in the western United States. From 1956 to 1963 she was an associate feature editor at Vogue *magazine, and during that time published widely in prominent national magazines. Her first book of essays,* Slouching Towards Bethlehem *(1968), compiles many of those early essays and focuses on America in the 1960s, particularly San Francisco. She has written four novels, including* Play It as It Lays *(1970) and* Book of Common Prayer *(1977), and collaborated with her husband on several screenplays. She is known for her incisive reflections and unique vision of American life-styles.*

On Keeping a Notebook

In this essay from Slouching Towards Bethlehem, *Joan Didion explains the purpose and importance, for her, of keeping a notebook. Though her analysis is primarily informational, it might also be considered directional for readers who are inclined to keep notebooks. She offers the process as a way for the writer to "keep in touch" with the people he or she "used to be."*

" 'That woman Estelle,' " the note reads, " 'is partly the reason why George Sharp and I are separated today.' *Dirty crêpe-de-Chine wrapper, hotel bar, Wilmington RR, 9:45 A.M. August Monday morning.*"

Since the note is in my notebook, it presumably has some meaning to me. I study it for a long while. At first I have only the most general notion of what I was doing on an August Monday morning in the bar of the hotel across from the Pennsylvania Railroad station in Wilmington, Delaware (waiting for a train? missing one? 1960? 1961? why Wilmington?), but I do remember

375

TEACHING SUGGESTIONS

In this essay the writer imaginatively discovers the writing process, engaging it by using her notes as a source of invention (accumulating information). Then she moves to drafting and revising, which for her requires an active imagination and memory, including "what some would call lies." She leaves out mention of the edited version, trusting that the essay readers hold in their hands will show that such a thing is possible.

You might want to discuss briefly the writing process, focusing on poetic license as it is used when writing drafts, according to this essay. Some students who have heard the expression "poetic license" seem to believe that it means "to write in any way you want because it's *your* writing."

"Poetic license" connotes departing from that which is acceptable as normal, but the departure must have its own defense. Didion uses "lies" in drafts of her essays, but her defense is that such a strategy gives her the creative latitude necessary to produce another kind of truth, universally interesting truth. Didion uses her notes to trigger her creative imagination.

You might want to have students bring to class and discuss an editorial or a story from the sports page of a newspaper, examining word choice. Do athletic teams "kill," "slaughter," "roll over," or "stomp" their opponents? Or do they merely "win"?

MARGINAL NOTES

The essay begins *in medias res,* "in the midst of things." Didion opens the story in the middle of an action and then adds information with flashbacks and other devices. *crêpe-de-Chine:* soft, crinkly fabric, usually silk.

The process of keeping a notebook has shaped Didion's life by helping her recollect general incidents. Her memory is jogged here, and the audience receives an anecdote replete with detail.

She develops the psychological details of the incident, expanding the note into a developing story. The 1960s New York stock character in the story represents Didion's imaginatively working out the details in her note.

The process is cyclic. The author reads one of her notes and then develops the note into a detailed fictional account. Then she moves to question herself about having written the note in the first place. Or about keeping a notebook, for that matter, which she justifies as being compulsive, growing from an impulse unique to some people.

The cyclic process moves autobiographically, giving the author a chance to remark that she

being there. The woman in the dirty crêpe-de-Chine wrapper had come down from her room for a beer, and the bartender had heard before the reason why George Sharp and she were separated today. "Sure," he said, and went on mopping the floor. "You told me." At the other end of the bar is a girl. She is talking, pointedly, not to the man beside her but to a cat lying in the triangle of sunlight cast through the open door. She is wearing a plaid silk dress from Peck & Peck, and the hem is coming down.

Here is what it is: the girl has been on the Eastern Shore, and now she is going back to the city, leaving the man beside her, and all she can see ahead are the viscous summer sidewalks and the 3 A.M. long-distance calls that will make her lie awake and then sleep drugged through all the steaming mornings left in August (1960? 1961?). Because she must go directly from the train to lunch in New York, she wishes that she had a safety pin for the hem of the plaid silk dress, and she also wishes that she could forget about the hem and the lunch and stay in the cool bar that smells of disinfectant and malt and make friends with the woman in the crêpe-de-Chine wrapper. She is afflicted by a little self-pity, and she wants to compare Estelles. That is what that was all about.

Why did I write it down? In order to remember, of course, but exactly what was it I wanted to remember? How much of it actually happened? Did any of it? Why do I keep a notebook at all? It is easy to deceive oneself on all those scores. The impulse to write things down is a peculiarly compulsive one, inexplicable to those who do not share it, useful only accidentally, only secondarily, in the way that any compulsion tries to justify itself. I suppose that it begins or does not begin in the cradle. Although I have felt compelled to write things down since I was five years old, I doubt that my daughter ever will, for she is a singularly blessed and accepting child, delighted with life exactly as life presents itself to her, unafraid to go to sleep and unafraid to wake up. Keepers of private notebooks are a different breed altogether, lonely and resistant rearrangers of things, anxious malcontents, children afflicted apparently at birth with some presentiment of loss.

My first notebook was a Big Five tablet, given to me by my mother with the sensible suggestion that I stop whining and learn to amuse myself by writing down my thoughts. She returned the tablet to me a few years ago; the first entry is an account of a woman who believed herself to be freezing to death in the Arctic night, only to find, when day broke, that she had stumbled onto the Sahara Desert, where she would die of the heat before lunch. I have no idea what turn of a five-year-old's mind could have prompted so insistently "ironic" and exotic a story, but it does reveal a certain predilection for the extreme which has dogged me into adult life; perhaps if I were analytically inclined I would find it a truer story than any I might have told about Donald Johnson's birthday party or the day my cousin Brenda put Kitty Litter in the aquarium.

So the point of my keeping a notebook has never been, nor is it now, to have an accurate factual record of what I have been doing or thinking. That would be a different impulse entirely, an instinct for reality which I sometimes envy but do not possess. At no point have I ever been able successfully to keep a diary; my approach to daily life ranges from the grossly negligent to the merely absent, and on those few occasions when I have tried dutifully to record a day's events, boredom has so overcome me that the results are mysterious at best. What is this business about "shopping, typing piece, dinner with E, depressed"? Shopping for what? Type what piece? Who is E? Was this "E" depressed, or was I depressed? Who cares?

In fact I have abandoned altogether that kind of pointless entry; instead I tell what some would call lies. "That's simply not true," the members of my family frequently tell me when they come up against my memory of a shared event. "The party was not for you, the spider was *not* a black widow, *it wasn't that way at all.*" Very likely they are right, for not only have I always had trouble distinguishing between what happened and what merely might have happened, but I remain unconvinced that the distinction, for my purposes, matters. The cracked crab that I recall having for lunch the day my father came home from Detroit in 1945 must certainly be embroidery, worked into the day's pattern to lend verisimilitude; I was ten years old and would not now remember the cracked crab. The day's events did not turn on

did not progress gradually through life. Instead, she went through stages, a concept that permits Didion to examine her five-year-old self as if that person were now external.

6 Didion's notebook, not factually accurate, nevertheless provides a psychological record of her experiences. The process of keeping the notebook holds her life together, but not necessarily in the austere, orderly way that would come from her keeping a record of each day's events.

7 The author's cyclic process of keeping and using a notebook, her way of recording experiences and then remembering them, grows from her imagination. Unlike the newspaper journalist or the keeper of a diary, Didion does not simply record experiences. She filters her experiences however she wishes. But when she looks back at what she has done to those experiences—adding a fictitious cracked crab to a lunch, for example—she remembers the details of their reality.

cracked crab. And yet it is precisely that fictitious crab that makes me see the afternoon all over again, a home movie run all too often, the father bearing gifts, the child weeping, an exercise in family love and guilt. Or that is what it was to me. Similarly, perhaps it never did snow that August in Vermont; perhaps there never were flurries in the night wind, and maybe no one else felt the ground hardening and summer already dead even as we pretended to bask in it, but that was how it felt to me; and it might as well have snowed, could have snowed, did snow.

How it felt to me: that is getting closer to the truth about a 8 notebook. I sometimes delude myself about why I keep a notebook, imagine that some thrifty virtue derives from preserving everything observed. See enough and write it down, I tell myself and then some morning when the world seems drained of wonder, some day when I am only going through the motions of doing what I am supposed to do, which is write—on that bankrupt morning I will simply open my notebook and there it will be, a forgotten account with accumulated interest, paid passage back to the world out there: dialogue overheard in hotels and elevators and at the hatcheck counter in Pavillon (one middle-aged man shows his hat check to another and says, "That's my old football number"); impressions of Bettina Aptheker and Benjamin Sonnenberg and Teddy ("Mr. Acapulco") Stauffer; careful *aperçus* about tennis bums and failed fashion models and Greek shipping heiresses, one of whom taught me a significant lesson (a lesson I could have learned from F. Scott Fitzgerald, but perhaps we all must meet the very rich for ourselves) by asking, when I arrived to interview her in her orchid-filled sitting room on the second day of a paralyzing New York blizzard, whether it was snowing outside.

I imagine, in other words, that the notebook is about other 9 people. But of course it is not. I have no real business with what one stranger said to another at the hatcheck counter in Pavillon; in fact I suspect that the line "That's my old football number" touched not my own imagination at all, but merely some memory

---

The cyclic process is explained here. The ostensible reason for her keeping a notebook is to have detailed descriptions of people, places, and events, so that on days when the imagination will not boil forth, Didion can summon the remembrances of things past from her notebook and then write.

But no. The notebook does not collect other people and events so much as it gathers Didion's reactions *to* other people and events. The notebook tells Didion about how she was, among the events, not about how the events were, with her looking, describing, and recording them.

Aperçus: quick insights or surveys.

F. Scott Fitzgerald (1896–1940) chronicled the extraordinary lives of wealthy Americans, especially in *The Great Gatsby* (1925).

of something once read, probably "The Eighty-Yard Run." Nor is my concern with a woman in a dirty crêpe-de-Chine wrapper in a Wilmington bar. My stake is always, of course, in the unmentioned girl in the plaid silk dress. *Remember what it was to be me:* that is always the point.

It is a difficult point to admit. We are brought up in the ethic that others, any others, all others, are by definition more interesting than ourselves; taught to be diffident, just this side of self-effacing. ("You're the least important person in the room and don't forget it," Jessica Mitford's governess would hiss in her ear on the advent of any social occasion; I copied that into my notebook because it is only recently that I have been able to enter a room without hearing some such phrase in my inner ear.) Only the very young and the very old may recount their dreams at breakfast, dwell upon self, interrupt with memories of beach picnics and favorite Liberty lawn dresses and the rainbow trout in a creek near Colorado Springs. The rest of us are expected, rightly, to affect absorption in other people's favorite dresses, other people's trout.

And so we do. But our notebooks give us away, for however dutifully we record what we see around us, the common denominator of all we see is always, transparently, shamelessly, the implacable "I". We are not talking here about the kind of notebook that is patently for public consumption, a structural conceit for binding together a series of graceful *pensées;* we are talking about something private, about bits of the mind's string too short to use, an indiscriminate and erratic assemblage with meaning only for its maker.

And sometimes even the maker has difficulty with the meaning. There does not seem to be, for example, any point in my knowing for the rest of my life that, during 1964, 720 tons of soot fell on every square mile of New York City, yet there it is in my notebook, labeled "FACT." Nor do I really need to remember that Ambrose Bierce liked to spell Leland Stanford's name "£eland $tanford" or that "smart women almost always wear black in Cuba," a fashion hint without much potential for practical

10   Didion herself is the "unmentioned girl in the plaid silk dress."

Didion's notebook causes her to remember Didion, rather than the events around her. She sees events, she writes them down colored by her own reactions to them or their effects on her, and she later processes them, adding her own details. Life processes life.

The author begins by admitting the obvious, that we are taught a particular way to affect behavior. But in the notebook of our minds we behave in quite another way, directed by "the implacable 'I'."

11   How we act and how we think while we act parallel the notions of appearance versus reality. Here, the reality is what Didion constructs from her notebook, fragments expanded by her imagination into newly minted events, giving old reality a new meaning and life of its own, a fiction.

Pensées: reflections or thoughts.

12   If the maker has difficulty with the meaning, even then the meaning remains. Everything in Didion's notebook either is later expanded in her imagination or is a point on her mental compass to remind her where she was or where she is. Nothing is useless that remains in her notebook.

Ambrose Bierce (1842–1914?): American journalist and short-story writer best known for *Devil's Dictionary* (1906), in which he defined *achievement,* for example, as "the death of endeavor and the birth of disgust."

Leland Stanford (1824–1893): Capitalist and politician. Governor of California (1861–1863). Promoted and financed Central Pacific Railroad, western link in transcontinental line. United States Senator (1885–1893). Founded Stanford University.

Ambergris: a gray waxy substance from the intestinal canal of sperm whales. It used to be the basis for the most expensive perfume extracts until a substitute was synthesized.

The Wall Street stock-market crash of 1929.

James Riddle Hoffa (1913–1975?): President of the International Brotherhood of Teamsters (1957–1971). Murder suspected—involved with gangsters; body never found.

Syndicate: A nationwide network of criminals.

John O'Hara (1905–1970): Journalist, realistic novelist—*Appointment in Samarra* (1934), *Butterfield 8* (1935), and *Pal Joey* (1940).

application. And does not the relevance of these notes seem marginal at best?:

> In the basement of the Inyo County Courthouse in Independence, California, sign pinned to a mandarin coat: "This MANDARIN COAT was often worn by Mrs. Minnie S. Brooks when giving lectures on her TEAPOT COLLECTION."

> Redhead getting out of car in front of Beverly Wilshire Hotel, chinchilla stole, Vuitton bags with tags reading:
> Mrs Lou Fox
> Hotel Sahara
> Vegas

Well, perhaps not entirely marginal. As a matter of fact, Mrs. Minnie S. Brooks and her MANDARIN COAT pull me back into my own childhood, for although I never knew Mrs. Brooks and did not visit Inyo County until I was thirty, I grew up in just such a world, in houses cluttered with Indian relics and bits of gold ore and ambergris and the souvenirs my Aunt Mercy Farnsworth brought back from the Orient. It is a long way from that world to Mrs. Lou Fox's world where we all live now, and is it not just as well to remember that? Might not Mrs. Minnie S. Brooks help me to remember what I am? Might not Mrs. Lou Fox help me to remember what I am not?

But sometimes the point is harder to discern. What exactly   13
did I have in mind when I noted down that it cost the father of someone I know $650 a month to light the place on the Hudson in which he lived before the Crash? What use was I planning to make of this line by Jimmy Hoffa: "I may have my faults, but being wrong ain't one of them"? And although I think it interesting to know where the girls who travel with the Syndicate have their hair done when they find themselves on the West Coast, will I ever make suitable use of it? Might I not be better off just passing it on to John O'Hara? What is a recipe for sauerkraut doing in my notebook? What kind of magpie keeps this note-

book? *"He was born the night the* Titanic *went down."* That seems a nice enough line, and I even recall who said it, but is it not really a better line in life than it could ever be in fiction?

But of course that is exactly it: not that I should ever use the line, but that I should remember the woman who said it and the afternoon I heard it. We were on her terrace by the sea, and we were finishing the wine left from lunch, trying to get what sun there was, a California winter sun. The woman whose husband was born the night the *Titanic* went down wanted to rent her house, wanted to go back to her children in Paris. I remember wishing that I could afford the house, which cost $1,000 a month. "Someday you will," she said lazily. "Someday it all comes." There in the sun on her terrace it seemed easy to believe in someday but later I had a low-grade afternoon hangover and ran over a black snake on the way to the supermarket and was flooded with inexplicable fear when I heard the checkout clerk explaining to the man ahead of me why she was finally divorcing her husband. "He left me no choice," she said over and over as she punched the register. "He has a little seven-month-old baby by her, he left me no choice." I would like to believe that my dread then was for the human condition, but of course it was for me, because I wanted a baby and did not then have one and because I wanted to own the house that cost $1,000 a month to rent and because I had a hangover.

It all comes back. Perhaps it is difficult to see the value in having one's self back in that kind of mood, but I do see it; I think we are well advised to keep on nodding terms with the people we used to be, whether we find them attractive company or not. Otherwise they turn up unannounced and surprise us, come hammering on the mind's door at 4 A.M. of a bad night and demand to know who deserted them, who betrayed them, who is going to make amends. We forget all too soon the things we thought we could never forget. We forget the loves and the betrayals alike, forget what we whispered and what we screamed, forget who we were. I have already lost touch with a couple of people I used to be; one of them, a seventeen-year-old, presents little threat, although it would be of some interest to me to know again

14   *Titanic:* A British luxury liner, supposedly unsinkable, which sank after hitting an iceberg in the North Atlantic on her maiden voyage in April 1912, with a loss of 1,517 lives.

The first exemplar paragraph. The woman who wanted to go back to Paris and the checkout clerk both have their stories, which Didion duly records. Later, upon reflection, she sees how those women's stories are, in themselves, not important. What matters is how those stories have affected Didion. Her aspirations mirror part of each woman's life.

15   Didion's keeping this kind of notebook amounts to the psychological process of recording her individuality as she moves from one phase in her life to the next. The value of this process is that it reminds Didion of her self as that self has evolved over the years. Rereading the notes that bring imaginatively to mind the former selves helps to contain the former selves.

what it feels like to sit on a river levee drinking vodka-and-orange-juice and listening to Les Paul and Mary Ford and their echoes sing "How High the Moon" on the car radio. (You see I still have the scenes, but I no longer perceive myself among those present, no longer could even improvise the dialogue.) The other one, a twenty-three-year-old, bothers me more. She was always a good deal of trouble, and I suspect she will reappear when I least want to see her, skirts too long, shy to the point of aggravation, always the injured party, full of recriminations and little hurts and stories I do not want to hear again, at once saddening me and angering me with her vulnerability and ignorance, an apparition all the more insistent for being so long banished.

It is a good idea, then, to keep in touch and I suppose that keeping in touch is what notebooks are all about. And we are all on our own when it comes to keeping those lines open to ourselves: your notebooks will never help me, nor mine you. *"So what's new in the whiskey business?"* What could that possibly mean to you? To me it means a blonde in a Pucci bathing suit sitting with a couple of fat men by the pool at the Beverly Hills Hotel. Another man approaches, and they all regard one another in silence for a while. "So what's new in the whiskey business?" one of the fat men finally says by way of welcome, and the blonde stands up, arches one foot and dips it in the pool, looking all the while at the cabana where Baby Pignatari is talking on the telephone. That is all there is to that, except that several years later I saw the blonde coming out of Saks Fifth Avenue in New York with her California complexion and a voluminous mink coat. In the harsh wind that day she looked old and irrevocably tired to me, and even the skins in the mink coat were not worked the way they were doing them that year, not the way she would have wanted them done, and there is the point of the story. For a while after that I did not like to look in the mirror, and my eyes would skim the newspapers and pick out only the deaths, the cancer victims, the premature coronaries, the suicides, and I stopped riding the Lexington Avenue IRT because I noticed for the first time that all the strangers I had seen for years—the man with the

16

The second exemplar paragraph. Baby Pignatari was a leader in the Syndicate. Our notebooks are for ourselves. The anecdote about the blonde reminds Didion heavily of how time affects other people's looks and fortunes, so strongly that she begins to avoid evidence of how time affects her.

Writing about the process of keeping her notebook benefits Didion: "It all comes back." She wrote a passage that amounts to an extended notebook entry about the process of keeping a notebook, which in turn led her to remember details of events entered in the original notebook. The process is complete.

seeing-eye dog, the spinster who read the classified pages every day, the fat girl who always got off with me at Grand Central—looked older than they once had.

It all comes back. Even that recipe for sauerkraut: even that brings it back. I was on Fire Island when I first made sauerkraut, and it was raining, and we drank a lot of bourbon and ate the sauerkraut and went to bed at ten, and I listened to the rain and the Atlantic and felt safe. I made the sauerkraut again last night and it did not make me feel any safer, but that is, as they say, another story.   17

Meaning and Purpose

1. After reading this essay, you know that a diary and a notebook differ. What is one big difference?
2. Do you keep a notebook or journal? If so, how does your method of writing in it, and the use you make of it, compare to Didion's?
3. What is one process the author discusses, and why does any writer need to become familiar with it?
4. In a line in paragraph 11, Didion says, "Our notebooks give us away." To whom do they give us away?
5. Several statements in the essay could be taken as versions of Didion's main point. What are some of them, and how are they related to one another?

Strategy

1. The essay begins in the middle of an action—Didion is reading a note she wrote in her notebook. Then, before she gives a context for the note, she talks about it and embellishes it. Why do you think she begins in this way?

2. The little stories about the notes tie together the progression of Didion's main points. She expands the context of the notes to lead herself to realize what she is really doing: remembering, and thereby keeping an account of herself. Paragraph 7 is a good example of this act when she talks about the cracked crab that "makes me see the afternoon all over again . . . that is what it [the incident] was to me." And then in paragraph 8 she solidifies this insight with, "*How it felt to me:* that is getting closer to the truth about a notebook."

3. Didion does in a sense bring the essay full circle by explaining the note about the sauerkraut recipe. But she has also gained insight here by going through the process of the notebook. "It all comes back" (paragraph 19)—the notebook is about bringing the past back, remembering who she was. And when she makes the sauerkraut "again last night," she suggests there is another story, one that perhaps won't be understood until she can look back later at what she recorded in her notebook.

Style

1. Didion's language is informal and conversational, as if she is thinking out loud. She is sharing something quite personal in her notebooks. The transition from paragraphs 7 to 8 shows this thinking-aloud voice. She is conjecturing here about the truth of one of her notes, and then she comes suddenly to a realization—"*How it felt to me*"—in paragraph 8.

2. An "Estelle" is "the other woman," the one who is responsible for breaking up a romantic relationship. (The name "Estelle" comes from a Latin word meaning "star.")

3. Students' answers will vary. They might include references to a suntan, sunstreaked hair—whatever else they believe the stereotype includes.

4. A predilection is a preconceived liking, a partiality. A "predilection for the extreme" describes a person who sees or imagines the exotic or extreme in a situation. This is Didion talking about herself as a writer.

2. In the structure of her essay, how does Didion make use of the little stories behind the brief notes she has written in her notebook?

3. Didion ends her essay with the story of the recipe for sauerkraut, another note expanded into an anecdote. Is she ending in the middle again, as she began? Discuss the effectiveness of the ending.

Style

1. What is Didion's tone in this essay—her attitude toward her subject?

2. In paragraph 3, the writer says she "wants to compare Estelles," using the noun metaphorically. What is an "Estelle"?

3. "California complexion," in paragraph 16, is an example of stereotyping. In your opinion, what is "California complexion"?

4. In paragraph 5, Didion mentions that she has a "predilection for the extreme." Explain this phrase.

Writing Tasks

1. Describe one of your dreams and discuss what it reveals about you, just as Didion discusses what her notebook reveals about her.

2. Didion describes a process linked to the creative imagination. Her notes themselves are not so important as what those notes suggest to her, imaginatively. Using a similar procedure, choose three related personal items. Write an informative process analysis in which you describe these items briefly, and then discuss what they mean emotionally to you.

❦ Jessica Mitford ❦

Born in England in 1917 to wealthy parents, Mitford was educated at home by her mother. She emigrated to the United States in 1939 at age twenty-two, later to become a naturalized citizen. She worked at several jobs before devoting herself to investigative journalism in her late thirties. She is known for her books of scathing social criticism and satire, including The American Way of Death *(1963), which brought her literary acclaim at age forty-six. Her articles have appeared in* Harper's, The Atlantic, *and other major periodicals and have been collected in an anthology covering twenty-two years of her work,* Poison Penmanship: The Gentle Art of Muckraking *(1979). Her eccentric family is the subject of her incisive commentary in her autobiographical works,* Daughters and Rebels *(1960) and* A Fine Old Madness *(1977).*

The American Way of Death

This essay is an excerpt from Mitford's book by the same title. The author describes in detail the process of embalming a corpse and making it presentable to viewers. She explains this procedure as it affects the financial gains it brings the embalmer as her way of commenting on the "business" of death in the United States.

The drama begins to unfold with the arrival of the corpse at the mortuary. [1]

Alas, poor Yorick! How surprised he would be to see how his counterpart of today is whisked off to a funeral parlor and is in short order sprayed, sliced, pierced, pickled, trussed, trimmed, creamed, waxed, painted, rouged, and neatly dressed—transformed from a common corpse into a Beautiful Memory Picture. This process is known in the trade as embalming and restorative art, and is so universally employed in the United States and Canada that the funeral director does it routinely, without consulting [2]

385

TEACHING SUGGESTIONS

Mitford's discussion of embalming is also a social commentary on an unexamined custom. If we had only this essay from which to reason, we would come away from it believing that embalmers are in business only to make money. But barbershops and beauty parlors too are in business to make money. Embalmers, barbers, hair stylists, and other provide a service, not a product.

Hair stylists and barbers profit from unexamined customs, another name for styles that change from season to season and from year to year and are apparent to everyone. The class might want to discuss other unexamined customs, including their humorous aspects. What comprises "psyching out" a teacher?

What steps are in the "education process," which is often discussed, but seldom defined? Are all those steps formal, or do some of them take place outside of class, in places like the library, a snack bar, or on the quad or the school lawn?

We often talk as if a custom were a block of thought, rather than a process with discrete steps. Breaking customs into steps, students think how much of their lives is "customized."

MARGINAL NOTES

Mitford's "drama" and "corpse" in paragraph 1 are followed, in paragraph 2, by Hamlet's graveyard remark to Horatio about Yorick. Hamlet's speech includes another line important in a later paragraph in this essay: "Here hung those lips that I have kissed I know not how oft" (*Hamlet*, V, i, 201).

Yorick was simply buried, without being embalmed. As staged, this scene usually features Hamlet holding aloft Yorick's skull as he speaks the line "Alas, poor Yorick!"

"Beautiful Memory Picture" is capitalized as it would appear in an advertisement by a funeral parlor.

The *balm* in "embalm" refers to anything soothing or healing. A thousand years ago in northern Europe, however, drastic measures were taken to prevent the dead from haunting the living. Often, the corpse was bound and the feet and head amputated.

We have come a long way. Neanderthals buried their dead ritually with food, weapons, fire charcoals, and flowers. The ancient Romans believed that funeral torches would guide the soul to its eternal resting place. The word *funeral* is from the Latin *funus,* "torch." Most of us know less about modern embalming than about Neanderthal and ancient Roman burial practices.

corpse or kin. He regards as eccentric those few who are hardy enough to suggest that it might be dispensed with. Yet no law requires embalming, no religious doctrine commends it, nor is it dictated by considerations of health, sanitation, or even of personal daintiness. In no part of the world but in Northern America is it widely used. The purpose of embalming is to make the corpse presentable for viewing in a suitably costly container; and here too the funeral director routinely, without first consulting the family, prepares the body for public display.

Is all this legal? The processes to which a dead body may be subjected are after all to some extent circumscribed by law. In most states, for instance, the signature of next of kin must be obtained before an autopsy may be performed, before the deceased may be cremated, before the body may be turned over to a medical school for research purposes; or such provision must be made in the decedent's will. In the case of embalming, no such permission is required nor is it ever sought. A textbook, *The Principles and Practices of Embalming,* comments on this: "There is some question regarding the legality of much that is done within the preparation room." The author points out that it would be most unusual for a responsible member of a bereaved family to instruct the mortician, in so many words, to "*embalm*" the body of a deceased relative. The very term "embalming" is so seldom used that the mortician must rely upon custom in the matter. The author concludes that unless the family specifies otherwise, the act of entrusting the body to the care of a funeral establishment carries with it an implied permission to go ahead and embalm.

Embalming is indeed a most extraordinary procedure, and one must wonder at the docility of Americans who each year pay hundreds of millions of dollars for its perpetuation, blissfully ignorant of what it is all about, what is done, how it is done. Not one in ten thousand has any idea of what actually takes place. Books on the subject are extremely hard to come by. They are not to be found in most libraries or bookshops.

In an era when huge television audiences watch surgical operations in the comfort of their living rooms, when, thanks to the animated cartoon, the geography of the digestive system has become familiar territory even to the nursery school set, in a land where the satisfaction of curiosity about almost all matters is a national pastime, the secrecy surrounding embalming can, surely, hardly be attributed to the inherent gruesomeness of the subject. Custom in this regard has within this century suffered a complete reversal. In the early days of American embalming, when it was performed in the home of the deceased, it was almost mandatory for some relative to stay by the embalmer's side and witness the procedure. Today, family members who might wish to be in attendance would certainly be dissuaded by the funeral director. All others, except apprentices, are excluded by law from the preparation room.

A close look at what does actually take place may explain in large measure the undertaker's intractable reticence concerning a procedure that has become his major *raison d'être*. Is it possible he fears that the public information about embalming might lead patrons to wonder if they really want this service? If the funeral men are loath to discuss the subject outside the trade, the reader may, understandably, be equally loath to go on reading at this point. For those who have the stomach for it, let us part the formaldehyde curtain. . . .

The body is first laid out in the undertaker's morgue—or rather, Mr. Jones is reposing in the preparation room—to be readied to bid the world farewell.

The preparation room in any of the better funeral establishments has the tiled and sterile look of a surgery, and indeed the embalmer-restorative artist who does his chores there is beginning to adopt the term "derma-surgeon" (appropriately corrupted by some mortician-writers as "demisurgeon") to describe his calling. His equipment, consisting of scalpels, scissors, augers, forceps, clamps, needles, pumps, tubes, bowls and basins, is crudely imitative of the surgeon's, as is his technique, acquired in a nine- or twelve-month post-high-school course in an embalming school. He is supplied by an advanced chemical industry with a bewildering array of fluids, sprays, pastes, oils, powders, creams, to fix or soften tissue, shrink or distend it as needed, dry it here, restore the moisture there. There are cosmetics, waxes and paints

6

7

8

We learn much about how our bodies function and how they are cared for, but little about how corpses are prepared for burial. We have distanced ourselves and our homes from deceased relatives.

French: "reason for being." Formaldehyde: HCHO, a colorless, pungent, irritant gas used as a preservative in an aqueous solution of 37 percent formaldehyde. A powerful disinfectant, it hardens and preserves tissue.

Part of the humorous introduction to the process, opening the metaphorical curtain begins the "drama" mentioned in paragraph 1.

The body is personified as the not-quite-anonymous "Mr. Jones."

derma-surgeon: The prefix *derma*, from Greek, means the "cutis vera," or true skin. demi-surgeon: the prefix *demi*, from Latin, means "half."

Just as the stage must be set for the drama, the preparation room must be set for the embalming.

to fill and cover features, even plaster of Paris to replace entire limbs. There are ingenious aids to prop and stabilize the cadaver: a Vari-Pose Head Rest, the Edwards Arm and Hand Positioner, the Repose Block (to support the shoulders during the embalming), and the Throop Foot Positioner, which resembles an old-fashioned stocks.

The author gives Mr. Eckels's description, another textbook's advice, and a third writer's comments, partly to provide a survey of the first stage in the process and partly to reveal the macabre humor accidentally transmitted to the readers of such information—humor that Mitford's commentary intensifies.

Mr. John H. Eckels, president of the Eckels College of Mortuary Science, thus describes the first part of the embalming procedure: "In the hands of a skilled practitioner, this work may be done in a comparatively short time and without mutilating the body other than by slight incision—so slight that it scarcely would cause serious inconvenience if made upon a living person. It is necessary to remove the blood, and doing this not only helps in the disinfecting, but removes the principal cause of disfigurements due to discoloration."   9

Another textbook discusses the all-important time element: "The earlier this is done, the better, for every hour that elapses between death and embalming will add to the problems and complications encountered. . . ." Just how soon should one get going on the embalming? The author tells us, "On the basis of such scanty information made available to this profession through its rudimentary and haphazard system of technical research, we must conclude that the best results are to be obtained if the subject is embalmed before life is completely extinct—that is, before cellular death has occurred. In the average case, this would mean within an hour after somatic death." For those who feel that there is something a little rudimentary, not to say haphazard, about this advice, a comforting thought is offered by another writer. Speaking of fears entertained in early days of premature burial, he points out, "One of the effects of embalming by chemical injection, however, has been to dispel fears of live burial." How true; once blood is removed, chances of live burial are indeed remote.   10

The process begins, with Mitford using the advertising claims for various embalming fluids to fortify the dry humor of her text. The right and left common carotid arteries are the principal blood supply to the head and neck. The

To return to Mr. Jones, the blood is drained out through the veins and replaced by embalming fluid pumped in through the arteries. As noted in *The Principles and Practices of Embalming,* "every operator has a favorite injection and drainage point—a fact   11 which becomes a handicap only if he fails or refuses to forsake his favorites when conditions demand it." Typical favorites are the carotid artery, femoral artery, jugular vein, subclavian vein. There are various choices of embalming fluid. If Flextone is used, it will produce a "mild, flexible rigidity. The skin retains a velvety softness, the tissues are rubbery and pliable. Ideal for women and children." It may be blended with B. and G. Products Company's Lyf-Lyk tint, which is guaranteed to reproduce "nature's own skin texture . . . the velvety appearance of living tissue." Suntone comes in three separate tints: Suntan; Special Cosmetic Tint, a pink shade "especially indicated for young female subjects"; and Regular Cosmetic Tint, moderately pink.

About three to six gallons of a dyed and perfumed solution of formaldehyde, glycerin, borax, phenol, alcohol, and water is soon circulating through Mr. Jones, whose mouth has been sewn together with a "needle directed upward between the upper lip and gum and brought out through the left nostril," with the corners raised slightly "for a more pleasant expression." If he should be bucktoothed, his teeth are cleaned with Bon Ami and coated with colorless nail polish. His eyes, meanwhile, are closed with flesh-tinted eye caps and eye cement.

12

The next step is to have at Mr. Jones with a thing called a trocar. This is a long, hollow needle attached to a tube. It is jabbed into the abdomen, poked around the entrails and chest cavity, the contents of which are pumped out and replaced with "cavity fluid." This done, and the hole in the abdomen sewn up, Mr. Jones's face is heavily creamed (to protect the skin from burns which may be caused by leakage of the chemicals), and he is covered with a sheet and left unmolested for a while. But not for long—there is more, much more, in store for him. He has been embalmed, but not yet restored, and the best time to start the restorative work is eight to ten hours after embalming, when the tissues have become firm and dry.

13

The object of all this attention to the corpse, it must be remembered, is to make it presentable for viewing in an attitude of healthy repose. "Our customs require the presentation of our dead in the semblance of normality . . . unmarred by the ravages of

14

femoral artery terminates behind the knee. The jugular vein receives blood from the brain and passes it down the neck. The subclavian is the large vein that drains the arm and unites with the internal jugular. Glycerin: $C_3H_8O_3$. A syrupy alcohol used as a solvent and preservative. Borax: Sodium borate. Chiefly used as a detergent, water softener, and weak antiseptic. Phenol: C_6H_5OH. A crystalline, colorless or light pink solid, melting at 43°C (109.4°F), phenol rapidly corrodes tissues. Synonym: carbolic acid. Bon Ami: A well-known, mildly abrasive household cleanser. (In French, *bon ami* means "good friend.") Trocar: From French *trois quarts*, "three quarters." A sharply pointed surgical instrument in a metal tube or sheath ("cannula"). After the trocar is withdrawn from the body, the cannula allows the body fluids to escape. After the embalming, Mr. Jones will be left "unmolested for a while."

Notice Mitford's sarcasm in "few people die in the full bloom of health," and "The funeral industry is equal to the challenge."

Apparent here and elsewhere in the essay is the amount of research Mitford has done. She often cites experts in the field.

"returns to the attack" / "seeks out and fills": Earlier, Mitford describes the process as if it resembles molesting, and now it resembles an attack. The tone suggests that one is describing work on an automobile in a body shop rather than on a human body in a mortuary.

illness, disease or mutilation," says Mr. J. Sheridan Mayer in his *Restorative Art*. This is rather a large order since few people die in the full bloom of health, unravaged by illness and unmarked by some disfigurement. The funeral industry is equal to the challenge: "In some cases the gruesome appearance of a mutilated or disease-ridden subject may be quite discouraging. The task of restoration may seem impossible and shake the confidence of the embalmer. This is the time for intestinal fortitude and determination. Once the formative work is begun and affected tissues are cleaned or removed, all doubts of success vanish. It is surprising and gratifying to discover the results which may be obtained."

The embalmer, having allowed an appropriate interval to 15 elapse, returns to the attack, but now he brings into play the skill and equipment of sculptor and cosmetician. Is a hand missing? Casting one in plaster of Paris is a simple matter. "For replacement purposes, only a cast of the back of the hand is necessary; this is within the ability of the average operator and is quite adequate." If a lip or two, a nose or an ear should be missing, the embalmer has at hand a variety of restorative waxes with which to model replacements. Pores and skin texture are simulated by stippling with a little brush, and over this cosmetics are laid on. Head off? Decapitation cases are rather routinely handled. Ragged edges are trimmed, and head joined to torso with a series of splints, wires and sutures. It is a good idea to have a little something at the neck—a scarf or high collar—when time for viewing comes. Swollen mouth? Cut out tissue as needed from inside the lips. If too much is removed, the surface contour can easily be restored by padding with cotton. Swollen necks and cheeks are reduced by removing tissue through vertical incisions made down each side of the neck. "When the deceased is casketed, the pillow will hide the suture incisions . . . as an extra precaution against leakage, the suture may be painted with liquid sealer."

The opposite condition is more likely to present itself—that 16 of emaciation. His hypodermic syringe now loaded with massage cream, the embalmer seeks out and fills the hollowed and sunken areas by injection. In this procedure the backs of the hands and fingers and the under-chin area should not be neglected.

Positioning the lips is a problem that recurrently challenges   17
the ingenuity of the embalmer. Closed too tightly they tend to
give a stern, even disapproving expression. Ideally, embalmers
feel, the lips should give the impression of being ever so slightly
parted, the upper lip protruding slightly for a more youthful appearance. This takes some engineering, however, as the lips tend
to drift apart. Lip drift can sometimes be remedied by pushing
one or two straight pins through the inner margin of the lower lip
and then inserting them between the two front upper teeth. If Mr.
Jones happens to have no teeth, the pins can just as easily be
anchored in his Armstrong Face Former and Denture Replacer.
Another method to maintain lip closure is to dislocate the lower
jaw, which is then held in its new position by a wire run through
holes which have been drilled through the upper and lower jaws
at the midline. As the French are fond of saying, *il faut souffrir
pour être belle*.

il faut souffrir pour être belle: French, literally, "One must suffer in order to be beautiful." This paragraph about the lips reminds one of the unstated remainder of Hamlet's "Alas, Poor Yorick!" quotation, in paragraph 2.

If Mr. Jones has died of jaundice, the embalming fluid will   18
very likely turn him green. Does this deter the embalmer? Not
if he has intestinal fortitude. Masking pastes and cosmetics are
heavily laid on, burial garments and casket interiors are color-
correlated with particular care, and Jones is displayed beneath
rose-colored lights. Friends will say, "How *well* he looks." Death
by carbon monoxide, on the other hand, can be rather a good
thing from the embalmer's viewpoint: "One advantage is the fact
that this type of discoloration is an exaggerated form of a natural
pink coloration." This is nice because the healthy glow is already
present and needs but little attention.

The staging is almost complete. The question is whether or not the corpse resembles himself when he was alive. Notice the distance established between the corpse and the embalmer, who treats the body as if it were only a cosmetic challenge, far from being human. For that matter, according to the embalmer, the corpse's kin do not recognize cosmetic changes, either. The embalming process is a matter of unexamined tradition.

The patching and filling completed, Mr. Jones is now shaved,   19
washed and dressed. Cream-based cosmetic, available in pink,
flesh, suntan, brunette, and blond, is applied to his hands and
face, his hair is shampooed and combed (and, in the case of Mrs.
Jones, set), his hands manicured. For the horny-handed son of
toil special care must be taken; cream should be applied to remove
ingrained grime, and the nails cleaned. "If he were not in the habit
of having them manicured in life, trimming and shaping is advised for better appearance—never questioned by kin."

Jones is now ready for casketing (this is the present participle   20
of the verb "to casket"). In this operation his right shoulder should

Notice the final irony: The embalmer must be careful to position the body as it lies in the box so that it does not create "the impression that the body is in a box" after it has been "cas- keted," as the jargon of the trade has it.

Finally and sadly, we see the only semblances of historical reality—the pipe, the book, or the Teddy bear—which serve to complement the corpse, the cosmetically alive but obviously dead, antiseptic reality that will be visited during the stated hours.

POSSIBLE ANSWERS

Meaning and Purpose

1. Mitford's purpose, or thesis, is the last sentence of paragraph 2. Evidence of her humorous and sarcastic attitude toward the subject of embalming lies in the sentence in words such as "presentable," "suitably costly container," "without first consulting the family," and "for public display."
2. Mitford is addressing lay readers, those who aren't embalmers and who know little or nothing about embalming. She wants to inform those readers about an unexamined custom. She includes quotations from textbooks and authorities on the subject for readers outside the profession.
3. Corpses are embalmed because of custom, which denotes "implied permission." Most people want to see a "presentable" (paragraph 1) corpse. Mitford disapproves of this custom, and her attitude is evident in her tone of irreverent humor and sarcasm. She thinks Americans and Canadians should spare themselves the expense ("hundreds of millions of dollars," paragraph 4) of embalming.
4. The prefix "derma" refers to skin. "Derma-surgeon" suggests medical expertise; it is a pleasing sounding term that masks reality, a euphemism.
5. Jones is a common name; calling the corpse "Mr. Jones" keeps him anonymous—yet gives him a name.

Strategy

1. Mitford takes six paragraphs to introduce her subject and establish her attitude of ma-

be depressed slightly "to turn the body a bit to the right and soften the appearance of lying flat on the back." Positioning the hands is a matter of importance, and special rubber positioning blocks may be used. The hands should be cupped slightly for a more lifelike, relaxed appearance. Proper placement of the body requires a delicate sense of balance. It should lie as high as possible in the casket, yet not so high that the lid, when lowered, will hit the nose. On the other hand, we are cautioned, placing the body too low "creates the impression that the body is in a box."

Jones is next wheeled into the appointed slumber room 21 where a few last touches may be added—his favorite pipe placed in his hand or, if he was a great reader, a book propped into position. (In the case of little Master Jones a Teddy bear may be clutched.) Here he will hold open house for a few days, visiting hours 10 A.M. to 9 P.M.

Meaning and Purpose

1. Where does Mitford state her purpose in this essay? Can you tell from the statement what attitude she takes toward her subject?
2. Whom is Mitford addressing in the essay, and how do you know?
3. According to Mitford, why are corpses embalmed in this country? Do you think she approves of this custom?
4. Why would an embalmer-restorative artist want to call himself or herself a "derma-surgeon," as Mitford says in paragraph 8?
5. Why do you think Mitford calls the corpse "Mr. Jones" in paragraph 7?

Strategy

1. Mitford doesn't begin giving us the actual process of embalming until paragraph 7. Why does she take this long? What is her strategy in the first six paragraphs?

2. Read again the first sentence in the essay and the last sentence in paragraph 6. Why is the first sentence alone in a paragraph? What frame does Mitford set up for the rest of the essay in these two sentences?
3. The essay shows evidence that the author did research before she wrote about the embalming process. What is one example of that evidence?
4. Has Mitford written a directive or an informative process analysis? Explain.
5. The author writes a long paragraph describing the part of embalming that affects lips. Why are lips so important in this process?

Style

1. Describe the tone of this essay, and point out statements that illustrate it.
2. In your opinion, why does the author use *geography* in paragraph 5 ("the geography of the digestive system")?
3. Paragraph 7 is only one sentence, saying the same thing twice, about what first happens to the body in the embalming process. Why did the author say the same thing in two ways?
4. At the beginning of paragraph 15, the author says, "The embalmer, having allowed an appropriate interval to elapse, returns to the attack." Why do you think Mitford uses *attack* here?

Writing Tasks

1. Research the process of cremation as an alternative to embalming. Write a directive or informative process analysis; talk also about cremation as a custom and about attitudes toward it.
2. Imagine that the process Mitford describes is required in your state. Write a proposal to the governor, suggesting that another embalming or burial process be required instead. Describe this other process in detail.

cabre humor and sarcasm toward it. She also establishes her authority to talk about embalming by quoting a textbook in paragraph 3 and giving facts about the widespread acceptance of the custom. By the time they get to the process itself, readers have sided with Mitford in her opinion that embalming is an unnecessary and rather barbaric ritual.
2. The first sentence is alone in a paragraph for emphasis and drama. Mitford calls embalming a "drama" about to "unfold" (paragraph 1) and frames the process as if it's acted on a stage. She takes readers with her into the embalming room by saying, "let us part the formaldehyde curtain . . . " (paragraph 6), a metaphorical curtain that until now has remained closed.
3. Answers will vary, but students usually cite one of the book titles in the essay or one of the experts Mitford quotes.
4. This essay is an informative process analysis. It does not take the form of specific instructions to embalmers; instead, it explains embalmers' activities to a lay audience.
5. Lips betray character, so the story goes. Smiles, frowns, smirks, grins—all tell us something about the person.

Style

1. Mitford's tone is one of irreverent humor and sarcasm. In paragraph 18, she asks about the corpse's turning green. "Does this deter the embalmer? Not if he has intestinal fortitude." The humorous reference here is to the cosmetic challenge and to intestines, which the embalmer possesses but the corpse no longer does. She also uses an almost textbooklike tone in, for instance, describing embalming fluid in paragraph 11. This tone is itself humorous because it makes a macabre process sound beautifying and clinical.
2. In health books, a digestive system looks a bit like a road map. And the cartoon presentations for the "nursery school set" often simplify concepts.
3. The first way states the reality; the second shows how the reality is euphemistically described by the embalmer. The effect is humor.
4. Mitford implies that a small war is being fought to make the corpse look lifelike. "Attack" adds to the macabre humor of the essay.

❦ Additional Writing Tasks ❦

Process Analysis

1. Develop one of these subjects (or one you create for yourself) through *directive process analysis.* Explain the process one step at a time and be sure to provide your reader with enough detail to make each step clear.

   a. how to prepare a vegetable garden
   b. how to live without an automobile
   c. how to domesticate a wild creature, such as a falcon or rabbit
   d. how to get rid of pests without using poisons
   e. how to prepare for an acting role
   f. how to prepare a canvas for paint
   g. how to show appreciation to others
   h. how to toss a Frisbee, football, baseball, and so on
   i. how to skateboard, roller blade, roller skate
   j. how to bluff at poker
   k. how to survive Muzak
   l. how to complain effectively
   m. how to overcome shyness
   n. how to write an effective essay
   o. how to take effective notes
   p. how to outsmart a video game
   q. how to survive a natural disaster, such as an earthquake or tornado
   r. how to meditate in a crowded setting
   s. how to ride a roller coaster
   t. how to attend a concert
   u. how to run for local elected office
   v. how to win others to your point of view
   w. how to buy a used motorcycle or car

2. Develop one of these subjects (or one you create for yourself) through *informative process analysis.* Remember that this technique does not explain "how to" do something; it explains how something happens—it informs, often using narrative and descriptive techniques.

a. how psychoanalysis works
b. how secret codes are broken
c. how to read detective, espionage, or suspense fiction
d. how to learn from past experience
e. how a stroke damages the brain
f. how Alzheimer's disease develops
g. how dreams work
h. how intuition works
i. how to taste wine
j. how to create a frightening film scene
k. how to create suspense
l. how to collect art, rare books, or something else
m. how to detect lies
n. how to overcome guilt
o. how to change community thinking
p. how to live as an outsider
q. how to become an insider
r. how an idea becomes accepted
s. how voodoo works

7

Classification and Division
Establishing Categories

The Method

Have you ever played Twenty Questions, a parlor game in which one participant selects a person, place, or thing and the other participants try to guess it? The participants have twenty yes-or-no questions to find the answer. To discover that answer is a difficult task—unless you understand the principles of **classification**.

The game usually begins with a series of questions that divide the world into three roughly drawn categories: animal, vegetable, or mineral. Once the correct category is determined—"animal," for our purposes—the interrogation begins, the participants moving logically from category to category.

"Does it live in water?" a questioner might ask. A sensible question, for the earth is easily divided into land and water.

"No," the person with the secret responds. But "No" means the animal lives on land, keeping in mind that birds may fly but may also nest on land. The process of elimination continues.

"Does it have two legs?" Another logical question, because animals can be classified by locomotion.

"No."

"Four legs?" The pace of questions quickens.

"No."

Aha! the questioner has it, "Is this creature an insect?"

"Nope!" Oops . . . must be a snake, right? But what snake? The only two large categories are venomous and nonvenomous. If the answer is venomous, the questions will take one direction, "Does it have rattles?" If the answer is nonvenomous, the questions will move in another direction, "Does it kill by coiling around and crushing its prey?" And so on, until the secret is revealed or twenty questions are exhausted.

To classify is to divide a large subject into components and sort them into categories with common characteristics, a principle that clearly guides the search in any round of Twenty Questions. Classification is so pervasive that it must be fundamental to the human way of perceiving and understanding experience. Few things, no matter how significant or insignificant, seem to escape classification. Think how chaotic your campus library would be without a clear classification system. Your supermarket trips are probably organized by the manager's way of classifying products—first the vegetables, on to dairy products, rush to meats, march to canned goods, stalled at the register. Television shows, books, actors, restaurants, fun-zone rides—the possibilities for classification are endless because of our desire to understand and organize experience.

Keep in mind, too, that most subjects can be classified in a number of ways, depending on the purpose and who's doing the classifying. Consider the subject *college students*. For statistical purposes, a registrar might classify college students by age, sex, major, grade-point average, or region. An art teacher might classify students by their talent: painters, sculptors, ceramicists, illustrators, and print makers. A political-science teacher might classify the same students by their politics: reactionary, conservative, liberal, or radical. Much of this kind of classification is done informally, but in writing, a classification system should be complete and follow consistent principles.

Writers using classification as a pattern of development begin by carefully analyzing their subject—that is, by breaking it into components. They look for qualities that some components share and that others don't share. Using the qualities they've identified, they create categories. They then sort through the various components to group them in the appropriate category. They are careful to be logical, sorting and grouping the parts in a consistent manner. They also keep in mind that their categories must be complete. It would not be complete if they divided voters into Republicans and Democrats, because some voters are registered in the Peace and Freedom and Libertarian parties, among others. But if a writer's subject is limited to elected senators, then the categories might indeed be Republicans and Democrats, because no other party is represented in the Senate. Writers also make sure their categories do not overlap. To classify a group of congresswomen as Republicans, Democrats, and politicians would not make much sense because all are politicians.

Professional writers distinguish between the terms *division* and *classification,* yet these categories are intellectual companions in the classification procedure. Writers begin by first *dividing* a subject into manageable categories. They then *classify* the components of the subject according to the shared qualities. Consider the subject *movies,* which can be broken down into such categories as mystery, romance, horror, musical, comedy, western, and war. This step is division. Once the categories are established, a writer might evaluate several films, and sort them according to the qualities of each category. This step is classification. Remember, division breaks one subject into categories; classification groups the parts of the subject into the categories. Although this distinction may be important for understanding the intellectual procedure of classification, it is less important in reaching the result, a system that shows the relationship between parts of a subject.

The simplest form of classification is **two-part**, often called **binary**, classification. This pattern divides a subject in two, usually into positive and negative categories, such as vegetarians and nonvegetarians; smokers and nonsmokers; television viewers and nontelevision viewers; deaf people and hearing people; or runners and nonrunners. But two-part classification is usually inexact and skirts the edge of comparison and contrast. Most classification systems, therefore, have at least three categories.

Strategies

Careful writers arrange their classifications in a straightforward division, usually in blocks and according to the order that seems most appropriate. Each block is a subclass and will usually be identified by a name or phrase to keep the reader on track. In the following paragraph, anthropologist Ruth Benedict divides the ceremonial societies of the Zuni. She clearly identifies each society—the priestly societies, the masked-god societies, and the medicine societies—before describing them.

This ceremonial life that preoccupies Zuni attention is organized like a series of interlocking wheels. The priesthoods have their sacred objects, their retreats, their dances, their prayers; and their year-long program is annually initiated by the great winter solstice ceremony that makes use of all the different groups and sacred things and focuses all their functions. The tribal masked-god society has similar possessions and calendric observances, and these culminate in the great winter tribal masked god ceremony, the Shalkado. In like fashion the medicine societies, with their special relation to curing, function throughout the year and have their annual culminating ceremony for tribal health.

These three major cults of Zuni ceremonial life are not mutually exclusive. A man may be, and often is, for the greater part of his life, a member of all three. They each give him sacred possessions "to live by" and demand of him exacting ceremonial knowledge.

Writers use one of two strategies to identify their categories. They either use ready-made categories or they create their own. In the next classification passage, from *Blood and Money,* Thomas Thompson uses subclasses to present his view of the personal characteristics that describe surgeons.

> Among those who train students to become doctors, it is said that surgeons find their niche in accordance with their personal characteristics. The orthopedic surgeon is medicine's carpenter—up to his elbows in plaster of Paris—and tradition holds that he is a gruff, slapdash sort of man whose labor is in a very physical area of healing. Away from the hospital, the orthopedists are often hunters, boaters, outdoorsmen.
>
> The neurosurgeon, classically, does not get too involved with his patients. Or, for that matter, with anybody. They are cool men, blunted, rarely gregarious.
>
> Heart surgeons are thundering egotists, star performers in a dazzling operating theater packed with assistants, nurses, paramedics, and a battery of futuristic equipment which could seemingly lift the room into outer space. These are men who relish drama, who live life on the edge of the precipice.
>
> And the plastic surgeon? He is, by nature, a man of art, and temperament, and sensitivity. "We are the artists who deal in beauty lost, or beauty that never was," said one plastic man at a national convention. "Our stitches are hidden, and so are our emotions."

Because Thompson is working with established categories, part of his task is to make his material fresh. Most readers know the professional qualities of surgeons, and so Thompson creates a sense of the person holding the scalpel by including descriptive details of each type's dominant personality trait.

In the next paragraph, Larry McMurtry uses established categories in a slightly different way. He classifies beer bars in the city of Houston according to their location: East side, West side, and North side.

> The poor have beer-bars, hundreds of them, seldom fancy but reliably dim and cool. Most of them are equipped with jukeboxes, shuffleboards, jars of pig's feet and talkative drunks. There are lots of bar burlesques, where from 3 P.M. on girls gyrate at one's elbow with varying degrees of grace. On the East side there are a fair number of open-air bars—those who like to watch the traffic can sit, drink Pearl, observe the wrecks, and listen to "Hello, Vietnam" on the juke box. Louisiana is just down the road, and a lot of the men wear Cajun sideburns and leave their shirttails out. On the West side cowboys are common. Members of the cross-continental hitch-hiking set congregate on Franklin Street, at places like The Breaking Point Lounge. Symbolic *latinos* slip over to the Last Concert on the North side; or, if they are especially bold, go all the way to McCarty Street, where one can view the most extraordinary example of Mexican saloon-and-whorehouse architecture north of the border.

McMurtry opens with a general description of Houston beer bars: They are dim and cool with jukeboxes, shuffleboards, jars of pig's feet, and drunks—a watering hole for blue-collar men. After rendering the general qualities of these bars, McMurtry presents the geographic categories, each with a brief description that characterizes it.

Writers often classify a subject that has no ready-made categories. They must, therefore, create their own categories and the labels that identify them. In this paragraph from "Here Is New York," E. B. White divides the population of New York into three categories according to a person's relation to the city.

There are roughly three New Yorks. There is, first, the New York of the man or woman who was born here, who takes the city for granted and accepts its size and its turbulence as natural and inevitable. Second, there is the New York of the commuter—the city that is devoured by locusts each day and spat out each night. Third, there is the New York of the quest of something. Of these three trembling cities the greatest is the last—the city of final destination, the city that is a goal. It is this third city that accounts for New York's high-strung disposition, its poetical deportment, its dedication to the arts, and its incomparable achievements. Commuters give the city its tidal restlessness; natives give it solidarity and continuity; but the settlers give it passion. And whether it is a farmer arriving from Italy to set up a small grocery store in a slum, or a young girl arriving from a small town in Mississippi to escape the indignity of being observed by her neighbors, or a boy arriving from the Corn Belt with a manuscript in his suitcase and a pain in his heart, it makes no difference: each embraces New York with the intense excitement of first love, each absorbs New York with the fresh eyes of an adventurer, each generates heat and light to dwarf the Consolidated Edison Company.

Commuters, natives, and settlers, these are White's three categories. He uses each category to present characteristics of New York City. The commuter gives the city a sense of restlessness; the native gives it solidarity; and the settler, the category he stresses, gives it passion.

Classification in College Writing

The physical sciences, social sciences, humanities, all make use of classification. In fact, you can expect to use the classification pattern across the academic curriculum. For example, Mark Freeman was assigned an informal classification paper in cultural anthropology. The subject was *leisure time*. His task was to observe people pursuing a leisure activity or hobby. Freeman narrowed his subject to offbeat hobbies and concentrated on comic-book collectors, a hobby he has pursued for years. He begins his essay with this classification paragraph that establishes the categories and the general characteristics of the collectors who comprise them.

Freeman opens with a sentence that identifies his subject—comic-book collectors. He follows with a generalized physical description of collectors.

To keep his reader on track, Freeman lists the categories he'll use to group collectors.

Freeman devotes most of the paragraph to grouping collectors into one of the categories according to their motivation for collecting. Notice that the categories are arranged in blocks.

One fascinating off-beat hobbyist is the comic book collector. Usually male, pale, wearing glasses, bushy-haired and disheveled, collectors can be found rummaging through pile after pile of unsorted, secondhand comics in magazine marts across the country. Comic book collectors, the serious ones, seem to fall into four major groups: Antiquarians, Mercenaries, Idolators, and Compulsive Completers. The Antiquarian cares only for age value; subject matter is of no concern. He is looking for a 1933 Funnies on Parade from the days when men were men and comics were comics. To the Mercenary, value is all-important. Certain numbers and titles ring a bell in his cash-register brain and start him furtively checking through a half dozen price sheets. A pristine first edition of Action Comics (value $4,000) would suit him just fine. The Idolator could not care less about age or value. He is looking for favorites: Sheena, a Flash Gordon, or an Incredible Hulk. Hiding in the corner, reading those he cannot afford to buy, the Idolator will be the last one out of the mart at night and the first one back in the morning. The most frustrated collector is the Compulsive Completer. He will examine and reject thousands of comics in his search for a badly needed Felix

He closes with a clincher that identifies a trait all collectors share.

the Cat to complete a year's set or the one Howdy Doody missing from his collection. But no matter what the reason for collecting, these hobbyists share a common trait: They love the thrill of the hunt.

Because no ready-made categories are available, Freeman creates his own—Antiquarians, Mercenaries, Idolators, and Compulsive Completers—and groups them according to their motivation for collecting. He arranges this paragraph in a common classification structure, opening with a general description of collectors, then listing the categories he'll group them in. Next, he discusses each category in detail, identifying the characteristics of the collector who falls into each group.

❦ Judy Syfers ❦

Judy Syfers was born in San Francisco in 1937. She studied painting at the University of Iowa, married and had children, and later worked as a secretary in San Francisco, having been discouraged by her male university professors from becoming a teacher. She later became very active in the feminist movement and has written numerous articles on women's roles in society and related subjects. In 1973 she went to Cuba to study social class relationships, having developed an interest in how societies change from her feminist political work. Now divorced and disenchanted with marriage, she has called herself a "disenfranchised and fired housewife."

I Want a Wife

This essay was published in the first issue of Ms. *magazine in 1971 and has been widely reprinted since. This biting description of the "ideal" wife has become a classic of feminist satire. Syfers first classifies herself as a wife, then proceeds to classify the work of a wife into five categories by explaining why she wants a wife of her own.*

TEACHING SUGGESTIONS

Though this essay is two decades old, it still triggers lively classroom discussions about the modern roles of husbands and wives. It can also lead to provocative discussions about to-day's roles of fathers and mothers.

　　One way to approach the division illustrated in this essay is to ask students to provide a label for the content of each paragraph from 3 to 7. When they have arrived at labels that satisfy them, it is easy to see that each paragraph is a division of the subject, "wife" (or wifely duties).

　　The essay is written from a feminist point of view, but most people will recognize the duties presented here as fairly accurate traditional expectations. What are the traditional expectations for husbands? Have both traditions changed in the years since the essay was written?

MARGINAL NOTES

The first sentence establishes the class the writer belongs to.

The encounter with a male friend triggers thoughts about the "duties" of a wife. The rest of the essay divides being a wife into five types of activities.

The first division includes complete care of the children as well as work outside the home.

I belong to that classification of people known as wives. I am A Wife. And, not altogether incidentally, I am a mother. 1

Not too long ago a male friend of mine appeared on the scene fresh from a recent divorce. He had one child, who is, of course, with his ex-wife. He is looking for another wife. As I thought about him while I was ironing one evening, it suddenly occurred to me that I, too, would like to have a wife. Why do I want a wife? 2

I would like to go back to school so that I can become economically independent, support myself, and, if need be, support those dependent upon me. I want a wife who will work and send me to school. And while I am going to school I want a wife to take care of my children. I want a wife to keep track of the children's doctor and dentist appointments. And to keep track of 3 mine, too. I want a wife to make sure my children eat properly and are kept clean. I want a wife who will wash the children's clothes and keep them mended. I want a wife who is a good nurturant attendant to my children, who arranges for their schooling, makes sure that they have an adequate social life with their peers, takes them to the park, the zoo, etc. I want a wife who takes care of the children when they are sick, a wife who arranges to be around when the children need special care, because, of course, I cannot miss classes at school. My wife must arrange to lose time at work and not lose the job. It may mean a small cut in my wife's income from time to time, but I guess I can tolerate that. Needless to say, my wife will arrange and pay for the care of the children while my wife is working.

I want a wife who will take care of *my* physical needs. I want a wife who will keep my house clean. A wife who will pick up after my children, a wife who will pick up after me. I want a wife who will keep my clothes clean, ironed, mended, replaced when need be, and who will see to it that my personal things are kept in their proper place so that I can find what I need the minute I need it. I want a wife who cooks the meals, a wife who is a *good* cook. I want a wife who will plan the menus, do the necessary grocery shopping, prepare the meals, serve them pleasantly, and then do the cleaning up while I do my studying. I want a wife who will care for me when I am sick and sympathize with my pain and loss of time from school. I want a wife to go along when our family takes a vacation so that someone can continue to care for me and my children when I need a rest and change of scene.

I want a wife who will not bother me with rambling complaints about a wife's duties. But I want a wife who will listen to me when I feel the need to explain a rather difficult point I have come across in my course of studies. And I want a wife who will type my papers for me when I have written them.

I want a wife who will take care of the details of my social life. When my wife and I are invited out by my friends, I want a wife who will take care of the babysitting arrangements. When I meet people at school that I like and want to entertain, I want a wife who will have the house clean, will prepare a special meal,

4   The second division includes housekeeping and cooking.

The third division involves being emotionally supportive without expecting the same support yourself.

5

6   The fourth division involves the duties of a social secretary.

serve it to me and my friends, and not interrupt when I talk about things that interest me and my friends. I want a wife who will have arranged that the children are fed and ready for bed before my guests arrive so that the children do not bother us. I want a wife who takes care of the needs of my guests so that they feel comfortable, who makes sure that they have an ashtray, that they are passed the hors d'oeuvres, that they are offered a second helping of the food, that their wine glasses are replenished when necessary, that their coffee is served to them as they like it. And I want a wife who knows that sometimes I need a night out by myself.

The fifth division involves being the ideal lover but also respecting the double standard.

I want a wife who is sensitive to my sexual needs, a wife who makes love passionately and eagerly when I feel like it, a wife who makes sure that I am satisfied. And, of course, I want a wife who will not demand sexual attention when I am not in the mood for it. I want a wife who assumes the complete responsibility for birth control, because I do not want more children. I want a wife who will remain sexually faithful to me so that I do not have to clutter up my intellectual life with jealousies. And I want a wife who understands that *my* sexual needs may entail more than strict adherence to monogamy. I must, after all, be able to relate to people as fully as possible. 7

If, by chance, I find another person more suitable as a wife than the wife I already have, I want the liberty to replace my present wife with another one. Naturally, I will expect a fresh, new life; my wife will take the children and be solely responsible for them so that I am left free. 8

When I am through with school and have a job, I want my wife to quit working and remain at home so that my wife can more fully and completely take care of a wife's duties. 9

My God, who *wouldn't* want a wife? 10

Meaning and Purpose

1. What are your ideas about what a wife is and does, and where do your ideas come from? How do they compare to what Syfers says she wants her "wife" to be and do?
2. Syfers repeats "I want a wife" many times throughout this essay. What is the purpose of that repetition?
3. Why does Syfers use "of course" in paragraph 2?
4. Can you find a thesis statement in the essay? What is Syfers's main point?
5. In listing a wife's duties, Syfers also lists a husband's needs. What are some of these needs, and do you think Syfers is fair to husbands in this essay?

Strategy

1. Do you think the first paragraph is effective as an opening? How does it serve Syfers's purpose?
2. A classification groups the parts of a subject into categories. Look at how Syfers has structured her categories. For each of paragraphs 3–7, label the category and tell which characteristics Syfers describes.
3. Classify this essay by labeling it with a name such as "informative," "political," "sarcastic," or "optimistic." Try to think of your own name—use one of those above if you must—and explain your reasons for labeling it as you have.

Style

1. Why is "A Wife" capitalized in the first paragraph?
2. What important attitude of Syfers toward her "wife" does the word "replace" in paragraph 8 suggest?
3. Paragraph 4 says that the wife will not go on vacation with the author. Instead, she will go "along" on vacation. What is

POSSIBLE ANSWERS

Meaning and Purpose

1. Let students explore their notions about what being a wife means, and where those notions come from. A comparison of their ideas with Syfers's should show how traditional or progressive your students are.
2. Repeating "I want a wife" emphasizes the focus of the essay, which is on the elements in Syfers's classification, rather than on a simple description. It also sounds demanding, and many men demand that their wives do all the things on Syfers's list.
3. Syfers's view is that men expect women to assume all domestic duties, so "of course" the duty to care for children stays with the wife after a divorce. The use is sarcastic.
4. No one statement asserts Syfers's main point. Instead, her thesis is implied in all her details about what a wife is and does: that it is ridiculous and grossly unfair to expect wives to be superwomen who see to the needs of husbands and families who do far less work than a wife—and yet they are expected to perform thus. In her last sentence she asks a rhetorical question that implies her thesis.
5. The husband's needs are implicitly stated with the wife's duties in sentences such as, "I want a wife who will keep my clothes clean, ironed, mended, replaced when need be, and who will see to it that my personal things are kept in their proper place so that I can find what I need the minute I need it" (paragraph 4). Students may think Syfers describes extremes when she stereotypes roles, but students probably know men who are this demanding and self-centered. Stereotypes are never fair, but these serve Syfers's point that wives are expected to do far too much for their husbands.

Strategy

1. The first paragraph announces the classification "wives" as the subject of the essay, and also establishes Syfers's authority to talk about wives because she is one. This opening is strong and direct, and it informs the reader, giving a context.

2. These are the labels and characteristics: Paragraph 3: label—worker outside the home and primary caretaker for the children; characteristics—organized, fastidious, thrifty. Paragraph 4: label—personal maid; characteristics—neat, good cook, patient. Paragraph 5: label—therapist; characteristics—patient, good listener. Paragraph 6: label—hostess; characteristics—organized, gracious. Paragraph 7: label—perfect lover; characteristics—selfless, responsible.

3. Answers will vary. Student should support their choice of label with statements from the essay. An appropriate label would be *sarcastic*.

Style

1. The expression "A Wife" is capitalized because it is used as a formal label of classification.

2. The word "replace" suggests that a Syfers wife is an expendable piece of equipment rather than a person. The word also suggests that husbands are fickle about wives and don't care about *who* they are, only about what they do.

3. When people are "going on" vacation, they are going together. The person who "goes *along*" with another person is not altogether that person's equal.

4. The question is rhetorical, which means that it requires no answer—it has already been answered. It emphasizes Syfers's sarcastic attitude about what men expect wives to do and her own frustrations about being expected to be such a wife. Questions are effective because they usually address readers directly and provoke thought.

the difference in meaning between "going" and "going along" on vacation?

4. Why does Syfers end her essay with a question? How is the question effective?

Writing Tasks

1. Syfers's "wife" is ideal, a stereotype. Who is your ideal person in some classification of people, such as mother, boyfriend, sister, teacher? Write a classification essay in which you create categories for this person and describe the characteristics of each category, or what the person in each category should do.

2. Give a man's counterpoint to Syfers's essay: "I Want a Husband." Write from a first-person male point of view and decide which categories to use. Try to imitate Syfers's sarcastic and exaggerated tone.

❦ Russell Baker ❦

Russell Baker has twice been awarded the Pulitzer Prize, once for journalism in 1979, and again in 1983 for his best-selling autobiography, Growing Up *(1982). Born in rural Virginia in 1925, Baker grew up in New Jersey and Maryland. He graduated from Johns Hopkins University and worked for several years as a reporter for the* Baltimore Sun *before taking a job with* The New York Times *in 1953. He covered the national political scene in Washington, D.C. for almost twenty years, and in 1962 began writing his now famous column, "Observer." He has also contributed to* Sports Illustrated, McCall's, Saturday Evening Post, *and other major periodicals. His columns have periodically been collected into books, including* Poor Russell's Almanac *(1972),* So This Is Depravity *(1980), and* The Rescue of Miss Yaskell and Other Pipe Dreams *(1983), and recently he published a continuation of his autobiography, entitled* The Good Times *(1989).*

TEACHING SUGGESTIONS

This is an excellent essay to use in discussing how humor can become an entertaining element of writing. In this essay the tone is always consistent and the examples are never overly exaggerated, always rooted in common experience.

The essay can also be used for discussing kinds of categories that can be created for the same subject, depending on the author's purpose. Here Baker wants to entertain his audience by playing with frustrations we all have experienced. What if he had wanted to categorize things according to their practical values? According to status values? According to any other value? How would the examples change?

The Plot Against People

This essay first appeared in The New York Times *in 1968. Typical of Baker, the essay is a humorous and satirical treatment of a very mundane subject. Baker classifies machines by the ways in which they inconvenience the human beings whose lives they are supposed to make easier.*

Inanimate objects are classified scientifically into three major categories—those that break down, those that get lost, and those that don't work.

The goal of all inanimate objects is to resist man and ultimately to defeat him, and the three major classifications are based on the method each object uses to achieve its purpose. As a general rule, any object capable of breaking down at the moment when it is most needed will do so. The automobile is typical of the category.

MARGINAL NOTES

1 Baker establishes his three broad categories in the opening sentence. He also establishes the essay's facetious tone by claiming that these categories have been established scientifically.

2 He states his thesis in the opening sentence and uses the automobile as a typical example.

411

He then personifies the automobile by calling it "cunning" and a member of a "breed." He cites an example of its behavior to demonstrate its cunning.

He now lists other inanimate objects that fit into his first category.

This is a transitional paragraph that carries the reader from the first category to the second.

He moves from a statement of what objects in this category do, to a claim that science cannot fathom their mysterious behavior, to the most "plausible theory" about their behavior.

Here Baker cites examples of the objects' mysterious behavior.

He now brings the first two categories together, claiming they seldom intrude on each other.

These next two paragraphs propose two explanations for the conundrum cited in paragraph 8, the second, more sinister explanation of course being the more probable.

3 With the cunning peculiar to its breed, the automobile never breaks down while entering a filling station which has a large staff of idle mechanics. It waits until it reaches a downtown intersection in the middle of the rush hour, or until it is fully loaded with family and luggage on the Ohio Turnpike. Thus it creates maximum inconvenience, frustration, and irritability, thereby reducing its owner's lifespan.

4 Washing machines, garbage disposals, lawn mowers, furnaces, TV sets, tape recorders, slide projectors—all are in league with the automobile to take their turn at breaking down whenever life threatens to flow smoothly for their enemies.

5 Many inanimate objects, of course, find it extremely difficult to break down. Pliers, for example, and gloves and keys are almost totally incapable of breaking down. Therefore, they have had to evolve a different technique for resisting man.

6 They get lost. Science has still not solved the mystery of how they do it, and no man has ever caught one of them in the act. The most plausible theory is that they have developed a secret method of locomotion which they are able to conceal from human eyes.

7 It is not uncommon for a pair of pliers to climb all the way from the cellar to the attic in its single-minded determination to raise its owner's blood pressure. Keys have been known to burrow three feet under mattresses. Women's purses, despite their great weight, frequently travel through six or seven rooms to find hiding space under a couch.

8 Scientists have been struck by the fact that things that break down virtually never get lost, while things that get lost hardly ever break down. A furnace, for example, will invariably break down at the depth of the first winter cold wave, but it will never get lost. A woman's purse hardly ever breaks down; it almost invariably chooses to get lost.

9 Some persons believe this constitutes evidence that inanimate objects are not entirely hostile to man. After all, they point out, a furnace could infuriate a man even more thoroughly by getting lost than by breaking down, just as a glove could upset him far more by breaking down than by getting lost.

Not everyone agrees, however, that this indicates a concilia-   10
tory attitude. Many say it merely proves that furnaces, gloves and
pliers are incredibly stupid.

The third class of objects—those that don't work—is the most   11
curious of all. These include such objects as barometers, car
clocks, cigarette lighters, flashlights and toy-train locomotives. It
is inaccurate, of course, to say that they *never* work. They work
once, usually for the first few hours after being brought home,
and then quit. Thereafter, they never work again.

In fact, it is widely assumed that they are built for the purpose   12
of not working. Some people have reached advanced ages without
ever seeing some of these objects—barometers, for example—in
working order.

Science is utterly baffled by the entire category. There are   13
many theories about it. The most interesting holds that the things
that don't work have attained the highest state possible for an
inanimate object, the state to which things that break down and
things that get lost can still only aspire.

They have truly defeated man by conditioning him never to   14
expect anything of them. When his cigarette lighter won't light or
his flashlight fails to illuminate, it does not raise his blood pressure. Objects that don't work have given man the only peace he
receives from inanimate society.

The "most curious" category is introduced.

Meaning and Purpose

1. What is the meaning of Baker's title? Where does he state his
   thesis?
2. In what three categories does Baker place all inanimate objects?
   Why do you think he chose these categories?
3. Baker says that one "theory" explaining why inanimate objects
   that break down very seldom get lost is that they are "incredibly
   stupid." Explain.

Possible Answers

Meaning and Purpose

1. In the essay, Baker takes the position that
all inanimate objects are in league against
man, that all the problems man has with inanimate objects happen because they plot
against him to defeat him. The thesis is the
first sentence in paragraph 2.

2. Baker chooses three broad categories, "those that break down, those that get lost, and those that don't work" (1). These categories represent the commonest problems we have with "things."

3. Baker cites two possible reasons why objects that break down seldom get lost. The first is that inanimate objects are not entirely hostile to man (9). The second and more probable reason is "that furnaces, gloves and pliers are incredibly stupid." If they had the intelligence to recognize that their getting lost "could infuriate a man even more thoroughly" (9), they would invariably get lost.

4. Although objects in the first two categories infuriate man (9), raise his blood pressure (7), and reduce his lifespan (3), the objects in the third category have utterly defeated him "by conditioning him never to expect anything of them" (14).

5. Baker plays humorously with the frustrations all of us have experienced with the everyday things we need to function. Although the essay has no real serious point, Baker does strike a chord that we can all recognize.

Strategy

1. Baker establishes his humorous intentions in sentence 1 when he claims that science established his three categories of inanimate objects. During the rest of the essay he consistently refers to scientific theories to explain seemingly unaccountable behavior by inanimate objects. And, of course, he personifies the objects so that they become a sensate and conscious force out to purposely frustrate and defeat man.

2. Baker orders his categories from least to most important. Objects breaking down at the least appropriate moment has become the commonest of frustrations. Objects that get lost have evolved "a different technique" (5), and are mysterious because they can never be

4. Explain the "scientific theory" that objects which simply don't work "have attained the highest state possible for an inanimate object" (13).

5. Is Baker merely silly in the essay, or is he making a serious or semiserious point?

Strategy

1. How has Baker made absolutely clear from the very beginning that his subject is facetious? How does he maintain humor throughout the essay?

2. Why does Baker order his categories in the way he does?

3. How does paragraph 5 function in the structure of the essay?

Style

1. What is Baker's attitude toward his subject? Where do you see it?

2. What is the effect of *not* addressing the reader as "you"?

3. If necessary, use a dictionary to determine the meanings of these words: *cunning* (3); *league* (4); *plausible* (6); *conciliatory* (10); *baffled* (13).

Writing Tasks

1. Write an essay using classification, in which you divide a subject you are familiar with into various categories. Select your categories so that they demonstrate a clear purpose and are not merely obvious or superficial. Make sure that your examples are specific and that you distinguish each category from the next. Your subject is limited only by your first-hand knowledge. Some possibilities are teachers, jobs, college students, high-school students,

records or tapes you own, families, rock bands, comic strips, or dates.

2. All of us have at one time or another been frustrated by mechanical devices that seem to have had minds of their own and, instead of functioning as we anticipated, did what appeared to be "their own thing." Using Baker's essay as a model, describe an experience you have had in which some mechanical device seemed to act on its own. Break down its "malfunctions" into categories.

seen doing so (6). Objects in the final category are so advanced that "science is utterly baffled" by them.

3. Paragraph 5 is a transition from the first category to the second.

Style

1. Baker's attitude is facetious and humorous toward his subject. To achieve this tone, he personifies inanimate objects throughout the essay ("they are a cunning breed" [3], actively hostile to man [9] with "single-minded determination" to raise man's "blood pressure" [7]). The effect of his approach is to acknowledge and yet make light of our common frustrations.

2. Not addressing the reader as "you" gives the essay a more formal, or pseudoacademic, feel that fits Baker's humor in describing "scientific" categories and theories.

3. *Cunning:* skill employed in a shrewd or sly manner, as in deceiving; *league:* working together, often secretly or for a harmful purpose; *plausible:* having an appearance of truth or reason; *conciliatory:* overcoming distrust or hostility; *baffled:* confused, bewildered, or perplexed.

🍎 Mary E. Mebane 🍎

Born in North Carolina in 1933, Mary Mebane studied at Carolina College and North Carolina University, where she earned her Ph.D. in English. She began her teaching career in North Carolina public schools and went on to become a professor of English, teaching in southern colleges and universities. She has written primarily about the lives of blacks in the South after 1960. Mebane's work has been anthologized in A Galaxy of Black Writing *(1970) and* The Eloquence of Protest *(1972), and she is the author of a two-act play, "Take a Sad Song" (1975).*

Shades of Black

This essay is from Mary Mebane's autobiography, Mary *(1981). The author explains how university students in the 1950s were "classified" by the color of their skin, and black university students were classified by the relative darkness of their skin. "Black black" women in particular were handicapped by a stereotypical stigma that began to change only in the 1970s.*

<table>
<tr>
<td valign="top" width="38%">

Teaching Suggestions

This is a good essay for demonstrating how different rhetorical methods can be used in one essay. After Mebane establishes her thesis that "social class and color were the primary criteria used in determining status on campus . . ." (3), she designates social categories (4) and how skin color determined faculty attitudes toward students. Later in the essay she classifies roles that dark-skinned women can choose in this racist system (16). Most of the rest of the essay consists of examples that dramatically demonstrate how this system affects real people.

</td>
<td></td>
</tr>
</table>

Marginal Notes

At the very beginning, Mebane connects authority with whiteness in her college setting.

Mebane establishes that power was always negative in her segregated society.

During my first week of classes as a freshman, I was stopped one day in the hall by the chairman's wife, who was indistinguishable in color from a white woman. She wanted to see me, she said.   1

This woman had no official position on the faculty, except that she was an instructor in English; nevertheless, her summons had to be obeyed. In the segregated world there were (and remain) gross abuses of authority because those at the pinnacle, and even their spouses, felt that the people "under" them had no recourse except to submit—and they were right except that sometimes a black who got sick and tired of it would go to the whites and complain. This course of action was severely condemned by the blacks, but an interesting thing happened—such action always got positive results. Power was thought of in negative terms: I can   2 deny someone something, I can strike at someone who can't strike back, I can ride someone down; that proves I am powerful. The concept of power as a force for good, for affirmative response to people or situations, was not in evidence.

When I went to her office, she greeted me with a big smile. "You know," she said, "you made the highest mark on the verbal part of the examination." She was referring to the examination that the entire freshman class took upon entering the college. I looked at her but I didn't feel warmth, for in spite of her smile her eyes and tone of voice were saying, "How could this black-skinned girl score higher on the verbal than some of the students who've had more advantages than she? It must be some sort of fluke. Let me talk to her." I felt it, but I managed to smile my thanks and back off. For here at North Carolina College at Durham, as it had been since the beginning, social class and color were the primary criteria used in determining status on the campus.

First came the children of doctors, lawyers, and college teachers. Next came the children of public-school teachers, businessmen, and anybody else who had access to more money than the poor black working class. After that came the bulk of the student population, the children of the working class, most of whom were the first in their families to go beyond high school. The attitude toward them was: You're here because we need the numbers, but in all other things defer to your betters.

The faculty assumed that light-skinned students were more intelligent, and they were always a bit nonplussed when a dark-skinned student did well, especially if she was a girl. They had reason to be appalled when they discovered that I planned to do not only well but better than my light-skinned peers.

I don't know whether African men recently transported to the New World considered themselves handsome or, more important, whether they considered African women beautiful in comparison with Native American Indian women or immigrant European women. It is a question that I have never heard raised or seen research on. If African men considered African women beautiful, just when their shift in interest away from black black women

3   The chair's wife expresses surprise that someone as dark-complected as Mebane should have done so well on a verbal exam. This reaction leads to Mebane's thesis, which she states in the final sentence of the paragraph.

4   Here Mebane divides the college students into hierarchic social classes, the first criterion of status.

5   Now she demonstrates how skin color determines faculty attitudes toward students.

6   Mebane uses this paragraph as a transition to the discussion of how racism is manifested in segregated education. She begins with speculation, which leads to a definitive final statement.

occurred might prove to be an interesting topic for researchers. But one thing I know for sure: by the twentieth century, really black skin on a woman was considered ugly in this country. This was particularly true among those who were exposed to college.

Hazel, who was light brown, used to say to me, "You are *dark,* but not *too* dark." This saved commiserating with the damned. I had the feeling that if nature had painted one more brushstroke on me, I'd have had to kill myself. 7

Black skin was to be disguised at all costs. Since a black face is rather hard to disguise, many women took refuge in ludicrous makeup. Mrs. Burry, one of my teachers in elementary school, used white face powder. But she neglected to powder her neck and arms, and even the black on her face gleamed through the white, giving her an eerie appearance. But she did the best she could. 8

I observed all through elementary and high school that for various entertainments the girls were placed on the stage in order of color. And very black ones didn't get into the front row. If they were past caramel-brown, to the back row they would go. And nobody questioned the justice of these decisions—neither the students nor the teachers. 9

One of the teachers at Wildwood School, who was from the Deep South and was just as black as she could be, had been a strict enforcer of these standards. That was another irony—that someone who had been judged outside the realm of beauty herself because of her skin tones should have adopted them so whole-heartedly and applied them herself without question. 10

One girl stymied that teacher, though. Ruby, a black cherry of a girl, not only got off the back row but off the front row as well, to stand alone at stage center. She could outsing, outdance, and outdeclaim everyone else, and talent proved triumphant over pigmentation. But the May Queen and her Court (and in high school, Miss Wildwood) were always chosen from among the lighter ones. 11

When I was a freshman in high school, it became clear that a light-skinned sophomore girl named Rose was going to get the 12

The author's personal example of hurt will lead to other examples of dark-skinned black students pained and demeaned by a racist system.

Mebane now cites behavior that is the logical consequence of the racist system. She first gives a general example and then a specific one.

Mebane offers a second example, which emphasizes the pernicious pervasiveness of a racist system that reaches all the way to elementary school.

She describes a third ironic example of a black black teacher at the school who enforces the racist standard of beauty.

Mebane turns to a personal example.

"best girl scholar" prize for the next three years, and there was nothing I could do about it, even though I knew I was the better. Rose was caramel-colored and had shoulder-length hair. She was highly favored by the science and math teacher, who figured the averages. I wasn't. There was only one prize. Therefore, Rose would get it until she graduated. I was one year behind her, and I would not get it until after she graduated.

To be held in such low esteem was painful. It was difficult not to feel that I had been cheated out of the medal, which I felt that, in a fair competition, I perhaps would have won. Being unable to protest or do anything about it was a traumatic experience for me. From then on I instinctively tended to avoid the college-exposed dark-skinned male, knowing that when he looked at me he saw himself and, most of the time, his mother and sister as well, and since he had rejected his blackness, he had rejected theirs and mine.

Oddly enough, the lighter-skinned black male did not seem to feel so much prejudice toward the black black woman. It was no accident, I felt, that Mr. Harrison, the eighth-grade teacher, who was reddish-yellow himself, once protested to the science and math teacher about the fact that he always assigned sweeping duties to Doris and Ruby Lee, two black black girls. Mr. Harrison said to them one day, right in the other teacher's presence, "You must be some bad girls. Every day I come down here ya'll are sweeping." The science and math teacher got the point and didn't ask them to sweep anymore.

Uneducated black males, too, sometimes related very well to the black black woman. They had been less firmly indoctrinated by the white society around them and were more securely rooted in their own culture.

Because of the stigma attached to having dark skin, a black black woman had to do many things to find a place for herself. One possibility was to attach herself to a light-skinned woman, hoping that some of the magic would rub off on her. A second was to make herself sexually available, hoping to attract a mate. Third, she could resign herself to a more chaste life-style—either

13   She now comments on the pain she felt because of her treatment as a black black. By extension, all the other people she cites as victims of this kind of discrimination must have suffered the same kind of pain.

14   Ironically, lighter-skinned males had not rejected their own blackness.

15   Men not molded by the racist educational system seem untouched by racist standards.

16   Mebane now classifies the options open to black black women.

(for the professional woman) teaching and work in established churches or (for the uneducated woman) domestic work and zealous service in the Holy and Sanctified churches.

In the next five paragraphs she cites examples—women who chose the roles she has just classified.

Even as a young girl, Lucy had chosen the first route. Lucy 17 was short, skinny, short-haired, and black black, and thus unacceptable. So she made her choice. She selected Patricia, the lightest-skinned girl in the school, as her friend, and followed her around. Patricia and her friends barely tolerated Lucy, but Lucy smiled and doggedly hung on, hoping that some who noticed Patricia might notice her, too. Though I felt shame for her behavior, even then I understood.

As is often the case of the victim agreeing with and adopting 18 the attitudes of oppressor, so I have seen it with black black women. I have seen them adopt the oppressor's attitude that they are nothing but "sex machines," and their supposedly superior sexual performance becomes their sole reason for being and for esteeming themselves. Such women learn early that in order to make themselves attractive to men they have somehow to shift the emphasis from physical beauty to some other area—usually sexual performance. Their constant talk is of their desirability and their ability to gratify a man sexually.

I knew two such women well—both of them black black. To 19 hear their endless talk of sexual conquests was very sad. I have never seen the category that these women fall into described anywhere. It is not that of promiscuity or nymphomania. It is the category of total self-rejection: "Since I am black, I am ugly, I am nobody. I will perform on the level that they have assigned to me." Such women are the pitiful results of what not only white America but also, and more important, black America has done to them.

Some, not taking the sexuality route but still accepting black 20 society's view of their worthlessness, swing all the way across to intense religiosity. Some are staunch, fervent workers in the more traditional Southern churches—Baptist and Methodist—and others are leaders and ministers in the lower status, more evangelical Holiness sects.

Another avenue open to the black black woman is excellence in a career. Since in the South the field most accessible to such women is education, a great many of them prepared to become teachers. But here, too, the black black woman had problems. Grades weren't given to her lightly in school, nor were promotions on the job. Consequently, she had to prepare especially well. She had to pass examinations with flying colors or be left behind; she knew that she would receive no special consideration. She had to be overqualified for a job because otherwise she didn't stand a chance of getting it—and she was competing only with other blacks. She had to have something to back her up: not charm, not personality—but training.

The black black woman's training would pay off in the 1970s. With the arrival of integration the black black woman would find, paradoxically enough, that her skin color in an integrated situation was not the handicap it had been in an all-black situation. But it wasn't until the middle and late 1960s, when the post-1945 generation of black males arrived on college campuses, that I noticed any change in the situation at all. *He* wore an afro and *she* wore an afro, and sometimes the only way you could tell them apart was when his afro was taller than hers. Black had become beautiful, and the really black girl was often selected as queen of various campus activities. It was then that the dread I felt at dealing with the college-educated black male began to ease. Even now, though, when I have occasion to engage in any type of transaction with a college-educated black man, I gauge his age. If I guess he was born after 1945, I feel confident that the transaction will turn out all right. If he probably was born before 1945, my stomach tightens, I find myself taking shallow breaths, and I try to state my business and escape as soon as possible.

21

22 Because of black awareness in the 1960s, things, she concludes, have changed for the generations born after 1945.

POSSIBLE ANSWERS

Meaning and Purpose

1. Mebane's primary purpose is to expose the devastating psychological and social consequences for black people, particularly black women, in a social value system that accepts as fact that skin pigmentation determines both intelligence and beauty—the lighter toned the skin the better. Her thesis is the last sentence in paragraph 3.

2. Mebane is addressing more than one audience: whites who discriminate against blacks; whites who do not discriminate but who should be informed about it; blacks who discriminate against blacks; blacks who do not discriminate but who should know what their fellow blacks are doing to each other; blacks who are victims of the discrimination Mebane describes. Mebane's information is relevant to all these groups.

3. Because black people's intelligence, beauty, and authority are judged by the lightness of their skin, it is significant that the woman's skin is indistinguishable from a white's.

4. Mebane was resentful of the racist, sexist educational system she describes. She felt cheated, demeaned, and powerless (13). Yet she recognized the injustices. She feels encouraged now that younger blacks, particularly males, are seeing black as beautiful.

5. Mebane avoided dark-skinned males because, having already rejected their own and their mothers' and sisters' blackness, they now would reject her also, causing her much pain.

6. The expression means a black girl who has a dark red tone to her skin.

Strategy

1. College students are put into social and economic categories according to who their parents are; children of doctors are considered superior to those of working-class parents (4). For all students, another measure of worth is skin color: "The faculty assumed that light-skinned students were more intelligent" (5). Black black women have difficulty being accepted, even by blacks. Mebane puts them into three categories for finding a place in society: those who attach themselves to light-skinned women; those who are sexually available; and those who take up teaching or church work (16). All these categories are unfairly limiting and demeaning, and the people in them are victimized by both white and black America (19).

2. Mebane's main subject is discrimination because of skin tone, not just skin color. In education, light skin was equated with intelligence; examples of this prejudice follow in

Meaning and Purpose

1. What is Mebane's primary purpose in the essay? Where does she state her thesis?
2. Who do you think Mebane's audience is? Why?
3. In the first paragraph Mebane says she was stopped in the hall of her college by a woman "who was indistinguishable in color from a white woman." Of what significance is this detail?
4. Describe Mebane's feelings about being black in her society.
5. Mebane says in paragraph 13 that she "instinctively tended to avoid the college-exposed dark-skinned man." Why did she do so?
6. Mebane calls a young student "a black cherry of a girl." What does she mean by that?

Strategy

1. Describe two sets of categories Mebane uses in this essay—one for college students and one for "black black women"—and their significance.
2. How are the two sets of categories related? What is the logic behind the essay's structure?
3. What is the purpose of the space break between paragraphs 5 and 6?
4. Mebane uses a rhetorical strategy besides classification and division. What is it, and how does it work in the essay?

Style

1. In paragraph 3, Mebane begins to use the label "black black women." What does each of the two "blacks" modify? What effect does this construction have?
2. What language in the essay creates its tone?

3. If necessary, use a dictionary to find the meanings of these words: *pinnacle* (2); *nonplussed* (5); *commiserating* (7); *stymied, outdeclaim* (11); *stigma* (16); *staunch, fervent* (20); *paradoxically* (22).

Writing Tasks

1. Mebane demonstrates how a class system worked in a black southern college. Write a classification paper in which you demonstrate the class system in your college or in the high school you attended. Make sure you give plenty of examples.
2. What can be classified by color other than people? Perhaps road signs? flowers? clothing? Choose something to classify by color and create appropriate categories. Give examples in each category. Try to use a humorous tone if the subject is suitable.

7–14. Mebane goes to her next categories about the darkest-skinned women (because college-exposed people were more likely to be prejudiced against this group [6]); examples follow. Mebane indicts both black and white America for victimizing black black women.

3. Paragraphs 1–5 are a long introduction. Paragraph 6 is transitional, carrying the reader from the class system described in 4 and the faculty's assumptions underlying that system (5) to examples of how that system worked (7–21).

4. Example is used heavily in this essay, with examples of people in all the categories (17–21). The examples support and further define the categories. A classification-and-division strategy almost always requires examples.

Style

1. With no comma between the two *blacks,* the first becomes the modifier of the second, and the second modifies *woman.* Putting the two words together emphasizes the blackness, or the darkest skin color.

2. Mebane's tone is serious and informative, and she speaks from the point of view of an insider subjected to the prejudice she describes: she is herself a black black woman (2). Here too is a hint of defiance: her authority to talk about her subject; her confidence in being morally right and in recognizing injustice (4). And, though pained by suffering discrimination, she is determined to rise above it.

3. *Pinnacle:* the highest or culminating point, as of success, power, fame; *nonplussed:* at a loss for what to say or do; *commiserating:* feeling or expressing sorrow or sympathy for; *stymied:* hindered, blocked, or thwarted; *outdeclaim:* to declaim is to speak or write in an oratorical manner; *stigma:* a mark of disgrace or infamy; *staunch:* firm or steadfast in principle; *fervent:* having or showing great warmth or intensity of spirit; *paradoxically:* a paradox is any person, thing, or situation exhibiting an apparently contradictory nature.

TEACHING SUGGESTIONS

In the essay Lurie classifies Americans according to their styles of dress and divides the country into five distinct regions that represent these styles. She offers historical, geographic, climatic, political, and economic explanations for the evolution of regional dress. You might begin by asking your students how valid these classifications appear to them. Is an element of stereotyping involved here? Does Lurie take into account other factors that might influence dress? What classifications in dress could be identified at your college or university?

The last question could lead to a discussion of how division and classification help us make sense of complex issues. Both methods separate large subjects into smaller and more comprehensible units. Both methods make large issues easier to understand.

Born in Chicago in 1926, Alison Lurie graduated from Radcliffe College. As a fiction writer, she has often been compared to Jane Austen, both for her style and for her subject matter, which has often been a particular segment of American society—that of the wealthy and educated. Since publication of her first novel, Love and Friendship, *in 1962, she has published seven more, the latest of which is* The Truth about Lorin Jones *(1988). She received a Pulitzer Prize for her novel* Foreign Affairs *(1984). She has also published three children's books and a nonfiction book on the social history of clothes.*

American Regional Costume

In this excerpt from her book The Language of Clothes *(1981), Lurie classifies American styles of dress by region, and the people of those regions by the clothes they wear. She traces the historical influences of climate, landscape, economy, and life-style on various regional "costumes."*

MARGINAL NOTES

Lurie begins with the immediate claim that America has no typical dress, that the varied histories of various regions have left an indelible mark on styles of dress.

After establishing where distinctions of regional dress can best be observed, Lurie states her thesis that five distinct styles of dress can be seen in the United States.

Even today, when the American landscape is becoming more 1 and more homogeneous, there is really no such thing as an all-American style of dress. A shopping center in Maine may superficially resemble one in Georgia or California, but the shoppers in it will look different, because the diverse histories of these states have left their mark on costume.

Regional dress in the United States, as in Britain, can best be 2 observed at large national meetings where factors such as occupation and income are held relatively constant. At these meetings regional differences stand out clearly, and can be checked by looking at the name tags Americans conventionally wear to conventions. Five distinct styles can be distinguished: (1) Old New England, (2) Deep South, (3) Middle American, (4) Wild West

424

and (5) Far West or Californian. In border areas, outfits usually combine regional styles.

Americans who do not travel much within their own country often misinterpret the styles of other regions. Natives of the Eastern states, for instance, may misread Far Western clothing as indicating greater casualness—or greater sexual availability—than is actually present. The laid-back-looking Los Angeles executive in his open-chested sport shirt and sandals may have his eye on the main chance to an extent that will shock his Eastern colleague. The reverse error can also occur: a Southern Californian may discover with surprise that the sober-hued, buttoned-up New Englander he or she has just met is bored with business and longing to get drunk or hop into bed.

Northeast and Southeast:
Puritans and Planters

The drab, severe costumes of the Puritan settlers of New England, and their suspicion of color and ornament as snares of the devil, have left their mark on the present-day clothes of New Englanders. At any large meeting people from this part of the country will be dressed in darker hues—notably black, gray and navy—often with touches of white that recall the starched collars and cuffs of Puritan costume. Fabrics will be plainer (though heavier and sometimes more expensive) and styles simpler, with less waste of material: skirts and lapels and trimmings will be narrower. More of the men will also wear suits and shoes made in England (or designed to look as if they had been made in England). The law of camouflage also operates in New England, where gray skies and dark rectangular urban landscapes are not unknown.

The distinctive dress of the Deep South is based on a climate that did not demand heavy clothing and an economy that for years exempted middle- and upper-class whites from all manual labor and made washing and ironing cheap. Today the planter's white suits and fondness for fine linen and his wife's and daughters' elaborate and fragile gowns survive in modern form. At our

3 She now explains how styles can be misinterpreted by someone alien to a region. This confusion bolsters her contention that dress styles reflect history, geography, and climate rather than social mores or personal morals.

4 Here Lurie begins the paragraph with its topic sentence and then cites examples to establish its validity.

5 She again begins with a topic sentence and proceeds with examples. Now, though, the often elaborate dress of the Deep South is contrasted with the severer dress of New England described in the preceding paragraph.

imaginary national meeting the male southerners will wear lighter-colored suits—pale grays and beiges—and a certain dandyism will be apparent, expressing itself in French cuffs, more expensive ties, silkier materials and wider pin stripes. The women's clothes will be more flowery, with a tendency toward bows, ruffles, lace and embroidery. If they are white, they will probably be as white as possible; a pale complexion is still the sign of a Southern lady, and female sun tans are unfashionable except on tourists.

Midwest and Wild West: Pioneers and Cowboys

Lurie uses the first two sentences to introduce her next classification, midwestern dress, and to lead to her topic sentence, the third. After describing midwestern dress, she compares it to dress in New England and the South to even more clearly distinguish it.

The American Midwest and Great Plains states were settled by men and women who had to do their own work and prided themselves on it. They chose sturdy, practical clothes that did not show the dirt, washed and wore well and needed little ironing, made of gingham and linsey-woolsey and canvas. From these clothes descends the contemporary costume of Middle Americans. This style is visible to everyone on national television, where it is worn by most news announcers, politicians, talk-show hosts and actors in commercials for kitchen products. A slightly dowdier version appears in the Sears and Montgomery Ward catelogues. But even when expensive, Middle American fashion is apt to lag behind fashion as it is currently understood back East; it is also usually more sporty and casual. The pioneer regard for physical activity and exercise is still strong in this part of the country, and as a result the Midwesterners at our convention will look healthier and more athletic—and also somewhat beefier—than their colleagues from the cold, damp Northeast and the hot, humid South. Their suits will tend toward the tans and browns of plowed cornfields rather than the grays of Eastern skies. More of them will wear white or white-on-white shirts, and their striped or foulard ties will be brighter and patterned on a larger scale than those purchased in sober New York and Boston.

She now describes dress in the Wild West and claims that the language as well as the dress of the Wild Westerners reflects a ranching background.

The traditional Western costume, of course, was that of the cowboy on the range. Perhaps because of the isolation of those wide-open spaces, this is the style which has been least influenced by those of other regions. At any national convention the Wild Westerners will be the easiest to identify. For one thing, they are apt to be taller—either genetically or with the help of boots. Some may appear in full Western costume, the sartorial equivalent of a "he-went-thataway" drawl; but even the more conservative will betray, or rather proclaim, their regional loyalty through their dress, just as in conversation they will from time to time use a ranching metaphor, or call you "pal" or "pardner." A man in otherwise conventional business uniform will wear what look like cowboy boots, or a hat with an enlarged brim and crown. Women, too, are apt to wear boots, and their jackets and skirts may have a Western cut, especially when viewed from the rear. Some may wear red or navy-blue bandanna-print shirts or dresses, or an actual cotton-print bandanna knotted round their necks.

The Far West:
Adventurers and Beach Boys

The men and women who settled the Far West were a mixed and rather raffish lot. Restlessness, the wish for excitement, the hope of a fortune in gold and sometimes a need to escape the law led them to undertake the long and dangerous journey over mountains and deserts, or by sea round Cape Horn. In more than one sense they were adventurers, and often desperadoes—desperate people. California was a territory where no one would ask about your past, where unconventionality of character and behavior was easily accepted. Even today when, as the country song puts it, "all the gold in California is in a bank in the middle of Beverly Hills in somebody else's name," the place has the reputation of an El Dorado. Men and women willing to risk everything on long odds in the hope of a big hit, or eager to put legal, financial and personal foul-ups behind them, often go west.

Present-day California styles are still in many ways those of adventurers and eccentrics. Whatever the current fashion, the California version will be more extreme, more various and—

8   First Lurie gives a brief historical background on California's development and then shows how the present reflects the past.

El Dorado was a legendary treasure city in South America sought by early Spanish explorers. By extension, then, it is any place promising great wealth.

9

possibly because of the influence of the large Spanish-American population—much more colorful. Clothes tend to fit more tightly than is considered proper elsewhere, and to expose more flesh: an inability to button the shirt above the diaphragm is common in both sexes. Virtuous working-class housewives may wear outfits that in any other part of the country would identify them as medium-priced whores; reputable business and professional men may dress in a manner which would lose them most of their clients back east and attract the attention of the Bureau of Internal Revenue if not of the police.

To emphasize the sometimes outlandish Californian dress, Lurie shows how that dress might be interpreted in other parts of the country.

Lurie now connects southern Californians with others in the Sun Belt and gives two more examples that distinguish them from those of other regions.

Southern Californians, and many other natives of what is now called the Sun Belt (an imaginary strip of land stretching across the bottom of the United States from Florida to Santa Barbara, but excluding most of the Old South), can also be identified by their year-round sun tans, which by middle age have often given the skin the look of old if expensive and well-oiled leather. The men may also wear the getup known as Sun Belt Cool: a pale beige suit, open-collared shirt (often in a darker shade than the suit), cream-colored loafers and aviator sunglasses. The female version of the look is similar, except that the shoes will be high-heeled sandals.   10

Regional Disguise:
Sunbelt Puritans and Urban Cowboys

In the last section of the essay, Lurie explains why some people who live in a region refuse to dress typically and why some styles are popular in all regions. She begins by giving some general examples of people who choose to dress outside the norm.

Some long-time inhabitants of California and the other sartorially distinct regions of the United States refuse to wear the styles characteristic of that area. In this case the message is clear: they are unhappy in that locale and/or do not want anyone to attribute to them the traits associated with it. Such persons, if depressed, may adopt a vague and anonymous mode of dress; if in good spirits they may wear the costume of some other region in order to proclaim their sympathy with it. In terms of speech, what we have then is not a regional accent, but the conscious adoption of a dialect by an outsider.   11

She now offers specific examples.

In the urban centers of the West and Far West bankers and financial experts of both sexes sometimes adopt an Eastern manner of speech and a Wall Street appearance in order to suggest   12 reliability and tradition. And today in Southern California there in the library stacks, avoid the beach and dress in clothes that would occasion no comment in Harvard Yard. New arrivals to the area sometimes take these men and women for visiting Eastern lecturers, and are surprised to learn that they have lived in Southern California for thirty or forty years, or have even been born there.

The popularity of the various regional styles of American costume, like that of the various national styles, is also related to economic and political factors. Some years ago modes often originated in the Far West and the word "California" on a garment was thought to be an allurement. Today, with power and population growth shifting to the Southwestern oil-producing states, Wild West styles—particularly those of Texas—are in vogue. This fashion, of course, is not new. For many years men who have never been nearer to a cow than the local steakhouse have worn Western costume to signify that they are independent, tough and reliable. In a story by Flannery O'Connor, for instance, the sinister traveling salesman is described as wearing "a broad-brimmed stiff gray hat of the kind used by businessmen who would like to look like cowboys"—but, it is implied, seldom succeed in doing so.

The current popularity of Western costume has been increased by the turn away from foreign modes that has accompanied the recent right-wing shift in United States politics. In all countries periods of isolationism and a belligerently ostrichlike stance toward the rest of the world have usually been reflected in a rejection of international modes in favor of national styles, often those of the past. Today in America the cowboy look is high fashion, and even in New York City the streets are full of a variety of Wild West types. Some are dressed in old-fashioned, well-worn Western gear; others in the newer, brighter and sleeker outfits of modern ranchers, while a few wear spangled, neon-hued Electric Cowboy and Cowgirl costumes of the type most often seen on Texas country-rock musicians.

13   Lurie introduces two other factors that influence the popularity of a regional style and offers examples from the past.

14   She concludes with an explanation of the current popularity of western costume and gives present-day examples.

POSSIBLE ANSWERS

Meaning and Purpose

1. Encourage students to examine their own ideas about what regional American dress is, as well as where those ideas come from and what attitudes they might reflect.
2. Attendees of national meetings generally come from similar occupational and economic backgrounds. Their dress would vary not because of social and economic status, but because of the regions they come from (3).
3. Lurie's thesis is that Americans have five distinct kinds of dress, as she states (2).
4. Regional styles are determined by the region's history and climate and do not reflect moral attitudes. Someone from outside a region may misinterpret the dress of that region by reading moral values into the style of dress (3).
5. She claims that history, local interests, geography, and climate account for the differences in regional dress styles.
6. The current popularity of western costume reflects recent far-right politics and isolationism and a turning away from foreign modes (14).

Strategy

1. Lurie's organizational scheme follows the historical development of the United States from the Northeast to the South, the Midwest to the Southwest, and, finally, to the Far West.
2. Lurie's first two subheadings pair adjacent regions, and the two style categories under each are markedly different. The Far West gets its own subheading because it is traditionally big and bold enough to stand alone. California is usually set apart from other regions.
3. To clearly distinguish the "sturdy and practical" dress of the midwesterner, Lurie compares this style to that of both the New Englander and the southerner (6). She empha-

Meaning and Purpose

1. If you were to classify American regional dress, would you choose Lurie's categories? Why or why not? If not, what would your categories be?
2. Why does Lurie claim that large, national meetings are best for observing regional dress?
3. What is Lurie's main point, and where does she state it?
4. Why is it possible to misinterpret the dress styles of different regions?
5. How does Lurie explain the differences in dress from region to region?
6. How does Lurie account for the current popularity of western costume? Do you agree with her?

Strategy

1. What scheme does Lurie use to organize her categories?
2. In paragraph 2, Lurie lists five categories of style of dress, but only three subheadings cover those five categories. Why do you suppose she puts the first two and the second two together, and gives the Far West its own subheading?
3. Lurie adds to classification and division other rhetorical strategies to support her categories. Look again at paragraphs 4 and 5, and paragraph 8 and paragraph 9. What strategies does she use in these places?
4. Lurie quotes a country song in paragraph 8 and the short-story writer and novelist Flannery O'Connor in paragraph 13. What is the purpose of these quotations?

Style

1. Lurie often juxtaposes formal sociological and anthropological language with the language of casual conversation and slang.

What are some examples of this mixture? What is the effect of such juxtapositions?

2. In her categories and descriptions, is Lurie making any judgments about regional dress, or is she neutral? Support your answer with language from the essay.

3. If necessary, check a dictionary for the meanings of these expressions: *homogeneous, superficially* (1); *Puritan* (4); *dandyism* (5); *gingham, linsey-woolsey, dowdier, foulard* (6); *sartorial* (7); *raffish* (8); *allurement* (13); *isolationism, belligerently* (14).

Writing Tasks

1. Analyze the styles of dress popular on your campus. Create four or five style categories and use as many specific examples as you can. In a classification-and-division essay, establish clearly the basis for your classifications.

2. Examine the ways in which popular entertainment—movies, television, rock music, and rock-music stars—affects dress, speech, or hair style. Write a classification essay in which you show how these influences have produced the styles you describe.

sizes the often outlandish California styles by showing how such dress would be interpreted in other parts of the country, particularly the more formally attired Northeast (9).

4. The quotations show that the kinds of dress she describes are reflected in popular and literary culture. These facts bolster the validity of her thesis.

Style

1. Some examples: "homogeneous" (1), "factors such as occupation and income are held relatively constant" (2), "laid-back-looking" and "hop into bed" (3). The casual language gives the impression that she's talking about real people.

2. Lurie makes no explicit judgments, but some of her descriptive language sounds opinionated or stereotypical.

3. *Homogeneous*: composed of parts or elements that are all of the same kind; *superficially*: externally or outwardly; *Puritan*: a member of a group of Protestants that arose in the sixteenth century within the Church of England, demanding simpler doctrine and worship and stricter religious discipline; many Puritans migrated to New England; *dandyism*: excessive attention to clothes and appearance; *gingham*: yarn-dyed, plain-weave cotton fabric, usually striped or checked; *linsey-woolsey*: a coarse fabric woven from linen warp, or sometimes cotton and coarse wool filling; *dowdier*: to be dowdy is to be out of style, drab, old-fashioned, untidy; *foulard*: a soft, lightweight silk, rayon, or cotton of plain or twill weave with printed design; *sartorial*: of or pertaining to clothing or style or manner of dress; *raffish*: mildly or sometimes engagingly disreputable or nonconformist; *allurement*: fascination, charm; *isolationism*: the policy or doctrine of isolating one's country from the affairs of other nations by declining to enter alliances, foreign economic commitments, international agreements, and so on; *belligerently*: warlike, aggressively hostile.

❦ John Holt ❦

John Holt is the author of, among other famous books, How Children Fail *(1964) and* How Children Learn *(1967). He was born in 1923 and studied at Yale University. His fourteen years of experience in elementary and high-school teaching led him to some radical and controversial conclusions about the ineffectiveness of the American educational system. In many of his books he addresses this problem and offers alternative methods for helping children learn. He was a visiting lecturer at Harvard University and the University of California at Berkeley. After 1969 he devoted himself primarily to writing, lecturing, social activism, and playing the cello, which he took up at age forty. He founded, edited, and published* Growing Without Schooling, *a magazine by and for families who choose to teach their children at home. He died in 1985.*

TEACHING SUGGESTIONS

The essay could be used for discussing both childrearing and learning. The students' own backgrounds will undoubtedly determine their attitudes toward each of the kinds of discipline Holt describes, especially that of Superior Force. Encourage students to give specific examples to back up their opinions, demonstrating that specifics are always needed to be convincing.

Three Kinds of Discipline

This tightly organized short essay offers a general prescription for the use of discipline by classifying it in three categories. Here and in the book where this passage first appeared, Freedom and Beyond *(1972), Holt argues that, in order to learn, children need to be left alone as much as they need to be disciplined.*

MARGINAL NOTES

Holt begins with examples that immediately illustrate the Discipline of Nature.

A child, in growing up, may meet and learn from three different kinds of disciplines. The first and most important is what we might call the Discipline of Nature or of Reality. When he is trying to do something real, if he does the wrong thing or doesn't do the right one, he doesn't get the result he wants. If he doesn't pile one block right on top of another, or tries to build on a slanting surface, his tower falls down. If he hits the wrong key, he hears the wrong note. If he doesn't hit the nail squarely on the head, it bends, and he has to pull it out and start with another. If he doesn't measure properly what he is trying to build, it won't open,   1 close, fit, stand up, fly, float, whistle, or do whatever he wants it to do. If he closes his eyes when he swings, he doesn't hit the ball. A child meets this kind of discipline every time he tries to *do* something, which is why it is so important in school to give children more chances to do things, instead of just reading or listening to someone talk (or pretending to). This discipline is a good teacher. The learner never has to wait long for his answer; it usually comes quickly, often instantly. Also it is clear, and very often points toward the needed correction; from what happened he can not only see that what he did was wrong, but also why, and what he needs to do instead. Finally, and most important, the giver of the answer, call it Nature, is impersonal, impartial, and indifferent. She does not give opinions, or make judgments: she cannot be wheedled, bullied, or fooled; she does not get angry or disappointed; she does not praise or blame; she does not re- member past failures or hold grudges; with her one always gets a fresh start, this time is the one that counts.

He then shows why this kind of discipline is important in schools: it is a good teacher.

The next discipline we might call the Discipline of Culture, of Society, of What People Really Do. Man is a social, a cultural animal. Children sense around them this culture, this network of agreements, customs, habits, and rules binding the adults to- gether. They want to understand it and be a part of it. They watch very carefully what people around them are doing and want to do the same. They want to do right, unless they become convinced they can't do right. Thus children rarely misbehave seriously in church, but sit as quietly as they can. The example of all those grownups is contagious. Some mysterious ritual is going on, and children, who like rituals, want to be part of it. In the same way, the little children that I see at concerts or operas, though they may fidget a little, or perhaps take a nap now and then, rarely make any disturbance. With all those grownups sitting there, neither moving nor talking, it is the most natural thing in the world to imitate them. Children who live among adults who are habitually courteous to each other, and to them, will soon learn to be courteous. Children who live surrounded by people who speak a certain way will speak that way, however much we may try to tell them that speaking that way is bad or wrong.

2 After explaining the Discipline of Culture, Holt gives examples to show that it works in the real world.

Holt begins the paragraph using the same format as the last, a brief explanation of the Discipline of Superior Force followed by examples.

The third discipline is the one most people mean when they speak of discipline—the Discipline of Superior Force, of sergeant to private, of "you do what I tell you or I'll make you wish you had." There is bound to be some of this in a child's life. Living as we do surrounded by things that can hurt children, or that children can hurt, we cannot avoid it. We can't afford to let a small child find out from experience the danger of playing in a busy street, or of fooling with the pots on the top of a stove, or of eating up the pills in the medicine cabinet. So, along with other precautions, we say to him, "Don't play in the street, or touch things on the stove, or go into the medicine cabinet, or I'll punish you." Between him and the danger too great for him to imagine we put a lesser danger, but one he can imagine and maybe therefore wants to avoid. He can have no idea of what it would be like to be hit by a car, but he can imagine being shouted at, or spanked, or sent to his room. He avoids these substitutes for the greater danger until he can understand it and avoid it for its own sake.

He now cautions that this kind of discipline should be used sparingly and goes on to explain why.

But we ought to use this discipline only when it is necessary to protect the life, health, safety, or well-being of people or other living creatures, or to prevent destruction of things that people care about. We ought not to assume too long, as we usually do, that a child cannot understand the real nature of the danger from which we want to protect him. The sooner he avoids the danger, not to escape our punishment, but as a matter of good sense, the better. He can learn that faster than we think. In Mexico, for example, where people drive their cars with a good deal of spirit, I saw many children no older than five or four walking unattended on the streets. They understood about cars, they knew what to do. A child whose life is full of the threat and fear of punishment is locked into babyhood. There is no way for him to grow up, to learn to take responsibility for his life and acts. Most important of all, we should not assume that having to yield to the threat of our superior force is good for the child's character. It is never good for *anyone's* character. To bow to superior force makes us feel impotent and cowardly for not having had the strength or courage to resist. Worse, it makes us resentful and vengeful. We can hardly wait to make someone pay for our humiliation, yield to us as we

3

were once made to yield. No, if we cannot always avoid using the discipline of Superior Force, we should at least use it as seldom as we can.

There are places where all three disciplines overlap. Any very demanding human activity combines in it the disciplines of Superior Force, of Culture, and of Nature. The novice will be told, "Do it this way, never mind asking why, just do it that way, that is the way we always do it." But it probably *is* just the way they always do it, and usually for the very good reason that it is a way that has been found to work. Think, for example, of ballet training. The student in a class is told to do this exercise, or that; to stand so; to do this or that with his head, arms, shoulders, abdomen, hips, legs, feet. He is constantly corrected. There is no argument. But behind these seemingly autocratic demands by the teacher lie many decades of custom and tradition, and behind that, the necessities of dancing itself. You cannot make the moves of classical ballet unless over many years you have acquired, and renewed every day, the needed strength and suppleness in scores of muscles and joints. Nor can you do the difficult motions, making them look easy, unless you have learned hundreds of easier ones first. Dance teachers may not always agree on all the details of teaching these strengths and skills. But no novice could learn them all by himself. You could not go for a night or two to watch the ballet and then, without any other knowledge at all, teach yourself how to do it. In the same way, you would be unlikely to learn any complicated and difficult human activity without drawing heavily on the experience of those who know it better. But the point is that the authority of these experts or teachers stems from, grows out of their greater competence and experience, the fact that what they do *works*, not the fact that they happen to be the teacher and as such have the power to kick a student out of the class. And the further point is that children are always and everywhere attracted to that competence, and ready and eager to submit themselves to a discipline that grows out of it. We hear constantly that children will never do anything unless compelled to by bribes or threats. But in their private lives, or in extracurricular activities in school, in sports, music, drama, art, running

4   With an extended example of ballet training Holt illustrates how all three disciplines often overlap.

a newspaper, and so on, they often submit themselves willingly and wholeheartedly to very intense disciplines, simply because they want to learn to do a given thing well. Our Little-Napoleon football coaches, of whom we have too many and hear far too much, blind us to the fact that millions of children work hard every year getting better at sports and games without coaches barking and yelling at them.

Meaning and Purpose

1. What does Holt set out to say in this essay?
2. What methods of discipline have you seen in practice, and how effective do you think they are?
3. Do you agree with the statement, "Thus children rarely misbehave seriously in church, but sit as quietly as they can" (paragraph 2). Does Holt make a good case for the truth of the statement? Why or why not?
4. What is Holt's attitude toward children? Where is this attitude evident in the essay?

Strategy

1. Holt divides discipline into three kinds. What is the basis for this division, and why does he identify only three kinds?
2. Does paragraph 4 describe a fourth kind of discipline? If so, does this category cause an imbalance in the essay's structure (Holt announces only three categories in the beginning)? Why or why not?
3. How does Holt make use of examples in this essay?

POSSIBLE ANSWERS

Meaning and Purpose

1. Holt means that children will "meet and learn" from discipline. His first sentence is his thesis. He goes into detail about three kinds of discipline and how children may learn best from them.
2. Give students time to talk about discipline they have observed and their opinions about it. Encourage them to compare their observations to some of Holt's descriptions.
3. Students will have their own opinions about this statement. Holt's point is that children usually imitate the adults around them and that example is the best teacher. He says, "They watch very carefully what people around them are doing and want to do the same" (paragraph 2). The evidence he offers is general and perhaps idealistic, but his argument is effective.
4. He believes children are basically good and easily trained, and also that they will naturally strive for the best. The penultimate sentence in the essay illustrates this attitude.

Strategy

1. Holt's classification system has to do with the kinds of things in the world outside the self that he thinks impose discipline on children. He chooses nature, culture, and force as three large areas of influence. Another social scientist might choose three other categories, or more than three. Holt's categories result from his own observations and opinions.
2. Paragraph 4 describes where his categories overlap. He doesn't say this is a fourth category, but rather sums up the three and brings them together. In practice, his kinds of discipline don't always occur in isolation. The essay is not imbalanced but balanced by this last paragraph, tied up neatly and brought to an end.

Style

1. Why do you think Holt capitalizes the names of the kinds of discipline he classifies?
2. What is Holt's attitude toward his subject? Is he neutral about it or is he advocating something? How do you know?
3. If necessary, look up the meaning of these words: *wheedled* (1); *contagious, fidget* (2); *impotent* (3); *novice, autocratic, suppleness* (4).

Writing Tasks

1. Write an essay in which you classify parents according to the kinds of discipline they use with their children. Speak from first-hand knowledge, and take Holt as a model for using specific examples.
2. Write an essay in which you classify students. You might want to use elementary, high-school, or college students, or you might show how each kind of student behaves at each of the three levels of education. Make sure you use typical examples and then demonstrate them in real life with specific examples.

3. Each paragraph contains a series of brief, typical examples illustrating Holt's general statements.

Style

1. The names are capitalized because they are formal labels of each division.
2. Holt appreciates the value of all three kinds of discipline while trusting the child to grow naturally without excessive adult interference. He is clearly advocating an approach to teaching in its broadest sense: allow the child to learn from hands-on experiences; provide good examples for the child to imitate; and protect the child from danger, but do not underestimate his or her ability to understand its real nature.
3. *Wheedled*: to have endeavored to influence a person by smooth, flattering, or beguiling words or acts; *contagious*: tending to spread from person to person; *fidget*: to move about restlessly, nervously, or impatiently; *impotent*: lacking power or ability; *novice*: a person who is new to the circumstances in which he is placed; *autocratic*: tyrannical, despotic, domineering; *suppleness*: the condition of being flexible, pliant.

Excepting a few who may have had a sociology or social anthropology course, students do not often encounter the social-scientific methods of classification used by Morris. Some say that humankind is not to be treated like other animals. But what of athletes? We classify them like tools—according to their uses, not their intrinsic worth as people. Tribal, family, and personal territories are often thought of as occupying the whole planet, a thought decried by ecologists.

Territory carries responsibility. Do we protect the territory that we display as ours? Or do we ruin it as part of our displaying that it is ours?

While Morris examines territorial behavior, it enlivens the class discussion to add the concept of responsibility to that behavior. Explore the question of whether we should protect for ourselves what is ours alone or whether we should keep our territory in trust. If we keep it in trust, how far are we willing to go to protect it? As far as war? War destroys territory. Are we willing to be constantly vigilant politically to protect territory? And from whom are we protecting it?

MARGINAL NOTES

Morris begins by dividing human territory into three classifications. Before he expands those classifications, he discusses their sociology. First, he describes the penalties for violating the territories of others. Next, he discusses briefly the healthy reasons for having "owned space." Then he tells how we mark our territories.

❦ Desmond Morris ❦

Born in England in 1928, Desmond Morris studied at Birmingham University and Oxford University. After receiving his doctorate from Oxford, he was a researcher in the zoology department there for a short time. He later worked for several years at the Zoological Society of London, first as curator of mammals and later as director of the society's television and film department. He has also been director of London's Institute of Contemporary Arts, and in 1950 had a one-man show in which he exhibited his own paintings. He is best known, however, as writer of popular—if sometimes controversial—books on human behavior, including The Naked Ape *(1967) and* The Human Zoo *(1969).*

Territorial Behavior

This essay is from Morris's book Manwatching *(1974), another of his works on human behavior. He supports his premise that human beings are "remarkably territorial animals" by classifying and describing three kinds of human territory, each of which induces its own form of territorial behavior.*

A territory is a defended space. In the broadest sense, there are three kinds of human territory: tribal, family and personal. 1

It is rare for people to be driven to physical fighting in defense of these "owned" spaces, but fight they will, if pushed to the limit. The invading army encroaching on national territory, the gang moving into a rival district, the trespasser climbing into an orchard, the burglar breaking into a house, the bully pushing to the front of a queue, the driver trying to steal a parking space, all of these intruders are liable to be met with resistance varying from the vigorous to the savagely violent. Even if the law is on the side of the intruder, the urge to protect a territory may be so strong that otherwise peaceful citizens abandon all their usual controls 2

438

and inhibitions. Attempts to evict families from their homes, no matter how socially valid the reasons, can lead to siege conditions reminiscent of the defense of a medieval fortress.

The fact that these upheavals are so rare is a measure of the success of Territorial Signals as a system of dispute prevention. It is sometimes cynically stated that "all property is theft," but in reality it is the opposite. Property, as owned space which is *displayed* as owned space, is a special kind of sharing system which reduces fighting much more than it causes it. Man is a co-operative species, but he is also competitive, and his struggle for dominance has to be structured in some way if chaos is to be avoided. The establishment of territorial rights is one such structure. It limits dominance geographically. I am dominant in my territory and you are dominant in yours. In other words, dominance is shared out spatially, and we all have some. Even if I am weak and unintelligent and you can dominate me when we meet on neutral ground, I can still enjoy a thoroughly dominant role as soon as I retreat to my private base. Be it ever so humble, there is no place like a home territory.

Of course, I can still be intimidated by a particularly dominant individual who enters my home base, but his encroachment will be dangerous for him and he will think twice about it, because he will know that here my urge to resist will be dramatically magnified and my usual subservience banished. Insulted at the heart of my own territory, I may easily explode into battle—either symbolic or real—with a result that may be damaging to both of us.

In order for this to work, each territory has to be plainly advertised as such. Just as a dog cocks its leg to deposit its personal scent on the trees in its locality, so the human animal cocks its leg symbolically all over his home base. But because we are predominantly visual animals we employ mostly visual signals, and it is worth asking how we do this at the three levels: tribal, family and personal.

First: the Tribal Territory. We evolved as tribal animals, living in comparatively small groups, probably of less than a hundred, and we existed like that for millions of years. It is our basic social

3

4

5

6 Returning to the first of his classifications, Morris develops it by the strategy of cyclic expansion. That is, he starts at the center, the

small group, and expands outward, each circle of expansion larger: The tribe's home base expands, finally, to become the capital city of a nation.

The nation itself, fixed by borders, holds so many people that individuals begin to lose their tribal identity. They compensate by forming subgroups, social tribes, to gain a sense of belonging, which includes the territorial signals such social tribes agree to use.

unit, a group in which everyone knows everyone else. Essentially, the tribal territory consisted of a home base surrounded by extended hunting grounds. Any neighbouring tribe intruding on our social space would be repelled and driven away. As these early tribes swelled into agricultural super-tribes, and eventually into industrial nations, their territorial defence systems became increasingly elaborate. The tiny, ancient home base of the hunting tribe became the great capital city, the primitive war-paint became the flags, emblems, uniforms and regalia of the specialized military, and the war-chants became national anthems, marching songs and bugle calls. Territorial boundary-lines hardened into fixed borders, often conspicuously patrolled and punctuated with defensive structures—forts and lookout posts, check-points and great walls, and, today, customs barriers.

Today each nation flies its own flag, a symbolic embodiment of its territorial status. But patriotism is not enough. The ancient tribal hunter lurking inside each citizen finds himself unsatisfied by membership of such a vast conglomeration of individuals, most of whom are totally unknown to him personally. He does his best to feel that he shares a common territorial defence with them all, but the scale of the operation has become inhuman. It is hard to feel a sense of belonging with a tribe of fifty million or more. His answer is to form sub-groups, nearer to his ancient pattern, smaller and more personally known to him—the local club, the teenage gang, the union, the specialist society, the sports association, the political party, the college fraternity, the social clique, the protest group, and the rest. Rare indeed is the individual who does not belong to at least one of these splinter groups, and take from it a sense of tribal allegiance and brotherhood. Typical of all these groups is the development of Territorial Signals—badges, costumes, headquarters, banners, slogans, and all the other displays of group identity. This is where the action is, in terms of tribal territorialism, and only when a major war breaks out does the emphasis shift upwards to the higher group level of the nation.

Each of these modern pseudo-tribes sets up its own special kind of home base. In extreme cases non-members are totally excluded, in others they are allowed in as visitors with limited rights and under a control system of special rules. In many ways they are like miniature nations, with their own flags and emblems and their own border guards. The exclusive club has its own "customs barrier": the doorman who checks your "passport" (your membership card) and prevents strangers from passing in unchallenged. There is a government: the club committee; and often special displays of the tribal elders: the photographs or portraits of previous officials on the walls. At the heart of the specialized territories there is a powerful feeling of security and importance, a sense of shared defence against the outside world. Much of the club chatter, both serious and joking, directs itself against the rottenness of everything outside the club boundaries—in that "other world" beyond the protected portals.

In social organizations which embody a strong class system, such as military units and large business concerns, there are many territorial rules, often unspoken, which interfere with the official hierarchy. High-status individuals, such as officers or managers, could in theory enter any of the regions occupied by the lower levels in the peck order, but they limit this power in a striking way. An officer seldom enters a sergeant's mess or a barrack room unless it is for a formal inspection. He respects those regions as alien territories even though he has the power to go there by virtue of his dominant role. And in businesses, part of the appeal of unions, over and above their obvious functions, is that with their officials, headquarters and meetings they add a sense of territorial power for the staff workers. It is almost as if each military organization and business concern consists of two warring tribes: the officers versus the other ranks, and the management versus the workers. Each has its special home base within the system, and the territorial defence pattern thrusts itself into what, on the surface, is a pure social hierarchy. Negotiations between managements and unions are tribal battles fought out over the neutral ground of a boardroom table, and are as much concerned with territorial display as they are with resolving problems of wages and conditions. Indeed, if one side gives in too quickly and accepts the other's demands, the victors feel strangely cheated and deeply suspicious that it may be a trick. What they are

9

Notice that this classification is as cyclic as the strategy Morris uses to describe it. As the tribe expands, members of the tribe circle back to making efforts to form a subgroup, keeping their own membership small enough to be comfortably identifiable.

missing is the protracted sequence of ritual and counter-ritual that keeps alive their group territorial identity.

Likewise, many of the hostile displays of sports fans and teenage gangs are primarily concerned with displaying their group image to rival fan-clubs and gangs. Except in rare cases, they do not attack one another's headquarters, drive out the occupants, and reduce them to a submissive, subordinate condition. It is enough to have scuffles on the borderlands between the two rival territories. This is particularly clear at football matches, where the fan-club headquarters becomes temporarily shifted from the club-house to a section of the stands, and where minor fighting breaks out at the unofficial boundary line between the massed groups of rival supporters. Newspaper reports play up the few accidents and injuries which do occur on such occasions, but when these are studied in relation to the total numbers of displaying fans involved it is clear that the serious incidents represent only a tiny fraction of the overall group behaviour. For every actual punch or kick there are a thousand war-cries, war-dances, chants and gestures.

Second: the Family Territory. Essentially, the family is a breeding unit and the family territory is a breeding ground. At the centre of this space, there is the nest—the bedroom—where, tucked up in bed, we feel at our most territorially secure. In a typical house the bedroom is upstairs, where a safe nest should be. This puts it farther away from the entrance hall, the area where contact is made, intermittently, with the outside world. The less private reception rooms, where intruders are allowed access, are the next line of defence. Beyond them, outside the walls of the building, there is often a symbolic remnant of the ancient feeding grounds—a garden. Its symbolism often extends to the plants and animals it contains, which cease to be nutritional and become merely decorative—flowers and pets. But like a true territorial space it has a conspicuously displayed boundary-line, the garden fence, wall, or railings. Often no more than a token barrier, this is the outer territorial demarcation, separating the private world of the family from the public world beyond. To cross it puts any visitor or intruder at an immediate disadvantage. As he crosses

Moving down as they read, from the tribe classification to the family classification, students are occasionally shocked to see the family defined as a "breeding unit" and the family's territory as a "breeding ground." They might be reminded that Morris is not being cavalier with the family unit; instead, he is using the neutral terminology of the social scientist.

Morris's "typical house" is typical for the author's area, but houses differ in this country, according to cost and location. Because his house can be described as "ideal Victorian," students from other kinds of homes might need to be reminded that he is using a model here to represent reality, not to define it.

the threshold, his dominance wanes, slightly but unmistakably. He is entering an area where he senses that he must ask permission to do simple things that he would consider a right elsewhere. Without lifting a finger, the territorial owners exert their dominance. This is done by all the hundreds of small ownership "markers" they have deposited on their family territory: the ornaments, the "possessed" objects positioned in the rooms and on the walls; the furnishings, the furniture, the colours, the patterns, all owner-chosen and all making this particular home base unique to them.

It is one of the tragedies of modern architecture that there has been a standardization of these vital territorial living-units. One of the most important aspects of a home is that it should be similar to other homes only in a general way, and that in detail it should have many differences, making it a *particular* home. Unfortunately, it is cheaper to build a row of houses, or a block of flats, so that all the family living-units are identical, but the territorial urge rebels against this trend and house-owners struggle as best they can to make their mark on their mass-produced properties. They do this with garden-design, with front-door colours, with curtain patterns, with wallpaper and all the other decorative elements that together create a unique and different family environment. Only when they have completed this nest-building do they feel truly "at home" and secure.

When they venture forth as a family unit they repeat the process in a minor way. On a day-trip to the seaside, they load the car with personal belongings and it becomes their temporary, portable territory. Arriving at the beach they stake out a small territorial claim, marking it with rugs, towels, baskets and other belongings to which they can return from their seaboard wanderings. Even if they all leave it at once to bathe, it retains a characteristic territorial quality and other family groups arriving will recognize this by setting up their own "home" bases at a respectful distance. Only when the whole beach has filled up with these marked spaces will newcomers start to position themselves in such a way that the inter-base distance becomes reduced. Forced to pitch between several existing beach territories they will feel a

12   Morris's comments on modern architecture can deeply affect students, particularly if they live in apartments, condominiums, or in some older tracts of homes that were built quickly and identically. Teachers often break here, to discuss with their students the ways in which we mark our property as our own, with plants, paint, lawns, fences, pets, trees, and so on. A stimulating question is: "How much do we mark our territory as being comfortably ours before we begin to mark it as a warning to others not to trespass?" It is one thing to build a white picket fence around our house, quite another to build a six-foot chain-link fence, for example.

13   So also with temporary territory: Here is a good place to discuss the worth of Morris's comments. Does it really happen as he describes it? Do we stake out territory in the mountains, at the park, the river, the lake, or near the ocean? What happens when our territory is violated? Does it make a difference what kind of people violate our territory? If an old woman and an old man sit quite near our territory, do we feel differently than we would if a teenage boy and girl violated our territory?

momentary sensation of intrusion, and the established "owners" will feel a similar sensation of invasion, even though they are not being directly inconvenienced.

The same territorial scene is being played out in parks and   14
fields and on riverbanks, wherever family groups gather in their clustered units. But if rivalry for spaces creates mild feelings of hostility, it is true to say that, without the territorial system of sharing and space-limited dominance, there would be chaotic disorder.

The third classification, the personal space, brings us to the subject many students call the "rights" of the individual. They should notice that Morris is not talking about rights; he is precisely describing the results of socio-scientific observations. Determining where we sit and how we protect our personal space is the cultural manifestation of our tribe's territorial habits.

Third: the Personal Space. If a man enters a waiting-room and   15
sits at one end of a long row of empty chairs, it is possible to predict where the next man to enter will seat himself. He will not sit next to the first man, nor will he sit at the far end, right away from him. He will choose a position about halfway between these two points. The next man to enter will take the largest gap left, and sit roughly in the middle of that, and so on, until eventually the latest newcomer will be forced to select a seat that places him right next to one of the already seated men. Similar patterns can be observed in cinemas, public urinals, aeroplanes, trains and buses. This is a reflection of the fact that we all carry with us, everywhere we go, a portable territory called a Personal Space. If people move inside this space, we feel threatened. If they keep too far outside it, we feel rejected. The result is a subtle series of spatial adjustments, usually operating quite unconsciously and producing ideal compromises as far as this is possible. If a situation becomes too crowded, then we adjust our reactions accordingly and allow our personal space to shrink. Jammed into an elevator, a rush-hour compartment, or a packed room, we give up altogether and allow body-to-body contact, but when we relinquish our Personal Space in this way, we adopt certain special techniques. In essence, what we do is to convert these other bodies into "nonpersons." We studiously ignore them, and they us. We try not to face them if we can possibly avoid it. We wipe all expressiveness from our faces, letting them go blank. We may look up at the ceiling or down at the floor, and we reduce body movements to a minimum. Packed together like sardines in a tin,

we stand dumbly still, sending out as few social signals as possible.

Even if the crowding is less severe, we still tend to cut down our social interactions in the presence of large numbers. Careful observations of children in play groups revealed that if they are high density groupings there is less social interaction between the individual children, even though there is theoretically more opportunity for such contacts. At the same time, the high-density groups show a higher frequency of aggressive and destructive behaviour patterns in their play. Personal Space—"elbow room"—is a vital commodity for the human animal, and one that cannot be ignored without risking serious trouble.

Of course, we all enjoy the excitement of being in a crowd, and this reaction cannot be ignored. But there are crowds and crowds. It is pleasant enough to be in a "spectator crowd," but not so appealing to find yourself in the middle of a rush-hour crush. The difference between the two is that the spectator crowd is all facing in the same direction and concentrating on a distant point of interest. Attending a theatre, there are twinges of rising hostility towards the stranger who sits down immediately in front of you or the one who squeezes into the seat next to you. The shared armrest can become a polite, but distinct, territorial boundary-dispute region. However, as soon as the show begins, these invasions of Personal Space are forgotten and the attention is focused beyond the small space where the crowding is taking place. Now, each member of the audience feels himself spatially related, not to his cramped neighbours, but to the actor on the stage, and this distance is, if anything, too great. In the rush-hour crowd, by contrast, each member of the pushing throng is competing with his neighbours all the time. There is no escape to a spacial relation with a distant actor, only the pushing, shoving bodies all around.

Those of us who have to spend a great deal of time in crowded conditions become gradually better able to adjust, but no one can ever become completely immune to invasions of Personal Space. This is because they remain forever associated with either

16 The higher the density, the less we socially interact. This behavior surprises students until they test its validity by observation. Notice the differences between "crowds and crowds": the spectator crowd has a special, collective goal. The rush-hour crowd has diverse goals, a fact that might lead to disputes.

17 Students are often interested in discussing this observation as it might be applied to driving their cars. Is rush-hour traffic more frenetic because the drivers are focusing on diverse goals? On freeways, expressways, thoroughfares, and toll roads, why does it seem that cars travel in packs, like crowds?

18 Adjusting to crowds takes a combination of practice, patience, and observation.

Morris is discussing *proxemics* here, both sociologically and linguistically. Sociologically, proxemics describes human spatial requirements and the effects of population density on behavior. Linguistically, proxemics describes how far apart people in conversation stand, depending on their degree of intimacy.

Students from Latin America usually stand closer to each other when talking than students from western Europe. You might want to ask your students to observe proxemics in practice throughout the campus or at their jobs.

powerful hostile or equally powerful loving feelings. All through our childhood we will have been held to be loved and held to be hurt, and anyone who invades our Personal Space when we are adults is, in effect, threatening to extend his behaviour into one of these two highly charged areas of human interaction. Even if his motives are clearly neither hostile nor sexual, we still find it hard to suppress our reactions to his close approach. Unfortunately, different countries have different ideas about exactly how close is close. It is easy enough to test your own "space reaction": when you are talking to someone in the street or in any open space, reach out with your arm and see where the nearest point on his body comes. If you hail from western Europe, you will find that he is at roughly fingertip distance from you. In other words, as you reach out, your fingertips will just about make contact with his shoulder. If you come from eastern Europe you will find you are standing at "wrist distance." If you come from the Mediterranean region you will find that you are much closer to your companion, at little more than "elbow distance."

Trouble begins when a member of one of these cultures meets   19
and talks to one from another. Say a British diplomat meets an Italian or an Arab diplomat at an embassy function. They start talking in a friendly way, but soon the fingertips man begins to feel uneasy. Without knowing quite why, he starts to back away gently from his companion. The companion edges forward again. Each tries in this way to set up a Personal Space relationship that suits his own background. But it is impossible to do. Every time the Mediterranean diplomat advances to a distance that feels comfortable for him, the British diplomat feels threatened. Every time the Briton moves back, the other feels rejected. Attempts to adjust this situation often lead to a talking pair shifting slowly across a room, and many an embassy reception is dotted with western-European fingertip-distance men pinned against the walls by eager elbow-distance men. Until such differences are fully understood, and allowances made, these minor differences in "body territories" will continue to act as an alienation factor which may interfere in a subtle way with diplomatic harmony and other forms of international transaction.

If there are distance problems when engaged in conversation,   20
then there are clearly going to be even bigger difficulties where
people must work privately in a shared space. Close proximity of
others, pressing against the invisible boundaries of our personal
body-territory, makes it difficult to concentrate on non-social matters. Flatmates, students sharing a study, sailors in the cramped
quarters of a ship, and office staff in crowded workplaces, all have
to face this problem. They solve it by "cocooning." They use a
variety of devices to shut themselves off from the others present.
The best possible cocoon, of course, is a small private room—a
den, a private office, a study or a studio—which physically ob-
scures the presence of other nearby territory-owners. This is the
ideal situation for non-social work, but the space-sharers cannot
enjoy this luxury. Their cocooning must be symbolic. They may,
in certain cases, be able to erect small physical barriers, such as
screens and partitions, which give substance to their invisible
Personal Space boundaries, but when this cannot be done, other
means must be sought. One of these is the "favoured object." Each
space-sharer develops a preference, repeatedly expressed until it
becomes a fixed pattern, for a particular chair, or table, or alcove.
Others come to respect this, and friction is reduced. This system
is often formally arranged (this is my desk, that is yours), but
even where it is not, favoured places soon develop. Professor
Smith has a favourite chair in the library. It is not formally his,
but he always uses it and others avoid it. Seats around a mess-
room table, or a board-room table, become almost personal property for specific individuals. Even in the home, father has his
favourite chair for reading the newspaper or watching television.
Another device is the blinkers-posture. Just as a horse that over-
reacts to other horses and the distractions of the noisy race-course
is given a pair of blinkers to shield its eyes, so people studying
privately in a public place put on pseudo-blinkers in the form of
shielding hands. Resting their elbows on the table, they sit with
their hands screening their eyes from the scene on either side.

A third method of reinforcing the body-territory is to use   21
personal markers. Books, papers and other personal belongings
are scattered around the favoured site to render it more privately

Libraries are sometimes crowded. Workers often are assigned carrels. Students often share apartments with roommates. They all "cocoon," carving out their own privacy in one way or another.

Morris thoroughly discusses by example each part of this classification. Students are often eager to investigate some of these examples. Do your students have their own territories, favorite chairs in the library or favorite tables in the cafeteria? Do they have favorite parking places that they feel territorially belong to them? How do they react when that territory is "invaded"?

You might want to discuss with students the various methods they use to let others know they have already claimed a space. Do they use the "favored object," the "personal marker," or the "reservation effect"? With what success? Do they have other peaceful ways of claiming their own territory?

Morris points out that we hear about the exceptions to territorial respect, that most of us respect the other person's "territory," be it the temporary space of a library chair or the more lasting space of a home.

Time permitting, you might want to ask your students whether their city or neighborhood is running out of space that each person or household can call its own. If space is becoming scarce, then you might want to discuss ways of redefining territory or creating respect for territory so that we can keep strife from getting out of hand.

owned in the eyes of companions. Spreading out one's belongings is a well-known trick in public-transport situations, where a traveller tries to give the impression that seats next to him are taken. In many contexts carefully arranged personal markers can act as an effective territorial display, even in the absence of the territory owner. Experiments in a library revealed that placing a pile of magazines on the table in one seating position successfully reserved that place for an average of 77 minutes. If a sports-jacket was added, draped over the chair, then the "reservation effect" lasted for over two hours.

In these ways, we strengthen the defences of our Personal Spaces, keeping out intruders with the minimum of open hostility. As with all territorial behaviour, the object is to defend space with signals rather than with fists and at all three levels—the tribal, the family and the personal—it is a remarkably efficient system of space-sharing. It does not always seem so, because newspapers and newscasts inevitably magnify the exceptions and dwell on those cases where the signals have failed and wars have broken out, gangs have fought, neighbouring families have feuded, or colleagues have clashed, but for every territorial signal that has failed, there are millions of others that have not. They do not rate a mention in the news, but they nevertheless constitute a dominant feature of human society—the society of a remarkably territorial animal.

22

Possible Answers

Meaning and Purpose

1. Morris's main point is that we are territorial animals, and territory by definition must be defended. The thesis is implicit in a general way in the very first sentence. The third sen-

Meaning and Purpose

1. What is the main point Morris makes in this essay? Does it have a thesis statement?
2. Can you tell from the title what kind of essay this will be?
3. In paragraph 11, the author says, "we feel at our most territorially secure" in our bedroom. Does this statement apply to you?

Where is another place in which you feel quite "territorially secure"?

4. What does Morris say we do in our large tribal territory to feel a sense of belonging?

5. Why is it "one of the tragedies of modern architecture" that so many new homes look alike?

6. In paragraph 11, Morris calls the family and its territory a "breeding unit" and "breeding ground." What does he mean by these expressions? Is he being sarcastic or judgmental?

Strategy

1. Morris begins his categories of territories in paragraph 6. How does he use the first five paragraphs?

2. What strategy does Morris use to develop the classification of "Tribal Territory"?

3. In the personal-space category, Morris has some subcategories. What are they, and how do they work in the structure of this category?

4. In paragraph 4, Morris mentions a "home base." If Morris had wanted, he could have classified several kinds of home bases. In your opinion, what are two kinds of home bases?

Style

1. How would you describe the tone of this essay? Where is the tone evident?

2. What is a "pseudo-tribe"?

3. Judging from the tone and style of this essay, whom do you think Morris has in mind for his audience?

tence in paragraph 3 is the thesis, and the last sentence in paragraph 5 narrows the thesis.

2. The title is neutral-sounding and could signal an academic and informative essay (which this is), or the title could be ironic or humorous, depending on the content of the essay. In other words, the title isn't much help in knowing the content of the essay absolutely before reading it.

3. A number of students mention the bathroom! Some include their place of work (the backroom or storage areas), and others specify attics, basements, garages, and the like.

4. We form subgroups (paragraph 7) in our large tribal territories to feel a sense of belonging. We choose a "splinter group" to identify with, such as a union or political party.

5. Because so many homes look alike, people have more difficulty displaying theirs as a particular home in an attempt to feel secure and "at home" (paragraph 12).

6. Morris's words are the neutral terminology of social science.

Strategy

1. Morris discusses the sociology of the three categories of territory, including the penalties for violating someone else's territory, and the reasons for having "owned space" (paragraph 3). The first five paragraphs give background and definitions so that readers know Morris's basis for classification.

2. The strategy of development is a kind of cyclic expansion. Morris starts with the small group at the center, expands it outward to hunting grounds, and eventually the home base becomes the capital city. When nations become too big for people to feel personal belonging, people circle back to form small groups that they can belong to.

3. Morris talks about the distances at which people stand from each other in conversation and labels three categories: fingertip, wrist, and elbow distance (paragraph 18). He also discusses how people in crowded places stake out personal space. He calls the strategy "cocooning" (paragraph 20), and names three kinds: small private office or studio, favored object such as a chair or alcove, and personal markers such as books or jackets. All these subdivisions help organize and order Morris's information so that it is clear and understandable to readers.

4. A home base can be one of a number of areas, depending on the student's perspective. It could be a play area, a favored street corner, one side of a fence, or a car.

Style

1. The tone is formal and academic, and people are labeled clinically—this is a social-science essay. Almost any sentence demonstrates this tone, such as the first in paragraph 3: "The fact that these upheavals are so rare is a measure of the success of Territorial Signals as a system of dispute prevention."

2. A "pseudo-tribe" is a modern imitation of the historical tribes mentioned earlier in the essay (paragraph 8). The prefix *pseudo* means "fictitious, pretending, or falsely seeming."

3. Morris's audience probably consists of readers who have read academic writing before, for he doesn't talk down to them. But they are not necessarily social scientists. His language is understandable and readable for lay readers, and he is careful to define his terms in context.

Writing Tasks

1. Classify your "tribe's territory." How does your neighborhood, town, city, parish, county, or other easily identifiable political territory differ from others in its display? How do its looks make it different? How do its people make it different? How does its economy make it different? In what other ways does classifying your territory show that it is different from other territories in the same class?

2. Personal space is becoming more and more difficult to enjoy. What is your own definition of "personal space"? How do you separate and protect your space? How do you handle intruders into your space? How would you instruct elementary-school children who tell you they would like to learn how to have more personal space?

❧ *Additional Writing Tasks* ❧
Classification and Division

1. Choose one of the following subjects and write an essay using division as the dominant pattern. Describe each component in some detail, distinguishing it from the other components. Keep your readers in mind by guiding them carefully from component to component.
   a. A musical performance
   b. A board game, like chess, Monopoly, Risk, or Clue
   c. The human mind
   d. A ceremonial event, like a wedding, funeral, campaign rally, banquet, religious service
   e. A week at a teenage vacation spot
   f. A novel
   g. A police drama, situation comedy, or national news broadcast
   h. Your monthly income
   i. Bargaining in a foreign marketplace
   j. A meal in an expensive restaurant

2. Write an essay using classification as the dominant development method. Sort one of the following subjects into categories. Be sure the basis for your classification is clear. To direct your readers' attention, make up names for each category.
   a. The books, records, and/or video tapes you own
   b. Unusual sports, like "earth games" or other sports seldom televised or reported in newspapers
   c. Talk-show hosts
   d. War toys, family-oriented toys, or intellectual toys
   e. People who like to hunt game
   f. Lies
   g. Ways to read a novel or poem
   h. Ways to watch a horror movie
   i. Kinds of photography
   j. Attitudes revealed by bumper stickers
   k. Trends in dating, marriage, or divorce
   l. Kinds of terror

451

m. Responses to a dramatic national or international event
n. New ways to learn
o. Kinds of good luck
p. Kinds of bad luck

8

Definition
Limiting Meaning

The Method

Think of how many words you hear in a day. Tens of thousands? Hundreds of thousands? Millions? Spoken words are plentiful. They are easy to produce: just open your mouth, activate your larynx, wag your tongue, and words will take flight. Of course, spoken words are often strung together thoughtlessly. If you have any doubts about this description, just turn your television dial to a talk show and listen to the relentless babble.

But written words are different. They require work. Serious writers select them with care. Some words are so technical that only technically trained readers understand them. Some words are so rarely used that few readers know what they mean. Some have meanings so ambiguous that readers understand them differently. That is why definition is indispensable in writing.

Strategies

Professional writers approach definition in three ways: etymological, or lexical, definition; stipulative definition; and extended definition.

Etymological Definition

An etymological definition is a dictionary definition. It defines a word in a narrow way by specifying its class and its distinguishing characteristics. Consider the word "thriller." A good college dictionary tells you that a thriller is a suspenseful work of fiction—a novel, play, or film—that deals with crime or detection. Sometimes an etymological definition includes synonyms: a "thriller" might be referred to as a "whodunit."

Rather than use a ready-made dictionary definition, writers often expand dictionary information to fit the interests of their audience and requirements that suit their purposes. Consider the dictionary definition of *bird:* "a warm-blooded, two-legged, egg-laying vertebrate with a wishbone, feathers, and wings." Now imagine that a writer wishes to define *bird* for a ten-year-old reader. The definition might read something like this:

> A bird is an animal. It has a backbone, is warm-blooded, and walks on two legs, but a human being does, too. It flies, but insects and bats do, too. It lays eggs, but salamanders, some snakes, and turtles do the same.
> What then makes birds different from all other animals? Only birds have feathers and a wishbone.

Stipulative Definition

Sometimes a writer uses a common word extensively in a special or limited way. The writer then usually stipulates the meaning of the word—that is, the writer explains how the word is to be understood as it appears throughout the essay. This explanation creates the *stipulative definition*. In this paragraph from *Amusing Ourselves to Death,* educator and communications critic Neil Postman stipulates the meaning of "conversation."

> I use the word "conversation" metaphorically to refer not only to speech but to all techniques and technologies that permit people of a particular culture to exchange messages. In this sense, all culture is a conversation or, more precisely, a corporation of conversations, conducted in a variety of symbolic modes. Our attention here is on how forms of public discourse regulate and even dictate what kind of content can issue from such forms.

And social critic Don Pierstorff stipulates a meaning for "suits" when examining Michael Levine's *Deep Cover,* an exposé of the Drug Enforcement Administration (DEA).

> Who are the "suits"? They are the men and women who crowd the corridors and sit behind the desks of the Drug Enforcement Administration. They are government bureaucrats and managers. According to Michael Levine, they are the people who have no first-hand experience of the drug war and are unwilling to listen to agents who do. They spend their days shuffling reports and briefing politicians.

Postman's paragraph stipulates the meaning of "conversation" by enlarging it to mean all the methods culture uses to communicate. Pierstorff's paragraph defines the commonly understood word "suits" by presenting its uncommon slang definition, the way in which DEA agents use it. Both authors anticipate that their readers will need to know these special definitions to understand what they are writing about.

Extended Definitions

Etymological and stipulative definitions usually are concisely written for the sole purpose of clarification. Extended definitions are much more detailed and usually employ various patterns of development to fully explain a word or concept. In this paragraph from *Hog on Ice,* C. E. Funk defines "white elephant." He uses examples to establish its class and a brief narration about the word's origin to differentiate it from others.

> That large portrait of your wealthy Aunt Jane, given by her and which you loathe but do not dare to take down from your wall; that large bookcase, too costly to discard, but which you hope will be more in keeping with your future home; these, and a thousand other like items, are "white elephants"—costly but useless possessions. The allusion takes us to Siam. In that country it was the traditional custom for many centuries that a rare albino elephant was, upon capture, the property of the emperor—who even today bears the title Lord of the White Elephant—and was thereafter sacred to him. He alone might ride or use such an animal, and none might be destroyed without his consent. Because of that latter royal prerogative, it is said that whenever it pleased his gracious majesty to bring about the ruin of a courtier who had displeased him, he would present the poor fellow with an elephant from his stables. The cost of feeding and caring for the huge animal that he might neither use nor destroy—a veritable white elephant—gave the term its present meaning.

In this two-paragraph passage from *Alligators in Sewers and Other Urban Legends,* Jan Harold Brunvand defines "urban legend." Brunvand first establishes the class to which "urban legend" belongs and then distinguishes it from other members of the class.

His definition goes beyond the etymological category because he develops the expression in greater detail, primarily with brief comparison and contrast and examples.

> Urban legends are realistic stories that are said to have happened recently. Like old legends of lost mines, buried treasure, and ghosts, they usually have an ironic or supernatural twist. They belong to a subclass of folk narratives that (unlike fairy tales) are set in the recent past, involving ordinary human beings rather than extraordinary gods and demigods.
>
> Unlike rumors, which are generally fragmentary or vague reports, legends have a specific narrative quality and tend to attach themselves to different local settings. Although they may explain or incorporate current rumors, legends tend to have a longer life and wider acceptance; rumors flourish and then die out rather quickly. Urban legends circulate by word of mouth, among the "folk" of modern society, but the mass media frequently help to disseminate and validate them. While they vary in particular details from one telling to another, they preserve a central core of traditional themes. In some instances these seemingly fresh stories are merely updatings of classic folklore plots, while other urban legends spring directly from recent conditions and then develop their own traditional patterns in repeated retellings. For example, "The Vanishing Hitchhiker," which describes the disappearance of a rider picked up on a highway, has evolved from a 19th-century horse-and-buggy legend into modern variants incorporating freeway travel. A story called "Alligators in the Sewers," on the other hand, goes back no further than the 1930s and seems to be a New York City invention. Often, it begins with people who bring pet baby alligators back from Florida and eventually flush them down the drain.

Both Funk's definition of "white elephant" and Brunvand's definition of "urban legend" involve much more than merely looking up the established meanings; nevertheless, they do make use of a common pattern of definition by placing a term in a class and distinguishing it from other members of the class. Funk and Brunvand can use this pattern because the words they define have been in common use for some time. But the strength of an extended definition is to introduce new terms to readers, or, more accurately, to introduce concepts represented by those terms. This kind of extended definition may be highly personal, embodying a writer's values and independent observation.

In this three-paragraph passage from *Zen and the Art of Motorcycle Maintenance,* Robert M. Pirsig defines "mechanic's feel." Clearly, his definition is based on close observation during personal experience.

> The mechanic's feel comes from a deep inner kinesthetic feeling for the elasticity of materials. Some materials, like ceramics, have very little, so that when you thread a porcelain fitting you're very careful not to apply great pressures. Other materials, like steel, have tremendous elasticity, more than rubber, but in a range in which, unless you're working with large mechanical forces, the elasticity isn't apparent.
>
> With nuts and bolts you're in the range of large mechanical forces and you should understand that within these ranges metals are elastic. When you take up a nut there's a point called "fingertight" where there's contact but no take-up of elasticity. Then there's "snug," in which the easy surface elasticity is taken up. Then there's the range called "tight," in which all the elasticity is taken up. The force required to reach these three points is different for each size of nut and bolt, and different for lubricated bolts and for locknuts. The forces are different for steel and cast iron and brass and aluminum and plastics and ceramics. But a person with mechanic's feel knows when something's tight and stops. A person without it goes right on past and strips the threads or breaks the assembly.
>
> A "mechanic's feel" implies not only an understanding for the elasticity of metal but for its softness. The insides of a motorcycle contain surfaces that are precise in some cases to as little as one ten-thousandth of an inch. If you drop them or get dirt on them or scratch them or bang them with

a hammer, they'll lose that precision. It's important to understand that the metal *behind* the surfaces can normally take a great shock and stress but that the surfaces themselves cannot. When handling precision parts that are stuck or difficult to manipulate, a person with mechanic's feel will avoid damaging the surfaces and work with his tools on the nonprecision surfaces of the same part whenever possible. If he must work on the surfaces themselves, he'll always use softer surfaces to work them with. Brass hammers, plastic hammers, wood hammers, rubber hammers and lead hammers are all available for this work. Use them. Vise jaws can be fitted with plastic and copper and lead faces. Use these too. Handle precision parts gently. You'll never be sorry. If you have a tendency to bang things around, take more time and try to develop a little more respect for the accomplishment that a precision part represents.

Pirsig's definition of "mechanic's feel" is unique. Readers have no resource to consult for a commonly accepted definition of an expression like that. Primarily relying on descriptive techniques, Pirsig carefully delineates the qualities of "mechanic's feel," right down to naming the degrees to which someone might tighten down a bolt: "fingertight," "snug," and "tight." Pirsig points out that metal has elasticity, and that someone with "mechanic's feel" must sense that quality or face the consequences—a broken assembly. Pirsig creates a sense of the soft, delicate surfaces of metal and names the tools someone should use when working on them—hammers of many materials varying in softness, as well as vise grips fitted with soft faces. Someone with mechanic's feel is precise; in fact, the need for precision seems to be the message beneath the detail.

Definition in College Writing

Definition is often used as a significant passage in essays with other dominant patterns of development. In the next example,

Chris Schneider opens an essay exploring the use of cultural myths in advertising with a definition of "myth," his key term. A thorough definition of "myth" is vital to the success of his essay because its meaning has been enlarged by social critics.

Schneider opens with several cultural myths in question form. He closes by pointing out how the questions reflect "myths" as semiologists use the term.

Do you believe that childhood is a time of innocence separated from the emotions and cares of the adult world? Do you count on science to solve the dangers of fossil fuel shortage, ozone depletion, and toxic pollution? Do you feel that men and women embody a set of opposing psychological and social characteristics; that men, for instance, are rational and women are intuitive? Men are active; women, passive? Men are ambitious; women, nurturing? If you do, then your perceptions have been influenced by common American "myths," as a group of contemporary scholars and social critics known as semiologists would claim.

Schneider illustrates what the term "myth" is commonly understood to mean. But semioticians do not use "myth" in this way.

To most of us, the term "myth" might call to mind marvelous Greek stories of disguised gods cavorting with humans. We might think of heroes wielding swords against dragons or of magicians mesmerizing entire armies. We might recall the story of Johnny Appleseed planting apple trees across the American landscape or of Rip Van Winkle sleeping for twenty years or of John Henry racing against a steam-powered spike driver. These myths are different from legends because they lack historical background and shade into the supernatural. They are also different from fables because they lack an overt moral intent. Like legends and fables they are stories, imaginative stories, that, according to one popular view, embody cultural patterns. Now semioticians are currently using the term "myth" in a different way.

In the final paragraph, Schneider explains how a semiotician uses "myth," and closes with a sentence that leads the reader into the rest of the paper.

To the semiotician "myth" refers to deeply rooted cultural beliefs, not to ancient stories. These beliefs are held by most members of any given society. Despite whatever evidence there might be to contradict the validity of a myth, semiologists do not judge it as right or wrong. They merely recognize its existence and analyze its social influence. Whether valid or invalid, a myth, therefore, is a psychological and social fact projected onto experience. We never clearly see things as they really are; we only see their reflections of our cultural beliefs. Nowhere is this reflection more pervasive than in advertising.

Schneider's three-paragraph passage is a straightforward extended definition. His strategy is relatively simple. In paragraph 1 he opens with questions to involve the reader before indicating that he will be defining the term "myth" as a group of social critics known as semiologists use it. In paragraph 2, Schneider refers to the way in which most readers would understand the meaning of "myth," which is based on its lexical definition. He concludes the paragraph by indicating that this is not the definition he intends, thus setting up the semiological definition revealed in paragraph 3. Here he explains that for the semiotician a myth is a deeply held cultural belief. As does any successful extended definition, this one goes beyond the dictionary to give the reader broader understanding of the word being defined.

Writers, unlike lexicographers, often define
concepts for special reasons. A political writer
might define a *liberal* as "a person who believes
in throwing money at social problems," or as
"a person who believes that a government must
be accountable to someone besides itself." The
writer's motive determines the definition.

Ehrlich's motive for defining *cowboy* is
the desire to counter the stereotypical definition of *cowboy* in story, song, and, above all,
advertising. The Marlboro man is not a cowboy; neither is the long-haul truck driver, although the latter often wears cowboy boots
and a cowboy hat.

Stereotypical definitions abound because
they are unexamined. Ehrlich sets out to hu-
manize the cowboy, to deny the stereotypical
definition.

A fruitful way to begin a class discussion
is by stereotypically defining groups or individuals. What characteristics define the stereotypical politician? athlete? sales clerk? After
the class has gathered defining characteristics
for several stereotypes, ask if anyone has had
experiences with a stereotypical group that
caused them to modify their definition of that
group. Then have the class read this essay, to
see how Ehrlich's experiences with cowboys
have caused her to define them realistically.

The Marlboro ads, stereotypically featuring a
rangy cowboy against a backdrop of majestic
mountains, have been around for more than
twenty years. Marlboro cigarettes, once featuring red tips so that lipstick would not show on
them, were originally targeted at women
smokers. Later, in an advertising appeal to
men, the Marlboro cowboy appeared.

❦ Gretel Ehrlich ❦

*Gretel Ehrlich is a journalist, poet, fiction writer, and documentary
film maker. She was born in California and studied at Bennington
College, UCLA Film School, and the New School for Social Research.
She went to Wyoming to make a documentary film and chose to live
there, doing various kinds of ranch work, including branding, herd-
ing sheep, and helping with the births of lambs and calves. Now a
ranch owner herself, she raises beef cattle. Her essays have been
collected in* The Solace of Open Spaces *(1985), and she has published two books of poetry and a book of short stories as well.*

About Men

Gretel Ehrlich's essay, from The Solace of Open Spaces, *defines the
word "cowboy," but, as the title suggests, her purpose is to challenge
some assumptions "about men" in general, not just cowboys in
particular. She achieves this intent by describing cowboys as she
knows them, dispelling some myths about one of America's favorite
stereotypes.*

When I'm in New York but feeling lonely for Wyoming I look 1
for the Marlboro ads in the subway. What I'm aching to see is
horseflesh, the glint of a spur, a line of distant mountains, brim-
ming creeks, and a reminder of the ranchers and cowboys I've
ridden with for the last eight years. But the men I see in those
posters with their stern, humorless looks remind me of no one I
know here. In our hellbent earnestness to romanticize the cowboy
we've ironically disesteemed his true character. If he's "strong and
silent" it's because there's probably no one to talk to. If he "rides
away into the sunset" it's because he's been on horseback since
four in the morning moving cattle and he's trying, fifteen hours
later, to get home to his family. If he's "a rugged individualist"
he's also part of a team: ranch work is teamwork and even the

462

glorified open-range cowboys of the 1880s rode up and down the Chisholm Trail in the company of twenty or thirty other riders. Instead of the macho, trigger-happy man our culture has perversely wanted him to be, the cowboy is more apt to be convivial, quirky, and softhearted. To be "tough" on a ranch has nothing to do with conquests and displays of power. More often than not, circumstances—like the colt he's riding or an unexpected blizzard—are overpowering him. It's not toughness but "toughing it out" that counts. In other words, this macho, cultural artifact the cowboy has become is simply a man who possesses resilience, patience, and an instinct for survival. "Cowboys are just like a pile of rocks—everything happens to them. They get climbed on, kicked, rained and snowed on, scuffed up by wind. Their job is 'just to take it,' " one old-timer told me.

A cowboy is someone who loves his work. Since the hours are long—ten to fifteen hours a day—and the pay is $30 he has to. What's required of him is an odd mixture of physical vigor and maternalism. His part of the beef-raising industry is to birth and nurture calves and take care of their mothers. For the most part his work is done on horseback and in a lifetime he sees and comes to know more animals than people. The iconic myth surrounding him is built on American notions of heroism: the index of a man's value as measured in physical courage. Such ideas have perverted manliness into a self-absorbed race for cheap thrills. In a rancher's world, courage has less to do with facing danger than with acting spontaneously—usually on behalf of an animal or another rider. If a cow is stuck in a boghole he throws a loop around her neck, takes his dally (a half hitch around the saddle horn), and pulls her out with horsepower. If a calf is born sick, he may take her home, warm her in front of the kitchen fire, and massage her legs until dawn. One friend, whose favorite horse was trying to swim a lake with hobbles on, dove under water and cut her legs loose with a knife, then swam her to shore, his arm around her neck lifeguard-style, and saved her from drowning. Because these incidents are usually linked to someone or something outside himself, the westerner's courage is selfless, a form of compassion.

The Chisholm Trail: Named after an American scout, Jesse Chisholm (1806–1868), this cattle trail led north from San Antonio, Texas, to Abilene, Kansas. It was used for about twenty years after the Civil War.

"cultural artifact": As generally used, this expression means an object made by human work, such as a primitive tool or weapon, which illustrates the ideas, customs, skills, or arts of a people during a specific period. Ehrlich suggests that we have defined the real cowboy as a stereotypical one, and then we have used that definition in a part of our culture.

The first half of this paragraph illustrates the figure of speech called *hysteron proteron,* used to describe a passage in which something that should logically come last comes first. According to Ehrlich, Americans have defined a cowboy first, and then fit the cowboy into the definition.

"manliness": Earlier in the essay, Ehrlich said that our society wanted the cowboy to be "the *macho,* trigger-happy man." Notice that she distinguishes between "macho" and "manliness," reserving "macho" for qualities we perceive outwardly, and "manliness" for qualities within a man.

"courage": This word's root is the Latin *cor,* "heart." Men of courage act with the heart.

The physical punishment that goes with cowboying is greatly   3
underplayed. Once fear is dispensed with, the threshold of pain
rises to meet the demands of the job. When Jane Fonda asked
Robert Redford (in the film *Electric Horseman*) if he was sick as
he struggled to his feet one morning, he replied, "No, just bent."
For once the movies had it right. The cowboys I was sitting with
laughed in agreement. Cowboys are rarely complainers; they show
their stoicism by laughing at themselves.

If a rancher or cowboy has been thought of as a "man's   4
man"—laconic, hard-drinking, inscrutable—there's almost no
place in which the balancing act between male and female, manliness and femininity, can be more natural. If he's gruff, handsome, and physically fit on the outside, he's androgynous at the
core. Ranchers are midwives, hunters, nurturers, providers, and
conservationists all at once. What we've interpreted as toughness—weathered skin, calloused hands, a squint in the eye and a
growl in the voice—only masks the tenderness inside. "Now don't
go telling me these lambs are cute," one rancher warned me the
first day I walked into the football-field-sized lambing sheds. The
next thing I knew he was holding a black lamb. "Ain't this little
rat good-lookin'?"

So many of the men who came to the West were southern-   5
ers—men looking for work and a new life after the Civil War—
that chivalrousness and strict codes of honor were soon thought
of as western traits. There were very few women in Wyoming
during territorial days, so when they did arrive (some as mail-
order brides from places like Philadelphia) there was a stand-
offishness between the sexes and a formality that persists now.
Ranchers still tip their hats and say, "Howdy, ma'am" instead of
shaking hands with me.

Even young cowboys are often evasive with women. It's not   6
that they're Jekyll and Hyde creatures—gentle with animals and
rough on women—but rather, that they don't know how to bring
their tenderness into the house and lack the vocabulary to express
the complexity of what they feel. Dancing wildly all night becomes
a metaphor for the explosive emotions pent up inside, and when
these are, on occasion, released, they're so battery-charged and

"Jekyll and Hyde": From Robert Louis Steven-
son's *The Strange Case of Dr. Jekyll and Mr.
Hyde*. The kind, gentle Dr. Jekyll discovers
drugs that he can use to transform himself into
the mean, vicious Mr. Hyde, and back again.

potent that one caress of the face or one "I love you" will peal for a long while.

The geographical vastness and the social isolation here make emotional evolution seem impossible. Those contradictions of the heart between respectability, logic, and convention on the one hand, and impulse, passion, and intuition on the other, played out wordlessly against the paradisical beauty of the West, give cowboys a wide-eyed but drawn look. Their lips pucker up, not with kisses but with immutability. They may want to break out, staying up all night with a lover just to talk, but they don't know how and can't imagine what the consequences will be. Those rare occasions when they do bare themselves result in confusion. "I feel as if I'd sprained my heart," one friend told me a month after such a meeting.   7

My friend Ted Hoagland wrote, "No one is as fragile as a woman but no one is as fragile as a man." For all the women here who use "fragileness" to avoid work or as a sexual ploy, there are men who try to hide theirs, all the while clinging to an adolescent dependency on women to cook their meals, wash their clothes, and keep the ranch house warm in winter. But there is true vulnerability in evidence here. Because these men work with animals, not machines or numbers, because they live outside in landscapes of torrential beauty, because they are confined to a place and a routine embellished with awesome variables, because calves die in the arms that pulled others into life, because they go to the mountains as if on a pilgrimage to find out what makes a herd of elk tick, their strength is also a softness, their toughness, a rare delicacy.   8

Meaning and Purpose

1. What is Ehrlich's thesis, and where does she state it?
2. Comment on the title's significance. Did you understand it differently before you read the essay than after?

POSSIBLE ANSWERS

Meaning and Purpose

1. Ehrlich's thesis is in the first paragraph: "This macho, cultural artifact the cowboy has become is simply a man who possesses resilience, patience, and an instinct for survival."

2. The title denotes a very broad subject. After reading the essay, however, you see that the word "men" has been placed in Ehrlich's context: they are people who possess both male and female qualities. "There's almost no place in which the balancing act between male and female, manliness and femininity, can be more natural" (4).

3. Many southerners went West because the South was devastated by the Civil War. Others went West to avoid possible capture and incarceration by armies of the North. Still others went simply to seek their fortune in a new land.

4. The word "aching" means "longing" in this sentence. Ehrlich uses a bit of cowboy diction.

5. The expression "emotional evolution" as used in this paragraph refers to our maturing abilities to rank and control our emotions in order of their social acceptance. Most of us learn as we grow that we can control impulse with logic, for example, or passion with convention.

6. The word "torrential," from "torrent," suggests violence, swiftness, that which overwhelms. Wyoming has violent, beautiful storms, swift rivers, and natural beauty that overwhelms its viewers.

Strategy

1. Some features of cowboys mentioned in the essay are being part of a team, softhearted, hardworking, compassionate, childlike, and tender.

2. "About Men" is an extended definition. Ehrlich uses descriptive techniques, covers var-

3. In paragraph 5, Ehrlich says that many of the men who went West were southerners. Why did so many southerners go West after the Civil War?

4. In paragraph 1, the author says that what she's "aching to see is horseflesh." Why does the author use "aching" in this sentence, and what does "aching" mean here?

5. From information in paragraph 7, write a definition for "emotional evolution."

6. Define "torrential" and tell why you think Ehrlich, in the last paragraph, describes Wyoming's beauty as "torrential."

Strategy

1. Imagine that you must write a concise definition for the word "cowboy." From the essay, list three features which cowboys have in common, and which you think you should include in your definition.

2. Is "About Men" a lexical, stipulative, or extended definition? Give examples from the essay that illustrate which kind it is.

3. You may have seen the Marlboro ads that the author mentions in paragraph 1. Why would a cigarette company advertise a cigarette by showing a cowboy riding a horse near a mountain range that resembles the Wyoming mountains?

4. In paragraph 1, why does Ehrlich define the stereotypical cowboy in the Marlboro ad when that is not the way cowboys really are?

Style

1. In paragraph 6, Ehrlich mentions "explosive emotions," but clearly the author is not talking about anger or jealousy. What "explosive emotions" does she probably mean?

2. The last sentence in paragraph 6 says in part that "one 'I love you' will peal for a long while." Why is "peal" used in that sentence?

3. In paragraph 4, Ehrlich says that a cowboy is "androgynous." In fact, an androgynous human being is rare. What does the author mean by that word in this essay?

Writing Tasks

1. Write an extended definition of "cowboy," based on the way in which Hollywood and television portray him. Refer to several specific movies and television roles to give examples for your definition.
2. Imagine that you have just inherited a ranch in Wyoming, so you must hire a few cowboys. Write an extended definition of the kind of cowboys that you want to hire. Your definition will become a job description that appears in the local newspapers.

ious characteristics, and gives examples of situations that define "cowboy." Some examples are: "For the most part his work is done on horseback and in a lifetime he sees and comes to know more animals than people" (2); and " 'Now don't go telling me these lambs are cute,' one rancher warned me . . . . The next thing I knew he was holding a black lamb. 'Ain't this little rat good-looking?' " (4).

3. Because cigarettes have been proven to be a grave health risk, cigarette companies associate their product with health, nature, youth, and vigor, and either masculinity or femininity.

4. As part of defining the "true character" of a cowboy, Ehrlich first defines the stereotype most people are familiar with. Saying what a cowboy is not helps define what it is.

Style

1. The author is probably talking about the explosive emotions having to do with repressed love and sexuality.

2. The word "peal" refers to the loud ringing of a bell or any prolonged sound, such as laughter or thunder. It has a sense of "echo." The "I love you" need not be repeated because once it has been said, it remains said, as if the listener can still hear its echo.

3. "Androgynous" means that a cowboy has both male and female characteristics. His tough exterior hides an "androgynous core."

Modern makers of dictionaries for general use try to remain unbiased when defining words—unlike writers, who often slant their definitions to make a point. Also, modern dictionaries are focused more on individual words than on concepts, and writers—Theroux, in this instance—often define concepts.

Theroux defines *being* a man, not just the word *man*. His definition is active and continuing, culturally determined for the present. To reinforce it, he points out how it affected him and other male writers.

The expressions "being born a male" and "being a man" differ significantly. The first has biological roots; the second has cultural roots. Students enjoy discussing the notion of socially *being*. They respond well to the questions, "What does it mean to you to *be a woman*?" and "What does it mean to you to *be a man*?" The discussion almost always leads to the discovery that social conditions affect social definitions.

The larger question is how we go about changing societal definitions. Teachers usually discuss Theroux's "Being a Man" and Ehrlich's "About Men" together, so that students can see that writers themselves do not always agree on definitions.

❦ Paul Theroux ❦

Paul Theroux was born in Medford, Massachusetts, in 1941 and attended the University of Massachusetts and Syracuse University. He began a life of extensive world travel by joining the Peace Corps at age twenty-two, spending almost ten years in the organization teaching English in faraway countries such as Malaysia, Uganda, and Singapore. He is a poet and essayist and has published numerous novels, but is best known for his travel writing. The Great Railway Bazaar *(1975),* The Old Patagonian Express *(1979), and most recently his bestseller,* Riding the Iron Rooster *(1988), describe traveling by train through Asia, Central and South America, and China, respectively. He has also published a collection of essays titled* Sunrise with Seamonsters: Travels and Discoveries, 1964–1984 *(1985).*

Being a Man

Theroux defines "being a man" by describing what he considers the prevailing attitudes about what it means to be "manly," attitudes with which he strongly disagrees. Though the essay is personal and subjective, Theroux's opinions are backed by plenty of pertinent examples. The essay originally appeared in The New York Times Magazine *in 1983.*

"Fetishism": This word denotes a form of mental illness in which one is sexually stimulated at the sight of a shoe, glove, some other article of apparel, or some part of the body. In psychiatry, a fetish is the love object of a person who suffers from fetishism. To the masochist, such objects indicate domination.

There is a pathetic sentence in the chapter "Fetishism" in Dr. Norman Cameron's book *Personality Development and Psychopathology*. It goes, "Fetishists are nearly always men; and their commonest fetish is a woman's shoe." I cannot read that sentence without thinking that it is just one more awful thing about being a man—and perhaps it is an important thing to know about us. 1

I have always disliked being a man. The whole idea of manhood in America is pitiful, in my opinion. This version of mas- 2 culinity is a little like having to wear an ill-fitting coat for one's entire life (by contrast, I imagine femininity to be an oppressive sense of nakedness). Even the expression "Be a man!" strikes me as insulting and abusive. It means: Be stupid, be unfeeling, obedient, soldierly and stop thinking. Man means "manly"—how can one think about men without considering the terrible ambition of manliness? And yet it is part of every man's life. It is a hideous and crippling lie; it not only insists on difference and connives at superiority, it is also by its very nature destructive—emotionally damaging and socially harmful

The youth who is subverted, as most are, into believing in the masculine ideal is effectively separated from women and he spends the rest of his life finding women a riddle and a nuisance. Of course, there is a female version of this male affliction. It begins with mothers encouraging little girls to say (to other adults) "Do you like my new dress?" In a sense, little girls are traditionally urged to please adults with a kind of coquettishness, while boys are enjoined to behave like monkeys towards each other. The nine-year-old coquette proceeds to become womanish in a subtle power game in which she learns to be sexually indispensable, socially decorative and always alert to a man's sense of inadequacy.

Femininity—being lady-like—implies needing a man as witness and seducer; but masculinity celebrates the exclusive company of men. That is why it is so grotesque; and that is also why there is no manliness without inadequacy—because it denies men the natural friendship of women.

It is very hard to imagine any concept of manliness that does not belittle women, and it begins very early. At an age when I wanted to meet girls—let's say the treacherous years of thirteen to sixteen—I was told to take up a sport, get more fresh air, join the Boy Scouts, and I was urged not to read so much. It was the 1950s and if you asked too many questions about sex you were sent to camp—boys' camp, of course: the nightmare. Nothing is more unnatural or prison-like than a boy's camp, but if it were not for them we would have no Elks' Lodges, no pool rooms, no boxing matches, no Marines.

Theroux defines with synonyms his version of America's cultural "masculinity": it's a destructive life, socially and emotionally unhealthy.

3

The female version of this cultural separation of the sexes, femininity, is introduced. Girls are taught how to grow into "proper" women; boys are taught how to grow into "proper" men.

4   Femininity implies needing men; masculinity celebrates excluding women. The effect is to deny natural bonding with the opposite sex.

5   At an age when it is natural for a boy to seek the company of a girl, society sends him in the other direction by forcing him to seek the company of other males. As a result, boys mature into men who have been schooled to believe that they should "hang out" together.

Theroux attacks competitive athletes, saying that the preparation, training, and competition in which they engage prepare them only to live physically in society. This kind of "manliness" is "philistine"; that is, smugly narrow, authoritarian, and indifferent to cultural and esthetic values.

When Theroux wrote this essay, Ronald Reagan was president. President Reagan was often photographed wearing clothing that looked as if it had been purchased from L. L. Bean, a mail-order company that specializes in high-quality merchandise such as plaid woolen shirts, canvas jackets, thick parkas, heavy denim pants, waterproof hunting boots—anything one needs to survive with style in the great outdoors.

A consequence of our culture's way of defining stereotyped "manliness" is that this stereotype does not accord with the American definition of male *writer,* and yet the male writer often succumbs to that stereotyped definition. This role playing greatly affected Theroux's early life.

6   And perhaps no sports as we know them. Everyone is aware of how few in number are the athletes who behave like gentlemen. Just as high school basketball teaches you how to be a poor loser, the manly attitude towards sports seems to be little more than a recipe for creating bad marriages, social misfits, moral degenerates, sadists, latent rapists and just plain louts. I regard high school sports as a drug far worse than marijuana, and it is the reason that the average tennis champion, say, is a pathetic oaf.

7   Any objective study would find the quest for manliness essentially right-wing, puritanical, cowardly, neurotic and fueled largely by a fear of women. It is also certainly philistine. There is no book-hater like a Little League coach. But indeed all the creative arts are obnoxious to the manly ideal, because at their best the arts are pursued by uncompetitive and essentially solitary people. It makes it very hard for a creative youngster, for any boy who expresses the desire to be alone seems to be saying that there is something wrong with him.

8   It ought to be clear by now that I have something of an objection to the way we turn boys into men. It does not surprise me that when the President of the United States has his customary weekend off he dresses like a cowboy—it is both a measure of his insecurity and his willingness to please. In many ways, American culture does little more for a man than prepare him for modeling clothes in the L. L. Bean catalogue. I take this as a personal insult because for many years I found it impossible to admit to myself that I wanted to be a writer. It was my guilty secret, because being a writer was incompatible with being a man.

9   There are people who might deny this, but that is because the American writer, typically, has been so at pains to prove his manliness that we have come to see literariness and manliness as mingled qualities. But first there was a fear that writing was not a manly profession—indeed, not a profession at all. (The paradox in American letters is that it has always been easier for a woman to write and for a man to be published.) Growing up, I had thought of sports as wasteful and humiliating, and the idea of manliness was a bore. My wanting to become a writer was not a flight from that oppressive role-playing, but I quickly saw that it

was at odds with it. Everything in stereotyped manliness goes against the life of the mind. The Hemingway personality is too tedious to go into here, and in any case his exertions are well-known, but certainly it was not until this aberrant behavior was examined by feminists in the 1960s that any male writer dared question the pugnacity in Hemingway's fiction. All the bullfighting and arm wrestling and elephant shooting diminished Hemingway as a writer, but it is consistent with a prevailing attitude in American writing: one cannot be a male writer without first proving that one is a man.

It is normal in America for a man to be dismissive or even somewhat apologetic about being a writer. Various factors make it easier. There is a heartiness about journalism that makes it acceptable—journalism is the manliest form of American writing and, therefore, the profession the most independent-minded women seek (yes, it is an illusion, but that is my point). Fiction-writing is equated with a kind of dispirited failure and is only manly when it produces wealth—money is masculinity. So is drinking. Being a drunkard is another assertion, if misplaced, of manliness. The American male writer is traditionally proud of his heavy drinking. But we are also a very literal-minded people. A man proves his manhood in America in old-fashioned ways. He kills lions, like Hemingway; or he hunts ducks, like Nathanael West; or he makes pronouncements like, "A man should carry enough knife to defend himself with," as James Jones once said to a *Life* interviewer. Or he says he can drink you under the table. But even tiny drunken William Faulkner loved to mount a horse and go fox hunting, and Jack Kerouac roistered up and down Manhattan in a lumberjack shirt (and spent every night of *The Subterraneans* with his mother in Queens). And we are familiar with the lengths to which Norman Mailer is prepared, in his endearing way, to prove that he is just as much a monster as the next man.

When the novelist John Irving was revealed as a wrestler, people took him to be a very serious writer; and even a bubble reputation like Erich (*Love Story*) Segal's was enhanced by the news that he ran the marathon in a respectable time. How

10

11

Ernest Hemingway (d. 1961), awarded the Nobel Prize in literature (1954), wrote *The Sun Also Rises* (1926), *For Whom the Bell Tolls* (1940), and *The Old Man and the Sea* (1952), among others. He died of a self-inflicted gunshot wound.

Wealth, drinking, hunting, killing—these are the worst traits of "manliness," according to Theroux.

Nathanael West, a novelist and screen writer whose best-known work is *The Day of the Locust* (1940). James Jones (d. 1977) wrote the bestseller *From Here to Eternity* (1951). William Faulkner (d. 1962), awarded the Nobel Prize in literature (1949), wrote *As I Lay Dying* (1930), *Absalom, Absalom!* (1936), and *The Hamlet* (1940), among others. Jack Kerouac (d. 1969) flourished from the mid-1950s to the mid-1960s. His best-known works are *On the Road* (1957) and *The Dharma Bums* (1958). Norman Mailer (b. 1923) probably is best known for *The Naked and the Dead* (1948) and *The Executioner's Song* (1979). For the latter he was awarded the Pulitzer Prize in literature. John Irving (b. 1942) said, "A writer uses what experience he or she has. It's the translating, though, that makes the difference." Eric Segal wrote the bestselling *Love Story* (1970). Joyce

Carol Oates (b. 1938) wrote *A Garden of Earthly Delights* (1967) and *You Must Remember This* (1988), among others. Joan Didion (b. 1934) wrote the acclaimed *Slouching Towards Bethlehem* (1968), a book of essays.

To strengthen his charge that "manliness" works against a man's being an unapologetic author, Theroux has run the gamut of twentieth-century American authors.

Notice the distinction Theroux draws between "man" and "manly." Being a "man" is biological; being "manly" (acting with "manliness") requires that a man live up to a socially imposed definition, at great personal cost.

POSSIBLE ANSWERS

Meaning and Purpose

1. Being born male is biological; "being a man," in Theroux's meaning, is cultural, learned, imposed.
2. Theroux's audience is certainly other men of his generation, who might agree or disagree with him, feel the cultural stereotype in themselves or not. He also speaks to women, especially mothers of boys, who can do something about the models their sons grow up with. Anyone in our society could appreciate this.
3. This phrase refers to American literature in general, including the learning and knowledge associated with it.
4. The image of the cowboy is a masculine one. People who are insecure about themselves may dress to portray what they would like to be, rather than what they believe they really are.
5. The so-called manly ideal stresses competition and teamwork; the creative arts stress solitude and individuality. Theroux thinks the two roles are incompatible.
6. Possible answers are that athletes have been accused of taking money and favors for attending a school, or that some athletes are allowed to attend a school even if they score low on entrance tests or maintain poor grades.

surprised we would be if Joyce Carol Oates were revealed as a sumo wrestler or Joan Didion active in pumping iron. "Lives in New York City with her three children" is the typical woman writer's biographical note, for just as the male writer must prove he has achieved a sort of muscular manhood, the woman writer—or rather her publicists—must prove her motherhood.

There would be no point in saying any of this if it were not generally accepted that to be a man is somehow—even now in feminist-influenced America—a privilege. It is on the contrary an unmerciful and punishing burden. Being a man is bad enough; being manly is appalling (in this sense, women's lib has done much more for men than for women). It is the sinister silliness of men's fashions, and a clubby attitude in the arts. It is the subversion of good students. It is the so-called "Dress Code" of the Ritz-Carlton Hotel in Boston, and it is the institutionalized cheating in college sports. It is the most primitive insecurity. 12

And this is also why men often object to feminism but are afraid to explain why: of course women have a justified grievance, but most men believe—and with reason—that their lives are just as bad. 13

Meaning and Purpose

1. In Theroux's essay, is "being a man" different from being born male? How?
2. Whom do you think Theroux imagines his audience to be?
3. In paragraph 9, what is the meaning of "American letters"?
4. Theroux says in paragraph 8 that former President Reagan dressed like a cowboy, and that this was a "measure of his insecurity and his willingness to please." How is dressing like a cowboy a measure of a man's insecurity?
5. All the creative arts are "obnoxious to the manly ideal" (7) according to the author. Why?
6. What do you think is meant by "institutionalized cheating in college sports" (12)?

Strategy

1. What kind of definition does Theroux write in this essay? Explain.
2. How does Theroux establish his authority for defining what it is to be a man?
3. Define "pugnacity." How does this word in paragraph 9 characterize Hemingway's fiction?
4. Where and how does Theroux bring up for contrast the definition of what it is to be a woman as a help in expressing what it is to be a man?

Style

1. Point out some of Theroux's language that establishes his unhappy and angry attitude toward being a man.
2. Compare Ehrlich's "men" in "About Men" with Theroux's "manly" and "being a man." How does the voice that defines differ in these essays?
3. Define these words: *connives* (2); *coquette* (3); *philistine* (7); *roistered* (10).

Writing Tasks

1. In an essay, define "being a woman" with the same critical eye Theroux uses in his essay. How does our culture define what it is to be a woman?
2. In paragraph 6, Theroux says that "the manly attitude towards sports" can lead to bad marriages and other problems in people's lives. Reread the essay to determine why Theroux made this remark, and then define an attitude toward sports that does not agree with Theroux's definition.

Strategy

1. This essay can be considered either a stipulative or an extended definition. It is stipulative because Theroux limits the meaning of "being a man" to the context of modern American culture. It is extended because Theroux paints a wide and seemingly all-encompassing picture of what "being a man" means.

2. Theroux has authority to define his term because he is, first, a man himself. He also grew up in the 1950s when much of the cultural pressure he describes influenced boys, and he participated in Boy Scouts, summer camp, and sports. And he is a writer who has experienced the insecurity of being a man in that profession.

3. The word "pugnacity" means being eager and ready to fight, being quarrelsome and combative. Hemingway writes with pugnacity to demonstrate that, though he is a fiction writer, he is also "manly."

4. Theroux describes a "female version of this male affliction" (3) early in the essay, establishing that "being a man" has a counterpart. He links the cultural definition of "manliness" inextricably to femininity when he says "there is no manliness without inadequacy—because it denies men the natural friendship of women" (4). The woman writer "must prove her motherhood" (11) as the male writer must prove his "muscular manhood" (11).

Style

1. Theroux's attitude is in these words, as well as others: "The whole idea of manhood in America is pitiful" (2); "It is a hideous and crippling lie" (2); "It is also by its very nature destructive—emotionally damaging and socially harmful" (2); "It is so grotesque" (4); "being manly is appalling" (12).

2. Let students compare the descriptions in the two essays.

3. *Connives*: cooperates secretly, or conspires; *coquette*: a vain young girl who tries to get men's attention and admiration; *philistine*: crass, and guided by material rather than artistic values; *roistered*: caroused, or engaged in noisy revelry.

❦ Michael Harrington ❦

Michael Harrington, a leading intellect on the American left, is a political scientist who has written and lectured widely, advocating democratic socialism. He was born in St. Louis in 1928 and studied at the Yale Law School and the University of Chicago. He has been an active and outspoken member of the Socialist Party since the 1950s and more recently served as cochair of the Democratic Socialists of America. His book The Other America: Poverty in the United States *(1962), was instrumental in developing the War on Poverty, a government movement initiated by President Lyndon Johnson in 1964. Harrington has published more than a dozen books, including* The Vast Majority: A Journey to the World's Poor *(1977), which won the National Book Award, and* The New American Poverty *(1984), in which he assesses the War on Poverty.*

A Definition of Poverty

Harrington's definition of poverty, excerpted from his very influential The Other America, *is a response to more abstract definitions that avoid the reality of "here and now." As social and economic standards and conditions change through history, the definition of poverty must change accordingly, he claims. Harrington ends by delineating how poverty should be defined.*

In the nineteenth century, conservatives in England used to argue against reform on the grounds that the British worker of the time had a longer life expectancy than a medieval nobleman. 1

This is to say that a definition of poverty is, to a considerable extent, a historically conditioned matter. Indeed, if one wanted to play with figures, it would be possible to prove that there are no poor people in the United States, or at least only a few whose plight is as desperate as that of masses in Hong Kong. There is starvation in American society, but it is not a pervasive social 2

474

problem as it is in some of the newly independent nations. There are still Americans who literally die in the streets, but their numbers are comparatively small.

This abstract approach toward poverty in which one compares different centuries or societies has very real consequences. For the nineteenth-century British conservative, it was a way of ignoring the plight of workers who were living under the most inhuman conditions. The twentieth-century conservative would be shocked and appalled in an advanced society if there were widespread conditions like those of the English cities a hundred years ago. Our standards of decency, of what a truly human life requires, change, and they should.

There are two main aspects of this change. First, there are new definitions of what man can achieve, of what a human standard of life should be. In recent times this has been particularly true since technology has consistently broadened man's potential: it has made a longer, healthier, better life possible. Thus, in terms of what is technically possible, we have higher aspirations. Those who suffer levels of life well below those that are possible, even though they live better than medieval knights or Asian peasants, are poor.

Related to this technological advance is the social definition of poverty. The American poor are not poor in Hong Kong or in the sixteenth century: they are poor here and now, in the United States. They are dispossessed in terms of what the rest of the nation enjoys, in terms of what the society could provide if it had the will. They live on the fringe, the margin. They watch the movies and read the magazines of affluent America, and these tell them that they are internal exiles.

To some, this description of the feelings of the poor might seem to be out of place in discussing a definition of poverty. Yet if this book indicates anything about the other America, it is that this sense of exclusion is the source of a pessimism, a defeatism that intensifies the exclusion. To have one bowl of rice in a society where all other people have half a bowl may well be a sign of achievement and intelligence; it may spur a person to act and to fulfill his human potential. To have five bowls of rice in

3   He first diminishes such arguments by calling them "abstract," removed from the cruel consequences such justifications have in the real world, and then concludes that "standards of decency" must change with time.

4   Harrington now offers his first definition of poverty.

5   As his first definition is tied to technological advances, his second involves social standards.

6   This paragraph and the two preceding deal in one way or another with psychological suffering by the poor in alienation, pessimism, and despair.

a society where the majority have a decent, balanced diet is a tragedy.

This point can be put another way in defining poverty. One of the consequences of our new technology is that we have created new needs. There are more people who live longer. Therefore they need more. In short, if there is technological advance without social advance, there is, almost automatically, an increase in human misery, in impoverishment.   7

And finally, in defining poverty one must also compute the social cost of progress. One of the reasons that the income figures show fewer people today with low incomes than twenty years ago is that more wives are working now, and family income has risen as a result. In 1940, 15 percent of wives were in the labor force; in 1957 the figure was 30 percent. This means that there was more money and, presumably, less poverty.   8

Yet a tremendous growth in the number of working wives is an expensive way to increase income. It will be paid for in terms of the impoverishment of home life, of children who receive less care, love, and supervision. This one fact, for instance, might well play a significant role in the problems of the young in America. It could mean that the next generation, or a part of it, will have to pay the bill for the extra money that was gained. It could mean that we have made an improvement in income statistics at the cost of hurting thousands and hundreds of thousands of children. If a person has more money but achieves this through mortgaging the future, who is to say that he or she is no longer poor?   9

It is difficult to take all these imponderables together and to fashion them into a simple definition of poverty in the United States. Yet this analysis should make clear some of the assumptions that underlie the assertions in this book: 10

Poverty should be defined in terms of those who are denied the minimal levels of health, housing, food, and education that our present stage of scientific knowledge specifies as necessary for life as it is now lived in the United States.   11

Poverty should be defined psychologically in terms of those whose place in the society is such that they are internal exiles who, almost inevitably, develop attitudes of defeat and pessimism   12

Harrington concludes this section of the essay by showing that technological and social advances must be made in tandem to avoid human misery.

The next two paragraphs demonstrate that a change some might consider an inroad against poverty (generally higher incomes) may have been bought at too dear a price (the future of our children).

Harrington's brief, four-paragraph conclusion simplifies and summarizes his definitions of poverty.

and who are therefore excluded from taking advantage of new opportunities.

Poverty should be defined absolutely, in terms of what man and society could be. As long as America is less than its potential, the nation as a whole is impoverished by that fact. As long as there is the other America, we are, all of us, poorer because of it.

Meaning and Purpose

1. Find Harrington's main points about poverty.
2. Harrington claims that "a definition of poverty is, to a considerable extent, a historically conditioned matter" (2). Explain what he means.
3. Harrington says that to compare the poverty of one time to that of another is an "abstract approach toward poverty" (3). Why does he find this approach objectionable?
4. What does Harrington mean in paragraph 8 when he says that "in defining poverty one must also compute the social cost of progress"?
5. In paragraphs 8 and 9, Harrington seems to suggest if women weren't in the work force in such numbers as they are, America's children would have fewer problems. What solutions can you think of for the "impoverishment of home life" other than women's staying at home?
6. Considering all that Harrington said before, explain what he means in the last sentence.

Strategy

1. How does Harrington's argument in the first three paragraphs lead to his definitions of poverty?
2. How would you categorize Harrington's definitions—lexical, stipulative, or extended—and why?

Meaning and Purpose

1. Harrington's main points are the last three paragraphs.

2. Our perceptions and definitions of poverty are determined by our place in history. The poverty of nineteenth-century England, for instance, would be totally unacceptable now. To argue against social reforms by claiming that the present poor are better off than the poor of another time or place is thus illogical and unacceptable.

3. Comparing the poverty of one historical time to another is purely an intellectual ("abstract") activity that has pernicious consequences in the real world. It allowed nineteenth-century conservatives to ignore inhuman conditions among the poor. And twentieth-century conservatives who would be appalled by the horror of nineteenth-century poverty use the same fallacious reasoning to ignore conditions today (3).

4. Families had higher incomes in 1962 when Harrington published *The Other America* than twenty years earlier because more wives were in the work force. The price of this progress may be that children have less care, love, and supervision. Thus, we may have mortgaged their futures—a high price to pay for "progress" (8, 9).

5. Some students may find Harrington's opinions in these paragraphs sexist. Other solutions would be for men and women to share equally the responsibility for taking care of children, and for companies to provide adequate day-care for children of working parents.

6. Any society that has the wealth to eliminate the horrors of poverty and doesn't is spiritually impoverished.

Strategy

1. Paragraph 1 gives the justification nineteenth-century British conservatives used to avoid change. In paragraph 2, Harrington cites similar arguments and implies their fallacious-ness. In paragraph 3, he shows explicitly how these arguments are flawed and concludes that our standards of decency must change with time.

2. Each of the definitions can be taken as stipulative. In paragraph 5, Harrington stipulates the "social definition of poverty." Each of the last three paragraphs defines a different aspect of poverty: quality of life (11), psychological (12), and moral (13). Together, these stipulative definitions, and all the other points Harrington makes in considering these definitions of poverty (such as "the social cost of progress" in paragraph 8), constitute an extended definition of poverty.

3. In paragraphs 2–7, Harrington uses the word "this" in the first sentence to clearly refer to ideas just stated. "Finally" indicates (8) that he will make his final point. "Yet" (9) indicates he will now make a distinction from what he has just said. And "all these imponderables" (10) clearly connects the paragraph with all that he has just said.

Style

1. Harrington's tone is formal and controlled, as in these sentences: "Indeed, if one wanted to play with figures . . . United States" (2); "Yet if this book . . . intensifies the exclusion" (6); and "if there is technological advance . . . in impoverishment" (7). The words in these sentences do not convey strong feelings; they sound academic.

2. "Internal exiles" here means that the poor are members of the society, are internal to the society, but they are outcasts because they "are dispossessed . . . had the will" (5).

3. *Pervasive:* spread through all parts of; *dispossessed:* having suffered the loss of expectations, prospects, relationships, and also disinherited, disaffiliated, alienated; *affluent:* having abundant wealth, property, and other material goods; *imponderables:* things that cannot be precisely determined, measured, or evaluated.

3. What transitions does Harrington use to connect paragraphs 1–10?

Style

1. Analyze the tone of the essay by looking closely at the language and word choices.
2. How does Harrington use the phrase "internal exiles" in paragraph 5?
3. Define these words: *pervasive* (1); *dispossessed, affluent* (5); *imponderables* (10).

Writing Tasks

1. In an essay, develop a definition, or definitions, of wealth. Take social and economic factors into account. Consider offering solutions to the problems of the wealthy.
2. Choose one word, such as "student" or "happiness," and write three kinds of definitions for it—lexical, stipulative, and extended.

❦ Victor B. Ficker and Herbert S. Graves ❦

Victor Ficker was born in 1937 in Illinois and attended the University of Florida. He has worked in education for most of his professional life and has published extensively about social problems in the United States. He is coauthor, with Carol Wines, of Man's Search for Himself (1972). Herbert Graves has been head of the Department of American Studies at Polk Junior College. Ficker and Graves have coauthored two books: Deprivation in America (1970) and Social Science and Urban Crisis, 2nd ed. (1978).

You're Asking Me What Deprivation Is?

In this essay, from their book Deprivation in America, *Ficker and Graves cite a young woman's first-person description of her own life of poverty as an extended definition of deprivation. Though a case study is an unusual way of presenting a definition, the young woman's story gives the reader an understanding of deprivation that a conventional definition cannot impart.*

While deprivation is not a respecter of race, religion, or national origin, it does befall the lower social and economic groups of our society. It is often said that anyone with the desire to do so can climb out of his environment and forever be rid of the deprivations of poverty and want. See if you agree with that thought after you read the case study that follows.

This case study is not fiction—it is the *true* story of a woman of twenty-eight or twenty-nine years of age who looks more nearly fifty. The story is in the subject's own words—slightly cleaned up to eliminate the profanity and some of her bitter resentment toward a society which does not include her. It is her report to case workers in a field office of the Office of Economic Opportunity.

TEACHING SUGGESTIONS

Ficker and Graves, in their introduction to the case study, cite a popular belief that those who want to badly enough can climb out of poverty. A paragraph later they say that the woman in the study seems trapped in a deep well with no way out. One way to get at this essay is to have students apply these two observations to the case study. Students can also be asked to compare their views of poverty before and after they read the case study.

To pursue the essay as an example of a definition paper, it might prove profitable to have students examine the structure of the essay: the two-paragraph introduction; the definition itself broken into ten parts; and the three-paragraph conclusion.

MARGINAL NOTES

1 The authors' first sentence connects with the woman's last sentence in the case study: "I'm here, now, and there are others like me all around you." The last sentence in this paragraph is almost a challenge: After reading this case study, see if you can still believe the cliché that one can climb out of poverty if one really wants to.

2 The authors emphasize that the story is true and claim they've eliminated some of the bitterness. There's irony here in that the story is full of bitterness, understandably.

Now the authors emphasize again that the problem of poverty is ubiquitous and this idea connects, again, with the woman's last sentence.

The first two paragraphs serve as the introduction. The first captures us with impressively concrete language. The second asks us to try to understand, again concretely.

Here the woman begins with the first part of her definition, a section primarily about the smell of poverty.

Considering the conditions she describes, the dog analogy is very effective here.

Read her story with compassion. It is one of desperation and utter hopelessness; it covers all categories of deprivation. This woman seems trapped in the bottom of a deep well with sides too steep to climb, with no handholes or ropes to grasp. If you feel no compassion for her, then think of her children, for she sees no way out for them either.

3

The authors have never read an account that better describes the many types of deprivation experienced by our disadvantaged citizens. Here in one package is what the present means for one family and what little hope exists for its future. The woman is white; the locale is Tennessee. She could just as easily have been black, Mexican-American, or Puerto Rican—families such as hers exist in each of our fifty states. As a matter of fact, families such as this exist in all of our communities. We can find them if we only will look; we can help if only we take the trouble to understand and decide to help. Can we do less?

4

A Case Study in Deprivation

Here I am, dirty, smelly, with no proper underwear beneath this rotting dress. I don't know about you, but the stench of my teeth makes me half sick. They're decaying, but they'll never be fixed. That takes money.

5

Listen to me without pity, now, for I don't need your pity; it won't help me at all, and it won't help my hungry children. Listen to me with understanding, if you can. Try to put yourself in my dirty, worn-out, ill-fitting shoes—if you can stand the thought, much less the reality.

6

What is poverty? Poverty is getting up every morning from a dirty and illness-stained mattress—a hard, lumpy mattress. Sheets? There are no sheets. They have long since been used for diapers, for there are no real diapers here, either.

7

That smell? That other smell? You know what it is—plus sour milk and spoiled food. Sometimes it's mixed with the stench of onions cooked too often. Onions are cheap.

8

We're like dogs in that we live in a world of smells and we've learned to identify most of them without searching them out. There is the smell of young children who can't make it down that

9

long path at night. There is the smell of the filthy mattress. There is the smell of food gone sour because the refrigerator doesn't work. I don't remember when the refrigerator did work. I only know it takes money to get it fixed. And there is the smell of garbage. I could bury it, but where do you get a shovel without money?

Poverty is being tired—dog tired all the time. I can't remember when I wasn't tired. When my last baby came, they told me at the hospital that I had chronic anemia caused by a poor diet, a bad case of worms, and the need for a corrective operation.

When they told me about my condition, I listened politely. The poor are always polite, you know. We can't afford to offend those who might decide to be big and give us something. The poor always listen, for there really isn't much we can say. If we were to say anything, it might prejudice somebody with a little money. What good would it do to say there is no money for iron pills, better food, or necessary medicine?

The idea of an operation is frightening even if you have the money required. IF I had dared, I would have laughed. Who would have taken care of my children while I was in the hospital for a prolonged period?

The last time I left my children with their grandmother was when I had a job. I came home to find the baby covered with fly specks and wearing a diaper that had not been changed since I left. When the dried diaper was removed, bits of my baby's flesh were on it. My middle child was playing with a sharp piece of glass, and my oldest was playing alone at the edge of an unprotected lake. On my job I made $22 a week. A nursery school charges $20 a week for three children. So I had to quit my job.

Poverty is dirt. You may say, in your clean clothes and coming from your clean house, "Anybody can be clean." Let me explain housekeeping with no money. For breakfast, I give my children grits with no margarine, or cornbread made without eggs or oleo. For one thing, that kind of food doesn't use up many dishes. What dishes there are, I wash in cold water. No soap. Even the cheapest soap has to be saved for washing the old sheets I use for the baby's diapers.

10   The woman begins the second part of her definition here. Paragraphs 10–13 are particularly coherent, each following naturally from the preceding.

11

12

13

14   Here she begins the third part of her definition.

Look at these cracked red hands. Once I saved up for two 15
months to buy a jar of Vaseline for my hands and for the baby's
diaper rash. When I had the money and went to buy the Vaseline,
the price had gone up two cents, and I didn't have another two
cents. Every day I have to decide whether I can bear to put these
cracked, sore hands into that cold water and strong soap. Why
don't I use hot water? It takes money to get something with which
you can heat it. Hot water is a luxury. We don't have luxuries.

You would be surprised if I told you my age. I look twenty 16
years older than I am; my back has been bent over tubs so long I
can't stand up straight any more. I can't remember when I did
anything but wash, but we're still dirty. I just can't seem to keep
up with all the washing. Every night I wash every stitch my
school-age child had on and just hope the clothes will be dry
enough to wear when morning comes.

The fourth part of the definition begins here. The discomforts and dangers of poverty favor no season over another.

Poverty is staying up all night when it is cold to guard the 17
one fire we have; one spark striking the newspaper we have on
our walls would mean my sleeping children would die in the
flames. In the summer, poverty is watching gnats and flies devour
my baby's tears when he cries, which is most of the time. I've
never been in an air-conditioned house. I've just heard folk talk
about them. Our screens are torn, but we pay so little rent that I
know it's foolish to even talk about getting them fixed. Poverty
means insects in your food, in your nose, in your eyes, and crawl-
ing over you while you sleep. Poverty is children with runny
noses, even in the summer. Paper handkerchiefs take money, and
you need all your rags for other things. Antihistamines are for
the rich.

She begins the next part of her definition here. After describing the physical travails of poverty, she now depicts some of the psychological suffering.

Poverty is asking for help. Have you ever had to swallow what 18
pride you had left and ask for help, knowing your children will
suffer more if you don't get it? Think about asking for a loan from
a relative, if that's the only way you can really understand asking
for help.

I'll tell you how asking for help feels: You find out where the 19
office is, the one from which paupers are supposed to get help.
When you find it, you circle that block four or five times trying
to get up nerve enough to go in and beg. Finally, the thought of

your children's need and suffering pushes you through the door. Everybody is very busy and official. After an eternity, a woman comes out to you and you tell her you need help, and you force yourself to look at her.

She isn't the one you need to see. The first one never is. She   20
sends you to see someone else and, after spilling your poverty and shame all over the desk, you find out this isn't the right office. Then you repeat the whole procedure. It doesn't get any easier.

You ask for help in two or three places, until you're sick   21
of the whole procedure, but you're always told to wait. You are told why you have to wait but you don't really hear, because the dark cloud of shame and despair deafens you with its roar of recrimination.

Poverty is remembering—remembering quitting school in   22   In this part she looks backward.
junior high school because the nice children from nice homes were so cruel about your clothes and your smell. (There have always been smells—you think you should have been a bloodhound.) I remember when I quit and the attendance teacher came to see my mother. She told him I was pregnant. I wasn't, but my mother knew they wouldn't make me go back to school if she told them that. She thought I could get a job and bring home some money. I had jobs off and on, but never long enough to earn much.

I remember mostly being married. I was so young. I'm still   23
young, but you can't tell it. In another town, for a little while we had most of the things you have; a little house with lights, hot water and everything. Then my husband lost his job. For a little while there was some unemployment insurance, but soon all our nice things were repossessed and we moved back here—I was pregnant at the time. This house didn't look so bad when we first moved in. Every week it got worse, though. Nothing was ever fixed. Soon we didn't have any money at all.

My husband got a few odd jobs, but everything went for   24
food—just as it does now. I'll never know how we lived through three years and three babies, but we did. After that last baby, I just plain destroyed my marriage. Would you want to bring another baby into this filth? I didn't, and birth-control measures

take money. I knew the day my husband left that he wasn't coming back, but neither of us said anything. What was there to say? I hope he has been able to climb out of this mess somewhere. He never could hope to do it here, with us to drag him down.

It was after he left that I first asked for help. I finally got it: $78 a month for the four of us. That's all we'll ever get. That's why there is no soap, no medicine, no needles, no hot water, no aspirin, no hand cream, no shampoo—none of those things ever. And forever, I pay $20 a month rent. The rest goes for food: grits, cornmeal, rice, beans and milk.   25

Poverty is looking into the future colored only the blackest black. There is no hope. Your children wouldn't play with my children; you wouldn't allow it. My boys will someday turn to boys who steal to get what they need. I can already see them behind prison bars, but it doesn't bother me as it would you. They'll be better off behind prison bars than they would be behind the bars of my poverty and despair. They'll find the freedom of alcohol and drugs—the only freedom they'll ever know.   26

My daughter? She'll have a life just like mine, unless she's pretty enough to become a prostitute. I'd be smart to wish her dead already.   27

You say there are schools? Sure there are, but my children have no paper, no pencils, no crayons, no clothes, no anything worthwhile or useful. All they have is worms, pinkeye, infections of all sorts all the time. They aren't hungry, but they are undernourished. There are surplus commodity programs some places, I hear, but not here. Our county said it would cost too much. There is a school lunch program, but I have two children who are already too damaged for that to do them any good.   28

Yes, I know there are health clinics. They are in the towns, and I live eight miles from any town. I can walk that far, but my little children can't, and I can't carry them.   29

I have a neighbor who will take me to town when he goes, but he expects to be paid one way or another. No thanks; at least the hungry children I have are legitimate. You may know my neighbor. He is the large fellow who spends his time at the gas station, the barber shop, and the corner complaining loudly about   30

Having looked at her bleak past, she now projects a future that is even bleaker because of her children.

the government spending money on the immoral mothers of illegitimate children.

Poverty is an acid that eats into pride until pride is burned out. It is a chisel that chips at honor until honor is pulverized. You might do something if you were in my situation—for a week or a month. Would you do it year after year, getting nowhere?

Even I can dream. I dream of a time when there is money—money for the right kind of food, for medicine, for vitamins, for a toothbrush, for hand cream, for a hammer and nails, for screens, for a shovel, for paint, for sheets, for needles, and thread and . . . but I know it's a dream, just like you know it's a dream when you see yourself as President.

Most, though, I dream of such things as not having wounded pride when I'm forced to ask for help. I dream for the peace of sincerely not caring any more. I dream of a time when the offices I visit for help are as nice as other government offices, when there are enough workers to get to you quickly, when those workers don't quit in defeat and despair just as poor folk quit hoping. I dream of the time when I have to tell my story just once each visit, to just one person. I'm tired of proving my poverty over and over and over.

I leave my despair long enough to tell you this: I did not come from another place, and I did not come from another time. I'm here, now, and there are others like me all around you.

31   She uses effective metaphors for the final part of her definition.

32

33

34

Meaning and Purpose

1. Evaluate the title. Is it appropriate for the essay? Is it effective? Explain.
2. What do Ficker and Graves want you to think about as you read the woman's story? Why?
3. Where else in the essay does the woman use the paragraph 9 analogy? How appropriately does the analogy seem to describe the condition of being poor?

Possible Answers

Meaning and Purpose

1. In speaking the title, we would emphasize "Me" for sarcasm and a sense of incredulity. The title is appropriately in the woman's voice, for she tells the story. And the question is effective because it's rhetorical. The title is ironic because, of course, this woman knows—better than any reader—what deprivation is. And the word "Deprivation" is more pointed, starker, than "poverty" would be.
2. Ficker and Graves want readers to think

about the glib attitude they might have—"it is often said that anyone with the desire to do so can climb out of his environment and forever be rid of the deprivations of poverty and want" (1)—and reevaluate it after reading the woman's story. The authors want readers to read the essay as a "*true* story" (2), to read it with compassion for the woman's children if not for her (3), and to read it with an open mind for taking action on behalf of the poor (4).

3. Because the poor live in a world where bad smells predominate (7–9), the woman makes the analogy that she and her family are like dogs (9). She begins the next paragraph, "Poverty is being tired—dog tired all the time."

4. The woman vividly describes the shame that makes her reluctant to ask for help, and the demeaning and hopeless ritual she is forced to go through to get it. She concludes this section pointedly: "You are told you have to wait but you don't really hear, because the dark cloud of shame and despair deafens you with its roar of recrimination" (21).

5. The woman dreams of the everyday necessities that most people take for granted. She has a sense of bitter irony knowing that these dreams are fantasies: "but I know it's a dream, just like you know it's a dream when you see yourself as President" (31–32).

Strategy

1. Ficker and Graves offer the woman's case study as their definition of deprivation and poverty, believing she can define these best with her own life story. The definition is an extended one because it includes many kinds of deprivation in different situations.

2. The essay is organized with an introduction (5–6), the body (7–31), and a conclusion (32–34). In the body of the essay, she defines poverty, each section describing an aspect of poverty.

3. The conclusion deftly reinforces the definition of poverty and its attendant despair. The woman begins her conclusion with the bitter irony that her dreams of the meagerest things can never be realized (32), and continues with

4. In paragraphs 18–21, she describes asking for help. Characterize her perception of how she was treated.

5. In part of her conclusion (paragraphs 32, 33), the woman says that she has dreams like everyone else. What are her dreams? What hope does she have of attaining them?

Strategy

1. What kind of definition of deprivation and poverty do Ficker and Graves offer, and why?

2. The woman organizes her definition of poverty around several aspects of being poor. What are these aspects, and how is the essay organized around them?

3. Discuss the effectiveness of the woman's conclusion. How does it reinforce her definition of poverty?

4. How is it significant that the woman is not named in her story?

Style

1. Compare the diction in this essay with that of Michael Harrington in "A Definition of Poverty." How is it different? How is the diction appropriate for each author's purposes?

2. How would you describe the tone of the woman's story? Cite passages that illustrate the tone.

3. Look closely at the sentence structure and language in these sentences: "They told me at the hospital that I had chronic anemia caused by a poor diet, a bad case of worms, and the need for a corrective operation." (10); "She sends you to see someone else and, after spilling your poverty and shame all over the desk . . ." (20); and "because the dark cloud of shame and despair deafens you with its roar of recrimination" (21). The woman tells us that she quit school in junior high (22). Do you think this language is hers? Why or why not?

Writing Tasks

1. This essay combines narration and definition. In your essay, develop a definition of something abstract, such as loyalty or heroism, by presenting a story that illustrates it. The narrator of the story should be the person you think best suited to tell it.

2. Choose a group you believe is underprivileged, discriminated against, or misunderstood, such as illiterate adults, paraplegics, or gay parents. Write a dialogue between a member of that group and someone who is not sympathetic toward or aware of the problems the group member lives with. The dialogue should define what it is to be a member of the group, and the reality of what the person's life is like. Use the two points of view to make the definitions sharper.

the dream "for the peace of sincerely not caring any more" in order to relieve her hurt (33). Her final point is that she, and others like her, are all around us. She is part of Michael Harrington's "other America" ("A Definition of Poverty") that the rest of us ignore or conveniently overlook.

4. Not giving the woman a name keeps her anonymous and representative of all poor people. It also distances her from the privileged (by comparison) audience she addresses, and doesn't require them to personalize her beyond what is comfortable for them. It's as if she and the authors know that poor people can be frightening and threatening if they get too close to those who don't share their world.

Style

1. Michael Harrington's diction is formal and scholarly, perfectly appropriate for developing a philosophical definition of poverty. The woman who speaks in "You're Asking Me What Deprivation Is?" lives in the dirt and suffering of poverty and her diction is vividly, and appropriately, concrete and specific.

2. The woman's tone is both bitter and despairing. Examples are "Look at these cracked red hands" (15); "Have you ever had to swallow what pride you have left and ask for help, knowing your children will suffer more if you don't get it?" (18); "All they have is worms, pinkeye, infections of all sorts all the time" (28).

3. These sentences and others (such as sentence 3 in paragraph 33) are sophisticated in construction, vocabulary, and figures of speech beyond the expression most junior-high dropouts (who are unlikely to be well read) would be capable of. It is likely that the case worker or the authors or all three have manipulated the language to appeal to an educated audience. Ask students whether, if this manipulation has been done, the story would have been more or less effective told just as the woman probably spoke.

❦ Barbara Ehrenreich ❦

A self-proclaimed socialist and feminist, Barbara Ehrenreich has been outspoken against social injustice, and sexism in particular. She was born in Butte, Montana, in 1941 and received her Ph.D. from Rockefeller University in 1968. She has held several positions in the health sciences and written extensively about male domination of the American health-care system. A political activist, she has served as cochair of the Democratic Socialists of America and has been a contributing editor to Ms. *magazine. Her books include* For Her Own Good: One Hundred Fifty Years of the Experts' Advice to Women *(1978) and* The Hearts of Men: American Dreams and the Flight from Commitment *(1983). Her latest book, a collection of essays about the years of the Reagan presidency, is called* The Worst Years of Our Lives: Irreverent Notes from a Decade of Greed *(1990). Her articles, essays, and book reviews have appeared in* Mother Jones, New Republic, *and* The New York Times Magazine.

Oliver North and the Warrior Caste

In Ehrenreich's definition of the Warrior Caste, she describes Oliver North's war mentality as typical of that group. Questioning and criticizing "love of war" from a feminist perspective in this essay, which originally appeared in Ms. *magazine in May 1987, she ends with a challenge to "end the millennia-old reign of the Warrior Caste."*

When I first saw Oliver North on television, testifying—or rather, declining to testify before the House Committee on Foreign Affairs—I was so taken by the expression on his face that I almost missed the main point. The expression was one of exaggerated attentiveness: eyebrows drawn up high into the center of his fore- 1

488

head, the corners of his mouth tucked down ceremoniously toward his chin. It was the kind of face you might wear for a solemn occasion where it would be tactless, if not incriminating, to break out into a grin.

The main point, however, is not that Oliver North may have enjoyed his role in Iranscam, or been amused by the feeble institution of Congress. The main point—the only real message of his silent testimony—was the uniform. This prince of Reagan's secret government had chosen to confront the public in a costume that proclaimed his license to kill—not just impersonally as a President may by pressing a button—but, if necessary, messily and by hand. A civilian official in a civilian government, he had chosen to come as a warrior.

I think that this may be one of the more useful ways to think of North and his cabal of collaborators: as members of the oldest male elite there is, the Warrior Caste. Not that, in the crafting of Iranscam, ideology was unimportant—or profiteering, or personal neurosis, or sheer hell-raising adventurism. But the same mixed motives have inspired the warrior elite throughout history, from the sacking of Troy to the raids of Genghis Khan and the Crusades against the Muslim world. What defines the Warrior Caste, and sets it apart from the mass of average military men, is a love of war that knows no bounds, accepts no peace, and always seeks, in the ashes of the last battle, the sparks that might ignite the next. For North and many of his key collaborators, the sequence was Vietnam, then Nicaragua, with detours into war-torn Angola and prerevolutionary Iran. The end of one war demanded the creation of the next.

I have been thinking about the Warrior Caste ever since a remarkable book, Klaus Theweleit's *Male Fantasies* (the English edition was just published by the University of Minnesota Press), introduced me to a group of men who might be considered the psychological prototype of the modern warrior elite, the German Freikorpsmen. These were officers who refused to disarm after World War I, but instead returned to Germany and organized private armies to battle the rebellious working class of their own nation. They went on, in the thirties, to become the core of Hitler's

2   She uses emotionally charged language to make negative comments on her subject. Calling his uniform a "costume," for instance, connotes that North is an actor on a stage and thus insincere.

3   Her diction continues her tone of disdain in this paragraph. Her use of "cabal" and her twice repeating "collaborators" emphasize the secretive scheming by North and the rest of his Warrior Caste, a label she defines in the paragraph's penultimate sentence.

4

Ehrenreich sets up the Freikorpsmen as the prototype of the Warrior Caste, whose behavior she compares to North's.

SA and, in some cases, key functionaries in the Third Reich. Thus for them, the period between 1914 and 1945 was continuous, almost uninterrupted, war, in no small part because they made it so. Historian Robert Waite quotes a Freikorpsman who had enlisted in the German army at the age of 16: "People told us that the War [World War I] was over. That made us laugh. We ourselves are the War. Its flame burns strongly in us. It envelops our whole being and fascinates us with the enticing urge to destroy. We obeyed . . . and marched onto the battlefields of the postwar world just as we had gone into battle on the Western Front: singing, reckless and filled with the joy of adventure . . . silent, deadly, remorseless in battle."

She uses examples that favorably compare North's behavior and motives to those of the Freikorpsmen.

We are a long way, of course, from the trenches of the Western 5 Front and the street battles of postwar Berlin, but some of the same "joy" and "enticing urge" seem to have driven Oliver North. The son of an army colonel and brother of two officers, North had been in such a hurry to get to Vietnam in 1968 that he skipped a summer leave. According to the Washington *Post,* friends said he didn't want to miss the war. In Vietnam, he was a hero, or, depending on your point of view, a maniac. "He burned inside," a Marine Corps buddy has said, unconsciously echoing the Freikorpsman quoted above. "He was a zealot."

Back from Vietnam in 1969, North poured his energies into 6 his job as a Marine instructor. Other instructors seem to have thought him a bit mad, coming to class in camouflage paint, bush hat, bandoliers across his chest, with four guns and three knives tucked about his person. "He was pumped up after Vietnam," a friend explained to the press, and dashed back to that unhappy country at his first chance—to testify in 1970 on behalf of a fellow Marine charged with murdering 16 Vietnamese women and children at Son Thang. While the trial dragged on, he passed the time by volunteering for "killer teams" on nighttime patrol. Even hardened Marines thought this was going a little far, "hiding behind trees and slitting throats on his own time."

The intimation here is that North and the others in the Warrior Caste will go insane if they have no war to fight. The implied irony, of course, is that to constantly fight wars is in itself insane behavior.

North could take anything, except, apparently, the stress of 7 peace. Assigned to a routine Marine Corps job in 1974, he experienced a psychotic episode. His superior officer reportedly found him in his quarters, "babbling incoherently and running around naked, waving a .45 pistol." He had nothing to live for, he explained, and he may have meant nothing to kill for.

That problem—the horror of peace—would be solved once he reached the dark inner core of Reagan's secret government. North had spent the rest of the 1970s in the Marines and then headed for the Naval War college, where he impressed enough higher-ups to get a White House appointment in 1981. From his post in the National Security Council, he designed the invasion of Grenada, abetted the South Africa–supported guerrillas in Angola, engineered the hijacking of the *Achille Lauro* hijackers, and seems to have almost single-handedly managed the covert war against Nicaragua. He no longer had to wait for wars or worry about getting to a war too late. He could make his own.

It matters, of course, that North has a specific ideology to defend. No doubt he sees himself as a steadfast crusader against Communism, and not as a macho thrill-seeker. But the thrill is there, and even temporary warriors, soldiers who gladly return to the routines of peacetime, often describe combat as the peak event of their lives. "I had the most tremendous experiences of all of life: of fear, of jubilance, of misery, of hope, of comradeship, and of the endless excitement, the theatrics of it," a World War II veteran told Studs Terkel in his book *The Good War*. After an experience like that, "everything," to quote another of Terkel's vets, "is anticlimactic."

I will admit that this is alien territory to me, the psychology of the warrior. In part, this is because his anticlimactic "everything" is all that I, and probably you the reader, have ever known or experienced: work, love, children, family, friends, and the peaceful struggles we wage in the name of love and children. As feminists, we may honor myths and tales of women warriors, but, overwhelmingly and throughout history, women have inhabited a world that warriors happily leave behind, or arrive at—only to destroy.

There is another reason for our ignorance of the warrior mentality. In our generation of feminist scholars, the history of war and warriors has taken second place to "social history"—the

8   Now Ehrenreich uses examples to establish a cause-and-effect relationship.

9   Here she contrasts ideology with the sheer thrill of war. Ideology comes off a distant second as the motivating force for North and other warriors.

10   Ehrenreich now moves away from North as emblematic of the Warrior Caste to consider the more general psychology of warriors and how that psychology has shaped social values. In paragraphs 10 and 11 the author establishes two reasons why she cannot fully understand that psychology.

11   The author cites authority to establish the link between militarism and patriarchy.

attempt to reconstruct how ordinary people have gone about their lives, producing what they need and reproducing themselves. We rejected the conventional history of "king and battles" for what Sheila Rowbotham has called the "hidden history" of everyday life, almost to the point of forgetting how much of everyday life has, for millennia, been shaped by battles and dominated by warrior elites.

Now Ehrenreich theorizes why the Warrior Caste has been so successful throughout history.

But I do not think we will ever understand either history or women's place in it without a *feminist* understanding of the Warrior Caste: history, because so much of it is made by warriors; women, because our very absence from the warriors' ranks must be understood, finally, as a profound clue to the mystery of male power and gender itself. The absence of women, I would argue, is not a mere "result" of patriarchy or a "consequence" of sexism; it is intrinsic to the psychology of the warrior, just as war itself—and the endless preparations and celebrations it demands—may be intrinsic to the perpetuation of patriarchy. 12

In his brilliant psychoanalytical study of the Freikorpsmen, Theweleit offers one of the links between militarism and patriarchy: war, to those permanent warriors, was a condition of life *because* it was an escape from women and all things female. The Freikorpsmen, whose letters and diaries Theweleit analyzes, did not just hate women; in a way they did not even *see* women, including their own wives—except as intruders, threats, yawning "swamps" in which a man could be engulfed. Nor was this a matter of "repressed homosexuality" or sexuality of any kind. For these prototypical warriors, the only resolution of the horror of women was the murder of women (as well as men), an act they describe not only with relish, but with relief. 13

Now, quite aside from Theweleit's thesis, I would argue that any prestigious, socially pervasive, all-male institution serves to perpetuate patriarchy, whether it is the men's longhouse of a tribal society or the executive class of an industrial society. The reason is simple: as long as the male career trajectory is a movement from a world centered on women (mothers) to a world in which there are no women, "growing up" for men will always mean growing away from women. And for the men who "grow up," women will 14 always be reminders of their own vulnerability and helpless infancy. Women will be feared, contemned, or perhaps merely patronized as incomplete and childish versions of men.

Some feminist theorists have suggested that the earliest such   15
institution of patriarchy was the male hunting band. But for most of recorded history, and in most of the world, the premier institution of male power has probably been the military, and especially the warrior elite. Not all societies hunt, and not all societies organize their religions around male-only hierarchies, but almost all societies that can make any claim to being "civilized" have cultivated the Warrior Caste. I think, for example, of the remarkable parallels, even in their style of warfare and codes of honor, between the samurai of feudal Japan and the knights of feudal Europe: as if their Warrior Caste had a kind of historical inevitability, transcending physical distance, language, and everything we know as "culture."

My guess is that the historical "success" of the Warrior Caste   16
rests on the fact that it is, in more than one sense, self-propagating. First, in a geographical sense: the existence of a warrior elite in City-State 1 called forth its creation in City-State 2—otherwise the latter was likely to be reduced to rubble and the memories of slaves. Natural selection, as it has operated in human history, favors not only the clever but the murderous.

Second, and quite apart from ordinary biology, the Warrior   17
Caste has the ability to reproduce itself from one generation to the next. Only women can produce children, of course; but—more to the point—only wars can produce *warriors*. One war leads to the next, in part because each war incubates the warriors who will fight the next, or, I should say, *create* the next. The First World War engendered the warrior elite that ushered in the Third Reich, and hence the Second World War. And Vietnam created men like Oliver North, who, through subterfuge and stealth, nourished the fledgling war in Central America.

But to return to North: the real point, it occurs to me, may   18   Her conclusion begins here where she ties all
not have been the uniform, after all. For the key characteristic of   her main threads together.
the Warrior Caste in its modern form is that it does *not* dress up
in battle costume or indulge in recreational throat-slitting. The

men of the true warrior elite in the United States today (and no doubt in the Soviet Union as well) wear tailored suits, kiss their wives goodbye in the morning, and spend their days at desks, plotting covert actions, megadeaths, and "low-intensity" interventions. They are peaceable, even genial, fellows, like the President himself. But still I would say, to the extent that they hoard the resources of the nation for the purposes of destruction, they live for war.

The real lesson of Iranscam, with its winding trail of blood   19
and money, guns and drugs, may be to remind us that we have not evolved so far at all from the most primitive barbarism of the Warrior Caste. That caste has institutionalized itself in the bureaucracy of the "national security" state—the CIA, the National Security Council, the Pentagon. But insofar as their business is still murder (and there can be no other name, I think, for the business of the contras and their American supporters), our modern, gray-flannel warriors are blood brothers to the mercenaries and thugs who made up North's "secret team"—and are spiritual descendants of that Freikorps officer who could say, in exultation, "We are the war."

Our task—we who cherish "daily life" and life itself—is to   20
end the millennia-old reign of the Warrior Caste. There are two parts to this task. One is to uproot the woman-hating, patriarchal consciousness that leads some men to find transcendence and even joy in war, and only war. That will take time, though we have made a decent start. The other part is to remember that war itself is the crucible in which new warriors are created. If we cannot stop the warriors' fevered obsessions, and bring these men back into the human fold, we can at least try to stop their wars.

POSSIBLE ANSWERS

Meaning and Purpose

1. The essay's thesis is stated in paragraph 3: "What defines the Warrior Caste, and sets it apart from the mass of average military men, is a love of war that knows no bounds, accepts no peace, and always seeks, in the ashes of the last battle, the sparks that might ignite the next."
2. The Freikorpsmen perfectly illustrate Ehrenreich's definition of the Warrior Caste. They so loved war that they refused to give up their arms after World War I and spent their time between the two world wars preparing the way for World War II (4). North, the author claims, was driven by the same "joy" and "enticing urge" as the Freikorpsmen. She gives his military history in paragraphs 5–8.
3. Ehrenreich offers two reasons for the warrior mentality being alien to her: all the things

Meaning and Purpose

1. How does Ehrenreich define "Warrior Caste"? Find her thesis.
2. Describe how the German Freikorpsmen were a prototype of the Warrior Caste, and how Ehrenreich says Oliver North is like them.
3. Ehrenreich says that the psychology of the warrior is alien to her. Why is it alien?
4. The author claims that we must have a "feminist" understanding of the Warrior Caste. Why? What is that understanding?
5. Those who cherish life, Ehrenreich claims, must abolish the reign of the Warrior Caste. How does she propose that we go about this task?

Strategy

1. The body of the essay is divided into two parts. Beginning with paragraph 10, Ehrenreich diverts from her discussion of Oliver North as an example of the Warrior Caste. What is her purpose in this diversion? How does it further her definition?
2. What rhetorical devices does Ehrenreich use to extend and explain her definition? Pay particular attention to paragraphs 5–9.
3. How does Ehrenreich's conclusion pull together both parts of the body of the essay?

Style

1. How does Ehrenreich's language show her attitude toward her subject? Cite some examples.
2. What audience does Ehrenreich appeal to, and how do you know?
3. If necessary, look up the meanings of these words in a dictionary: *cabal* (3); *prototype, functionaries* (4); *bandoliers* (6); *abetted*

in life that the warrior finds "anticlimactic"—work, love, children, friends—are the only things she has ever known and experienced (10); in our generation of feminist scholars the history of war and warrior have been supplanted by social history (11).

4. A "feminist" understanding of the Warrior Caste is needed to understand history, because so much history is made by warriors, and to understand women because they are excluded from the warrior ranks (12). War, for the Freikorpsmen, was an escape from women (13). And any "prestigious, socially pervasive, all-male institution" such as the military perpetuates patriarchy because men who "grow up" in such an institution grow away from women who are "feared, contemned, or perhaps merely patronized as incomplete and childish versions of men" (14).

5. Ehrenreich says the two tasks in abolishing the Warrior Caste are to eliminate the "women-hating patriarchal consciousness" that produces war, and war itself (20). She does not say how we should accomplish these tasks.

Strategy

1. The first part of Ehrenreich's discussion shows how her definition fits one individual. The second part demonstrates how warriors have dominated our history and consciousness, thus extending her definition. Paragraphs 4–8 set up the Freikorpsmen as the prototype of the Warrior Caste (5) and then demonstrate how Oliver North fits that prototype (6–8). Paragraphs 9–17 explore the Warrior Caste in a more general sense.

2. Paragraph 5 compares North to the Freikorpsmen described in paragraph 4. Paragraph 6 cites examples of North as a zealot. Paragraph 7 cites an example demonstrating the validity of the topic sentence. Paragraph 8 uses examples to create a cause-and-effect relationship. Paragraph 9 contrasts ideology with the sheer thrill of war.

3. The essay's last three paragraphs bring together the Freikorpsmen, Oliver North, and

the rest of the Warrior Caste in order to condemn their "primitive barbarism."

(8); *millennia* (11); *intrinsic* (12); *longhouse, trajectory* (14); *samurai, feudal* (15); *mercenaries* (19); *transcendence* (20).

Style

1. Ehrenreich at once makes clear her disdain for North and the Warrior Caste he represents and how dangerous she thinks he is. Some examples of negatively charged language are "prince of Reagan's secret government," "costume" (2); "cabal of collaborators," "profiteering," "personal neurosis" (3); "the horrors of peace" (8); and "Iranscam, with its winding trail of blood and money, guns and drugs," "primitive barbarism," "mercenaries," "thugs" (19).

2. Ehrenreich wants to reach an audience of women and feminists who are men or women. Throughout she says "we" to include her audience in her thinking about military patriarchy. In the final paragraph she identifies "we" as those "who cherish 'daily life' and life itself."

3. *Cabal*: a small group of secret plotters, as against a government or person in authority; *prototype*: someone or something that illustrates the typical qualities of a class; *functionaries*: people who function in a special capacity, especially in government service; *bandoliers*: broad belts worn over the shoulders by soldiers and having small loops or pockets for holding cartridges; *abetted*: encouraged, supported, or countenanced by aid or approval, usually in wrongdoing; *millennia*: periods of one thousand years; *intrinsic*: belonging to a thing by its very nature; *longhouse*: a communal dwelling consisting of a wooden, bark-covered framework, often as much as one hundred feet in length; *trajectory*: the curved path of a projectile or rocket in its flight; *samurai*: members of a hereditary warrior caste of feudal Japan; *feudal*: pertaining to the political, military, and social system in the Middle Ages, based on the holding of land in fief and on the resulting relations between lord and vassal; *mercenaries*: professional soldiers hired to serve in foreign armies; *transcendence*: the quality or state of going beyond ordinary limits.

Writing Tasks

1. In the essay Ehrenreich tries to show how Oliver North and the rest of the Warrior Caste differ from other men and even from other soldiers. Choose a group of people you are familiar with and write a paper defining the group and showing how the people in it differ from other people and from similar groups. Use specific examples and choose one member of the group as representative of it.

2. Examine a stereotype often found in movies or on television—the housewife, perhaps, or the soldier, or the private detective, or the doctor. Write a definition of the stereotype, using as many examples as you can. You might try writing a double definition: one definition for the stereotype in movies or on television prior to 1970, compared to the definition of the same stereotype in movies or television after 1970.

❧ Shari Miller Sims ❧

Born in New York in 1956, Shari Sims, soon after graduating from Kenyon College, joined the staff at McCall's magazine, where she was an associate editor. She then spent six years as a staff writer and editor for Vogue. She began working for Self magazine in 1987 and is executive editor of Health and Beauty there. She is coauthor, with Lia Schorr, of two beauty books: Lia Schorr's Skin Care Guide for Men *(1985) and* Seasonal Skin Care *(1988). She has also contributed to* Working Woman *magazine.*

Violent Reactions

Domestic violence, reports Sims in an essay from the March 1989 issue of Self, *appears increasingly to be considered an "acceptable" form of communication within families and couples. In her essay she probes the changes in sex roles for possible causes, seeking a new definition for "violence."*

A thirty-year-old man moved out of a New York City apartment it had taken him months to find. Nothing unusual, except for the reason: the couple, just about his age, who lived next door. Their fights were getting progressively louder, more intense, and what he'd heard was more than words. The shouting seemed to have escalated into all-out warfare, and lately additional noises—breaking glass, the crash of objects being thrown echoed into his apartment. What was even more disturbing to him was their source: He was convinced it was the woman who was starting the fights, who was screaming the words of abuse and hurling things across the apartment—all aimed at the man.

A reporter recently asked a karate champion how she happened to choose her sport. "I tried running and I tried cycling. Then," she paused, "I tried karate. And I discovered how good it felt to hit someone."

497

The author contrasts the reactive definition—what the word "violence" suggests to American women—with an academic discovery that violence has become socially acceptable, circumstantially, as a form of communication.

When most American women hear the word "violence," they think of criminals armed with knives or guns, or tragic tales of cruelty, psychiatric troubles, alcohol and drug use that lead to headline-making cases of wife or child abuse. But those who study America's social landscape also recognize a more hidden—perhaps even more frightening—side: the emergence of violence as a socially acceptable means of communication, a way of grabbing, or holding on to, power, a way of speaking up for oneself.   3

The paragraph moves from a lexical definition of *violence* to a socially realistic modification of that definition, which includes general examples drawn from life.

In its narrowest sense, violence is defined as an act carried out with the intention of causing physical pain or injury to another. But in real life, severe physical violence is only one extreme of a whole spectrum of aggressive behavior that ranges from "verbal violence"—screaming, shouting, saying vicious, spiteful things—to banging one's fist on the table and slamming doors to actually pushing, hitting, kicking, throwing things at or beating another person.   4

The main topic is introduced in paragraph 5, following the anecdotes and their appropriate definitions, which, combined, form a "hook" introduction, designed to engage readers by piquing their interest.

Wherever one looks—in newspapers, on television, in social- and psychological-science journals—there is evidence that America in the late 1980s is a decidedly aggressive society. What's also showing up in the statistics, but is missing from the headlines: Women, contrary to most of our wishes and stereotypes, may not only be as aggressive as men, they may also, in certain situations, be just as violent. And this violence cuts across barriers of education, race and economic class.   5

The Urge Toward Anger

Paragraph 4 defines *violence* lexically; paragraph 6 defines it as "levels of violence," drawing attention to responsive violence, particularly in human beings, while showing that society has hitherto denied women the reasons for responsive violence.

At the most basic level, violence is an effort to subdue another person, the most extreme sort of control. In the animal kingdom, there is rarely, if ever, random violence; when violence does occur, it's generally in response to a threat, actual or implied, to an animal's family or home. Among people, aggressive impulses also arise in response to threats—to one's power, position, to the possibility that someone else may not follow orders. Women, traditionally, have been thought of as the less aggressive (even nonaggressive) sex. They have also been out of the seats of power   6 and been trained, in a male-dominated society, to deny, rather than express, anger.

"Young girls are given the message, incredibly early in life, that it's 'not nice' to get angry," says Jay Lefer, M.D., associate professor of psychiatry at New York Medical College. "Studies in which tape recorders were put in families' homes revealed that as soon as a little girl sounded angry, her parents—and most often the father—would tell her to stop. Ironically, anger that is not expressed, that's bottled up, may be most dangerous, to oneself and to society."

7   An important reason that encourages women to contain the anger that leads to violence is cultural, as shown by psychological studies in the home, where parents, mostly fathers, tell daughters that anger is "not nice."

Traditional psychological theory has it that men hit out in anger, women hit in. Depression, or melancholia as Freud called it, is thus thought to be the inward turning of aggression—and, again not coincidentally, is also thought to be primarily a woman's problem. Modern psychoanalysts, while acknowledging that some depressed patients do have a great deal of anger, see other possibilities. "A young girl who is taught to deny her feelings, who takes this lesson to heart, can eventually become so good at denial that she becomes alexithymic—which means not being able to put words to one's feelings, to a point at which one stops feeling," says Dr. Lefer. "This is the type of person who can say 'I'm furious' without the slightest hint of heat—or fury—in her voice."

8   Traditional, male-dominated psychology takes one stance; modern psychology accepts other, more inclusive, possibilities, including a girl's accepting the kind of denial that causes her to have profoundly severe psychological difficulties. "alexithymic": From "alexithymia," the inability to verbalize feelings.

Suppressing one's emotions, most of us are taught, is the "civilized" way to behave. Expressions such as "keeping a stiff upper lip" or "keeping one's cool" epitomize polite society. But human beings are a passionate species. And in the case of an emotion like anger, suppression may only intensify a feeling. Many mental-health experts believe that a significant amount of violence erupts from pent-up hostility, from anger so tightly bound up that it intensifies to a point at which it bursts out, literally beyond control.

9   In psychoanalytical theory, especially Freudian theory, *suppression* means pushing down painful memories so that they are not available in consciousness. Psychiatrists believe, however, that these memories may persist in some form in the unconscious, occasionally creating psychological havoc.

"Anger may be the starting point for violence," says Dr. Lefer, "but true physical violence is usually an expression of anger at a much deeper level, of a truly helpless kind of rage. That point at which a person feels helpless is usually when violence occurs—when there's a sense of no longer being able to master a situation.

10

A definitive connection links the inability to master a situation and the onset of violent behavior.

Just about everyone has fantasies of violence—of punching out the guy at the motor vehicle bureau who sends you to the end of yet another line after a two-hour wait, or of hurling your briefcase at the ninth person who tells you 'It's not my job'—but we normally don't act on these fantasies. The norms of civilized behavior just don't allow it."

Verbal Violence: Women as Expert?

Notice that the author moves from Lefer's "norms of *civilized* behavior" to her own "norms of *proper* behavior," thereafter introducing the notion of society's control over women's behavior.

The norms of proper behavior do allow women to express 11 their feelings in words—and the angry barb, the rapier-sharp put-down have long been considered women's special province. It also sheds light on how much of what we assume to be natural differences between the sexes often starts with society's molding and controlling of our impulses.

"Most human behavior results from a combination of biolog- 12 ical and societal factors," explains Estelle Ramey, M.D., who is professor emeritus of physiology at Georgetown University School of Medicine in Washington, D.C. "In a historical sense, women, being smaller in structure and musculature than the male of the species, would be more vulnerable to retaliation after physical expressions of anger. So it would be more to a woman's advantage to choose verbal weaponry, an area in which she would safely be on equal footing with a man, over physical force.

Structurally and muscularly smaller than most men, most women vent their anger verbally instead of physically. Verbally, women and men are more evenly matched.

Estelle Ramey offers the historical reason that women are often portrayed in literature as being more verbal than physical.

"Women have become, in one sense, masters of verbal vio- 13 lence. It's no accident that women are often portrayed in literature as nagging, whining or screaming, or that the expression 'sharp-tongued' is usually applied to a female."

Sims, with the expert's aid, dispenses with the argument that men are more physically violent just because of testosterone.

What of the much-touted "testosterone factor" in male aggres- 14 sion? Biological determinism, in this case, has been given far too much credence, argues Dr. Ramey. "It is true that testosterone, when given in abnormally high amounts, can induce aggressive behavior," she says. "A normal, healthy man, though, is not a victim of his hormones, any more than a woman is. Males and females, in fact, both respond to physical threats in the same way, with the release of adrenaline, corticosteroids and other stress

"corticosteroids": Hormonal steroids, including the sex hormones, of the adrenal cortex.

hormones. While it's true that a woman's hormonal system may need a slightly greater stimulus to elicit the same biochemical level of response, as a practical matter this isn't a big difference. The vast majority of men in civilized cultures don't use physical violence—and women, on the other hand, can be trained to be incredibly ruthless soldiers. The biggest differences come in what boys and girls are taught: Women are sometimes so socialized not to express negative emotions that they are even afraid to hit back when faced with someone else instigating violence."

Sims preserves her definition by strengthening her argument that how girls are taught, their "socialization," determines their responses to violence.

This socialization is confirmed by ground-breaking research into aggressive behavior. In an exhaustive review of fifty psychological studies conducted during the past twenty years, researchers Alice H. Eagly, Ph.D., and Valerie Steffen, Ph.D., concluded that the biggest deterrent to physical aggression for a woman was her concern about the consequences of her actions. 15

"Research supports the conclusion that women worried about the harm they could cause another person, the guilt or anxiety they would feel themselves, or the danger they would put themselves in by their actions. Interestingly, the studies that conclude that males are much more aggressive than females really apply primarily to children; by the time we're adults, the differences are smaller," notes Dr. Eagly, who is professor of psychology at Purdue University in Indiana. 16

Mention how the studies confirm that as we mature, we modify our behavior socially.

Power and Physicality

The social roles ascribed to men—the military, sports, the competition of the business world—as well as the superior status of men over women may all help to explain the positive way most men view aggressive behavior. These are spheres, Drs. Eagly and Steffen note, in which the "masculine values" of strength and controlled aggression are especially valued. 17

Our views are shaped by our behavior, as that behavior is endorsed by society.

These are also spheres into which women have made highly visible, much publicized and encouraged moves within the last two decades. While in the past, women's traditional roles—homemaker, mother, wife—emphasized nurturance and passivity, 18 feminists have put a high value on assertiveness and on challenging the long-held view of women as "the weaker sex." Adopting masculine roles, sociologists have observed, also has meant for many women endorsing masculine values. "This is a highly charged topic, politically," acknowledges Jackie Macaulay, Ph.D., a former researcher at the University of Wisconsin in Madison who is now a lawyer. "There is just no scientific evidence that women are innately more peaceful than men. If women's non-violence is a learned behavior, then we have to recognize the possibility that, as we change that learning, we may change women's behavior in ways that aren't all for the better. That's a message feminists don't want to hear."

It's also a message that is showing up in subtle and not so 19 subtle ways every day. As women have sought power in the workplace, in relationships and in society at large, they have also sought to claim physical power through fitness and sports. Women in exercise classes, says one observer, rarely seem happier than when doing the punching movements in aerobic dance routines. Fitness marketers seem to have noticed; they're appealing to women with a much more hard-edged approach. In an ad for Nike shoes, triathlete Joanne Ernst talks as tough as the guys: "Just do it," she snaps, staring down her audience.

Female wrestlers are now featured weekly on TV, while *People* 20 magazine trumpets the fact that the motorcycle magazine *Harley Women* now has nine thousand female readers. Even radio psychotherapists, normally empathetic, are said to be getting meaner—in a *New York Times* column, West Coast writer Anne Taylor Fleming says they now deliver "karate chops to the soul . . . over the airwaves."

And women are delivering more than figurative karate chops. 21 Enrollment in martial-arts classes is way up among women all across the country, as are the numbers of women taking boxing classes at once-all-male bastions like Gleason's Gym in New York City. While self-defense is a motive for some, many more are there for the physical challenge. In 1983, when dancer/choreographer Twyla Tharp took lessons at Gleason's in preparation for the ballet *Fait Accompli*, she was an anomaly; today, Gleason's

When socially acceptable learning is changed, behavior is changed in ways that may not have been predicted.

Recent, socially acceptable learning is reflected in advertising. See also the Virginia Slims cigarette advertisements in magazines, with its slogan directed toward women: "You've come a long way, Baby."

These examples reinforce Sims's exploratory remarks on how changing social attitude will change social behavior.

has nearly two hundred women regularly jabbing and feinting and "working out on the bags"—up from two women regulars just five years ago.

Few people would argue that gaining a sense of power in oneself—physically as well as emotionally—isn't a good thing. Or that women's testing themselves against male standards hasn't led to very real benefits for society as a whole. But there may be a fine line between relishing physical power and using it for not so positive ends—and it's a line that, the latest studies suggest, many women in America may be dangerously close to crossing. Recent statistics, for example, suggest that twelve million women in the U.S. own guns—a number that increased 50 percent in the last decade. Even more disturbingly, at a time when the study of family violence is shattering many of our illusions about the sanctity of our homes, research is revealing that on the home front, women's physical aggressiveness may not be the rarity it's assumed to be.

22   More than 100 years ago, Susan B. Anthony said, in a women's suffrage newspaper, "Make [your employers] understand that you are in their service as workers, not as women" (*The Revolution,* October 8, 1868).

Love and Violence

The popular notion of violence is something that happens "out there"—a random shooting in the street, an explosion from afar—but the reality is that "all intimate relationships have a higher propensity to violence than do encounters among strangers or even acquaintances. The sad fact is that the family is the most violent social institution, with the single exception of the army in times of war," says Murray A. Straus, Ph.D., professor of sociology and director, Family Research Laboratory, University of New Hampshire.

23   As used here, *violence* has two meanings: First, it refers to physical force used to injure, damage, or destroy. Second, it refers to unjust or callous use of force or power, as in violating another's rights or sensibilities.

Perhaps the most controversial finding of all, says Dr. Straus, is that when it comes to violence against one's spouse, women participate in equal numbers to men. And while three fourths of the violence committed by women against their husbands is in acts of self-defense, one fourth is not. And it is that one fourth that Dr. Straus finds especially worrisome: "It's important to understand that men's greater size and strength means that a man's punch will usually produce more injury and pain than a woman's.

24

But that doesn't mean that violence by women should be hidden or overlooked. It is part of the hidden violence of American family life."

Unfortunately, socially derived facts can be used politically, to "prove" whatever a clever manipulator of the language wants to prove.

One reason the data on women's violence hasn't been publicized: fears of misinterpretation of the facts. In 1976, when Dr. Straus announced the results of the first National Survey on Family Violence, the statistics on women's aggression toward their husbands were seized by antifeminist groups in efforts to argue against the need for shelters for battered women. Their claims were that if women were violent, then they didn't need protection against men's violence. Other reports raised false alarms via greatly inflated estimates of the number of battered husbands. In 1985, when the survey was repeated, the number of women aggressors within couples actually increased slightly. But there was no rush to publicize the finding. Experts hesitated to discuss the statistics lest they be used against women.

Notice that Sims carefully includes the results of studies and remarks by specialists. She does not simply make statements about aggression; she lets the experts do that.

In the last ten years, however, a growing number of studies have come to the same conclusion: An average of one third of unmarried men and women—whether dating, engaged or living together—have been involved in physical aggression with the opposite sex. In studies of couples living together before marriage, Patricia A. Gwaitney-Gibbs, Ph.D., associate professor of sociology at the University of Oregon, found that women were even slightly more likely than men to have thrown something, pushed, grabbed, shoved, slapped, kicked, beaten or punched their living-together partners. "Only in the truly severe areas of assault—beating up, threatening with a knife or gun or actually using a knife or gun—were the men more likely to have inflicted these acts on women," said Dr. Gwaitney-Gibbs.

These conclusions are echoed by other researchers. When psychologist K. Daniel O'Leary, Ph.D., of the State University of New York at Stony Brook, and his colleagues studied over two hundred fifty couples during their engagement periods and the first two years of marriage, they found that 44 percent of the women and 31 percent of the men reported pushing, slapping or shoving their partner at least once during the year before marriage—and that, eighteen months later, the number who pushed, slapped or shoved their spouses were still "at a rate that warrants very serious concern.

"In contrast to cases of serious physical abuse, in which the aim is to truly inflict hurt," says Dr. O'Leary, "much of this violence is seen almost as a means of communication. These couples seem to view physical aggression as a permissible means of expression—a fact our society needs to be very concerned about."

In fact, that acceptance of aggressive behavior in general may be the real cause for concern, say experts in the field. While it is true that couples who are younger, poorer and have less education do seem to experience more violence as a group than those who are older, wealthier and more educated, violent relationships exist at all levels of society. It is the observation of violence as a child—along with social class, educational background and being a victim of violence oneself—that is the strongest predictor of becoming a violent adult, claim Dr. Straus and his coauthor, Richard J. Gelles, Ph.D., professor of anthropology and sociology at the University of Rhode Island, in their new book, *Intimate Violence.* The learning experience of being physically punished is most significant, they note, but seeing your mother and father strike one another also teaches a child three lessons: that those we love are those who hit us or are people we can hit; that it is morally right to hit those we love; and that if other means of getting one's way, dealing with stress or expressing oneself don't work, violence is permissible.

28   These comments deal with *perception,* sensory experience that has meaning or significance. Because of learning, one understands relationships among objects. When learning includes aggression or violence, then aggression or violence is perceived as part of a relationship.

29   G. H. Mead at the University of Chicago early in this century devised a theory linking society, the development of personality, and communication. Mead's statement is famous: To be able to communicate is to be able to "take the role of the other" toward one's own vocalizations and behavior. Nowadays, some people find it possible to take the role of the other, when the other is a fictitious character in film or on television.

Thresholds of Aggression

This sanctioning of violence can go on not only within the family but in society as well. And for women especially, there seems to have been an explosion of hyperaggressive role models in the seventies and eighties. "On television and in the movies, women certainly seem to be hitting out more," says New York City psychologist Loretta Walder, Ph.D. "In fifties shows like *The Honeymooners,* when Ralph got angry, he yelled, 'Bam! Zoom!' but what did Alice do? She just stood there with her hands on her

30

The actions on television shows can be seen as condoning societally centered activities that in fact were not all condoned before those actions were presented on television to a broad spectrum of the population.

hips and said 'Ralph.' In the seventies, we started seeing women in gun-toting cop roles, as in *Police Woman* or *Charlie's Angels*, but the level of violence and danger was nothing like the eighties' *Cagney & Lacey*. There are also other messages now, as in *Moonlighting*. Maddie slams her door, David slams his—the door-slamming is one of the show's trademarks, and Maddie and David's means of communication. In the movie *Fatal Attraction,* a clearly psychotic woman tries to kill her lover and the entire American population seemingly can't get enough of the story."

While most experts emphasize that there is no proof that the portrayal or even glorification of violence in the media can actually incite similar actions in the public, many experts do worry that, as with the observation of violence in the family, it can raise a person's "comfort-zone" of physical aggression. 31

Seeing Sigourney Weaver wield a flame-thrower in *Aliens* can't make a woman run out of the movie theater and do something violent. "Human beings are clearly more intelligent than that. But it does add to society's message that violence is appropriate," says Jan Stets, Ph.D., assistant professor of sociology, Washington State University. "There is an attitude toward violence that's built up over time, out of observation and experience, that can increase a person's chances of using violent behavior in a moment of heightened emotion. Just as social learning goes on from one generation to the next within a family, there are messages that are passed on within a culture as well." In some studies, for example, dating couples who were verbally abusive toward each other were more likely to become physically aggressive later on; it was as if their threshold of aggression shifted upward. 32

If, in fact, women are being given the message by society that they need to be more and more assertive, to seize control, to be in charge, our society needs to examine where that will take us. Research into violence by men reinforces the notion of physical aggression as a means of control, of getting the other person to do what they wouldn't otherwise do. It also confirms that the most egalitarian of relationships—in society and within a family—are also the least violent. It shouldn't come as a total surprise, then, that women struggling with unresolved issues of intimate 33

This paragraph opens with a conditional clause, an "if" clause, indicating that all the facts remain to be sifted and examined.

Sims draws a possible parallel, however: That which has been shown in research into violence done by men may also be shown in research into violence done by women. As used in this paragraph, *vulnerable* means being affected by a specified influence, in this case that of irrationality.

relationships and control may be most vulnerable to the powerful and often irrational emotions that can so quickly make verbal violence turn physical.

Meaning and Purpose

1. Seeing a word can cause you to picture elements of its definition. What elements in its definition do you think of when you see the word "violence"?
2. Sims says in paragraph 5 that "Wherever one looks . . . there is evidence that America in the late 1980s is a decidedly aggressive society." In our opinion, what is one current piece of evidence that shows America is a decidedly aggressive society, so far, in the 1990s?
3. What does Sims mean by "seats of power," in paragraph 6?
4. Why have women become, in one sense, "masters of verbal violence"?
5. In your own words, define "concern about the consequences of her actions," in paragraph 15, *based on the comments* in paragraph 16.

Strategy

1. What kind of definition of violence does Sims give in paragraph 4? Why?
2. How does Sims structure her definition of violence, and why? What aspects of the meaning of the word does she include in her definition?
3. In your opinion, what are the differences in the definitions of the expression "civilized behavior," in paragraph 10, and the expression "proper behavior," in paragraph 11?
4. Several examples are included in paragraphs 20 and 21. What do these examples help the author illustrate?

POSSIBLE ANSWERS

Meaning and Purpose

1. Varied examples of violence are rape, murder, aggression, some sports, fire, child abuse, emotional abuse, and so on.
2. Answers to this question may depend upon your students' degree of social awareness; some examples are alcohol and drugs and firearms.
3. Historically, the "seats of power" include high-profile government positions and executive-level management positions. The expression describes any jobs that include the power to make serious, important, far-reaching decisions.
4. Throughout history women have been smaller than men in stature and musculature; they have therefore chosen verbal weaponry as a counterbalance (12).
5. The consequences of violent actions include fear of harming another person and worry about being in a dangerous position, physically.

Strategy

1. Sims gives a lexical, or dictionary, definition of violence in paragraph 4. She begins with this narrow but "official" definition before she extends the definition to a larger, and at the same time more specific, perspective.
2. Sims divides her definition into five sections, each with a subheading indicating that section's content. Because she wants to cover so much territory in her definition, from the "basic level" (6) to the "Threshold of Aggres-

sion" (30), the sections help organize her information and guide the reading.

3. "Civilized behavior" is behavior that keeps people living together in relative harmony and that most people in a society understand tacitly. "Proper behavior" is temporary behavior that is fitting, seeming, or right for the occasion.

4. These examples help the author to illustrate how women have become more assertive physically and emotionally by gaining a sense of strength.

Style

1. The journalistic anecdotes in the first two paragraphs are specific and interesting stories that grab readers' attention and ease them into the topic.

2. Sims has obviously done research on her subject. Her tone is academic and factual, and she quotes numerous authorities—as in paragraph 12—to back her assertions.

3. The pronoun *it* refers to "the portrayal or even glorification of violence in the media," earlier in the paragraph.

Style

1. Why do you think Sims begins her essay with two journalistic anecdotes?
2. What gives Sims authority to talk about women and violence? Where do you see this authority in the essay?
3. In paragraph 31, Sims says, "it can raise a person's 'comfort zone' of physical aggression." What does the pronoun *it* refer to in that clause?

Writing Tasks

1. A "working definition" is one that defines a word or a phrase simply, for a specific occasion. Your car may have an "automatic drive," which is the "working definition" for a torque-conversion unit that converts and transfers power from the engine to the drive wheels.

   Select a recent issue of a newsmagazine such as *Time, Newsweek, Insight, U.S. News & World Report,* or *The Economist.* Leaf through the issue, listing all references to violence. Then write a "working definition" of the word *violence,* followed by examples of violence from the newsmagazine that illustrate your definition.

2. Based on the readings in this chapter, write a short essay in which you define a "definition essay." Use the readings as examples, and organize your essay according to what you see as the range of elements in a definition essay.

❦ *Additional Writing Tasks* ❦
Definition

1. Write an essay that defines one of the following terms. Explore the subject beyond its dictionary meaning, using a variety of methods to develop your definition. As part of this or any extended definition, you can state what the subject *excludes* as a way to clarify your definition.
   a. humanity
   b. education
   c. Armageddon
   d. terror
   e. leadership
   f. honesty
   g. fad
   h. evil
   i. female liberation
   j. male liberation
   k. corruption
   l. intuition
   m. liberation theology
   n. social responsibility
   o. obsession
   p. team player
   q. sociopath
   r. maverick
   s. imagination
   t. tragedy
   u. confidence
   v. luck
   w. glamour
   x. scorched earth
   y. genocide
   z. blindsided

2. From the following list of seldom-used slang terms, select one and define it in several paragraphs. After you explain the term, create a situation in which it might apply, using the term in

several sample sentences as a speaker might. Also include current slang that has a similar meaning.
a.   hoodwink
b.   greenhorn
c.   whoopee
d.   scam
e.   boob
f.   folknik
g.   bamboozled
h.   boodle
i.   macho
j.   bonehead

3. As a representative of a student rights organization, you have accepted the responsibility to convince a campus grievance committee composed of students, faculty, and administrators that a sexual harassment policy should be adopted as official college policy. Your first task is to define "sexual harassment" and to illustrate at least three different ways it manifests itself in behavior.

4. a. You are an environmentalist living in a major metropolitan area. You have formed an action group committed to protect all the natural landscapes that still exist in your city, even to the point of taking militant action against developers. You have used the phrase "urban environmentalist" to describe people who think and act as you do. In an essay, define "urban environmentalists" and describe what developers can expect from them.

    b. A group of self-designated "urban environmentalists" are disrupting development in the city. They see themselves as saviors of natural settings that exist within the urban landscape, but you regard them as "environmental terrorists." In an essay, define "environmental terrorists" and predict what city officials can expect from them.

5. Look up the medical explanation of a debilitating ailment such as Alzheimer's disease, Down's syndrome, or Hodgkin's disease. Once you understand the medical terminology, write a definition essay that explains the disease to someone who has no background in medicine. Create a case study of a person who has the disease to further explain its debilitating effects.

9

Persuasion and Argument

Convincing a Reader

The Method

An argumentative essay is an attempt to change or reinforce someone's opinion or to move someone to take action. On the one hand, the essay may be emotionally charged, appealing to a reader's feelings with emotional detail and biased language. The writing is then called *persuasion* or *persuasive argument*. On the other hand, an argumentative essay may be highly rational, appealing to a reader's intellect with logical explanation. This writing is called *argument* or *logical argument*. Political writing relies heavily on persuasion, and scientific writing on argument. Rarely, however, does an argumentative essay appeal only to emotion or only to reason. Usually, writers appeal to both, striving to convince their readers that their position is valid.

Imagine that you want to convince your readers of the merits of a vegetarian diet. You might begin by appealing to reason. First, you might contrast the high cost of meat with the low cost of grains that provide comparable protein. Second, you might point out that the grains grown for animal feed would be better used to feed the world's hungry. You might continue by presenting the danger highly marbled meat poses to health. You might then shift the appeal to emotion. You might construct an emotional description of animals being raised in pens, relating examples of force feeding and chemical injections, and describing slaughterhouse procedures. While composing the essay, you would keep an eye on your readers, anticipating their responses to your appeals by asking yourself if you are being too emotional or even too rational.

Throughout an argumentative essay a writer must carefully balance reason and emotion. A writer whose essay is so self-righteous that it ignores reason or so rational that it ignores feelings will alienate most readers. A general rule to follow is that an argumentative essay should be primarily rational or it may fail to convince critical readers. Consequently, writers of effective arguments usually present their opinions persuasively but develop ample and strong evidence throughout their essays. This practice will impress upon readers that the writer is *ethical;* that is, a well-informed, reasonable person committed to his or her position—and, therefore, worthy of being believed.

Assertions and Evidence

An argumentative essay is predicated on an *assertion;* that is, the opinion you want a reader to accept or an action you want your reader to take. When stated in a sentence the assertion is referred to as a *proposition* or *thesis:* "The high-fashion fur industry should be curtailed"; "The state should resume capital punishment"; "Magazines featuring nudity, such as *Playboy, Penthouse,* and *Playgirl,* should be banned from community magazine stands." The writer then supports the proposition with evidence.

It is the quality of evidence that persuades the reader to agree with an assertion and reject an opposing assertion. Keep in mind that the evidence writers use in an argumentative essay is the same as that any of us uses in oral arguments: personal experience, the experience of others, and authoritative sources.

First, personal experience can be used to support a proposition. Suppose you wanted to develop the argument that police are harassing college-age drivers. You, yourself, have had first-hand experience. Several times a patrol car has pulled you over while you were driving near campus. Each time an officer initiated a search of your car. Once one even required you to take a field sobriety test, which you passed. At none of these times did any officer issue a traffic citation. These personal experiences could serve as legitimate evidence to support your opinion.

Second, the experience of others can also be used as evidence to support an argument. You might narrate a story of a friend who had a similar experience. You might also include observations by a passenger or bystander to corroborate your friend's experience. When using the experience of others, do all you can to be sure that the information is accurate. You know how accurate a description of your experience is because you lived it, but when you use the experience of others, you are, in effect, vouching for its veracity. It is wise, therefore, to include more than one account of the same event.

Finally, authoritative sources can also be used to support an opinion. An argument gains its strength from the quality of authoritative evidence a writer can marshal. You can develop some authoritative information yourself. Once again consider the argument supporting the proposition that police are harassing college-age drivers. To support your opinion even more thoroughly, you might research police records. If the research revealed that police stopped and searched a significantly larger number of college-age drivers than older drivers, than you would use the information as evidence.

Sometimes, however, you must rely on other authoritative sources, such as encyclopedias, dictionaries, handbooks, digests, journals, and scientific research as well as people who are recognized as having extensive knowledge about a subject. When citing knowledgeable people to support an argument, be sure their expertise is in the subject you are discussing. It will not do your argument much good to quote a well-known nuclear physicist's opinion on gun control; your reader won't accept that specialist's word as authoritative.

Facts and statistics from authoritative sources can lend a great deal of credibility to any argument. Facts are irrefutable. No matter what the source, a fact is a fact: The Earth revolves around the sun. John F. Kennedy, the thirty-fifth president of the United States, was assassinated on November 22, 1963. When facts are corroborated by statistics, they exert a powerful influence on a reader. The United States has more homicides each year than Japan, Taiwan, and the combined countries of Western Europe. But what does this statistical fact mean? Should the government execute all convicted murderers? Do we need stricter handgun laws? Should every citizen arm for self-protection? Answering these questions involves interpretations of fact based on personal feelings and beliefs—that is, it involves opinions.

Strategies

Writers of argumentative essays will use any rhetorical method that is appropriate to their presentations: narration, description, examples, comparison and contrast, cause and effect, process analysis, and definition. Generally, however, effective argumentative essays do have five elements:

1. A clear statement of the writer's assertion;
2. An orderly presentation of the evidence;
3. A clear connection between the evidence and the argument;

4. A reasonable refutation of evidence that is counter to the writer's assertion;
5. A conclusion that emphasizes the assertion.

No doubt the most important of these elements is clear presentation of the evidence. To be convincing, evidence in an argumentative essay must be arranged in logical sequence or readers will reject the writer's conclusion. When composing an argument, writers reason from evidence to a conclusion through one of two processes: induction or deduction.

Inductive Reasoning

Through *inductive reasoning* writers accumulate enough specific evidence to justify a *general conclusion*. In other words, inductive reasoning moves from the *specific* to the *general*. While growing up we all learned to use induction. A child may bite into a hard green apple and discover that it tastes bitter. When the child tastes a hard green pear, he finds that it, too, is bitter. At another time the child bites into a hard green plum and an apricot. Both are bitter. By induction, he draws the general conclusion that hard green fruit is bitter and should not be eaten.

Argumentative essays written with inductive reasoning follow a similar pattern but with one difference: they usually begin with a *hypothesis* or question that embodies the conclusion the writer wants the reader to accept as valid. To argue that a city named Glenwood is environmentally responsible, a writer will have to present evidence that leads directly to that conclusion.

Hypothesis: Glenwood is an environmentally responsible city. (or: Is Glenwood an environmentally responsible city?)

Evidence: Glenwood has instituted these environmental programs:
Curbside recycling for glass, newspaper, aluminum, and plastics;
Disposal of household toxic waste;

Law prohibiting release of ozone-depleting chlo-
rofluorocarbons from air conditioners;
Refuse landfill designed to protect ground water
from toxic pollution and to generate methane
gas;
A wetlands bird habitat preserved as open space.
Conclusion: Glenwood is environmentally responsible.

Conclusions drawn from the inductive reasoning procedure
are usually referred to as *probable conclusions,* or *inferences,*
for they are reached with incomplete evidence. The reader's acceptance of a conclusion that follows from inductive reasoning is
often referred to as the *inductive leap.* To establish a clear connection between the evidence and the conclusion, you must be
sure that the evidence you present is *relevant, sufficient,* and
representative.

To be relevant, the evidence must support the hypothesis and
contribute directly to the conclusion. To be sufficient, the evidence must amply support the conclusion. And to be representative, the evidence must represent the full range of information
related to the hypothesis, not just one side or the other. By following these criteria, a writer increases the probability that the conclusion is valid, thus bridging the distance from evidence to
conclusion and making the reader's passage easier.

Deductive Reasoning

Deductive reasoning is the opposite of inductive reasoning.
Deductive reasoning moves from general assumptions, called
premises, to a specific conclusion that follows from the general
premises. In formal logic, this deductive instrument is called a
syllogism, a form of organization that includes a *major premise,* a
minor premise and a *necessary conclusion,* one that is the logical
result of the two premises. The classic example of syllogistic form
comes down to us from Aristotle:

Major premise: All humans are mortal.
Minor premise: Socrates is human.
Conclusion: Therefore, Socrates is mortal.

The conclusion of a syllogism is always drawn from the major and minor premises, both of which must be accurate for the conclusion to be accurate. If the premises are drawn from relevant, sufficient, and representative evidence—the same criteria used to draw sound conclusions in inductive reasoning—the conclusion of a syllogism will probably be accurate. But syllogisms can be illogical. An inaccurate major premise may make the syllogism illogical:

Major premise: Professional gamblers carry large quantities of cash and drive expensive cars.
Minor premise: John Murphy is a professional gambler.
Conclusion: Therefore, John Murphy must carry large quantities of cash and drive an expensive car.

The major premise is inaccurate. Ask yourself, Are all professional gamblers successful enough to have large quantities of cash on their person and drive expensive cars? Because the major premise is inaccurate the conclusion is inaccurate.

Sometimes the language of a syllogism is deceptive. Consider the use of "good American," "accept," and "change" in this flawed syllogism.

Major premise: Every good American accepts the United States Constitution.
Minor premise: Martin Luther King did not accept the United States Constitution because he worked to change it.
Conclusion: Therefore, Martin Luther King was not a good American.

The phrase "good American" is vague, too vague to describe a class of people accurately. What do "accept" and "change" mean in this context? The United States Constitution has provisions for change. In fact, it has been amended many times. Anyone who accepts the Constitution accepts the possibility of changing it. Because language is used deceptively in the premises, the conclusion is meaningless.

Sometimes a syllogism is illogical because it is constructed improperly. First, examine this properly constructed syllogism:

Major premise: All artists rely on intuition.

In a properly constructed syllogism, the subject of the major premise, in this example "artists," must appear in the minor premise and be narrowed.

Minor premise: John is an artist.

The conclusion then follows necessarily from the major and minor premises.

Conclusion: Therefore, John relies on intuition.

This syllogism is properly constructed and is valid. Now examine this invalid syllogism:

Major premise: All artists rely on intuition.
Minor premise: All psychics rely on intuition.
Conclusion: Therefore, all psychics are artists.

This syllogism is improperly constructed because the minor premise does not repeat the subject of the major premise. The conclusion, therefore, is invalid.

Like inductive reasoning, deductive reasoning can help organize an argument. But using deduction is never quite as simple as the skeletal form of syllogisms used to illustrate it.

Imagine that the Sierra Club has established a *representative sample* of environmentally responsible cities. By extensive inductive reasoning, the Sierra Club finds several cities, including Glenwood, from our previous example, operating effective environmental programs. Based on its analysis of these programs, the Sierra Club defines the environmentally responsible city. A syllogism showing that a city is environmentally responsible might be constructed in this sequence:

Major premise: Cities with ecologically beneficial programs for disposal of waste, conservation of energy, and preservation of open space are environmentally responsible.

Minor premise: San Lorenzo has ecologically beneficial programs for disposal of waste, conservation of energy, and preservation of open space.

Conclusion: Therefore, San Lorenzo is environmentally responsible.

In an argumentative essay, a syllogism seldom appears in such clear form, but often its deductive structure is embedded in an argumentative essay. If a writer wanted to argue that San Lorenzo is environmentally responsible, he or she might first construct a syllogism such as the one above, analyze the evidence needed to support the proposition, and then arrange the argument, incorporating syllogistic reasoning in the structure.

In the first section of the essay, the writer would address the questions raised in the major premise.

1. What is an ecologically beneficial program for disposing of waste?
2. What is an ecologically beneficial program for conserving energy?
3. What is an ecologically beneficial program for preserving open space?

To answer these questions would take several paragraphs, and the writer would have to rely on the authority of the Sierra Club's definition. An ecologically beneficial program for disposing of waste would probably require recycling usable trash, disposing of toxic waste, and stringent restrictions on use of landfills. An ecologically beneficial program for conserving energy would probably mean reducing use of automobiles to save fuel and increasing use of solar energy to save electricity. An ecologically beneficial program for preserving open space would probably include protection for unique land formations and wildlife habitats. This discussion would be rather broad because the definition is based on a representative sample of many cities that may vary dramatically in size and geographic location.

To develop the second section of the essay, the writer would address the questions raised by the minor premise:

1. What specific actions has San Lorenzo taken to implement an ecologically beneficial waste-disposal program?
2. What specific actions has San Lorenzo taken to implement ecologically beneficial programs for conserving energy?
3. What specific actions has San Lorenzo taken to implement an ecologically beneficial program for preserving open space?

The purpose of this section is to present evidence that San Lorenzo does indeed meet the definition of environmentally responsible cities. In this section, which would also require several paragraphs to fully develop, the writer would present as evidence the specific environmental programs San Lorenzo has implemented, thus demonstrating the validity of the syllogism's minor premise.

In the last section of the essay, by far the shortest, the writer would conclude that San Lorenzo is an environmentally responsible city. The writer might choose to summarize the key points of the argument, but here the force of deductive reasoning would be irresistible, making it unnecessary to rearticulate the argument in abbreviated form. But whether to develop a conclusion fully or to leave it implied is the decision of the writer, who is responsible for the argument's coherence and consistency. Risks lie in both strategies.

Logical Fallacies in Writing

Logical fallacies are common mistakes in reasoning, and an argument tainted by them is ineffective. The word *fallacy* means "deception," or "a fault in reasoning." Fallacies deceive by distorting the truth and making logical conclusions unattainable. Using fallacies consciously signifies dishonesty; using them inadvertently demonstrates muddled thinking.

Study this list of eight most common fallacies. Remember that writers must scrutinize their arguments to avoid slipping into fallacious reasoning.

Overgeneralization: Writers overgeneralize when they draw a conclusion from insufficient or unrepresentative evidence.

> During the last year three of five award-winning films concentrated on family violence. An examination of family violence was just broadcast on national television. No doubt these events indicate that family violence is on the rise.

A handful of films and a television program do not constitute a trend. The conclusion that family violence is rising could be substantiated with statistics and reports from authorities such as psychologists, sociologists, and law-enforcement officers.

Oversimplification: To oversimplify is to ignore essential information from which a conclusion is drawn. Be careful to avoid this fallacy when writing about complicated subjects. You might become too eager to offer a simple explanation to a complicated problem.

> The problems of air pollution, ozone depletion, and global warming are not really problems at all. They are

merely manifestations of our educational system. We have too many scientists working in universities with nothing to do but study our environment.

Faulty either/or reasoning: The either/or fallacy is a type of oversimplification in which a writer assumes only two alternatives, black or white, when there are others, including gray. The slogan, "America, love it or leave it," implies that love of country must be unqualified, which has the effect of excluding constructive criticism.

> Everyone would agree that America is being severely damaged by the sale and use of illegal drugs. The only two courses of action are these: the country's leaders can ignore the problem, or they can enforce the law to its maximum limits.

Of course, other actions are possible—initiate public education, fund rehabilitation for former drug users, develop agreements with other countries to curtail manufacturing of drugs, and even legalize use of drugs. The choice is not between doing nothing or joining a law-and-order crusade.

***Post hoc* argument**:   The complete Latin phrase is *post hoc, ergo propter hoc,* which means "after this, therefore because of this." The assumption in this fallacious argument is that one event causes another event simply because the second follows the first in time.

> For more than a year, I have been meditating nightly for one hour. Although I usually have the flu at least once each year, I didn't have it last year. No doubt the meditation prevented me from catching the flu.

As stated, the only relationship between meditation and catching the flu is that one followed the other. Other explanations could be found: perhaps that year had no flu epidemic, or perhaps the person was lucky enough to avoid a deadly sneeze. Time sequence alone cannot prove that a cause-and-effect relationship applies.

Non sequitur: In Latin, *non sequitur* means "it does not follow." A *non sequitur* is a conclusion that does not logically follow from its premises.

> The city in this county that has the most crime also has the highest-paid police force. The city with the least crime has the lowest-paid police force. It does not make sense for our city to pay higher salaries to our police when doing so will not reduce crime.

The reasons for high crime rates are many, a high incidence of poverty being one of them. But we doubt that high police salaries contribute to a rising crime rate. In fact, dangerous working conditions could lead to higher wages for police.

False analogy: Someone using a false analogy assumes that if two things are similar in one or more characteristics, then they are similar in other characteristics.

> We should not forget the lessons of Grenada and Panama, when our leaders tried to negotiate settlements and failed. Once we sent in the Marines, peace and a working relationship were restored. The best way to deal with renegade countries who act against our interests is to invade them to show other hostile governments we will not be bullied.

We are not living in the same world we lived in even five years ago. The break-up of communist-bloc countries, the danger of renegade terrorist action, the proliferation of nuclear weapons, all make the international scene too complex for rash action based on a false analogy.

Ad hominem argument: When a writer attacks a person associated with an issue rather than the argument supporting the issue, then the writer is committing an *ad hominem* fallacy, which in Latin means "to the man."

> Councilman Hunt has made a strong argument against raising the gasoline tax for revenue to build more roads. Why shouldn't he? He takes the bus to work each day, and he has the money to fly to any part of the country where he might want to vacation.

This statement ignores the argument for a tax increase and concentrates instead on the person making the argument.

Association fallacy: To commit the association fallacy is to claim that an act or belief is worthy or unworthy simply because of the people associated with it.

> Congressman Will is supported by some of Hollywood's leading figures. Because actors, directors, and producers know talent when they see it, you should support Congressman Will too.

Do Hollywood figures know any more about the qualities necessary to serve as an effective congressman than most other voters?

Argument in College Writing

Often you will be asked to take a position and convince a reader of its validity. In the next example, Rhonda Burris responds to an assignment in a mass-communications class. Her task is to convince a reader that movies featuring characters who smoke should carry a warning much like the one the law requires cigarette companies to place in magazine advertisements. She leads her reader to the general conclusion, which she states directly in the closing paragraph.

The opening is indirect but interesting. It ends with the author's hypothesis: films that feature appealing actors smoking may encourage viewers to smoke.

Among college students Humphrey Bogart is still a popular actor. Films he starred in, such as The Maltese Falcon, The Harder They Fall, and To Have and Have Not still flicker every weekend in fraternity houses and dormitories across America. Just last Saturday my college sponsored a Bogart film retrospective. Probably for the fifteenth time in my life, I watched Casablanca, a film that could be classified as a cult favorite. It has become more romantic each time I view it, capturing an exotic place and time, featuring mysterious supporting characters, and concentrating on the dilemma the beautiful heroine faces when trying to decide between two men who love her, a political idealist and a world-weary cynic, whom Bogart plays. Bogart is suave, his style dominating the film, but during this viewing I saw something I had not noticed before: No actor could handle a cigarette better than Bogart. Hanging from the corner of his mouth as he talks or held between two fingers as he drinks, the burning cigarette is part of the suave image Bogart projects to the viewer. The truth that is not part of the image is that he died, at the relatively young age of fifty-eight, of lung cancer. Toward the end of the film, I asked myself how many people Bogart's suave handling of a cigarette influenced in their decision to smoke?

Specific examples illustrate how one cigarette manufacturer associates its products with appealing actors. The assumption is that if Phillip Morris is willing

Apparently the power of association to influence someone's decision to smoke has not been lost on cigarette manufacturers. Recently the Phillip Morris Company, the people who sell such popular brands as Benson and Hedges ("For people who love to smoke"), Virginia Slims ("You've come *to pay producers to feature Lark and Marlboro, then the association must have some influence on viewers.*

a long way, Baby"), and Merit ("For those who want marital bliss") paid $350,000 to have secret agent 007 James Bond smoke Lark Cigarettes in License to Kill. Why? Many young men, Phillip Morris seems to believe, are too immature to make the obvious connection between smoking and death, and so they make the ridiculous connection between smoking and the adventurous life James Bond leads, even though that life is only a movie life, not a real one.

A couple of years earlier, it was the Phillip Morris Company who paid $42,000 to have Lois Lane smoke Marlboro cigarettes in Superman II. The payment went unnoticed until one movie critic raised the question that if characterization of Lois Lane required that she smoke, why feature a brand of cigarette so prominently? Now the answer is clear. Phillip Morris must have been counting on the power of association even then. Will every immature young woman who sees Superman II come to believe that if she smokes Marlboro cigarettes, sooner or later her own Man of Steel will arrive? Probably not consciously, but the subconscious might associate smoking and sex appeal. What more could a cigarette advertiser expect?

The reader is led to conclude that if viewers are warned that some films are violent then they should also be warned that smoking, an established health hazard, is also featured.

Movies are rated according to who should be allowed to see them. The National Coalition on Television Violence discovered that cigarette smoking appears in 100 percent of PG-13 films, which are approved for people over thirteen who have parental permission to view them. Clearly, young people who attend films (what young people do not?) are exposed to actors smoking in varied situations and from various stations in life. Even if they come from families who do not smoke, they are exposed to powerful images that show smoking as accepted behavior. But where is the warning that smoking is hazardous to health?

The writer draws a parallel between cigarette advertisements in magazines and indirect advertisements in movies. The reader will reasonably conclude that both should carry health warnings.

Cigarette advertisements have been banned from television and radio. When they appear in magazines, cigarette advertisements must by law include the Surgeon General's warning that smoking can result in cancer, heart disease, or fetal injury in pregnant women. This requirement is a sensible public-health policy, but where does such a warning appear in films that feature characters who smoke? Clearly one cigarette manufacturer believes that by associating its cigarettes with appealing characters it will influence a person's decision to smoke. Why else would Phillip Morris pay movie producers to feature their products?

Burris concludes with an emotional allusion to Bogart's death.

The practice of featuring characters who smoke in films is disturbing enough, but when cigarette manufacturers actually pay to have their brands featured in a film, the practice goes beyond being disturbing to being criminal. It is time government put a stop to this kind of indirect advertising, or at the very least, require that films featuring characters who smoke announce the dangers of smoking before the plot begins. Then the next time someone watches Humphrey Bogart raise a glass, squint through a cloud of cigarette smoke at Ingrid Bergman, and say, "Here's looking at you, Kid," the viewer will not concentrate on the romantic image but on the excruciating pain Bogart must have felt while dying of lung cancer.

Rhonda Burris begins her argument indirectly by discussing Humphrey Bogart. She refers to *Casablanca,* one of Bogart's most popular movies, and creates an impression of the suave Bogart style. In the closing sentences she sets up her hypothesis by revealing that Bogart, usually portrayed with a cigarette in hand, died of lung cancer. She maintains that films that feature appealing actors smoking may influence viewers by leading them to smoke.

In paragraphs 2 and 3, Burris develops her argument with examples of the Phillip Morris Company actually paying to have its cigarettes prominently displayed in films. The goal, she argues, is to associate its products with appealing characters, hoping that the association will benefit sales. In paragraph 4, Burris presents an interesting observation: movies are evaluated for the violence they display, but nothing is done to warn viewers that smoking, a clear hazard to health, is displayed in appealing ways. At the end of the paragraph she raises a question that echoes her conclusion: "Where is the warning that smoking is hazardous to health?"

In paragraph 5, Burris points out something we all know: cigarette advertisements in magazines must carry the Surgeon General's warning, a sensible public-health policy. Burris's reasoning clearly leads us to one conclusion. In the final paragraph, Burris completes the inductive sequence and states her thesis: "It's time the government put a stop to this kind of indirect advertising, or at the very least, require that films featuring characters who smoke announce the dangers of smoking before the plot begins." She closes with an emotional reference to *Casablanca* and Bogart's painful death from lung cancer.

❦ Ron Karpati ❦

Ron Karpati is a pediatrician involved in cancer research. Born in Los Angeles, California, in 1961, he did his undergraduate studies at the University of California, Los Angeles, and then attended UCLA Medical School. He did his medical residency at Children's Hospital of Los Angeles. The essay reprinted here reflects his views about the use of animals in medical research. Employed by the National Cancer Institute in Bethesda, Maryland, he did research on using the body's immune system to fight cancer, known as the "immunotherapy" of cancer. In 1991 he became a clinical fellow at the University of California at San Francisco, where he works in pediatric oncology and transplantation of bone marrow.

A Scientist:
"I Am the Enemy"

A physician reacting against animal-rights activists, Karpati attempts to convince the reader of the need for animal research. In this essay, first published in Newsweek's *"My Turn" column in December 1989, he uses both factual information and emotional appeals to rouse the "apathetic majority" to action.*

I am the enemy! One of those vilified, inhumane physician-scientists involved in animal research. How strange, for I have never thought of myself as an evil person. I became a pediatrician because of my love for children and my desire to keep them healthy. During medical school and residency, however, I saw many children die of leukemia, prematurity and traumatic injury—circumstances against which medicine has made tremendous progress, but still has far to go. More important, I also saw children, alive and healthy, thanks to advances in medical science such as infant respirators, potent antibiotics, new surgical

TEACHING SUGGESTIONS

This essayist argues against the radical side of recently debated questions. Should we become more aware of the arguments used by a radical group within a larger group, and should we more actively examine our own opinions about whether or not to use animals in medical research and scientific experimentation? In fact we "use" animals in many ways without thinking about their comfort or possible death.

A fruitful way to begin the discussion is with such provocative questions as "Should animals be captured, trained, and caged for the pleasure of circus audiences?" "Should seeing-eye dogs have their movements severely limited so that they can function as guides for the blind?" "Should chicks be dyed and sold as Easter gifts?" "Should sled-dog races be banned?" "Should people who want dogs and cats as pets be required to have a psychological evaluation before being permitted to have those pets?"

Can some animals be used for scientific research? Can some human beings better the world by doing scientific research that involves animals? These are the questions to ask after the class has established that the world of morality has more gray than first meets the eye.

MARGINAL NOTES

Karpati starts not with a declaration but with an exclamation. But then we see that he does not subscribe to his "confession"; he feels slandered, "vilified."

A chronic or acute disease causing unrestrained growth of white blood corpuscles. The patient develops anemia, infections, and fatigue, among other symptoms. An infant born at any time before completing the thirty-seventh week of gestation (time from conception to birth) is premature. *Trauma* is a physical injury or wound caused by external force or violence.

1

techniques and the entire field of organ transplantation. My desire to tip the scales in favor of the healthy, happy children drew me to medical research.

My accusers claim that I inflict torture on animals for the sole purpose of career advancement. My experiments supposedly have no relevance to medicine and are easily replaced by computer simulation. Meanwhile, an apathetic public barely watches, convinced that the issue has no significance, and publicity-conscious politicians increasingly give way to the demands of the activists.

We in medical research have also been unconscionably apathetic. We have allowed the most extreme animal-rights protesters to seize the initiative and frame the issue as one of "animal fraud." We have been complacent in our belief that a knowledgeable public would sense the importance of animal research to the public health. Perhaps we have been mistaken in not responding to the emotional tone of the argument created by those sad posters of animals by waving equally sad posters of children dying of leukemia or cystic fibrosis.

Much is made of the pain inflicted on these animals in the name of medical science. The animal-rights activists contend that this is evidence of our malevolent and sadistic nature. A more reasonable argument, however, can be advanced in our defense. Life is often cruel, both to animals and human beings. Teenagers get thrown from the back of a pickup truck and suffer severe head injuries. Toddlers, barely able to walk, find themselves at the bottom of a swimming pool while a parent checks the mail. Physicians hoping to alleviate the pain and suffering these tragedies cause have but three choices: create an animal model of the injury or disease and use that model to understand the process and test new therapies; experiment on human beings—some experiments will succeed, most will fail—or finally, leave medical knowledge static, hoping that accidental discoveries will lead us to the advances.

Some animal-rights activists would suggest a fourth choice, claiming that computer models can simulate animal experiments, thus making the actual experiments unnecessary. Computers can simulate, reasonably well, the effects of well-understood princi-

Notice the radically opposite points of view in the last sentence in paragraph 1 and sentence 1 in paragraph 2.

Karpati distinguishes three groups in paragraph 2: his group, the activist-accusers' group, and the apathetic-public group.

"Animal fraud" is an example of emotive speech used to persuade an audience by appealing to its emotions.

"cystic fibrosis": An inherited, incurable disease that affects the pancreas, respiratory system, and sweat glands.

Paralleling the triangle in paragraph 2 comes this triangle of debatable choices: test on animal models of injuries, test on human beings, or hope for accidental medical discoveries.

Karpati anticipates and rejects the fourth choice, offering his argument against it.

ples on complex systems, as in the application of the laws of physics to airplane and automobile design. However, when the principles themselves are in question, as is the case with the complex biological systems under study, computer modeling alone is of little value.

One of the terrifying effects of the effort to restrict the use of animals in medical research is that the impact will not be felt for years and decades: drugs that might have been discovered will not be; surgical techniques that might have been developed will not be, and fundamental biological processes that might have been understood will remain mysteries. There is the danger that politically expedient solutions will be found to placate a vocal minority, while the consequences of those decisions will not be apparent until long after the decisions are made and the decision makers forgotten.

Fortunately, most of us enjoy good health, and the trauma of watching one's child die has become a rare experience. Yet our good fortune should not make us unappreciative of the health we enjoy or the advances that make it possible. Vaccines, antibiotics, insulin and drugs to treat heart disease, hypertension and stroke are all based on animal research. Most complex surgical procedures, such as coronary-artery bypass and organ transplantation, are initially developed in animals. Presently undergoing animal studies are techniques to insert genes in humans in order to replace the defective ones found to be the cause of so much disease. These studies will effectively end if animal research is severely restricted.

In America today, death has become an event isolated from our daily existence—out of the sight and thoughts of most of us. As a doctor who has watched many children die, and their parents grieve, I am particularly angered by people capable of so much compassion for a dog or a cat, but with seemingly so little for a dying human being. These people seem so insulated from the reality of human life and death and what it means.

Make no mistake, however: I am not advocating the needlessly cruel treatment of animals. To the extent that the animal-rights movement has made us more aware of the needs of these

6

7 This is the status quo or "existing-condition" argument, which says that many of us now enjoy good health because of animal research.

8 In this paragraph he argues for compassion. Animals and human beings die, but some human beings live because some animals die.

9 Karpati attempts to dispose his audience toward his argument by pointing out that not everyone in the animal-rights movement is his

accuser. On the contrary, the movement itself has done much good work. The fact remains that the more radical members of the movement might get their way.

With this question, he urges the audience to action.

animals, and made us search harder for suitable alternatives, they have made a significant contribution. But if the more radical members of this movement are successful in limiting further research, their efforts will bring about a tragedy that will cost many lives. The real question is whether an apathetic majority can be aroused to protect its future against a vocal, but misdirected, minority.

POSSIBLE ANSWERS

Meaning and Purpose

1. Let students articulate their own opinions about animals used in research. Karpati, of course, does not believe that he is an "inhumane physician-scientist."
2. Karpati is not very tolerant of the extremists' opinion against using animals in medical research. He says activists misunderstand him and might succeed in their efforts to restrict animal research (2). Karpati says he is "particularly angered by people capable of so much compassion for a dog or a cat, but with seemingly so little for a dying human being" (8). He calls the activists' success "a tragedy that will cost many lives," and the activists themselves a "misdirected minority" (9).
3. He specifies the kind of activist in the animal-rights movement whom he argues against (3). He compliments many activists for the good they have done (9).
4. "Insulated" means placed in a detached situation. In this sentence it means such people are not in touch with "the reality of human life and death," and that they shut themselves off from understanding "what it means."
5. The first sentence of paragraph 2 implies that Karpati himself uses animals for medical research.

Meaning and Purpose

1. Do you agree or disagree with the animal-rights activist opinion that Karpati declares in the first two sentences? Why or why not?
2. How tolerant is Karpati of the animal-rights activist opinion that he presents in the first two sentences? What does he think might happen if the activists are successful? Support your answers with statements from the essay.
3. How do you know that Karpati is not totally against the animal-rights movement?
4. Paragraph 8 has a sentence that says people seem "insulated from the reality of human life and death and what it means." Define "insulated" as it is used in that sentence.
5. Can you find a sentence implying that Karpati himself uses animals for experiments relevant to medicine?

Strategy

1. What is one of Karpati's arguments for using animals in medical research?
2. What is one of the animal-rights activists' arguments against using animals for medical research?
3. Does Karpati appeal mainly to emotion or reason in his argument? Find statements that illustrate his appeal.

4. What kind of evidence does Karpati offer to support his argument: personal experience, the experience of others, or authoritative sources? Is his choice effective for his argument?

Style

1. How do animal-rights activists give a strongly emotional tone to their argument against experimentation?
2. Modern essayists often follow a classical arrangement including a part called *explicatio,* in which they define terms and explain issues. Why aren't the issues explained thoroughly in Karpati's essay?
3. What is the effect on readers of Karpati's describing himself as the enemy in the first two sentences?

Writing Tasks

1. Whether you subscribe to this viewpoint or not, take the position of animal-rights activists against Karpati. Write an essay in response to "A Scientist: 'I Am the Enemy'" arguing against using animals in research. Be sure you respond to each of Karpati's arguments first.
2. Write a brief dramatic dialogue with an argument between two people: one is an animal-rights activist who has just toured a research lab where conditions for the animals are cruel, appalling. The other person is the parent of a child who is about to have surgery for a life-or-death ailment, a procedure that was made possible by animal research.

Strategy

1. One argument is that "vaccines, antibiotics, insulin and drugs to treat heart disease, hypertension and stroke are based on animal research" (7).
2. One argument is sentence 1 in paragraph 4.
3. Karpati appeals mostly to reason when he says that stopping animal research will mean that drugs and surgical procedures will not be discovered (6), that much in medicine now is based on animal research (7), and that using computers instead of animals is often inadequate (5). Some of his words are emotional, such as "terrifying effects" (6) and "a tragedy" (9), but overall he appeals to reason.
4. Karpati's evidence is experience—"I also saw children alive and healthy, thanks to advances in medical science such as infant respirators, potent antibiotics, new surgical techniques and the entire field of organ transplantation" (1). He is an authoritative source because he is a physician-scientist.

Style

1. The emotional tone is apparent in description ("malevolent and sadistic nature"), in waving "sad posters of animals," and in accusing Karpati of inflicting "torture on animals."
2. The issues are not explained thoroughly for at least two reasons: (1) Most of the public has already heard of the issues, even though they are probably not "familiar" with them in any depth. (2) Karpati argues against radical animal-rights advocates more than he argues the animal-rights issue.
3. The first two sentences grab readers because the language is emotional and startling. First Karpati castigates himself as activists do, then he defends himself. His accusers cannot say worse of him than he's said of himself; the technique undermines their argument.

❦ Willard Gaylin ❦

A practicing psychiatrist and psychoanalyst, Willard Gaylin is also a prolific writer. He was born in Cleveland, Ohio, in 1925 and studied at Harvard University and Columbia University. He has been a professor and supervising psychoanalyst at Columbia University and a visiting lecturer at colleges and universities throughout the United States and in Paris. He has written several books on psychiatry and the law, including The Killing of Bonnie Garland: A Question of Justice *(1982), in which he raises questions about the insanity defense as it was used in the case of a Yale University student who was murdered by her boyfriend. Gaylin has contributed numerous articles to both scholarly journals and general-interest periodicals such as* Harper's, The Atlantic, Saturday Review, The New York Times, *and* The Washington Post.

What You See Is the Real You

In this article from the October 7, 1977, issue of The New York Times, *Gaylin argues against the idea that in each of us is an "inner person," who may be very different from the "outer person." He points out ways in which this theory can be used to absolve people of responsibility.*

TEACHING SUGGESTIONS

In paragraph 1, Gaylin quotes Father Flanagan as saying he "never met a bad boy." You might want to discuss this quotation with the class. Have members of the class ever met a "bad boy"? If so, what are the characteristics that make a "bad boy"? On the other hand, can members of the class name a noted living person who is "good"? If so, what are the characteristics that make that person "good"?

The characteristics of the "bad boy" and the "good person" will undoubtedly be based on observable behavior. You might ask if it is possible to misjudge a person by his or her observed behavior. Perhaps some will suggest that we should not judge unless we know that person's motives and circumstances or psychological health, which may have been influenced by any number of experiences.

Such a discussion should serve as reasonable preparation for Gaylin's essay. He argues simply that probing for the psychological inner person may be informative, but that insights gleaned in such a way should not be used alone as excuses for observable behavior.

MARGINAL NOTES

Edward Joseph Flanagan (1886–1948), a Roman Catholic clergyman born in Roscommon, Ireland, founded Boys' Town in Nebraska (1917), a home for wayward boys. Here the boys live in a democratic environment. Gaylin quickly distinguishes between Flanagan's outlook and his own, demeaning neither.

It was, I believe, the distinguished Nebraska financier Father Edward J. Flanagan who professed to having "never met a bad boy." Having, myself, met a remarkable number of bad boys, it might seem that either our experiences were drastically different or we were using the word "bad" differently. I suspect neither is true, but rather that the Father was appraising the "inner man," while I, in fact, do not acknowledge the existence of inner people. 1

Since we psychoanalysts have unwittingly contributed to this confusion, let one, at least, attempt a small rectifying effort. Psy- 2

534

choanalytic data—which should be viewed as supplementary information—are, unfortunately, often viewed as alternative (and superior) explanation. This has led to the prevalent tendency to think of the "inner" man as the real man and the outer man as an illusion or pretender.

While psychoanalysis supplies us with an incredibly useful tool for explaining the motives and purposes underlying human behavior, most of this has little bearing on the moral nature of that behavior.

Like roentgenology, psychoanalysis is a fascinating, but relatively new, means of illuminating the person. But few of us are prepared to substitute an X-ray of Grandfather's head for the portrait that hangs in the parlor. The inside of the man represents another view, not a truer one. A man may not always be what he appears to be, but what he appears to be is always a significant part of what he is. A man is the sum total of *all* his behavior. To probe for unconscious determinants of behavior and then define *him* in their terms exclusively, ignoring his overt behavior altogether, is a greater distortion than ignoring the unconscious completely.

Kurt Vonnegut has said, "You are what you pretend to be," which is simply another way of saying, you are what we (all of us) perceive you to be, not what you think you are.

Consider for a moment the case of the ninety-year-old man on his deathbed (surely the Talmud must deal with this?) joyous and relieved over the success of his deception. For ninety years he has shielded his evil nature from public observation. For ninety years he has affected courtesy, kindness, and generosity—suppressing all the malice he knew was within him while he calculatedly and artificially substituted grace and charity. All his life he had been fooling the world into believing he was a good man. This "evil" man will, I predict, be welcomed into the Kingdom of Heaven.

Similarly, I will not be told that the young man who earns his pocket money by mugging old ladies is "really" a good boy. Even my generous and expansive definition of goodness will not accommodate that particular form of self-advancement.

Those who investigate mental processes and treat neuroses and other disorders of the mind, using methods developed by Freud, Jung, and others. Gaylin says their data supplement rather than replace other explanations, but many still cherish the "inner-man" view.

3 Social scientists often use this expression to mean "norms that govern social behavior in a group or society." Gaylin implies later that the idea carries a nonnegotiable code of religion-inspired ethics.

4 Gaylin refers to a person as a *Gestalt,* an organized whole in which the parts, though distinguishable, are interdependent, yet the whole has some characteristics independent of the parts.

5 Kurt Vonnegut (born 1922) is the author of *Cat's Cradle* (1963) and *Slaughterhouse-Five; or The Children's Crusade* (1969), among other works.

6 A compilation of Jewish oral law and rabbinical teachings separate from the Hebrew Bible, or Old Testament. It includes the *Aggada,* which is devoted to legends and stories.

7

The argument here hinges on this word's meaning "in reality," a notion that what you see is not necessarily what is. Gaylin argues that the exterior is indeed the reality.

"psychohistories": Of American coinage, this word means studying historical people and events by applying psychological theories and methods. "egalitarianism": The belief that all people should have equal political, social, and economic rights; Gaylin includes in context the notion that all people "at heart" are equally good and bad.

Francis of Assisi (1182–1226) renounced his wealth, consecrated himself to poverty, gathered a few companions, and founded the Franciscan order. He was canonized by Pope Gregory IX in 1228.

The Oedipus complex is the allegedly universal sexual desire of the son for the mother and his sexual conflict with the father figure.

Attila (406?–453), King of the Huns, was known as "the Scourge of God."

It does not count that beneath the rough exterior he has a heart—or, for that matter, an entire innards—of purest gold, locked away from human perception. You are for the most part what you seem to be, not what you would wish to be, nor, indeed, what you believe yourself to be.   8

Spare me, therefore, your good intentions, your inner sensitivities, your unarticulated and unexpressed love. And spare me also those tedious psychohistories which—by exposing the goodness inside the bad man, and the evil in the good—invariably establish a vulgar and perverse egalitarianism, as if the arrangement of what is outside and what inside makes no moral difference.

Saint Francis may, in his unconscious, indeed have been compensating for, and denying, destructive, unconscious Oedipal impulses identical to those which Attilla projected and acted on. But the similarity of the unconscious constellations in the two men matters precious little, if it does not distinguish between them.

I do not care to learn that Hitler's heart was in the right place. A knowledge of the unconscious life of the man may be an adjunct to understanding his behavior. It is *not* a substitute for his behavior in describing him.

The inner man is a fantasy. If it helps you to identify with one, by all means, do so; preserve it, cherish it, embrace it, but do not present it to others for evaluation or consideration, for excuse or exculpation, or, for that matter, for punishment or disapproval.

Like any fantasy, it serves your purposes alone. It has no standing in the real world which we share with each other. Those character traits, those attitudes, that behavior—that strange and alien stuff sticking out all over you—*that's the real you!*

Meaning and Purpose

1.   What is Gaylin's thesis?
2.   Why does Gaylin believe the ninety-year-old man will be "welcomed into the Kingdom of Heaven"?
3.   Why does Gaylin argue that the young man mentioned in paragraph 7 is not "really" a good boy?
4.   In paragraph 9, Gaylin says "Spare me . . . your good intentions." To whom is he speaking, and why?
5.   Defining his terms before he presents his argument, Gaylin differentiates between "outer man" and "inner man." What is the most significant difference between the two?

Strategy

1.   Father Flanagan was a priest. After you consult a reference book to read about Flanagan, tell how Gaylin's calling him a "financier" in the first paragraph helps Gaylin's argument.
2.   In paragraph 4, Gaylin talks of substituting "an X-ray of Grandfather's head for the portrait that hangs in the parlor." Why is this a good analogy for Gaylin's argument?
3.   How does quoting Kurt Vonnegut in paragraph 5 help Gaylin's argument?
4.   Willard Gaylin is himself a psychoanalyst. How does this qualification strengthen his argument?

Style

1.   What is the tone of Gaylin's argument, or his attitude toward his subject? Give some examples of language that illustrates his tone.
2.   Look up the definition of "fantasy." Why does Gaylin say that the inner man is a fantasy?
3.   What does "exculpation" mean (paragraph 12)?

POSSIBLE ANSWERS

Meaning and Purpose

1. Gaylin's thesis is in paragraph 4: "A man may not always be what he appears to be, but what he appears to be is always a significant part of what he is."

2. All external evidence says that the man lived a saintly life, despite his inner anguish, and Gaylin believes that behavior shows the real person.

3. Throughout the essay, Gaylin argues that actions take precedence over conjecture about the "inner" person. The boy mugged a woman; therefore, in the real world, he is "bad."

4. Gaylin addresses his readers, those whom he suspects believe the commonplace notion that traits of the "inner" person somehow should be the final evidence by which we judge someone.

5. From Gaylin's point of view, "inner" people do not exist and have "no standing in the real world which we share with each other" (13).

Strategy

1. Outwardly, Father Flanagan was a financier who worked hard to get financial backing from a number of sources to fund Boys' Town. Inwardly, he was a pious person. By acknowledging the outward person, Gaylin establishes his argument that the outward person, to him, is the real one.

2. The outside of grandfather is all that you will remember; you will not be prodded to reminiscence by a black-and-white view of a cranium. Therefore, the outer person is more important than the inner one.

3. Kurt Vonnegut's quotation supports Gaylin's argument, and Vonnegut is a respected author whose authority in human behavior complements Gaylin's.

4. Gaylin argues from the standpoint of the informed expert, rather than the laity.

Style

1. Gaylin's tone is authoritarian, and at times he sounds almost impatient or flip. Some examples of this tone are: (paragraph 3); "Consider for a moment the case of . . ." (6); "I will not be told that the young man who earns his pocket money by mugging old ladies is 'really' a good boy" (7); and "I do not care to learn that Hitler's heart was in the right place" (11).
2. "Fantasy" refers to the imagination's working hard to construct an entire "inner" world, far from the philosopher's "empirical reality," that which can be tested by observation. Gaylin's attitude is that the "inner" person is imaginary.
3. "Exculpation" in paragraph 12 means "being free from blame" or "being declared or proved innocent."

Writing Tasks

1. Gaylin's argument against the "inner" person is offered from the expert's standpoint. In your paper, argue against Gaylin. Give evidence to support the claim that in fact an "inner" person exists, even though that person cannot be seen or felt. Choose three of Gaylin's supporting points and show why they are in fact weak bits of evidence for saying that we have no "inner" person.
2. The irony of the title, "What You See Is the Real You," is that you never see the real you. Your image in a mirror is not the "real you," nor is your photograph. Other people, however, see the "real you," by Gaylin's definition, all the time. Based on five things that you have done, witnessed by at least one other person, argue that you are a "good" person in Gaylin's sense of "good."

❧ Francine du Plessix Gray ❧

Born in France in 1930, Francine du Plessix Gray came to the United States at age eleven. She attended Bryn Mawr College and Barnard College and, in the summers, Black Mountain College, where she studied writing and painting. She was dedicated to both of these creative arts, but eventually decided to focus on writing. She has been a reporter for United Press International, an editorial assistant for a French magazine, Realités, *in Paris, and a staff writer at* The New Yorker. *As a freelance writer since 1955, she has contributed stories and articles to major periodicals, including* Vogue, The New Yorker, Saturday Review, New Republic, *and* New York Times Book Review. *Her novels include* Lovers and Tyrants *(1976) and* October Blood *(1985).*

In Praise of Idleness

Francine du Plessix Gray argues against a popular belief of Western culture, that idleness is the root of evil. Expressing solicitude for the health of the English language, she proposes that idleness may offer a source for its rejuvenation. The essay was first published in Harper's *in April 1990, but was written as a sermon delivered at the New York City Cathedral of St. John the Divine in November 1989.*

Hold aloof from every Christian brother who falls into idle habits.

> —From the second letter of Paul
> to the Thessalonians

I plan this morning to challenge St. Paul to a public debate: I shall counter the apostle's attack against idleness by exalting, in the broadest possible way, the indispensable riches and rewards of leisure.

539

1

Aristotle (384–322 B.C.), a Greek philosopher, pupil of Plato, and tutor of Alexander the Great.

She then immediately establishes her position, part of the mainstream of western thought.

Plato (427–347 B.C.), a Greek philosopher and a pupil of Socrates.

Gray concludes this section by quoting from Christ's "Sermon on the Mount": Matthew 6:26.

She states the possible consequences of taking St. Paul too seriously.

Now Gray spends two paragraphs explaining why taking the work ethic too seriously might be so disastrous.

Jiddu Krishnamurti (1895–1986), an Indian spiritual leader who attained fame by presenting a unique version of Hindu philosophy and mysticism. During a time of spiritual purga-

To begin with, let us recall that in Aristotle's *Ethics,* leisure is a far more noble, spiritual goal than work. Unlike work, which is pursued for our financial advancement or for our egos, leisure is pursued solely for its own sake. The Greek word for leisure is telling: It is *skole,* the pursuit of true learning, our absorption in activities desirable for their own sake—highest of these being the pleasures of music and poetry, the exchange of conversation with friends, and the joy of gratuitous, playful speculation. The same esteem of leisure prevailed among the Romans: The Latin words for leisure and work are also notable—leisure, the ultimate good, is *otium;* and the verbal opposite, formed by a negative prefix, is *negotium,* or gainful work.

Which leads me to think that St. Paul might well have freaked out at those symposia or banquets described by Plato that were the highest educational forums of ancient times, those indolent round-the-clock dinner parties at which—over the passing of the libation cup—some of our earliest definitions of freedom, liberty, and love were born. And how would he have reacted to Matthew's adage: "They sow not, neither do they reap, nor gather into barns; yet your Heavenly Father feedeth them"?

And so I ask you to consider the possibility that we have sought too much counsel in the proto-Calvinist work ethic preached by St. Paul and that many of us constantly run the risk of losing our compassion, if not our souls and our very selves, by channeling our energies too exclusively into useful, gainful toil.

For it is only during the cessation of work that we nurture our family bonds, educate our children, nourish our friendships; it is in "recreation" that we literally re-create, renew, restore ourselves after the wear of labor. And those of us who are painters, writers, and musicians know that it is in a particular form of idleness, in the suspension of everyday, routine work, in loafing and inviting our souls, that most of our innovations and breakthroughs, our best inspiration, come; only then can we enjoy what the Hindu philosopher Krishnamurti called a Blessed Freedom from the Known. It is in the essential lazing offered by the Sabbath ritual that prayer and recollection proceed; it is only in our ungainful unemployed time that we can tune in to God's Word by dimming out the static created by our egos and our drive to excel. And it is only in our moments of deepest repose and just plain loafing that we are offered those miraculous peak moments in which we're suddenly startled to realize that we exist, that anything exists in which the gift of existence suddenly shines out at us, like chalk on a blackboard, against the possibility of not existing at all.

Finally, one might also say that it is only in a certain kind of idling that true compassion begins. For compassion is the art of acute selfless listening, of becoming alert and mindful to the needs of others by listening to them unconditionally with what St. Benedict called the "ear of our hearts." Compassion is an acuteness of attention difficult indeed to cultivate at the workplace and most readily reached over leisurely talk or a shared walk or cup, or during visits to jails, shelters, hospitals, wherever our social concerns draw us during our time off. So I would argue against Paul that the routine of our daily work has too often served as deep, dumb, deaf sleep, a refuge from two of life's most crucial states of being—keen awakedness to the needs of others and equal awakedness to the transcendent, which only comes in some state of loitering, dallying, tarrying, goofing off.

I'd like to move on to the literary implications of good idleness. For beyond the human community, if there is one thing on our planet most oppressed by soul-killing labor, by a dearth of recreation, it is the medium of my craft and of all human communication—language—which has been subjected to a round-the-clock shift as a drudge of media hype and of mass communication.

For here I must comment on a dilemma central and unique to that terrifyingly versatile symbolic system we call language: Compared to the mediums of music and painting, language has precious little Sabbath time in which to renew and re-create itself. Unlike the serenely abstract, leisured notations of music, or those means as free from daily labor as the visual artist's paint, canvas, and clay, our poor medium of language works like a slave in a salt mine. Look how vast a spectrum is covered by that one entity "word": From denoting the Word of God, "word" descends to

6

tion that came to be known as "The Process," his "higher self" departed from his body and entered a state that to his followers appeared to be a transcendent state of consciousness.

St. Benedict (A.D. 480?–543?), an Italian monk who founded the Benedictine order about A.D. 530.

7   Gray shifts her argument to address the necessity of idleness for writing.

8

those menial symbolic signs with which we holler and whimper our most primitive needs and fears, with which we execute our crassest commercial transactions. Compare the tranquillity of the musician's or painter's means to the incessant laboring of that verbal idiom we might use, within the span of a few hours, to say such diverse things as I love you unto death; please pass the horseradish; the Dow Jones went up 17 points at closing; Winston tastes good like a cigarette should. This is the exhausted, plodding dray horse—language—we prose writers are stuck with, and our central task is to air it and freshen it and reinfuse it with playfulness and honor and integrity in order to spiritualize it into art. In sum, our vocation, as writers, is the vacation of language; our task is to liberate words from their mercantile, pragmatic, everyday labor and usher them into the frolicking idleness of a perpetual Sunday; and, hopefully, to craft them into units of sound and meaning as free from everyday toil as James Agee's phrase "His eyes had the opal lightings of dark oil," or Vladimir Nabokov's "I stared at the window whence the wounded music came," or Joyce's "riverrun, past Eve and Adam's, from bend of bay to swerve of shore . . ."

James Agee (1909–1955), an American author, scenarist, and film critic. Vladimir Nabokov (1899–1977), an American novelist and short-story writer born in Russia. James Joyce (1882–1942), an Irish novelist and short-story writer.

How to resuscitate the exhausted word after relieving it of the   9
drudgery of full-time employment? Few writers have answered that question more eloquently than St. Augustine, whose entire process of conversion to Christianity was marked by his rebellion against the mass media of his time. For St. Augustine spent his early adulthood—when he was still a pagan—as a rhetorician, as a salesman of gross commercial language. And in late antiquity rhetoricians were the PR magnates and advertising tycoons and TV anchors of their society. Employed by politicians to write their speeches, using the techniques of eloquence to win friends and influence people, they were very dangerous precisely because they were so powerful.

St. Augustine (A.D. 354–430), one of the Latin fathers in the early Christian Church.

So a fair part of Augustine's conversion to Christianity is   10
based on his realization that the art of rhetoric has turned his colleagues into a society of corrupt hot-air artists, on his disillusionment with what he calls "the peddling of tongue science."

And a crucial step in his spiritual progress was to drop out of the work force, to abandon his lucrative peddling job, to liberate himself and his language into the gratuitous idleness of reading and talking about philosophy. Eventually, during that famous conversion scene in the garden, St. Augustine picks up the book nearest at hand and happens upon the chapter from St. Paul's Corinthians telling him to put on the *word* of Christ. That is the moment when Augustine, former taskmaster of enslaved words, is reborn into the truth and freedom of the absolute Word, thereby liberating his own verbal idiom and crafting the "language of the soul" that he will use to write his great *Confessions.*

11 The implications of St. Augustine's conversion to the higher Word are as deeply literary as they are religious: Once he's given up the practice of commercial writing, he begins to see his former sin, in part, as an addiction to debased and fettered language, to any discourse in which sheer technique prevails over ethics or genuine emotion.

12 Those passages of St. Augustine's *Confessions* that deal with his conversion to a purified language intimate, as few moments in literature have, that there is a particular form of grace to be sought by all writers; that, as we parole words from their perennial salt mines, it is our spiritual duty to follow an ethic of the written sign—or, to use the phrasing of the Commandments, "Honor thy medium as thyself." St. Augustine suggests that all those devices that he and his predecessors in the art of rhetoric pioneered—simile, irony, metaphor—must be used with care and precision and never with excess or with undue striving for a flamboyant effect.

13 Which is why I turn to another writer who saw the perils of any language engaged in daily gainful employment—our beloved contemporary Flannery O'Connor. In her book *Mystery and Manners,* O'Connor left us a small treasure house of literary ethics. And although her thoughts were often couched in theological terms, they have been decoded by even the most hardheaded agnostics as some of the most precious literary advice of our time.

Flannery O'Connor (1923–1954), an American novelist and short-story writer.

Gray has totally turned the tables on St. Paul's work ethic. A writer must have leisure to work and that work is ultimately religious.

St. Thomas Aquinas (1225?–1274), an Italian scholastic philosopher, a major theologian of the Roman Catholic Church.

Father Thomas Merton (1915–1968), a Trappist monk, and an American poet and religious writer.

For instance, O'Connor believed that the highest purpose of literature is "the accurate naming of the things of God"—as good a metaphor as any for a fastidiously responsible, selfless, nonexploitative attitude toward language. She often turns to another injunction she has learned from St. Thomas Aquinas: The artist, she tells us, must solely be concerned with the good of that which he makes, not with the good that it can bring into his life, for only thus can his work enlarge the glory of God's creation. 14

O'Connor went on to remind us that whatever talent we have comes from the Holy Spirit. This gift is given to us to plumb the mystery of evil, the mystery of personality, the mystery of our incompleteness. It is a considerable responsibility, a mystery in itself, something gratuitous and totally undeserved whose real uses will probably always be hidden from us. 15

To which I would add: Like the spirituality of our Sabbath, our fragile, beleaguered, exhausted language—the preserver of our civilization and the vehicle for most of our gifts—thrives on attitudes of release, of labor suspended. It will best endure not on the work ethic preached by St. Paul but rather on that message expressed by Thomas Merton in the following words: "The Lord plays and diverts Himself in the garden of His creation, and if we could let go of our own obsessions with what we think is the meaning of it all, we might be able to hear His call and follow Him in His mysterious, cosmic dance. . . . For the world and time are the dance of the Lord in emptiness. The silence of the spheres is the music of a wedding feast." 16

POSSIBLE ANSWERS

Meaning and Purpose

1. Give students time to discuss the meanings of both work and leisure in their lives, and where their attitudes toward these come from. **2.** The title announces the subject and the au-

Meaning and Purpose

1. In your own life, and considering time for attending school, what has been the balance of work and leisure? Which are you encouraged to pursue?
2. Comment about the appropriateness and effectiveness of the title. What is the connotation of "idleness"? of "leisure"?

3. What is du Plessix Gray's purpose in the essay, and where does she state it?
4. What does du Plessix Gray mean by the "proto-Calvinist work ethic" in paragraph 4?
5. Why does Gray call language "that terrifyingly versatile symbolic system" in paragraph 8?
6. How does the discussion of St. Augustine's "conversion to the higher Word" (11) serve the author's purpose?

Strategy

1. Do you think du Plessix Gray appeals more to reason or emotion in her argument? Show places in the essay that support your answer.
2. Explain whether the reasoning in paragraphs 13 and 14 is inductive or deductive.
3. Find some references to religion, spirituality, and religious people. How do these references serve du Plessix Gray's purpose, or strengthen her argument?
4. The essay begins and ends with quotations from religious leaders. How does this strategy help structure the essay?

Style

1. What is the tone of this essay? How do words like "the passing of the libation cup" (3) and "our task is to liberate words from their mercantile, pragmatic, everyday labor and usher them into the frolicking idleness of a perpetual Sunday" (8) work with words like "freaked out" (3), or "loitering, dallying, tarrying, goofing off" (6)? To whom does du Plessix Gray appeal?
2. In the language that she uses, du Plessix Gray tries to "spiritualize [language] into art" (8). Give some examples of figures of speech that illustrate this intent.
3. The first sentences in paragraphs 3, 9, 13, and 16 are fragments. How do these sentences work stylistically in the essay?

thor's persuasion about it. The phrase "In Praise of Idleness" ties in stylistically to much of the formal and religious writing quoted in the essay. "Idleness" usually has the negative connotation of time spent in unproductive laziness; "leisure" is more positive and connotes time spent at some recreational or relaxing activity.

3. The purpose is to debunk the Calvinist-like superior status of the work ethic over that of leisure time by showing the merits of and need for leisure, particularly for leisure spent raising language to an art. She states her purpose clearly in paragraph 1.

4. "Proto" means beginning or giving rise to. The Calvinist work ethic says that the measure of one's worth and productivity, and one's service to God, is in work, not leisure. Leisure time is the playground of the devil.

5. She means that language can be used for everyday purposes in society without people's ever seeing it as art; thus, the versatility is "terrifying" because it includes using language "like a slave in a salt mine" (8) and might mean the demise of language as art.

6. St. Augustine's conversion is an example of a person changing from a "salesman of gross commercial language" (9) to one who crafts the "language of the soul" (10). This discussion strengthens the author's point about the need for writers to use leisure time to raise language to an art, and so enrich us all.

Strategy

1. The author appeals to reason when she cites authorities, such as a Hindu philosopher (5) and St. Augustine (10). She also appeals to emotion, and to a higher spiritual state that she believes human beings are capable of, as in 5, and in her discussion of compassion (6). She appeals about equally to emotion and to reason.

2. The reasoning in 13 and 14 is deductive; that is, general to specific. The general premise is that language becomes drudgery with full-time "employment" and that it needs to be "re-suscitated." Flannery O'Connor believes in this careful treatment of language and accomplishes it in her own writing.

3. Some references to religion and spirituality: "it is only in our ungainfully employed time that we can tune in to God's Word" (5); "equal awakedness to the transcendent" (6); " 'Honor thy medium as thyself' " (12); and "Like the spirituality of our Sabbath" (16). Du Plessix Gray carries a religious theme throughout.

4. The beginning and ending quotations tie together the theme of spirituality in the use of leisure time. The first quotation is the work ethic that the author argues against, and the last is the one she argues for. The structure of the essay goes through refuting the first work ethic and comes out asserting the second.

Style

1. The tone is reverent, authoritative, and conversational, as seen in the varied formal and informal language. The essay is a speech (she addresses listeners directly in sentence 1) to a modern, well-educated audience probably disposed to agree with her.

2. Some "artistic language" in the essay itself is: "dimming out the static" (5)—*metaphor;* "our poor medium of language works like a slave in a salt mine" (8)—*simile;* "How to resuscitate the exhausted word after relieving it of the drudgery of full-time employment?" (9)—*personification.*

3. The fragments are effective transitions between paragraphs because they carry over unfinished thoughts. They also make the tone conversational and informal.

4. *Libation cup:* used for ceremonial drinking; *adage:* a saying that embodies a common observation; *resuscitate:* to revive from apparent death; *beleaguered:* beseiged or beset.

4. What do these words mean: *libation cup* (3); *adage* (3); *resuscitate* (9); *beleaguered* (16)?

Writing Tasks

1. Write an argument titled "In Praise of _____" (fill in the blank). Address your audience directly, as if you were giving a speech. Organize the main points you want to both make and refute. Decide which kind of evidence to give in support of your argument: personal experience, experience of others, authoritative sources.

2. Illustrate each of these fallacies in a separate paragraph: faulty either/or reasoning; post hoc; false analogy. Consult the chapter introduction for explanations of the fallacies.

❦ Alice Walker ❦

Born in Eatonton, Georgia, in 1944, Alice Walker studied at Sarah Lawrence College. She has published short stories, novels, poetry, children's fiction, and two collections of essays. Though the themes of sexism and racism are predominant in her work, critics praise her writing for its universal relevance. She has taught literature and Afro-American Studies and has been writer in residence at several colleges and universities, including Wellesley College, Brandeis University, and the University of California, Berkeley. In 1983 she won both the Pulitzer Prize and the American Book Award for her novel, The Color Purple, *which was made into a feature film, directed by Steven Spielberg, in 1985. Her most recent book is a novel,* The Temple of My Familiar *(1989).*

Am I Blue?

In this essay Alice Walker uses narrative and description to further a very general argument in favor of freedom and justice. She chooses a horse as an example to illustrate her point, but her subject is all living things. This selection is from her book of essays, Living by the Word: Selected Writing 1973–1987 *(1988).*

For about three years my companion and I rented a small house in the country that stood on the edge of a large meadow that appeared to run from the end of our deck straight into the mountains. The mountains, however, were quite far away, and between us and them there was, in fact, a town. It was one of the many pleasant aspects of the house that you never really were aware of this.

It was a house of many windows, low, wide, nearly floor to ceiling in the living room, which faced the meadow, and it was from one of these that I first saw our closest neighbor, a large white horse, cropping grass, flipping its mane, and ambling

1

2

At least since Aesop, people have been attracted to stories that have a moral, and this narrative has a kind of moral—an ethical argument that depends a great deal on the writer's credibility.

Indirect arguments are used for the sake of harmony. To avoid confronting readers directly, she disarms them first, here by telling about her experiences with Blue. Gradually, however, readers come to see her argument: all of us, other animals and human beings alike, have feelings and ability to communicate—and therefore have rights. It is dangerous and unethical to believe otherwise.

You could begin by asking students to think about pets. Do we "have" them or do we "own" them or do we "live with" them? How do we perceive our relationships with pets? How do we communicate with pets? How do they communicate with us? Do animals have feelings akin to ours, or is that a foolish belief?

Above all, do animals have rights? What sort of rights? And do we classify living things on a vertical line, with human beings at the top and microorganisms at the bottom, and every other living creature somewhere between? If we do, then human beings are in charge. What then are we charged with? Taking care of those "beneath" us, or are they simply here to serve us?

MARGINAL NOTES

Walker opens with an idyllic description: the small house opens to a view of majestic unspoiled nature unobstructed by society; society is near, but it is not visible.

547

about—not over the entire meadow, which stretched well out of sight of the house, but over the five or so fenced-in acres that were next to the twenty-odd that we had rented. I soon learned that the horse, whose name was Blue, belonged to a man who lived in another town, but was boarded by our neighbors next door. Occasionally, one of the children, usually a stocky teenager, but sometimes a much younger girl or boy, could be seen riding Blue. They would appear in the meadow, climb up on his back, ride furiously for ten or fifteen minutes, then get off, slap Blue on the flanks, and not be seen again for a month or more.

Feeding apples to Blue sparks Walker's reminiscence about her childhood experiences riding horses. Because of these experiences, she has an affinity for horses, recognizing their great qualities.

There were many apple trees in our yard, and one by the fence that Blue could almost reach. We were soon in the habit of feeding him apples, which he relished, especially because by the middle of summer the meadow grasses—so green and succulent since January—had dried out from lack of rain, and Blue stumbled about munching the dried stalks half-heartedly. Sometimes he would stand very still just by the apple tree, and when one of us came out he would whinny, snort loudly, or stamp the ground. This meant, of course: I want an apple. 3

It was quite wonderful to pick a few apples, or collect those that had fallen to the ground overnight, and patiently hold them, one by one, up to his large, toothy mouth. I remained as thrilled as a child by his flexible dark lips, huge, cubelike teeth that crunched the apples, core and all, with such finality, and his high, broad-breasted *enormity*; beside which, I felt small indeed. When I was a child, I used to ride horses, and was especially friendly with one named Nan until the day I was riding and my brother deliberately spooked her and I was thrown, head first, against the trunk of a tree. When I came to, I was in bed and my mother was bending worriedly over me; we silently agreed that perhaps horseback riding was not the safest sport for me. Since then I have walked, and prefer walking to horseback riding—but I had forgotten the depth of feeling one could see in horses' eyes. 4

I was therefore unprepared for the expression in Blue's. Blue was lonely. Blue was horribly lonely and bored. I was not shocked that this should be the case; five acres to tramp by yourself, 5 endlessly, even in the most beautiful of meadows—and his was—cannot provide many interesting events, and once rainy season turned to dry that was about it. No, I was shocked that I had forgotten that human animals and nonhuman animals can communicate quite well; if we are brought up around animals as children we take this for granted. By the time we are adults we no longer remember. However, the animals have not changed. They are in fact *completed* creations (at least they seem to be, so much more than we) who are not likely to change; it is their nature to express themselves. What else are they going to express? And they do. And, generally speaking, they are ignored.

After giving Blue the apples, I would wander back to the house, aware that he was observing me. Were more apples not forthcoming then? Was that to be his sole entertainment for the day? My partner's small son had decided he wanted to learn how to piece a quilt; we worked in silence on our respective squares as I thought. . . .

Well, about slavery: about white children, who were raised by black people, who knew their first all-accepting love from black women, and then, when they were twelve or so, were told they must "forget" the deep levels of communication between themselves and "mammy" that they knew. Later they would be able to relate quite calmly, "My old mammy was sold to another good family." "My old mammy was _____ _____." Fill in the blank. Many more years later a white woman would say: "I can't understand these Negroes, these blacks. What do they want? They're so different from us."

And about the Indians, considered to be "like animals" by the "settlers" (a very benign euphemism for what they actually were), who did not understand their description as a compliment.

And about the thousands of American men who marry Japanese, Korean, Filipina, and other non–English-speaking women and of how happy they report they are, *"blissfully,"* until their brides learn to speak English, at which point the marriages tend to fall apart. What then did the men see, when they looked into the eyes of the women they married, before they could speak English? Apparently only their own reflections.

The phrasing "human animals and nonhuman animals" and the reminder that children assume the ability to communicate with other animals express a natural link between human beings and animals. The link is too often broken as we grow older.

6   In this transition and the next four paragraphs, Walker moves from the horse's ability to communicate with her to the larger consideration of human beings and their communication with one another, weaving an argument into her narrative: In many relationships we are not truly communicating because we are not truly listening; we are not sensitive to each other.

7

8

9

I thought of society's impatience with the young. "Why are 10
they playing the music so loud?" Perhaps the children have listened to much of the music of oppressed people their parents
danced to before they were born, with its passionate but soft cries
for acceptance and love, and they have wondered why their parents failed to hear.

Walker returns to her narrative about Blue.
Only when the white horse has a mate does it
see itself as free. The irony is that being alone
is not the same as being independent.

I do not know how long Blue had inhabited his five beautiful, 11
boring acres before we moved into our house; a year after we had
arrived—and had also traveled to other valleys, other cities, other
worlds—he was still there.

But then, in our second year at the house, something hap- 12
pened in Blue's life. One morning, looking out the window at the
fog that lay like a ribbon over the meadow, I saw another horse, a
brown one, at the other end of Blue's field. Blue appeared to be
afraid of it, and for several days made no attempt to go near. We
went away for a week. When we returned, Blue had decided to
make friends and the two horses ambled or galloped along together, and Blue did not come nearly as often to the fence underneath the apple tree.

When he did, bringing his new friend with him, there was a 13
different look in his eyes. A look of independence, of self-possession, of inalienable *horse*ness. His friend eventually became pregnant. For months and months there was, it seemed to me, a
mutual feeling between me and the horses of justice, of peace. I
fed apples to them both. The look in Blue's eyes was one of
unabashed "this is *it*ness."

After the other horse has been taken back to
her owner, Blue reacts much like a person
whose loved one is taken away. Walker sees the
affinity between the horse's feelings and how
slaves must have felt—she compares the common features of relationships treated with
callousness, which strengthens her later
argument.

It did not, however, last forever. One day, after a visit to the 14
city, I went out to give Blue some apples. He stood waiting, or so
I thought, though not beneath the tree. When I shook the tree
and jumped back from the shower of apples, he made no move. I
carried some over to him. He managed to half-crunch one. The
rest he let fall to the ground. I dreaded looking into his eyes—
because I had of course noticed that Brown, his partner, had
gone—but I did look. If I had been born into slavery, and my
partner had been sold or killed, my eyes would have looked like
that. The children next door explained that Blue's partner had
been "put with him" (the same expression that old people used, I

had noticed, when speaking of an ancestor during slavery who had been impregnated by her owner) so that they could mate and she conceive. Since that was accomplished, she had been taken back by her owner, who lived somewhere else.

Will she be back? I asked.   15

They didn't know.   16

Blue was like a crazed person. Blue *was*, to me, a crazed   17
person. He galloped furiously, as if he were being ridden, around and around his five beautiful acres. He whinnied until he couldn't. He tore at the ground with his hooves. He butted himself against his single shade tree. He looked always and always toward the road down which his partner had gone. And then, occasionally, when he came up for apples, or I took apples to him, he looked at me. It was a look so piercing, so full of grief, a look so *human,* I almost laughed (I felt too sad to cry) to think there are people who do not know that animals suffer. People like me who have forgotten, and daily forget, all that animals try to tell us. "Everything you do to us will happen to you; we are your teachers, as you are ours. We are one lesson" is essentially it, I think. There are those who never once have even considered animals' rights: those who have been taught that animals actually want to be used and abused by us, as small children "love" to be frightened, or women "love" to be mutilated and raped. . . . They are the great-grandchildren of those who honestly thought, because someone taught them this: "Woman can't think" and "niggers can't faint." But most disturbing of all, in Blue's large brown eyes was a new look, more painful than the look of despair, the look of disgust with human beings, with life, the look of hatred. And it was odd what the look of hatred did. It gave him, for the first time, the look of a beast. And what that meant was that he had put up a barrier within to protect himself from further violence; all the apples in the world wouldn't change that fact.

And so Blue remained, a beautiful part of our landscape, very   18
peaceful to look at from the window, white against the grass. Once a friend came to visit and said, looking out on the soothing view: "And it *would* have to be a *white* horse; the very image of freedom." And I thought, yes, the animals are forced to become for us merely

Animals suffer, Walker argues. They share our temperaments and have joys and sorrows. Because we have forgotten that animals communicate, we do not bother to listen to them. We see them as beneath us on a vertical scale of animal life. Where we have cast animals, we have sometimes cast other people. How we treat animals parallels our way of treating other people, especially those who are seen as "beneath us." Subtly but inexorably, Walker has argued in this narrative essay that people and other animals alike are to be treated with compassion, empathy, and respect.

Blue moves from center stage in an argument to an image in a narrative. At the very time he has come to symbolize freedom to Walker's friend, however, he has lost his own freedom. He is now an advertisement for freedom, not the real thing.

"images" of what they once so beautifully expressed. And we are used to drinking milk from containers showing "contented" cows, whose real lives we want to hear nothing about, eating eggs and drumsticks from "happy" hens, and munching hamburgers advertised by bulls of integrity who seem to command their fate.

As we talked of freedom and justice one day for all, we sat down to steaks. I am eating misery, I thought, as I took the first bite. And spit it out.

The hypocrisy of discussing freedom and justice for *all*, while eating a steak, overwhelms the narrator.

POSSIBLE ANSWERS

Meaning and Purpose

1. Evidence that Walker is empathetic is in these statements, among others: "Blue was horribly lonely" (5); and "Blue *was*, to me, a crazed person" (17).
2. Walker's main point is that we are insensitive to animals, just as we are to people we think of as no more than animals. Her thesis is in words she ascribes to Blue: " 'Everything you do to us will happen to you; we are your teachers, as you are ours. We are one lesson' " (17).
3. The title questions whether people and animals are the same in having feelings and needs and being connected creatures on the same planet. She discusses how some animals and people are treated by those who have more power. The title is also that of an old blues song.
4. "*Horse*ness" means that Blue had become the most horse he could be and had all the horse identity he could have in being properly treated as a horse. "*It*ness" means that bliss and peace were achieved and Blue's life was what it should be, the ultimate, with no abuse or neglect.
5. These are false images. The reality is that cows are slaughtered and hens lay eggs to feed people. We like to imagine these animals "contented" and "happy" and not to be aware that they are treated cruelly for our advantage.

Meaning and Purpose

1. Have you ever felt empathy for an animal as Walker does for Blue? How do you know she is empathetic?
2. What is the main point Walker is making? Can you find a statement of it?
3. How does the title fit the meaning of the essay?
4. What does Walker mean by "*horse*ness" and "*it*ness" in paragraph 13?
5. In paragraph 18, what is the meaning of "contented" cows and "happy" hens?

Strategy

1. Both narration and description appear in Walker's argument. How do all three rhetorical strategies work together?
2. In paragraphs 7–10, Walker talks about a group of people with whom those in power have poor or misdirected communication, and about whom they have a low opinion. What is the connection between these paragraphs and the rest of the essay?
3. What kind of appeal does Walker make in her argument? Give evidence of it in the essay.

Style

1. Explain the irony in paragraph 18.
2. Look up the word "anthropomorphize" and comment on how Walker uses it, and how effective you think it is.
3. The last paragraph is about "talking of freedom and justice," and about Walker's reaction to eating steak. How is this paragraph relevant to the rest of the essay and Walker's purpose?

Writing Tasks

1. Develop an argument for or against something and write it into a narrative. Be sure the story illustrates the argument. You might argue for the rights of a group on campus while telling the story of their demonstrating or petitioning.
2. How do you think Walker would respond to Karpati's argument for using animals in medical research in "A Scientist: 'I Am the Enemy' "? How do you think Karpati would respond to Walker's assertions about animals' feelings and to her reaction to eating steak? In a paragraph or two for each, write what you think these responses would be, in a voice appropriate to each author.

Strategy

1. Walker's argument is embodied in her narrative about Blue's life in the meadow. She uses the story to frame her argument and give it appeal and a familiar context. The description enhances the narrative and makes the scene real and alive—and this effect makes readers empathize with Blue as Walker does.

2. The people Walker refers to—enslaved Negroes, American Indians, foreign brides, young people—are considered like "lower" animals by some. This is what Walker thinks while she quilts and connects to the following thoughts: Blue depending on people's goodness for the quality of his life; how meaningful communication is possible between human beings and other animals; and how lack of empathy for other animals leads us also to the abuses she describes in paragraphs 7–10.

3. Walker makes an emotional appeal to readers: "Blue was lonely. Blue was horribly lonely and bored" (5); "It was a look so piercing, so full of grief, a look so *human*" (17); and "those who have been taught that animals actually want to be used and abused by us, as small children 'love' to be frightened, or women 'love' to be mutilated and raped" (17).

Style

1. That a white horse is an image of freedom is ironic because Blue is not free; he is trapped. It is ironic that our image of other animals is of " 'contented' cows," and "bulls of integrity who seem to command their fate," when really they are raised for slaughter.

2. "Anthropomorphize" means to attribute human form and traits to something not human, as when she says Blue is lonely and bored (5), he wonders "Were more apples not forthcoming then?" (6), and he had "the look of disgust with human beings, with life; the look of hatred" (17). This appeal to emotion is effective to the degree that readers identify with her feelings or think she is overly dramatic.

3. Freedom and justice are connected to Walker's purpose of recognizing the rights of animals and human beings. Her reaction to eating steak connects to the paragraph before, where she talks about image versus reality of animals' lives.

TEACHING SUGGESTIONS

Buckley, long recognized as a leading conservative, argues that we have become helpless to the point of apathy. This grave form of helplessness, he argues, accounts for our giving control of our personal lives to others, which results in our having "a powerful government whose hold upon us continues to increase."

A lively classroom discussion comes from questions like these: When do you take personal responsibility, when do you take social responsibility, and when do you depend on "the experts"? If your neighbors play a radio so loudly that it disturbs you in your own home, do you ask them to turn it down, or do you call the police instead? If you plan a party at home, do you consider your neighbors' comfort as the party progresses? When a salesperson telephones you at home, do you listen to the sales pitch because she or he has a right to give you that pitch? Or do you hang up because you have a right to privacy? Do you believe the federal government should financially assist students? Or do you believe that if students want an education, they should work for it?

Establish whether members of the class are thoughtfully involved or whether they "let the experts decide."

MARGINAL NOTES

Buckley begins anecdotally, presenting an autobiographical vignette that engages readers (1). When developing an argument, authors often write a beginning paragraph that will establish a friendly link with their audience, the better to later sway the audience to the writer's point of view.

❧ William F. Buckley, Jr. ❧

Born in New York in 1925, Buckley is the founder and editor-in-chief of National Review *and the host of "Firing Line," a Public Television forum of political commentary. He is an avowed conservative whose belief in the value of capitalism and democracy fuels his many activities, not the least of which is writing. He has published mystery, crime, and suspense novels, numerous essays, and many books of commentary on politics and national affairs. In 1983 he published an autobiography called* Overdrive *that records one week in his life and work in 1982. He frequently contributes essays of political and social commentary to magazines with national circulation.*

Why Don't We Complain?

This essay first appeared in Esquire *in January 1961. Buckley cites example after example of people (himself included) accepting unpleasant situations rather than complaining about them. By inductive reasoning, he then reaches a general conclusion about the passivity of Americans.*

It was the very last coach and the only empty seat on the entire train, so there was no turning back. The problem was to breathe. Outside, the temperature was below freezing. Inside the railroad car the temperature must have been about 85 degrees. I took off my overcoat, and a few minutes later my jacket, and noticed that the car was flecked with the white shirts of the passengers. I soon found my hand moving to loosen my tie. From one end of the car to the other, as we rattled through Westchester County, we sweated; but we did not moan. 1

I watched the train conductor appear at the head of the car. "Tickets, all tickets, please!" In a more virile age, I thought, the passengers would seize the conductor and strap him down on a 2 seat over the radiator to share the fate of his patrons. He shuffled down the aisle, picking up tickets, punching commutation cards. *No one addressed a word to him*. He approached my seat, and I drew a deep breath of resolution. "Conductor," I began with a considerable edge to my voice. . . . Instantly the doleful eyes of my seatmate turned tiredly from his newspaper to fix me with a resentful stare: What question could be so important as to justify my sibilant intrusion into his stupor? I was shaken by those eyes. I am incapable of making a discreet fuss, so I mumbled a question about what time we were due in Stamford (I didn't even ask whether it would be before or after dehydration could be expected to set in), got my reply, and went back to my newspaper and to wiping my brow.

The conductor had nonchalantly walked down the gauntlet of eighty sweating American freemen, and not one of them had asked him to explain why the passengers in that car had been consigned to suffer. There is nothing to be done when the temperature *outdoors* is 85 degrees, and indoors the air conditioner has broken down; obviously when that happens there is nothing to do, except perhaps curse the day that one was born. But when the temperature outdoors is below freezing, it takes a positive act of will on somebody's part to set the temperature *indoors* at 85. Somewhere a valve was turned too far, a furnace overstocked, a thermostat maladjusted: something that could easily be remedied by turning off the heat and allowing the great outdoors to come indoors. All this is so obvious. What is not obvious is what has happened to the American people.

It isn't just the commuters, whom we have come to visualize as a supine breed who have got on to the trick of suspending their sensory faculties twice a day while they submit to the creeping dissolution of the railroad industry. It isn't just they who have given up trying to rectify irrational vexations. It is the American people everywhere.

A few weeks ago at a large movie theatre I turned to my wife and said, "The picture is out of focus." "Be quiet," she answered. I obeyed. But a few minutes later I raised the point again, with mounting impatience. "It will be all right in a minute," she said

3 Buckley has long been established as a master of diction, using the most appropriate word or phrase in the most appropriate place. Notice "virile" ("manly strength or vigor"), "breath of *resolution*" (a breath that is "fixed and firm"), and "*sibilant* intrusion" (a "hissing act of illegal entry").

Used in the eighteenth century, this label applied to a person not in slavery or bondage, who had full civil and political rights. Being sarcastic, Buckley wonders why freemen have been "consigned to suffer" a punishment. The last sentence in this paragraph hints at a point in his later argument.

4 Buckley introduces his thesis: Americans have given up "trying to rectify irrational vexations"; that is, they have quit trying to set right not only the things which make no sense in the first place but also those which combine to make the country a place of annoyances, irritations, and disturbances.

5

He cannot make a "discreet fuss" (2); here, he says that his wife would go to great lengths to avoid one of his "infrequent scenes." Evidently, when Buckley does become angry, his anger goes beyond normal social bounds.

In Homer's *Iliad,* Hector was the Trojan hero killed by Achilles to avenge the death of Patroclus, Achilles' friend. In early popular drama, Hector was portrayed as a swaggering bully. Hence, *hectoring* means "browbeating or bullying."

Buckley's second anecdote ends here. Notice that he sandwiches between two anecdotes ("proofs") his thesis that Americans have given up trying to change their surroundings, giving his thesis the appearance of obvious fact.

In this conditional summary, Buckley reveals the probable cause, based on his evidence: everybody expected some other person to act.

He outlines his thesis in detail, that regardless of our discomfort, we hesitate to act positively on behalf of ourselves and others because we fear confrontation with those in authority.

apprehensively. (She would rather lose her eyesight than be around when I make one of my infrequent scenes.) I waited. It was *just* out of focus—not glaringly out, but out. My vision is 20-20, and I assume that is the vision, adjusted, of most people in the movie house. So, after hectoring my wife throughout the first reel, I finally prevailed upon her to admit that it *was* off, and very annoying. We then settled down, coming to rest on the presumption that: (a) someone connected with the management of the theatre must soon notice the blur and make the correction; or (b) that someone seated near the rear of the house would make the complaint in behalf of those of us up front; or (c) that—any minute now—the entire house would explode into catcalls and foot stamping, calling dramatic attention to the irksome distortion.

What happened was nothing. The movie ended, as it had begun *just* out of focus, and as we trooped out, we stretched our faces in a variety of contortions to accustom the eye to the shock of normal focus.   6

I think it is safe to say that everybody suffered on that occasion. And I think it is safe to assume that everyone was expecting someone else to take the initiative in going back to speak to the manager. And it is probably true even that if we had supposed the movie would run right through the blurred image, someone surely would have summoned up the purposive indignation to get up out of his seat and file his complaint.   7

But notice that no one did. And the reason no one did is because we are all increasingly anxious in America to be unobtrusive, we are reluctant to make our voices heard, hesitant about claiming our rights; we are afraid that our cause is unjust, or that if it is not unjust, that it is ambiguous; or if not even that, that it is too trivial to justify the horrors of a confrontation with Authority; we will sit in an oven or endure a racking headache before undertaking a head-on, I'm-here-to-tell-you complaint. That tendency to passive compliance, to a heedless endurance, is something to keep one's eyes on—in sharp focus.   8

I myself can occasionally summon the courage to complain, but I cannot, as I have intimated, complain softly. My own instinct   9 is so strong to let the thing ride, to forget about it—to expect that someone will take the matter up, when the grievance is collective, in my behalf—that it is only when the provocation is at a very special key, whose vibrations touch simultaneously a complexus of nerves, allergies, and passions, that I catch fire and find the reserves of courage and assertiveness to speak up. When that happens, I get quite carried away. My blood gets hot, my brow wet, I become unbearably and unconscionably sarcastic and bellicose; I am girded for a total showdown.

He portrays himself as every person, intimating that he represents us all, in that when we finally react, we overreact, almost entirely losing control. This loss of control might well be the result of not releasing our frustration when we should, each time we are vexed.

Why should that be? Why could not I (or anyone else) on that railroad coach have said simply to the conductor, "Sir"—I take that back: that sounds sarcastic—"Conductor, would you be good enough to turn down the heat? I am extremely hot. In fact, I tend to get hot every time the temperature reaches 85 degr—" Strike that last sentence. Just end it with the simple statement that you are extremely hot, and let the conductor infer the cause.

10   This moment of calm self-examination reminds readers of how they themselves should have reacted in such situations. How many times have we had just the right reply or just the right comeback—but only after we have removed ourselves from a situation and have had time to reflect?

Every New Year's Eve I resolve to do something about the Milquetoast in me and vow to speak up, calmly, for my rights, and for the betterment of our society, on every appropriate occasion. Entering last New Year's Eve I was fortified in my resolve because that morning at breakfast I had had to ask the waitress three times for a glass of milk. She finally brought it—after I had finished my eggs, which is when I don't want it any more. I did not have the manliness to order her to take the milk back, but settled instead for a cowardly sulk, and ostentatiously refused to drink the milk—though I later paid for it—rather than state plainly to the hostess, as I should have, why I had not drunk it, and would not pay for it.

11   Caspar Milquetoast is a cartoon character in a comic strip drawn by H. T. Webster (1885–1952). Milquetoast was timid, apologetic, and cowering.

Buckley's resolution is fortified by his episode with the waitress, strengthening his resolve to change, to start defending his rights.

So by the time the New Year ushered out the Old, riding in on my morning's indignation and stimulated by the gastric juices of resolution that flow so faithfully on New Year's Eve, I rendered my vow. Henceforward I would conquer my shyness, my despicable disposition to supineness. I would speak out like a man against the unnecessary annoyances of our time.

12   He sets the stage, framing the episode that shows him in action, putting into practice his New Year's resolution to speak out for his rights.

Forty-eight hours later, I was standing in line at the ski repair store in Pico Peak, Vermont. All I needed, to get on with my skiing, was the loan, for one minute, of a small screwdriver, to

13

tighten a loose binding. Behind the counter in the workshop were two men. One was industriously engaged in servicing the complicated requirements of a young lady at the head of the line, and obviously he would be tied up for quite a while. The other—"Jiggs," his workmate called him—was a middle-aged man, who sat in a chair puffing a pipe, exchanging small talk with his working partner. My pulse began its telltale acceleration. The minutes ticked on. I stared at the idle shopkeeper, hoping to shame him into action, but he was impervious to my telepathic reproof and continued his small talk with his friend, brazenly insensitive to the nervous demands of six good men who were raring to ski.

Suddenly my New Year's Eve resolution struck me. It was now or never. I broke from my place in line and marched to the counter. I was going to control myself. I dug my nails into my palms. My effort was only partially successful.   14

Determined to put his New Year's resolution into action, Buckley utters the first line of the small drama.

"If you are not too busy," I said icily, "would you mind handing me a screwdriver?"   15

Work stopped and everyone turned his eyes on me, and I experienced that mortification I always feel when I am the center of centripetal shafts of curiosity, resentment, perplexity.   16

The other character's response to Buckley's line, totally unpredictable, is followed by the equally unpredictable dénouement, or unraveling of the plot in this small drama.

But the worst was yet to come. "I am sorry, sir," said Jiggs deferentially, moving the pipe from his mouth. "I am not supposed to move. I have just had a heart attack." That was the signal for a great whirring noise that descended from heaven. We looked, stricken, out the window, and it appeared as though a cyclone had suddenly focused on the snowy courtyard between the shop and the ski lift. Suddenly a gigantic army helicopter materialized, and hovered down to a landing. Two men jumped out of the plane carrying a stretcher, tore into the ski shop, and lifted the shopkeeper onto the stretcher. Jiggs bade his companion goodby, was whisked out the door, into the plane, up to the heavens, down—we learned—to a near-by army hospital. I looked up manfully—into a score of man-eating eyes. I put the experience down as a reversal.   17

We discover that Buckley has written a reflective piece. He brings us into the present, saying that in his life nothing has changed; he remains the Milquetoast when he has an opportunity to act.

As I write this, on an airplane, I have run out of paper and need to reach into my briefcase under my legs for more. I cannot do this until my empty lunch tray is removed from my lap. I   18 arrested the stewardess as she passed empty-handed down the aisle on the way to the kitchen to fetch the lunch trays for the passengers up forward who haven't been served yet. "Would you please take my tray?" "Just a *moment,* sir!" she said, and marched on sternly. Shall I tell her that since she is headed for the kitchen *anyway,* it could not delay the feeding of the other passengers by more than two seconds necessary to stash away my empty tray? Or remind her that not fifteen minutes ago she spoke unctuously into the loudspeaker the words undoubtedly devised by the airline's highly paid public relations counselor: "If there is anything I or Miss French can do for you to make your trip more enjoyable, *please* let us—" I have run out of paper.

I think the observable reluctance of the majority of Americans to assert themselves in minor matters is related to our increased sense of helplessness in an age of technology and centralized political and economic power. For generations, Americans who were too hot, or too cold, got up and did something about it. Now we call the plumber, or the electrician, or the furnace man. The habit of looking after our own needs obviously had something to do with the assertiveness that characterized the American family familiar to readers of American literature. With the technification of life goes our direct responsibility for our material environment, and we are conditioned to adopt a position of helplessness not only as regards the broken air conditioner, but as regards the overheated train. It takes an expert to fix the former, but not the latter; yet these distinctions, as we withdraw into helplessness, tend to fade away.

Our notorious political apathy is a related phenomenon. Every year, whether the Republican or the Democratic Party is in office, more and more power drains away from the individual to feed vast reservoirs in far-off places; and we have less and less say about the shape of events which shape our future. From this alienation of personal power comes the sense of resignation with which we accept the political dispensations of a powerful government whose hold upon us continues to increase.

An editor of a national weekly news magazine told me a few years ago that as few as a dozen letters of protest against an

19 An argument on the issues as they involve readers. One result of technology ("technification") is that people have distanced themselves from their surroundings, losing their "hands-on" attitude toward solving their day-to-day problems.

Having offered autobiographical evidence earlier in the essay, Buckley argues that we all have lost our ability to distinguish between what we can do and what experts must do. Thus, we approach almost all our day-to-day problems feeling helpless because we have conditioned ourselves to accept helplessness as a result of living in a technological society.

20 Apathy in politics follows helplessness in problem solving. Buckley extends his argument to take in its political ramifications. Any individual power we do not exercise, we lose to political experts, and then we rely on them to make our decisions for us.

21 Buckley supports his political argument with evidence provided by the editor of a news magazine.

"plenipotentiary": Having or conferring full power or authority.

Because this hypothetical outcome carries Buckley's argument to only one of several possible conclusions, the conclusion is not ensured. A proposition is not true just because it cannot be proved false. Nevertheless, the paragraph warns readers of what may happen if we grow even more apathetic.

Nikita Sergeevich Khrushchev (1894–1971) was first secretary of the Communist Party (1953–1964) and premier of the Soviet Union (1958–1964).

Buckley's final sentence brings the essay back to the personal level; we have read one person's opinion, restated after he has offered evidence and outlined an argument.

editorial stance of his magazine was enough to convene a plenipotentiary meeting of the board of editors to review policy. "So few people complain, or make their voices heard," he explained to me, "that we assume a dozen letters represent the inarticulated views of thousands of readers." In the past ten years, he said, the volume of mail has noticeably decreased, even though the circulation of his magazine has risen.

When our voices are finally mute, when we have finally suppressed the natural instinct to complain, whether the vexation is trivial or grave, we shall have become automatons, incapable of feeling. When Premier Khrushchev first came to this country late in 1959 he was primed, we are informed, to experience the bitter resentment of the American people against his tyranny, against his persecutions, against the movement which is responsible for the great numbers of American deaths in Korea, for billions in taxes every year, and for life everlasting on the brink of disaster; but Khrushchev was pleasantly surprised, and reported back to the Russian people that he had been met with overwhelming cordiality (read: apathy), except, to be sure, for "a few fascists who followed me around with their wretched posters, and should be horsewhipped." 22

I may be crazy, but I say there would have been lots more posters in a society where train temperatures in the dead of winter are not allowed to climb to 85 degrees without complaint. 23

POSSIBLE ANSWERS

Meaning and Purpose

1. Encourage students to discuss complaining and apathy and offer anecdotes about times when they did or did not speak up.
2. The thesis appears first in brief form when he says all Americans "have given up trying to rectify irrational vexations" (4). The thesis is more fully explained in paragraph 8.

Meaning and Purpose

1. Do you agree with Buckley that most people have "given up trying to rectify irrational vexations"? Can you think of an instance when you spoke up and complained about something? What would you have done as a passenger on Buckley's 85-degree train? in the theater with the out-of-focus movie?
2. Where does Buckley state his thesis?
3. In paragraph 2 is the sentence, "No one addressed a word to him." Why is the sentence italicized?

4. What does "supine" mean, and who is the "supine breed" mentioned in paragraph 4?
5. Why is New Year's Eve important in this essay?
6. Whom is Buckley addressing in this essay?

Strategy

1. The stories about the overheated train, the out-of-focus movie, the waitress, the ski resort, and the stewardess are all personal anecdotes. Why do you think Buckley includes them, and how do they affect his argument?
2. What kind of reasoning does Buckley use in paragraph 7? Explain.
3. In paragraph 20, Buckley makes a transition to talking about political apathy. How does he accomplish this transition, and do you think he has established that political apathy has something to do with apathy on a smaller scale?

Style

1. What examples from the essay can you give displaying the tone of Buckley's argument? How effective is his tone?
2. What definition of "crazy" best fits the word as used in the last paragraph of this essay?
3. What do the last and first paragraphs of this essay have in common?

Writing Tasks

1. Buckley's thesis is that we Americans are eager to be unobtrusive, hesitant to claim our rights. According to him, when we have a reason to speak out, we don't, because we believe our case to be unjust, ambiguous, or too trivial "to justify the horrors

3. The sentence is Buckley's strong mental response to the episode, which he emphasizes graphically. Italics also indicate disbelief that we should be so compliant.
4. The "supine breed" are commuters who ride the train twice daily ("supine": apathetically passive or mentally or morally slack).
5. Buckley's resolution, of course, makes New Year's Eve appropriate. New Year's Eve also symbolizes a beginning, and Buckley wants to begin anew by starting to do something about being vexed.
6. Buckley addresses an intelligent audience of anyone who has ever been guilty of silence when a complaint was appropriate. He also warns apathetic people about the political danger in not complaining.

Strategy

1. The anecdotes first make a personal, friendly connection with readers, leaving them more likely to be swayed by what he says. The anecdotes strengthen his argument by reporting his experience of people "reluctant to make [their] own voices heard," and including himself in the group he criticizes.
2. An example of inductive reasoning (7). Buckley has just described a specific episode of reluctance to complain; from that he draws the general conclusion that everyone is guilty of thinking someone else will speak up.
3. Buckley has moved from the stewardess anecdote (18) to the larger problem of "helplessness in an age of technology and centralized political and economic power" (19), and then to "our notorious political apathy" (20). The transition is clear. Apathy about out-of-focus movies happens because we feel helpless to see to our own needs (19); how can we take on politicians and government if we can't even voice a complaint to a theater manager?

Style

1. Buckley's tone in these examples is sarcastic: "What question could be so important as to justify my sibilant intrusion into his stupor?" (2); sentence 1 in paragraph 4; and "we stretched our faces in a variety of contortions to accustom the eye to the shock of normal focus" (6). Sarcasm is effective because it mimics the ridiculousness of apathy and also emphasizes his strong feelings about what we settle for when we don't complain.

2. "Crazy" here means being "temporarily unbalanced." Buckley carefully uses the word before establishing a condition that has not been met, then conjectures about that condition as if it might have been met.

3. The last and first paragraphs are about train temperatures. In paragraph 1, he states what we do about our discomfort (nothing), and in the last paragraph wonders what would happen if we took a strong stand about train temperatures, metaphorically considered as taking such a stand about anything that vexes us.

of a confrontation with Authority." Write a paper in which you argue that Buckley's thesis is either well supported or weakly supported, by agreeing or disagreeing that the evidence proves his thesis or his purpose in the essay.

2. In an essay, tell one or more personal anecdotes to support a general assertion. You might talk about a childhood experience with an inept babysitter and argue that babysitters should be licensed as nurses and electricians are. Be sure your anecdotes support your argument; avoid overgeneralization.

❦ Elizabeth M. Whelan ❦

Born in New York City in 1943, Elizabeth Whelan has studied at Connecticut College, Yale School of Medicine, where she earned a master's in public health, and Harvard School of Public Health, where she earned a second master's degree and a doctoral degree. Currently she is president of the American Council on Science and Health. She is the author and coauthor of twenty books, including, most recently, Panic in the Pantry *(1975);* The Hundred Percent Natural, Purely Organic, Cholesterol-Free, Megavitamin, Low-Carbohydrate Nutrition Hoax *(1983),* Toxic Terror *(1985), and* Balanced Nutrition *(1989). Whelan has received the Walter Alvarez Award from the American Writers Association and an Early Career Award from the Public Health Association.*

Big Business vs. Public Health:
The Cigarette Dilemma

Whelan's analysis touches on many aspects of the "cigarette dilemma" in the United States, from the physical pain of individuals with cigarette-related diseases to the influence on government elections of the tobacco industry. First published in U.S.A. Today *in May 1984, this article is as relevant today as it was then.*

What do the following have in common: dioxin in Missouri; chemical seepage at Love Canal; radioactive contamination at Three Mile Island; saccharin; hairdyes; formaldehyde; coffee; Red Dye #2? All of these topics have been extensively, and emotionally, covered by the media in recent years. All have been indicted as possible causes of cancer, birth defects, and other human maladies.

In recent months, we have witnessed dozens of television documentaries, magazine cover stories, and unsettling headlines focused on the theme, "America, the Poisoned." We have seen a

563

TEACHING SUGGESTIONS

This important essay easily engenders interest because of its relevant topic, particularly the parts about advertising and about "cognitive dissonance," people's response when they acquire information that clashes with their behavior or firm belief.

You might begin the discussion with questions that cause cognitive dissonance: Where is "Marlboro country"? What does the Virginia Slims slogan, "You've come a long way, Baby" suggest? One Virginia Slims advertisement says, "A long, elegant, feminine light. Because women are equal, not the same." What does that advertising copy suggest?

A package of Lucky Strike filter cigarettes says, "SURGEON GENERAL'S WARNING: Smoking Causes Lung Cancer, Heart Disease, Emphysema, and May Complicate Pregnancy." On the front is "LOW TAR—RICH TASTE." This is an advertising ploy that relies on cognitive dissonance. If you smoke, you rely on the "information" on the front of the package. If you do not smoke, you believe the Surgeon General on the side. You believe what you want to believe; otherwise, you have cacophony, a "disharmony" between one statement and another.

What else do we "believe because we want to believe"? How much do we believe without questioning the sources of our evidence? When what we believe clashes with facts and statistics, why do we often cling to our beliefs? Here is life-or-death evidence that we had better take ourselves seriously, which means honestly.

MARGINAL NOTES

This rhetorical question engages the audience, which immediately becomes involved in thinking about the topic, particularly because the answer to the question is potentially devastating.

dramatic increase in the use of scare verbs like "ooze," "seep," "brew," and "foul," and scare adjectives like "ominous," "sinister," and "horrific." We have come to believe that there is an environmental time bomb ticking, and that what we see today is only the tip of the iceberg. We are left with a guilt-provoking and anxiety-producing feeling that modern American technology is just now catching up with us, that we will ultimately pay the highest price for the conveniences we now enjoy—environmentally induced premature death.

The Environmental Protection Agency, Consumer Product Safety Commission, Food and Drug Administration, consumer groups, and home owners' associations have responded to—and indeed contributed to—this escalating fear of environmental sources of disease by demanding the banning of pesticides, food additives, urea formaldehyde foam insulation, and other products of modern industrial know-how. In the case of the Love Canal, Pres. Carter went so far as to declare an official state of emergency and order the costly relocation of more than 700 homeowners. In Missouri, the EPA was the subject of bitter criticism, and damning press coverage, for not evacuating families sooner from the dioxin-contaminated areas.

It is no surprise, then, that national surveys indicated that, in the 1980s, Americans are significantly more supportive than ever before of environmental legislation, efforts to clean up toxic wastes, and more stringent government control of food additives, pesticides, and a vast array of consumer products. All of this is *allegedly* in the interest of promoting health through the application of preventive measures to remove the suspected disease-causing agents.

Those topics listed above have something else in common as well. Although in some cases there was suggestive evidence to indicate a *potential* threat to human health, and there was just reason for vigilance, there is no solid evidence that exposure to these substances has caused either deaths or any deleterious long-term impact on human health! In other words, in retrospect, the swell of American anxiety about environmental contaminants,

Paragraphs 2 and 3 provide the extensive background information needed to follow her forthcoming argument and set up the causes for the effect that is stated in paragraph 4.

The effect of the documentaries, cover stories, headlines, and presidential actions: Americans are environmentally conscious, more than ever before.

The transitional paragraphs, 5 and 6, surprise readers who had expected to read just another article expressing the proposition that the environment threatens people's health. Instead, Whelan reminds them of the facts, shorn of connotation.

and the apparent mandate for action to control them, is based on very little evidence of the existence of a real problem.

Dioxin in Missouri was not the cause of any human disease. Indeed, the only known human effect to have occurred in other circumstances when humans have been exposed to dioxin is chloracne, a severe form of acne. Even chloracne was not noted in Missouri. New York Gov. Hugh Carey's blue ribbon physician panel, which examined the health status at Love Canal, concluded that "There has been no demonstration of acute health effects linked to exposure to hazardous wastes at Love Canal . . . chronic effects of hazardous waste exposure at Love Canal have neither been established nor ruled out. . . ." The same panel found no evidence to support claims of higher rates of miscarriage or birth defects among Love Canal residents. Rep. Mike McCormack (D. Wash.), chairman of a subcommittee that prepared a report on Three Mile Island, summed up the general feeling among scientists when he said, "the greatest harm from the TMI accident was its severe emotional impact on an ill-informed and easily frightened public." Saccharin, hairdyes, Red Dye #2, and formaldehyde have been shown in a limited number of experiments to increase cancer risk in laboratory animals. There is no evidence from human studies that these substances cause disease. Coffee consumption was linked with pancreatic cancer in one controversial epidemiological study, but other human studies have not confirmed this finding.

It is in this context that the cigarette stands out as the ultimate paradox in American society. While magazines, newspapers, and the electronic media focus almost daily on *hypothetical* risks posed by environmental chemical contamination and the techniques of modern food production and processing, and the American public is demanding that the government "do something" to prevent environmentally induced disease, there is a near complete lack of interest in the leading cause of premature death in the U.S.—the cigarette. *While no one died at Love Canal or Three Mile Island, some 400,000 Americans this year alone will die prematurely from diseases directly associated with cigarette smoke.*

6

7   The thesis paragraph, in which Whelan states the point that she will prove. The italicized statement shocks us into reexamining our assumptions by comparing those assumptions with a fact.

A Malevolent Web

The series of rhetorical questions is designed to involve us intimately as readers. Whelan will attack each of these questions in the order she outlines here. The outline can help her readers immensely because it predicts sequentially each subtopic that will follow in the essay.

How can a product as dangerous as the cigarette continue to be accepted—and indeed be heavily promoted by advertising—in such a health-conscious and demanding society? Why are there no frequent television documentaries, investigative reporting, outraged citizens groups, and concerned legislatures dealing with what is arguably the most dramatic and far-reaching public health threat of this century? Why do we have anxious scrutiny over traces of dioxin, yet apathy about cigarettes as a cause of disease? How, 30 years after it was definitely shown to be a health hazard, does the cigarette remain triumphant in its knowledge of a secure future? The answer lies in a malevolent web of five extrinsic and intrinsic factors:

- The happenstance of a cruel and unpredictable backfire in human innovation.
- The physically addictive nature of cigarettes, which keeps smokers hooked despite a desire to quit.
- The human tendency to reject the premise that, under some circumstances, we may be responsible for causing our own illness or death—the adaptive psychological defense mechanisms which allow the smoker to sublimate, repress, and disassociate himself from the bad news about cigarettes.
- The related reluctance of nonsmokers to bring up grim statistics when they know that the smoker is already overburdened with guilt and anxiety.
- The enormous and unprecedented economic clout exerted by the tobacco industry. Those dependent on it for their livelihood take great pains to ensure that their addicted and potentially addicted customers be shielded from frequent onslaughts of information about how harmful cigarette smoking is.

Examining the first factor, the author explores "backfire" in 1950, when the public learned

Backfire. It goes without saying that, if the cigarette were being considered for introduction today, there is no way it would

8

9

meet the safety criteria of either the Food and Drug Administration or the Consumer Product Safety Commission, the two agencies which would seem most logical for approving and regulating it. Even without the dozens of human studies which we have today, the agencies would reject cigarettes because burned tobacco contains a significant number of cancer-causing agents and the immediate effects of tobacco inhalation (increased heart rate, increase in blood carbon monoxide levels, inhibition of stomach contractions) would be sufficient sources for concern. Whether it was the small businessman trying to have cigarettes approved or a large corporation's research department which had come up with this "brainstorm," today, the cigarette would not make its way out of the Federal testing laboratories, and the economic impact of the non-approval of cigarettes would be negligible.

However, the cigarette is *not* just being introduced; it has been around for approximately 100 years. (Tobacco, of course, has been used for generations, but it was the invention of the cigarette manufacturing machine in the 1880s which resulted in a new and devastating form of behavior—inhalation of smoke on a regular basis, directly into the lungs.) 10

Through the first 60 years of its 100-year existence, the cigarette and the marketing techniques that went with it represented a stellar success for those who worked hard and cleverly in a free enterprise environment to sell a product that gave pleasure, prestige, and relaxation to millions of eager customers. During the first six decades, there was, of course, "controversy" about cigarettes, and eventually some impressive scientific evidence that cigarettes were hazardous. In general, however, the time period between 1890 and 1950 marked the golden age of the cigarette, the birth of a new symbol of the all-American man and, eventually, the all-American woman. That was the dream: the carefree life; the glamorous ads; the hints that cigarettes might not only be pleasurable, but even healthful; and the development of a major, successful economic base for millions of people, directly or indirectly financially dependent on the production, manufacture, sales, and advertising of cigarettes. 11

about the enormous health risks associated with smoking. Growing, promoting, and selling tobacco were well-intentioned businesses that backfired when medical science showed that smoking kills consumers.

Then, in 1950, the dream became a nightmare. In a near   12
explosion of medical data, smokers and nonsmokers alike were
jolted by the reports of the devastating health impact of the plea-
sure-giving cigarette. The news was, quite decidedly, too frightening to fully digest, and indeed, through much of the 1950s, the
most prevalent reaction of the medical profession, the press, and
the general public was to downplay the evidence, demand "further
data," point to alleged gaps and limitations of the "statistics," and
run as far from the reality as possible. Human innovation had
backfired, and people did not know what to do about it. For years,
honest, hard-working, enterprising Americans had grown tobacco, manufactured cigarettes, and promoted and distributed the
product in a clever (and well-intentioned) manner. The tragedy
here is that, by the time the bad news about cigarettes had accumulated, the cigarette had become socially desirable, enormous
segments of the economic system—including the U.S. government—were dependent on the cigarette as a source of revenue,
and a sizable portion of the American population was physically
addicted to the product.

Addiction. Most Americans are well aware of the addictive   13
properties of illegal "recreational" drugs like heroin. Many would
be shocked to learn that Dr. Williams Polin, director of the National Institute on Drug Abuse, terms cigarette smoking "the most
widespread drug dependence in our country." In general, the
number of cigarettes consumed by the average smoker is 30 per
day. Each inhaled puff delivers a dose of drug to the brain, resulting in 50,000 to 70,000 such doses per person every year. There
is no other form of drug use which occurs with such frequency
and regularity.

The evidence on the addictive nature of smoking is evident   14
in national surveys which indicate that 90 percent of smokers
would like to quit and that 85 percent have tried to quit, but
failed. Cigarette smokers are physiological prisoners, their
bodies in need of the substances in cigarette smoke in order to
perform efficiently. Repeated studies indicate that tobacco is more
addictive than heroin, producing very strong physical dependence. Cigarette withdrawal symptoms include significant body
changes leading to decrease in heart rate, increase in appe-

In examining the second factor, addiction,
Whelan uses a wealth of statistics to support
her argument, thereby appealing to readers'
sense of logic. Notice the irony in the last line
in paragraph 15: The "tobacco industry's recipe for survival," which includes the essential
component of addiction, causes death, the very
opposite of human "survival."

tite, disturbances in sleep patterns, anxiety, irritability, and aggressiveness.

When a smoker tells you that he has tried to stop smoking, but just can't, he really means it. Moreover, of those who *are* able to give up smoking, some 70 percent resume the habit within three months—about the same recidivism rate as heroin. One cannot overstate the contribution that this addictive nature has made to the continued use of the cigarette; indeed, it is an essential component of the tobacco industry's recipe for survival.

Psychological blackout. The survival of the cigarette in the 1980s is a classical testimony to the existence of the psychological mechanisms which protect us from facts with which we cannot cope. The classic response to cognitive dissonance, which occurs when people acquire new information that clashes with their current behavior or firmly held belief, was vividly evident during the 1950s, when retrospective and prospective human epidemiological studies around the world confirmed the extraordinary rates of lung cancer, heart disease, emphysema, and other ailments among smokers. People simply refused to incorporate this new information into their consciousness. During that entire decade, there was enormous resistance on the part of the media, legislators, and even physicians to believe the new findings, and a tendency to dismiss what was unacceptable. During the early 1950s, some 70 percent of American men from all walks of life smoked, had previously thought it was at worst only slightly harmful, and could not deal with a different assessment.

Today's surveys show that 90 percent of Americans know cigarette smoking is hazardous to health (although most of them "know" it only in the rhetorical sense, unaware of the specific dangers). The clash here is between the reality of smoking and the evidence available that it is harmful. The two beliefs cannot exist together, so it is the evidence that is repressed and in some cases sublimated. (For example, when the smoker declares his "health consciousness" by joining an exercise club or shopping at a "health food" store.)

In plain English, smokers do not want to talk or think about the dangers of their habit. Currently, public service advertisements about the hazards of smoking are few and far between, so

15

16   Examining the third factor—the psychological response to cognitive dissonance—Whelan explains the emotional attachment people have had to tobacco. The attachment has been so strong that it could not be broken, even by overwhelming evidence showing it to be lethal. As used in this essay, *cognitive* describes all the aspects of knowing, including perception, judgment, reasoning and remembering, and thinking and imagining; and *dissonance* refers to incongruity, a lack of harmony. What the consumer "knows" does not harmonize with the irrefutable scientific evidence canceling that causal knowledge, so that the consumer buries, in a way, the evidence that refutes what he or she "knows."

17

18

most smokers find it relatively easy to avoid mental dissonance. Cigarette smoking literally becomes an involuntary, automatic form of behavior, with no incentive for the smoker to reevaluate his decision to smoke from week to week.

Examining the fourth factor shows that it, too, is psychological, effectively canceling the logic that one ordinarily associates with rational thinking. Social pressures come into play here: No one wants to lose a friend in the social sense; ironically therefore, a person may lose a friend who dies from smoking.

Nonsmokers' reluctance. It would seem logical that the non- 19 smoker, unencumbered by the physiological addiction to cigarettes, would be an ideal source of encouragement for smoking cessation. However, it generally does not work that way, because some basic human psychological mechanisms are at work.

First, disease data on smoking are so horrifying that it may 20 be difficult for a wife, for example, to allow herself to even imagine her husband experiencing an excruciating death from lung cancer, and a type of "secondhand" denial may set in. Second, she might meet major resistance and strike a chord of marital dissension should she attempt to focus her smoking husband on the subject. Third, in dealing with a friend, relative, or anyone else who smokes, many nonsmokers sense the smoker's depression, guilt, and unhappiness, sometimes masked by one-liners and grim humor, and feel reluctant to make a bad situation worse by bringing up a topic which is so depressing. There are, inevitably, many relatives, friends, and employers seriously concerned about the health of their smoking friends, but simply baffled about how to tactfully, graciously, and effectively bring the topic up without incurring the wrath of the person they are trying to help. The irony today is that cigarette smoking is socially acceptable, while discussions of the health hazards of smoking are not.

The combination of the "guilt-ridden smoker's phenomenon" 21 and the helplessness of the nonsmoker in giving the advice may be one reason why certain institutions—like churches and synagogues—have generally ignored the topic. This is ironic since, while religious organizations across the country may differ widely in their codes of theology, all are united in their belief that human life is precious. Most probably would agree that it is a sin, however defined, to take one's own life. Many have taken formal stances on potentially life-threatening aspects of life-style. For example, the National Council of Churches of Christ has issued official policy statements on drug abuse, health care, and alcohol use, but it and almost all other formal religious sects in this country maintain silence on the subject of cigarettes and health. (A vivid exception here is the Seventh-Day Adventist Church, which issues a substantial quantity of literature about the dangers of smoking, complete with photographs of diseased lungs.)

Why would a clergyman who grimly warned you that shooting yourself in the head with a loaded pistol would be contrary to God's wishes not warn you that slow-motion suicide was equally unacceptable and immoral? Why would the National Council of Churches take on the issue of infant formula in the Third World, claiming that it was life-threatening, and then turn their heads on an issue which kills hundreds of thousands of Americans—and is about to kill millions of new smokers in developing nations? The answer again indicates the physiological addiction process; the fact that a sizable minority of clergymen, like everyone else, smokes cigarettes; and that the smoking problem seems so deep-rooted and hopeless that no effort is made to address the subject.

Part of the psychological cover-up on the subject of smoking might be explained by the human eagerness to blame misfortune on anyone but ourselves. In the case of Third World-feeding practices, the "enemy" was the infant formula manufacturers; in the case of the anxiety about the health effects of dioxin or Red Dye #2, the "villain" was a chemical or a food company; in the case of the cigarette, the "villain" is the smoker or, as the cartoon figure Pogo once said, "We have met the enemy and he is us." It is far easier to focus one's attention and ire on health risks imposed by outside forces than it is to become introspective about one's own role in human disease. This rejection of introspection may, for example, explain the total lack of interest in the subject of cigarettes among the "women's movement," as represented by the National Organization for Women (NOW), *Ms.* magazine, and other groups which have a commitment to improving the quality of women's lives. The movement has been both active and successful in reducing on-the-job discrimination, fostering equal opportunity in advanced education, reducing the gap in compensation between males and females, proclaiming women's rights to control of their own bodies by encouraging availability of birth

22

23 "psychological cover-up": We transfer our misfortunes, blaming anyone but ourselves, which is true to form for any person having an addiction. Avoiding the act of facing ourselves and taking control of our own health, we focus on the outside world, where we find ways to avoid looking into our own minds and analyzing our own feelings.

control services and abortion, and developing novel ways of effectively combining careers with family life. It thus seems a bit strange that there is a peculiar silence on the subject of women's smoking in feminist circles.

The feminist health "bible," *Our Bodies, Ourselves,* has only a   24
passing reference to the subject of smoking. When asked about this, Judy Norsigian, a member of the Boston Women's Health Collective, which produced the original book, explained that they had intended to include a chapter on smoking, alcohol, and drugs, but "there was not sufficient room in the book, and we did not have the resources to do the research." NOW, which has taken a very active role in many women's health issues, has no comment on smoking, and in its 40-page submission to the 1979 Kennedy hearings on women's health, did not make a single reference to the problem. The National Women's Health Network, which represents about 1,000 American women's health organizations, has "no formal position on smoking." The San Francisco Women's Health Collective, an organization which describes itself as devoted to "women's health education," does not address the smoking issue because "it [is] not a priority in terms of health education."

Even the magazines of "liberated" women stand mute on this   25
subject. *Ms.,* which claims to "serve women as people, not roles," has distinct opinions about what advertising they should accept and are on record as saying they will not accept advertising that is offensive to women (for example, they turned down ads for vaginal deodorants), but they freely advertise cigarettes and, since they began publication a decade ago, have *never* carried an article on smoking and health.

Why the silence here? In the case of the magazines, it is clear   26
that the advertising revenue from tobacco companies plays some role, but there must be more to it than that. Feminist groups have a tradition of focusing on problems which they feel are unique to women, and perhaps they unconsciously decided that the cigarette problem affected everyone. However, in the 1980s, with lung cancer replacing breast cancer as the leading cause of cancer death in women and cigarettes being the major controllable threat to

Whelan cites feminist groups that do not focus on what women are doing to their health. She puts forth strong evidence for her position before recommending that the feminist movement become introspective, at least about the problem of smoking. Her appeal rests on the kind of evidence she offers, which leads to an ethical recommendation, not an emotional one.

the health of unborn children, should not priorities be reexamined? That is where the addiction and "self-inflicted" nature of the cigarette nightmare come in. Once again, the major thrust of the women's movement has always been focused on what others (particularly the male of the species) are doing to women, as opposed to what they are doing to themselves. In order to effectively address the growing calamity of cigarettes in women's death and morbidity, the leaders of the feminist movement must for once become introspective, acknowledging that the cigarette problem is largely self-induced.

Economic clout. With some 35,000 medical citations in the literature indicting tobacco use, particularly cigarette smoking, for a vast array of human diseases, and with 90 percent of their customers, although physiologically hooked, desirous of giving up their product, it is necessary for the tobacco industry to be constantly vigilant to ensure the survival of its business. Tobacco, particularly in the form of cigarettes, *is* Big Business in the U.S. With 640,000,000,000 cigarettes smoked in 1982 at a cost to smokers of over $21,200,000,000, the economic stakes are very high. Not only is tobacco grown in 22 American states and our sixth largest cash crop, but there is a vast and complex tobacco supply network which extends the chain of economic dependence on tobacco to include a full spectrum of industries, including manufacturers of farm supplies and equipment, transportation, advertising, and, in turn, those who depend on these suppliers. Thus, the economic ripple effect extends from the tobacco manufacturers, to Madison Avenue ad agencies, and finally to newspapers and magazines which derive over $1,000,000,000 annually in revenues from cigarette ads. In addition, any list of "cigarette dependents" must include Federal, state, and local governments, which receive more than $6,000,000,000 in cigarette sales and excise taxes each year.

There are four major ways that tobacco interests flex their economic muscle when they perceive any threat to their most important product—cigarettes. First, they rely on the corporate clout of their family companies. By buying soft drink, insurance, food, and alcoholic beverage companies, they have succeeded in

27   The fifth factor, economics, explains the countrywide effects of tobacco as big business with big muscle. Whelan outlines, with verifiable examples, the four ways in which the industry flexes its economic muscle: business mergers, business clients, business alliances, and business advertising.

28

spreading even further the economic dependency on cigarettes, thus extending the reach of their corporate teeth. For example, Del Monte, which operates canneries and specialty plants, beverage operations, and seafood and frozen food plants around the world, seemingly would have no interest in the sales of cigarettes. However, Del Monte is part of the R. J. Reynolds family and thus has a very definite interest in the success of the parent company. Similarly, it is all-in-the-family for Miller beer and Seven-Up, with their "father," Philip Morris; and there is a partnership of Saks Fifth Avenue, Gimbels department stores, and Brown and Williamson—all members of the Batus family. Some of the family members seem most incompatible. American Brands—makers of Lucky Strikes, Pall Mall, and Tareyton—owns the Franklin Life Insurance company, which offers discounts on policies to non-smokers! There is no doubt that, when the tobacco men are feeling pressure (for example, from Congress), they rally the "sibling" companies around the cigarette flag.

Second, tobacco executives know that businesses need clients, and the tobacco empire is a very valuable client, one which businesses which need accounts would do nothing to displease. Thus, a major chemical company which produces agricultural chemicals is part of the tobacco "family" too, because, if it became outspoken on the dangers of cigarettes, it might lose these affluent customers. The roots go even deeper; the suppliers of family companies (glass and container manufacturers) for Seven-Up, cans for Miller beer, sugar for Hawaiian Punch, flavoring agents for Patio Mexican foods and Chun King Oriental food) are dealing indirectly, but still significantly, with the tobacco empire. 29

Third, by teaming up with the manufacturers of other products that might be the subject of bad press or inhibiting government regulation, the cigarette manufacturers are constantly seeking potential allies who will stand by them in the name of Big Business and free enterprise. An analysis of the affiliation of the directors of the top tobacco companies is revealing, as it demonstrates how cigarette manufacturers have been successful in making corporate officers of other industries members of the 30 tobacco team. For example, the R. J. Reynolds board includes Herschel H. Cudd, retired senior vice president of Standard Oil, Ronald Grierson from General Electric, John D. Macomber from Celanese, and John W. Hanley of Monsanto.

Fourth, the cigarette manufacturers demonstrate their economic clout through the use of some of the most elaborate and extravagant advertising and promotional budgets in American history. Although they deny publicly that cigarettes are devastating to health, there is no possibility that the decision-makers at the big five tobacco companies are unaware of the risk associated with their product. Thus, they have made a conscious decision that their own economic well-being is far more important than the health of Americans. Advertising is their primary mechanism for neutralizing the medical fears among smokers and keeping the "pleasures" of smoking in the public's mind.

31   Whelan shows that when scientific evidence is countered with clever, continuous advertising, the effect in the minds of the public is to neutralize such evidence.

For years, cigarette apologists have defended their advertising practices by claiming that they advertise only to foster competition among various brands, not to mislead smokers about the effects of their habit, or to lure new smokers to the ranks. However, an analysis of the current advertisements for cigarettes strongly suggest that what the ads are selling is not cigarettes, but the *social acceptance of cigarettes*. While smokers today are understandably very nervous and unsure of the legitimacy of their smoking behavior, cigarette advertising reinforces them by giving them reassurance when they need it and communicating that lots of goodlooking, healthy, young people smoke.

32   Tobacco advertisements, according to Whelan, are not printed and aired to "prove" that one cigarette is superior to another. Instead, they share the economic feature of trying to "prove" that smoking is a socially acceptable habit.

The heavy reliance on the low tar and low nicotine statistics represents an attempt to convey the misleading message that "everything is all right now," but, beyond that, tobacco industry documents reviewed by the FTC indicate that many cigarette advertising techniques are aimed at denigrating or undercutting the health warning. Documents from Brown and Williamson and one of its advertising agencies, Ted Bates and Company, Inc., focused on means of reducing the concern about health effects. As a result of its research, Bates reported to B&W that many smokers perceive the habit as "dirty" and dangerous, a practice followed only by "very stupid people." The report concludes:

33

Notice the psychological approach taken by one advertising firm that handles the public's perception of smoking.

So far, Whelan has gained the audience's involved interest by presenting facts, statistics, and other solid evidence that shows how grave is the problem of tobacco addiction. Now she outlines four specific courses toward a possible solution to that problem: beginning a plan of action, stepping up agencies' attempts to warn the public, questioning the tobacco companies' advertising approaches, and attending more to the fact of addiction.

Each of the following sections includes consciously employed rhetorical strategies: Whelan states the course, develops the facts, supports the course, answers possible arguments, urges the audience to become involved, and then summarizes.

The audience is directly addressed, thereby becoming directly involved in the problem.

Thus, the smokers have to face the fact that they are illogical, irrational, and stupid. People find it hard to go throughout life with such negative presentation and evaluation of self. The saviours are the *rationalization* and repression that end up and result in a defense mechanism that, as many of the defense mechanisms we use, has its own logic, its own rationale. (Emphasis theirs.)

The report goes on to recommend that good ad copy will "deemphasize the objections" to smoking. With specific regard to health issues, the Bates report recommends: "Start out from the basic assumption that cigarette smoking is dangerous to your health—try to go around it in an elegant manner, but don't try to fight it—it's a losing war." 34

Coping with Disaster

The complexity of the cigarette's ongoing devastation to public health in America sometimes appears overwhelming because of its intermeshing of human frailties with the existence of a dominant industry and many sub-industries which seem committed to serving the needs of that human frailty, no matter what the cost. However, there are a number of specific courses this country could take to begin to cope with this national health disaster. 35

First, and foremost, before we as a country can begin a plan of action to deal with the cigarette, we must face up to the enormity of the problem that cigarettes now pose. We have to cast aside that sense of resignation to cigarettes and death and recognize cigarettes for what they are—a unique problem that merits a unique solution. 36

One might initially be tempted to argue that cigarettes are not any different from alcohol or even food; that anything can be overused to the point of becoming a health threat. Actually, unlike other forms of legal recreation such as alcohol consumption, there is, for all practical purposes, no known safe level of use for cigarettes or any known health benefit. While there are those who abuse alcohol, either by drinking to the point it is physically 37 damaging or combining drinking with driving an automobile, the majority of people who use alcohol consume it at levels that are harmless. The overwhelming majority of smokers, however, smoke at levels which are definitely detrimental to health. Due to their addictive nature, it is for all practical purposes not possible to smoke a "safe" number of cigarettes per day. Indeed, alcohol may offer some health benefits. Recently, a number of investigators have shown that moderate consumption of alcohol—one or two drinks a day—may offer some protection against coronary heart disease by contributing to the elevation of high density lipoproteins.

Let us, as a country, make a policy decision one way or another on cigarettes. Given our experiences with Prohibition in the 1920s, a government attempt to deny access to a commodity that people want, the outlawing of cigarettes seems like an unrealistic option. However, we *can* remove our heads from the sand and face the ultimate question: Are the economic benefits of cigarettes important enough to this country that they justify the premature deaths of 400,000 Americans each year? [Smoking costs the nation about $11,000,000,000 in direct medical expenses and $36,000,000,000 in lost productivity due to illness and premature death each year. Cigarette smokers pay only $7,000,000,000 annually in excise taxes, however, and, even with the tobacco industry's direct contributions to the economy (about $22,000,000,000 per year), we still come up short.]

Even if the answer is yes, do we choose to continue to disperse the enormous costs of smoking throughout the entire population and, indeed, to subsidize the production of tobacco? Or, will we adopt the policy of letting people smoke cigarettes as they please, but no longer make the nonsmoking population foot the bill in terms of the costs of extensive medical care, lost workdays, fire damage, and increased life insurance costs?

Were we to face up to that question and familiarize American nonsmokers with the enormous amounts of money they are paying for the smoker's "right" to light up, we might have one of the answers to the cigarette dilemma in America—let those who wish to smoke do so, but also let the smokers and companies that

38

39 An "if . . . then" strategy. If people want to smoke, then society as a whole should not have to pay the consequences.

40

market cigarettes assume all the economic responsibilities of the habit.

Second, both voluntary and government agencies should es- 41 calate their attempts to bring the warnings on the danger of smoking both to smokers and nonsmokers. In waging this war against more detailed cigarette health warnings, Sen. Wendell H. Ford (D.-Ky.) maintained that there was an "exceptionally high level of awareness" on the issue of smoking and the American public is bombarded with information on smoking." Indeed, a superficial look at recent Roper and Gallup polls seems to back him up, given that 90 percent of those surveyed knew that smoking could be "dangerous." However, the more-in-depth questions in these surveys noted that 30 percent of Americans were unaware that a 30-year-old man reduces his life expectancy by smoking a pack a day; 43 percent were unaware that smoking is a major cause of heart disease; and up to 80 percent of the population did not know that smoking causes most bronchitis and emphysema. Many anecdotal accounts from physicians indicate that nearly every patient who receives a diagnosis of lung cancer is shocked, angry, and indignant, claiming that he or she just didn't know that "only" a pack a day would cause this disease.

Although it would only be a small part of the effort to deal 42 with the effects of cigarettes, strengthening the warning label on the pack—and varying it occasionally to refer to specific diseases caused by cigarettes—would serve the function of triggering some cognitive dissonance among smokers and might lead them to reevaluate their decision to continue smoking. Beyond that, a cigarette label which noted that the product was physiologically addictive would give the smoker the knowledge he needs for a true "freedom of choice." The best evidence that stronger labels might work is the fact that the tobacco industry and their spokesmen in Congress are dead set against it. For the tobacco business, the best consumer is an uninformed one.

Third, we could give some serious consideration to whether 43 our society should encourage the production of increasingly brazen tobacco advertisements which associate smoking with glamour, youth, and good clean fun. It might be argued that cigarette

Whelan counters general poll results with specific statistical results.

Another use of the "if . . . then" strategy. If cigarette advertisements perform a serious function, then they should not include social pleasantries masking that function.

advertisements perform a function by providing tar and nicotine levels, but this could be done without the Satin Doll, the macho cowboy, and the athlete putting his socks on in the locker room. Toning down the ads, and perhaps eliminating them entirely except at point of purchase, might have the additional benefit of removing the editorial hesitancy to cover the topic of cigarettes in popular magazines.

Fourth, the concept of cigarette addiction needs more attention than it has received. It is theoretically possible that a substance—a type of methadone for cigarettes—could be developed which could, when used with behavior modification, have a significant success rate in getting smokers unhooked. Such research—and the approval of any product that would break cigarette addiction—would no doubt be inhibited by the tobacco lobby. However, if we do truly believe in "freedom of choice," the suppression of such a life-saving measure would be inconsistent and indeed immoral.

The cigarette has been maligned by a series of critics through the ages, but, until 30 years ago, the attacks were primarily emotional, with heavy moral overtones. In the 1980s, we should not be moralizing about cigarettes, but simply facing up to the realities and asking ourselves, if we really want to win the war against environmental disease, why don't we start by identifying the number-one enemy?

It Takes Clout to Keep a Harmful Product on the Market

- A major American company which supplies processing materials to the cigarette industry [the company asked not to be named, lest it be the target of further ire from the tobacco companies] recently released a booklet on environmental causes of cancer. Naturally, the publication focused a good deal of attention on cigarettes as the cause of many different malignancies and prominently featured a graph showing the enormous increase in lung cancer in the past 10 years. Shortly after the release of the publication, the chief executive officer of the chemical company received a letter from

44   Whelan shows how the concepts of "freedom of choice" and wanting to win the war against environmental disease should be expanded.

45   The dangers of cigarette smoking are not moral; they are scientific, based on enormous accumulations of data. Moral issues are debatable; data of this kind are not.

46   "Clout": Instead of backing her argument with examples to prove her final statement, Whelan uses a far more startling strategy: Without further commentary, she presents seven bulleted examples of what "clout" means in this context, which combine to shock the audience into realizing that the tobacco industry's clout is far stronger than ordinarily perceived. Whelan's crescendo ending for this essay makes a powerful emotional appeal to her audience.

his counterpart at a large tobacco company, chastising him for citing cigarettes as a cause of disease and requesting that the publication be withdrawn. When the executive did not respond to the tobacco man's request, that cigarette company made it clear that it would look elsewhere for its supplies.

- Since 1964, there has been no major story on the health impact of cigarette smoking in any major U.S. popular publication (with the exception of *Reader's Digest, Good Housekeeping,* and *The New Yorker*). Freelance medical writers know well the rule, "it is not fair game to discuss cigarettes." Some 10–40 percent of advertising revenues for U.S. magazines comes from tobacco advertisements.   47

- Paul Maccabee, a reporter for the *Twin Cities Reader* in Minneapolis, covered a press conference announcing Brown and Williamson Tobacco Corporation's annual Kool Jazz Festival and inserted an unexpected twist in his story—a list of jazz greats who had died of lung cancer. The next day, he was fired.   48

- Joseph Califano, an outspoken critic of cigarettes while he was Secretary of Health, Education, and Welfare under Pres. Carter, reports in his book, *The Governing of America,* what happened when he invited the wife of Rep. Fred Rooney (D.-Pa.), who had been a "classmate" of Califano's at SmokeEnders, to join him on the stage during one of his speeches: "When a Tobacco Institute lobbyist saw her, he told her husband that he would never get another dollar from the industry." Rooney lost his bid for reelection.   49

- In the U.S. each year, thousands of people successfully sue major industries to collect damages resulting from everything from their exposure to asbestos, tampons, and cotton dust to injuries incurred while using toys and household products. Although numerous damage suits have been initiated against the tobacco industry for chronic health problems caused by smoking cigarettes, only 10 have ever made it to court and only two have ever gone to jury. Even though cigarettes—in contrast to those other products—are dan-   50 gerous when used as intended, the cigarette industry has never lost a case or paid out one cent in compensation for tobacco-induced injuries.

- In September, 1976, 12,000,000 British viewers saw "Death in the West," frequently called "the most powerful anti-smoking film ever made." The film intercuts three types of footage: Marlboro commercials with cowboys lighting up around a camp fire; Philip Morris executives claiming that no one really knows if cigarettes cause cancer; and, finally, interviews with six real cowboys who have lung cancer and emphysema caused, their physicians say, by smoking. Philip Morris sued Thames Television, producers of the film, in British courts and obtained a court order preventing the film from being shown or even discussed by filmmakers. The court ordered that all copies of the film be destroyed or confiscated.

- "Death in the West" did, however, show up in San Francisco in mid-1982 and was shown on local television in that city. It stirred up a good deal of interest, so much so that the *Journal of the American Medical Association* commissioned a respected California public health authority, Dr. David Fletcher, to write a story on the documentary and the tobacco company's efforts to suppress it. As soon as it was submitted, however, the piece was killed because, in the words of a *JAMA* editor, "It was felt by the legal department that publication of a story on such a controversial subject would render the AMA vulnerable to legal action, possibly by Philip Morris, and that is not a chance that anyone here wanted to take."

POSSIBLE ANSWERS

Meaning and Purpose

1. Let students talk about the facts and opinions they have about cigarette smoking and either be critical of or agree with Whelan's argument.

2. *Malevolent* means intending harm. The "malevolent web" is woven of the five related reasons that Whelan gives for cigarettes remaining "triumphant in [their] knowledge of a secure future" (8).

3. One statement of purpose would be: Whelan intends to expose the uncompromising and harsh facts about cigarettes, and those who promote them, in an attempt to stir readers to take action.

4. All Whelan's facts are part of the cigarette dilemma, the "malevolent web": a history of cigarettes puts what is happening now into perspective; companies in the tobacco "family" have their hands tied about doing something to lessen the cigarette problem; and the women's movement is one place readers might think much attention would be given to cigarettes, but it is not.

5. "Backfire" means that we have critical information too late to reverse the damage already done. For instance, because of what we now know about the health risks of cigarettes, "the cigarette would not make its way out of the Federal testing laboratories" (9).

6. Whelan excuses smokers themselves when she acknowledges the difficulty of kicking cigarette addiction, the psychological mechanism that keeps people from admitting the risks, and the ruthlessness of advertising that goes after a market of young people.

Strategy

1. In the first six paragraphs, Whelan describes the controversies over environmental toxins that caused groups to act, then undercuts this action by declaring that all the anxiety "is based on very little evidence of the existence of a real problem" (5). By contrast, it is ironic that almost nothing has been done about cigarettes, which are a real and proven health problem.

2. This sentence is in italics because it states an irrefutable fact that Whelan wants to emphasize about a proven health risk at the end of a section in "hypothetical" risks of other environmental toxins.

3. Whelan's evidence consists of facts, statistics, and other authoritative sources. She stays away from personal experience and others' experience because she believes that "we should not be moralizing about cigarettes, but simply facing up to the realities . . . why don't we start

Meaning and Purpose

1. Did any information in the essay surprise you? Did you see any that you didn't know before, or didn't believe? Has Whelan convinced you of the magnitude of the "Cigarette Dilemma" as she describes it?
2. What does Whelan mean by a "malevolent web" in paragraph 8?
3. State Whelan's purpose in a sentence of your own.
4. Besides giving the medical and health facts about cigarettes, Whelan gives lots of other information, such as a brief history of cigarettes, facts about companies in the tobacco "family," and how the women's movement has ignored the problem. How do all these related facts serve Whelan's purpose?
5. What does "backfire" mean in paragraphs 9–12?
6. What responsibility does Whelan place on smokers themselves for using cigarettes?

Strategy

1. Whelan's title indicates that her subject is cigarettes, yet she doesn't mention them until paragraph 7. What do you learn in the first 6 paragraphs that sets you up for her discussion of cigarettes?
2. Why does Whelan italicize the last sentence in paragraph 7?
3. What kind of evidence does Whelan use to support her argument, and why?
4. Why does the author include the seven bulleted paragraphs that stand alone at the end of the essay?
5. How does Whelan use classification to organize her argument?

Style

1. What is the tone of the essay, and what are some sentences that illustrate it?

2. Whelan begins and ends her essay with a question, and also asks questions in paragraphs 8, 22, 26, and elsewhere. How does she use questions in her argument?
3. Point out some instances of irony in the essay and explain them.

Writing Tasks

1. Imagine you are a spokesperson for the tobacco industry. Write an essay in which you argue that the industry is necessary to the economic well-being of the country, and that it practices responsible advertising. Include other assertions that come to mind. You may need to do some research.
2. Give examples of the non sequitur and ad hominem fallacies in two separate paragraphs.

by identifying the number-one enemy?" (45). Her argument gets strength from its appeal to reason in this otherwise emotion-laden issue.

4. These seven paragraphs leave the reader with overwhelming evidence of the power of the tobacco industry.

5. Whelan uses classification in part to keep her argument sounding rational and reasoned. Paragraphs 9–27 describe the five factors she lists in paragraph 8. Paragraphs 28–31 divide the tobacco industry's influence into four categories. In the "Coping with Disaster" section (35–45), she proposes four courses of action. And in the final section she lists examples of the clout the tobacco industry has. All this organizing gives her argument clarity and order and strength.

Style

1. Whelan's tone is unflinchingly direct and authoritative, with underlying impatience and anger. Examples are: "It goes without saying that . . . regulating it" (9) *direct;* "the classic response to cognitive dissonance . . . among smokers" (16) *authoritative;* and "Why would a clergyman . . . unacceptable and immoral?" (22) *angry.* Whelan addresses an educated lay audience who might be smokers or know smokers, work for the tobacco industry, or just be ignorant about some of the facts she brings to light.

2. Questions engage readers directly and sometimes challenge them (8). Questions keep the pace fast and set up facts that Whelan gives as answers. Questions also give stylistic variety to the sentences.

3. There is irony in the last sentence in paragraph 7 because this is the unavoidable fact about which people are *not* taking enough action. The last sentence in paragraph 17 is ironic, as it is that the women's movement has not spoken out about cigarettes even though they are harmful to fetuses and claim more lives than breast cancer does.

Teaching Suggestions

We suggest giving students background in Swift's use of irony and Anglo-Irish relations.

Ireland was reduced almost to subjection after the Norman Conquest (circa A.D. 1160) and Elizabeth I's armies finished the job by suppressing Irish rebellions. The English then gave the Irish Catholic nobility's lands to English Protestants in the sixteenth century. Hearing of atrocities by Irish Catholics against English Protestants in the Rebellion of 1641, Oliver Cromwell led an English army, killing thousands of native Irish. By 1653 Cromwell's forces had subjected all Ireland. By Swift's time, 10 percent of Ireland's population was Protestant, controlling 90 percent of the land. This Protestant Ascendancy lasted into the last quarter of the nineteenth century.

Nine years before publication of "A Modest Proposal," the English dropped all pretext of home rule and made the English Parliament Ireland's governing body, the English House of Lords Ireland's Supreme Court. England used Ireland as a source of raw material and discouraged industrial development that could have alleviated abject poverty.

Swift wrote "A Modest Proposal" primarily to protest against the barbaric conditions imposed on the Irish (though he gets his licks in at the Irish as well). Some of the essay's irony is created by the persona Swift adopts, whose voice is steady, rational, disciplined, and interested. Help students see that the contrast between this absolutely logical and reasonable voice and the absolutely mad plan is the key to both humor and gravity.

Marginal Notes

"great town": Dublin, Ireland.

Paragraphs 1–7 introduce the problems Swift's proposal addresses and some of the calculations on which it is based.

❦ Jonathan Swift ❦

Born in Ireland in 1667 to English parents, Swift attended Trinity College in Dublin and Oxford University in England and was ordained an Anglican priest in 1694. While in England he was active in both religion and politics and worked as a pamphlet writer for the Tory party. Frustrated for many years in his attempts to gain advancement in the church, however, Swift returned to Ireland in 1713 as Dean of St. Patrick's Cathedral in Dublin. Increasingly he devoted himself to writing satire that exposed England's injustices against the Irish. His Drapier Letters (1724), in which he openly attacked the English for their abuses, made him a national hero in Ireland. The satirical allegory, Gulliver's Travels (1726), is his most famous work. When he died in 1745, three years after being declared of unsound mind, his estate went to found a hospital for the insane.

A Modest Proposal

The barbaric conditions of English rule over Ireland in the 1720s and England's blatant refusal to help the Irish poor is the subject of this biting satire, first published anonymously in 1729. Logic, hard facts, tone, and emotional appeal all contribute to the power of this argument.

It is a melancholy object to those who walk through this great town or travel in the country, when they see the streets, the roads, and cabin doors, crowded with beggars of the female sex, followed by three, four, or six children, all in rags and importuning every passenger for an alms. These mothers, instead of being able to work for their honest livelihood, are forced to employ all their time in strolling to beg sustenance for their helpless infants, who, as they grow up, either turn thieves for want of work, or leave their dear native country to fight for the Pretender in Spain, or sell themselves to the Barbados.

I think it is agreed by all parties that this prodigious number of children in the arms, or on the backs, or at the heels of their mothers, and frequently of their fathers, is in the present deplorable state of the kingdom a very great additional grievance; and therefore whoever could find out a fair, cheap, and easy method of making these children sound, useful members of the commonwealth would deserve so well of the public as to have his statue set up for a preserver of the nation.

But my intention is very far from being confined to provide only for the children of professed beggars; it is of a much greater extent, and shall take in the whole number of infants at a certain age who are born of parents in effect as little able to support them as those who demand our charity in the streets.

As to my own part, having turned my thoughts for many years upon this important subject, and maturely weighed the several schemes of other projectors, I have always found them grossly mistaken in their computation. It is true, a child just dropped from its dam may be supported by her milk for a solar year, with little other nourishment; at most not above the value of two shillings, which the mother may certainly get, or the value in scraps, by her lawful occupation of begging; and it is exactly at one year old that I propose to provide for them in such a manner as instead of being a charge upon their parents or the parish, or wanting food and raiment for the rest of their lives, they shall on the contrary contribute to the feeding, and partly to the clothing, of many thousands.

There is likewise another great advantage in my scheme, that it will prevent those voluntary abortions, and that horrid practice of women murdering their bastard children, alas, too frequent among us, sacrificing the poor innocent babes, I doubt, more to avoid the expense than the shame, which would move tears and pity in the most savage and inhuman breast.

The number of souls in this kingdom being usually reckoned one million and a half, of these I calculate there may be about

2

"Pretender": James Stuart. In 1718, many Irishmen joined an army dedicated to restoring Stuart to the crown.

"Barbados": Other Irish, wanting to emigrate, bound themselves as indentured servants to work for a number of years in the Barbados, a West Indies island, or other British colonies to pay for their passage.

3

4

"projectors": planners, people who develop projects or schemes. Swift takes on this persona in the essay.

"shilling": At the time a shilling was worth less than twenty-five cents in today's United States currency.

5

6

Swift uses process analysis here to develop his argument, describing his method of calculation.

two hundred thousand couples whose wives are breeders; from which number I subtract thirty thousand couples who are able to maintain their own children, although I apprehend there cannot be so many under the present distress of the kingdom; but this being granted, there will remain an hundred and seventy thousand breeders. I again subtract fifty thousand for those women who miscarry, or whose children die by accident or disease within the year. There only remain an hundred and twenty thousand children of poor parents annually born. The question therefore is, how this number shall be reared and provided for, which, as I have already said, under the present situation of affairs, is utterly impossible by all the methods hitherto proposed. For we can neither employ them in handicraft nor agriculture; we neither build houses (I mean in the country) nor cultivate land. They can very seldom pick up a livelihood by stealing till they arrive at six years old, except where they are of towardly parts; although I confess they learn the rudiments much earlier, during which time they can however be looked upon only as probationers, as I have been informed by a principal gentleman in the county of Cavan, who protested to me that he never knew above one or two instances under the age of six, even in a part of the kingdom so renowned for the quickest proficiency in that art.

I am assured by our merchants that a boy or a girl before 7
twelve years old is no salable commodity; and even when they come to this age, they will not yield above three pounds, or three pounds and half a crown at most on the Exchange; which cannot turn to account either to the parents or the kingdom, the charge of nutriment and rags having been at least four times that value.

I shall now therefore humbly propose my own thoughts, 8
which I hope will not be liable to the least objection.

I have been assured by a very knowing American of my ac- 9
quaintance in London, that a young healthy child well nursed is at a year old a most delicious, nourishing, and wholesome food, whether stewed, roasted, baked, or boiled; and I make no doubt that it will equally serve in a fricassee or a ragout.

I do therefore humbly offer it to public consideration that of 10
the hundred and twenty thousand children, already computed,

"are of towardly parts": Have innate ability.

"Cavan": a county in north central Ireland.

"three pounds and half a crown": A pound was twenty shillings, a crown five shillings.

Paragraphs 8–16 present the proposal, more calculations to demonstrate its potential, and a few ideas about how it would work.

"ragout": A highly spiced French stew.

twenty thousand may be reserved for breed, whereof only one fourth part to be males, which is more than we allow to sheep, black cattle, or swine; and my reason is that these children are seldom the fruits of marriage, a circumstance not much regarded by our savages, therefore one male will be sufficient to serve four females. That the remaining hundred thousand may at a year old be offered in sale to the persons of quality and fortune through the kingdom, always advising the mother to let them suck plentifully in the last month, so as to render them plump and fat for a good table. A child will make two dishes at an entertainment for friends; and when the family dines alone, the fore or hind quarter will make a reasonable dish, and seasoned with a little pepper or salt will be very good boiled on the fourth day, especially in winter.

I have reckoned upon a medium that a child just born will weigh twelve pounds, and in a solar year if tolerably nursed increaseth to twenty-eight pounds.   11

I grant this food will be somewhat dear, and therefore very proper for landlords, who, as they have already devoured most of the parents, seem to have the best title to the children.   12

Infant's flesh will be in season throughout the year, but more plentiful in March, and a little before and after. For we are told by a grave author, an eminent French physician, that fish being a prolific diet, there are more children born in Roman Catholic countries about nine months after Lent, than at any other season; therefore, reckoning a year after Lent, the markets will be more glutted than usual, because the number of popish infants is at least three to one in this kingdom; and therefore it will have one other collateral advantage, by lessening the number of Papists among us.   13

I have already computed the charge of nursing a beggar's child (in which list I reckon all cottagers, laborers, and four fifths of the farmers) to be about two shillings per annum, rags included; and I believe no gentleman would repine to give ten shillings for the carcass of a good fat child, which, as I have said, will make four dishes of excellent nutritive meat, when he hath only some particular friend or his own family to dine with him. Thus the   14

Paragraphs 10–15 compose a process analysis, the workings of the proposal. Paragraph 10 itself is cause-and-effect analysis.

Instead of the narrator's voice here, we get the voice of Swift himself, evident because the narrator has no quarrel with landlords and no sympathy with tenants. The pun on "devour" ironically gives away the stratagem because the humorless narrator would never have punned.

"French physician": François Rabelais (1494–1553), Swift's favorite French writer and a broad humorist, and thus not a grave author at all.

"among us": The narrator addresses the chief landowners and administrators of Ireland, who are Anglo-Irish (Englishmen who became Irish citizens) and Protestant. His views of Catholicism in Ireland and abroad reflect theirs.

"artificially": artfully.

"shambles": butcher shops or slaughter houses.

Paragraphs 17 and 18 present and reject a possible refinement of the proposal.

"Psalmanazar": Georges Psalmanazar, a Frenchman who passed himself off as a native Formosan in a totally fictional *Description of the Isle of Formosa* (1705). He became a celebrity of sorts in a gullible English society.

squire will learn to be a good landlord, and grow popular among the tenants; the mother will have eight shillings net profit, and be fit for work till she produces another child.

Those who are more thrifty (as I must confess the times require) may flay the carcass; the skin of which artificially dressed will make admirable gloves for ladies, and summer boots for fine gentlemen.   15

As to our city of Dublin, shambles may be appointed for this purpose in the most convenient parts of it, and butchers we may be assured will not be wanting; although I rather recommend buying the children alive, and dressing them hot from the knife as we do roasting pigs.   16

A very worthy person, a true lover of his country, and whose virtues I highly esteem, was lately pleased in discoursing on this matter to offer a refinement upon my scheme. He said that many gentlemen of his kingdom, having of late destroyed their deer, he conceived that the want of venison might be well supplied by the bodies of young lads and maidens, not exceeding fourteen years of age nor under twelve, so great a number of both sexes in every country being now ready to starve for want of work and service; and these to be disposed of by their parents, if alive, or otherwise by their nearest relations. But with due deference to so excellent a friend and so deserving a patriot, I cannot be altogether in his sentiments; for as to the males, my American acquaintance assured me from frequent experience that their flesh was generally tough and lean, like that of our schoolboys, by continual exercise, and their taste disagreeable; and to fatten them would not answer the charge. Then as to the females, it would, I think with humble submission, be a loss to the public, because they soon would become breeders themselves; and besides, it is not improbable that some scrupulous people might be apt to censure such a practice (although indeed very unjustly) as a little bordering upon cruelty; which, I confess, hath always been with me the strongest objection against any project, how well soever intended.   17

But in order to justify my friend, he confessed that this expedient was put into his head by the famous Psalmanazar, a native of the island Formosa, who came from thence to London above   18 twenty years ago, and in conversation told my friend that in his country when any young person happened to be put to death, the executioner sold the carcass to the persons of quality as a prime dainty; and that in his time the body of a plump girl of fifteen, who was crucified for an attempt to poison the emperor, was sold to his Imperial Majesty's prime minister of state, and other great mandarins of the court, in joints from the gibbet, at four hundred crowns. Neither indeed can I deny that if the same use were made of several plump young girls in this town, who without one single groat to their fortunes cannot stir abroad without a chair, and appear at the playhouse and assemblies in foreign fineries which they never will pay for, the kingdom would not be the worse.

"groat": a coin worth a few pennies. "chair": A sedan chair, on which a person is carried by two men. Swift's own voice surfaces again to attack the costs for "foreign fineries."

Some persons of a desponding spirit are in great concern about that vast number of poor people who are aged, diseased, or maimed, and I have been desired to employ my thoughts what course may be taken to ease the nation of so grievous an encumbrance. But I am not in the least pain upon that matter, because it is very well known that they are every day dying and rotting by cold and famine, and filth and vermin, as fast as can be reasonably expected. And as to the younger laborers, they are now in almost as hopeful a condition. They cannot get work, and consequently pine away for want of nourishment to a degree that if any time they are accidentally hired to common labor, they have not strength to perform it; and thus the country and themselves are happily delivered from the evils to come.

19 Paragraph 19 dispenses with a possible remaining problem.

I have too long digressed, and therefore shall return to my subject. I think the advantages by the proposal which I have made are obvious and many, as well as of the highest importance.

20 Paragraphs 20–28 describe the proposal's numerous advantages.

For first, as I have already observed, it would greatly lessen the number of Papists, with whom we are yearly overrun, being the principal breeders of the nation as well as our most dangerous enemies; and who stay at home on purpose to deliver the kingdom to the Pretender, hoping to take their advantage by the absence of so many good Protestants, who have chosen rather to leave their country than to stay at home and pay tithes against their conscience to an Episcopal curate.

21 Swift uses cause-and-effect development in paragraphs 21–28. The advantages of the proposal are the positive effects showing that the plan will benefit both the poor (24–26) and the rich (21–23, 25, 27–28). In paragraph 21 Swift attacks the current prejudice against Irish Catholics as well as the motives of many Protestant dissenters from the Church of England.

"liable to distress": subject to seizures by creditors.

Paragraphs 24–33 anticipate objections to the proposal and dispose of them.

"receipts": recipes.

Secondly, the poorer tenants will have something valuable of their own, which by law may be made liable to distress, and help to pay their landlord's rent, their corn and cattle being already seized and money a thing unknown. 22

Thirdly, whereas the maintenance of an hundred thousand children, from two years old and upwards, cannot be computed at less than ten shillings a piece per annum, the nation's stock will be thereby increased fifty thousand pounds per annum, besides the profit of a new dish introduced to the tables of all gentlemen of fortune in the kingdom who have any refinement in taste. And the money will circulate among ourselves, the goods being entirely of our own growth and manufacture. 23

Fourthly, the constant breeders, besides the gain of eight shillings sterling per annum by the sale of their children, will be rid of the charge for maintaining them after the first year. 24

Fifthly, this food would likewise bring great custom to taverns, where the vintners will certainly be so prudent as to procure the best receipts for dressing it to perfection, and consequently have their houses frequented by all the fine gentlemen, who justly value themselves upon their knowledge in good eating; and a skillful cook, who understands how to oblige his guests, will contrive to make it as expensive as they please. 25

Sixthly, this would be a great inducement to marriage, which all wise nations have either encouraged by rewards or enforced by laws and penalties. It would increase the care and tenderness of mothers toward their children, when they were sure of a settlement for life to the poor babes, provided in some sort by the public, to their annual profit instead of expense. We should see an honest emulation among the married women, which of them could bring the fattest child to the market. Men would become as fond of their wives during the time of their pregnancy as they are now of their mares in foal, their cows in calf, or sows when they are ready to farrow; nor offer to beat or kick them (as is too frequent a practice) for fear of a miscarriage. 26

Many other advantages might be enumerated. For instance, the addition of some thousand carcasses in our exportation of barreled beef, the propagation of swine's flesh, and improvements 27 in the art of making good bacon, so much wanted among us by the great destruction of pigs, too frequent at our tables, which are no way comparable in taste or magnificence to a well-grown, fat, yearling child, which roasted whole will make a considerable figure at a lord mayor's feast or any other public entertainment. But this and many others I omit, being studious of brevity.

Supposing that one thousand families in this city would be constant customers for infants' flesh, besides others who might have it at merry meetings, particularly weddings and christenings, I compute that Dublin would take off annually about twenty thousand carcasses, and the rest of the kingdom (where probably they will be sold somewhat cheaper) the remaining eighty thousand.   28

I can think of no one objection that will possibly be raised against this proposal, unless it should be urged that the number of people will be thereby much lessened in the kingdom. This I freely own, and it was indeed one principal design in offering it to the world. I desire the reader will observe, that I calculate my remedy for this one individual kingdom of Ireland and for no other that ever was, is, or I think ever can be upon earth. Therefore, let no man talk to me of other expedients: of taxing our absentees at five shillings a pound: of using neither clothes nor household furniture except what is of our own growth and manufacture: of utterly rejecting the materials and instruments that promote foreign luxury: of curing the expensiveness of pride, vanity, idleness, and gaming in our women: of introducing a vein of parsimony, prudence, and temperance: of learning to love our country, in the want of which we differ even from Laplanders and the inhabitants of Topinamboo: of quitting our animosities and factions, nor acting any longer like the Jews, who were murdering one another at the very moment their city was taken: of being a little cautious not to sell our country and conscience for nothing: of teaching landlords to have at least one degree of mercy toward their tenants: lastly, of putting a spirit of honesty, industry, and skill into our shopkeepers; who, if a resolution could now be taken to buy only our native goods, would immediately unite to cheat and exact upon us in the price, the measure, and the   29

Many of these proposals Swift himself had made in earlier works.

"Topinamboo": A district in Brazil inhabited by primitive tribes and notorious for barbarism and ignorance.

Refers to the fall of Jerusalem to the Romans (A.D. 70), during which time many prominent Jews were executed on charges of collaborating with the enemy.

goodness, nor could ever yet be brought to make one fair proposal of just dealing, though often and earnestly invited to it.

Therefore, I repeat, let no man talk to me of these and the like expedients, till he hath at least some glimpse of hope that there will ever be some hearty and sincere attempt to put them in practice. 30

But as to myself, having been wearied out for many years with offering vain, idle, visionary thoughts, and at length utterly despairing of success, I fortunately fell upon this proposal, which, as it is wholly new, so it hath something solid and real, of no expense and little trouble, full in our own power, and whereby we can incur no danger in disobliging England. For this kind of commodity will not bear exportation, the flesh being of too tender a consistence to admit a long continuance in salt, although perhaps I could name a country which would be glad to eat up our whole nation without it. 31

After all, I am not so violently bent upon my own opinion as to reject any offer proposed by wise men, which shall be found equally innocent, cheap, easy, and effectual. But before something of that kind shall be advanced in contradiction to my scheme, and offering a better, I desire the author or authors will be pleased maturely to consider two points. First, as things now stand, how they will be able to find food and raiment for an hundred thousand useless mouths and backs. And secondly, there being a round million of creatures in human figure throughout this kingdom, whose sole subsistence put into a common stock would leave them in debt two millions of pounds sterling, adding those who are beggars by profession to the bulk of farmers, cottagers, and laborers, with their wives and children who are beggars in effect; I desire those politicians who dislike my overture, and may perhaps be so bold to attempt an answer, that they will first ask the parents of these mortals whether they would not at this day think it a great happiness to have been sold for food at a year old in this manner I prescribe, and thereby have avoided such a perpetual scene of misfortunes as they have since gone through by the oppression of landlords, the impossibility of paying rent without money or trade, the want of common sustenance, with neither 32

"country": England. Swift again allows his own voice to intrude where he says the English may as well eat Irish children, for they are already glad to eat up the nation.

POSSIBLE ANSWERS

Meaning and Purpose

1. The persona writes as an efficient, rational man who sincerely wants to solve the problems of Ireland in a reasonable and humane way. Swift offers real solutions to the problems house nor clothes to cover them from the inclemencies of the weather, and the most inevitable prospect of entailing the like or greater miseries upon their breed forever.

I profess, in the sincerity of my heart, that I have not the least personal interest in endeavoring to promote this necessary work, having no other motive than the public good of my country, by advancing our trade, providing for infants, relieving the poor, and giving some pleasure to the rich. I have no children by which I can propose to get a single penny; the youngest being nine years old, and my wife past childbearing.   33

Meaning and Purpose

1. Swift uses the persona of a "projector," a person who suggests plans for social and economic change (see paragraph 9) to put forth a "modest proposal." Describe the character of this projector. How do his views differ from those of Swift? Where do you find Swift's voice and beliefs coming to the surface?
2. Exactly what is Swift's "modest proposal"? What problems is it designed to solve? In what ways would it solve those problems?
3. What, primarily, does Swift condemn in the essay?
4. Underneath all the irony, what is Swift arguing for?
5. What objections to Swift's proposal can you think of?

Strategy

1. What does Swift do in paragraph 1 to set the reader up for the text that follows?
2. What means does Swift use to establish the narrator as reasonable, ethical, and trustworthy?
3. Where does Swift first give the reader a clue that his plan is horrible, not modest?
4. What purpose does the final paragraph serve?

(29). He voices exasperation, however, that the real solutions have never been tried (30, 31).
2. The essay's persona proposes to kill one-year-old Irish infants and sell their flesh as meat to the wealthy. Because the Irish poor are oppressed by their landlords and have no reliable source of income, they have no way to escape their poverty. His proposal would remedy this social ill.
3. Swift condemns the cruel exploitation and oppression of the Irish by the English.
4. Underneath his irony, Swift pleads for charity and compassion. He sets forth reasonable and compassionate solutions (29).
5. Ask students to try to be serious about answering this question, perhaps in the same rational voice Swift uses.

Strategy

1. By vividly depicting poor women and their children, he creates sympathy for them so that the reader will react with horror to his proposal.
2. Swift, calling his proposal "modest," repeatedly describes the time and care he spent pondering the problem (4), and uses first person with verbs of consideration: "I calculate," "I subtract," "I apprehend," and so on (6). He cites authorities and experts, such as the "very knowing American" (9). He puts forth his proposal with modesty and humility (8, 10). His attitude is respectful throughout: "as I must confess," (15); "although I rather recommend" (16); "But with due deference" (17). He piously objects to cruelty (5, 17). He refers repeatedly to the good of the nation (2, 7, 19, 21, 23, 29, 33). He carefully lists the advantages of the proposal (21–28). He fears the flesh would spoil if exported (31). And he ironically professes at the end that he wouldn't make a penny from the proposal.
3. The first clue is language that is too outrageous to be taken seriously.
4. The final paragraph serves at least two subtle purposes: Swift takes one last poke at those

whose sole motivation is profit, and he aligns himself with the oppressed, the implication being that if he had infants they also would be for sale.

Style

1. The livestock expressions dehumanize the Irish poor, making the narrator's proposal more palatable—and Swift's satire more horrifying. These expressions also reflect and thus satirize English attitudes toward the Irish poor.

2. Some students undoubtedly will object to Swift's somewhat archaic language ("increaseth," paragraph 11; "how well soever intended," 17), to his formality, and to his often complicated sentences. Others may find that initial difficulties soon fade. Some others may recognize that Swift's formal style perfectly fits the narrator's rather pompous persona.

3. *Importuning:* pressing or besetting with solicitations; *prodigious:* extraordinary in amount; *rudiments:* elements or first principles of a subject; *fricassee:* meat browned lightly, stewed, and served in a sauce made with its own stock; *ragout:* a highly spiced French stew; *prolific:* producing abundant offspring; *papists:* Roman Catholics; *repine:* complain; *deference:* respectful submission or yielding to another's judgment, opinion, or will; *mandarins:* members of an elite or powerful class; *gibbet:* a gallows with a projecting arm at the top, from which the bodies of criminals were formerly hung in chains and left suspended after execution; *desponding:* depressed from loss of hope; *tithes:* the tenth part of agricultural products or income paid in support of the church or priesthood; *vintners:* people who make or sell wine; *farrow:* to bring forth young; *parsimony:* extreme or excessive economy or frugality; *animosities:* feelings of strong dislike; *disobliging:* giving offense or affront to; *inclemencies:* severities or harshnesses of weather; *entailing:* causing.

Style

1. How does Swift's choice of words enforce the barbarity of his proposal? Pay particular attention to his referring to Ireland's poor in language usually reserved for livestock, such as "breeders" (paragraph 6) and "fore or hind quarter" (10). Find other such expressions or sentences.

2. How would you describe Swift's writing style? Support your opinion by giving examples. Do his style and diction inhibit your understanding and appreciation of the essay? Why or why not?

3. If necessary, check the meanings of these words in a dictionary: *importuning* (paragraph 1); *prodigious* (2); *rudiments* (6); *fricassee, ragout* (9); *prolific, papists* (13); *repine* (14); *deference* (17); *mandarins, gibbet* (18); *desponding* (19); *tithes* (21); *vintners* (25); *farrow* (26); *parsimony, animosities* (29); *disobliging* (31); *inclemencies, entailing* (32).

Writing Tasks

1. Think of a personal, social, or economic problem that you have an opinion about, and write an outrageous solution to it in a rational and responsible voice. Share your essay with other students to see if you have made your point effectively with irony.

2. Take the same problem you discussed in task 1 and propose a real, not an outrageous, solution to it. Consider your audience and whether to appeal to emotion or reason.

❦ Martin Luther King, Jr. ❦

Born in Atlanta, Georgia, King was the son of a Baptist minister. At age eighteen he was an ordained minister himself. He went on to study at Morehouse College, Crozer Theological Seminary, and Boston University, where he earned a Ph.D. Until his assassination in Memphis, Tennessee, in 1968, he was the acknowledged leader of the American civil-rights movement, having gained national recognition in 1955 by organizing a successful boycott of the segregated busing system of Montgomery, Alabama. He was arrested and jailed more than a dozen times as a civil-rights leader, once for eight days, during which time he wrote the now-famous letter reprinted here. He founded and acted as president of the Southern Christian Leadership Conference, through which he promoted a philosophy of nonviolent resistance to racial discrimination that has often been compared to Gandhi's. In 1964 he was awarded the Nobel prize for peace.

Letter from Birmingham Jail

King's letter is written in response to a public statement by Birmingham clergymen who opposed the demonstrations King was leading to protest against the city's segregated transportation system. The argument is backed by examples from history, philosophy, theology, and literature, but the power of the writing lies equally in King's rich rhetorical style.

MY DEAR FELLOW CLERGYMEN:

While confined here in the Birmingham city jail, I came across your recent statement calling my present activities "unwise and untimely." Seldom do I pause to answer criticism of my work and ideas. If I sought to answer all the criticisms that cross my desk, my secretaries would have little time for anything other than such correspondence in the course of the day, and I would have

595

Some students may have seen and heard King speak on television, particularly the "I have a dream" speech, but the 1950s and 1960s civil-rights movement will be ancient history to most. Give them some history of the movement before they read the essay.

In 1955, Mrs. Rosa Parks, a seventy-two-year-old black woman, was arrested for breaking Montgomery, Alabama's segregation laws by refusing to give up her seat on a city bus to a white passenger. The outraged blacks organized the Montgomery Improvement Association to boycott the city's public-transit system. King, pastor of a Montgomery Baptist Church, was elected leader of the Association. In a difficult year it successfully desegregated transportation. King, greatly influenced by the New Testament teachings of Jesus, Thoreau's views on civil disobedience, and Gandhi's principle of nonviolent civil disobedience, then formed the Southern Christian Leadership Conference, which was committed to using nonviolent resistance to accomplish desegregation.

King put Birmingham, Alabama, the most segregated city in the South, in world news in 1963 when he led a campaign to desegregate the city's lunch counters and hiring. To the demonstrations and sit-ins, the Birmingham police responded by turning firehoses and dogs on the demonstrators and jailing King and 2,400 other civil rights workers. Eight local clergymen issued a public letter agreeing with the aims of the movement but deploring the methods used. King's letter is a response to theirs. King uses both logical argument and persuasion to convince readers that his actions are morally compelling. And his argument is complex enough to warrant a paragraph-by-paragraph analysis. You or one of your students might read paragraph 14 aloud to demonstrate its rhetorical power.

In 1964, Martin Luther King, Jr., was awarded the Nobel Peace Prize, at 34 the youngest person ever to receive that prestigious honor. He was murdered on April 14, 1968, in Memphis, Tennessee.

Paragraphs 1–4 explain King's presence in Birmingham, proceeding from immediate and practical causes to more philosophical, ultimate causes.

The first reason for his presence in Birmingham, he explains, is that he is president of the Southern Christian Leadership Conference, an interstate organization that has business there. He was, therefore, invited.

The second reason he is there is that injustice is there, and like the Apostle Paul and other religious prophets, he must respond.

The third reason for his presence is that we are all inextricably related, and injustice anywhere in our society affects us all. King, therefore, cannot be an "outside agitator." He is there because he is needed.

no time for constructive work. But since I feel that you are men of genuine good will and that your criticisms are sincerely set forth, I want to try to answer your statement in what I hope will be patient and reasonable terms.

2 I think I should indicate why I am here in Birmingham, since you have been influenced by the view which argues against "outsiders coming in." I have the honor of serving as president of the Southern Christian Leadership Conference, an organization operating in every southern state, with headquarters in Atlanta, Georgia. We have some eighty-five affiliated organizations across the South, and one of them is the Alabama Christian Movement for Human Rights. Frequently we share staff, educational, and financial resources with our affiliates. Several months ago the affiliate here in Birmingham asked us to be on call to engage in a nonviolent direct-action program if such were deemed necessary. We readily consented, and when the hour came, we lived up to our promise. So I, along with several members of my staff, am here because I was invited here. I am here because I have organizational ties here.

3 But more basically, I am in Birmingham because injustice is here. Just as the prophets of the eighth century B.C. left their villages and carried their "thus saith the Lord" far beyond the boundaries of their home towns, and just as the Apostle Paul left his village of Tarsus and carried the gospel of Jesus Christ to the far corners of the Greco-Roman world, so am I compelled to carry the gospel of freedom beyond my own home town. Like Paul, I must constantly respond to the Macedonian call for aid.

4 Moreover, I am cognizant of the interrelatedness of all communities and states. I cannot sit idly by in Atlanta and not be concerned about what happens in Birmingham. Injustice anywhere is a threat to justice everywhere. We are caught in an inescapable network of mutuality, tied in a single garment of destiny. Whatever affects one directly, affects all indirectly. Never again can we afford to live with the narrow, provincial "outside agitator" idea. Anyone who lives inside the United States can never be considered an outsider anywhere within its bounds.

You deplore the demonstrations taking place in Birmingham. But your statement, I am sorry to say, fails to express a similar concern for the conditions that brought about the demonstrations. I am sure that none of you would want to rest content with the superficial kind of social analysis that deals merely with effects and does not grapple with underlying causes. It is unfortunate that demonstrations are taking place in Birmingham, but it is even more unfortunate that the city's white power structure left the Negro community with no alternative.

In any nonviolent campaign there are four basic steps: collection of the facts to determine whether injustices exist; negotiation; self-purification; and direct action. We have gone through all these steps in Birmingham. There can be no gainsaying the fact that racial injustice engulfs this community. Birmingham is probably the most thoroughly segregated city in the United States. Its ugly record of brutality is widely known. Negroes have experienced grossly unjust treatment in the courts. There have been more unsolved bombings of Negro homes and churches in Birmingham than in any other city in the nation. These are the hard, brutal facts of the case. On the basis of these conditions, Negro leaders sought to negotiate with the city fathers. But the latter consistently refused to engage in good-faith negotiation.

Then, last September, came the opportunity to talk with leaders of Birmingham's economic community. In the course of the negotiations, certain promises were made by the merchants—for example, to remove the stores' humiliating racial signs. On the basis of these promises, the Reverend Fred Shuttlesworth and the leaders of the Alabama Christian Movement for Human Rights agreed to a moratorium on all demonstrations. As the weeks and months went by, we realized that we were the victims of a broken promise. A few signs, briefly removed, returned; the others remained.

As in so many past experiences, our hopes had been blasted, and the shadow of deep disappointment settled upon us. We had no alternative except to prepare for direct action, whereby we would present our very bodies as a means of laying our case

5 King uses paragraphs 5–9 to dispose of the clergymen's first objection, their deploring that Birmingham is the site of the demonstrations. Blacks, he explains, had "no alternative." His argument in this section is circular: There must be direct action after three more moderate steps have been taken; those three steps have been taken; there must, therefore, be direct action. The major premise is stated as a given. The minor premise, that all necessary steps have been taken, King fully documents.

6 King outlines the "four basic steps" in paragraph 6 and demonstrates how the first step, establishing that racial injustices exist in Birmingham, has been taken.

7 The second step, negotiation, was a failure.

8 King describes the third step, self-purification.

before the conscience of the local and the national community. Mindful of the difficulties involved, we decided to undertake a process of self-purification. We began a series of workshops on nonviolence, and we repeatedly asked ourselves: "Are you able to accept blows without retaliating?" "Are you able to endure the ordeal of jail?" We decided to schedule our direct-action program for the Easter season, realizing that except for Christmas, this is the main shopping period of the year. Knowing that a strong economic-withdrawal program would be the by product of direct action, we felt that this would be the best time to bring pressure to bear on the merchants for the needed change.

Then it occurred to us that Birmingham's mayoral election was coming up in March, and we speedily decided to postpone action until after election day. When we discovered that the Commissioner of Public Safety, Eugene "Bull" Connor, had piled up enough votes to be in the run-off, we decided again to postpone action until the day after the run-off so that the demonstrations could not be used to cloud the issues. Like many others, we waited to see Mr. Connor defeated, and to this end we endured postponement after postponement. Having aided in this community need, we felt that our direct-action program could be delayed no longer.

You may well ask, "Why direct action? Why sit-ins, marches, and so forth? Isn't negotiation a better path?" You are quite right in calling for negotiation. Indeed, this is the very purpose of direct action. Nonviolent direct action seeks to create such a crisis and foster such a tension that a community which has constantly refused to negotiate is forced to confront the issue. It seeks so to dramatize the issue that it can no longer be ignored. My citing the creation of tension as part of the work of the nonviolent-resister may sound rather shocking. But I must confess that I am not afraid of the word "tension." I have earnestly opposed violent tension, but there is a type of constructive, nonviolent tension which is necessary for growth. Just as Socrates felt that it was necessary to create a tension in the mind so that individuals could rise from the bondage of myths and half-truths to the unfettered

The final step, demonstration, has become inevitable.

In paragraphs 10 and 11 King argues the need for direct action, basing his argument primarily on Socrates.

Socrates (469?–399 B.C.) was an Athenian philosopher.

9

10

realm of creative analysis and objective appraisal, so must we see the need for nonviolent gadflies to create the kind of tension in society that will help men rise from the dark depths of prejudice and racism to the majestic heights of understanding and brotherhood.

The purpose of our direct-action program is to create a situation so crisis-packed that it will inevitably open the door to negotiation. I therefore concur with you in your call for negotiation. Too long has our beloved Southland been bogged down in a tragic effort to live in monologue rather than dialogue.

One of the basic points in your statement is that the action that I and my associates have taken in Birmingham is untimely. Some have asked: "Why didn't you give the new city administration time to act?" The only answer that I can give to this query is that the new Birmingham administration must be prodded about as much as the outgoing one, before it will act. We are sadly mistaken if we feel that the election of Albert Boutwell as mayor will bring the millennium to Birmingham. While Mr. Boutwell is a much more gentle person than Mr. Connor, they are both segregationists, dedicated to maintenance of the status quo. I have hoped that Mr. Boutwell will be reasonable enough to see the futility of massive resistance to desegregation. But he will not see this without pressure from devotees of civil rights. My friends, I must say to you that we have not made a single gain in civil rights without determined legal and nonviolent pressure. Lamentably, it is an historical fact that privileged groups seldom give up their privileges voluntarily. Individuals may see the moral light and voluntarily give up their unjust posture; but, as Reinhold Niebuhr has reminded us, groups tend to be more immoral than individuals.

We know through painful experience that freedom is never voluntarily given by the oppressor; it must be demanded by the oppressed. Frankly, I have yet to engage in a direct-action campaign that was "well timed" in the view of those who have not suffered unduly from the disease of segregation. For years now I have heard the word "Wait!" It rings in the ear of every Negro

11

12 Paragraphs 12–14 refute the clergymen's second charge, that the demonstrations are untimely, by demonstrating the opposite.

Reinhold Niebuhr (1892–1971), an American Protestant theologian and philosopher.

13

with piercing familiarity. This "Wait" has almost always meant "Never." We must come to see, with one of our distinguished jurists, that "justice too long delayed is justice denied."

We have waited for more than 340 years for our constitutional 14 and God-given rights. The nations of Asia and Africa are moving with jetlike speed toward gaining political independence, but we still creep at horse-and-buggy pace toward gaining a cup of coffee at a lunch counter. Perhaps it is easy for those who have never felt the stinging darts of segregation to say, "Wait." But when you have seen vicious mobs lynch your mothers and fathers at will and drown your sisters and brothers at whim; when you have seen hate-filled policemen curse, kick, and even kill your black brothers and sisters; when you see the vast majority of your twenty million Negro brothers smothering in an airtight cage of poverty in the midst of an affluent society; when you suddenly find your tongue twisted and your speech stammering as you seek to explain to your six-year-old daughter why she can't go to the public amusement park that has just been advertised on television, and see tears welling up in her eyes when she is told that Funtown is closed to colored children, and see ominous clouds of inferiority beginning to form in her little mental sky, and see her beginning to distort her personality by developing an unconscious bitterness toward white people; when you have to concoct an answer for a five-year-old son who is asking, "Daddy, why do white people treat colored people so mean?"; when you take a cross-country drive and find it necessary to sleep night after night in the uncomfortable corners of your automobile because no motel will accept you; when you are humiliated day in and day out by nagging signs reading "white" and "colored"; when your first name becomes "nigger," your middle name becomes "boy" (however old you are) and your last name becomes "John," and your wife and mother are never given the respected title "Mrs."; when you are harried by day and haunted by night by the fact that you are a Negro, living constantly at tiptoe stance, never quite knowing what to expect next, and are plagued with inner fears and outer resentments; when you are forever fighting a degenerating sense of "nobodiness"—then you will understand why we find it difficult to wait. There comes a time when the cup of endurance runs over, and men are no longer willing to be plunged into the abyss of despair. I hope, sirs, you can understand our legitimate and unavoidable impatience.

You express a great deal of anxiety over our willingness to break laws. This is certainly a legitimate concern. Since we so diligently urge people to obey the Supreme Court's decision of 1954 outlawing segregation in the public schools, at first glance it may seem rather paradoxical for us consciously to break laws. One may well ask: "How can you advocate breaking some laws and obeying others?" The answer lies in the fact that there are two types of laws: just and unjust. I would be the first to advocate obeying just laws. One has not only a legal but a moral responsibility to obey just laws. Conversely, one has a moral responsibility to disobey unjust laws. I would agree with St. Augustine that "an unjust law is no law at all."

Now, what is the difference between the two? How does one determine whether a law is just or unjust? A just law is a man-made code that squares with the moral law or the law of God. An unjust law is a code that is out of harmony with the moral law. To put it in the terms of St. Thomas Aquinas: An unjust law is a human law that is not rooted in eternal law and natural law. Any law that uplifts human personality is just. Any law that degrades human personality is unjust. All segregation statutes are unjust because segregation distorts the soul and damages the personality. It gives the segregator a false sense of superiority and the segregated a false sense of inferiority. Segregation, to use the terminology of the Jewish philosopher Martin Buber, substitutes an "I-it" relationship for an "I-thou" relationship and ends up relegating persons to the status of things. Hence segregation is not only politically, economically, and sociologically unsound, it is morally wrong and sinful. Paul Tillich has said that sin is separation. Is not segregation an existential expression of man's tragic separation, his awful estrangement, his terrible sinfulness? Thus it is that I can urge men to obey the 1954 decision of the Supreme Court, for it is morally right; and I can urge them to disobey segregation ordinances, for they are morally wrong.

15   With this biblical allusion to Psalms 23:4–6, King reinforces his point that he is walking "through the valley of the shadow of death" and, because of his faith, "will fear no evil." He thus uses a biblical reference to enforce the point that he is impatient.

In paragraphs 15–22, King refutes the next objection by the clergymen, that he and the civil-rights demonstrators are breaking the law by arguing that it is their moral responsibility to break unjust laws.

St. Augustine (A.D. 354–430) was one of the Latin fathers of the early Christian Church.

16   In paragraphs 16–20, King distinguishes between just and unjust laws and offers substantial support to the idea that the laws they are breaking are unjust.

St. Thomas Aquinas (1225?–1274) was an Italian Catholic philosopher and a major theologian of the Roman Catholic Church.

Martin Buber (1878–1965) was a Jewish philosopher and theologian.

Paul Tillich (1886–1965), born in Germany, was an American Protestant philosopher and theologian.

Let us consider a more concrete example of just and unjust   17
laws. An unjust law is a code that a numerical or power majority
group compels a minority group to obey but does not make
binding on itself. This is *difference* made legal. By the same token,
a just law is a code that a majority compels a minority to follow
and that it is willing to follow itself. This is *sameness* made legal.

Let me give another explanation. A law is unjust if it is in-   18
flicted on a minority that, as a result of being denied the right to
vote, had no part in enacting or devising the law. Who can say
that the legislature of Alabama which set up that state's segregation laws was democratically elected? Throughout Alabama all
sorts of devious methods are used to prevent Negroes from becoming registered voters, and there are some counties in which,
even though Negroes constitute a majority of the population, not
a single Negro is registered. Can any law enacted under such
circumstances be considered democratically structured?

Sometimes a law is just on its face and unjust in its applica-   19
tion. For instance, I have been arrested on a charge of parading
without a permit. Now, there is nothing wrong in having an
ordinance which requires a permit for a parade. But such an
ordinance becomes unjust when it is used to maintain segregation
and to deny citizens the First-Amendment privilege of peaceful
assembly and protest.

I hope you are able to see the distinction I am trying to point   20
out. In no sense do I advocate evading or defying the law, as
would the rabid segregationist. That would lead to anarchy. One
who breaks an unjust law must do so openly, lovingly, and with
a willingness to accept the penalty. I submit that an individual
who breaks a law that conscience tells him is unjust, and who
willingly accepts the penalty of imprisonment in order to arouse
the conscience of the community over its injustice, is in reality
expressing the highest respect for law.

Of course, there is nothing new about this kind of civil dis-   21
obedience. It was evidenced sublimely in the refusal of Shadrach,
Meshach, and Abednego to obey the laws of Nebuchadnezzar, on
the ground that a higher moral law was at stake. It was practiced
superbly by the early Christians, who were willing to face hungry

In paragraphs 21 and 22, King presents several
historical examples to justify the idea that they
not only have the right but indeed the responsibility to break unjust laws.

Shadrach, Meshach, and Abednego, Jews living
in Babylon, refused to worship a golden idol as

lions and the excruciating pain of chopping blocks rather than submit to certain unjust laws of the Roman Empire. To a degree, academic freedom is a reality today because Socrates practiced civil disobedience. In our own nation, the Boston Tea Party represented a massive act of civil disobedience.

We should never forget that everything Adolf Hitler did in Germany was "legal" and everything the Hungarian freedom fighters did in Hungary was "illegal." It was "illegal" to aid and comfort a Jew in Hitler's Germany. Even so, I am sure that, had I lived in Germany at the time, I would have aided and comforted my Jewish brothers. If today I lived in a Communist country where certain principles dear to the Christian faith are suppressed, I would openly advocate disobeying that country's anti-religious laws.

I must make two honest confessions to you, my Christian and Jewish brothers. First, I must confess that over the past few years I have been gravely disappointed with the white moderate. I have almost reached the regrettable conclusion that the Negro's great stumbling block in his stride toward freedom is not the White Citizen's Counciler or the Ku Klux Klanner, but the white moderate, who is more devoted to "order" than to justice; who prefers a negative peace which is the absence of tension to a positive peace which is the presence of justice; who constantly says, "I agree with you in the goal you seek, but I cannot agree with your methods of direct action"; who paternalistically believes he can set the timetable for another man's freedom; who lives by a mythical concept of time and who constantly advises the Negro to wait for a "more convenient season." Shallow understanding from people of good will is more frustrating than absolute misunderstanding from people of ill will. Lukewarm acceptance is much more bewildering than outright rejection.

I had hoped that the white moderate would understand that law and order exist for the purpose of establishing justice and that when they fail in this purpose they become the dangerously structured dams that block the flow of social progress. I had hoped that the white moderate would understand that the present tension in the South is a necessary phase of the transition from an

demanded by the King of Babylon, Nebuchadnezzar. For punishment they were thrown into a fiery furnace. Daniel 3:1–30.

22 Socrates was tried by the Athenians for corrupting their youth with his skeptical, questioning method of teaching. He refused to change and was condemned to death.

In 1956, an anticommunist revolution in Hungary was put down quickly by the Soviet army.

23 In paragraphs 23 and 24, King digresses from his logical argument to criticize white moderates.

24

obnoxious negative peace, in which the Negro passively accepted his unjust plight, to a substantive and positive peace, in which all men will respect the dignity and worth of human personality. Actually, we who engage in nonviolent direct action are not the creators of tension. We merely bring to the surface the hidden tension that is already alive. We bring it out in the open, where it can be seen and dealt with. Like a boil that can never be cured so long as it is covered up but must be opened with all its ugliness to the natural medicines of air and light, injustice must be exposed, with all the tension its exposure creates, to the light of human conscience and the air of national opinion, before it can be cured.

In paragraph 25, King takes on the next charge, that the demonstrations "precipitate violence." He shows this position is illogical by again citing historical precedents.

In your statement you assert that our actions, even though peaceful, must be condemned because they precipitate violence. But is this a logical assertion? Isn't this like condemning a robbed man because his possession of money precipitated the evil act of robbery? Isn't this like condemning Socrates because his unswerving commitment to truth and his philosophical inquiries precipitated the act by the misguided populace in which they made him drink hemlock? Isn't this like condemning Jesus because his unique God-consciousness and never-ceasing devotion to God's will precipitated the evil act of crucifixion? We must come to see that, as the federal courts have consistently affirmed, it is wrong to urge an individual to cease his efforts to gain his basic constitutional rights because the quest may precipitate violence. Society must protect the robbed and punish the robber. 25

In paragraph 26, King addresses the issue of whether the time is right for demonstrations.

I had also hoped that the white moderate would reject the myth concerning time in relation to the struggle for freedom. I have just received a letter from a white brother in Texas. He writes: "All Christians know that the colored people will receive equal rights eventually, but it is possible that you are in too great a religious hurry. It has taken Christianity almost two thousand years to accomplish what it has. The teachings of Christ take time to come to earth." Such an attitude stems from a tragic misconception of time, from the strangely irrational notion that there is something in the very flow of time that will inevitably cure all ills. Actually, time itself is neutral; it can be used either destruc- 26 tively or constructively. More and more I feel that the people of ill will have used time much more effectively than have the people of good will. We will have to repent in this generation not merely for the hateful words and actions of the bad people, but for the appalling silence of the good people. Human progress never rolls in on wheels of inevitability; it comes through the tireless efforts of men willing to be co-workers with God, and without this hard work, time itself becomes an ally of the forces of social stagnation. We must use time creatively, in the knowledge that the time is always ripe to do right. Now is the time to make real the promise of democracy and transform our pending national elegy into a creative psalm of brotherhood. Now is the time to lift our national policy from the quicksand of racial injustice to the solid rock of human dignity.

You speak of our activity in Birmingham as extreme. At first I was rather disappointed that fellow clergymen would see my non-violent efforts as those of an extremist. I began thinking about the fact that I stand in the middle of two opposing forces in the Negro community. One is a force of complacency, made up in part of Negroes who, as a result of long years of oppression, are so drained of self-respect and a sense of "somebodiness" that they have adjusted to segregation; and in part of a few middle-class Negroes who, because of a degree of academic and economic security and because in some ways they profit by segregation, have become insensitive to the problems of the masses. The other force is one of bitterness and hatred, and it comes perilously close to advocating violence. It is expressed in the various black national-ist groups that are springing up across the nation, the largest and best-known being Elijah Muhammad's Muslim movement. Nour-ished by the Negro's frustration over the continued existence of racial discrimination, this movement is made up of people who have lost faith in America, who have absolutely repudiated Chris-tianity, and who have concluded that the white man is an incor-rigible "devil."

I have tried to stand between these two forces, saying that we need emulate neither the "do-nothingism" of the complacent nor the hatred and despair of the black nationalist. For there is the

27 King now answers the final charge, that the demonstrators are extremists, by showing that they are, in fact, taking the middle road that will prevent a "racial nightmare" in the future (paragraphs 27–31).

28

more excellent way of love and nonviolent protest. I am grateful to God that, through the influence of the Negro church, the way of nonviolence became an integral part of our struggle.

If this philosophy had not emerged, by now many streets of the South would, I am convinced, be flowing with blood. And I am further convinced that if our white brothers dismiss as "rabble-rousers" and "outside agitators" those of us who employ nonviolent direct action, and if they refuse to support our nonviolent efforts, millions of Negroes will, out of frustration and despair, seek solace and security in black-nationalist ideologies—a development that would inevitably lead to a frightening racial nightmare.   29

Oppressed people cannot remain oppressed forever. The yearning for freedom eventually manifests itself, and that is what has happened to the American Negro. Something within has reminded him of his birthright of freedom, and something without has reminded him that it can be gained. Consciously or unconsciously, he has been caught up by the *Zeitgeist,* and with his black brothers of Africa and his brown and yellow brothers of Asia, South America, and the Caribbean, the United States Negro is moving with a sense of great urgency toward the promised land of racial justice. If one recognizes this vital urge that has engulfed the Negro community, one should readily understand why public demonstrations are taking place. The Negro has many pent-up resentments and latent frustrations, and he must release them. So let him march; let him make prayer pilgrimages to the city hall; let him go on freedom rides—and try to understand why he must do so. If his repressed emotions are not released in nonviolent ways, they will seek expression through violence; this is not a threat but a fact of history. So I have not said to my people, "Get rid of your discontent." Rather, I have tried to say that this normal and healthy discontent can be channeled into the creative outlet of nonviolent direct action. And now this approach is being termed extremist.   30

But though I was initially disappointed at being categorized as an extremist, as I continued to think about the matter I gradually gained a measure of satisfaction from the label. Was not Jesus   31

"Zeitgeist": German. The spirit of the time; the general trend of thought or feeling characteristic of a period.

an extremist for love: "Love your enemies, bless them that curse you, do good to them that hate you, and pray for them which despitefully use you, and persecute you." Was not Amos an extremist for justice: "Let justice roll down like waters and righteousness like an ever-flowing stream." Was not Paul an extremist for the Christian gospel: "I bear in my body the marks of the Lord Jesus." Was not Martin Luther an extremist: "Here I stand; I cannot do otherwise, so help me God." And John Bunyan: "I will stay in jail to the end of my days before I make a butchery of my conscience." And Abraham Lincoln: "This nation cannot survive half slave and half free." And Thomas Jefferson: "We hold these truths to be self-evident, that all men are created equal. . . ." So the question is not whether we will be extremists, but what kind of extremists we will be. Will we be extremists for hate or for love? Will we be extremists for the preservation of injustice or for the extension of justice? In that dramatic scene on Calvary's hill three men were crucified. We must never forget that all three were crucified for the same crime—the crime of extremism. Two were extremists for immorality, and thus fell below their environment. The other, Jesus Christ, was an extremist for love, truth, and goodness, and thereby rose above his environment. Perhaps the South, the nation, and the world are in dire need of creative extremists.

I had hoped that the white moderate would see this need. Perhaps I was too optimistic; perhaps I expected too much. I suppose I should have realized that few members of the oppressor race can understand the deep groans and passionate yearnings of the oppressed race, and still fewer have the vision to see that injustice must be rooted out by strong, persistent, and determined action. I am thankful, however, that some of our white brothers in the South have grasped the meaning of this social revolution and committed themselves to it. They are still all too few in quantity, but they are big in quality. Some—such as Ralph McGill, Lillian Smith, Harry Golden, James McBride Dabbs, Anne Braden, and Sarah Patton Boyle—have written about our struggle in eloquent and prophetic terms. Others have marched with us down nameless streets of the South. They have languished in filthy,

---

Here King cites several precedents in the history of extremism that have now become respectable.

Amos was a prophet in the eighth century B.C. A book in the Old Testament bears his name. Martin Luther (1483–1546) was a German theologian who led the Protestant Reformation in Germany. John Bunyan (1628–1688) was an English writer and preacher. His refusal to bow to royal edicts banning nonconformist preaching led to his imprisonment from 1660 to 1672.

32 King's rebuttal of the clergymen's charge and his argument for direct action end here. Paragraphs 32–44 are primarily devoted to chastising white moderates and the Jewish and Christian churches for being defenders of the status quo.

roach-infested jails, suffering the abuse and brutality of policemen who view them as "dirty nigger-lovers." Unlike so many of their moderate brothers and sisters, they have recognized the urgency of the moment and sensed the need for powerful "action" antidotes to combat the disease of segregation.

Let me take note of my other major disappointment. I have been so greatly disappointed with the white church and its leadership. Of course, there are some notable exceptions. I am not unmindful of the fact that each of you has taken some significant stands on this issue. I commend you, Reverend Stallings, for your Christian stand on this past Sunday, in welcoming Negroes to your worship service on a nonsegregated basis. I commend the Catholic leaders of this state for integrating Spring Hill College several years ago. [33]

But despite these notable exceptions, I must honestly reiterate that I have been disappointed with the church. I do not say this as one of those negative critics who can always find something wrong with the church. I say this as a minister of the gospel, who loves the church; who was nurtured in its bosom; who has been sustained by its spiritual blessings and who will remain true to it as long as the cord of life shall lengthen. [34]

When I was suddenly catapulted into the leadership of the bus protest in Montgomery, Alabama, a few years ago, I felt we would be supported by the white church. I felt that the white ministers, priests, and rabbis of the South would be among our strongest allies. Instead, some have been outright opponents, refusing to understand the freedom movement and misrepresenting its leaders; all too many others have been more cautious than courageous and have remained silent behind the anesthetizing security of stained glass windows. [35]

In spite of my shattered dreams, I came to Birmingham with the hope that the white religious leadership of this community would see the justice of our cause and, with deep moral concern, would serve as the channel through which our just grievances could reach the power structure. I had hoped that each of you would understand. But again I have been disappointed. [36]

I have heard numerous southern religious leaders admonish their worshipers to comply with a desegregation decision because [37] it is the law, but I have longed to hear white ministers declare: "Follow this decree because integration is morally right and because the Negro is your brother." In the midst of blatant injustices inflicted upon the Negro, I have watched white churchmen stand on the sideline and mouth pious irrelevancies and sanctimonious trivialities. In the midst of a mighty struggle to rid our nation of racial and economic injustice I have heard many ministers say: "Those are social issues, with which the gospel has no real concern." And I have watched many churches commit themselves to a completely otherworldly religion which makes a strange, un-Biblical distinction between body and soul, between the sacred and the secular.

I have traveled the length and breadth of Alabama, Mississippi, and all the other southern states. On sweltering summer days and crisp autumn mornings I have looked at the South's beautiful churches with their lofty spires pointing heavenward. I have beheld the impressive outlines of her massive religious-education buildings. Over and over I have found myself asking: "What kind of people worship here? Who is their God? Where were their voices when the lips of Governor Barnett dripped with words of interposition and nullification? Where were they when Governor Wallace gave a clarion call for defiance and hatred? Where were their voices of support when bruised and weary Negro men and women decided to rise from the dark dungeons of complacency to the bright hills of creative protest?"   38

Yes, these questions are still in my mind. In deep disappointment I have wept over the laxity of the church. But be assured that my tears have been tears of love. There can be no deep disappointment where there is not deep love. Yes, I love the church. How could I do otherwise? I am in the rather unique position of being the son, the grandson, and the great-grandson of preachers. Yes, I see the church as the body of Christ. But, oh! How we have blemished and scarred that body through social neglect and through fear of being nonconformists.   39

There was a time when the church was very powerful—in the time when the early Christians rejoiced at being deemed worthy to suffer for what they believed. In those days the church was not merely a thermometer that recorded the ideas and principles of   40 popular opinion; it was a thermostat that transformed the mores of society. Whenever the early Christians entered a town, the people in power became disturbed and immediately sought to convict the Christians for being "disturbers of the peace" and "outside agitators." But the Christians pressed on, in the conviction that they were "a colony of heaven," called to obey God rather than man. Small in number, they were big in commitment. They were too God-intoxicated to be "astronomically intimidated." By their effort and example they brought an end to such ancient evils as infanticide and gladiatorial contests.

Things are different now. So often the contemporary church   41
is a weak, ineffectual voice with an uncertain sound. So often it is an archdefender of the status quo. Far from being disturbed by the presence of the church, the power structure of the average community is consoled by the church's silent—and often even vocal—sanction of things as they are.

But the judgment of God is upon the church as never before.   42
If today's church does not recapture the sacrificial spirit of the early church, it will lose its authenticity, forfeit the loyalty of millions, and be dismissed as an irrelevant social club with no meaning for the twentieth century. Every day I meet young people whose disappointment with the church has turned into outright disgust.

"Ekklesia": The Greek New Testament word for the church.

Perhaps I have once again been too optimistic. Is organized   43
religion too inextricably bound to the status quo to save our nation and the world? Perhaps I must turn my faith to the inner spiritual church, the church within the church, as the true *ekklesia* and the hope of the world. But again I am thankful to God that some noble souls from the ranks of organized religion have broken loose from the paralyzing chains of conformity and joined us as active partners in the struggle for freedom. They have left their secure congregations and walked the streets of Albany, Georgia, with us. They have gone down the highways of the South on tortuous rides for freedom. Yes, they have gone to jail with us. Some have been dismissed from their churches, have lost the support of their bishops and fellow ministers. But they have acted in the faith that right defeated is stronger than evil triumphant.

Their witness has been the spiritual salt that has preserved the true meaning of the gospel in these troubled times. They have carved a tunnel of hope through the dark mountain of disappointment.

I hope the church as a whole will meet the challenge of this decisive hour. But even if the church does not come to the aid of justice, I have no despair about the future. I have no fear about the outcome of our struggle in Birmingham, even if our motives are at present misunderstood. We will reach the goal of freedom in Birmingham and all over the nation, because the goal of America is freedom. Abused and scorned though we may be, our destiny is tied up with America's destiny. Before the pilgrims landed at Plymouth, we were here. Before the pen of Jefferson etched the majestic words of the Declaration of Independence across the pages of history, we were here. For more than two centuries our forebears labored in this country without wages; they made cotton king; they built the homes of their masters while suffering gross injustice and shameful humiliation—and yet out of a bottomless vitality they continued to thrive and develop. If the inexpressible cruelties of slavery could not stop us, the opposition we now face will surely fail. We will win our freedom because the sacred heritage of our nation and the eternal will of God are embodied in our echoing demands.

44

Before closing I feel impelled to mention one other point in your statement that has troubled me profoundly. You warmly commended the Birmingham police force for keeping "order" and "preventing violence." I doubt that you would have so warmly commended the police force if you had seen its dogs sinking their teeth into unarmed, nonviolent Negroes. I doubt that you would so quickly commend the policemen if you were to observe their ugly and inhumane treatment of Negroes here in the city jail; if you were to watch them push and curse old Negro women and young Negro girls; if you were to see them slap and kick old Negro men and young boys; if you were to observe them, as they did on two occasions, refuse to give us food because we wanted to sing our grace together. I cannot join you in your praise of the Birmingham police department.

45   In paragraphs 45–46, King responds to the clergymen's praise of the Birmingham police.

It is true that the police have exercised a degree of discipline   46
in handling the demonstrators. In this sense they have conducted
themselves rather "nonviolently" in public. But for what purpose?
To preserve the evil system of segregation. Over the past few years
I have consistently preached that nonviolence demands that the
means we use must be as pure as the ends we seek. I have tried
to make clear that it is wrong to use immoral means to attain
moral ends. But now I must affirm that it is just as wrong, or
perhaps even more so, to use moral means to preserve immoral
ends. Perhaps Mr. Connor and his policemen have been rather
nonviolent in public, as was Chief Pritchett in Albany, Georgia,
but they have used the moral means of nonviolence to maintain
the immoral end of racial injustice. As T. S. Eliot has said, "The
last temptation is the greatest treason: To do the right deed for
the wrong reason."

I wish you had commended the Negro sit-inners and dem-   47
onstrators of Birmingham for their sublime courage, their willingness to suffer, and their amazing discipline in the midst of great
provocation. One day the South will recognize its real heroes.
They will be the James Merediths, with the noble sense of purpose
that enables them to face jeering and hostile mobs, and with the
agonizing loneliness that characterizes the life of the pioneer. They
will be old, oppressed, battered Negro women, symbolized in a
seventy-two-year-old woman in Montgomery, Alabama, who rose
up with a sense of dignity and with her people decided not to ride
segregated buses, and who responded with ungrammatical pro-
fundity to one who inquired about her weariness: "My feets is
tired, but my soul is at rest." They will be the young high school
and college students, the young ministers of the gospel and a host
of their elders, courageously and nonviolently sitting in at lunch
counters and willingly going to jail for conscience' sake. One day
the South will know that when these disinherited children of God
sat down at lunch counters, they were in reality standing up for
what is best in the American dream and for the most sacred values
in our Judaeo-Christian heritage, thereby bringing our nation
back to those great wells of democracy which were dug deep by

T. (Thomas) S. (Stearns) Eliot (1888–1965)
was a British poet and critic born in the United
States. He won the Nobel prize for poetry in
1948.

In paragraph 47, King makes the point that the
demonstrators, not the police, should have
been praised.

James Meredith was the first black to register
at the University of Mississippi.

the founding fathers in their formulation of the Constitution and the Declaration of Independence.

Never before have I written so long a letter. I'm afraid it is much too long to take your precious time. I can assure you that it would have been shorter if I had been writing from a comfortable desk, but what else can one do when he is alone in a narrow jail cell, other than write long letters, think long thoughts, and pray long prayers?

If I have said anything in this letter that overstates the truth and indicates an unreasonable impatience, I beg you to forgive me. If I have said anything that understates the truth and indicates my having a patience that allows me to settle for anything less than brotherhood, I beg God to forgive me.

I hope this letter finds you strong in faith. I also hope that circumstances will soon make it possible for me to meet each of you, not as an integrationist or a civil-rights leader but as a fellow clergyman and a Christian brother. Let us all hope that the dark clouds of racial prejudice will soon pass away and the deep fog of misunderstanding will be lifted from our fear-drenched communities, and in some not too distant tomorrow the radiant stars of love and brotherhood will shine over our great nation with all their scintillating beauty.

Yours for the cause of Peace and Brotherhood,
MARTIN LUTHER KING, JR.

Meaning and Purpose

1. Of what significance is it that King writes his letter from jail?
2. In paragraph 1, King says that he seldom pauses "to answer criticism." Why does he do so here?
3. How does King justify the demonstrations? Why does he claim that the time for negotiation is past?

48 In paragraphs 48–50, King sarcastically apologizes to the clergymen for taking so much of their "precious time." He also goes through the appropriate formalities for his Jewish and Christian colleagues and "brothers."

49

50

POSSIBLE ANSWERS

Meaning and Purpose

1. Jail usually silences and intimidates people, making them powerless. King is not silent or powerless as he puts pen to paper in his jail cell, working for civil rights.
2. King claims that, though mistaken, his critics are "men of genuine good will" and that their criticisms are sincere. They deserve an answer.
3. King outlines the four steps a nonviolent campaign must take to effect social change (6). Negotiation, the second, has already failed. All three first steps have been accomplished, leaving only the inevitable fourth: direct action, or demonstrations.
4. He discusses waiting for racial equality (13,

14). Freedom must be demanded because it is never voluntarily given over by an oppressor (13). He catalogues segregationist human abuses that legitimate immediate action (14).

5. King distinguishes between just and unjust laws (15–22). An unjust law is "out of harmony with the moral law" (16); is not rooted in eternal and natural law (16); "degrades human personality" (16); "is inflicted upon a minority that, as a result of being denied the right to vote, had no part in enacting or devising the law" (18). He shows historical and biblical precedents for breaking unjust laws (21, 22). A person who breaks an unjust law but is willing to suffer the penalty expresses highest respect for the law (20).

6. King establishes himself as "in the middle of opposing forces in the Negro community" (27), each of which is an extreme. Then he cleverly puts himself in the same camp as other "extremists" admired by the clergymen he addresses (31).

Strategy

1. Emphasizing that he writes from a jail cell, King hopes to create sympathy. He further ingratiates himself by complimenting the audience. He also intimates their importance, for he answers their criticisms, which he would not normally do.

2. King structures his letter around rebuttals to the clergymen's charges. He answers the first in paragraphs 5–9, the second in 10–11, the third in 12–14, the fourth in 15–22, the fifth in 25, the sixth in 26, and the last in 27–31.

3. King appeals to both reason and emotion. He reasons that a law is unjust and democracy thwarted if the minority has no voice in "enacting or devising the law" (18). His language is rational, not emotional. The logic is deductive: if democracy means the people participate in making the law, and a large group of people is denied this right, then the law does not meet the terms of a democracy and is unjust. He appeals to emotion by listing the horrible injustices that blacks suffer every day; he says to

4. How does King respond to the admonition that the time for racial equality is not now, that he should "wait" until the time is right?
5. Describe King's distinction between just and unjust laws. What justifications does he use to advocate breaking unjust laws?
6. How does King turn the accusation of being an extremist from a criticism to praise?

Strategy

1. In paragraph 1, King clearly establishes the setting in which he is writing the letter and addresses his intended readers as "men of genuine good will." Why?
2. Where does King address the clergymen's objections to his activities in Birmingham? How does he refute them? How do his refutations figure in the construction of his own essay?
3. Does King appeal to reason or emotion in his argument? Explain the effectiveness of his appeal, and give examples from the essay.
4. The last three paragraphs don't further King's argument. What do they do?

Style

1. Reread paragraph 14. The sentence beginning "But when you have seen" is more than 300 words long. Discuss its effectiveness and its emotional effect. What does King do to keep such a long sentence clear?
2. Find some metaphors in King's letter and explain how he uses them.
3. If necessary, check a dictionary for the meanings of these words: *provincial* (4); *gainsaying* (6); *gadflies* (10); *millennium, lamentably* (12); *abyss* (14); *anarchy* (20); *elegy* (26); *incorrigible* (27); *sanctimonious* (37); *interposition, clarion* (38); *laxity* (39); *mores* (40); *inextricably* (43); *scintillating* (50).

Writing Tasks

1. Write a persuasive essay illustrating King's statement in paragraph 4: "Injustice anywhere is a threat to justice everywhere." Think of an example of injustice and argue that it has implications beyond that case.

2. Think of a situation in which you feel that some person or group is being unjustly opposed, such as freshman students not being allowed some privilege that upperclassmen are allowed. In a brief essay, argue for a course of action that resolves the injustice. Who is your audience? What kind of appeal will you choose, and with what kind of evidence will you support your argument?

whites that the time has come for change (14). His language here is laden with emotion.

4. With sarcasm and subtlety King apologizes to the clergymen for taking too much of their "precious time." And he goes through the formalities appropriate to his "Christian brothers," to reestablish a harmonious relationship with them.

Style

1. The periodic sentence that begins "But when you have seen" is masterful. He withholds its full meaning until the last words, keeping the reader in suspense about how the sentence will come out, both structurally and semantically. The 300-word catalogue is organized into eleven parallel subordinate clauses, enforcing order and clarity. Repeating "when" connects the clauses and contributes to the drama in the switch to "then" in the short independent clause concluding the sentence. The long sentence emphasizes how long blacks have waited for justice.

2. King uses metaphors to achieve an eloquent and poetic style and to enhance his appeal to emotion.

3. *Provincial:* having the manners, viewpoints, and so on considered characteristic of unsophisticated inhabitants of an outlying province; *gainsaying:* denying, disputing, contradicting; *gadflies:* people who persistently annoy or provoke others with criticism, schemes, demands, requests; *millennium:* a period of general righteousness and happiness; *lamentably:* unfortunately; *abyss:* a deep, immeasurable pit or cavity; *anarchy:* without government or law; *elegy:* a mournful, melancholy, or plaintive poem, especially a funeral song or lament for the dead; *incorrigible:* beyond correction or reform; *sanctimonious:* making a hypocritical show of religious devotion or piety; *interposition:* barrier or obstacle; *clarion:* clear and shrill; *laxity:* carelessness or negligence; *mores:* folkways accepted without question and embodying a group's fundamental moral views; *inextricably:* incapable of being disentangled; *scintillating:* animated, vivacious, effervescent.

❦ Lewis H. Lapham ❦

TEACHING SUGGESTIONS

You will certainly find high feelings among your students for this one. Lapham is not moderate in either his opinion or language. We guess your students will be as volatile, albeit less controlled and organized. It might be a good idea, after an initial free-response discussion, to divide students into groups according to their feelings: the pros, the cons, and those who can see merit on both sides. Have each group develop a list of reasons to justify their opinions.

A more formal approach would be to examine the form the essay takes, how Lapham uses an introduction, a three-part body, and a conclusion. Implicit in the discussion, too, should be an examination of Lapham's language. Do his bitter accusations and name-calling help or hinder his argument?

Born in San Francisco in 1935, Lewis Lapham was educated at Yale University and at Cambridge University in England. He has had a long career as a journalist, starting as a reporter for the San Francisco Examiner. *He has also been a reporter for the* New York Herald Tribune *and a writer for* Saturday Evening Post *and* Life. *In 1971 he took an editing position at* Harper's.

A Political Opiate:

The War on Drugs Is a Folly and a Menace

Essentially, this essay is an argument refuting George Bush's argument in favor of the war on drugs. It was first published in the December 1989 issue of Harper's. *Lapham takes his emotional appeal from both the controversial subject and the heated rhetoric. The author challenges some views and assumptions dear to many Americans.*

MARGINAL NOTES

Lapham begins with a form of hypothetical syllogism. If, he says, the first clause of the first sentence is true, then the validity of the second clause logically follows. He spends the rest of the paragraph establishing the validity of the first clause. Then, instead of stating the conclusion as in a formal syllogism, he allows readers to draw their own conclusions. He clinches his charges with formal documentation.

If President Bush's September address to the nation on the topic of drugs can be taken as an example of either his honesty or his courage, I see no reason why I can't look forward to hearing him declare a war against cripples, or one-eyed people, or red geraniums. It was a genuinely awful speech, rooted at the beginning in a lie, directed at an imaginary enemy, sustained by false argument, proposing a policy that already had failed, playing to the galleries of prejudice and fear. The first several sentences of the speech established its credentials as a fraud. "Drugs," said Bush, "are sapping our strength as a nation." "The gravest domestic threat facing our nation," said Bush, "is drugs." "Our most serious problem today," said Bush, "is cocaine." None of the statements meets the standards either of minimal analysis or casual observation. The government's own figures show that the addic-

1

616

tion to illegal drugs troubles a relatively small number of Americans, and the current generation of American youth is the strongest and healthiest in the nation's history.*

In the sixth paragraph of his speech, the President elaborated his fraud by holding up a small plastic bag, as distastefully as if he were holding a urine specimen. "This is crack cocaine," he said, "seized a few days ago by Drug Enforcement Administration agents in a park just across the street from the White House. It could easily have been heroin or PCP." But since nobody, ever, has been known to sell any kind of drug in Lafayette Park, it couldn't possibly have been heroin or PCP. The bag of cocaine wasn't anything other than a stage prop: The DEA was put to considerable trouble and expense to tempt a dealer into the park in order to make the arrest at a time and place convenient to the President's little dramatic effect.

Bush's speechwriters ordered the staging of the "buy" because they wanted to make a rhetorical point about the dark and terrible sea of drugs washing up on the innocent, sun-dappled lawns of the White House. The sale was difficult to arrange because the drug dealer in question had never heard of Lafayette Park, didn't know how to find the place on a map, and couldn't imagine why anybody would want to make such complicated travel arrangements in order to buy rocks of low-grade crack.

Two days later, confronted by the press with the mechanics of his sleight of hand, Bush said, "I don't understand. I mean, has somebody got some advocates here for this drug guy?" The surprised and petulant tone of his question gave away the nature of the political game that he was playing, playing on what he assumed was the home field of the nation's best-loved superstitions. After seven months in office, he had chosen to make his first televised address on a topic that he thought was as safe as mother

He then cites an example of the president using a lie to justify his drug-war policy. That lie, then, becomes emblematic of the entire policy.

2 In the next three paragraphs he elaborates on the "fraud."

3

4

*In 1983, for the first time since anybody began keeping records, the death rate among youths aged fifteen to twenty-four dropped below 100 in 100,000. The truth of the statistic should be apparent to anyone who has taken the trouble to look at the crowd in the stands during a televised broadcast of a college football game.

and the undesecrated flag. He had politely avoided any and all of the "serious problems facing our nation today" (the deficit, say, or the environment, or the question of race) and he had done what he could to animate a noncontroversial platitude with a good visual. He expected people to be supportive and nice.

Apparently it never occurred to him that anybody would complain about his taking a few minor liberties with the facts. Nor did he seem to notice that he had seized upon the human suffering implicit in the drug trade as an occasion for a shabby political trick. He had exploited exactly the same device in his election campaign by transforming the image of Willie Horton, a black convict who committed violent crimes after being released on furlough from a Massachusetts prison, into a metaphor for all the world's wickedness. I can imagine his speechwriters explaining to him that the war on drugs was nothing more than Willie Horton writ large.

The premise of the war is so patently false, and the hope for victory so obviously futile, that I can make sense of it only by asking the rhetorical question *cui bono*? Who stands to gain by virtue of Bush's lovely little war, and what must the rest of us pay as tribute?

The question is a political one. But, then, the war on drugs is a political war, waged not by scientists and doctors but by police officers and politicians. Under more fortunate circumstances, the prevalence of drugs in American society—not only cocaine and heroin and marijuana but also alcohol and tobacco and sleeping pills—would be properly addressed as a public-health question. The American Medical Association classifies drug addiction as a disease, not as a crime or a moral defeat. Nor is addiction contagious, like measles and the flu. Given the folly and expense of the war on drugs (comparable to the folly and expense of the war in Vietnam), I expect that the United States eventually will arrive at some method of decriminalizing the use of all drugs. The arguments in favor of decriminalization seem to me irrefutable, as do the lessons of experience taught by the failed attempt at the prohibition of alcohol.

Because the premise of the war is false, Lapham asks who benefits from it.

Lapham doesn't at first directly answer his own questions. Rather, because the real problem is medical, the answer to his question, as well as the question itself, must be political.

But for the time being, as long as the question remains primarily political, the war on drugs serves the purposes of the more reactionary interests within our society (i.e., the defenders of the imagined innocence of a nonexistent past) and transfers the costs of the war to precisely those individuals whom the promoters of the war say they wish to protect. I find it difficult to believe that the joke, although bitter, is unintended.

To politicians in search of sound opinions and sustained applause, the war on drugs presents itself as a gift from heaven. Because the human craving for intoxicants cannot be suppressed—not by priests or jailers or acts of Congress—the politicians can bravely confront an allegorical enemy rather than an enemy that takes the corporeal form of the tobacco industry, say, or the Chinese, or the oil and banking lobbies.* The war against drugs provides them with something to say that offends nobody, requires them to do nothing difficult, and allows them to postpone, perhaps indefinitely, the more urgent and specific questions about the state of the nation's schools, housing, employment opportunities for young black men—i.e., the conditions to which drug addiction speaks as a tragic symptom, not a cause. They remain safe in the knowledge that they might as well be denouncing Satan or the rain, and so they can direct the voices of prerecorded blame at metaphors and apparitions who, unlike Senator Jesse Helms and his friends at the North Carolina tobacco auctions, can be transformed into demonic spirits riding north across the Caribbean on an evil wind. The war on drugs thus becomes the perfect war for people who would rather not fight a war, a war in which the politicians who stand so fearlessly on the side of the good, the true, and the beautiful need do nothing else but strike

8

9   Now he gives a partial answer to his question: reactionaries benefit.

Lapham elaborates his point by claiming politicians can gain popularity by challenging a nonexistent enemy, thus freeing them from having to face real problems.

*Even governments with all the means of fascist repression at their command cannot force human nature into the molds made for prime-time television comedy. In Turkey in the nineteenth century, the authorities slit the nostrils of anybody caught smoking cigarettes. Czarist Russia punished the crime of smoking with death. Although I suspect that both punishments might be heartily endorsed by certain members of the Bush administration, neither of them eliminated the use of tobacco.

noble poses as protectors of the people and defenders of the public trust.

Their cynicism is implicit in the arithmetic. President Bush in 10
his September speech asked for $7.9 billion to wage his "assault on every front" of the drug war, but the Pentagon allots $5 billion a year to the B-2 program—i.e., to a single weapon. Expressed as a percentage of the federal budget, the new funds assigned to the war on drugs amount to .065 percent. Nor does the government offer to do anything boldly military about the legal drugs, principally alcohol and tobacco, that do far more damage to the society than all the marijuana and all the cocaine ever smuggled into Florida or California.*

The drug war, like all wars, sells papers, and the media, like 11
the politicians, ask for nothing better than a safe and profitable menace. The campaign against drugs involves most of the theatrical devices employed by *Miami Vice*—scenes of crimes in progress (almost always dressed up, for salacious effect, with the cameo appearances of one or two prostitutes), melodramatic villains in the Andes, a vocabulary of high-tech military jargon as reassuring as the acronyms in a Tom Clancy novel, the specter of a crazed lumpenproletariat rising in revolt in the nation's cities.

Like camp followers trudging after an army of crusader 12
knights on its way to Jerusalem, the media have in recent months displayed all the garish colors of the profession. Everybody who was anybody set up a booth and offered his or her tears for sale—not only Geraldo and Maury Povich but also, in much the same garish language, Dan Rather (on *48 Hours*), Ted Koppel (on *Nightline*), and Sam Donaldson (on *Prime Time Live*). In the six weeks between August 1 and September 13, the three television networks combined with *The New York Times* and the *Washington Post* to produce 347 reports from the frontiers of the apocalypse—crack in the cities, cocaine in the suburbs, customs agents seizing

He cites statistics to validate his previous assertion and concludes again with formal documentation.

Lapham introduces the second beneficiary of the war, the media. They can make money from it and so package and sell it like a popular cops-and-robbers television show.

He compares media personalities to prostitutes.

*In 1988, American hospitals counted 3,308 deaths attributed to cocaine, as opposed to 390,000 deaths in some way attributable to the use of tobacco and 100,000 deaths directly related to the excessive use of alcohol.

pickup trucks on the Mexican border, smugglers named Julio arriving every hour on the hour at Key West.

Most of the journalists writing the dispatches, like most of the columnists handing down the judgments of conscience, knew as much about crack or heroin or cocaine as they knew about the molecular structure of the moons of Saturn. Their ignorance didn't prevent them from coming to the rescue of their own, and the President's, big story. On *World News Tonight* a few days after the President delivered his address, Peter Jennings, in a tone of voice that was as certain as it was silly (as well as being characteristic of the rest of the propaganda being broadcast over the other networks), said, "Using it even once can make a person crave cocaine for as long as they [sic] live."

13 He now claims that the reporters are ignorant about the subject they report. He emphasizes this vacuity by formally citing Peter Jennings's error in noun-pronoun agreement in the paragraph's final sentence.

So great was the media's excitement, and so determined their efforts to drum up a paying crowd, that hardly anybody bothered to question the premises of the drug war, and several of the more senior members of the troupe took it upon themselves to write diatribes against any dissent from the wisdom in office. A. M. Rosenthal, on the op-ed page of *The New York Times,* denounced even the slightest show of tolerance toward illegal drugs as an act of iniquity deserving comparison to the defense of slavery. William Safire, also writing in *The New York Times,* characterized any argument against the war on drugs as an un-American proof of defeatism. Without notable exception, the chorus of the big media tuned its instruments to the high metallic pitch of zero tolerance, scorned any truth that didn't echo their own, and pasted the smears of derision on the foreheads of the few people, among them Milton Friedman and William Buckley, who had the temerity to suggest that perhaps the war on drugs was both stupid and lost.

14

The story of the drug war plays to the prejudices of an audience only too eager to believe the worst that can be said about people whom they would rather not know. Because most of the killing allied with the drug trade takes place in the inner cities, and because most of the people arrested for selling drugs prove to be either black or Hispanic, it becomes relatively easy for white

15 Lapham begins the next part of his argument as an explanation of why the media can so easily sell the drug show: they play on public prejudices.

people living in safe neighborhoods to blur the distinction between crime and race. Few of them have ever seen an addict or witnessed a drug deal, but the newspapers and television networks keep showing them photographs that convey the impression of a class war, and those among them who always worried about driving through Harlem (for fear of being seized by gangs of armed black men) or who always wished that they didn't feel quite so guilty about the socioeconomic distance between East 72nd Street and West 126th Street can comfort themselves, finally, at long last, and with a clear conscience, with the thought that poverty is another word for sin, that their BMW is a proof of their virtue, and that they or, more likely, their mothers were always right to fear the lower classes and the darker races.

Lapham cites the vicious circle of the political war. As government takes money away from slum programs to fight the drug war, the slums come to look and become even more menacing, thus threatening the law-abiding citizens who live there.

As conditions in the slums deteriorate, which they inevitably   16
must because the government subtracts money from the juvenile-justice and housing programs to finance its war on drugs, the slums come to look just the way they are supposed to look in the suburban imagination, confirming the fondest suspicions of the governing and possessing classes, justifying the further uses of force and repression. The people who pay the price for the official portrait turn out to be (wonder of wonders) not the members of the prosperous middle class—not the journalists or the academic theorists, not the politicians and government functionaries living behind hedges in Maryland and Virginia—but (mirabile dictu) the law-abiding residents of the inner cities living in the only neighborhoods that they can afford.

It is in the slums of New York that three people, on average,   17
get killed every day—which, over the course of a year, adds up to a higher casualty rate than pertains in Gaza and the West Bank; it is in the slums that the drug trade recruits children to sell narcotics, which is not the result of indigenous villainy but of the nature of the law; it is in the slums that the drug trade has become the exemplary model of finance capitalism for children aspiring to the success of Donald Trump and Samuel Pierce; and it is in the slums that the police experiment with the practice of apartheid, obliging residents of housing projects to carry identity cards

See Pete Hamill's "T. Without Sympathy" in Chapter 5, p. 306, for a treatment of Trump as the symbol of 1980s greed.

and summarily evicting the residents of apartment houses tainted by the presence of drug dealers.*

To the extent that the slums can be seen as the locus of the nation's wickedness (i.e., a desolate mise-en-scène not unlike the Evil Empire that Ronald Reagan found in the Soviet Union), the crimes allied with the drug traffic can be classified as somebody else's moral problem rather than one's own social or political problem. The slums become foreign, alien nations on the other side of the economic and cultural frontiers. The deliberate confusion of geography with metaphysics turns out, again to nobody's surprise, to be wonderfully convenient for the sponsors of the war on drugs. The politicians get their names in the papers, the media have a story to tell, and the rest of us get off the hooks that otherwise might impale us on the questions of conscience or the obligation of higher taxes. In New York last week, I overheard a woman in an expensive restaurant say that she didn't understand why the government didn't arrange to put "arsenic or something" in a seized shipment of cocaine. If the government (or "the CIA or the FBI or whoever does that sort of thing") allowed the poisoned cocaine to find its way back onto the streets, then "pretty soon we'd be rid of the whole damn thing." 18

If the folly of the war on drugs could be understood merely as a lesson in political cynicism, or simply as an example of the aplomb with which the venal media can play upon the sentiments of a mob, maybe I would rest content with a few last jokes about the foolishness of the age. But the war on drugs also serves the interests of the state, which, under the pretext of rescuing people 19

19 Lapham uses this paragraph as a transition to the final segment of his argument. He reminds the reader of the first two beneficiaries of the war on drugs, politicians and the media, and now adds a third, the interests of the state, which enhances its powers of repression and control.

*The government's own statistics indicate that the middle classes no longer recognize the drug problem as one of their own. Doing lines of cocaine hasn't been hip for at least five years, and among college and high school students, the use of drugs has declined markedly over the same period of time. In fact, the number of current cocaine users has gone down from 5.8 million in 1985 to 2.9 million in 1988. A July poll conducted by the mayor's office in Washington, D.C., showed that the white residents in town worried more about potholes than about cocaine.

from incalculable peril, claims for itself enormously enhanced powers of repression and control.

He first cites an opinion poll on the public's acceptance of their own political oppression.

An opinion poll conducted during the week following President Bush's September address showed 62 percent of the respondents "willing to give up some freedoms" in order to hold America harmless against the scourge of drugs. The government stands more than willing to take them at their word. The war on drugs becomes a useful surrogate for the obsolescent Cold War, now fading into the realm of warm and nostalgic memory. Under the familiar rubrics of constant terror and ceaseless threat, the government subtracts as much as possible from the sum of the nation's civil liberties and imposes de facto martial law on a citizenry that it chooses to imagine as a dangerous rabble.   20

His second form of evidence is the language of William Bennett, the United States "Drug Tsar." He follows with a comparison and formal documentation of his charge in the next paragraph. From here to the essay's conclusion (paragraphs 26–28) Lapham cites the results of governmental repression.

Anybody who doubts this point has only to read the speeches of William Bennett, the commander-in-chief of the Bush administration's war on drugs. Bennett's voice is the voice of an intolerant scold, narrow and shrill and mean-spirited, the voice of a man afraid of liberty and mistrustful of freedom. He believes that it is the government's duty to impose on people a puritanical code of behavior best exemplified by the discipline in place at an unheated boarding school. He never misses the chance to demand more police, more jails, more judges, more arrests, more punishments, more people serving more millennia of "serious time."   21

Reading Bennett's speeches, I am reminded of the Ayatollah Khalkhali, appointed by the authorities in Iran to the office of executioner without portfolio. Khalkhali was blessed with the power to order the death of anybody whom he found in the company of drugs, and within a period of seven weeks he killed 176 people. Still he failed to suppress the use of opium, and he said, "If we wanted to kill everybody who had five grams of heroin, we would have to kill 5,000 people." And then, after a wistful pause, he said, "And this would be difficult."   22

In line with Bennett's zeal for coercion, politicians of both parties demand longer jail sentences and harsher laws as well as the right to invade almost everybody's privacy; to search, without a warrant, almost anybody's automobile or boat; to bend the rules of evidence, hire police spies, and attach, again without a warrant,   23 the wires of electronic surveillance. The more obviously the enforcement of the law fails to accomplish its nominal purpose (i.e., as more drugs become more accessible at cheaper prices), the more reasons the Supreme Court finds to warrant the invasion of privacy. In recent years, the Court has granted police increasingly autocratic powers—permission (without probable cause) to stop, detain, and question travelers passing through the nation's airports in whom the police can see a resemblance to a drug dealer; permission (again without probable cause) to search barns, stop motorists, inspect bank records, and tap phones.

The polls suggest that a majority of the American people   24
accept these measures as right and proper. Of the respondents questioned by an ABC/*Washington Post* poll in September, 55 percent supported mandatory drug testing for all Americans, 82 percent favored enlisting the military in the war on drugs, 52 percent were willing to have their homes searched, and 83 percent favored reporting suspected drug users to the police, even if the suspects happened to be members of their own family. In October, *Newsweek* took note of an inquisition in progress in Clinton, Iowa. The local paper had taken to printing cutout coupons that said, "I've had enough of drugs in my neighborhood! I have reason to believe that (blank) is using/dealing drugs." The paper collected the coupons for the town police, who reported the response as "excellent."

The enforcement of more and stricter laws requires additional   25
tiers of expensive government, and of the $7.9 billion that President Bush allotted to the war on drugs in September, the bulk of the money swells the budgets of the fifty-eight federal agencies and seventy-four congressional committees currently engaged, each with its own agenda and armies to feed, on various fronts of the campaign. Which doesn't mean, of course, that the money will be honestly, or even intelligently, spent. As was demonstrated all too plainly by the Reagan administration (cf. the sums misappropriated from HUD and the Pentagon), the government has a talent for theft and fraud barely distinguishable from the criminal virtuosity of the drug syndicates it wishes to destroy.

Even so, and notwithstanding its habitual incompetence and greed, the government doesn't lightly relinquish the spoils of power seized under the pretexts of apocalypse. What the government grasps, the government seeks to keep and hold. The militarization of the rhetoric supporting the war on drugs rots the public debate with a corrosive silence. The political weather turns gray and pinched. People who become accustomed to the arbitrary intrusions of the police also learn to speak more softly in the presence of political authority, to bow and smile and fill out the printed forms with the cowed obsequiousness of musicians playing waltzes at a Mafia wedding.   26

And for what? To punish people desperate enough or foolish enough to poison themselves with drugs? To exact vengeance on people afflicted with the sickness of addiction and who, to their grief and shame, can find no other way out of the alleys of their despair?   27

As a consequence of President Bush's war on drugs, society gains nothing except immediate access to an unlimited fund of resentment and unspecific rage. In return for so poor a victory, and in the interests of the kind of people who would build prisons instead of schools, Bush offers the nation the chance to deny its best principles, to corrupt its magistrates and enrich its most vicious and efficient criminals, to repudiate its civil liberties and repent of the habits of freedom. The deal is as shabby as President Bush's trick with the bag of cocaine. For the sake of a vindictive policeman's dream of a quiet and orderly heaven, the country risks losing its constitutional right to its soul.   28

The final paragraph of the conclusion brings the reader back to paragraph 1 and Bush's "trick" and projects the possible dire consequences of that trick and what the trick has become emblematic of.

POSSIBLE ANSWERS

Meaning and Purpose

1. The title is Lapham's thesis. He will describe how the war on drugs is a political opiate—and he injects criticism and irony by describing the drug war with "opiate." "Folly" and "menace" are a clue to his anger and sarcastic voice.

Meaning and Purpose

1. Which elements in the essay does the title alert you to?
2. According to Lapham, the entire drug war is a sham. Who profits from the war? Who pays for it?
3. The author claims the drug war is political. What does he say it should be?

4. How do the popular media treat the drug war? Why?
5. Lapham is obviously angry about the war on drugs. Is his anger justified? Explain.

Strategy

1. Lapham uses the first five paragraphs to describe and comment on a presidential speech on the war on drugs. How does he connect an incident in the speech to the drug war itself?
2. The essay is in six sections. What is the purpose of each section, and how do they work together to organize Lapham's argument?
3. The author cites Milton Friedman and William Buckley to bolster his argument in paragraph 14. Why does he cite these authors in particular?
4. How does Lapham's discussion of American slums in paragraphs 16–18 help further his argument?
5. Lapham formally documents several of his assertions. How effective is that documentation? Explain.

Style

1. Some people might consider Lapham's language excessively nasty and flip. Is it? Does his language detract from his argument? Explain.
2. Explain the simile Lapham uses in the first sentence of paragraph 12. Is it effective? Why?
3. Lapham develops a theatrical metaphor in paragraph 11. How accurately does the metaphor describe the real situation?
4. If necessary, look up these words in a dictionary: *platitude* (4); *cui bono* (6); *salacious, lumpenproletariat* (11); *apocalypse* (12); *diatribes* (14); *mirabile dictu* (16); *mise-en-scène, metaphysics* (18); *venal, aplomb* (19); *rubrics, de facto* (20); *autocratic* (23); *obsequiousness* (26).

2. The war on drugs benefits politicians who need applause and who assume noble poses about drugs to avoid real issues (7–10); the media, which use the drug war to play on common fears (11–15); and the state, which uses repression and control (19–25). It is the poor who pay (16–18).

3. Use of drugs is a medical problem that should be attacked by scientists and doctors, not by politicians and police officers.

4. The drug war sells papers. The popular media dramatize and sensationalize it and play on common fears (11–15).

5. Some students who agree with Lapham that the war on drugs is a sham and that the American public is manipulated and repressed will see his anger as justified. Others who believe drugs are a threatening menace will see his anger as overly polemical or paranoid.

Strategy

1. The president's speechwriters manufactured a story and he presented it as fact to justify the war on drugs. This fiction and the war on drugs are empty and meaningless.

2. Section 1 describes Bush's speech that launches Lapham into his scathing review of the drug war; section 2 shows how politicians profit from the war; section 3 indicts the media; section 4 describes the nation's victimized slums; section 5 accuses the state; section 6 points out the cost of the war, the power of government, the condition of addicts, and the immorality of the war. The sections work together to build his argument and create a bigger and more monstrous picture of the drug war.

3. To avoid being dismissed as a raging liberal, Lapham cites Friedman and Buckley, both very outspoken, very conservative, and in agreement with him.

4. All three paragraphs demonstrate the sham of the war on drugs.

5. The footnotes appear to document Lapham's argument effectively. They are even consistent with the essay's sarcastic tone.

Style

1. Rhetorically, Lapham may appear excessively polemical. He uses devices such as name-calling that might be frowned upon but feels he has just cause for his anger and accusations.

2. Media personalities, like the prostitutes (camp followers) who followed the crusading knights (politicians, especially the Bush administration) have sold themselves ("set up a booth and offered his or her tears for sale").

3. Lapham lists theatrical techniques that the media have certainly used. By connecting these to *Miami Vice* he emphasizes one theme: the stories on the drug war are, like the war itself and like *Miami Vice,* full of style but almost totally lacking in substance.

4. *Platitude:* a flat, dull, or trite remark, especially one uttered as if it were fresh or profound; *cui bono:* for whose benefit? *salacious:* lustful or lecherous; *lumpenproletariat:* the lowest level of the working class, composed of unskilled workers, vagrants, and criminals and lacking class identification and solidarity; *apocalypse:* any universal or widespread disaster; *diatribes:* bitter, sharply abusive denunciations; *mirabile dictu:* strange to say; *mise-en-scène:* the procedure of setting a stage; *metaphysics:* philosophy, especially in its more abstruse branches; *venal:* open to bribery, mercenary; *aplomb;* self-possession, poise, or assurance; *rubrics:* rules of conduct and procedure; *de facto:* in fact, in reality; *autocratic:* absolute power; *obsequiousness:* state of being servilely compliant or deferential.

Writing Tasks

1. In an essay, compare the subtle sarcasm and wit in "A Modest Proposal" with the angry sarcasm and name-calling in Lapham's essay. Analyze how the language in each essay is effective or not in presenting the argument. Consider who each author's audience is. Could Swift have used Lapham's style, and Lapham have used Swift's, and been effective?

2. In a short essay, argue whether studying essays of argument in a textbook such as this one is useful or not. Your audience is the next group of freshmen who will take a composition course.

❦ Additional Writing Tasks ❦
Persuasion and Argument

1. Write an argument in which you express one of your own deeply felt opinions. If the subject you select has undergone extensive public discussion, assume that your reader is familiar with the general elements of the debate and develop specific evidence based on your own observations, reading, and experience. Use the following list to stimulate your thinking, but do not feel bound by the subjects.
   a. Fraternities
   b. Sororities
   c. Hiring quotas
   d. Euthanasia
   e. Prayer in schools
   f. Giving birth control advice to teenagers
   g. Sex education
   h. Legalized drugs
   i. Capital punishment
   j. Smoking in public buildings
   k. Public profanity
   l. Disruptive behavior in public places
   m. Requiring people on public assistance to work for the city
   n. Animal rights
   o. Student code of conduct
   p. Violence on television
   q. Movie ratings
   r. Subliminal messages in music
   s. Emotional advertising in political campaigns
   t. Censorship
2. Plastic disposable diapers are becoming a significant problem. Each year Americans toss approximately eighteen billion diapers—containing an estimated 2.8 million tons of excrement and urine—in the trash each year. Every one of these disposable diapers takes up to five hundred years to decompose. Aside from the solid waste issue, there are also growing concerns about infectious material seeping into our soil and ground water,

wasted natural resources, the rising costs of diaper production, "disposal," and increasing risks of severe rashes and toxic shock syndrome in children.

Write an argument essay in opposition to disposable diapers. Direct your essay to new parents.

3.   Many people find junk mail entertaining, something to thumb through during a leisure moment. You, however, believe junk mail is not only a nuisance but also a hazard. For example, all the junk mail you receive this year will have consumed the equivalent of one and a half trees. One year's junk mail sent in the United States amounts to a hundred million trees.

Write an essay arguing against junk mail. Here are some commonly known facts you might want to use:

a.   Almost two million tons of junk mail are sent each year.
b.   Over 40 percent of all junk mail is never opened.
c.   Junk mail receives special postage rates—currently 10.1 cents per piece if arranged in presorted batches.
d.   The average American will spend eight months of his or her life just *opening* junk mail.
e.   The junk mail sent to a million people means the destruction of 1.5 million trees.

4.   A radical counterculture has emerged in Germany's inner cities. They are the *autonomen,* a term that means the same as "autonomous" in English. The *autonomen,* who wear masks at demonstrations, are composed of squatters and street people. They see themselves as the last hope of revolutionary activism. The group refuses to participate in any political or social system, and its brand of activism is usually spontaneous, unorganized, and often violent.

The *autonomen* have no counterpart on the American social scene, but some social psychologists predict our government's failure to solve the problems of homelessness, drug abuse, and street gangs will lead to the formation of groups like the *autonomen* to express the anger and alienation the inner-city underclass already feels.

Write an essay in which you argue that inner-city life must be improved or city governments will soon be dealing with groups like Germany's *autonomen*. You might begin by using the *Reader's Guide to Periodic Literature* to find background information on these groups.

Glossary

Abridgment A shortened version of a work, but one in which the compiler attempts to include all pertinent parts of the longer work.

Abstract Abstract words or terms describe ideas, concepts, or qualities, as opposed to **concrete** entities. Sample abstract words and expressions are *philosophy, remorse, happiness, beauty, honor, peace, organizational climate, achievement motive,* and *burden of proof.*

Acronym A word formed by combining the first letters or syllables of words, to form a new word. An example is BASIC, the word that names a computer language; it is an acronym meaning "Beginner's All-purpose Symbolic Instruction Code."

Ad hominem argument *See* **Logical fallacies.**

Allusion An allusion briefly and often casually refers to something the writer believes is common knowledge. If you write that your neighbor's fence "looks like the Berlin Wall," you allude to the state of the Berlin Wall, which is in ruins. "Future Schlock," the title of the Neil Postman essay in Chapter 3, is an allusion to Alvin Toffler's *Future Shock,* a book about what to expect in the future. A Robert Frost poem about the sudden death of a boy is titled, " 'Out, Out—,' " an allusion to lines from Shakespeare's *Macbeth:*

> Out, out, brief candle!
> Life's but a walking shadow, a poor player
> That struts and frets his hour upon the stage,
> And then is heard no more (V,v,23).

Analogy An analogy is an imaginative comparison between two things, one less familiar than the other, usually intended to clarify a description of the less familiar one. In his novel *The Red and the Black,* the French author Stendhal (Marie Henri Beyle) wrote, "A novel is a mirror that strolls along a highway. Now it reflects the blue of the skies, now the mud puddles underfoot," clarifying his concept of the novel by imaginatively comparing it to a common, familiar item.

Analysis   In an analysis, a writer examines a piece of writing by paying special attention to its elements of thought. An analysis is based on the premise that some ideas or concepts are actually combinations formed of other ideas or concepts. An analysis of an idea or concept as incorporated in an extended piece of writing often shows that many smaller thoughts have been combined into larger thoughts. Analyzing the Pledge of Allegiance to the Flag shows that it includes a definition of an ideal republic, which has its roots in classical Greek philosophy.

Anecdote   An anecdote is an incident, or **narration**, which reveals a facet of character, most often about a well-known person.

Argument   An argument is meant to persuade an audience to accept the qualities of a proposition (a statement to be supported), so that the audience will be convinced of the proposition's truth or falsity. In his commentary on rhetoric, Aristotle spoke of "artistic proofs," so called because they are invented in the sense of being thought up or devised for the specific purpose of swaying an audience to an orator's point of view.

Aristotelian proofs as they are used when writing arguments appeal to the audience in one of three ways: rationally, emotionally, or ethically. A rational appeal (*logos*) appeals to the audience's reason: an emotional appeal (*pathos*) appeals to the audience's emotions or passions; an ethical appeal (*ethos*) appeals to the audience's confidence in the writer's character or credentials. Today, an argument commonly includes more than one of these proofs, and may also embody such nonartistic proofs as statistics, results of polls, scientific data, and other scientifically verifiable statements.

Association fallacy   *See* **Logical fallacies.**

Audience   An audience is a reader or a class of readers whom writers keep in mind while they write and particularly while they revise their writing. Writers determine as much as they can about their audiences, including their expertise, their education, their biases, their political and cultural background, their assumptions, and their interests. Writers deal with many kinds of audiences, including those who already share the writer's convictions. Each audience affects the writer's way of casting the writing.

Knowing as much as they can about their audiences helps writers determine which **strategies** to use, such as sentence structure, reasoning, **definition, emphasis,** organization, and **style.**

Audiences also affect writers' **diction.** A writer aiming at an audience of experienced amateur sailors would use words like *pulpit* and *roach,* but for an audience knowing nothing of nautical terminology, the writer would use "the platform on the forward part of the ship from which sailors handle and change sails," instead of *pulpit,* and "the curved portion of a sail closest to the rear end of the ship," instead of *roach.*

Body The main part of a piece of writing is its body. Here, events are dramatized, dialogue is sustained, **conflicts** are developed, and other **strategies** are applied to sustain the reader's involvement.

Categories Classes or divisions in an organized **classification.** Under the classification *general education requirements,* a writer could list the categories humanities, foreign languages, and sciences. Further, the writer could subcategorize by listing *foreign languages* such as French, Latin, German, and Japanese.

Cause and effect A cause is that which came before an effect, the effect being the result of that cause. Combined, *cause and effect* is a useful way of analyzing reasons for actions and for the results of those actions. In the sentence, "Because Gwen did not study, she failed the calculus examination," one can see the immediate cause and the immediate effect. But what ultimate cause was behind Gwen's not studying? Not even Gwen can be absolutely sure, because most causes in our daily lives are probable, not certain. Aware of this uncertainty, writers use with caution the cause-and-effect strategy.

Circumlocution Circumlocution in writing fails to make a point clearly or evades a point because many words are used where fewer would have sufficed. The sentence, "What is the cause of the source of his pain cannot be other than his appendix, which seems to be less than healthy," illustrates circumlocution. The sentence could have been recast as, "His pain is probably caused by appendicitis."

Claim The philosopher and rhetorician Stephen Toulmin devised a model of reasoning similar to the **syllogism.** One of the Toulmin model's primary elements is *claim,* which is the conclusion. The other two elements are *data,* which form the evidence, and *warrant,* which is the supporting argument. This sentence briefly illustrates the Toulmin model: Jasmah is a physicist *(data);* therefore, Jasmah is intelligent *(claim)* because all physicists are intelligent *(warrant).*

Classification Classification is a system for sorting things into distinct categories, or classes. A music lover might want to organize her cassettes. After sorting them, she sees that she can classify them into these categories, according to types of music: jazz, classical, and country and western. Later, perhaps when she wants to write a paper about her jazz cassettes, she can classify them into categories according to the musical styles of the featured artists on her tapes, making sure that each category is described clearly so that it is distinct from other categories.

Cliché In French, the *cliché* is an outmoded system for making metal printing plates with which to print the same thing again and again. In English, the name describes words and phrases that have been used again and again so that they have become worn out, tired. Examples abound: A person can be "as old as the hills." A night can be "as black as coal." We can be "afraid of our own shadow." Someone can have "an ax to grind." A child can be "a chip off the old block," "here today; gone tomorrow," "a square peg in a round hole," "start from scratch," and so on. When revising, writers "keep an eye peeled" for clichés so that they can replace those with fresh, colorful expressions of their own **invention.**

Climax   In a **narration** essay, the climax is the conclusion, the highest point of interest. In other kinds of writing the climax, or peak of interest, marks the turning point in the action.

Coherence   Coherence clearly, consistently, and logically connects the parts in a piece of writing. It is the glue that holds together all vigorous, effective writing. Among other techniques, coherence invokes **transitions** to show introductory relationships among ideas, paragraphing to signal shifts in thought, sentences that follow reasonably from those which came before them, and **diction** appropriate to the **audience**.

Colloquial expressions   Colloquial expressions, such as "Don't even try to psych out Professor Sherman," and "Ralph crammed all his stuff into his closet" characterize informal (and often playful) speaking and writing. Therefore, they have limited use in formal writing because their very casualness can distract readers.

Comparison and contrast   A comparison involves similarities; a contrast, differences. Combining these two ways of judging qualities can lead to discoveries about two things formerly thought to be ordinarily alike or unalike. A writer who compares and contrasts an electric typewriter and a computer discovers that whatever an electric typewriter can do, a computer with a word-processing program and printer can do more efficiently (a comparison). The writer will also discover the many things that a computer, equipped with various programs, can do that a typewriter cannot possibly do, such as maintaining a continuous record of household expenditures (a contrast). On the other hand, the writer will discover that both machines can be used for writing brief informal notes, but a computer can also retain easily correctable copies of those notes on a disk (comparison and contrast).

Conclusions   Conclusions are ways of ending essays. The way in which an essay is concluded depends in great part on the content of the essay itself. An essay arguing for or against gun control is likely to end by restating the reasons for taking one position or another. An essay explaining one of the complex relationships between human beings and nature might conclude by warning the reader that the relationship is endangered. An essay with several examples of how the world's economies are intertwined might end with one sterling example of an economy that is vitally connected to our own. An essayist offering information about an inexpensive medicine for a common disease might conclude by recommending that readers consult their personal physicians for more information.

Conclusions do not drift into other topics, nor do they shift an essay's emphasis away from its own topic. A writer would not end an essay taking a firm stand against showing pornographic movies on television by writing something like, "It all depends on each person's tastes."

So-called cute conclusions suggest to the audience that the writer was not deeply involved in thinking about the essay's content. They should be avoided.

Conclusions grow logically and sufficiently from the essay, and they should content the **audience**.

Concrete   Concrete words or expressions refer to things experienced by the senses, as opposed to **abstractions**. These words and expressions are concrete: *chair, perfume, music, automobile, bitter, cardboard box, dictionary, window,* and *refrigerator.*

Conflict   In writing, a conflict is a struggle that grows from two opposing beliefs, values, characters, and so on, which are developed in the **body** of the piece.

Connotation   The word "connotation" describes the implied meanings that become attached to words, *Skinny* and *slender* both mean thin or slight, but the first has negative connotations (emaciation and perhaps ill health), and the latter implies grace, even elegance.

The descriptive phrase *cheap furniture* carries connotations of shoddy workmanship and poor quality. The phrase *inexpensive furniture,* however, implies only the furniture's low cost. Although *cheap* and *inexpensive* are dictionary synonyms, the meaning implied in *cheap* sets it apart from *inexpensive.* Careful writers keep in mind what words mean according to dictionaries and what those same words may imply beyond their dictionary definitions.

Data   The proofs in Stephen Toulmin's model of reasoning are *data*. They are the evidence that supports the model's **claim**, or conclusion.

Data are also nonartistic proofs (see **argument**) used in other models of reasoning. These kinds of data come from scientific observations, record keeping, or statistics—facts or figures from which conclusions can be inferred, and information from credible, reliable sources.

Deduction   A deduction is the result of reasoning from a general statement to a specific instance. If your college requires that all prospective students be tested in a foreign language before they are enrolled, then you can reason that Pat, who sits next to you in English class, has taken a test in a foreign language. Deductions are not always that clear-cut, though.

One might think that all small cars get good gas mileage and then buy a small car to save money on fuel, only to find that this car gets poor mileage. The original assumption, then, was false.

Definition   A definition outlines, limits, or states the meaning of a word, term, phrase, or concept.

A formal definition puts a term into a class and then shows how it differs from other members of the same class. A trumpet (term) is a brass musical wind instrument (class) consisting of a tube in an oblong loop or loops, with a flared bell at one end, a curved mouthpiece at the other, and three valves for making tonal changes (difference).

An extended definition, a form of **exposition**, not only defines in the senses above but also explains issues by including **strategies**, such as **narration**, **description**, **example**, and **evidence.** One example of an extended definition in this book is Paul Theroux's "Being a Man."

Denotation   The term *denotation* applies to the literal, lexical meaning of a word—that which is explained in a good dictionary.

Description   The technique of making pictures with words is *description*. An effective description includes clear evidence that appeals to one or more of the senses—sight, touch, taste, smell, or hearing—as well as **explanation**. Henry David Thoreau's "The Battle of the Ants," in Chapter 4, demonstrates this combination of description and explanation: "his own breast was all torn away, exposing what vitals he had there to the jaws of the black warrior, whose breastplate was apparently too thick for him to pierce; and the dark carbuncles of the sufferer's eyes shone with ferocity such as only war could excite."

Diction   Diction is deliberate choice of words. Writers conscientiously choose words and the ways in which they use them, being guided by their audience and their purpose. Writers make their selections from various levels of usage, including **standard English, slang,** conversational expressions, regionalisms (choosing among "spigot," "tap," and "faucet"), and scientific and technical **jargon**.

Consider these sentences:

1. "Christine resigned her position."
2. "Chris quit her job."
3. "Chris told him he could take his job and shove it!"

What determines which of these sentences is correct? The audience and the purpose.

Sentence 1 is appropriate for a formal audience and a formal purpose: perhaps the writer's audience was college-level readers and the purpose was to describe her best friend's employment difficulties.

Sentence 2 might have been for a semiformal audience and a semiformal purpose, such as writing an essay for the readers of a college alumnae newsletter to help graduates keep track of their classmates.

Sentence 3 might have been for an informal audience and purpose, such as writing an essay for other members of a composition class to explain how one of them had reacted to being treated poorly by the manager of a local pizza parlor.

Whoever the audience and whatever the purpose, writers are guided by their own sense of propriety and by dictionaries and a thesaurus. They rarely use a thesaurus, however, without also consulting a dictionary to be sure that the words they have chosen from the thesaurus are in fact appropriate for their audience and purpose.

Directive process analysis   A directive process analysis tells how to do something. It is a sequence of directions to guide a reader who wants to complete a specific task. Such an analysis tells how to plant a tree, but *not* how a tree grows, the latter topic being an **informative process analysis**.

Division   Division is a subclass of **classification**. Writers divide a classification into logical parts, usually for description or explanation. Let's say that a writer wanted to describe a personal computer. First, you would classify it, telling how it differs from mainframe computers, from large industrial computers, and from laptop computers. Then you would divide the home computer into its logical parts: the keyboard, the central processing unit, and the video monitor. After making that division, you would describe each of these components. By your division, you help the reader to see one component at a time, rather than try to imagine an entire home computer all at once.

Dominant impression   The dominant impression is the main sensation or conception that the author strives to fix in the reader's mind, by carefully shaping the details of a **description**.

Effect   It is part of **cause and effect,** the result or outcome of an occurrence or action, but the word *effect* also refers to the impression that writing—whether a word, sentence, paragraph, essay, or larger work—makes on its audience.

Emphasis   With emphasis, writers stress or highlight the things they want their readers to see as most important in their writing. Writers use such **strategies** as **diction**, sentence structure, position, active voice, repetition, and mechanics to emphasize their main points.

   Diction: A writer who wanted to emphasize a negative opinion of a newly opened restaurant could write, "This restaurant has food fit to eat only if you are starving."

Sentence structure: If you wanted to emphasize your opinion of the food itself, you could write a periodic sentence, which moves from supporting details to the main idea. "With lukewarm coffee, half-cooked cold chicken, salty mashed potatoes, and burned vegetables, my meal was barely edible." You could emphasize your description of the food by writing a loose sentence, in which the supporting details follow the main idea: "I had a barely edible meal of lukewarm coffee, half-cooked cold chicken, salty mashed potatoes, and burned vegetables."

Position: That which we read last, we remember longest, whether chapters in a book, groups of words in a sentence, or paragraphs in an essay. Commenting on an unsavory experience in a restaurant, you might begin a paper by describing how you had read about the restaurant in a respectable tourist guide, where it had been awarded three stars. Then you might devote a short paragraph to the small problem you had in finding the place because it was in a part of the city unfamiliar to the taxicab driver, who had been profusely apologetic. You then might describe the restaurant's décor, a delightful amalgam of French Provincial and Early American, and your waitress, a pleasant young lady dressed in a peasant frock, who was also attending law school at the nearby university. Finally, because you had been shocked at the poor quality of the food, in utter contrast to the treat you had been expecting, you might conclude the essay with a paragraph meant to shock your readers as well, thus emphasizing the most important point in your experience by putting it last.

Active voice: Verbs in active voice—"This restaurant serves poorly prepared food"—are more emphatic than those in passive voice: "Poorly prepared food is served by this restaurant."

Repetition: "I spent a valuable hour of my vacation sipping the lukewarm coffee at Harry's Restaurant, chewing Harry's half-cooked chicken, tasting the salty mashed potatoes at Harry's, and staring at the vegetables Harry burned. Never again will I eat in Harry's Restaurant."

Mechanics: Usually the least appropriate way to emphasize formal writing, mechanics include underlining, quotation marks, and exclamation points: "When I was served the 'food' I had ordered in this 'restaurant,' I was *shocked* to see how *poorly* it had been prepared!" Such devices must be used sparingly. Your emphasis will be more successfully communicated with diction, sentence structure, position, active voice, and repetition.

Essay   The word *essay* is from the French *essai,* meaning "attempt" or "experiment." In English, an essay is a relatively short piece of nonfiction prose on a specified topic. It is an attempt by a writer to persuade, inform, explain, argue, describe, narrate, expose, or in some other way organize and develop a topic to interest an **audience**.

Essays are occasionally defined as informal or formal, although the definitions admittedly are vague. Generally, however, a formal essay includes **diction** appropriate to a serious audience, has a serious **tone,** and is focused on a serious topic. An informal essay, on the other hand, often has a light, perhaps humorous tone and informal language, and is focused on a personal, perhaps frivolous topic.

Evaluation   An evaluation determines the worth or quality of a work. If you are revising your own work or reading someone else's, you try to evaluate it objectively, to see how well it fulfills its purpose. Usually, those who evaluate a work look to see how well its thesis is stated and supported, how strongly its proofs support its claims, how clearly it is organized, whether or not its language is clear, and whether or not it is appropriately written for its intended audience.

Evidence   Evidence is support for a theory, claim, or **thesis.** The commonest kinds of evidence are obvious evidence, manifest evidence, and clear evidence. Obvious evidence, usually scientific, is readily perceived or easily inferred. If $6 + 2 + x = 9$, then the evidence is obvious that $x = 1$. Manifest evidence is immediately clear to the understanding, often by intuition. If you see water in its solid state, then you know almost without thinking that it is frozen. Clear evidence, the kind essayists use most often, supports and clarifies a reader's understanding of the writer's thesis. If the writer's thesis is that marriage vows are hopelessly outmoded, then you must offer clear evidence to support that thesis. You must examine and clarify the vows, compare them with the spousal responsibilities in modern marriages, illustrate how those vows conflict with reality, and so on.

Examples   An example is an instance that follows and illustrates the content of your statement. Among the more usual are specific examples, typical examples, and hypothetical examples. Specific examples amplify one experience, event, incident, or fact. They clarify in detail your earlier statement. Typical examples illustrate many experiences, events, incidents, or facts. They clarify generally your earlier statement, so that they will be representative. Hypothetical examples are imagined or supposed representations. They clarify the probability of your earlier statement.

Exposition   An exposition is a detailed explanation of the content of an idea, an object, an attitude, or a position. An exposition exposes, makes something accessible to a reader, by using any of a number of **strategies**, including examples, comparisons and contrasts, analogies, and classifications. Most essays in this book are expository, as are most essays written in college.

False analogy   *See* **Logical fallacies.**

Faulty either/or reasoning   *See* **Logical fallacies.**

Figures of speech   Tropes, or figures of speech, make a clear style vivid by adding **connotations** to statements, which appeal to the reader's imagination. The most used figures of speech are metaphor, simile, personification, hyperbole (overstatement), litotes (understatement), synecdoche, metonymy, and paradox.

A *metaphor* is an implied comparison between two dissimilar things: "Jamie is the tiger on the team." Tigers are noted for their speed, intelligence, and strength—the attributes that this metaphor gives to Jamie.

A *simile* is an explicit comparison between two dissimilar things, using the word *as* or *like:* "Jamie is as southern as Georgia."

Personification gives human qualities to inanimate objects or abstract ideas: "Six tall, menacing pine trees guard our campus at night."

Hyperbole (overstatement) is deliberate exaggeration used for emphasis: "It was raining so hard that I almost drowned while driving to school."

Litotes (understatement) is deliberate understatement used for emphasis: "Getting a D on my history test was not my greatest birthday present."

Synecdoche substitutes part of something for the whole: "Two hands left the ship just before it sailed." In this example, *hands* substitutes for "sailors."

Metonymy substitutes the whole for a part of something: "The Pentagon said today that, except for Near Eastern flareups, fewer troops will be needed in the next decade." In this example, *The Pentagon* substitutes for "a spokesperson for the army."

A *paradox* appears to be contradictory, but in fact carries some truth: "The wealthier you are, the poorer you may be." Wealth is not always measured by money. It is also measured by wisdom, knowledge, morality, love, and other qualities.

Focus   In photography, a subject that is in focus is sharply defined. That is also true in writing. Writers who focus on their subject bring it into sharp detail. They begin by thinking about a large unfocused topic, such as "crime in the streets." Then they may decide to focus on some part of crime in the streets—"street crime in our city." After they have found their focus, they may narrow it even more—to "street crime in my neighborhood." How sharply they focus on a subject often depends on their **audience** and **purpose**.

General and specific   General words are names for broad classes of things, from which you can move to words that designate members of those classes. One broad class is *automobiles*. A term that designates a member of that class is *sports car*. A designation for a more specific member of the sports-car class is *Alfa Romeo*. Writers are guided by their **audience** and by their **purpose** when they choose among general and specific names.

Generalization   A generalization is a broad statement that rests on personal observation or acquired information. The sentence "Children usually follow their parents' advice" suggests that its writer has experience with raising children and from that experience has written a generalization that includes all children.

Writers sometimes begin with generalizations and then move toward conclusions based on their generalizations. But to avoid hasty generalizations, they often use qualifiers in their conclusions: "She has a degree in English, and so she *probably* knows a lot about Shakespeare." Or, "She has a degree in English, and so she *might* know *something* about Shakespeare." See also **induction**.

Hyperbole   *See* **Figures of speech**.

Hypothetical examples   *See* **Examples**.

Image   An image appeals to the imagination through the senses. It is a **strategy** many writers apply to help readers "see" what they are reading. The sentence, "Her ancient face was a sheaf of small etched road maps to nowhere," is an image that describes an old and wrinkled countenance. The sentence, "He sings the songs of an old man's childhood, the golden past that never was," describes a person who reminisces about former times, which seem far more attractive now ("the golden past") than they were then.

Induction   An induction is the result of reasoning that interprets limited evidence to arrive at a general truth. A person who has owned three or four friendly and alert cocker spaniels over the years may reason that all cocker spaniels are friendly and alert.

Inductive reasoning is useful in writing because it is a powerful persuader. Writers who want to persuade readers of a general truth use enough sound evidence to make their claims reasonably acceptable. If you wanted to persuade readers of the benefits in jogging, you might offer as evidence all your healthy friends who jog, newspaper articles that endorse jogging as a healthy activity, well-known athletes who jog, your doctor's saying that jogging promotes health, and so on. The more sound evidence you present, the more apt the reader is to accept your persuasive **argument**.

Informative process analysis   With an informative process analysis, you tell how something is done. You describe sequentially the steps in a natural procedure that does not involve intervention. An informative process analysis might tell how a tree grows, but *not* how to plant a tree, the latter topic being a **directive process analysis**.

Introduction   An introduction begins a piece of writing. An effective introduction establishes the essay's topic, tone, and territory.

It leads directly into the main idea or issue discussed in the **body** of the paper. Its purpose is to engender readers' interest. To achieve that purpose, writers include such **strategies** as **rhetorical questions**, unusual facts, **anecdotes**, and personal comments.

The length of an introduction depends on the essay's **purpose** and its intended **audience**.

Invention   Writers use invention to develop their subjects. It includes planning the piece of writing, thinking of ways of organizing material, of presenting material, and of deciding how to handle questions that you anticipate readers will raise.

Irony   A difference between appearance and reality creates irony. When it compliments, it is ironically condemning. When it condemns, it is ironically complimenting. The sentence "What a magnificent car," when used to describe a rusting hulk sitting in a junkyard, is ironic. The sentence "It's not a bad paint job," when used to describe Michelangelo's Sistine Chapel ceiling, is ironic. When the irony is not subtle but is intended to cause deliberate harm, it is called **sarcasm**. If someone says, "Thank you. It's just what I've always wanted," when reacting to the ketchup stain you accidentally put on her new blouse, she is using sarcasm.

When they are contrary to our anticipation, situations can also be ironic. You might discover that you were not hired for a job because you failed a company's mandatory typing test, only to learn that the job for which you applied required no typing at all.

Jargon   Jargon is technical vocabulary that is appropriate only among experts in a field. As a kind of shorthand, it saves time in their communication. Among themselves lawyers use such expressions as "caveat," "entrapment," "estoppel," "the M'Naghten Rule," and "mens rea," knowing that they all understand legal jargon. To a lay listener, however, the words mean little. For lay audiences, writers use jargon sparingly, and when they do use it, they include definitions.

Another kind of jargon, sometimes called bureaucratese, is nothing more than pompous **diction** used more to impress readers than to inform them. The sentence "Our consumer demand analysis precludes our implementation of the proposed planning stage"—which means, by the way, "We don't need to plan to produce something that no one wants to buy"—typifies the jargon of pomposity.

Litotes   *See* **Figures of speech**.

Logical fallacies   Mistakes in reasoning that lead to faulty conclusions are logical fallacies or fallacious reasoning.

An *ad hominem argument* attacks a person rather than the issue that is being considered.

The *association fallacy* suggests that an act or belief is worthy or unworthy merely because of the people who are associated with it.

A writer falls into *false analogy* by presuming that if two things are alike in one or more ways, then they must be alike in other ways as well.

The *either/or fallacy* is a type of oversimplification in which a writer assumes only two alternatives are possible when in fact many others should be considered.

A *non sequitur* is a conclusion that does not follow from the premise.

A writer making an *overgeneralization* draws a conclusion from insufficient or unrepresentative evidence.

With an *oversimplification,* we draw a conclusion while ignoring information essential to the subject.

Someone who accepts the *post hoc* argument assumes that if one event occurred before another, then the second event was caused by the first.

Metaphor   *See* **Figures of speech**.

Metonymy   *See* **Figures of speech**.

Narration   A narration tells a story and often includes extensive **description**. Narrations, usually chronological, include among their purposes entertaining, informing, and instructing. Some narrations have a plot, a story line that moves toward an insight about the principal character in the narration.

Narrative effect   The main **effect** from reading a **narration** is named the *narrative effect*. Each narration incorporates a reason for being. Writers decide the main effect that their narrative should have on their readers, and then form the narrative so as not to depart from their decision.

Non sequitur *See* **Logical fallacies.**

Nonstandard English Words and expressions that are often spoken but rarely written except when the writer has a clear reason for using them sometimes include nonstandard English. Some examples are *ain't, nohow, irregardless, theirselves, hisself, we'uns, could care less* (for "could not care less"), and *them* (instead of *those*), as in *Them people ain't got no smarts,* instead of "Those people do not seem intelligent."

Objective and subjective Objective writing is designed to be a distanced, factual account presented in language that is plain, direct, and free of value judgments. Pure objectivity is hard to achieve because people's perceptions are almost always colored by their experiences, their values, and their biases. But in writing such as scientific papers and technical reports, authors strive for objectivity. Subjective writing is more personal, more indicative of the writer's thoughts, feelings, and attitudes. The emphasis here is on the writer's relationship to the topic rather than the topic itself. Very few essays are exclusively objective or subjective. Most often, writings combine the two.

Opening An opening is the first part of a three-part narrative essay. The other two parts are the body and the climax. The beginning sentences usually capture the reader's attention without giving away the outcome. The opening may hint at the purpose of the story about to unfold, but may not actually reveal it.

Order of ideas Ideas can be arranged in various ways, but all are derived from the subject and the writer's purpose. The order may be spatial, moving from top to bottom, side to side, or background to foreground. Or the order may simply be chronological, as in a narrative. The writer may work from least important to most important. The sequence of ideas should always be well thought out, chosen for its greatest effect.

Overgeneralization *See* **Logical fallacies.**

Oversimplification *See* **Logical fallacies.**

Paradox *See* **Figures of speech**.

Paragraph   The paragraph is the basic unit in an essay. It is composed of a group of closely related sentences that together develop one of the essay's main ideas. The main or unifying idea of a paragraph is often stated in a topic sentence, often found at the beginning of the paragraph. All other sentences in the paragraph relate directly to the topic sentence, thus establishing unity and coherence. But occasionally a unified and coherent paragraph has no topic sentence. The paragraph then undoubtedly has a leading idea that is strongly implied in every sentence. Paragraphs also work visually in an essay, graphically demonstrating the progress of ideas and also providing visual relief to the reader.

Parallel structure   The repetition of similar grammatical elements within or between sentences makes a parallel structure. Logic dictates that grammatical elements with equal value in a sentence be constructed in the same grammatical form. Thus, "I prefer running, jumping, and to swim" does not exhibit parallelism, but does have awkwardness. "I prefer running, jumping, and swimming" demonstrates parallelism and logic. Parallel structure is also a stylistic technique often used to create emphasis and drama. The long fourth sentence in paragraph 14 of Martin Luther King's "Letter from Birmingham Jail" (Chapter 9) is a particularly effective example of parallel structure.

Paraphrase   A paraphrase is a restatement of another person's words in your own words. This technique is particularly necessary when writing any essay in which you use others' ideas or words as evidence supporting your own argument. Often, you paraphrase instead of using a direct quotation in order to more easily mold the idea to fit your argument. The sense of the original, as well as the tone and order of ideas, remains the same. In either a paraphrase or a direct quotation you must give credit to your source. In a more informal paper you incorporate the credit into your text: "According to Charles Neerland, being a Minneapolitan means being cold much of the year." In more formal writing, such as a research paper, footnoting is required.

Person   The grammatical distinction between the speaker (first person: I, we); the person spoken to (second person: you, singular and plural); and the subject spoken about (third person: he, she, it, or they) is labeled *person.*

Persona   A fictional speaker is an essay or the fictional narrator of a story is its persona. The character, attitudes, and ideas of the persona are often different from those of the author. In fact, it is often the persona's character, attitudes, and ideas that are held up for criticism. The persona of Swift's "A Modest Proposal" voices ideas that Swift obviously finds abhorrent.

Personification   *See* **Figures of speech.**

Persuasion or persuasive argument   Persuasive writing is an attempt to win readers to a point of view and, often, move them to action. It appeals primarily to the emotions, as opposed to *argument,* which is meant to win the reader by reason and logic. Most often, the two are used together.

Plagiarism   Presenting someone else's words or ideas as if they were your own is plagiarism. It is a serious offense in the academic world and can lead to consequences such as failure and expulsion from school. Whenever you use someone else's words or ideas you must give that person credit in your own text or by footnoting (see **paraphrase**).

Point-by-point and subject-by-subject development   These are the two basic methods for developing a comparison-and-contrast essay. Point-by-point development alternately presents each point being considered. Subject-by-subject development presents all the details about one side of the argument first and follows with all the details about the other side.

Point of view   In an argumentative essay the point of view is the author's opinion or the thesis the writer hopes to advance. In expository essays it is the physical or mental vantage point from which the author views the subject. An essay on professional football told from a player's first-hand experience would be approached differently from that of the team's owner (whose interest may be exclusively financial) or from that of a newspaper reporter. Each would approach the subject with a different kind of authority. And that authority would mean a difference in vocabulary, style, and tone. The player might use first **person** to capture immediacy. The owner might want to involve the reader in experiencing her financial woes and so use second person. Or, to create a mood of objectivity, the reporter might use the third person. The point of view in an essay must remain consistent. An inconsistent point of view can leave the reader confused and disconcerted.

Post hoc argument   *See* **Logical fallacies.**

Premise   A deductive **syllogism** is composed of two premises and a conclusion. The first or major premise is an assumption and the second or minor premise is a fact or another assumption based on evidence: All mammals are animals (first premise is an assumption). Raccoons are mammals (second premise is a fact). Therefore, all raccoons are animals (conclusion is logically deduced from the two premises).

Prewriting   All the activities a writer goes through before actually beginning to write are part of *prewriting*. These might consist of brainstorming for a subject, doing background reading, narrowing the subject, devising a thesis, planning the essay—everything, in other words, that leads to the actual writing.

Probable conclusions   Conclusions arrived at by inductive reasoning and from incomplete evidence are *probable conclusions*. The reader's acceptance of a conclusion that follows from inductive reasoning is often referred to as the *inductive leap*. To establish a clear connection between the evidence and the conclusion, the writer must be sure to present **relevant evidence**, **sufficient evidence**, and **representative evidence.**

Proposition or thesis   In argument, the proposition or thesis is a written assertion, the opinion the writer wants a reader to accept, or an action the writer wants a reader to take.

Psychological time   Arranging events in a narrative so as to show how they are connected in memory, shifting back and forth in time while keeping a sense of forward movement, creates *psychological time*.

Purpose The goal the writer wants to achieve is the *purpose*. The clearer the writer's purpose, the more clarity, coherence, and unity the essay will have. If the writer's purpose is muddled, the essay too will be muddled. All kinds of purposes are possible: to entertain with an amusing story; to inform; to convince readers of a point of view and move them to action. These purposes can be achieved by using the modes of prose: narration, description, exposition, and argument. In an essay you may use them alone or in combination.

Qualification Tempering broad statements to make them more logically acceptable is the technique called *qualification*. In qualifying a statement the writer admits that exceptions to that assertion are possible or probable, thereby indicating that the statement is not oversimplified. In these days with much emphasis on physical fitness, the statement "Physical exercise is good" might, at first blush, seem valid. But exercise may, in fact, be detrimental to some people. Therefore the statement needs qualifying. "Exercise is good for most people" might be a more acceptable statement.

Reason and result Another way of saying **cause and effect**.

Refutation The attempt to counter an opposing argument by revealing its weaknesses is called *refutation*. You must refute the opposition's argument if it is obvious and is strong or logical enough to be a real alternative to your own. The refutation usually is done early in an argumentative essay to get it out of the way so that you can proceed with your own argument. The three most usual strategies are pointing out weaknesses in the opposition's evidence, questioning the argument's relevance, and pointing out errors in logic. Refutation indicates that the writer is aware the issue is complex and is willing to consider opposing opinions. To be effective, refutation must always be done in a moderate tone and must always be accurate in representing the opposing argument. To do otherwise is to risk being judged harshly by the reader for sounding intemperate and for treating the opposition unfairly.

Relevant evidence You can directly support the essay's thesis and contribute directly to its conclusion with relevant evidence (see **representative evidence** and **sufficient evidence**).

Representative evidence Representative evidence covers the full range of information related to an essay's thesis, not just one side or the other. An argument cannot be convincing unless evidence from every point of view is admitted (see **relevant evidence** and **sufficient evidence**).

Representative sample A representative sample is a typical example chosen from among examples that exhibit similar characteristics.

Rhetoric Rhetoric is the study and art of using prose effectively. The various methods of prose discourse described and exemplified in this textbook—narration, description, exposition, and argument—are rhetorical forms.

Rhetorical question A rhetorical question is posed for effect and no answer is expected. It is a question meant to provoke thought or to launch the writer into the subject to be discussed in the writing.

Satire The form of writing using wit, irony, and ridicule to attack foolish and vicious human behavior and the institutions and customs that promote such behavior is *satire*. Two main types of satire are at the writer's disposal: social satire, which is used to attack foolish, but not dangerous, behavior and does it by invoking laughter and sympathy; ethical satire, which is far sharper and points with anger and indignation at social corruption and evil (see Jonathan Swift's "A Modest Proposal" in Chapter 9).

Sentimentality Sentimental writing overemotionalizes its subject and thus becomes ineffective. Sentimentality is often emotion displayed for the sake of emotion, losing connection with the actuality of the thing that supposedly caused the emotion. Sentimental writers risk readers' ridicule because they don't fully acquaint the reader with the actuality and thus appear to overreact.

Simile   *See* **Figures of speech.**

Slang   Colorful and humorous expressions, mostly short-lived and often peculiar to a group of people, are called *slang*. Almost always informal, slang is unacceptable in formal writing except in quotations and for creating special effects.

Specific examples   *See* **Examples.**

Standard English   The English language in its most widely accepted form, written and spoken by educated people in both formal and informal contexts, and having universal currency though it incorporates regional differences, is *standard English*.

Strategy   The means by which writers effectively accomplish their purpose in a piece of writing form their *strategy*. This planning includes evaluating the audience, narrowing the subject, choosing a dominant rhetorical pattern such as narration, description, examples, comparison and contrast, and definition, among others.

Style   The distinctive way in which a writer writes creates an individual *style*. Choice of words, structure of sentences, use or non-use of figurative language—all contribute to a writer's style. Two writers may write about the same subject, have the same attitude toward the subject (see **tone**), and yet "sound" distinctly different. Style is a writer's writing personality and can be developed with practice.

Subject-by-subject development   *See* **Point-by-point development.**

Sufficient evidence   In an argumentative paper you must supply ample evidence to convincingly support your conclusion (see **relevant evidence** and **representative evidence**).

Summary   A summary is a comprehensive and usually brief recapitulation of previously stated facts or statements. Summarizing your main points is one way of concluding a paper.

Suspense   The pleasurable uncertainty or excitement we feel when anticipating what will happen next as we read a story is *suspense*. This tactic is most evident in mystery or detective stories but is less dramatically present in much narration.

Syllogism   A form of deductive reasoning composed of two premises and a conclusion is the *syllogism*. The first premise (major premise) is an assumption and the second (minor premise) is a fact or another assumption based on **evidence.** The conclusion is logically deduced from the two premises: All human beings are animals (major premise is an assumption). Ephraim is human (minor premise is a fact). Therefore, Ephraim is an animal (conclusion is logically deduced from the two premises).

Symbol   A symbol is any concrete thing that means something beyond itself. Many symbols are, on the surface, clear-cut and readily acceptable. The flag, of course, represents country and elicits patriotic feeling. But ideas and attitudes differ about what constitutes patriotism and what things conjure patriotic feelings. Some people become proud when their country asserts itself militarily. Others find their patriotic values in freedom, tolerance, fairness, and compassion. The flag, a rather simple symbol as symbols go, therefore has a complex of powerful meanings beyond itself. Symbols are employed most in fiction and poetry, less in exposition and argument. But they can be used in the latter to express meaning concisely and palpably.

Synecdoche   *See* **Figures of speech.**

Thesis   The thesis is the main point in any piece of prose writing, an idea that all the other ideas and facts in an essay should point to and support. A thesis can be either clearly stated or implied. It is most commonly found at the end of an early paragraph. A thesis cannot be a statement of fact, because facts do not need proving. A thesis, therefore, must have an argumentative edge, a point of view that will be proven or demonstrated in some way somewhere in the paper.

Tone   Diction, sentence variety, figurative language, and anything else that establishes the writer's attitude toward the subject forms the tone, which can vary extensively. The writing's tone can be amused, angry, exasperated, approving, surprised, sarcastic. It can, in other words, run the gamut of human emotions. But tone should be consistent, for it must inform the entire essay and lead the reader to the response the writer desires.

Topic sentence   A topic sentence states the main idea of a paragraph. All other sentences in the paragraph support the topic sentence. Most often it appears at the beginning but can be placed anywhere in the paragraph.

Transitions   Transitions are words, phrases, sentences, and paragraphs that link ideas. Because a reader cannot get into the writer's head, it is the writer's responsibility to make sure that the ideas are clearly stated and that relationships between the ideas are clear. The first way to ensure that clarity is to organize ideas so that they flow logically from one to another. But even sturdier bridges are needed to carry the reader from sentence to sentence and from paragraph to paragraph. For this continuity you will need to use transitional devices such as these:

1. In the first sentence of a paragraph repeat some words or phrases from the last sentences in the preceding paragraph.
2. Use pronouns to refer back to nouns in the preceding paragraph. You must be careful here to make precisely clear which words the pronouns refer to.
3. Use transitional expressions to carry the reader.

    Addition: also, in addition, too, moreover, and besides, further, furthermore, equally important, next, then, finally.

    Example: for example, for instance, thus, as an illustration, namely, specifically.

    Contrast: but, yet, however, on the other hand, nevertheless, conversely, in contrast, on the contrary, still, at the same time.

    Comparison: similarly, likewise, in like manner, in the same way, in comparison.

    Concession: of course, to be sure, certainly, naturally, granted.

    Result: therefore, thus, consequently, so, accordingly.

    Summary: as a result, hence, in short, in brief, in summary, in conclusion, finally, on the whole.

> *Time sequence:* first, second, third, fourth, next, then, finally, afterward, before, soon, later, during, meanwhile, subsequently, immediately, at length, eventually, in the future, currently.
>
> *Place:* at the front, in the foreground, at the back, in the background, at the side, adjacent, nearby, in the distance, here, there.

Two-part classification   Often called *binary,* two-part classification is the simplest way of breaking a subject down. This pattern divides the subject in two, usually into positive and negative categories, such as vegetarians, nonvegetarians; smokers, nonsmokers; television viewers, nonviewers of television, and so on. But two-part classification is usually inexact and skirts the edge of comparison and contrast. Most classification systems, therefore, have at least three categories.

Typical examples   *See* **Examples.**

Understatement (Litotes)   *See* **Figures of speech.**

Unity   In a paragraph, every idea and every sentence relates directly to and helps support the main idea, usually stated in the topic sentence. Likewise, in the essay as a whole, every unified paragraph points to and supports the essay's main idea expressed in the thesis.

Warrant   Warrant is the supporting argument in Toulmin's model of reasoning (see **Claim**).

Writing process   The various tasks a writer must perform to produce a piece of writing are called the writing process. **Prewriting** entails a series of activities that pave the way for the actual writing. Only after this stage can the writer make the first draft, revise it into a number of subsequent drafts, and polish to achieve the final product.

A Guide to Editing
and Revising Sentences

This guide will help you revise your sentences to make them more readable and interesting. Unfortunately, no one has invented a clear procedure to follow when editing and revising prose. Some writers revise as they carefully work their way through a first draft; others swoop through the first draft and then revise during a second or third draft. Each writer, it seems, devises his or her own approach.

Two preliminary steps in revision do seem to be adopted by all writers. First, they must learn what makes writing effective. We offer this guide as a source of suggestions you can use to gain that knowledge. Second, they must pick up a pencil and go to work on their sentences. We must now stand aside and wish you the best of luck.

Eliminate pretentious language.

Pretentious writing draws attention to itself. The vocabulary is unnecessarily complex, perhaps because the writer has thumbed through a thesaurus replacing simple words with difficult words. Always try to select simple words over fancy ones. If you want to indicate that dogs make good pets, do not write, "Domesticated canines will contribute felicity to anyone's life."

659

The earthquake ~~struck with a malignant force that~~ *killed*

~~destroyed the lives of~~ more than than four thousand villagers.

Children ~~frolicking~~ *playing* ~~with their companions exhibit~~ *with friends demonstrate*

these fears.

Eliminate obsolete, archaic, and recently invented words.

Over the years some words and their meanings change or fall from common use. A good dictionary labels these words and meanings "obsolete" or "archaic." Obsolete words or meanings should not be used at all. "Yestereen," meaning last evening, is obsolete. Archaic words still occur in special contexts, especially in literary or religious works. "Thou" and "thee," "brethren," and "kine" appear in the King James version of the Bible and are identified as "archaic" in dictionaries. Unless you have a special reason for using archaic words, they too should be eliminated from your writing.

Recently invented words, or *neologisms,* are so new to the language that they may be unacceptable in college writing. Often neologisms, such as "teleplay," "floppy disk," and "aerobics" become part of our common vocabulary because they are the clearest way of referring to the things they stand for. But neologisms may quickly fall from use, as "usership," "time frame," and "palimony" may do any day. If a neologism is in common usage, then feel free to use it, but if it was created very recently, then use another word or phrase or risk confusing your reader.

Eliminate sexist language.

Rid your sentences of sexual bias. Traditionally, the masculine pronouns "he," "him," and "his" have been used to refer to members of either sex when gender is indefinite. Today, such usage leads to gender stereotyping, and we have a number of simple ways of eliminating sexist language in writing. One option is to change "his" to "his or her."

Faulty: Every attorney must prepare *his* closing remarks with care.

Revised: Every attorney must prepare *his or her* closing remarks with care.

This solution may generate wordiness and become awkward if applied throughout a longer passage. An alternative solution is to revise the sentence with the plural "attorneys," which would call for the plural pronoun "their" and eliminate the suggestion of gender.

Revised: Attorneys must prepare their closing remarks with care.

"Man" and "men" are used to refer to both men and women. With some thought you can change this practice in your writing. "Policeman" can be changed to "police officer"; "mailman" to "mail carrier"; "congressman" to "member of Congress"; "mankind" to "humanity," "people," or "human beings."

Eliminate slang and regional expressions.

Slang can be the colorful vocabulary that arises from the experience of a group of people with common interests, such as teenagers, rock stars, jazz musicians, actors, baseball fans, street gangs, and truck drivers. Unfettered by dictionary definitions, slang changes rapidly, reflecting each group's perceptions. Most slang expressions, such as "awesome," "bummer," "downer," "sleezoid," "rad," "bro," and "stoked" appear, increase in use, and then either become trite or shift in meaning. When slang words such as "jazz" and "A-bomb" become part of the general vocabulary, you may use them freely. Generally in college writing, however, revise your sentences to eliminate slang because it is imprecise and may be confusing.

As a type, comedians are ~~trippy, bummed~~ *unpredictable, depressed* out one moment and ~~flying~~ *elated* the next.

The reviewers ~~ragged on~~ *criticized* Kaufmann's poetry collection for

being sentimental.

Regional expressions are associated with a geographical area. A "soda pop" in one part of the country is a "tonic" in another. A "skillet" in one region is a "frying pan" in another. Generally, you should eliminate regional expressions from your college writing for the same reason as you should avoid slang: you may confuse the reader.

The vice squad had been ~~fixing~~ *preparing* to arrest Hawkins for months.

Use technical language, or jargon, with care.

When writing for a group of computer specialists, you may use such terminology as "hard disk," "modem," "user area," and "megabyte" with confidence that your readers will understand; these are technical terms, or jargon, which computer specialists use freely.

Most occupations and special activities have technical vocabularies. A person in advertising uses "story board," "outsert," "keyline," and "live tag" with ease. A ballet dancer feels equally at ease with "adagio," "barre," "sickle foot," and "pointe." Such language, however, is inappropriate for most readers.

Technical language is especially insidious when taken from its proper field and used in a broader context. Technical vocabulary from psychiatry is inappropriate when used to describe the behavior of any animals other than human beings.

The whale seemed ~~traumatized~~ *stunned* as it floundered in the

shallow surf, struggling to beach itself and ~~fulfill~~ *die*.

~~its unconscious death wish.~~

Consider the denotation and connotation of words.

Denotation is a word's literal definition, found in a dictionary. *Connotation* describes the emotional colorings that surround the word and influence how a reader might respond to it.

According to one dictionary, the word "apple" denotes "a round, firm, fleshy, edible fruit with a green, yellow, or red skin and small seeds." For some of us the word "apple" also connotes health ("an apple a day keeps the doctor away") and knowledge (the apple is often referred to as the forbidden fruit in the Garden of Eden, and the apple is the gift left on the teacher's desk). No wonder the name "Apple" seemed appropriate for the country's first popular personal computer (the logo even features an apple with a bite taken from it, "a little bite (byte) of knowledge is healthy for you"). It became "the apple of the consumer's eye"!

As a writer you must consider both the denotation and connotation of the words you use. If you do not, you may create a meaning you did not intend, as the writer of the next sentence does in attempting to describe how the company president moved through a crowded room to sit down and start a meeting.

> *Faulty:* Robert Rice, the company president, maneuvered himself to the chair at the head of the table.

Inadvertently, the writer creates a feeling that Robert Rice manipulated his way into the presidency of the company.

> *Revised:* Robert Rice, the company president, sat in the chair at the head of the table.

When selecting one of several words that have nearly the same meaning, you must take special care. Consider the words "emulate," "copy," and "mimic." Their denotations are similar, but they differ in connotation.

Beginning writer Jane West ~~mimics~~ *emulates* romance novelist

Rosemary Rogers's style.

The connotation of "mimic" is too negative for the sense this writer wants to convey, which is that West strives to achieve quality equaling that of Rogers.

Select concrete and specific words rather than abstract and general ones.

Abstract words name qualities, ideas, and concepts we experience in our feelings and our thoughts: "freedom," "love," "hate," "hope," "democracy," "honesty," and so on. Concrete words label things we experience through our senses: "smack," "kiss," "laugh," "smoke," "dance," "shout," and so on.

General words cover relatively large groups of things: "food," "places," "people." Specific words name specific things, a more limited segment of a large group: "pizza," "Boston," "Tom Cruise." "General" and "specific" are relative words. Language becomes more specific as it moves from the general group to a unique example of the group, as from "athlete" to "professional athlete," to "baseball player," to "Babe Ruth."

General	*Specific*	*More specific*
weapon	pistol	.45 automatic
fish	shark	hammerhead
food	pasta	linguini
music	popular music	rock and roll
Native Americans	Plains Indians	Sioux

College writers are inclined to overuse abstract and general words. Their sentences, therefore, can be vague, leaving their writing drab and lifeless. As you revise your sentences, replace vague wording with more concrete and specific wording wherever you can.

The subway ~~was frightening.~~ *smelled of fear.*

A crowd ~~waited~~ *restlessly milled* in the square.

The night ~~was dark.~~ *turned black as clouds swept in from the north.*

Envy ~~brings out the worst in people.~~ *makes people scheme, manipulate, and steal.*

You should also replace *euphemisms* with specific language. A euphemism is a word or phrase substituted for another word that is harsh or blunt. The funeral industry substitutes "loved one" or "the deceased" for "corpse," "vault" for "coffin," and "final resting place" for "grave site."

Euphemisms often may be necessary for tactfulness. No doubt most of us prefer to ask a stranger to guide us to the restroom rather than the toilet. Euphemisms may, however, distract us from the realities in experiences such as poverty, unemployment, and war. We have become accustomed to the euphemism of "low income," "inner city," and "correctional facility" as substitutes for "poor," "slum" or "ghetto," and "jail." Euphemisms are pervasive in the language of "polite society" and so you must guard against their slipping into your finished papers. If you find euphemistic phrasing when revising your sentences, consider rewriting the phrase in more specific language.

The *decline* ~~deterioration of his economic status~~ began when he ~~became unemployed.~~ *lost his job, car, and house.*

Military officials seem to believe that ~~misrepresenting the facts~~ *lying* is acceptable ~~behavior.~~

Use figurative language with care.

Figurative language draws a comparison between two things that are essentially different but alike in some underlying and surprising way. The two commonest figures of speech are simile and metaphor.

A *simile* expresses a comparison directly by connecting two ideas with "like" or "as."

> His face was like the sky, one minute overcast, the next minute bright.
>
> —*Joseph Conrad*

> The bowie knife is as American as the half-ton pickup truck.
>
> —*Geoffrey Norman*

A *metaphor* expresses a comparison indirectly, with neither "like" nor "as."

> Roads became black velvet ribbons with winking frost sequins.
>
> —*Hal Borland*

> A sleeping child gives me the impression of a traveler in a very far country.
>
> —*Ralph Waldo Emerson*

To be effective, a simile or metaphor must create a verbal image or clarify a writer's thought by making it understandable in other words. When a simile or metaphor is trite or overblown, it must be revised.

> When he leaned toward the audience and smiled, his gold
> tooth ~~shined like a bright star.~~ *reflected the light.*

Mixed metaphors create confusion by combining two or more incompatible comparisons.

Thought is restless, soaring and diving before ~~coiling~~ *circling* ~~around~~ an idea.

"Soaring" and "diving" suggest a bird in flight. "Coiling" suggests a snake, leaving the metaphor mixed and in need of repair.

Eliminate trite expressions.

Trite expressions are phrases that have become stale by overuse. They include clichés ("He ran around the neighborhood *like a chicken without a head*"), wedded adjectives and nouns ("They made a *lifelong commitment*"), and overused phrases ("We all know that *the rich get richer and the poor get poorer*"). Many trite phrases appear in early drafts of college papers, especially if the writing has been rushed. When revising, strike out trite expressions and reword them in a more direct way.

He was guilty *undeniably* ~~beyond a shadow of doubt.~~

The business was ~~sinking in a sea of red ink.~~ *almost bankrupt.*

~~To make a long story short,~~ The widow married the banker.

To make you more aware of trite phrases, here are some of the most exhausted ones.

a crying shame	in the final analysis
a thinking person	in the nick of time
after all is said and done	last but not least
at this point in time	method in his madness
depths of despair	never a dull moment
drop in the bucket	none the worse for wear
face the music	pay the piper
flat as a pancake	quick as a flash
in this day and age	sadder but wiser

Eliminate wordiness.

Empty phrases make your writing unnecessarily wordy. Often one word will do the work of an entire empty phrase.

Barthes ~~is of the opinion~~ *believes* that culture can be understood

by reading the "signs" it generates.

~~It is usually the case that~~ *D*iet books *usually* encourage the dieter's

fantasies about being slim.

Study this list to become familiar with common empty phrases and substitutes for them.

Empty phrase	Substitute
at all times	always
at this point in time	now
at any point in time	then
by means of	by
due to the fact that	because
for the purpose of	for
give consideration to	consider
give encouragement to	encourage
in order to	to
in the event that	if
in the final analysis	finally
make contact with	call
of the opinion that	that
regardless of the fact that	although
the fact that	that
until such time as	until or when

Repetition of key words is often necessary for parallel structure or for emphasis, but needless repetition leads to boring, wordy sentences.

The Pacific ~~rattlesnake~~ *rattler* is California's most dangerous

snake.

I ~~continue to~~ *still* believe that government will not survive

unless the Attorney General acts.

Redundancy is similar to needless repetition in that it conveys the same meaning twice, as in the phrases "visible to the eye" and "large in size." Like needless repetitions, redundancies make your sentences wordy and should be eliminated during revision. At times, an entire sentence or passage may need to be rewritten.

If researchers probe the fac~~tual truth deeply~~*s*, they

will find the solution.

Millions of ~~people who~~ vote*rs* support national health

insurance.

Though suffering from malaria, he continued ~~on~~ his journey

to the Mayan temple.

These are some common redundancies.

advance forward	continue to go on
autobiography of her life	disappear from sight
basic fundamentals	factual truth
circle around	important essential
close proximity	refer back
combine together	repeat again
consensus of opinion	round in shape

Eliminate unnecessary expletive constructions.

The word "there" followed by a form of the plain verb "to be" is an *expletive,* a word used to fill out a sentence. An expletive signals that the subject of the sentence will follow the verb. This construction is unnecessarily wordy and lacks the vigor of subject-verb constructions.

~~There are~~ /T wo horses trott~~ing~~ ed in the meadow.

~~There is no hope for~~ /T he rain forests, *face destruction*.

The pronoun "it" often functions as an expletive in similar constructions.

~~It is difficult to~~ /A nalyz ing poetry, *is difficult*.

At times, however, "it" often is needed as an expletive, as in "It is raining."

Revise passive sentences.

Voice is the quality in verbs that shows whether a subject is the actor or is acted upon. "The arroyos were flooded by rain" is a passive sentence because the subject, "arroyos," is acted upon. In contrast, "Rain flooded the arroyos" is an active sentence because the subject, "rain," is the actor. Active constructions are more concise, direct, and forceful than passive constructions.

The tornado left death
~~Death~~ and despair ~~was left by the tornado.~~

~~The western world's attention was captured by~~ Nelson

Mandela's speeches, *captured the western world's attention.*

Scientists consider astrology
~~Astrology is considered by scientists~~ to be a mere

superstition.

Although generally in revising you should eliminate unnecessary passive constructions, at times the passive may be necessary. Passive constructions are appropriate when the subject is ambiguous or when you wish to emphasize the receiver of an action.

The mysterious rumor was received from New York.

In this example, the writer does not know who started the rumor.

His self-esteem was damaged by years of severe criticism.

In this example, the writer wishes to emphasize the thing that received the action, "self-esteem."

Revise for proper coordination.

Clauses that have equal importance in a sentence are *coordinate* and should be connected by a coordinating word or punctuation mark. To show the relationship between equal clauses you need to select the proper coordinator.

Coordinating conjunctions

and   but   for   nor   or   so   yet

Correlative conjunctions

both . . . and   either . . . or   neither . . . nor
not only . . . but also   whether . . . or

Conjunctive adverbs

consequently	furthermore	however	meanwhile
moreover	nevertheless	therefore	thus

Different coordinators show different relations. The common kinds of relations are addition, contrast, choice, and result.

Addition: Reviewers criticized his paintings, *and* collectors stopped buying them.

Contrast: Once novels were the primary home entertainment, *but* today television predominates.

Choice: *Either* we human beings will stop polluting the earth, *or* we will perish amid our waste.

Result: Advertising campaigns sell products; *therefore,* manufacturers are willing to pay for them.

Writers sometimes use semicolons to give equal emphasis to main clauses when the main clauses they connect are closely related in meaning and structure.

In Irish folklore, spirits sometimes appear as men or women; at other times they appear as birds and beasts.

When revising a paper, correct faulty coordination that gives equal emphasis to unequal or unrelated clauses.

Faulty: John Fowles is the author of three bestsellers, and he lives in England.

The clause "he lives in England" has little connection to the clause "John Fowles is the author of three bestsellers." These two clauses therefore should not be coordinated. Still, the writer might want to include the information, even though it does not relate directly to the main idea.

Revised: John Fowles, who lives in England, is the author of three bestsellers.

Revised: John Fowles, an English writer, is the author of three bestsellers.

You should also revise to eliminate excessive coordination; that is, stringing main clauses together for no apparent purpose. This practice can become monotonous for the reader and fails to show the proper relation between clauses. A sentence with excessive coordination must be untangled and rewritten.

Excessive: Americans desire heroes, and they find them in films, sports, and politics, but sometimes the real-life behavior of hero figures is disappointing, and then they must find new ones.

Revised: Americans desire heroes, whom they find in films, sports, and politics, but sometimes the real-life behavior of hero figures is disappointing, which means they must find new ones.

Revised: Americans desire heroes, whom they find in films, sports, and politics. Sometimes the behavior of real-life hero figures is disappointing, which means they must find new ones.

Revise for proper subordination.

Clauses deserving less emphasis in a sentence are dependent and should be introduced by a subordinating word. To establish the correct relation between a main clause and a dependent clause, you must use the proper subordinating word.

Common subordinating conjunctions

after	although	as	as if
as soon as	because	before	if
in order that	since	so that	though
unless	until	unless	when
whenever	where	wherever	while

Relative pronouns

that	what	whatever	which	whichever
who	whoever	whom	whomever	whose

Choosing which clause to subordinate depends, of course, on your intention, but writers commonly subordinate a clause to show concession, identification, time, cause, condition, and purpose.

Concession ("as if," "though," "although")

> *Although the evidence clearly called for a guilty verdict,* the jury found him innocent.

Identification ("that," "when," "who")

> Medical researchers, *who came from around the world,* gathered in San Francisco for the convention.

Time ("before," "while," "as soon as")

> The attacks continued *as soon as the troops withdrew.*

Cause ("because")

> *Because historians know how events turned out,* they study the causes of those events.

Condition ("if," "unless," "provided")

> *If bombastic masculinity hides fear of inferiority,* many police officers lack feelings of self-worth.

Purpose ("so that," "in order that")

> Following a catastrophe, people must accept reality *so that healing can begin.*

When revising your sentences, check to see if you have faulty or excessive subordination. If so, rewrite the sentences.

Professor Clark, ~~who is~~ noted for her work in *reproductive cell* ~~the~~ chemistry, ~~of cells when they reproduce has~~ *prestigious* received the Louis Pasteur Award, ~~which is highly prestigious.~~

Place modifiers with care.

A writer can confuse a reader by misplacing a modifier in a sentence. When revising your sentences, be sure to place modifiers so that a reader will be certain which words they modify.

Revise sentences with a *dangling modifier,* a phrase or clause not clearly attached to any word in the sentence. To correct a dangling modifier, see that it clearly relates to the intended word.

As he ran
~~Running~~ through the meadow, his breathing made steamy clouds.

a writer must keep
To complete a screen play, a daily schedule ~~must be kept.~~

he spent   *his*
After six months in therapy, ~~the~~ psychiatrist pronounced him cured.

I was
When a student at Reed, Ken Kesey was the student body's favorite writer.

For clarity, revise sentences to place modifiers as close as possible to the words they modify.

in Hollywood restaurants
Many beginning actors wait on tables to support themselves ~~in Hollywood restaurants.~~

An aging athlete who exercises occasionally hurts himself.

Be particularly aware of where you place limiting modifiers, such as "only," "hardly," "just," "nearly," "almost," and "ever." They can function in many positions in a sentence, but they modify the expression immediately following them. As these limiting modifiers change position in a sentence, the meaning of the sentence also changes.

> I will go *only* if he asks me. [Otherwise I will stay.]
> *Only* I will go if he asks me. [The others will stay.]
> I will go if *only* he asks me. [Please ask!]
> I will go if he asks *only* me. [If he asks others, I will stay.]

Revise sentences with lengthy modifiers placed between important sentence elements.

~~Inner-city crime~~, Because of the increase in drug

inner-city crime

use and reduced law-enforcement budgets, is rising.

~~The winning candidate appeared~~, To the surprise

the winning candidate appeared

of his supporters, unprepared.

~~The rescue team has been~~, With the help of local

the rescue team has been

scouts, searching for the lost teenagers all night.

Revise sentences with modifiers that split infinitives awkwardly. An infinitive consists of "to" plus the simple form of a verb: "to dance," "to moan," "to study," and so on. Usually, a split infinitive can be revised effectively by placing the modifier more accurately.

When oil was discovered, even conservative bankers began

to (frantically) invest in land.

Sometimes a sentence with a split infinitive cannot be revised without creating a misreading. Rewrite the sentence.

Faulty:	His inability to *clearly* explain the issues cost him the election.
Faulty revision:	His inability to explain the issues *clearly* cost him the election.
Rewritten:	His inability to explain the issues *in clear language* cost him the election.

Eliminate faulty pronoun reference.

Pronoun reference is the relation between a pronoun and its *antecedent*—that is, the word to which it refers. If a pronoun's reference is unclear, the sentence will confuse or misinform a reader. Revise sentences so that a pronoun refers clearly to one antecedent.

After Duff had studied Shakespeare for a decade,

he realized that ~~he~~ *Shakespeare* was a master psychologist.

Revise sentences that use "this," "that," or "it" to make a broad reference to an entire sentence.

While watch~~ing~~ *ed* *I* *Friday the 13th* on television, my cat

howled and sprang onto my lap, ~~This~~ *which* frightened me.

Revise sentences that use "it," "they," and "you" without specific antecedents. In conversation these pronouns are often used to make vague reference to people and situations in general. In writing, this practice should be avoided.

During the "Six O'Clock News," ~~it~~ *one reporter* gave a

special report on intelligence testing.

School policy does
~~They do~~ not allow soliciting on campus.

a police officer
In law enforcement, ~~you~~ must stay alert to a

community's changing values.

Using "you" to refer to "you the reader" is perfectly appropriate in all but the most formal writing.

If *you* major in accounting, then *you* should find a job easily.

Revise sentences with pronouns ending in "-self" and "-selves" in place of other personal pronouns.

The philosophy professor tried to convince Robin and

me
~~myself~~ that Albert Camus was fundamentally an optimist.

Pronouns ending in "-self" and "-selves" should refer to words within the sentence.

To stay calm, *I* talked to *myself*.

Nick Ufre is such a sly character, *he* tricked *himself*.

Eliminate inconsistencies in sentences.

Revise your sentences for faulty shifts that indicate your thinking is not clear. Often a faulty shift in consistency takes place in pronoun reference.

they
If students properly prepare for their tests, ~~you~~ will

not fear failing.

you
If you stretch your muscles before a workout, ~~a runner~~

will not face injury.

Faulty shifts also afflict verb tenses, which can confuse time sequences.

The dancer rehearsed for six months, but finally master*ed*

the movement and was ready to perform.

Sometimes shifts in the *mood* of a verb confuse a writer's intent.

Study the causes of World War I, and then you should study

World War II.

A common inconsistency befalls a writer who shifts from active to passive voice, thus dropping from the sentence someone or something performing the action.

In the game of curling a player slides a heavy stone

over the ice toward a target, and *a teammate sweeps* the ice in front of

the stone ~~is swept~~ to influence its path.

You should also revise sentences with shifts between direct and indirect discourse. *Direct discourse* includes a direct quotation: "Dr. Jones said, 'Life, my friends, is boring.' " *Indirect discourse* rephrases a direct quotation and therefore does not require quotation marks: "Dr. Jones had indicated that life is boring."

Faulty shift:	The judge said to pay the fine and "Never return to my court again."
Revised:	The judge said to pay the fine and never return to his court again.
Revised:	The judge said, "Pay the fine and never return to my court again."

Finally, revise sentences with *faulty predication,* which occurs when the information that follows a linking verb does not rename or describe the subject of the verb. In the sentence, "Dr. Brown is a full professor," both "Dr. Brown" and "full professor" refer to the same person. And in the sentence, "Dr. Brown is short," "short" clearly describes "Dr. Brown." In both sentences the predication is logically consistent; that is, the information following the linking verb "is" clearly renames or describes the subject. When the sentence's predication is faulty, however, you must revise it.

> *Faulty:*   The issue of gun control is an easy solution to a complicated problem.

The predication is faulty because the subject "issue" is not a "solution," as the sentence indicates. The "issue," however, is "complicated."

> *Revised:*   The issue of gun control is complicated.

> *Revised:*   Gun control is an easy solution to a complicated problem.

Sometimes predication is faulty because "when" is misused; the word should be used to indicate time.

> *Faulty:*   Nepotism is when officials appoint their relatives to desirable positions.

> *Revised:*   Nepotism is the appointing of relatives to desirable positions.

> *Revised:*   Nepotism takes over when relatives are appointed to desirable positions.

Complete your sentences.

Some sentences are incomplete because they lack words a reader needs to understand them. Often comparisons are not complete. Revise your comparisons to make them clear and logical.

Dr. Casey treats students better / *than other professors*.

Mystery novels are easier to read than romance novels / *are*.

The silence of the streets was more frightening
a wail from
than ₐ a siren.

In some sentence constructions writers omit words that are under-stood, and this practice is correct.

> *Correct:*   Two people control the city government: one is the mayor; the other, the mayor's wife.

But if omitted words do not fit consistently into the structure, the omission is faulty and the sentence must be revised.

In the woods I feel the peace of nature; now, ₐ the *I feel*

violence of the city.

Humans have a strong belief *in* and desire for love.
                          ₐ

Maintain parallelism.

When you revise a paper, maintain *parallel structure* by keep-ing similar ideas in the same grammatical form. In a pair or a series, you must make items parallel to avoid awkward shifts in construction. A noun must be matched with a noun, a verb with a verb, a phrase with a phrase, and a clause with a clause. Revise your sentences to make coordinate ideas parallel.

She loved reading Anne Tyler's novels and ₐ ~~the~~ poetry ~~of~~ *Anne Sexton's*

~~Anne Sexton.~~

His summer activities were ₐ ~~the dances~~ at Hotspur's *dancing*

and sleeping until noon.

Words such as "by," "in," "to," "a," "the," and "that" should usually be repeated when they apply to both elements in a parallel construction.

By not developing their land and ~~by~~ ignoring tax-reporting

requirements, the family found itself bankrupt.

Revise your sentences to make compared and contrasted ideas parallel.

Ms. Lauko would prefer ~~to~~ work~~ing~~ on her physics project rather

than playing chess.

Zen masters are materially poor, but they are rich ~~in spirit~~ *spiritually*.

Revise correlative constructions to make them parallel. The ideas joined by correlative conjunctions, such as "either . . . or," "rather . . . than," and "not only . . . but also," should be parallel.

The law applies not only to people but also *tr* corporations.

Cosmo is either dreaming about the future or ~~in a deep~~

examin~~ation of~~ *ing* the past.

Provide variety in your sentences.

One way to create varied sentences is to revise sentence beginnings. Most inexperienced writers start their sentences with a subject. Unyielding repetition of this pattern can become monotonous, but if you frequently vary your sentence beginnings, you can offset the monotony.

Begin with an adverb.

~~The~~ ^t^ answer came (unexpectedly) in a dream.

~~A~~ ^a^ low moan (suddenly) echoed through the empty mansion.

Begin with a prepositional phrase or verbal phrase.

(v Victory) ^F^ for most politicians justifies any behavior.

(a A banker) ~~who wants~~ ^T^ to be successful must speak Japanese

and "computerese."

(Allen Bates) ~~rubbed~~ *Rubbing* his hands together, ~~and~~ studied the

photograph.

Begin with descriptive phrases.

Hanging in the air like a heavy mist,
v Violence, ~~which~~ was the only solution left, ~~hung in the~~

~~air like a heavy mist.~~

His hand trembling, he
~~He~~ picked up the pencil ~~and felt his hand tremble.~~

~~The~~ basics necessary for a secure childhood ~~include~~ ^F^ food,

shelter, and love; *these are the*

You can also vary sentences by mixing their structures. In an early draft you might rely too heavily on one kind of structure. When you revise your paper, include varied structures.

Simple sentences have only one main clause and no dependent clauses, although they may have several modifiers and modifying phrases.

A crucial function in writing advertisements is manipulating clichés. They help involve consumers.

Compound sentences have two or more main clauses but no dependent clauses.

> Puns are said to be the lowest form of humor, but ad writers breathe new life into them.

> Consumers must analyze an ad writer's techniques, and ad writers must create new ones.

Complex sentences have one main clause and at least one dependent clause.

> When ad writers sit at their word processors, they must rely on their understanding of the popular imagination.

> Ad writers who work at major advertising firms are dramatically influencing public perceptions.

Compound-complex sentences have at least two main clauses and at least one dependent clause.

> If you are curious about commercial influences in society, examining advertisements critically will reveal the desires ad writers stimulate, but be careful because the examination may stimulate your desire for a new car, a trip to exotic islands, or merely time with "people who like beer."

You should also consider revising your sentences to vary their form. You might include an inverted sentence now and then, but not often. Inverted sentences reverse typical subject-verb structures by moving the verb ahead of the subject.

~~The vault is~~ *At* the bottom of a winding staircase

that leads into the cellar*, is the vault* .

Occasionally use a question to create sentence variety.

What does the ~~The~~ word "persona" mean*s* *?* ~~"mask."~~ *means "mask" and* It refers to a

theatrical mask that Greek actors wore on stage.

"The Frontier" from *Legends, Lies and Cherished Myths of American History* by Richard Shenkman. Copyright ©1980 by Richard Shenkman. Reprinted by permission of William Morrow & Co.

"Marrying Absurd" and "On Keeping a Notebook" from *Slouching Towards Bethlehem* by Joan Didion. Copyright ©1966, 1967, 1968 by Joan Didion. Reprinted by Permission of Farrar, Straus and Giroux, Inc.

"Tools of Torture" reprinted by permission of Georges Borchardt, Inc., for the author. Copyright ©1986 by Phyllis Rose.

"Future Shlock" from *Conscientious Objections* by Neil Postman. Copyright ©1988 by Neil Postman. Reprinted by permission of Alfred A. Knopf, Inc.

"Sexism in English: A 1990s Update" ©1990 by Alleen Pace Nilsen. Reprinted by permission of the author.

"Grant and Lee: A Study in Contrasts" by Bruce Catton. Copyright U.S. Capitol Historical Society. Reprinted with permission.

"Erotica and Pornography" from *Outrageous Acts and Everyday Rebellions* by Gloria Steinem. Copyright ©1984 by East Toledo Productions, Inc. Reprinted by permission of Henry Holt and Company, Inc.

"Beauty and the Beast" from *The Human Animal* by Phil Donahue. Copyright ©1985 by Multimedia Entertainment, Inc., and Woodward/White, Inc. Reprinted by permission of Simon & Schuster, Inc.

"Female Athletes" originally titled "Sex Differences in Sports" by P. S. Wood. Reprinted with permission from the October 1980 Reader's Digest. Copyright ©1980 by The New York Times Company. Reprinted by permission.

"A New Game for Managers to Play" by Robert Keidel, copyright ©1985 by The New York Times Company. Reprinted by permission.

"My Wood" from *Abinger Harvest,* copyright 1936 and renewed 1964 by Edward Morgan Forster, reprinted by permission of Harcourt Brace Jovanovich, Inc.

"Severing the Human Connection" by H. Bruce Miller from the *San Jose Mercury News,* August 4, 1981. Reprinted with permission from the *San Jose Mercury News.*

"It Is Time to Stop Playing Indians," from the *Los Angeles Times,* November 25, 1987, reprinted by permission of the author, Arlene B. Hirschfelder.

"T. Without Sympathy" copyright 1989 by Pete Hamill. First appeared in *Esquire,* December 1989. Reprinted by permission of the author.